PERSONNEL
LAW

FOURTH EDITION

PERSONNEL LAW

Kenneth L. Sovereign, J.D.

Former Vice President of Industrial Relations
Hoerner Waldorf Corporation
and
Associate Counsel
Champion International Corporation

 Prentice Hall, Upper Saddle River, NJ 07458

Acquisitions Editor: David Shafer
Editorial Assistant: Shannon Sims
Editor-in-Chief: Natalie Anderson
Marketing Manger: Tami Wederbrand
Production Editor: Tara Ruggiero
Permissions Coordinator: Monica Stipanov
Managing Editor: Dee Josephson
Manufacturing Buyer: Ken Clinton
Manufacturing Supervisor: Arnold Vila
Design Manager: Patricia Smythe
Cover Design: Kiwi Design

Copyright ©1999, 1994, 1989, 1984 by Prentice Hall, Inc.
A Simon & Schuster Company
Upper Saddle River, New Jersey 07458

Library of Congress Cataloging-in-Publication Data

Sovereign, Kenneth L.
    Personnel law/Kenneth L. Sovereign.–4th ed.
        p.   cm.
    Includes bibliographical references and index.
    ISBN 0-13-020038-7 (pbk.)
    1. Labor laws and legislation–United States.   2. Personnel management–Law and
    legislation–United States.   3. Employee rights–United States.   4. Discrimination
    in employment–Law and legislation–United States.   I. Title.
    KF3455.S68   1998
    344.7301–dc21   98-34088
                                                        CIP

Prentice-Hall International (UK) Limited, London
Prentice-Hall of Australia Pty. Limited, Sydney
Prentice-Hall Canada, Inc. Toronto
Prentice-Hall Hispanoamericana, S.A., Mexico
Prentice-Hall of India Private Limited, New Delhi
Prentice-Hall of Japan, Inc. Tokyo
Simon & Schuster Asia Pte. Ltd., Singapore
Editora Prentice-Hall do Brasil, Ltda., Rio De Janeiro

Printed in the United States of America
10 9 8 7 6 5 4 3 2 1

To my wife, Janet, and sons, David and Jeff, who care

CONTENTS

4

DISCRIMINATION UNDER CIVIL RIGHTS ACT OF 1866 AND TITLE VII   33

5

SELECTING QUALIFIED APPLICANTS   46

6

ACCOMMODATION FOR RELIGION AND PHYSICAL HANDICAPS   67

7

WORKING CONDITIONS
BASED ON SEX 89

13
BALANCING EMPLOYEE PRIVACY RIGHTS AND EMPLOYER'S RIGHT TO KNOW   186

14
THE FAIR LABOR STANDARDS ACT AND INDEPENDENT CONTRACTORS   210

15
SAFETY LAW   228

16
CONTROL OF WORKERS'
COMPENSATION COSTS   238

20

MANAGEMENT MALPRACTICE   301

21

THE DIRECTION OF PERSONNEL
LAW IN THE LATE 1990s
AND 2000   315

PREFACE

In all things, success depends upon previous preparation, and without such preparation there is sure to be failure.

CONFUCIUS

Employment law is a blend of well-established principals that are unlikely to change as new cases find their way into the courts.

When the first edition of this book was published, U.S. Supreme Court justice William Brennan stated that pregnancy was not sex related under Title VII (*General Electric v. Gilbert,* 429 U.S. 125 [1976]). There was no drug testing, a disabled person was not in the protected class under federal law, whistle-blowing was not a popular statute, and there was no legal definition of sexual harassment, it just happened. Statutes and court decisions have changed all this. The third edition included these changes. Since the publication of the third edition, many companies have realized the importance of safety and OSHA compliance. Chapter 15, "Safety Law," has been added to reflect this change. This chapter states the author's philosophy of a good safety program and OSHA compliance. The author has 18 years of experience as a safety director (one of many assignments as a personnel executive) and 10 years as counsel representing management in OSHA cases. More than 18 years as a member and chair of the Minnesota OSHA Review Board are also reflected in this philosophy.

Another chapter has been added to the fourth edition; Chapter 3 reflects the new trend being used by regulatory agencies to ease the ever increasing loads (EEOC has already adopted it [HR2977 and S1224], and more will follow). Chapter 2 was split into two chapters. Chapter 4 shows a distinction between physical handicaps and those brought on by habits.

Commonly used personnel terms such as *man, attitude, sexual conduct, probationary period, personality defects,* and *old* have different meanings under the law. Some of these terms not only are obsolete but are now legally challengeable. Past practice must be reviewed and many habits changed. A clear definition of sexual harassment is needed, and clear definitions are especially needed from the Supreme Court or legislatures in the environmental area (too many lawsuits).

The book is a comprehensive and practical text. It tells what to do, how to do it, when to do it, and why. The author has been a personnel executive, consultant, and corporate counsel; has practiced law; and, since 1965, has taught personnel law to managers. The text is unintentionally management oriented. With this background, it is difficult to write anything else.

Business failures, to a large extent, are caused by people's problems. Although the law prohibits discrimination, there is no law that prohibits good management. You can't legislate good management, but nothing prevents the employer from practicing it. In the "litigation-happy society" in the United States, a devastating lawsuit with high damage awards and large legal fees can have an important effect on the bottom line. This book is a reference for practitioners who have the responsibility of the personnel function and for in-house counsel who deal with employment law.

This book is also designed for use in colleges and universities. A course in personnel law should be as important to a management and legal curriculum as business law. The trend in employee litigation will not cease unless preventive personnel law courses are required of future managers and lawyers.

The understandable, nonlegal language and humor will help the reader maintain an interest in the subject matter. The book will put the college student into the real world. It is especially useful to the beginner in personnel work who lacks training in the law when performing the personnel function.

Although there is an increasing intrusion of the law into the personnel function, it is better not to be a lawyer to be successful in human relations. A real danger would exist if the contributions of the personnel function to corporate goals were replaced by legal counsel. A strictly legal approach to the solution of a personnel problem is devastating to organizational survival and employee well-being. The legal counsel must understand the employee relations consequences of a decision. The manager must have some knowledge of the law before making a decision. Unless the manager and legal counsel recognize their roles, employee litigation will continue to increase.

The fourth edition of *Personnel Law* continues to recognize the term *human resource manager* as the most common title for the person performing the personnel function. This modern title is as controversial as the previously used terms *industrial relations director, personnel director,* and *employee relations manager.* The term *personnel* as used throughout this book includes past, present, and future job titles of persons who are assigned the personnel or human resource responsibility. The term *personnel* is a dated term that does not include employment law or its principles.

Personnel Law, fourth edition, is not concerned with the "latest fad" of the proper job title for the personnel function. The corporate profits are best protected by preventing exposure to lawsuits. Good employee relations and legal practices are more important to corporate survival than the job title of the person performing the personnel or human resource function.

The fourth edition of *Personnel Law* continues the third edition's focus on trying to solve the turmoil in the workplace caused by the courts and legislation of the 1960s and 1970s attempting to balance management interests with employee rights. It is impossible for the reader to comprehend and apply all the existing legal principles. Setting priorities is necessary.

The objective of the fourth edition is to find a way for personnel law to live with its partner—employment law—whose principles are laid down by legislation and interpreted by the courts. A balance must be reached between employee rights and the law (created by persons who know nothing about good management).

The text is not intended to replace the legal counsel but to help the manager know the permissible activity and make economic use of counsel.

The book is the author's interpretation of the subjects covered. It is not intended to constitute legal advice or consulting services. The cases cited are illustrative of the legal principles developed by the courts and their interpretation of the existing statutes. Editing and production schedules prevent research beyond July 1997.

ACKNOWLEDGMENTS

The author is deeply indebted to personnel practitioners, legal associates, clients, and employees for their suggestions and encouragement. Combining the law with the personnel function is a task that involves many different backgrounds and training. Special thanks to the 1,000 or more personnel practitioners and attorneys who attended seminars conducted by the author, sponsored by management associations or educational institutions. The participants' practical suggestions and questions when field-testing in this complicated area were most helpful.

As the late Professor H.G Heneman, Jr., said in the forward of the first edition, "It takes both experience and formal education to be a personnel professional. A book of this kind is best written by one who has studied, taught, and practiced labor law and personnel and industrial relations. The author of this book meets this requirement handsomely. The book's problem-centered approach reads as if written by someone who has been there and who speaks the language of the plant. This approach enlivens and enriches the pages that follow."

Special recognition is given to Debbie Napiorkowski, who pioneered the first edition while carrying her first child. Very special thanks go to Sue Moro, without whom subsequent editions would not have been possible. Her work habits and expertise in the use of the computer made the author's job easier.

The author takes full responsibility for any selection of the wrong case law or legal principles. Reaching the wrong conclusions from often confusing case law and statutes and setting wrong priorities is a risk that the author must accept.

The references are as current, accurate, and authoritative as possible. The unrestricted use of the State of Minnesota Law Library and University of Minnesota Industrial Relation Reference Library was most helpful. The extensive research required by the subject matter would have been impossible without the cooperation of excellent staff from these two libraries.

Kenneth L. Sovereign

CHAPTER

1

MERGING OF THE LAW INTO THE PERSONNEL FUNCTION

In the past four decades there has been considerable restraint on the traditional personnel functions. The law has caused many employers to "play dead" and comply regardless of the effect upon the business. Some employers ignore the law and wait until they get caught. When the enforcement agency moves in, the employer challenges the law, and a lawsuit often results.

Neither reaction is correct. Both reactions will reduce profits and could result in additional legislation that neither the employee nor the employer will like.

The law's encroachment into the personnel office has forced the personnel administrator to consider not only the traditional employee relations consequences but also a new problem of legal implications. That does not mean that man-

agement is restricted in carrying out its function,[1] but it does result in more administrative tasks.

EVOLUTION OF THE PERSONNEL FUNCTION

The personnel function as a part of the organization developed from necessity. Somebody was needed to hire employees, process terminations, expedite paperwork, administer employee

---

[1]Leah H. Maguire, "Employment and Labor Law," *Wayne Law Review,* 42 (1996), 757. Also "Recent Developments in Employment Law (Annual Survey of Tort and Insurance Law)" Robert B. Fitzpatrick and Marlissa S. Brigget. *Tort and Insurance Law Journal,* 30 (1993), 316-339.

insurance, and act as a liaison between management and the employee. Personnel practitioners were originally semiprofessional do-gooders; as organizations became larger, the function grew from an administrative task to one that involved decision making in human relations. The personnel director took a place in the "management cabinet" and was largely responsible for people problems. In this intermediate stage of development, personnel was basically a technical function. As more regulations were passed and human resources became more expensive and important to the organization, the personnel director was regarded as a practical but professionally results-oriented person who worked closely with the chief executive officer on the people aspects of the business. At this stage of development the law began to merge with the personnel function.[2]

MERGING OF THE LAW INTO THE PERSONNEL FUNCTION

The merging of the law into the personnel function was a gradual process, accelerated by enforcement of discrimination laws, federal control of pension plans, welfare problems, and safety regulations, all of which seemed to come into focus in the middle 1980s. With the enactment of several laws dealing with employee relations in the 1960s and 1970s, the personnel function had another stage of development, whereby the law must be considered in almost every decision made by the personnel practitioner. Employee relations laws have had a profound effect on policies and practices of both large and small organizations. Their policies and practices are now subject to an external audit by a government regulatory agency. In order to pass this external audit, personnel administration must be more objective and develop job-related policies.

---

[2]Vida G. Scarpello, James Ledvinka, and Thomas J. Bergmann, *Human Resource Management: Environments and Functions.* (Cincinnati, OH: Southwestern College Publishing, 1995; Robert L. Mathias and John H. Jackson, *Personnel and Human Resource Management,* 6th ed. (St. Paul, MN: West, 1991).

EFFECT OF THE MERGER

It was only a short time ago that the employment manager would hear a familiar phrase from a supervisor: "Don't send me a black because I can't fire him." This was a common belief among supervisors when civil rights legislation was first passed. It was a fear caused by a misunderstanding of the application of the antidiscrimination laws to the workplace. No court of law has ever said that you must hire any person who is not, in management's opinion, the best qualified. No court of law has ever said that you must promote somebody who is not qualified or that you cannot discharge an employee for poor performance.

The law does not say that management has to change the standards of performance required of an employee, but it does say that you cannot discriminate in applying those standards to an individual because of race, sex, color, religion, age, disability, and nationality.[3]

Elimination of Pseudo Practices

Management had many "pseudo" practices that not only were discriminatory but also were ineffective personnel practices. When the author was in graduate school, his professor, Dale Yoder, told the class never to use a test unless there is some assurance that it will predict performance on the job. Twenty-five years later the Supreme Court in *Griggs* v. *Duke Power Co.,* 401 U.S. 424 (1971), told management the same thing. In the interim, many tests that had no relationship to job performance were used to reject applicants. Application forms required answers to questions that were not job related. When a regulatory agency asked the purpose of the question, nobody knew, except that it was on the form that was purchased from a professional organization—another pseudo practice. When a worker was retired, the reason was that he or she was 65. Everybody should retire at 65 regardless of performance or knowledge of the job. When a person was discharged and somebody asked the

---

[3]John S. Donahue and Peter Siegalman, "The Changing Nature of Employment Discrimination Litigation," *Stanford Law Review,* 43 (May 1991), 983.

reason, the answer very often would be "poor performance," but there was no objective measurement of that performance. Often when an employer was questioned under oath how performance was measured, the answer would be that it couldn't be measured except by subjective observation. Some of these practices are the reason for civil rights legislation and lawsuits. As the law moved into the personnel function, these practices were externally audited. Management began to realize that maybe some demands of the regulatory agency were also good personnel practices.

For many years the personnel practitioner was frustrated because there was no professionalization of personnel practitioners. The law moving into the personnel function made great strides in professionalizing this area of management activity, where other efforts have failed. The law forced objectivity. What is wrong in forcing a test to predict success on the job? Why is it wrong for a question on an application form to be job related or to reject subjectivity in the measurement of performance?

Management Resistance

In the chapters that follow, managers and personnel practitioners will be shown how compliance with the law often made the personnel function more useful. The law does not interfere with good management, but it does require a change in practices. It also increases the administrative workload of the personnel function. It is understandable that management often would be hostile to changes necessary to comply with regulatory decisions. This is a normal reaction. Management also resisted the National Labor Relations Act when it became effective in 1938. This resistance will disappear when personnel law is better understood.

The philosophy of top management or its belief concerning the reasonableness of the particular law often influences management's decision on whether the law should be violated. The value of the law is overlooked because of management resistance. Management in the decision-making process seeks legal counsel, but lawyers often differ on the application of the law to a given set of facts. Legal counsel is seldom asked to consider the employee relations consequences of a legal decision; thus the input of the personnel practitioner at this stage of the decision-making process is highly important.

The entry of the law into the personnel function does not mean that personnel administrators must be lawyers, but they must be aware of possible legal implications and permissible activities. Because contemporary personnel administration must consider the legal implications before action is taken, more knowledge of the law is required than in the past.

EDUCATION OF WORKERS AS TO THEIR RIGHTS

The problems that the contemporary personnel practitioner faces today are so much greater than those of two decades ago that often it is difficult for top management to realize it.[4] The government cannot be blamed for this mess; the cause is demographics. The aged are increasing—they want better health care; the young are increasing—they want better education; middle-aged workers are becoming vocal—they want better pensions; criminals are on the rise—they want better prisons.

The change is caused not only by the existence of regulations and laws but also by the worker being better educated about his or her rights and obligations. Most federal laws and regulations promote communication to the employee by requiring the employer to post official notices of employee rights. Many states also have similar posting requirements where federal laws do not apply. These statutes require the regulatory agency to impose a penalty for failure to meet the posting requirements. The regulatory agency will usually supply the poster on request. Posting provisions generally require that the notice be posted in a conspicuous place so as to permit ready observance. For some laws both applicants and employees must be communicated with;

---

[4]Every year more than 64 percent of all employers have at least one complaint filed. See Richard Reminger, "At Risk," *Personnel Journal* 70 (March 1991), 52.

accordingly, the employment or personnel office is the logical place for the postings. The employer who posts next to the time clock or at an exit complies with the requirements of a conspicuous place, but the posting is seldom read. Communications to employees should be placed where the employee will take time to read them, such as in the lunchroom. An entrance, an exit, or a time clock is not usually one of those places.

When the law became a part of the personnel function, as with any merger, new problems were created. At the time of the merger employees were well-educated; for those who wanted more educational opportunities, the state-supported university labor education centers were available.

Worker Education Programs

In addition to communication via government posters, the labor unions have publicized the workers' rights under the laws and regulations in their periodicals and at meetings. They hold training seminars on the law to give their members and leaders information on how to exercise their rights. Labor education centers on university campuses work with labor organizations to provide educational opportunities to union members. (Most universities also have management education centers.) These labor education centers have a full-time staff who work with an advisory committee of union leaders. They develop a curriculum and course material in a wide variety of subjects. The centers are usually supported in part by the legislative budget, the remainder coming from tuition.

Some of the subjects taught in labor education are basic steward training, bargaining for health care, union leadership, discrimination and harassment, video production, and workers' compensation.

A function of labor education centers at universities is to communicate to the union membership what their rights are under the law. Each year over 200 union members will attend these classes on a given campus.[5]

Legal Advertising

The Supreme Court in 1977[6] held that lawyers could not be prevented from advertising. Since then there has been a rise in the use of the media to encourage the public to see a lawyer about any problem from personal injury to a fight with a spouse. Before 1983, 13 percent of the lawyers advertised; by 1995,[7] more than 25 percent were advertising. Lawyers who do not advertise state that it is unprofessional and that they have enough work without it.[8]

The rapid increase in advertising of legal services indicates that it must work. The employee hears over the radio or on television that he or she can consult a lawyer about any problem without paying a fee. This increases lawsuits. In the past, employees who had claims of potential employer liability would often refrain from seeing a lawyer because they were not sure how good a case they had or how much it would cost. They didn't want to pay an unknown fee to the lawyer for talking about their case. With the advent of advertising free legal assessment, there is bound to be an increase in litigation.

The media, notice-posting requirements, lawyer advertising, labor education centers, and the high level of education among the workers have increased lawsuits. An employee who knows his or her rights is more likely to sue than the less-educated employee of the past, although some of the statutes granting those rights have existed for many years.

The material in this text may appear to be written from the employer's point of view. The reader must remember that a right or remedy the employer has, the employee or union often has. In many situations, the term *employer* is synonymous with *union*.

There are several reasons why employees file lawsuits against their employers according to the case law. The reasons are:

---

[5]*Union Leadership Academy* (Labor Education Service, University of Minnesota, 1992–93). Also 1995-96.

[6]*Bates* v. *State Bar of Arizona,* 97 S.Ct. 2691, 433 U.S. 384 (1977).

[7]Some law firms' advertising budgets are over $900,000 a year.

[8]Paul McEnroe, "Lawyer Advertising—Making a Fool of Ourselves," *Bench & Bar of Minnesota,* February 1992, p. 16.

1. Secrecy in hiring and promotion practices. Failure to inform interested employees of a vacancy or to list the requirements of vacant jobs.
2. Playing favorites, but not violating the law. Prejudices, likes, or dislikes of the supervisor.
3. Subjective or inaccurate performance appraisals. Some employers never tell the employee what level of performance is expected.
4. Failure to treat employees as humans. This not only creates litigation but fails to motivate the employee to work for the good of the organization. It is difficult to work for somebody who is not fair or considerate.

RELATIONSHIP OF PERSONNEL PROBLEMS TO LEGAL PROBLEMS

Problems Encountered in Personnel Administration

The personnel practitioner may be aware of the legal consequences of an employment decision, but often other members of management are not. Management is sometimes hostile to the changes necessary to comply with government regulations. Hostile management considers them interference with employment decisions. It is the duty of the manager to make other managers aware of the legal consequences of the regulations and applicable laws and obtain legal counsel when necessary. As the personnel function of management attempts to solve legal problems, solutions must be weighed in light of employee relations consequences. The hypothetical situations shown in Exhibit 1-1 point out the dilemma of the personnel practitioner.

Whether the solutions of these problems should be based on legal considerations or employee relations considerations or both depends on the law and factual situations:

1. Do the facts fit into a well-established principle of law, or is this a gray area, where there is a choice?
2. Is the employee relations consequence so severe that it is worth the cost of challenging the law to get a court interpretation or hope the employee will not file a lawsuit?
3. What are the problems if the employer complies?

In the past, determinations in employment decisions were made on instinct and had no basis except a certainty by the decision maker. They would be accepted by management as right.

The examples in Exhibit 1-1 point out that such decisions can, and often do, have legal consequences. When such a decision was made in the past, only management reviewed it. Now there is an external audit of policies and procedures.

Employee relations consequences are a consideration only if there is uncertainty about the interpretation of the statute or regulation. Management is responsible for compliance where there is no doubt about interpretation. The reasonableness of the statute or regulation also affects top management's decision on whether to challenge the law. The personnel practitioner's opinion of whether the company can live with the law must be considered. The efficient employment of human resources demands that solutions be found to employee relations problems that do not result in lawsuits.

Exposure to a Lawsuit

Throughout this book the text will refer to *exposure* to a lawsuit. Nothing can stop an employee from seeking a lawyer to represent him or her in a lawsuit. However, if the facts of the case show that the employee has a good chance of winning, the lawyer will take the case on a contingency (usually one third of what is collected). If the facts show it will be a difficult case to win, the lawyer either will refuse to take the case or will demand an up-front fee before taking it.

Exposure as used in this book means that the employer's actions have developed facts that give the employee a good chance of winning. The lawyer will take it on a contingency fee and inflict the legal and court costs on the employer.

When the policies and procedures of the employer are legally in place, there is little chance of winning. This fact causes the lawyer to demand a fee. There will not be a lawsuit because the employee will not take the risk of losing and paying a fee. This is common in discharge cases where the employee's income has stopped. The only person who wins a lawsuit is the person who avoids it.

EXHIBIT 1-1   *A Personnel Practitioner's Day*

Situation	An employee has been dating a co-worker for two years. Production manager instructs both to cease dating in off-duty hours. They refuse. No evidence that relationship interfered with their work. Both are discharged. Female files a lawsuit—discharged for invasion of privacy.
Legal considerations	Case law supports company right to stop off-duty dating. Courts say that employer problems with nepotism stronger than employees' privacy.
Employee relations considerations	What harm is there in allowing cupid in the workplace? May lose two well-trained workers. Relationship does not affect their work, but may in the future.
Situation	Worker discharged for excessive absenteeism. Caused by work-related injury. Sues—retaliation for filing a workers' compensation claim.
Legal considerations	Employer must show discharge was not for filing a workers' compensation claim, but for absenteeism. May legally discharge for excessive absenteeism although due to work-related injury. Separate remedies.
Employee relations considerations	Makes the safety program a police action. Defeats the no-fault liability concept of workers' compensation. Poor public relations. Company a big cruel bear. Would cause a union problem if organized.
Situation	Worker is intoxicated on the job. Manager pours him in his car. While driving home worker has an accident. Gets a drunken driving ticket. Causes a fatal injury to a little girl. Parents sue the company for allowing worker to drive home intoxicated.
Legal considerations	Majority rule is that company is not liable. An activity outside work site. Same result if employee became intoxicated at a company-sponsored sales meeting where company furnished the liquor.
Employee relations considerations	It was the company's fault that the little girl was killed. Could have been avoided if they hired a taxi. Does company have a conscience? Legally correct to drink liquor on company time?
Situation	Employee has AIDS, and co-workers refuse to work with him. They fear contracting the disease.
Legal considerations	Employee with AIDS in the protected class. Considered handicap under federal and most state laws. Workers can strike, although nonunion, but company can hire permanent replacements.
Employee relations considerations	Education is only legal remedy. Must convince workers medically there is no chance of contracting AIDS. Company must have a position statement that explains what they will do on a case when problems occur. Must respect rights of both parties.

Living Economically with the Law

The employer must prevent exposure to lawsuits by putting policies and practices legally in place so the employee is discouraged from starting a lawsuit.[9] Once the lawsuit is started it is too late, because management time and legal fees have been expended. The personnel practitioner must find a way to communicate to operating management that it may not have a full range of choices about how it deals with employees.

However, the manager is not prevented from acting in the best interests of the organization.

Changing Personnel Practices

The use of such terms as *probationary period, permanent employee, merit increases, white collar, gold collar, steel collar, annual salary* in a job offer, and *personality problems* on the termination form now causes serious exposure to a lawsuit. The use of these terms never did fit into good professional human resource management.

Personnel administrators are faced with an increasing number of seemingly conflicting legal and employee relations implications. Therefore, they must have enough knowledge of the law to be

---

[9]The author knew the boss was in violation. He wrote a memo and forgot about it after placing it in the files. The next day the law was complied with.

EXHIBIT 1-2

> Statute → Enforcement agency → Agency goes beyond statutory authority → The challenge
> by management → for Enforcement agency to comply with statute

aware of the legal implications and when to seek legal counsel.

A vital part of personnel administration involves advising management of the consequences of failure to apply the law as interpreted by a regulatory agency. As new laws have been enacted and government agencies created to enforce them, challengeable gray areas have been created.

The many uncertainties in the law have resulted from regulatory agencies issuing guidelines or interpretative bulletins that are challenged as shown in Exhibit 1-2.

To comply with or challenge new laws and guidelines that are not judicially interpreted is a business decision. The personnel practitioner, with the assistance of legal counsel, must advise the management of the alternatives. Costs and employee relations have to be balanced with the effect upon the operation.

ESTABLISHMENT OF WRITTEN POLICIES

The law has merged with the personnel function, causing a need for personnel administration to become more legally aware. The law demands more exactness when dealing with people. The best policy is no policy at all, but unfortunately this is no longer advisable or realistic. The legal approach is seldom the best approach when solving people problems. However, courts demand that we become more legal and have more policy. This is essential if the employer is to be protected from lawsuits.

The term *policy manual* as used in the text is synonymous with the term *handbook*. Legally they are the same. Some employers have both, although it is not necessary. This is no problem legally unless they conflict.

In our litigation-happy society it is necessary to have more policy to prevent exposure to lawsuits.

It is essential to have policies on sexual harassment, discharge, searches, and, if needed, on drug testing and life-threatening diseases.[10]

When the manager reads about a large jury award, the first reaction is to have more policy to prevent such an award. This approach is not always the answer. A small organization may need very little policy. If the appeal period has not expired, the decision could still be reversed. The cherished informal approach in dealing with employees in small companies sometimes creates more problems than it solves. Some policy may be necessary to correct the balance. A policy manual should be drafted if management decides to become more formal. The policy manual should be drafted only when it becomes necessary because of the increased number or frequency of people problems.

How Much or How Little Policy?

The first objective in reviewing existing policies or writing new ones is to make them as short, as unambiguous, and as simple as possible. These criteria are important from both legal and employee relations standpoints. If you include too much, the policy will not be followed by even the most conscientious managers. It also runs the risk of lawsuits that the policy was intended to avoid. If you have too little detail, you may also invite litigation to interpret the meaning of the statement.

It is not uncommon for managers to use policy to justify a position that already has been decided upon. They may ignore a policy that they do not like. Neither approach should be encouraged. In most small organizations only a few specific policies are necessary to avoid lawsuits, unless a compelling operating need or a statute requires more.

---

[10]These will be discussed in subsequent chapters.

Drafting a Policy Manual or Handbook

As a practical matter the statements in a policy manual should be limited to those employment-related situations where uniform administration is necessary to avoid lawsuits. For example, when one department requires employees to sign out when leaving the facility during meal periods and another department in the same organization does not, the immediate consequences may be minimal. However, if one department has a different leave of absence policy from that of another—possibly because the decision has been left up to the supervisors—the exposure to litigation under the discrimination laws may be serious and a policy may be necessary.

The real test for deciding whether you should have a policy in a given area is whether you can give an affirmative answer to the following questions:

1. Does the policy aid in solution of people problems?
2. Is the policy absolutely necessary for the smooth and efficient operation of the organization?
3. Are you seriously exposed to lawsuits or frequent employee relations problems if you do not have a policy?

The first two questions can be answered on the basis of past problems that arose because of the lack of policy.

The answer to the third question is not as simple. An element of uncertainty always surrounds dealing with possible legal considerations. Certain policies may be necessary for selected job categories, such as antitrust violation restrictions for sales-related jobs, and conflict of interest policies.

Often the policy manual becomes the repository for benefits, such as vacations and severance pay. These are benefits that tell employees what they have a right to expect. They belong in a separate book—not in the policy manual or handbook. In determining what should be communicated to employees, management should keep in mind that once the communication is issued, it can't be changed immediately. Employees have a right to depend upon the statement. This is not to say that policy cannot be changed, but change must come before the fact. For example, if the organization is threatened with unionization, it legally is too late to communicate changes after the union activity commences.

To comply with the various discrimination laws and with the federal Wage-Hour Law and other federal statutes, certain written policies are necessary. Present practices may be in conflict with various state or local laws. The organization may have grown to the point where managers and supervisors need guidance to ensure uniform administration of procedures in dealing with employees.

One employer included a discussion of severance pay in a policy manual drafted in 1962. In 1971, the manual was changed. The court held that the obligation did not cease upon the modification in 1971 but that severance pay accrued on a different basis from 1971 on.[11]

This case also illustrates the danger of having a policy on severance pay. Why not give severance pay as the occasion arises? That procedure allows management to retain its flexibility. Some selling points may be lost in not telling the employees what a fine organization they are working for, and lack of a policy statement may cause some difficulty in recruiting. But other ways can be found to emphasize good working conditions without granting the employee a right that can be the basis for a lawsuit later.[12] A policy on a matter such as severance pay should not be put in writing unless no other alternative exists. Management must be willing to accept the problems that may result.

Drafting Policy Manuals or Handbooks

Management should start with the assumption that the best policy is no policy at all. When communications become necessary, a decision should be made: Should it be a manual or a guideline? A communicated manual can be interpreted by the employee as a contract. A guideline for supervisors can be enforced by

---

[11]*Johnson* v. *Allied Stores Corp.,* 679 P.2d 640 (Idaho 1984).

[12]Why tell the employees what the company will do for them? Just do it.

selected discipline. Statutes and case law may limit flexibility and informality contrary to the best interests of the organization.

Top management should always make one person responsible for original drafting. A committee should be appointed to work on revisions. A deadline for completion should be set. If a deadline is not set, the manual will seldom get completed before it is too late to avoid a lawsuit.

Recommendations for Drafting Policies

1. Have a written policy only for those procedures that involve substantial legal exposure and must be uniformly enforced throughout your organization.

Decide what you want the policy to accomplish. Is it intended to outline standard operating procedures? Is it an aid to managers in solving people problems or handling interdepartmental relationships? Is it a communication from management about what must be done in certain situations? Or is it intended to solve most of the employee problems?

2. Polices affecting people can be relatively general, but others must be procedure oriented.

Many personnel practitioners believe that statements in policy manuals should be limited to those relating to people. All other matters should be covered by statements in an internal procedures manual. From a legal point of view this approach has many desirable features.

A common mistake of some practitioners is to go to a seminar or purchase a "how to" book and then proceed to copy policies written by professionals. Those with such an inclination might look at the apparent inverse correlation between the number of policies and the success of the organization.

Policies that are not uniformly administered, or that are used in place of intelligent management, are worse than no policies at all. Those who have the responsibility for writing policy manuals must be aware of pitfalls. The drafting committee or the approving authority cannot know how the policy will work until it is field tested.

3. Make the proposed policy an internal guideline before stating it as policy and communicating it to the employees.

The legal difference between an internal guideline and a policy is that an internal guideline tells management what they should do about a problem. A policy, after it is communicated, tells employees what they can expect management to do. The policy may become a contract. When management tells employees something, the employees have a legal right to depend upon management to follow through. It becomes a condition of employment that the employee considers when deciding to seek employment elsewhere or to remain with the present employer.

4. Make every policy as flexible as possible. Provide an escape hatch as wide as possible. Stay within the legal limits and organizational objectives.

This statement might sound like double-talk at first, and an example might help in clarification. Suppose that a supervisor decides to do something about the poor quality of the output. The supervisor announces a policy of progressive discipline. The first offense will result in a written warning, the second in a layoff, and the third in discharge. After the warning and discipline, an employee turns in a poor-quality product for the third time. The policy calls for discharge. The supervisor faces a situation where one operator is ill and another is on vacation. If the employee is discharged as the policy requires, no one will be available to run the machine. The supervisor has to meet a deadline for an important customer.

The dilemma could have been avoided if the statement had been more flexible for the third offense. It might have stated that severe disciplinary action would be given, up to and including discharge.

Personnel practitioners who are strict constructionists might say that a flexible statement is not definite enough. Such a policy would not stand up under judicial scrutiny. The courts would not agree. Subjectivity is not illegal per se if objective standards are involved, according to case law.

EXHIBIT 1-3

> This manual contains the most recent operating and staff policies for ABC company. I urge you to review them so that if you have any questions you can put them through the proper channels. I hope you will find this policy manual useful in carrying out your responsibilities.

Where management often goes astray in writing policies is in attempting to find easy ways to solve people problems. Too often the result is that some time after the policy is written, they find that there is no easy way to avoid people problems and still be legally sound.

5. Keep the language simple and nonlegal. Such terms as "we have the right to" when you already have the right may raise a question about whether you are giving away part of the right or retaining part of it. Similarly if you state that "exceptions may be made for," you raise unnecessary questions. In the absence of a statement that "there will be no exceptions," you imply that you can make them. If exceptions are necessary, you do not need a policy to make them. Do it. Normally this does not set a precedent.

6. Clear, concise, and straightforward wording with few syllables is essential. All persons the policy affects must understand it. Nothing is more damaging to effectiveness than a disagreement over what the statement means.

7. Indicate that the authority is coming from top management and that the policy is not changing this. When you start telling what management will do, you open exposure to lawsuits. A policy statement is not a union contract.

Once the few policies are drafted, they should be reviewed by upper management and then revised on the basis of the comments received. The second draft should be reviewed at the next level of management and again revised. The process should be repeated on a step-by-step basis until everyone from top management to the first-line supervisors has had an opportunity to review and contribute to the policies.

The next step is to "field-test" the statements for a period of time as guidelines before they are finally adopted as policy. It is recognized that this is not always possible. This development process is often necessary to make sure that they have as much acceptance as possible. During the entire review and testing, the substance of the statements as decided by top management will probably not be changed, although the wording may be.

Revision of Present Polices

In many cases policies already exist in some form. However, to comply with the laws and court decisions, revision is necessary. Present policies may be in conflict with state or federal laws, the company may have been organized by a union since the last policy was written, or the organizational structure may have changed. Whatever the reason, the important point to remember is that the change should not become effective for a period of time. The employee should always be allowed enough time to look for a new job if he or she does not like the new conditions imposed by revisions. This avoids exposure to a charge of invasion of privacy. Where there is a union, employees have a right to challenge the reasonableness of the policy.

ESSENTIAL PROCEDURES TO AVOID EXPOSURE TO LAWSUITS

Have counsel review the document and give a legal opinion, not a personal belief. This is good defensive procedure. It shows that the employer made a good faith effort to draft a policy that is legal, to avoid a lawsuit. A key question here is the willingness of management to enforce the policy. Management must make a decision that it is going to do so. The first step in enforceability is a clear statement from top management. All too often, this statement has a tone that seems to ask for cooperation rather than one of giving direction and indicating an intention of enforcement. Exhibit 1-3 is language that merely asks for cooperation. It is

EXHIBIT 1-4

> The purpose of these rules is to clearly inform you of the terms and conditions of employment that we all are required to work under. These rules will also promote our desired customer image by the behavior and appearance of our personnel.

difficult to enforce because it indicates that compliance is voluntary.[13]

This statement from the CEO does not imply that management will enforce the policies. Instead it seems to allow the managers to enforce the policies if they wish to do so. This approach creates the greatest possible exposure to lawsuits. The managers who do enforce the policies expose those who do not. A manual with this type of statement from the CEO is merely a guideline. It should not be communicated to the employees involved. Doing so opens the possibility that the manual will be considered a contract.[14]

Assert in the manual that top management will use its authority to support and enforce the provisions of the manual. State strongly what is expected of the employees. As soon as the manual states what management will do for the employees, there is exposure to a lawsuit.[15] Exhibit 1-4 reflects language that not only communicates, but also is enforceable.

Avoiding violations of antidiscrimination laws does not necessarily require a written policy. Any employer can follow a nondiscriminatory course without one. Policies that cannot—or will not—be enforced should not be communicated to employees. Management may wish to establish internal procedures that managers may follow or not, depending upon the circumstances and the direction of their superiors. These procedures may be written, and inevitably some of them may come into the hands of employees other than the managers for whom they were intended. The important point is that employees would not be

permitted to depend upon them as conditions of employment. In one typical case, the discharge of the employee was unquestionably justified, but the written policy in the handbook was not followed, and as a result the employee was awarded damages.[16]

All manuals or handbooks should have a sign-off statement by the employee whereby it is agreed that the manual or handbook will be followed and that its provisions are understood. Exhibit 1-5 contains some recommended wording.

Since John Marshall was chief justice of the Supreme Court (1801), the U.S. judicial system has attempted to fit the Constitution into contemporary economic and social situations. This is a momentous task for the courts, yet it is no more difficult than that faced by management in trying to write policies that will fit all employees.

The policy often does not fit the individual employee or the facts surrounding the specific situation. As a result, personnel practitioners are always bumping the employee's head on the policy doorway as they attempt to push through. The law does not interfere with the end result of effective personnel administration; however, it does require some extra caution in many areas. The drafting or revision of policies is one of them.

IS DIVERSITY A CAN OF WORMS?

An Affirmative Action (AA) program is not only the right thing to improve the bottom line, but the government says if you are to get along with us you had better have one. The employer does not have the luxury of ignoring over 80 percent of the gainfully employed. However, companies have hired people who were not qualified in order to

---

[13]See W. Hartsfield, "How to Write Your Employee Handbook" (Madison, CT: Business & Legal Reports, Inc., 1991), Sect. 110–1104.

[14]Also, *Morton v. Care Marketing,* 1994 U.S. Appl. (US 5830)

[15]Tell them not what the company will do for them, but what they will do for the company.

[16]*Pine River State Bank* v. *Richard F. Mettille Sr.,* 333 N.W. 2d 622 (Minn. 1983).

EXHIBIT 1-5

I, _____ , have read, understand, and have in my possession the company's policies and procedures. I agree to abide by policies in the manual and if there is at any time something that I do not understand I agree to ask a company representative.

Signature _____   SS# _____

Date _____

---

satisfy their AA programs. There is no law that states you must hire someone who is not qualified to do the work. The "in" companies all had AA programs, and the literature was full of how to start and complete an AA program. Diversity is a by-product of the AA program.

To set aside one group of persons in the workforce to be trained is no more right than the City of Richmond setting aside contracts to be awarded to minorities. Now (1996), not much is seen about AA programs, but one cannot pick up a management magazine and not see something about diversity.

This is not to say that one should not recognize diversity, but what about merit? What difference does the color of skin make if the person can do the job? To be sure, there are cultural differences that the manager has to contend with, but who said that the manager's job was easy?[17] There has to be some intensive training programs for the diverse workforce.[18] Displacement of the worker by technology also demands training. Training of one group demands different training from another group. The point is that diversity is overplayed. Other than considerations of consumer demands and relationship between individuals to get a better bottom line, hire or train qualified people and forget diversity. Management has enough problems without creating more.

Consumer Considerations

The consumer demand is radically changing. Women spend over 85 percent of the consumer dollar. Older Americans control more than 50 percent of all spendable dollars and discretionary income, and spend more than $800 billion annually. According to the American Management Association, over 50 percent of companies will increase their diversity programs, but if they keep the bottom line on the back burner, they will fail. By the year 2000, African-Americans, Hispanics, and Asian-Americans will spend over $600 billion annually. The demographics of the new American workforce will change consumer demand. The white non-Hispanic will still dominate the workforce, but their numbers will be reduced by 2005. Women will enter the workforce in increasing numbers. These are figures that cannot be ignored by an aggressive company. Some companies are convinced that minorities are better employees than nonminorities, and they may be for that company. If so, hire and train them.

Diversity within the company will be necessary to sell the products. From this aspect diversity initiatives are important. Over 50 percent of companies have diversity training. The diversity consumer must be satisfied. The more diverse the market becomes, the greater the sensitivity to tastes and differences. Management can learn about the consumer from the cultural differences in the workforce. The consumer expects the people they do business with to have like values. This was not the case in 1952. The diversity was

---

[17]Like the story of the patient who went to the doctor for a physical. Doctor to patient, "You are in good shape. How old was your father when he died?" Patient to doctor, "Who said he was dead?" Doctor to patient, "How old was your grandfather when he died?" Patient to doctor, "Who said he was dead – he's going to be married next week." Doctor to patient, "Why would he want to get married at his age?" Patient to doctor, "Who said he wants to?"

[18]*Personnel Journal*, Aug 1991, pp. 60-65.

always there, but it is being exercised more and more. It is a business matter to have a diverse workforce.

When focusing only on diversity, the emphasis is in the wrong place. If a person cannot do the job, get or train someone who can. The employer is there to make money, not institute a social change. If a person remembers this, there will not be trouble with antidiscrimination laws as long as it can be proven that the profit motive was the reason for employer actions.

2

EXPLANATION OF THE COURT STRUCTURE

Structure of the Federal Courts
Supreme Court
Explanation of Legal Documents
Increase in Litigation
Attorney Fees—Reasonable or Unreasonable?
Use of Legal Counsel
Making A Risk Analysis

It is important for the reader to know a little about the court structure for two reasons. When the attorney talks to management about a procedure, management will have some idea of what he or she is talking about, and the reasonable cost and quality of service are more easily determined. Furthermore, when management receives a legal document it will know what to do with it.

The person in charge of personnel records will often receive a legal document and do exactly what the documents say, without consulting an attorney. Sometimes this is correct; other times it is not. When management receives a legal document the first thing to be done is to call an attorney.

One of the problems created when the law moved into the personnel function is the overreaction of management when it is reported in the news media that a company of 50 employees had to pay a million dollars in damages for a wrongful discharge. The CEO immediately calls his lawyer and wants some guidance to be certain the company is not exposed to any liability but will still be permitted to discharge undesirable employees. The mistake the CEO makes is that this is only a decision of a lower court (unless it is a Supreme Court decision) and there are two more chances that the decision will be reversed on appeal.

STRUCTURE OF THE FEDERAL COURTS

The following exhibit shows the court structure for both state and federal government.

Federal	State
District Court	District Court
Appeals Court	Appeals Court
Supreme Court	Supreme Court

The Supreme Court in both federal and state structure is the last court of appeal.

Some statutes allow an administrative ruling to be appealed. If so, most of them provide the district court to hear the matter first, then move up the ladder. Some statutes allow the appellate court or Supreme Court to hear the dispute, thus omitting the lower courts.[1]

The federal courts of the United States are structured at three levels: district court, appellate court, and Supreme Court. The district court is where the case starts. All the evidence is recorded and witnesses testify. In certain cases the jury will participate, while in other cases the judge makes the decision. The federal district court decisions are cited in this text as West's Federal Supplement Reports. (Sometimes they are cited as, for example, *1995 D.C. Mont. Lexis 560.)* An example of citation would be 560 F. Supp. 820 (D.C. Mont. 1993). 560 is the volume number, F. Supp. is Federal Supplement Reports, and 820 is the page number. D.C. Mont. is the district court of Montana where the case was decided, and 1995 is the year of the decision.

Although district court decisions are important, they are not considered precedent setting. If not appealed, they apply only to the area where the court has jurisdiction. The employer must decide, after consulting an attorney, whether the district court decision necessitates changing a policy.

Within a certain time after a decision is rendered (usually 30 days), either party may appeal the decision to the next higher court, which must consider the appeal. It is called the appellate court and considers whether the decision of the lower court was proper as to the law and the facts presented. The appellate court will usually not hear new evidence. These cases are cited in this text as __F.2d__ (5th Cir. 1993). The F.2d stands for West's Publishing Federal Reporter 2d series, and the 5th Circuit is where the case was decided. (Lexis is another reporting system, similar to West, so it would cite as 1993 US App. Lexis ___.) There are 11 circuit courts of appeal in the United States, and a Federal Court (9 Federal Courts) which are divided into geographic areas. The D.C. Circuit is the 12th and has jurisdiction over the entire country. Most lawyers respect circuit court opinions because less than 20 percent are appealed to the U.S. Supreme Court (the highest court in the system), which hears a little over 1 percent of the appeals filed.

SUPREME COURT

The Supreme Court does not have to grant review of the appellate court decision (the petition for review is called a writ of certiorari). If the Supreme Court refuses to review, the decision of the appellate court becomes the law in the circuit where it was decided. The Supreme Court will not hear any new evidence but will make its decision based on the oral arguments, case law, statutes, and legal reasoning of the lower courts. Both the appellate court and the Supreme Court review whether the rules of procedure were followed in the district court.

All federal judges are appointed for life by the president with the consent of the Senate. Presidents tend to appoint judges of their own political philosophy, so one president in office may appoint most of the judges in a certain court and another president of a different philosophy may appoint those in a higher court. Often the philosophy influences the interpretation of the law. As a result upper courts will often reverse lower courts.

Employment law generated but a handful of decisions during the Court's 1994 term, unlike 10 years before when employment law cases figured prominently in term after term.[2]

---

[1]See *Wicken* v. *Morris,* 523 N.W. 2d 415 (Minn. 1995). Also *Malley* v. *Ulland Bros.,* 529 N.W. 2d 735 (Minn. Ct. App. 1995), MSA 26 et seq. as amended in 1995.

[2]See Eileen Kaufman, "Employment Discrimination: Recent Developments in the Supreme Court," *Touro Law Review,* 12 (1996), 389. Also Ramona Mariana, "Student survey. Labor law." *Villanova Law Review,* 40 (1995), 957.

Most state courts have basically the same structure as the federal, only they interpret the state laws. The court where the case starts is the state district court; then there is the appellate court and the state Supreme Court. As in the federal system, the appellate court must consider the appeals from the district court, but the Supreme Court can decide what cases it will hear.[3]

EXPLANATION OF LEGAL DOCUMENTS

The personnel executive should become familiar with the basic legal terms. Often service of court proceedings against the company is made to the persons in the personnel office when the matter involves employees.

Most legal documents have a time limit in which they have to be acted on; it is highly important that the documents are expedited promptly. Failure to act within the time limits can result in liability by default or other serious legal consequences. In all legal documents the time limits are clearly stated. The court serving the papers and the attorneys involved are clearly stated on the documents.

Interrogatories. Interrogatories are a set or series of written questions served on one party in a proceeding. The purpose is a factual examination of a prospective witness. They are used mostly in pretrial discovery to obtain information, to aid the attorney in preparing the case, and to help in selecting witnesses.

The personnel practitioner will sometimes receive the interrogatories from an opposing attorney to obtain information about employees. An attorney should always review the information before it is released. Answers to interrogatory questions are not done under oath but are often used as a basis for questions that are answered under oath. Answers can also determine how the attorney will try the case.

---

[3]The employment law output of the 1996 term included two cases under Title VII of the 1964 Civil Rights Act, and one case under the Fair Labor Standards Act.

The request for interrogatories comes directly from the attorney requesting them; they do not need court approval unless objected to by the opposing party.

Exhibit 2-1 is an interrogatory served on a company where the personnel department would supply the answers. In the interest of brevity, only enough questions are included to show a typical interrogatory.

1. Describe the nature of the supervision of your premises employed to maintain control over employees on the job, in the cafeterias, and in any other areas of the premises to which the employees have access.
2. Had you received any complaints in 1992 by nonunion workers that they were being harassed by union workers?
3. If the answer to interrogatory No. 2 is yes, identify all persons who made such complaints.
4. Did any security unit, the foreman, or any other of your employees investigate such complaints?

Deposition. The deposition is a pretrial discovery procedure whereby the testimony of a witness is taken outside of open court, pursuant to permission by the court to take testimony from a witness.

Most questions are based on, but not restricted to, the interrogatories. A deposition differs from interrogatories in that it is under oath and it is used under certain conditions in court proceedings for questioning the witness.

When a deposition is taken, it is contemplated that the person will be a witness in the trial, but this is not always the case.

When an employee is requested to give a deposition, often there is a sense of insecurity; although the other attorneys may be present, the employee requests the legal counsel from the company to be present.

This is a policy matter for management and legal counsel to determine. Some companies consider it good employee relations to give security to an employee when giving a deposition; others feel that the presence of one attorney representing the employee's interest is enough.

Subpoena. The subpoena is an order directed to a certain person to appear at a certain time and

EXHIBIT 2-1

| STATE OF _____ | DISTRICT COURT |
| COUNTY OF _____ | SECOND JUDICIAL DISTRICT |

LEO SMITH,　　　　　　　　　　)
　　　　　　　　　　　　　　　)
　　　　　Plantiff,　　　　　　)
　　　　　　　　　　　　　　　)
　　　v.　　　　　　　　　　　)　INTERROGATORIES
　　　　　　　　　　　　　　　)
ABC COMPANY　　　　　　　　　)
　　　　　　　　　　　　　　　)
　　　　　Defendant.　　　　　)

TO: DEFENDANT ABC COMPANY AND ITS ATTORNEY JOHN ROE,
(ATTORNEY'S ADDRESS)

　　　PLEASE TAKE NOTICE that Plaintiff, Leo Smith, requests, pursuant to Rule 33 of the Rules of Civil Procedure, that the Defendant ABC Company answer the following Interrogatories within the time prescribed by law. These Interrogatories shall be deemed continuing in nature and should the answers require modification or supplementation it is demanded that you so advise Plaintiff and his attorney.

DEFINITIONS

　　　Unless conclusively altered by the context of a specific Interrogatory, the following definitions are to be considered to apply to all the Interrogatories contained herein.

　　　A.　　You and Your means ABC Company, present and former directors, officers, employees, attorneys, agents, representatives, and any and all other persons, firms, corporations, or entities acting or purporting to act on behalf of ABC Company.

　　　B.　　Identify or Identification
　　　　　1.　　When used in reference to a person, means her or his:
　　　　　　　a.　　Full name
　　　　　　　b.　　Present or last known residence address
　　　　　　　c.　　Position and job description at the time in question

INTERROGATORIES

1. Describe the nature of the supervision of your premises employed to maintain control over employees on the job, in the cafeterias, and in any other areas of the premises to which the employees have access.
2. Had you received any complaints in 1992 by nonunion workers that they were being harassed by union workers?
3. If the answer to interrogatory No. 2 is yes, identify all persons who made such complaints.
4. Did any security unit, the foreman, or any other of your employees investigate such complaints?

LAW OFFICES OF RICHARD ANDERSON

By _____
　　Richard Anderson
　　(Address)
　　(Telephone)

Dated _____

give testimony on a certain matter.[4] The most common subpoena in the personnel department is to appear and bring all documents and written materials related to the subject matter of the case. This is called a subpoena duces tecum. Often the records are all that the attorney wants. Production of the records satisfies the subpoena. It is not necessary for the person in charge of the records to testify. However, permission from the attorney signing the subpoena not to appear is required. When receiving a subpoena duces tecum, the attorney requesting the documents should always be asked whether only the records are wanted or whether the person subpoenaed has to testify. A lot of time will be saved if only the documents must be produced. Also, it is not advisable for the personnel practitioner to appear in the courtroom and be called as a witness. He or she will be subject to cross-examination. Any personnel document marked confidential, as between company counsel and the employee, need not be produced.

Exhibit 2-2 is a typical subpoena duces tecum, often received in workers' compensation and divorce suits. Subpoena duces tecum is also used in criminal proceedings.

Summons. A summons is an order served on the defendant to appear in court, to give an answer within a specified time. The nature of the lawsuit is stated in the complaint.

It is important to note the time and date when the summons is received because the answer must be within a specified time (usually 20 or 30 days).

Complaint. A complaint in a civil proceeding is the first or initial pleading by the plaintiff. The complaint is usually served with the summons. Under the rules of civil procedure, it must contain certain information about the case, such as the alleged wrong, the names of the parties, county and name of the court where the action is brought, and relief sought. The complaint also states why the defendant is being sued, and the relief requested by the plaintiff.

The personnel department should not respond to a complaint but refer it to legal counsel.

---

[4]*Black's Law Dictionary* 6th ed. (St. Paul, MN: West, 1990) p. 1026.

INCREASE IN LITIGATION

The entry of the law into the management function is not a phenomenon particular to the personnel function, but it is indicative of the growth of law in all business and social activities. Beginning in the early 1970s there was a growing concern for people to be protected legally from every problem, even from their own gullibility. Litigation has been growing so fast that it is difficult to know the total number of pending cases on the dockets of the courts. The unfriendly stigma of a lawsuit has almost disappeared. Doctors are sued by patients, lawyers by clients, parents by their children; brothers sue brothers and sellers sue their customers. As the mother said to the father, "If I make Johnny eat his spinach, he will sue us." Social legislation such as antidiscrimination laws, the Occupational Safety and Health Act, the Civil Rights Act of 1991, the Employee Retirement Insurance Act, the Immigration Reform and Control Act, Consolidated Omnibus Budget Reconciliation Act, and Americans with Disabilities Act has given added legal opportunities to individuals never before experienced in judicial history. The alphabet soup of government regulatory agencies creates a thriving climate for the litigation-happy individual.

When to Use Legal Counsel

When legal documents require an answer, they should be referred to legal counsel. Sometimes these documents can be interpreted as admitting liability, which should never be admitted without advice of counsel. Once liability is admitted or implied, there is nothing left to mitigate. The person is at the mercy of the court or regulatory agency.

Written agreements that can be interpreted as enforceable contracts should be either drafted or reviewed by an attorney. If a lay person drafts a contract, it is more likely to be challenged. In the event of latent liability, the drafter is protected if the contract is reviewed by an attorney. One should not sign a document without understanding the terms or having it explained by counsel. When the corporation is involved, there should be some control on who has authority to sign, because any

EXHIBIT 2-2

No. 2072—Subpoena Duces Tecum. (Rev. 1980)

State of Minnesota,

County of .... Smithson ....

DISTRICT COURT

.... 1st .... *Judicial District*

.... John Doe ....

....

Plaintiff ....

.... vs. ....

.... Homer Smith ....

....

Defendant ....

SUBPOENA
DUCES TECUM

THE STATE OF MINNESOTA TO .... ABC Corp., Milltown, Minnesota .... :

You are hereby commanded to appear in the above named court at the Court House, in the
County .... *of* .... Smithson .... *, on the* .... 22nd ....
day of .... August .... *, 19* 92 *, at* .... 9:00 .... *o'clock* .... *fore* .... *noon, then and*
there to testify on behalf of .... John Doe .... *in*
above entitled proceeding.

You are further directed and commanded to bring with you the following papers and documents
now in your possession or under your control, viz.:

All Personnel Records, including wages paid during the last two years,

days absent during said period, all medical records and work performance

records and appraisals.

WITNESS, The Honorable .... RONALD E. HACH .... *Judge of said*
Court, and the seal thereof this .... 2nd .... *day of* .... July .... *, 19* 92

HAZEL G. ART

Clerk

By .... *(signature)* ....

Deputy

State of Minnesota,

County of .... Smithson ....

I hereby certify and return that I served the within Subpoena on the within named
.... Personnel Director ....

.... *by reading the same to him and delivering to him*
a true copy thereof, at .... ABC Corp., 415 Jones St., Milltown, Minnesota ....
in said County and State, on this .... 15 .... *day of* .... Aug. .... *, 19* 92

SHERIFF'S FEES:

Arnold Anderson

Sheriff of said County

Service, ... 15.00 ....

By .... *(signature)* ....

Mileage, $ .... 12.00 ....

(All names and places are fictitious)

member of management can bind the corporation if there is reason to believe that the person signing has authority to do so. The erosion of the at-will doctrine caused many astute employers to have legal counsel review all discharges. The lawyer would determine whether there is a possible exposure to a lawsuit. This is a good procedure when there is any doubt. Voluntary quits in some situations can be constructive discharge,[5] and if that possibility exists, it should be reviewed by counsel.

A Litigation-Happy Society

To illustrate how people are suing each other in civil rights cases, the EEOC caseload has increased more than 30 percent since 1981.[6] The number of charges filed under the ADA grew from 20.7 percent in the previous year to 22.6 percent in fiscal 1995, while charges under the ADEA decreased from 18.7 percent to 16.7 percent. Charges under Title VII continued to occupy the majority of the EEOC's charges, accounting for about 60% of all charges. Congress avoids hard choices, so it writes vague laws. The courts fell into this pattern and will hear almost any claim. We have over 750,000 lawyers in the United States, and most of them have started practicing in the last 10 years. Lawyers like to keep busy by taking disputes to court rather than solving them peacefully.[7]

Some social scientists fear that the willingness to sue is destroying the personal relationships and trust between individuals that has made our society so pleasant.

Growth of the Legal Profession

The increase in litigation has created a demand for more attorneys, and once the trend has started it is difficult to stop. When the demand is there, everybody enters law school.

There has been no sincere attempt to limit the number of law students. As long as the students can meet the academic and economic standards, they are admitted. They become lawyers when the field is already overcrowded.

In 1994 there was one lawyer for every 100 persons; in 1973 there was one lawyer for every 1,250 persons.[8]

The increase in litigation caused an increase in attorneys, and now, with the surplus, the number of attorneys has caused an increase in litigation. This problem is made evident by the amount of advertising they now do.

Economic Use of Legal Counsel

There has been a growing dependency of the personnel function on the legal counsel. The social legislation of the late 1960s, 1970s, and 1980s increased employee rights to the extent that the law has become an external auditor of the personnel function. The personnel practitioner must have enough knowledge of the law to make a determination of when legal advice is necessary. Managers must find an economical way to obtain this advice.

It is too expensive and not practical for the practitioner to become a lawyer, or for the lawyer to become a personnel practitioner. Although both disciplines are needed at times, merging them is not only unnecessary but at times could be very disruptive. The legal approach to personnel problems is rarely the best approach.

It is often said that the only thing an attorney has to sell is his or her time.[9] So when using legal counsel, the objective is to take the least time possible and still get the information and guidance necessary. Review what you are going to ask. Organize the references that you think you will need and have them in front of you. It is expensive

---

[5]This doctrine is explained in Chapter 11.

[6]U.S. EEOC Annual Report, 1997.

[7]For a good discussion of this problem, see John G. Kester, "Too Many Lawyers," *The Washington Magazine,* February, 1984.

[8]American Bar Association, Chicago; also *Employment and Earnings,* Department of Labor, Bureau of Labor Statistics, January 1992.

[9]A client once asked a woman in a law office to get him a cup of coffee. When she returned she asked him what she could do for him. Realizing he had mistaken his attorney for a secretary, he apologized. She said she didn't mind taking her time at $200 an hour. The cup of coffee cost him $50.

to go to the file and find a document while the attorney is holding the line.

Be prompt in supplying information. Tell the attorney all the facts, including the bad facts. It is very damaging if the bad facts come out after the case is prepared or in court through the opposing attorney. Often the attorney will have to ask for a continuance and prepare the case all over again. Amended pleadings and new witness preparations are very expensive for the employer. This expense would have been avoided if the bad facts had been told originally.

If in your reading you come across a certain case and you want to talk to your attorney about it, get the citation if it is available. Before the issue can be considered, the attorney has to look up the case. It often takes a great deal of time to find the citation, for which you are charged, especially if one of the names of the parties to the case is spelled wrong.

ATTORNEY FEES—REASONABLE OR UNREASONABLE?

The late Chief Justice Burger once said that the lawyer has gone from professionalism to commercialism. In Warren Burger's time of practicing law the client saw a lawyer and never asked about the fee. It was unethical to do so. It did not make much difference compared to the quality of service one received. In the late 1980s fees became a substantial part of the lawsuit and the client needs to know. (See Exhibit 2-3.)

The practicing attorney wants a good public image,[10] which he or she has until a bill is sent charging $250 an hour.[11] This is hard to swallow for a person with just as much education making $20 an hour. Certainly the attorney has office expenses, a library to keep up and a computer to write wills and deeds on, but not that much office expense. The lawyer has an obligation to explain the hour cost to the client before the bill is sent,

otherwise the bill comes as a surprise, especially if the case is lost. This destroys the client-attorney relationship and the public image of all attorneys.[12] The plaintiff has an obligation to determine what is reasonable.

Office expenses for an attorney run about one-half of the fee. The Supreme Court and subsequent cases say that the fee must be reasonable. Are they reasonable when the client gets $1,000,000 and the attorney fees are over $700,000? The attorney says they are, and this was upheld by the Supreme Court. The only thing an attorney has to sell is his or her time. The client should ask for the fees and judge the quality of service. If they are not reasonable it is not practical to go to court because the judge was once an attorney who charged, in his mind, reasonable fees.

The client gets a fairer deal by going to the Professional Responsibility or Professional Conduct board and stating that a rule has been violated. There are two reasons for not going to court other than getting an attorney to take the case. First, it is too expensive because the department does all the legal work. Second, it is a matter of discipline and the Professional Conduct Board (acting under the state Supreme Court) is in a better position than the lower court to give discipline. Perhaps the judge charged unreasonable fees and got away with it. Some attorneys charge what "the traffic will bear."

Some states have arbitration committees that act under the Supreme Court, which is not as effective as giving discipline. It is better to find out who did the work, the hourly charge, and whether the charge was reasonable based on the case. If a manager as a lay person does not know what is reasonable, it is not unethical to ask another attorney. Most attorneys charge over $100 per hour. The partners receive a portion (unless they are a sole practitioner), some is used for advertising (in certain firms), and so forth. The associate is usually on a salary and must get so many fee hours or leave the firm.

---

[10]Attorneys ranked second in having the worst public image; a used car salesman is first.

[11]Does not violate state or federal equal protection or due process guarantees, or separation of powers doctrine (*Newton* v. *Cox*, 115 S.Ct. 189 (1994).

[12]For a good discussion on attorney fees see Yilek, "Interest and Late Charges," *Bench and Bar*, Minn. Bar Assn., March 1991; Johnson, "Interest on Attorney Fees," *Bench and Bar*, May/June 1993; Johnson, "Dollars and Sense," *Bench and Bar*, Nov. 1995.

Contingent Fees

The contingent fee is charged by an attorney only if he or she wins. If the case is lost, no fee is charged and the plaintiff often pays only the court costs. The contingent fee is used mostly by the plaintiff's bar in personal injury cases. Most plaintiff's attorneys are quite sure of prevailing before they take the case (about 80 percent are turned down). Attorneys often advertise, "Come and see us—you have nothing to lose." The contingent fee has caused the employer to put in policies in order to avoid exposure to a lawsuit. If the employee wins the employer pays the fee. In my judgment the extensive use of the contingent fee has greatly increased the caseload for the courts.

Referral Fees

A referral arises when the case is referred by one lawyer to another, and is used mostly in personal injury cases. The referring lawyer can collect a fee without doing any work for the client, except retaining responsibility for the case. Responsibility, under ABA Code 86-1514, means financial as well as other responsibility. There must be a written agreement under most rules and the client must be informed. The client cannot object to the fee splitting because this is a matter between the attorneys involved.

Nonrefundable Retainers

Some states allow nonrefundable retainers if the client agrees, and this is not prohibited by the rules of professional conduct. The money is usually held in a trust account and withdrawn as earned. If the client discharges one of the attorneys the money usually goes to the other attorney, not the client. In all situations, the fees must be reasonable.

It is no reflection on your ability as a practitioner to seek legal advice. If it becomes unnecessarily expensive, it will then be avoided at times when it is needed. It is not unprofessional to question an attorney's fee statement. The fee hours charged, who performed the service, and the time charge should be itemized. A statement that says "for services rendered" should not be accepted. It should be detailed enough to allow, if necessary,

EXHIBIT 2-1 *What Lawyers Bill*

Year lawyer admitted to practice	Low hourly rate	High hourly rate	Mean rate	
1960 and earlier	$100	$350	$198	
1961-65	$90	$360	$190	
1966-70	$80	$350	$200	
1971-75	$100	$320	$193	
1976-80	$85	$265	$177	
1981-85	$55	$240	$161	
1986	$95	$215	$148	
1987	$83	$180	$140	
1988	$70	$175	$133	
1989	$90	$185	$134	
1990	$80	$170	$120	
1991	$65	$170	$111	
1992	$66	$190	$105	
1993	$65	$220	$96	
1994	$0	$120	$96	
				Number of Respondents
All attorneys	$40	$360	$157	1,818
Law clerks	$30	$105	$63	66
Legal assistants	$20	$150	$70	433

Source: Robert Hayden, Minnesota Consultants for Law firms.

another attorney to assess the reasonableness of the charges.

The practitioner must learn how to use legal counsel economically. The more you can do to help the attorney, the less time it will take to give an opinion.[13] That saves money. Like it or not it is a necessary expense in certain situations.

USE OF LEGAL COUNSEL

One of the most common errors of managers is not seeking legal advice early enough in the decision-making process. The counsel should be asked: What are the legal consequences of my decision? What are the legal alternatives? What can I do to prevent my decision from being challenged in the courts? Where there are no

---

[13]Legal advice is used to make a business decision whether to take the exposure to a lawsuit or comply. Compliance eliminates all possible chance of a lawsuit, even though the company may legally be right. The exposure to a lawsuit is more adventurous and could be very expensive.

alternatives within the law, that fact should be determined after every possible avenue has been explored.

Whether to take the adventurous approach or the conservative one depends upon management philosophy. How much does the regulation interfere with economical operation of the enterprise? What are the chances of prevailing?

Legal counsel should be expected to give an uncompromised legal opinion, which may not satisfy the person seeking it. The practitioner should be able to distinguish between a legal opinion and a personal prejudice toward the problem. Often managers will not ask legal counsel, because of the fear that the answer will be no. If this situation exists, the legal counsel is failing in the assigned tasks of advising management. Managers do not want to know what they cannot do but what they can do and still be legal. If they decide to be contrary to the established law this is a business risk for top management to take, and many often do so.

Distinction between Personnel and Legal Function

The personnel function is top management status. It is exposed to an avalanche of layers that brought them into an area with which they were often unfamiliar. The lawyer looks at a personnel problem in a legal context. Decisions are based solely upon what the lawyer believes the law says one must do or not do. The human relations manager must consider the conflicting considerations between a personnel decision and legal decision. For example, it is a legal determination that only those employees who filed a claim for disability pay due to pregnancy should be paid when the court determines that the state law was violated. It is an employee relations consideration whether to pay all employees who became disabled from pregnancy whether they filed a claim or not.

The legal counsel determines only what is required under the law. The personnel practitioner in considering the employee relations consequences may go beyond what the law requires. In another example, the courts have stated that a safety inspector from the Department of Labor cannot enter an employer's premises without a search warrant unless the employer agrees.[14] It is a policy decision whether the employer wants to agree.

Relationship of Legal Counsel to Employees

When an attorney is acting on behalf of a corporation on a legal matter involving an employee, the client is the corporation. There is no attorney-client relationship with the employee unless the employee obtains a different attorney.

Information that an attorney obtains when acting for the corporation belongs to the corporation. The employee as an individual has no right to see the information or to use it.[15] It is immaterial whether the employee gave the information to the attorney at the direction of a superior or obtained the information elsewhere. If the information was obtained while performing a function on behalf of the corporation and is relevant to the case, it belongs to the corporation.[16] A corporation has a right to any information that the employee obtained in the course of employment that is job related. The employee can be disciplined or discharged for refusing to disclose it. However, it is good employee relations to inform the employee how the information is going to be used. The employee has no constitutional right under the Fourth or Fifth Amendment to take immunity when the employer requests information.[17] Corporate counsel also can look at all the files concerning the employee. The employee has no remedy under the common law to prevent it.

---

[14]*Marshall* v. *Barlow's, Inc.*, 436 U.S. 307 (1978). Also *Justin* v. *Martin*, 951 F.2d 121 (7th Cir. 1991), affirm'd 113 S.Ct. 55 (1992).

[15]Most states have statutes requiring the employer to show the employee his or her own records.

[16]*Diversified Industries* v. *Meredith*, 572 F.2d 596 (8th Cir. 1977).

[17]*U.S.* v. *Solomon*, 509 F.2d 863 (2nd Cir. 1975).

Use of In-House Counsel

Often employees seek personal advice of the in-house counsel or company attorney. The corporation, as a matter of policy, must determine whether the attorneys should be used to give advice to employees when they have personal problems. Some personnel practitioners take the position that one hires the whole person. Employees' legal problems are company problems. The company should give them initial aid in the same manner that the company nurse does when an employee has a head cold.

Other practitioners take the position that getting too involved legally in an employee's personal problems can have an adverse effect. A policy followed by many companies is to refuse legal advice to employees on matters not related to their job duties. This may require an initial conference to determine whether the legal problem is job related. If it is determined that it is not, the employee is advised to seek his or her own lawyer. It is advisable not to assess the merits of the case in this situation, because the employee's lawyer may have a different opinion.

Some companies will permit the in-house counsel to do "first echelon" legal work. Legal counsel will look over a deed for an employee buying a house. Advice could be given as to cost on an automobile accident as to alternatives and court procedure. Or a local attorney might be assessed or recommended. Companies that use their in-house counsel in this manner believe that it is good employee relations. However, they do not get involved in the employee's personal legal problems; do not give advice for which the company may be responsible. This is a good policy for companies with in-house counsel if it is restricted to nonunion management personnel. The benefits to the company outweigh the adverse results as long as discretion is used.[18]

Obtaining Legal Opinions

The opinion of counsel can be valuable to the practitioner, depending on how it is obtained and used. An opinion should be requested before taking any questionable action that may result in legal implications.

The outside legal counsel or the law department should get the problem as early as possible. The more lead time before the legal opinion must be rendered, the more time for research and the more complete the opinion. Often a considerable amount of research is necessary: A half-page memo or letter may be the result of 8 hours of research.

When an opinion is requested, the problem should be properly framed. Asking further questions takes time, which increases the cost of legal services. When requesting an opinion, the personnel executive should do the following:

1. Give the attorney all known facts. Facts should not be condensed or digested. Do not be reluctant to disclose all the facts, even those that are damaging.[19]
2. When giving the facts, be prepared to provide documents such as memos, letters, or other written support.
3. Always identify assumptions and state those separately from the facts.
4. Be prompt in returning information requested. When the attorney must call twice for the same information, the company is charged for two telephone calls.
5. When calling for advice, have all the documents available and think out the questions beforehand.

These five points are so important that some have been repeated to encourage economical use of counsel. Management must find a way to use counsel economically, or advice will not be requested when needed.

Sometimes a person will receive two different legal opinions on the same issue or problem. There are several reasons why legal opinions differ:

---

[18]Those benefits could include saving management time of the employee seeing a lawyer or increasing employee satisfaction. A troubled employee is often a poor producer, and you hire all his or her problems.

[19]In this author's experience as an in-house counsel, failure to disclose damaging facts was a common practice among managers.

EXHIBIT 2-4

> The enclosed matters are communicated to you in confidence and constitute or contain legal services given to you by legal counsel. There are to be no duplications distributed or otherwise disclosed except through the attorney rendering them.

1. A slight difference in the facts or circumstances may have a different legal result.
2. There may be some changes in the laws between the time the first opinion and the second opinion are received.
3. Different lawyers may come to different conclusions when they weigh various facts and interpret statutes or court decisions. Experience, background, and personal beliefs often affect the interpretation of the law.
4. In gray areas of the law there are legal risks that cannot be avoided. Different attorneys may give different advice. Some attorneys will be more adventurous than others in assessing a legal problem.

Oral versus Written Opinions

Many practitioners telephone legal counsel and ask for an immediate oral opinion. An oral opinion has many pitfalls. It should not be used to solve important legal problems. This is especially true where legal counsel is not familiar with the subject matter. Even where the counsel is considered an expert, oral opinions can be misleading. They should be used only when the problem is routine and an immediate answer is essential. The pitfalls of an oral opinion are these:

1. The attorney has to remember the facts and apply them to the law with little thought.
2. There is a danger that the recipient of the opinion may misunderstand it.
3. There is no record of the opinion. If the consequences are adverse, there is always a question of what facts were given and the content of the opinion.
4. Because oral opinions lack research, they may not reflect the most current law.

Written opinions take longer and are more costly, but they are easily understood. They can be retained in the file for future reference. However, when using a written opinion in another situation, take care that the facts are exactly the same.

Information that an attorney receives or gives to any company employee is privileged. It cannot be used by a third party or subpoenaed.[20] It is important to identify that the information was received through the attorney as an employee of the company. It should be classified as confidential in the file. One way to do this is to have an attorney mark all legal opinions confidential. An example of how documents should be marked when received from an attorney is shown in Exhibit 2-4.

A statement similar to this should be marked on all documents given to the counsel, as shown in Exhibit 2-5. Usually the counsel will do so, but if not, then the person sending them should do it.

MAKING A RISK ANALYSIS

When management is considering whether to challenge a law or to comply, it should have a conference with legal counsel. A number of risk considerations can be explored.[21]

1. Is the desired course of action likely to bring a lawsuit?
2. Can the company financially risk the lawsuit or is compliance less expensive?
3. What consequences may result from an adverse decision—in the marketplace, with corporate goodwill, on employee relations, on corporate objectives and priorities?
4. Is the company in line with other companies in the same industry?

---

[20]*Upjohn* v. *U.S.,* 101 S.Ct. 677 (1981).

[21]There is never a sure case. All an attorney can do is give the possibility of prevailing.

EXHIBIT 2-5

> This document contains legal matters that are given to an attorney for his or her own use and is not to be disclosed to other persons unless upon the advice of the attorney receiving it.

The next consideration is the approximate cost of the case. In determining the cost it should be decided how far the company will appeal the case. Then the costs for attorneys at the first level of the hearing are determined, as well as cost of appeal to the next court.

When considering the attorney's costs, these cannot be exact figures; an attorney can only estimate the time involved.[22] For example, in research sometimes an attorney can find a case that serves as authority for the client's position in an hour or two. Other times research may require half the day. Because all the attorney has to sell is time, a two-page opinion can cost $900 or $200 depending on the time for the research and drafting.

When considering the cost of a case, the company should always ask the price per hour of the attorney's time, plus an estimate of what the case will cost.[23] Also when considering the cost, management time must be considered. Litigating a lawsuit involves the time of management personnel.

Cost Compared to Importance of Issue

Once the estimated cost of the case is determined, an assessment of winning should be made. The parties must look at the strengths and weaknesses of both the plaintiff and the defendant. They should be prepared for a surprise decision. The role of the legal counsel in assessing the chances of winning is to consider the facts in light of research and legal expertise. The final decision, after advice of counsel, on whether to take the risk belongs to the client.

Once it is decided to take the matter to court, a management representative should be assigned to the case. That person should become involved as much as possible. A lot of the attorney's time can be saved by client availability. Another reason to be involved is that settlement is always a possibility at any stage of the proceedings. Counsel cannot settle without the consent of the client. Sometimes settlement possibilities exist only for a short time; if the management representative is not available, that opportunity is lost.[24]

When assessing whether to litigate or settle, the economic considerations must be weighed with the employee relations or operational consequences.

For example, suppose a testing program is being challenged by EEOC. Management is convinced that because of the low educational level of the local labor market, tests must be given in order to select qualified applicants. The cost of litigation must be considered against the operational consequences if the test is eliminated as a selection tool.

Statistics show that American society is litigation happy. Everybody is suing, and there is no end in sight. The increase in litigation of all types, including employee relations cases, means that legal implications of employment decisions will not go away. The human resource or personnel executive must become involved with legal concepts.

The personnel practitioner must develop policies and procedures that will avoid exposure to lawsuits. Legal advice, when necessary, should be economically used to prevent exposure to lawsuits. Preventive legal advice is much more economical than a lawsuit.

---

[22]Some clients get the estimate and then double it to be more realistic.

[23]A 42-year-old attorney was at St. Peter's gate asking why he died so *young*. He said he didn't smoke or drink, exercised regularly, and lived a very healthy life. St. Peter looked at the record and said, "According to the time you charged your clients, you are more than 90 years old."

---

[24]The author once had a strike agreement. It was Saturday night at a bar. Nobody had a pen to sign the agreed-upon contract. A strike resulted.

3

ALTERNATIVE DISPUTE RESOLUTION? (ADR)

What is Alternative Dispute Resolution?
Definition of Mediation
Unsuccessful ADR
Settlement Documents
Federal Courts Enforce ADR

WHAT IS ALTERNATIVE DISPUTE RESOLUTION?

Alternative Dispute Resolution (ADR) is a variety of processes that are designed to assist the parties in resolving disputes. Most scholars believe that all the processes result in a quick and cheaper settlement than going to court. The parties in the dispute resort to it because it is quicker and chapter than litigation.[1]

In a speech to a law school class, Abraham Lincoln encouraged the use of ADR. He said, "Discourage litigation. Persuade your neighbors to compromise whenever you can. Point out to them how a nominal winner is often a real loser— in fees, expenses and waste of time. ..."[2] Lincoln said this over 125 years ago, and the reasons for using ADR have not changed.

Litigation is expensive. The average cost in 1994 was over $4 million. Litigation is often complex and involves many witnesses and documents. There is usually discovery and considerable investigation, which often precludes the parties with legitimate claims from pursuing their claims because a part is required to pay their own attorney fees. Even in contingent fee cases one party or the other is typically required to pay all or some of the costs. Costs are sometimes negotiable, but this is difficult. Both the Americans with Disabilities Act (42 U.S. 12 et al.) and the Civil Rights Act of 1991 (42 U.S.C. § 1981) encourage the use of ADR

---

[1]For a good discussion of mediation and settlement, see D. Reder, "Mediation as a Settlement Tool for Employment Disputes," *Labor Law Journal,* 43, no. 9 (September 1992). 602.

[2]See B. Cogan, "Alternative Dispute Resolution and Judicial Immunity: A Potential Retail Pitfall?" *Labor Law Journal,* (November 1994), 722.

procedures, including mediation, to resolve employment disputes.

Why ADR?

The parties want a quick settlement. Litigation is not designed for quick settlement. The parties have to relive the case, and they find it difficult to go on with their lives with the lawsuit pending. The long discovery process does not help. It was wisely said, "justice delayed is justice denied."

With long delays the public also begins to lose faith in the court system. Attorneys agree that when they encourage the use of ADR there is a fear that the particular process will cause more problems than litigation. This is caused by lack of knowledge and inexperience with the process. As the parties gain experience and education, the obstacles will be removed.

Types of ADR

1. *Mediation.* This is a process of voluntary negotiation between the parties in an informal and flexible setting. The parties select a neutral to assist them in a settlement.
2. *Arbitration.* This is a process that can be binding or nonbinding, depending upon what the parties agree to. Arbitration is less structured than court procedures, and is much faster. If nonbinding, the parties select the neutral; if binding, the parties will use a third resource and the decision is final and binding.[3]
3. *Mini-Trial.* This process is close to a court presentation. It is an abbreviated version of the case that is presented to a panel of decision-makers and a neutral. The decision rendered (usually by the neutral) either is binding or may be used for further settlement discussions. In this situation it is an advisory process.
4. *Summary Jury Trial.* Here the parties present expedited evidence to a mock jury that is either selected by the parties or impaneled by a judge. The opinion rendered is advisory and is used for further discussions.

5. *Moderated Settlement Conference.* The parties present an expedited version of their case to a panel of neutrals (usually retired judges or arbitrators) who preside over judicial process and make a binding decision. The opinion is used in further settlement discussions.
6. *Neutral Fact-Finding.* Here the parties select a neutral to issue a report or finding regarding a complex issue. The report can be binding but usually is nonbinding.
7. *Private Judging.* The parties select a neutral (usually retired judge or arbitrator) to preside over the process and make a decision. The decision is usually binding and the parties give up control of the case.

All of the preceding processes are used in different cases. The process selected depends on the facts in the case. What names are given to the process or whether or not it is used depends upon the parties. Generally, outside counsel is more likely to use ADR than in-house counsel.

Selection of the Process

Mediation is used primarily in the United States. Some companies have used ADR in international disputes, particularly in Canada, Great Britain, and France. About 25 percent of company counsel use ADR internationally.[4]

The process selected depends upon the parties and the facts of the case. Mediation is the most used process with arbitration running a close second.[5]

The selection of the proper process must satisfy a client's objective. Will the process lead to a settlement? The article (note 5) encourages the selection of mediation as the preferred method. In some cases mediation is not advised, such as on constitutional issues, where legal precedent is important, or where one party or the other thinks it

---

[3]See Deloitte & Touche Litigation Services, 1993 Survey–MN, CLE 40 Milton St., Suite 101, St. Paul, MN 55104-7094.

[4]See Deloitte & Touche Litigation Services, 1993 Survey–MN, CLE. Ibid.

[5]For a good article on the selection process see "Fitting the Forum to the Fuss: A User Guide to Selecting an ADR Procedure," *Negotiation Journal,* January 1994. This article gives a sophisticated method that is important to settlement of a dispute.

has no liability, or if it is a summary case and will likely be granted.

Effectiveness of ADR

ADR is not as effective as it could be, but most users are satisfied with it and use it wherever possible.[6] The two most important reasons the parties use ADR are to reduce costs and to save time. Sometimes it does neither. Other motivating factors are less important. (Maintaining the relationship between the parties is the least important among users; this should be higher.)

ADR is most likely to be effective in routine cases where the involvement of top management is presumed not to be necessary. This is unfortunate because top management should be involved in all decisions, especially in settlements. Most users are satisfied with the result if the process is entered into voluntarily, but if it is involuntary, users are much less satisfied. The attorney gives an overview of the processes and assists the parties in discussing methods with which they are most comfortable.

A Successful ADR

Mediation is used in over one-half of the cases. Most users are also the most satisfied with it, and resort to ADR wherever possible.[7] If the parties take a hard-line position, the success of the process is in jeopardy. A successful ADR does not just happen—it requires preparation. The neutral, the lawyer (if any), and the parties are all a necessary part of the process. ADR makes possible the use of creativity in a way that litigation or binding arbitration cannot.

All the processes have some form of mediation, but do not have the flexibility. When the decision is nonbinding and is used for further discussions, mediation is used to settle. Mediation is used before a suit is filed, in pre-discovery, after the trial, or in any other stage of the legal proceedings.

------

[6]See William B. Gould study, *Report and Recommendations of the Commission on the Future of Worker-Management Relations*, Washington, D.C.: U.S. Dept. of Labor and U.S. Dept. of Commerce, (Jan. 1995) 70.

[7]Task Force and EEOC. However, EEOC started using ADR in 1996.

DEFINITION OF MEDIATION

Mediation is defined as a structured process in which the parties to a dispute or conflict negotiate its resolution with the assistance of a neutral party. It is used in over half of the disputes or conflicts. Because of its cooperative problem-solving nature, mediation is helpful in identifying and articulating serious concerns that might otherwise be dismissed, derogated, or, more likely, left unexpressed and unresolved.

The focus of mediation and mediating training is to shift from the usual emphasis on an adversarial method of problem solving to a cooperative approach of conflict management.

Mediation Training

Mediation is structured negotiations with the help of a neutral. There are seven stages of mediation. Questions and listening will help the mediator understand the issues of the parties. These stages are very important: (1) introduction, (2) problem determination, (3) summarization, (4) issue identification, (5) generation and evaluation of alternatives, (6) selection of approriate alternatives, and (7) conclusion.

Role-Playing

The next component of mediation training is the use of case simulations, which typically involve three students playing roles under the supervision of an experienced mediator. Two students play the roles of opposing disputants, each having been assigned certain attitudes, positions, goals, or negotiating techniques. The third student, acting as the mediator, is provided with very limited information regarding the dispute. The trainer provides guidance to the other two trainees.

An advantage of mediation over other methods of dispute resolution is that all decision-making authority remains with the disputants, who are in the best position to make their own creative settlements and will more likely follow the agreements.

The parties must choose a good mediator, one who knows the personality of the judge. If the judge has the personality that aggressive mediation demands, the mediator should know this and act accordingly. The mediator has a tougher job when the judge has a low-key approach. Successful mediators have the training and skills to be a neutral and know the judge.

A good mediator establishes rapport very early in the session. He meets with the parties early to discuss various issues and tells a little bit about himself. Unless an element of trust is established, there is no way the mediator can get all the facts.

This process is usually the one referred to when talking about ADR. Co-mediators are often considered when several issues are involved or some party considers it important to have a person with a similar racial, ethnic, or protected class background. Often the parties want a second opinion. This is especially true where there is little agreement on a single mediator.

The Impasse

Often the problem is communications, which do not have to be verbal. A good neutral can watch the eyes or body language of the parties and can often determine their position. The telegram is clear to a good neutral.

It is the author's experience that an impasse should be reached before the mediation is started. After an impasse is reached, there is no right time to mediate; it may start anytime. If there is no impasse the mediator will not be useful. The parties involved know their business better than the mediator does. His or her main objective is to keep the parties talking until an agreement is reached.

UNSUCCESSFUL ADR

If no settlement is reached, the process can be very costly to the parties because they still have to litigate. Another negative result is that the relationship between the parties is often destroyed. Mediation requires disclosing facts that ordinarily would not be disclosed. If one of the parties undress themselves and there is no settlement, then the relationship is hurt. Some obstacles to settlement are poor communications, different view of the facts or the law, pressure from the boss or constituent, and different interests (common in labor disputes). An unsuccessful ADR creates an adverse situation that does neither party any good. The potential of bad blood becomes real, and this can take a long time to heal. If ADR is unsuccessful the parties may have picked the wrong avenue to avoid litigation.

There Is Not a Settlement

In any human endeavor there is always possibility of failure. In ADR, if there is no settlement the process will still be worth the effort. If ADR fails, then the parties must go to court to get the matter resolved. After ADR, the issues will be narrowed, the witnesses will be better informed, and there is still the possibility that it can be settled with the judge's help. The negotiation process has been started and the parties probably have made concrete offers. Maybe after another ADR method, such as a mini-trial, a better risk analysis may be made. The court proceedings can start from there. Scheduling for the discovery process starts at the unsuccessful meeting. All of these factors will save management time and legal fees when the parties go to court. The time and money spent on ADR will be returned many times over.

Unions and employers must find some way to avoid delays in getting a dispute resolved, expensive court procedures, and waste of lawyers' fees and management's time. Mediation of employment-related disputes is one method that is worth a trial.

SETTLEMENT DOCUMENTS

When a settlement is reached, the neutral should not let the parties leave the room until a settlement agreement is drafted. This essential document should state the issues and how they were settled. Later, a more definitive document can be drafted and be more binding. The original agreement should state clearly who is agreeing to what, when, and how. Wherever possible, the disputants' wording should be used. It is signed by all parties.

Contents of a Definitive Document

A definitive document is more specific in that it sets times and deadlines. It is a balanced document that is positive and provides for resolution of future disputes. (Agreement may not always be reached in this area.)

This document is drafted as a contract and is a legal document. In this respect the definitive agreement differs from the agreement signed at the process session. It states that the neutral has no obligation to protect the interests of the parties and that the signing could affect their legal rights. (The settlement cannot violate public policy.) The process is stated to be voluntary or ordered by a judicial body. The parties agree to a voluntary settlement or that the decision was binding on both parties. The court of law can set aside the agreement if appropriate, but it cannot act in an arbitrary manner.

The settlement agreement constitutes waiver of any right, statutory or common law, that is inconsistent with what was agreed upon. The parties should consult an attorney for signing. Often an attorney will draft the definitive agreement but not the settlement.

FEDERAL COURTS ENFORCE ADR

The U.S. Supreme Court's decision in *Gilmer* v. *Interstate/Johnson Lane Corp.,* 500 U.S. 20 (1991) opened the floodgates for the use of arbitration, mediation, and other forms of alternative dispute resolution (ADR) for employment disputes in nonunion settings.[8] Subsequent court decisions have recently added force to the *Gilmer* decision.[9]

Before *Gilmer,* it was unclear whether any form of private agreement could require the arbitration of a statutory employment discrimination claim. In *Williams* v. *Katten, Muchin & Zavis,* 837 F. Supp. 1430 (N.D. Ill. 1993), a federal district court affirmed the report and recommendation of a magistrate who applied *Gilmer* to require arbitration of statutory discrimination claims under an employment agreement.

The incentives have never been greater to use a procedure to settle a dispute out of court. It is not uncommon for one lawsuit involving a wrongful discharge to cost more than $100,000. With the advent of the CRA91 and ADA there is no doubt that the frequency of lawsuits will increase.

Court decisions have suggested that ADR will be fully accepted by the courts. Judicial attitudes about ADA have changed drastically since *Alexander* v. *Gardner-Denver,* 415 U.S. 36 (1974). The vast backlog of cases, the lack of arbitrators to resolve statutory claims, and Congress's intent that statutory claims do not have to be resolved in judicial forums are probably the reasons for this change in attitude.

The strong trend of recent cases is to give the widest possible role to alternative dispute resolution procedures in the employment context. In view of the costs that can be incurred even in successfully defending against a lawsuit, as well as the uncertainties inherent in the ever-expanding availability of jury trials and punitive damages, most employers should at least consider whether adopting some form of alternative dispute resolution would be appropriate. A formal ADR program may not be appropriate for all employers. The nature of the workforce, experience with claims, willingness to abide by procedures that will be considered fair, and many other issues need to be considered before adopting ADR.

Ethics in ADR

An attorney or any other advisor is ethically bound to discuss the various processes available to the parties to resolve the dispute.[10] Rule 114 of the General Rules of Practice for the District Courts in Minnesota requires attorneys to confer with their respective clients regarding ADR and then confer with opposing counsel regarding the section of an

---

[8]See "Key Developments," *Employment Relations Today,* Summer 1993.

[9]*Gilmer* v. *Interstate/Johnson Lane Corp.,* 111 S.Ct. 1647 (1991).

[10]For a good discussion of ADR see E. Pauer and C. Meunie, "New Rules on ADR." *Colorado Lawyer,* 21 (1992), 820. Also Burnhardt, "Ethical Duty to Consider Alternative Dispute Resolution," *California Lawyer,* 19 (Feb. 1994), 241.

ADR process, the timing of the process, and the selection of the neutral.

An attorney is ethically bound to discuss with his or her client the various ADR processes available to resolve the client's dispute in lieu of traditional litigation. In addition, in order to meet this obligation, the attorney must be sufficiently knowledgeable and skillful in the most basic procedures of each type of ADR to competently discuss and advise the client. Failure to address ADR with the client and lack of competence in ADR are no longer options for today's attorney.

Some of the rules that a lawyer must follow are: "A lawyer shall provide competent representation to a client. Competent representation requires the legal knowledge, skill, thoroughness and preparation reasonably necessary for the representation." "A lawyer shall abide by a client's decisions concerning the objects of representation, … and shall consult with the client as to the means by which they are to be pursued. A lawyer shall abide by a client's decision whether to accept an offer of settlement of a matter. …" "In representing a client, a lawyer shall exercise independent professional judgment." "A lawyer shall explain a matter to the extent reasonably necessary to permit the client to make informed decisions regarding the representation.

4

DISCRIMINATION UNDER THE CIVIL RIGHTS ACT OF 1866 AND TITLE VII

The Law of Discrimination
Application and Coverage of Civil Rights Act of 1866 and Its Amendments
Discrimination under Title VII
Out-of-Court Settlements

Chapter 1 described how the law moved into the personnel function and drastically changed personnel management. These traditional practices of adopting attitudes, beliefs, and ideas about political or ethnic background for an employment decision are now restricted by antidiscrimination laws.

Many of these well-accepted practices and policies are no longer advisable. A key reason has been the impact of antidiscrimination legislation. This legislation outlaws policies and practices that result in disparate treatment of or disparate impact on any protected class of applicants or employees.

State and federal statutes affect all phases of the employment process, from initial advertising of a job vacancy through hiring, promotion, discipline, discharge, and retirement of the employee.

Title VII was the first major antidiscrimination legislation that drastically affected employment decisions. If the employment decisions resulted in a person's being treated differently because of race, color, religion, sex, or national origin, Title VII would cause the employer to restore the employee to his or her original status, including reimbursement for any monetary losses.

Although Title VII had the greatest impact on the employment relationship, it was not the first antidiscrimination statute passed by Congress. In 1866 Congress passed a civil rights act that prohibited discrimination because of race. In 1870 and 1871 the act was amended to plug the loopholes in the 1866 statute. This statute was not applied to the employment relationship until 1971, but it is now used in discrimination cases as much as Title VII.

This chapter will discuss the application to the employment relationship of Title VII, the 1866 statute (42 U.S.C. Sect. 1981–83), and the Civil Rights Act of 1991 (CRA91). The CRA91 amended Title VII, the 1866 statute, the Age

Discrimination in Employment Act (ADEA), and the Americans with Disabilities Act (ADA) and voided several state statutes. The ADEA and the ADA as amended will be given consideration in subsequent chapters. The effect of CRA91 upon state statutes will be referred to when applicable. Since 1992 no antidiscrimination law has been passed by Congress; only court decisions have been made.

THE LAW OF DISCRIMINATION

It is a violation of antidiscrimination statutes if by some employment action or inaction an employee is treated less favorably than another because of sex, race, age, disability, and the like. The mere showing of a difference in treatment does not prove discrimination. There must be a discriminatory purpose or result. The action taken by the employer must be based on a prohibitive provision of the statute.

In *St. Mary's Honor Ctr.* v. *Hicks,* 113 S.Ct. 2742 (1993) the U.S. Supreme Court held that a plaintiff who establishes a prima facie case of intentional discrimination is not entitled to judgment as a matter of law, even if the fact finder rejects the employer's nondiscriminatory reasons for the adverse employment action. Instead, the plaintiff must still prove that the adverse action was based on discriminatory conduct prohibited by Title VII.

When the employee alleges discrimination, the employee must show that a statute has been violated. This is done by showing:

1. That the employee is protected by a statute.
2. That action was taken because the employee was a member of the protected class.
3. That the employee was qualified,[1] but was replaced by someone else.

The procedure in court is that the employee alleges discrimination. The employer states that the action was nondiscriminatory and there was no violation of a statute. The employee then alleges that this is pretext and the real reason for the action was discrimination. This raises the issue for the court or a jury to decide.

APPLICATION AND COVERAGE OF CIVIL RIGHTS ACT OF 1866 AND ITS AMENDMENTS

The original statute was passed shortly after the Civil War to support the Thirteenth Amendment. It gave blacks the same rights under the law as whites. Because it did not cover all activities, such as right to sell, purchase, lease, or inherit real and personal property where the state has jurisdiction, the act had to be amended. The 1871 amendment, which is presently the most widely used, asserts that when acting under the "color of the state" (any local, state, or federal governmental units) all persons must be given the same rights.[2] The 1871 amendment made the employer or the employee acting in behalf of the employer personally liable for violating the act.[3]

Personal Liability

In *Vinard* v. *King,* 728 F.2d 428 (10th Cir. 1984), the director of a municipal-owned hospital discharged an employee without a hearing, contrary to the procedure in the handbook. The court held the director personally liable but not the hospital, because it was part of the municipality, which couldn't be sued. Even if it could be sued, the city could be liable only if an employee's action is based on policy that is unconstitutional. This makes it much harder for employees who have been wrongfully discharged to sue the city. When a prison guard placed an inmate in a cell with another inmate whom he knew to be dangerous and the plaintiff was assaulted, the guard was held personally liable.

---

[1]Whether the employee is qualified is a factual matter. A court will not force an employer to tolerate a low-level performer: *Lucero* v. *Hart,* 915 F.2d. 1367 (9th Cir. 1990).

[2]The statute is codified in 42 U.S.C. Sect. 1981–83.

[3]See Shari Weinman, "Supervisory Liability under 42 U.S.C., Sect. 1983: Searching for the Deep Pocket," *Missouri Law Review,* 56 (1991), 1041.

This personal liability extends to judges of state courts who in an administrative action violate the statute.

Differences from Other Antidiscrimination Laws

Another difference between the 1866 statute and Title VII, in addition to individual liability, is that the plaintiff does not have to show intent[4] under Title VII and CRA91 amendment[5] when punitive or compensatory damages are asserted.[6] If the plaintiff's attorney uses both statutes and intent cannot be shown, it is still a violation of Title VII where the only remedy is to make the employee whole (unless compensatory or punitive damages can be shown under CRA91).

Another difference between the 1866 statute and most other antidiscrimination statutes is that there is no limitation on retroactivity. The act goes back to the date of the incident.

Another distinction is an exclusive remedy. You do not have to go through the Equal Employment Opportunity Commission (EEOC) or other administrative agencies; you can go directly into court. This is sometimes a great advantage when the plaintiff wants to get the case adjudicated quickly. Because it is exclusive remedy, if the plaintiff fails under other antidiscrimination statutes, he or she can still bring an action under the 1866 statute.

The 1866 statute does not cover sex discrimination. However, the statute was amended by CRA91 to include all members of the protected class. Before, under CRA91, intent was not required in a Title VII action as it was under Section 1981. CRA91 somewhat narrowed this major difference by requiring intent[7] under Title VII if compensatory or punitive damages are asserted. This is also true of trial by jury. Before the CRA91 amendment, jury trial was allowed and intent had to be shown in any action under the 1866 statute.

If possible the employee will always choose jury trial over a judge's decision. Juries (most of whom are employees or have been at one time) are more sympathetic to employees than a judge who must follow the law more closely and is not as emotionally influenced as a jury.

The unequivocal right of jury trial and ability to make an individual personally liable are two great incentives for the plaintiff to sue under the 1866 act and CRA91.

DISCRIMINATION UNDER TITLE VII

The broadest antidiscrimination statute is the 1964 Civil Rights Act and CRA91 Amendment (commonly called Title VII).[8] It is the principal source of antibias rules for employment practices. The act and its amendments prohibit discrimination in all employment decisions on the basis of race, color, religion, national origin, disability, or sex, including pregnancy, childbirth, or abortion. Title VII applies to employers, labor unions, apprenticeship committees, employment agencies, and federal, state, and local governments. It covers all employees from the part-time office boy to the chief executive officer. Before a business is subject to the act, it must affect interstate commerce and employ 15 or more individuals for at least 20 weeks during the current or preceding calendar year.[9]

Section 101 of CRA91 specifically amended Section 1981. The old clause in Section 1981 that referred to making and enforcing contracts now includes making, performance, modification, and termination of contracts. It also includes the

---

[4]Under Americans with Disabilities Act no intent is required, but discrmination has to be shown, *Mayberrey* v. *von Valtier,* 62 N.W.252 (E.D. Mich. 1994).

[5]Discussed in chapter 3.

[6]*Compensatory damages* as used in this text mean actual loss suffered. *Punitive damages* (sometimes called *exemplary*) are punishment for outrageous conduct and are given to deter future wrongdoing; they are often in addition to compensatory damages.

[7]Under ADA intent is required.

---

[8]In 1993, 15 percent of the charges filed with EEOC resulted in a finding of discrimination. In the other words, 15 percent of employers had to pay defensive fees.

[9]If an employer is not covered by federal law, state or municipal laws fill in the void. Employers should not seek jurisdictional shelter under federal law because some other law will cover them.

enjoyment of all benefits, privileges, terms, and conditions of a contractual relationship. The effect of this amendment is to allow more individuals complaining of discrimination to sue for actual compensatory and punitive damages to enforce their rights. Section 3 of CRA91 states the purposes of the amendments to the various antidiscrimination statutes:

1. To provide appropriate remedies for intentional discrimination and unlawful harassment in the workplace.
2. To codify business necessity and job-related concepts. To reinstate the *Griggs* decision and reverse *Wards Cove Packing Co.* v. *Atonio,* 409 U.S. 642 (1989).
3. To confirm statutory authority and provide statutory guidelines adjudication of disparate impact suits under Title VII.

The effect of this statute was to invalidate the holding of the Supreme Court in six cases.

In *EEOC* v. *American Arabian Oil Co.,* 111 S.Ct. 1227 (1991), the workers in a foreign country employed by an American company were not covered by Title VII. Under Section 109 of CRA91 workers are now covered.

In *West Virginia University Hospitals, Inc.* v. *Casey,* 111 S.Ct. 1138 (1991), the court held that expert witness fees could not be collected by the losing party. Under Section 113 of CRA91 expert witness fees are now included within the definition of attorney's fees.

In *Patterson* v. *Mclean Credit Union,* 491 U.S. 164 (1989), the court held that adverse employment actions including racial harassment were not covered in Section 1981 of the Civil Rights Act of 1866. There was no breach of contract. Section 101 of CRA91 allowed coverage in all benefits in the contractual relationship as well as termination.

In *Wards Cove Packing Co.* v. *Atonio,* 409 U.S. 642 (1989), the court increased the burden on the plaintiff in disparate impact cases. It stated that statistical imbalance does not necessarily establish a prima facie case to allow the plaintiff to get into court. The controlling factor was the relevant labor market rather than the imbalance. Section 105 of

CRA91 rejects this doctrine and returns to the concept in *Griggs* v. *Duke Power Co.,* 401 U.S. 424 (1971), that puts the burden on the defendant to prove business necessity or show that the policy was not discriminatory. In effect this legislation brings us back to the Griggs doctrine.[10]

Section 107 of CRA91 also changes the concept in mixed discharge cases. Now if the plaintiff can show that a prohibited motive led to an employment action even though a nonprohibited motive was also involved, the plaintiff is entitled to recover. This changes the concept announced in *Price Waterhouse* v. *Hopkins,* 409 U.S. 228 (1989), and many subsequent mixed discharge cases, such as *NLRB* v. *Transportation Management Corp.,* 103 S.Ct. 2469 (1983), and the NLRB precedent found in *NLRB* v. *Wright Lines,* 662 F.2d 899 (1st Cir. 1981). Before the plaintiff could recover there had to be a showing that the employer would have discharged the employee for the offense and that the protected activity did not influence the discharge. Under Section 107 of CRA91 it will be more difficult to discharge where there exists a protected activity.

In *Lorance* v. *AT&T Technologies, Inc.,* 490 U.S. 900 (1989), the Supreme Court prevented a challenge to an affirmative action seniority system if it was not challenged when the system was adopted. Section 112 of CRA91 expressly overrules this doctrine and allows a challenge at any relevant time.[11]

Most legal scholars agree that CRA91 will not require quotas. It will, however, make it tougher for employers to defend themselves against discrimination charges. Jury trial and punitive and compensatory damages will increase the exposure to lawsuits and boost the price that employers will pay for intentional discrimination. However, it must be remembered that CRA91 has several gray areas that will need court interpretation. The cost-conscious employer will not overreact and rush into major policy changes. These would only

---

[10]Not all scholars agree. C. Ray Gullet, " The Civil Rights Act of 1991: Did It Really Overturn Wards Cove?" *Labor Law Journal,* 43 (July 1992), 462.

[11]ADEA and Section 1981 cases are not protected: *EEOC* v. *City Colleges of Chicago,* 944 F.2d 339 (7th Cir. 1991).

EXHIBIT 4-1

Applicants	Number of Minority Rejected	Number of Nonminority Rejected
100	53	30

Rate of selection = 100 − rate of rejection

$$\frac{\text{Selection rate for minorities (47\%)}}{\text{Selection rate for nonminorities (70\%)}} = 67\%$$

result in exposure to litigation. If possible, it is much more economical to let somebody else pay the legal costs to develop the case law.

There are several guidelines that the employer can follow to avoid exposure to litigation as a party to an expensive lawsuit:

1. Do not in any way indicate or even suggest an intent to discriminate. You can treat employees differently, but don't discriminate.
2. Be knowledgeable on the provisions of Title VII, and draft policies and procedures accordingly.
3. Have accurate and current job descriptions. These will document your business necessity.
4. Always investigate an alternative practice that is just as good but has less discriminatory implications.
5. Make sure that practices and procedures as well as business-necessity beliefs are not based on stereotyped thinking.
6. Document everything that is questionable, and maintain objective records.

The Equal Employment Opportunity Commission enforces the objectives of the act. All charges under Title VII must begin with the EEOC or a state referral agency whose decision is not binding on the EEOC.

Definition of Discrimination Under Title VII

Title VII did not define discrimination. The first task of the courts was to define it. Discrimination exists, according to the Supreme Court in the landmark case of *Griggs* v. *Duke Power Co.*, 401 U.S. 424 (1971), if there was disparate treatment of the protected class. If an employment policy resulted in the treatment of employees or individuals in the protected class differently from those in another class, this is *discrimination* or *disparate impact*. The term *disparate treatment* is usually used when less than the entire class is affected. Business necessity is a defense for both.[12]

In order for an employer to determine whether employment practices would result in discrimination on a member of the protected class, the EEOC issued guidelines. One formula enables the employer to determine mathematically whether a disparate impact on a certain class of employees existed. This formula is not a statutory definition of a violation but only evidence of violation. When discrimination is found, the employer must give a nondiscriminatory reason why it exists. Exhibit 4-1 illustrates how an employer can determine whether a disparate impact exists.

If the selection rate for minorities is less than 80 percent of the selection rate for the remaining applicants, a disparate impact is demonstrated. To make this computation, divide the selection rate for the minorities (or covered group) by the selection rate for the remaining applicants. In this example 67 percent is below 80 percent; therefore a disparate impact would exist.[13]

---

[12]For a legal approach to discrimination see John J. Donohue III and Peter Siegalman, "The Changing Nature of Employment Discrimination," *Stanford Law Review*, 43 (1990), 983.

[13]The court in *Albemarle Paper Co.* v. *Moody*, 422 U.S. 1343 (1975) gave judicial approval to the formula.

When the term *disparate treatment* is used, an employee alleges that she or he has been treated less favorably than others because of sex, race, etc., or employment action. Sometimes the term *disparate impact* is used in place of the term *disparate treatment,* but the meaning is not the same. *Disparate treatment* is a term used by employees when the employer has treated one person differently from another because of statutorily protected class. The disparate treatment complaints are individual cases, and the plaintiff must show that the employer had an unlawful motive or intended to discriminate. The basis for a violation under this theory can be found in *Furnco Construction Co.* v. *Waters,* 438 U.S. 567 (1978), and *Texas Community Affairs* v. *Burdine,* 450 U.S. 248 (1981).

Disparate impact is a term used when the plaintiff challenges the policies of management as being discriminatory toward a group of employees who are members of the protected class. The employer's intent to discriminate is irrelevant. The disparate impact theory was defined in *Griggs* v. *Duke Power Co.,* 401 U.S. 424 (1971).

The distinction is important to employers because if the complaint is disparate treatment and only one person is involved, intent or unlawful motive must be shown. Often employers become concerned about treating one employee differently from another. These concerns are not well founded because many times the person involved is not a member of a protected class. Even if he or she is, if a nondiscriminatory reason can be shown and there is no intent to discriminate, the action is legal.

Under disparate impact, although the plaintiff does have to show intent, the plaintiff must show by statistical evidence that the policy or procedure had the effect of discriminating against several members of the protected class. In *Watson* v. *Fort Worth Bank & Trust,* 108 S.Ct. 2777 (1988), the court held that although there may have been disparate treatment of a black female (who was refused four promotions by subjective decisions of white males), the plaintiff failed because she brought the suit under the disparate impact theory. She could not prove that a protected class was intentionally affected by an employer's policy.

However, under the disparate treatment theory she would have had a strong case for individually being treated differently as a member of the protected class. It must be remembered that an employer can always treat a member of the protected class differently (although it may be disparate treatment) as long as there is no intent to discriminate, a nondiscriminatory reason can be shown, and there is no alternative that is less objectionable.

Prima Facie Evidence

It is a legal principle that before a person can go to court, it must be shown that a wrong has been committed by stating certain facts. In discrimination lawsuits this is called a prima facie case (will establish a fact until rebutted). In alleging discrimination in employment the Supreme Court said that the charging party must establish a prima facie case by showing the following:[14]

1. The applicant is a member of a class protected by the statute alleged to be violated.
2. The applicant applied for the vacancy and is qualified to perform the job. (Where the employer requested specific questions be answered in a résumé and the applicant refused to answer those questions, the court held that the plaintiff had not completed the application process and therefore was not an applicant and failed to establish a prima facie case.)[15]
3. Marginally qualified, the applicant was rejected.
4. After rejection, the job vacancy remained open. The employer continued to seek applications from persons of equal qualifications.

Distinction between Equal Employment and Equal Opportunity

It is a common belief among managers that there is no discrimination when a minority is rejected and another minority is accepted. This was considered in *Connecticut* v. *Teal,* 102 S.Ct.

---

[14]*McDonnell Douglas Corp.* v. *Green,* 411 U.S. 792 (1973).

[15]*Tagupa* v. *Board of Directors Research Corp., U. of Hawaii,* 633 F.2d 1309 (9th Cir. 1980).

2525 (1982). The court stated that Title VII is designed not only to protect groups but to protect individuals as well. In this particular case, the selection procedures show no disparate impact upon the group, but individuals were denied an equal opportunity to be employed because of an identifiable pass/fail test barrier. Those individuals are entitled to protection under Title VII. If the individuals are deprived of employment opportunities or if their status is affected, then Title VII is violated. The law guarantees members of the protected class the opportunity to compete equally on the basis of job-related criteria. The fact that others were not discriminated against in the hiring process does not mean that certain individuals have not been wronged.

It was clear from this decision that there is a difference between equal employment and equal opportunity. Title VII requires that an employee be given an equal opportunity to be employed. Prior to the *Teal* decision, employers could review their hiring and promotion procedures according to the number hired.

The procedures would pass scrutiny by EEOC if the final result did not show a disparate impact. The courts and EEOC did not inquire into the disparate impact or disparate treatment of the process.

The Supreme Court in the *Teal* decision stated that the "bottom-line" approach is not a defense if in the process individuals have been adversely affected. In this case certain individuals were disqualified for promotion because they failed to pass a test that had not been validated. The results of the test had a disparate impact; therefore, business necessity had to be shown by validating the test.

The fact that the final selection rate did not show a disparate impact was immaterial. The *Teal* decision clearly establishes the difference between equal employment and equal opportunity to be employed.

Discrimination can take place at any step in the employment process. The individual must be given an opportunity to show that she or he is qualified. Elimination from consideration for a promotion or to fill a vacancy for non-job-related reasons denies the opportunity to be considered according to qualifications. An equal opportunity employer is one who gives the opportunity to become employed. Any barrier that is not job related or a business necessity is discrimination under Title VII.[16]

Protection from Retaliation

Most statutes have a provision that prohibits the employer from retaliating against an employee who attempts to aid in the enforcement of a statute. The legislative purpose of the provision is to encourage the employee to use the protection of the statute by reporting a violation and enhancing its enforcement.[17]

Title VII has a retaliation provision that is similar to those of other statutes.[18] Retaliation is defined by the courts as an unlawful practice of an employer whereby the employer discriminates against the employee for participating in the enforcement of a statute or a right.[19]

The application of these principles can be found in *Donnellon* v. *Fruehauf Corp.*, 796 F.2d 598 (11th Cir. 1986). The employee filed a discrimination complaint with the EEOC alleging that she was denied the sales representative position because of her sex. Three weeks later she was discharged. Four days after her discharge she filed an additional retaliation charge with the EEOC alleging that she was discharged in retaliation for filing her original claim. The court held that there was no sex discrimination but that

---

[16]Feminist remarks were given great weight by the court in *Price Waterhouse* v. *Hopkins*, 109 S.Ct. 1775 (1989).

See also *Sherman* v. *Burke Contracting*, 891 F.2d 1527 (11th Cir. 1990).

[17]*EEOC* v. *Ohio Edison*, 1 F.3d 541 (6 Cir. 1993).

[18]42 U.S.C. Sect. 2000(e)(3) provides that an employer cannot discriminate against an employee "because he has opposed any practice made an unlawful employment practice by this subchapter or because he has made a charge, testified, assisted, or participated in any manner in an investigation or hearing under this chapter."

[19]A retaliatory discharge of a at-will employee is a tort action in state courts as contrary to public policy, although other statutory remedies are available: *Tate* v. *Browning-Ferris Inc.*, 833 P.2d 1218 (Okla Sup. Ct. 1992).

she was discharged in retaliation for filing a claim.[20]

In order to get into court for a retaliation case (prima facie proof of retaliation), the employee must show

1. That she or he has engaged in statutorily protected activity.
2. That the employer has taken an adverse employment action.
3. That there is a causal connection between the protected activity and adverse action.
4. That the employer would not have taken the adverse action, "but for" the employee's good faith belief that the practice under the law was wrongful, and he or she was seeking to enforce it.

Retaliation Defense

It is up to the employer to show that the adverse action had nothing to do with the filing of the charge. If the employee's conduct was unlawful, excessively disloyal, hostile, disruptive, or damaging to the employer's business, then she or he cannot claim protection under the statute's discrimination clause.

In *Donnellon* there was no question that the plaintiff could meet the requirements to get into court. It then became a question of why she was discharged. The employer, according to the court, could not give an articulated, clear, and consistent reason for the discharge. Each witness gave a different reason. (An inconsistent reason is always damaging in any discharge case.) The court put great weight on the fact that she was discharged a month after filing the sex discrimination charge.

In *Alberty v. Tyson Foods,* 986 F.2d 1426 (10th Cir. 1992) the court found retaliation when a worker filed a workers' compensation claim.

Sometimes the employer will give clear reasons for discharge but they are not very persuasive. Such reasons as "generally poor work performance," "failure to cooperate," or "gross insubordination" usually will not be accepted by the court as legitimate, nondiscriminatory reasons, but will be considered a pretext for the retaliation.

The reason for the discharge must stand on its own. If the employee would not have been discharged for the offenses committed or if other employees committed the same offenses and were not discharged, then the courts could conclude it was retaliation. This also applies to former employees under Title VII.[21]

The retaliation on the part of the employer must be intentional. Showing that the employer treated the plaintiff differently from the way the firm would have treated other employees under similar circumstances is usually considered intentional.[22] The most important element in the defense of retaliation cases is that the discipline or employment decision is applied to all employees when the situation is the same. The mistake that employers often make is to treat a person who has filed a charge either more leniently or more strictly. Either policy is troublesome in retaliation charges. The more lenient policy reaches the point of no return; when enforcement takes place, retaliation is alleged. The overly strict policy will cause retaliation charges unless it is consistent.

Proper procedures for discharge are the best defenses to retaliation charges. If the employer's discipline, grievance, and discharge procedures are uniformly applied, violation of statutory retaliation provision will seldom be found.

Role of Trade Unions Under Title VII

A labor organization is defined under Title VII as any organization, agency, or employee representation committee that exists to deal with the employer.[23] Any conference or joint board that is subordinate to a national or international labor organization is also subject to the act. The labor organization must have at least 15 members for coverage under Title VII. The union cannot exclude from membership or otherwise discriminate

---

[20]*Ayoub* v. *Texas A&M University,* 927 F.2d 834 (5th Cir. 1991). Also in *Alberty* v. *Tyson Foods,* 986 F.2d 1426 (10th Cir. 1992), the court found retaliation in a workers' compensation claim.

[21]*Robeson* v. *Shell Oil Co.,* 66 FEP Cases (BN) 1284 (1994).

[22]The employee is adversely treated when a right is asserted; there does not have to be a statute involved. *Quiroga* v. *Hasbro, Inc.,* 934 F.2d 497 (3rd Cir. 1991), cert. denied.

[23]See *EEOC Compliance Manual,* Sect. 1.89, Part III.

against members because of race, color, religion, disability, sex, national origin, or age. It cannot cause the employer to discriminate against an individual. A labor organization cannot maintain segregated locals or discriminate as to referrals for acceptance in apprenticeship training programs.

Labor unions have a special duty under Title VII to represent fairly all employees apart from the requirements of the National Labor Relations Act. They must attempt to eradicate any discriminatory practices.

For more than 30 years the National Labor Relations Act was the only legislation concerned with labor management relationships except for some occasional disputes under the Fair Labor Standards Act.

In 1972, when Title VII was amended, a third party entered the relationship. EEOC could sue both the union and the employer for discrimination. The problem immediately arises: Who has jurisdiction, the National Labor Relations Board or EEOC, especially when procedures are different. If the union discriminates, the board will not hold a representation election under the act. The employee's right to strike over discriminatory practices of both the company and the union is supported by the NLRB after a grievance is processed.

For the purpose of this section it is important only to review a few basic principles concerning the role of the union in discrimination cases.

1. The Supreme Court, long before Title VII, held that a collective bargaining agreement between a union and an employer that discriminated against blacks is a violation of the duty of fair representation. Under the act all classes of employees must be represented.[24] Based on this decision the courts refuse to enforce an unfair labor practice against a union where it discriminates.[25]

2. Because the employees have elected the union to be their bargaining representative, they cannot discuss discrimination matters directly with the employer but must go through the union. If there is evidence that the union approves of employer discriminatory practices, the employees must still go through the union before going to EEOC. Where the employees went out on strike over discriminatory practices without going through the grievance procedure, it is not a protected activity; therefore, discharging the employees is not an unfair labor practice.[26] (Discharge because of strike activity is otherwise unlawful.) The court said that although employees have a right to be free from discrimination under Title VII, the right cannot be pursued at the expense of orderly collective bargaining.

When employees are represented by a union, the employer should not entertain complaints about discrimination unless they are discussed with the union first. The National Labor Relations Board and the courts strictly hold the employer to this rule. Regardless of whether the union is discriminating, the employees are represented by the union and therefore they must act through their representative.

Business Necessity as a Reason for Discrimination

Business necessity is a term originated by the Supreme Court in the *Griggs* case.[27] The employer's burden to prove was reinstated in CRA91. In the *Griggs* case the court stated that business necessity is justification for a policy that discriminates against a member of a protected class. Business necessity has been defined as "that which is reasonably necessary to the safe and efficient operation of the business." Business necessity has not been as useful as a defense to the employers as it might appear because of the narrow interpretation by the courts of what is efficient (or normal) and safe operation of the business.

[24]*Steele* v. *Louisville & Nashville Co.,* 323 U.S. 192 (1944).

[25]In *Chicago Tribune Co.* v. *NLRB,* 943 F.2d 791 (7th Cir. 1992) the court refused to enforce an NLRB order to bargain with a union that was guilty of racial discrimination.

[26]*Emporium Capwell Co. and Western Addition Community Organization* v. *NLRB,* 420 U.S. 50 (1973).

[27]*Griggs* v. *Duke Power,* 401 U.S. 424 (1971). CRA91 codifies the *Griggs* principle as to business necessity. Some legal scholars believe that the defense of business necessity will be even more difficult after CRA91.

The courts have held that business necessity cannot be used as a defense unless there is a showing of no other acceptable alternative that will serve the employer equally well and has a lesser impact on members of protected groups. With a defense of business necessity, the employer admits discrimination but argues that there is a reason for it.

Bona fide occupational qualification (BFOQ) differs from business necessity in that it is defined by 703(e) of Title VII and originally referred only to sex. Section 703(e) states that sex discrimination is valid in certain circumstances where sex is "a bona fide occupational qualification reasonably necessary to meet the normal operation of that particular business or enterprise." As a practical matter there is very little difference between the two, and often they are interchanged when used as a defense for discrimination in an employment decision. If the employer's perception of business necessity is not supported by objective data, the courts will reject it. The objective data must show that the discriminatory action was necessary for the efficient operation of the business. The courts demand evidence that the traditional qualifications for hiring or promotion are necessary to the safe and efficient performance of the job.

The employer often fails to sustain this burden because of subjective beliefs of what is necessary for the safe and efficient operation of the business.

Where the employer alleged business necessity in promoting a white over a black because the white had supervisory experience, the court found that the need for supervisory experience in order to perform the job was subjective.

The one area in which the employer has been able to show business necessity is where the safety of the employee or safety of others is involved. Business necessity has been accepted as a good reason for discrimination in airline cases where flight attendants become pregnant and are removed from duty.[28] In *Levin* v. *Delta Airlines*, 730 F.2d 994 (5th Cir. 1984), the court had little trouble in holding that removal of the flight attendants as soon as it was known that they were pregnant was a business necessity. However, the employees argued that there was available a less-discriminatory alternative that would cushion the adverse consequences of the discriminatory policy. The court held that the employer need only adopt the alternative when it is a customary practice in similar situations.[29] Failure to use the customary alternative does not indicate that the policy was a pretext.

Other than for the safety factor, business necessity is very difficult to prove. Where customers in South America would not deal with a female sales representative and the employer removed her, the court said as a matter of law the reason was insufficient defense of business necessity for the sex discrimination.[30] Because discrimination is admitted when using business necessity, the employer should not use it unless there are very strong facts to support the defense.

A Nondiscriminatory Reason for the Employment Decision

It is well-settled law that when an employee alleges that she or he has been discriminated against, the employee must establish a prima facie case as previously defined in this chapter. Once that is accepted by the court, the employer has to show a nondiscriminatory reason for the employment decision. This principle was established by the Supreme Court in two landmark decisions. CRA91 did not change it.

In the first situation, *Furnco Construction Corp.* v. *Waters*, 438 U.S. 567 (1978), the employer had to defend what appeared to be a discriminatory action of refusing to hire three black bricklayers who were fully qualified. The firm had a policy of hiring only bricklayers known to be experienced and competent or recommended by other contractors as skilled workers. The evidence showed that this policy was consistently

---

[28]In *International Union UAW* v. *Johnson Controls*, 111 S.Ct. 1196 (1991), the Court held that an EEOC directive is not a BFOQ and employer action was discriminatory.

[29]It is not certain that CRA91 will change this. Most legal scholars believe it will. The Supreme Court will have the final word.

[30]*Fernandes* v. *Wynn Oil Co.*, 653 F.2d 1275 (9th Cir. 1982).

followed with all applicants. Under this policy some blacks were hired.

The court held that the employer only had to give a legitimate nondiscriminatory reason for not hiring the blacks and that there is no requirement for the hiring procedure to maximize the hiring of minorities.

In the second case a female alleged that she was discharged because of her sex and a male was hired in her place.[31] The issue before the court was the kind of proof necessary to prove to the court that the action was nondiscriminatory.

The court held that once a prima facie case was established, the employer had to articulate a nondiscriminatory reason for the action. The employee could rebut the reason as being a pretext (not the real reason), but it must be shown by strong evidence that discrimination was the real reason. It then became a question of fact for the trial court to decide. The court in *Burdine* said there was no burden on the employer to persuade the court that the reason was not a pretext. This was up to the employee to do.[32]

The employer can rebut an assumption by giving nondiscriminatory reasons why the condition exists. For example, recruiting is broadly based, few minorities applied for the jobs, and there were few minorities unemployed in the labor market area.

It is now well-settled law that in any situation where the employer's action is alleged to be discriminatory it can be defended by showing a nondiscriminatory reason. The burden is on the employee to show that it was discrimination and that the nondiscrimatory reason was a pretext.

To prevent exposure to lawsuits under Title VII or any other antidiscrimination statute, the employer should always ask the question: Was the reason for the action a nondiscriminatory one? If the answer is in the affirmative, then there is good defense in the event it is challenged as being discriminatory.

OUT-OF-COURT SETTLEMENTS

When an employer receives a discrimination charge, there are three approaches to take. One is to adopt an aggressive, adversarial advocacy and take the offensive. The second approach is to adopt a passive but adversarial position. This approach is a defensive one where the employer lets the employee be the aggressor. The third approach is to pursue settlement as soon as possible.[33] (More than 90 percent of all claims are settled without a trial or any other hearing.) None of these approaches is proper until several factors are considered.

Factors to Be Reviewed

1. The problems created by administrative and/or judicial proceedings: the length of time it takes to get a decision, the necessity for testimony from witnesses who later have to work with the employee, the emotional stress for some management members, and the management time to process the case. This is a hidden cost of litigation and is seldom considered.

2. The chances of prevailing. This is a judgment factor that is better determined by legal counsel, who can only make an educated guess. Some cases that should never be lost *are* lost, and sometimes all the facts point to losing and the case is won. If there are "gray areas" in the law it becomes more difficult to assess the case.

3. The out-of-pocket cost of taking the charge through the judicial process. In discrimination cases if the employer loses he or she must pay the employee's attorney's fees, which are sometimes more than the damages.[34]

These factors should be considered in the early stages of the case. As the case progresses, these factors become less important, and if the case is

---

[31]*Texas Department of Community Affairs* v. *Burdine*, 450 U.S. 248 (1981).

[32]Court interpretation of CRA91 may change this as employee is getting rights through statute and court decisions.

[33]The author once knew a manager who would immediately offer to settle the case, regardless of the facts, for the cost of transportation for a corporate Equal Opportunity Office representative to investigate the charge.

[34]In *City of Riverside* v. *Rivera*, 106 S.Ct. 2686 (1986), the court upheld attorney fees of $245,000 while plaintiff received $33,350. See also *Malarkey* v. *Texaco, Inc.*, 794 F.Supp. 1248 (S.D. N.Y. 1992).

settled "on the courthouse steps," most of the economic advantages of settlement are gone.

Alternative Dispute Resolution

One approach that has increasing popularity, in the early stages of the dispute, is a process called the Alternative Dispute Resolution, commonly referred to as ADR. The parties can select seven mediation processes as an alternative to a full-blown trial. ADR is effective when the parties have not communicated to each other the reasons for their disagreement. Sometimes the parties are in agreement but they do not know it, or there is a minor disagreement that somehow got expanded. In these situations ADR could be helpful.[35] Some attorneys and practitioners believe that it weakens a case to make an approach to settle. If ADR is suggested as an alternative to an expensive trial, however, it is difficult to see how this would weaken the case.[36]

Considerations for Out-of-Court Settlements

A settlement in a civil rights case is compromise that is voluntarily agreed upon by the parties. Both parties accept a little less than they believe they are entitled to. The incentive to settle is that each party believes that the compromise is more advantagous than taking the risks and costs involved in pursuing the claim. Before either party decides to enter into a settlement the disadvantages and advantages should be carefully considered. The courts encourage settlements without consideration of the consequences. It must be shown that the parties have had opportunity to read and understand the contents of the settlement agreement that is usually drafted by a lawyer. If these facts are present the courts have little sympathy with a person who wants to rescind or modify the settlement.

Considerations as to out-of-court settlements should contain legal as well as employee consequences. Another consideration is a settlement that does not prevent a retaliation charge if the employee has been reinstated. Therefore, in the settlement negotiations, whether reinstatement is a "must position of the employee" has considerable influence on the decision. The employee will often propose reinstatement along with full back pay, but that is sometimes a starting point for negotiations. To accept would be capitulation.

As to employee relations considerations, the first problem is with the supervisor involved. Any monetary settlement implies discrimination regardless of the settlement agreement. With some managers and supervisors, this stigma is difficult to overcome, especially in a sex discrimination case when their wives are active in the feminist movements. Often a member of management feels that settlement is an admission of guilt. Settlement could cause problems, especially when there is no believed discrimination. Settlement for economic reasons is a mistake, unless management determines that economic reasons override all other considerations.[37]

The effect of lump-sum payment on other employees is an important consideration. It has little effect unless the employee is reinstated. With reinstatement, the exposure to adverse employee relations is present, but it does not always have an adverse effect. One way to mitigate an adverse effect on employee relations is to prohibit disclosure of the terms in the settlement agreement.

Settling a case where there is little evidence of discrimination is not advisable when consideration is given to the long-range economic and employee relations consequences. In situations where the legal assessment of winning in the courts is assessed at more than 50 percent, the long-range economic and employee relations benefits are maybe worth risking a court decision, although the immediate cost may not justify it.

The Settlement Agreement

When it appears that both parties want to settle, no final agreement should be reached until a

---

[35]Mediation process is especially suited for discrimination cases.

[36]See chapter 3 for more details on ADR.

[37]See *Miller* v. *Staats,* (D.C. Cir. 1983).

settlement agreement is drafted. The language of the settlement agreement is as important as the award agreed upon. This written agreement should be reviewed by an attorney. When the attorney drafts the agreement the practitioner should be certain that it contains certain nonmonetary elements, including the following:

1. The charging party or regulatory agency (if involved) should release any and all rights it has to further pursue the case, including participating in a class action. In some cases the parties involved may want to get releases from other possible members of the class.
2. The parties should agree to keep the terms of the settlement confidential.
3. There should be no determination of who is right or wrong.
4. Payment of the charging party's attorney's fees should be agreed upon. A settlement agreement does not prevent the prevailing party from later collecting attorney's fees unless there is previous agreement.

5. In regard to conduct after the case is closed, the employer should agree to take steps so the situation will not be repeated. However, nothing should be agreed upon that will interfere with the economical operation of the business or that is administratively burdensome.
6. Because retaliation is always a possibility, there should be a clause that states that settlement terms will not prevent the employer from treating the charging party any differently from other employees.

Unreasonable provisions can be prevented by hard negotiations. Usually the parties will agree rather than not settle when there is disagreement over language. It is the amount of the award and demands for reinstatement that often prevent a settlement.

CHAPTER
5
SELECTING QUALIFIED APPLICANTS

The Civil Rights Act of 1991 (CRA91)
Preemployment Procedures
Selection Process
National Origin Discrimination
Immigration Reform and Control Act of 1986 (IRCA)
The Selection Audit

THE CIVIL RIGHTS ACT OF 1991 (CRA91)

The Civil Rights Act of 1991 (CRA91) was signed into law on November 21, 1991. This is the most sweeping revision of the existing framework of federal discrimination laws since Title VII was passed in 1964.[1] Throughout this text various provisions will be referred to. The law does somewhat reduce the predictability of conflict over discrimination claims. It not only gives the present lawyers a tactical look at the discrimination laws, but also will generate considerable litigation over its interpretation.[2]

The act for the first time in discrimination law opens the door for punitive and compensory damages with dollar ceilings. It allows jury trial, sets up a glass ceiling committee (wasn't effective), repeals several 1989 Supreme Court decisions, and requires many procedural and substantive changes in dealing with discrimination at the workplace. Before any existing antidiscrimination law is considered, CRA91 should be researched. The EEOC has given their position in many areas, and if any area is overlooked, this author believes they will, upon request, explain their interpretation of the law. In 1993 EEOC issued discrimination guidelines (20 CFR 1609). The EEOC's policy on compensory and punitive damages can be found in "Guidance Enforcement: Compensatory and Punitive Damages Available under Section 102." Guidance for the charge processing can be found in "Revised Enforcement Guidance on Recent Developments in Disparate

---

[1]See Fair Employment Practices Manual Sect. 407, 1995.

[2]See Mark S. Dichter and A. M. Foran, "Implementing the Civil Rights Act of 1991," *The Human Resources Yearbook, 1992/93* (Englewood Cliffs, NJ: Prentice Hall), p. 174, also EEOC Annual Report, Sect. 407, 1993.

Treatment." Both policy statements were published in July 1992. Employers should acquaint themselves with these commission views as well as any other position that the EEOC has taken or may take in the future. It may not be the same as the court interpretation, but at least it will keep the government's primary regulatory agency off the employer's back. In the past the courts have given great weight to the EEOC's interpretation, and CRA91 will be no exception.

PREEMPLOYMENT PROCEDURES

The antidiscrimination laws described in chapter 4 have considerable impact on the entire management function. One of personnel's major areas of activity is the recruitment and selection of qualified applicants. These areas were especially affected by antidiscrimination laws. The selection process deeply involves all members of management who interview job candidates and make decisions on selection.

Members of management must be aware of the exposure to costly and time-consuming charges of discrimination even though they may be acting in good faith.

The antidiscrimination statutes do not specifically state what type of recruitment or selection is in compliance. We must look to court decisions, policies, and agency guidelines for direction.[3] More often than not, employers learn later that a dispute could have been avoided if they had taken a hard look at their application form, the screening process, and selection process. An employer should always check both state and federal laws before making a selection of an applicant.

Recruitment

The recruitment procedure is the preliminary step to the selection procedure; unless designed properly, it will have a devastating effect on the selection of qualified applicants. The place to prevent disparate impact is in recruitment procedure.

Some employers have said that it is not possible to select a qualified candidate because of the restrictions of antidiscrimination laws. This statement simply is not true. The supervisor who says, "Don't send me a minority or a female because I cannot refuse to hire them," does not understand the purpose and objective of the antidiscrimination laws.

Recruitment is a two-step process. First, the employer must announce a job opening to a labor market area that contains applicants capable of responding. Second, those capable of responding must become aware of and be encouraged to answer the announcement.

Relying on One Method

Where only one or two sources of recruitment are relied upon, state and federal agencies will attack the method as not being broad enough to attract all segments of the labor market. It is essential that a broad recruiting base be used.[4]

The key question in all recruitment procedures is whether the method limits qualified applicants from applying. There are certain inquiries that may have sex limitations, with such gender-based terminology as busboy, bartender, directress, or pressman. These have all been popular terms in the past, but now they can cause problems with the regulatory agencies. This type of ad limits the number of persons applying for the vacancy and could result in a disparate impact in the selection process. You don't have to be a boy to bus dishes or to tend bar.

Perhaps a more serious effect of an ad that limits the number of persons replying is that the ad is not serving the legitimate business purpose of seeking the best-qualified applicants available. Even if one were to disregard the legal restrictions of a gender-based ad, it still is not a sound recruitment practice.[5]

---

[3]EEOC Guidance on Interview Process (1993).

[4]See *Stacks* v. *Southwestern Bell Yellow Pages*, 27 F.3d 316 (8th Cir. 1994).

[5]D. Arthur, *Recruiting, Interviewing, Selecting, and Orienting New Employees*, 2nd ed. (New York: American Management Association, 1991), p. 52; R. Gatewood and H. Feild, *Human Resource Selection*, Chapter 10 (Chicago: Dryden Press, 1990), p. 421.

Word of Mouth Recruiting

Another common recruiting method is word of mouth (sometimes called an informal contact or employee referral). Many employment managers rightfully believe this to be the best source of qualified applicants. Courts closely examine this procedure because experience indicates that one worker will rarely refer another of a different race, nationality, religion, and so on. As a result, a "built-in headwind" limits the hiring of minorities if this is the sole source of applicants.[6] If the employee referral approach to recruiting is accompanied by an affirmative action program to encourage minorities and females to apply, the recruiting package would probably be acceptable to the courts.[7]

An affirmative action program to encourage minorities and females to apply would be to seek applicants actively from such sources as the Urban League, minority-oriented media, local Hispanic organizations, women's organizations, and schools with large minority populations.

Recruitment procedures that require listing all new job openings with state employment agencies and advertising in media with an adequate minority and female audience are seldom challenged by regulatory agencies.

If the employer chooses word-of-mouth or walk-in as the sole method of recruiting or any other single method of recruitment, the procedure will not be questioned unless the workforce has a statistical imbalance.[8] Such factors as commuting time and fluency requirements affect an applicant's job preference and must be considered, according to the court in the *Chicago Lamp* case.

The traditional methods of recruiting should not be eliminated because of antidiscrimination laws; the same resources should be used for protected classes in the same manner as for other applicants. However, the employer should be alert to possible disparate impact. If several sources are used, a disparate impact would be unlikely.

Preemployment Inquiries on Application Forms

The application form is an important document from which hiring decisions are made, but it presents potential discrimination problems and can form the basis for successful lawsuits. Some questions can be asked orally in the interview. They are as subject to litigation on the application form.[9]

There is nothing in the federal statutes, guidelines, or court decisions that prevents making preemployment inquiries either on the application forms or orally after a conditional offer is made, except for convictions or arrests. The inquiries are required to have a job-related purpose, and the information must not be used for discriminatory purposes.

If the application form has a disparate impact upon the hiring process, then it will be considered wrongful and will be challenged. These challenges will be indefensible where it can be shown that few applicants are placed after information is received.

Unstructured preemployment inquiries such as "What do you expect in salary in five years?" present the greatest exposure to liability in the selection process.[10]

All questions on the application form have one rule—they must have a job-related purpose. It is not advisable to use a form that other professionals have designed. However, the use of questions on such forms is helpful in designing your own form to meet your particular needs and to comply with

---

[6]In *EEOC* v. *Detroit Edison Co.,* 512 F.2d 301 (6th Cir. 1975), the court concluded that employee referrals would perpetuate the imbalance in the workforce in favor of white males that already existed at the facility.

[7]*Diggs* v. *Western Electric,* 587 F.2d 1070 (10th Cir. 1978); *United States* v. *Georgia Power Co.,* 474 F.2d 906 (5th Cir. 1973).

[8]*EEOC* v. *Chicago Miniature Lamp Works,* 947 F.2d 292 (7th Cir. 1991). Some courts will hold that if it is the most efficient and economical method, word-of-mouth recruiting is legal notwithstanding statistical imbalance: *EEOC* v. *Consolidated Service Systems, Inc.,* No. 91–3530 and 92–1879, unpublished opinion (7th Cir. 1993).

[9]See *Supervision,* vol. 53, Professional Training Association, 210 Commerce Blvd., Round Rock, TX 78664, February 12, 1992.

[10]The author once knew of a manager who would ask when "the War of 1812 was fought?" If the applicant didn't know, he would reject the applicant.

EXHIBIT 5-1

Name, address, telephone number, social security number.

Person to contact in case of an emergency.

Are you prevented by law from becoming employed in the United States? (Proof of immigration status will be required upon employment.)

Application for the known vacancy(ies) of _____ .

Previous employment. (Previous five years is long enough.)

Highest wages on previous job.

Previous training or experience related to present known job vacancies.

Availability to work: full-time, shifts, reasonable overtime, part-time, temporary, or all of those mentioned.

Permission to contact previous employer as to skills or knowledge in the former jobs held.

If laid off from previous job, are you subject to recall?

---

the law. The interviewer can get the same answer by asking a question in a different way. For example, in most states and under the Americans with Disabilities Act, it is illegal to ask whether you ever made a workers' compensation claim. There would be no problem in asking, after the job offer is made, whether the applicant is physically capable of performing the job-related functions of the vacancy applied for. If in doubt the employer can require a physical. The job offer would be conditional on passing the physical. Often the answer to a question will depend upon how it is worded.[11]

Many state statutes, Title VII, and the Age Discrimination in Employment Act prohibit the use of certain questions on the application form before a conditional job offer has been made. A conditional job offer is made after it has been determined that the applicant has the knowledge or skill to perform all functions of any job vacancy. This two-stage selection procedure is effective in selecting qualified applicants. Why should the employer care about anything else if the applicant does not have the skills to perform the job? This procedure will avoid exposure to a challenge by the regulatory agencies. Information necessary before a job offer is to be made will not be challenged. An example of this information is shown in Exhibit 5-1.

The interviewer can now decide whether the applicant is qualified as to skills and knowledge. If not, the employer should reject and tell why. If the applicant is qualified, then a *conditional* offer should be made. The applicant is informed that failure to meet or agree to any one of the conditions may result in a rejection. The applicant is required to answer only those questions that are asked.

The questions related to the conditional offer are in Exhibit 5-2. They are merely suggestions. Many other questions could be asked. The questions to be included would depend upon the vacancies under consideration and whether the information is necessary to determine that the applicant is suitable for the vacancies available.

To protect the employer from exposure to lawsuits the application form must have a closing section signed by the employer and applicant that includes

---

[11]An insurance defense attorney questioning a witness asked, "Is it not true that you told the sheriff immediately after the accident that you felt fine." The witness did not give a direct yes or no answer, but started to relate how the accident happened. The insurance attorney appealed to the judge, who, after several attempts to get a yes or no answer, let the witness tell the story he had started so many times. It seems that the witness was approaching an intersection with his dog in the front seat and his cow in the back of a pickup truck. At the impact the dog flew into the ditch, as did the cow. The sheriff came and looked at the cow, pulled out his gun, and shot the cow. He looked at the dog and shot it. He then came to the witness and asked how he felt.

EXHIBIT 5-2

1. Do you have any responsibilities that conflict with the job vacancy?
2. How long have you lived at present address?
3. Do you have any relatives working for this company?
4. Do you have any physical defects that would prevent you from performing certain jobs where, to your knowledge, vacancies exist?
5. Do you have adequate means of transportation to get to work?
6. Have you had any major illness (treated or untreated) in the past 10 years?
7. Have you ever been convicted of a felony or have a history of being a violent person? (This is a very important question to avoid a negligent hiring or retention charge.)
8. Educational background. (The information required here would depend on the job-related requirements of the position.)

1. A statement by the employer that the information requested is necessary to determine the best-qualified candidate and will not in any way be used for discriminatory purposes. Suggested wording could be: "We consider applicants for all positions without regard to race, color, creed, sex, national origin, age, disability, veteran status, or other legally protected status." (Takes care of state laws.)
2. An authorization by the applicant that all statements can be investigated if necessary to reach any employment decision.
3. The applicant's agreement that in the event of employment, and at all times thereafter, if any written or oral statements are false or misleading this is just cause for discharge.

The unanimous Supreme Court in *McKennon* v. *Nashville Banner*, 66 FEP 1192 (1995) held that after-acquired evidence that would have justified a termination nonetheless will not act as a bar to bringing a discrimination claim. The Court noted that the purpose of discrimination law is to force employers to examine the motives for their actions and to penalize them if they acted discriminatorily. The Court also felt that after-acquired evidence of wrongdoing could not simply be ignored, thus not allowing reinstatement because of plaintiff's now revealed misconduct.

At least four circuits had held that after-acquired evidence of prior employee misdeeds, such as false statement on résumés, automatically bars employment discrimination claims. The past misdeeds are often uncovered during the dis-covery phase of job bias litigation. Two other circuits had ruled that after-acquired evidence does not shield an employer from liability for discrimination but may limit the relief available.

The Court ruled unanimously in an Age Discrimination in Employment Act case that employees cannot be denied all relief under the antidiscrimination laws just because the employer discovers prior wrongdoing by the employee that would justify termination. Of some solace to employers, however, the Court limited the remedies available in such instances.

Some circuit courts said if the defendant could establish that the plaintiff would not have been hired if the false information was known, this resulted in dismissal. In those cases established recovery was barred. This was consistent with the Supreme Court expectation that the defendant must establish that the after-acquired evidence standing alone would not result in an adverse decision.[12]

The Court in the *McKennon* case adopted the tenth circuit position that held in *Summers* v. *State Farm Mutual Automobile Insurance*, 864 F.2d 700 (CA 10, 1988) that after-acquired evidence would not bar the wrongful discharge suit, but would preclude any relief or remedy. The sixth and seventh circuits followed his rule while others said

---

[12]*Welch* v. *Liberty Machine Works, Inc.*, 23 F.2d 1403 (8th Cir. 1994), *Frey* v. *Ramsey County Community Human Services*, 517 N.W. 2d 591 (Minn. Ct. App. 1994).

it does not bar the lawsuit and after-acquired evidence should be taken into consideration when giving a remedy. The *Summers* court and other circuits said there is no remedy. The Supreme Court adopted the *Summers* rule, which is now the rule in all courts.

The *McKennon* case was brought under ADEA, but in *Wallace* v. *Dunn Construction Co., Inc.,* 62 F.2d 374 (11th Cir. 1995) the action was brought under Title VII and Equal Pay Act.

The court will almost always support a discharge for falsifying information when applying for work. In *Johnson* v. *Honeywell Systems,* 955 F.2d 409 (6th Cir. 1992) the court upheld a discharge where the misrepresentation was unknown at the time of discharge. The misrepresentation was found during discovery in preparing for a wrongful discharge suit.

4. A statement that applicant understands and agrees, if employed, to abide by all reasonable rules and policies of the employer.

5. A statement that if the applicant is employed, this employment relationship is at will and may be terminated at any time by either party with or without cause. (This clause is optional, but enforceable.)[13]

The law does not restrict any question that has a job-related purpose. However, the information must be used for a nondiscriminatory purpose. The author feels that the preceding information should be on a separate form and placed on file. If the applicant is not hired, a nondiscriminatory reason should be placed in the file and kept for at least one year, unless a charge is filed.

SELECTION PROCESS

The Use of the Weighted Application Form

One of the problems that employers have with regulatory agencies is that the application form has questions that are not job related. When asked why a question is on the form, employers cannot give a business-related answer. One way to be sure the application form is not discriminatory is to use a technique called the Weighted Application Blank (WAB).

This is a technique that for many years was used to control turnover by the selection of job applicants according to defined personal history factors that were found controlling. WAB is more accurately defined as a structured method for determining which characteristics and other variables found in a job applicant are important for success on certain specified jobs.[14]

The concept on which this method was developed is that certain quantitative and objective information is found in each applicant that will determine behavior for a particular job category. For many years employment managers and supervisors have subjectively determined that a certain type of person will or will not succeed in a certain job. (For example, a supervisor believed that all persons from Wisconsin are lazy). It was usually based on limited experience that employees who lived far away, had high wages on previous jobs, did not have a car, were divorced, or either quit or were discharged from the previous job were all turnover applicants. The WAB seeks to establish a profile by the use of statistical techniques and analysis that with some degree of accuracy predicts whether certain factors have any influence on job tenure.[15]

Exhibit 5-3 shows some of these factors. The data are taken from a sample of employees on the payroll for a period of three months or less and from another group of employees with one or more years of service. The purpose of this study was to control turnover in the unskilled and semiskilled job categories.[16]

---

[14]"Development and Use of Weighted Application Blanks," rev. ed., no. 55 (Industrial Relations Center, University of Minnesota, Minneapolis, 1971).

[15]Although there is not an absolute correlation between tenure and success on the job, for the purpose of WAB analysis, tenure of one or more years on the job is predictive of some degree of success based on the assumption that if an employee lasts one year or longer, performance has been rated as acceptable.

[16]The WAB technique assumes that there is an opportunity to select from the labor market. In a tight labor market, as in some areas during the Korean War, the employer moved the employment office upstairs; if applicants could walk up the stairs, they were hired.

---

[13]The at-will clause is discussed in chapter 12.

EXHIBIT 5-3

The following factors were used in a weighted application blank survey of the paper stock division:

1. Location
2. Age hired
3. Weight
4. Height
5. Marital status
6. Number of children
7. Freinds or relatives employed here
8. Referred by
9. Prior job injury
10. Military service
11. Education
12. Length of last job
13. Number of jobs in last three years
14. Reasons for leaving last job
15. Wages before hire
16. Type of last job

The factors numbered 2, 4, 6, 9, 10, 14, and 16 were discarded because they did not differentiate between the active group and the terminee group.

The original list of factors was based on the opinions of the employment manager and over 30 supervisors on what characteristics determine the ideal employee. Of 16 original factors, only 9 were found to differentiate between active groups and terminee groups. This outcome is illustrative of what regulatory agencies are referring to when they insist that a question on the application form have a business purpose rather than reflect subjective thinking of the employer. Exhibit 5-4 shows the ideal employee for the paper stock division.

The calculation is the correlation of the personal histories with the tenure on the job. It is a mathematical formula that provides relative weighing of each significant independent characteristic. The characteristics are given a point value, and a cutting score is developed by drawing a line between the number that shows where the most terminees would be eliminated and the most actives would have been hired.

Exhibit 5-4 shows in graphic form that for the paper stock division a cutting score of 11 would be effective in eliminating hires who will be terminated within a year. In this study of actives and terminations, no data were compiled as to the reason for termination except that an applicant with certain (point value) characteristics of less than 11 would be more likely to be terminated than an applicant above 11.

The WAB is most effective in the factory and office semiskilled jobs. It has little or no use with higher skilled jobs or managerial jobs because factors other than personal characteristics, such as job assignment, supervision, training, and work experience, would outweigh the personal characteristics used in WAB. Most personnel practitioners can develop the WAB to fit their needs with some research and a little training. More sophisticated WABs can be found in the literature, and study of this literature may be advisable.[17] Some feel that WAB is discriminatory because of the sample used. They adopt the

---

[17]Abraham and E. Flippo, *Managing a Changing Workforce,* Chapter 6 (Chicago: Commerce Clearing House, 1991), p. 169; also D. Arthur, *Recruiting, Interviewing, Selecting, and Orienting New Employees,* 2nd ed. (New York: American Management Association, 1991), p. 52.

EXHIBIT 5-4

The ideal employee in the paper stock division had the following characteristics at the time of hire:

1. Is from local or labor market area within approximately 20 miles of plant site
2. Weighs between 151 and 170 pounds
3. Is married
4. Has friends or relatives who work here
5. Was a walk-in
6. Has education of eight years or less or is a high school graduate
7. Last job was 12 to 23 months in duration
8. Had one to two jobs in the last three years
9. Wages before hire were less than or equal to employer's starting rate

A cutoff score of 11 or better was arrived at by using the greatest differentiation between the active group and the terminee group. This would mean that 72 percent of the actives would have been hired and 4 percent of the terminees would have been hired.

Source: All exhibits relating to the WAB method are from personnel files of Hoerner Waldorf Corporation, St. Paul, Minnesota.

Biographical Data Method. The theory is the same; the name is different.[18]

The system described in this chapter is a simplified one that works; if a method works, it should be used without becoming too academic.

WAB as Defense to Questions Asked

The WAB replaces the possible subjective interviewer's biases, which are often artificial barriers in the selection and promotion of the protected classes. It is certainly more defensible in showing nondiscriminatory reasons than the less objective measures used by many interviewers. Like any other selection device, it should first be determined whether the WAB has any adverse impact in the selection of protected classes; if so, then the method used to develop it should be changed or modified for validation purposes. The experience of those who use WAB has been that

there is no disparate impact provided that the characteristics used and sample come from all classes of employees.

If the present workforce that is used as a sample has a statistical imbalance, then WAB would probably be challenged as perpetuating discrimination. The WAB also serves to establish reasons for asking certain questions in the interview that have been found to be predictive of tenure and success on the job.

Affirmative action compliance officers and EEOC have consistently stated that there must be a legitimate purpose for asking questions in the interview. Questions to determine characteristics used to score the WAB would have a legitimate nondiscriminatory purpose.

The WAB should be used in the initial screening interview; if the applicant fails at this level, further interviews would not be necessary. This would eliminate the opportunity for supervisor and manager bias at the second level of the hiring process.

For several years practitioners have been using the weighted application technique as an effective

---

[18]See R. Gatewood and H. Feild, *Human Resource Selection: Weighted Application Blank and Biographical Data* (Chicago: Dryden Press, 1990), p. 421.

EXHIBIT 5-5

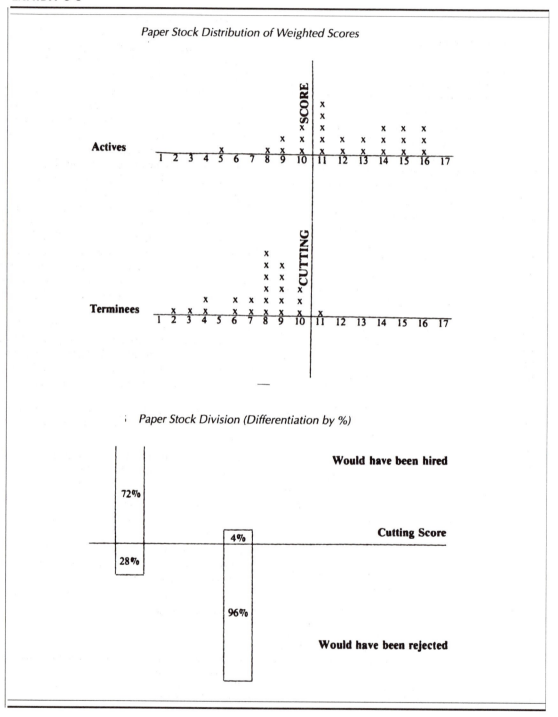

Paper Stock Distribution of Weighted Scores

Paper Stock Division (Differentiation by %)

way to predict turnover; this is an additional use of WAB.

Preemployment Testing

The most significant change in the selection process as a result of antidiscrimination laws is in the area of preemployment testing.[19] The field of industrial testing grew substantially after World War II to the extent that it was considered by many personnel practitioners a necessity in the selection process. Most testing programs were instituted with little or no knowledge of the jobs for which the selection tests were given. Often the tests determined only whether the applicant was an average American. Testing programs, whether valid or invalid, became popular because they afforded a crutch for the selection of an applicant. It was an easy way for the nonprofessional interviewer to screen and select applicants.

For more than five decades professors were advising their students not to use a test as a selection tool unless it was validated to determine whether the test could predict job performance. However, this pseudopsychological method of selecting applicants continued with increasing popularity. The failure of personnel practitioners to validate tests was contrary to sound selection practice. It was doomed to fall under the ax of antidiscrimination laws. When the ax did fall, many employers abandoned tests altogether.[20] This result was unfortunate because a properly validated test is one of the least discriminatory means of selecting employees. It reduces the need to rely on the unconscious, illegal, subjective judgment of the interviewer. This is probably the reason testing is becoming more popular in the later 1990s.[21]

Restrictions on Testing

Although antidiscrimination laws do not prohibit the use of tests[22] in the selection process, they do limit their use.[23] Some employers feel that the requirement of antidiscrimination laws for validation and the risk of being in violation are too great compared to the accuracy of predicting success on the job. For this reason many small employers chose not to use the test as a selection tool, or if they do use it the scores are a very small part of the decision-making process.

Judicial requirements for valid testing can be found in the leading and most-quoted case in antidiscrimination law, *Griggs* v. *Duke Power Co.,* 401 U.S. 424, decided by the Supreme Court in 1971. The selection test used by Duke Power Company was the Purdue Vocational Test form B for initial testing and form A for retesting purposes. The time limits were disregarded. It was considered a work test. Applicants protected by Title VII were affected adversely as shown in Exhibit 5-6.

Fifty-two percent of Caucasians tested were enrolled in a training program, but only 13 percent of blacks and 5 percent of Hispanic-Americans were enrolled. The *Griggs* case stands for the following principles in preemployment testing:

1. A test must be job related. If verbal ability is not required to perform functions of the job, one should not test for it.

2. An employer's intent not to discriminate is irrelevant. This is applicable only to Title VII and CRA91; other statutes require intent.

3. If a practice (training school in the *Griggs* case) is fair in form but discriminatory in operation, it is in violation.

4. The defense for any existing program that has adverse impact is *business necessity.* Business necessity was not defined by the court.

5. Title VII does not forbid testing, only tests that do not measure job performance.

---

[19]For a detailed analysis of preemployment testing, see Mary F. Cook, "The Effectiveness and Legality of Preemployment Testing," *The Human Resources Yearbook, 1992/93* (Englewood Cliffs, NJ: Prentice Hall), p. 432.

[20]In a survey in 1963, 90 percent of employers were using tests; in 1971 only 55 percent used tests of one kind or another. "Personnel Testing," *Bulletin to Management,* ASPA-BNA Survey no. 12 (Washington, DC: Bureau of National Affairs, 1971).

[21]*Olsen Report,* September 1991, The Olsen Corporation, One Merrick Ave., Westbury, NY 11590.

[22]See C. Allen, "Black and White Controversy," *Insight,* 8, no. 2 (January 13, 1992), 4.

[23]See Uniform Guidelines of Employee Selection Procedures, 29 CFR Sect.

EXHIBIT 5-6

Number Tested	Mean Score	Race	Enrolled in Training School
108	38.75	Caucasian	52
41	24.92	Negro	13
1	—	Oriental	1
1	—	American Indian	0
14	29.53	Spanish-American	5

Source: Court records, *Griggs* v. *Duke Power,* 401 U.S. 424 (1971). Race terms are actual terms used in the case.

6. The test must measure the person for the job and not the person in the abstract.

7. Less-qualified applicants should not be hired over those better qualified because of minority origins. There is no requirement to hire unqualified persons.

A test that has an identifiable pass/fail score denies an employment opportunity to a disproportionately large number of the protected class. This prevents an individual from proceeding to the next step in the selection process. It would be in violation of Title VII.[24]

In determining whether the procedure has an adverse impact, statistical evidence should be considered; however, a statistically unbalanced workforce (disproportionate number of non-minorities or females) does not necessarily mean that the selection procedure is in violation. The reason for the condition may not be the selection procedure but a characteristic of the labor market.

Validation of Tests

If a test has an adverse impact on the selection process as was the case in *Griggs,* it must be validated as to whether it is

1. Job related

2. Predictive of performance

3. Necessary because no less-discriminatory methods are available; then business necessity is required[25]

---

[24]*Connecticut* v. *Teal,* 102 S.Ct. 2525 (1982).

[25]CRA91 permits the employee to show that a less-discriminatory practice can be used.

Good faith effort or neutrality in placing applicants is irrelevant if an adverse impact results. The court in *Griggs* did not say how the test should be validated, but at the time of the *Griggs* decision *Albemarle Paper Co.* v. *Moody,* 422 U.S. 405, was working its way through the lower courts. In June 1975 the Supreme Court put to rest the question of what constituted the proper validation of a preemployment test as well as the backpay issue.

In 1963, Albemarle Paper Company adopted the Wonderlic Test A and B series as a screening program for selection of employees. General population norms were used to set cutoff scores until the *Griggs* decision; after that Albemarle hired an expert in industrial psychology to validate the test. He used ratings of job performance from three different supervisors, which were correlated with test scores. After the validation 96 percent of the white applicants passed the test and 64 percent of the blacks. The test scores were primarily used to select and place employees in 11 separate departments where 17 training lines of progression were established.

Exhibit 5-7 shows the placement of employees in the wood yard, which is an unskilled job category.

The skilled lines of progression were in the paper mill. To be placed in this line of progression it was necessary to have a certain score in the Wonderlic test. In Exhibit 5-7 there were a large number of African-Americans in unskilled jobs, while in Exhibit 5-8 there are very few. To defend this disparate impact it was necessary to validate

EXHIBIT 5-7

A. Wood Yard Department	Negro[27]	White
Yard Crew		
Crane Operator (Large)	0	9
Long Log Operator	0	4
Log Stacker Operator	0	4
Small Equipment Operator	0	4
Bulldozer Operator	0	1
Oiler	0	4
Chip Unloader	1	3
Chain Operator	0	4
Chipper Operator No. 2		
Chipper Operator No. 1	4	0
Tractor Operator	5	0
Chip Bin Operator	4	0
Laborers	12	0
Service Crew		
Dempster-Dumpster	1	0
Winch Truck Operator	3	0
Winch Truck Operator Helper	1	0
Laborer	6	0

Source: Appendix to brief of appellants, *Albemarle Paper* v. *Moody,* No. 74-389.

EXHIBIT 5-8

C. Paper Mill Department	Negro[27]	White
Paper Machine Line of Progression		
Machine Tender No. 1	0	4
Machine Tender No. 2	0	4
Back Tender No. 1	0	4
Third Hand No. 1	0	4
Third Hand No. 2	0	4
Fourth Hand No. 1	0	4
Fourth Hand No. 2	0	4
Front Plugger No. 1	0	4
Back Plugger No. 1	1	4
Back Plugger No. 2	0	4
Beaterman	0	4
1st Helper	0	4
Brokeman	4	0
Stock Puller	0	0
Laborer	1	0

Source: Appendix to brief of appellants, *Albemarle Paper* v. *Moody,* No. 74-389.

[27]Term used in Appendix of *Albemarle Paper Co.* v. *Moody,* No. 74-389, is "negro." It is used in Exhibits 5-7 and 5-8 referring to that case in its historic context. The term is now considered improper in antidiscrimination documents. The preferred term now is "African-American."

the tests. The validation of the tests by Albemarle was improper to show business necessity because:

1. The validation process used was not related to the job being applied for. Subjective supervisors' ratings were compared to test scores. The study focused on experienced employees in upper-level jobs; high scores of that group are not predictive of qualifications for new workers to perform lower-level jobs.
2. The supervisors rated older whites and experienced workers, whereas tests were given to job applicants who were younger, unexperienced, and nonwhite.

Particular attention has been paid to these two cases because a substantial part of the EEOC Employee Selection Procedures Guidelines of 1978 as related to testing had their origin in the *Griggs* and *Albemarle* cases. Legal principles in the guidelines have had little change in subsequent years.

Determination of Disparate Impact Threshold

The EEOC Uniform Guidelines (which have judicial acceptance) use a "4/5 or 80 percent" test to determine whether a disparate impact exists. The disparate impact threshold for females is therefore 0.8 times (x) the selection rate for males. For minority applicants, the disparate impact threshold is 0.8 times (x) the selection rate for nonminority applicants. This formula could be safely used for any protected class. However, it would not work if the job class contained only a small number of employees.

Types of Test Validation

There are three types of test validation that are stated in the EEOC Uniform Guidelines and have been judicially accepted.

1. *Criterion-related validity* is a collection of data that measure job performance and establish statistical relationships between measure of job performance and test scores. This is the traditional method of validation of preemployment tests, which has been used for more than 30 years. Supervisor ratings must

be objective or will fail to meet the criteria in the *Albemarle* case (the most popular case).

2. *Content validity* correlates certain aspects of the job performance with test scores to measure job performance. This differs from the criterion validation in that the job performance is measured in the specific job for which the applicant is being tested. This method of validation relies heavily on job analysis methods alluded to by the appellate court in the *Albemarle* case.[26]
3. *Construct validation* is a psychological method of validation based on research that identifies a psychological trait as essential to the successful performance of the job and develops a selection procedure to measure the presence and degree of that trait. Examples of a trait would be leadership ability and ability to work under pressure (not used very often).

An important requirement of the EEOC Uniform Guidelines that has been judicially accepted is found in Section 5(I), where it is stated that procedures to select for a higher-skilled job would not be appropriate if three conditions existed:

1. The majority of the applicants selected do not progress to a higher-level job within a short time after being placed on lower-level job.[28]
2. There is no real distinction between the higher- and lower-level jobs, or selection procedures measure skills not necessary to perform the higher-level job.
3. Knowledge could be acquired on the higher-level job without the employee's being trained on the lower-level job.

The validation process is expensive and time consuming and even when completed may not be accepted by the courts. In view of this lack of certainty in judicial acceptance, the employer should seriously consider whether testing is

---

[26]Job analysis as used by the court is a statement that provides basic information about job requirements and characteristics of persons who can successfully perform the job.

[28]A short period is a matter of judgment of the enforcement agency and the courts. The length of time would be somewhat related to the degree of skill required.

necessary to predict job performance. Testing is especially subject to exposure if it has an adverse impact; however, a test is permitted if given to all applicants, job-related, not of medical in nature, and consistent with business needs.

Preemployment Physicals

Questions about physical ability to perform the job being applied for can lead into questions about medical history and preemployment physical examinations. Many preemployment physical examinations given by employers are not related to the physical requirements of the job. A job-related preemployment physical should not be given until a conditional job offer is made.[29] This federal procedure eliminates any exposure from state handicap laws.

An audit of company preemployment physical examinations is advisable in light of the requirement that any prerequisite to hiring must be job related.

An important step in making a preemployment physical job related is to be assured that the doctor has knowledge of the physical requirements of the job. Often this is difficult because either the doctor does not want to take the time to study the job or the job content changes so rapidly that it makes the study obsolete in a short time. It is best for the doctor to observe the various jobs. If this observation is not possible, a good job description will be sufficient.

In the job description the essential physical requirements of the job should be noted; when the job is changed, the job description should be updated and communicated to the doctor. Preemployment inquiries as to the applicant's physical condition can be justified in determining job placement after the job offer has been made.

If the applicant is handicapped, it is necessary for the employer to know his or her physical condition in order to accommodate under the ADA. This need justifies a preemployment physical after the job offer has been made.[30]

Although questions about medical history and physical or mental disabilities are not specifically prohibited by the law after a job offer has been made, they are hazardous unless a specific business purpose can be shown.

Often the same information can be obtained without a discriminatory emphasis that may trigger an investigation or a complaint. For example, as has been noted, instead of asking whether an applicant has any disabilities, one should ask whether any disabilities would interfere with the ability to perform the job for which application is being made.

If an applicant does not know, further inquiry as to the physical condition is justified. However, to protect the applicant's right to privacy, disclosure of medical information should be only to persons who have a need to know.

This discussion on preemployment inquiries has been directed to those involved in screening applicants; however, as a practical matter interviews are conducted on all levels of management. To avoid exposure to discrimination and to eliminate prejudice by management personnel, those who interview should not be allowed the discretion of the past. Written guidelines to standardize preemployment inquiries are helpful. All preemployment inquiries should have the specific purpose of determining the qualifications of the individual applicant as required by the job and not necessarily what the interviewer subjectively believes will make a good employee.

The advent of Title VII caused changes in the selection of applicants for many organizations. The key new element was that the evaluation of the applicant must be objective. The practice of selecting candidates by the instincts of the supervisor, prejudices—often based on single experience—or other subjective criteria will no longer withstand judicial scrutiny. It is questionable whether these subjective methods were ever effective in selecting the best-qualified person. The courts do not force the employer to select a low-level performer.[31] (The author knew a supervisor who would not accept applicants who

---

[29]ADA allows employers to require if certain conditions are met.

[30]Treatment of handicapped workers is found in chapter 6.

[31]*Lucero* v. *Hart*, 915 F.2d 1367 (9th Cir. 1990).

were too fat because he believed that they were all lazy!) The day of the supervisor who said that he could determine the physical strength of applicants by looking at the applicant is over. As one court said, an "eyeball test" is not valid for determining the strength of an applicant.[32]

The major objective of the selection procedure is to hire qualified applicants. It is necessary to establish appropriate job specifications and to structure at least part of the interview. Before antidiscrimination laws, employers were not required to establish job specifications. If they did, their validity or accuracy was never questioned by anyone except internal management, which often aided in drafting them. Under antidiscrimination laws the selection procedure is subject to the EEOC Uniform Guidelines on Employee Selection Procedures, enforcement agencies, and scrutiny of the courts.[33] Selection procedures must be modified to eliminate exposure but still be effective in selection of the best-qualified applicant.

Establishing Criteria for Selection

Most companies either formally or informally establish some criteria for selection. When establishing these criteria the labor market conditions must be taken into consideration. When the criteria are not supported by the labor market conditions, the employer must either lower the criteria for selection or not be able to fill the vacancy.

What usually happens is that the criteria are lowered. For example, the employer establishes a qualification of a college degree in chemistry and four years of experience for the position of a chemist. When nobody can be found on the labor market with those qualifications, the standards are lowered to three years of college and three years of experience.

A white male applies with those qualifications and gets the job. One week previous to filling the

vacancy a black female with three years of college and four years of experience was turned down because she did not meet the criteria. She finds out that the white male with less experience was hired and files a charge under Title VII. The employer now has an extremely difficult defense.

This practice of lowering the standards and not notifying the turn-downs is common and can result in a lawsuit, not because the employer intended to discriminate but because the selection procedure did not consider the discriminatory problem when standards were lowered.

When a particular job category is short in supply and the manager is forced to go without help for a period of time, she or he becomes desperate and crisis hiring results. The following case history illustrates this point.

Use of Job Descriptions and Job Analysis: What Are They?

Job descriptions are detailed listings of job duties and expectations attached to the performance of a particular position. They present a picture of why the job exists and the work it involves. Job descriptions can range from a formal listing used to identify job responsibilities and provide a basis for evaluation to an advertisement. They establish hiring specifications, communicate performance standards and expectations to employees, and provide documentation for staff planning.

Job descriptions became a hot topic after the enactment of the American with Disabilities Act (ADA) in January 1990. Employment lawyers and human resource professionals debated the relative legal and business-related advantages and risks attributed to maintaining written job descriptions. Employers were advised to review and update all job descriptions in advance of the ADA's July 26, 1992, effective date. "Essential function" became the menu of the day as employers re-evaluated their employee's duties and responsibilities in a more concrete way. Now several years later, experience has shown that job descriptions are useful tools in the workplace. They do require attention to detail to retain their accuracy and credibility.

---

[32]*EEOC* v. *Spokane Concrete Products,* 534 F.Supp. 518 (E.D. Wash. 1982).

[33]For application and interpretation of Uniform Guidelines see Gatewood and Feild, *Human Resource Selection,* p. 674.

Crisis Hiring—A Case History

The department head requests a quality control supervisor. The market for experienced quality control supervisors is extremely tight. A month goes by and the department head completely discredits the personnel department to the CEO for failure to fill the vacancy. The CEO calls in the vice president of personnel, who relieves the pressure by agreeing to recruit a quality control supervisor, because the employment manager has been unable to do so and if anybody is to be accountable it must be the department head. Another two weeks pass, and top management continues to apply the pressure. A well-dressed, fast-talking person (wearing a tie with ducks on it) applies for the job. The vice president of personnel interviews him and gives him the standard skill reading rule test that is given to all machine operators. His answer to a 2 3/4-inch measurement is "2 inches one big mark, and one small one." The intelligence test score shows the mind of an 8-year-old. The personnel vice president sends him to the production manager, who, after shooting thousands of ducks through conversation with the applicant, hires him. The vice president of personnel, out of professional pride, tells the production manager that the person he has hired can neither read a rule nor come up to the intelligence level of a high school education, which is one of the qualifying requirements of the job. His answer is "He can learn by my training."

This type of crisis hiring could later cause problems when "the duck-hunting trip is over" and the production manager is faced with the problem of too many rejects.

This focus is on the who, what, when, where, and why of the development of a job description that may be used by an employer to identify the essential functions of the job and provide relevant evidence in the event of litigation. No law requires job description or job analysis, but they are good personnel tools.

Qualifications for the job are determined by job analysis from current job descriptions. These techniques are subject to judicial suspicion. Many times they are developed for ad hoc purposes, as a method to justify the wage and salary or promotion decisions. An audit of the current job analysis and job descriptions often discloses that any resemblance between what the employee is doing and what the job analysis or job description states is purely coincidental.

Obsolete Job Descriptions

Job descriptions should be reviewed by asking certain questions: Are the functions described in the job description still a part of the actual job? Are all essential functions of the job included in the job description? Have the physical requirements listed been reviewed by a doctor? Do the employees currently doing the job have the skills or education listed in the job description? Is the job description written in simple and understandable language? Does the job content demand greater or less technical knowledge that is actually needed to perform all the job functions? Are realistic educational requirements listed? An affirmative answer to these questions, as well as others, will often determine whether the job description is current and accurate.

Litigation and Job Descriptons

Often job descriptions are valuable for exhibits in EEOC hearings or disputes under the Fair Labor Standards Act.[34] However, they can be damaging when they are not kept up to date, are developed to get an employee a raise, or are intended to other-

---

[34]*Henchey* v. *Town of North Greenbush,* 831 F.Supp. 960 (ND NY 1993).

wise upgrade the job content on paper. Actual observance of job content for purposes of job analysis and job descriptions is legally necessary if they are to be used as a basis for employment decisions.

When the job analysis and job descriptions are developed by objective methods,[35] the employer is then in a position to establish an applicant pool of qualified candidates.[36]

Use of Applicant Pool to Eliminate Crisis Hiring

The applicant pool is a technique by which the employment manager has made an attempt to have available qualified candidates to fill future vacancies.[37] It is developed by predicting (through experience) job vacancies in the next six-month period (or whatever period is appropriate) in certain job categories. After determining the need or size of the pool, the employment manager immediately recruits and selects the best-qualified applicants for that job category. When all the candidates have been selected for the anticipated vacancies, recruiting and selection stops until placements are made to those in the applicant pool.

In selecting candidates for the applicant pool, those selected are told that when a vacancy occurs they will be hired; if they are not available when a vacancy occurs, other candidates in the pool will be selected according to their qualifications and the order in which they were accepted in the pool.[38]

The courts often require quotas to correct discriminatory practices. An offer of a job that is refused is the same as a hire to satisfy the judicial quota requirements.[39] This concept is reinforced by the Supreme Court, where it held that a job offer after discriminatory refusal to hire stops liability even though retroactive seniority of six years was not included in the job offer.[40] In view of the rule in the courts that a job offer is the same as a hire, one criticism of the applicant pool is eliminated, that is, that once placed in the pool the best qualified may not be available when the vacancy occurs and the underutilized category is not filled. Whether the vacancy is filled or not, as long as the offer is made, the good faith effort has been made to correct the underutilization.

The applicant pool gives almost zero exposure to affirmative action problems and still allows the employer to hire the best-qualified applicant. The applicant pool must be properly structured to include qualified persons of all classes. Where the employer established an applicant pool that had a height requirement[41] that excluded more women than men, the court held that although some women were not discriminated against by the requirement, others were.[42]

NATIONAL ORIGIN DISCRIMINATION

Unlawful discrimination occurs when an employment decision is based on the national origin of the person adversely affected by that

---

[35]Karstens, Schroeder, Surrett, "Impact of the Americans with Disabilities Act on Job Evaluation," *Labor Law Journal*, July 1995, p. 436.

[36]Job analysis and job descriptions should be developed by persons who are not supervisors or members of the personnel staff. In the author's experience, industrial engineers or outside consultants are persons most likely to develop unbiased job analyses and job descriptions.

[37]Given judicial approval by Justic Powell in *Albermarle* case.

[38]The practice of telling applicants that their application blank will be kept on file and if a vacancy occurs they will be called for an interview is troublesome because all too often they are not called and a less-qualified person is hired through normal recruiting sources.

[39]A remedy for a statistical imbalance caused by discriminatory practices is a court order to require the employer to hire a certain percentage of the protected class discriminated against. The employer therefore must take the best qualified within those classes to comply with court order.

[40]*Ford Motor Co.* v. *EEOC,* 102 S.Ct. 3057 (1982).

[41]*Shutt* v. *Sandoz Crop Protection Corp.,* 944 F.2d 1431 (9th Cir. 1991). A 21-member labor pool was used, and 106 members of all the sales representatives were available; the court said it was not a representative labor pool. For further information on the applicant pool concept, see Justice Powell's appendix opinion in *Regents of University of California* v. *Bakke,* 438 U.S. 265 (1978). In *Johnson* v. *Transportation Agency,* 107 S.Ct. 1442 (1987), the court in approving the applicant pool concept stated that an affirmative plan that requires all applicants in the pool to compete with all other applicants is acceptable.

[42]*Costa* v. *Markey,* 677 F.2d 1582 (1st Cir. 1982).

decision.[43] Although national origin discrimination under Title VII has not been popular and case law is scarce compared to other protected classes such as race, religion, and sex, it can be troublesome.[44] National origin bias is unlawful in hiring and promotion, the same requirement to get into court as in race, religion, and sex. However, it has one additional feature: where the employee cannot speak English. To require the employee to do so can be violative of Title VII if knowledge of English is not required for successful performance of the job. However, a foreign accent is a legitimate reason for rejecting where the job requires the applicant to deal with the public.[45] The EEOC has issued guidelines.

Labor unions may be required to publish collective bargaining agreements in a foreign language in order to ensure adequate representation of their members when a large proportion of the membership speak only a foreign language.

Discrimination because of national origin is unlawful if physical requirements such as height tend to exclude certain nationalities, unless business necessity can be shown.[46]

National origin under Title VII has nothing to do with citizen status: The employer may refuse to hire noncitizens provided the refusal is applied to noncitizens of all national origins.[47]

Dress and Grooming Codes

Prohibition of dress and grooming customs can be a violation of national origin if native appearance does not interfere with the job. However, the courts give very liberal interpretation to this section of the act. Employers can prescribe any dress code that does not show intentional discrimination because of nationality or sex. This is true whether it be requiring males to wear neckties and not females, prohibiting males from wearing earrings, requiring males to shave off a beard, or specifying hair lengths. Company requirements on grooming and dress must be stated as a job necessity and should not be adopted for the sake of appearance. This is the position of most courts.

Title VII was originally interpreted to mean that many dress and grooming codes were discriminatory, but subsequent court decisions changed this interpretation.

National origin discrimination is also a violation of the Immigration Reform and Control Act, discussed in the next section. Many observers believe that there is greater potential of exposure under this act than under Title VII.

IMMIGRATION REFORM AND CONTROL ACT OF 1986 (IRCA)

The Immigration Reform and Control Act of 1986 [IRCA; 8 U.S.C. 1324(a)] substantially changes the employer's right to hire undocumented or illegal aliens. Previous to the act it was not considered illegal to knowingly hire an undocumented alien. Congress, in all its wisdom, concluded that the only way to stop illegal entry into the United States was to prevent the employer from hiring undocumented aliens.[48] For this reason there is a substantial burden on the employer to know whether an applicant is legally qualified to work in the United States.[49]

The act imposes sanctions not only on the employer but also on the individual within the company who knowingly hires an unauthorized alien without complying with the statute. It is also unlawful to knowingly continue to employ an alien.[50] The Immigration and Naturalization Service (INS), which is responsible for enforce-

---

[43]*Butros* v. *Canton Reg. Transit Authority,* 997 F.2d 196 (6th Cir. 1992).

[44]It is more difficult to show hostile environment under national origin: *Daemi* v. *Church's Fried Chicken,* 931 F.2d 1379 (10th Cir. 1991).

[45]*Fragrante* v. *City & County of Honolulu,* 888 F.2d 591 (9th Cir. 1991).

[46]For a good discussion of language problems as they relate to nationality discrimination, see Eric Matusewitch, "Language Rules Can Violate Title VII," *Personnel Journal,* October 1990, p.98.

[47]*Fortino* v. *Ousar,* 950 F.2d 389 (7th Cir. 1991).

[48]The act has caused considerable litigation, is difficult to enforce, and has not been successful in stopping illegal entry.

[49]The 1990 amendment relaxed some of the problems created by original act.

[50]*Mester Mfg. Co.* v. *INS,* 879 F.2d 561 (9th Cir. 1989).

ment, has issued regulations implementing the act [8 CFR Sect. 274a (2)]. It is important that the employer have a copy of these regulations because they are a good guide for compliance.[51]

The IRCA is not violated by a simple mistake in hiring. The employer must have failed to know or to make a reasonable effort to find out that the alien hired was not authorized to work in the United States.[52]

Verification of Employability

The employer must have sufficient documentation, before hiring, that the applicant is authorized to work in the United States. The documentation must reasonably appear to be genuine. A passport, certificate of citizenship, naturalization or resident card (green card), valid work authorization card, or birth certificate would establish employment authorization. A driver's license or a state-issued ID card would only establish identity, and further documentation of authorization to work, such as an unexpired work permit or a Social Security card, would be required. Both the applicant and the employer are required to fill out an I-9 form. The employer is required to inspect the applicant's part and make certain that the questions answered on the I-9 form appear to be accurate. Verification is required for all applicants, not just those believed to be aliens.[53] Hiring without verification may constitute harboring an alien and be in violation. Verification requirements if not followed create an exposure to a fine under the terms of the statute.[54]

Penalties

Penalties are in the form of a fine ranging from $250 to $2,000 per illegal alien hired. If there is a second violation the fines are increased from $250 to $3,000. A pattern practice or a complete disregard for the act would result in a criminal violation, which permits up to $10,000 in fines and six months in prison.

The employer is required to retain employment records for three years or one year after termination, whichever is sooner. Failure to do so carries a fine of $1,000.[55] The wording of the statute indicates that the enforcement provisions leave little room for discretion.[56]

Discrimination Provisions of IRCA

The statute (Sect. 102) provides for a remedy when discriminating because of nationality in the same manner as Title VII, but it is broader, because it covers employers with three or more employees. (Title VII covers 15 or more.) When requiring identity, the employer under the terms of the statute must be cautious not to appear to use nationality as a factor in the hiring decision. The employer, under specific provisions, may not favor one nationality over another but may give preference to U.S. citizens.[57] If the INS adopted the EEOC position, verification requirements would force the employer to justify the reason for asking certain questions. "Where born" was a "red flag" under EEOC rules, but it may be necessary for verification under the statute. Courts have held that illegal aliens are protected by other statutes.[58]

---

[51]The INS also has a handbook (revised) that gives instructions on how to complete I-9 form.

[52]*Furr's* v. *INS,* 976 F.2d 1366 (10th Cir. 1992).

[53]In *Food International Corp.* v. *INS,* 948 F.2d 549 (9th Cir. 1991), the court held that failure to check the signature on a Social Security card according to INS handbook for filling out I-9 form did not establish willful intent to violate the act. However, in *El Rey Sausage, Inc.* v. *INS,* 925 F.2d 1153 (9th Cir. 1991), the same court required intent.

[54]These verification requirements have been relaxed (8 CFR Sect. 274a et seq., 1991).

[55]This is an unusual provision. Most statutes requiring record keeping do not provide for a penalty when the statute is violated.

[56]To allow more skilled immigrants to enter the United States, Congress passed the Immigration Act of 1991.

[57]In *Patel* v. *Quality Inn South,* 846 F.2d 700 (11th Cir. 1988), the court held that an undocumented alien had the protection of the Fair Labor Standards Act. Also see *NLRB v. Town & Country,* 116 S.Ct. 450 1995.

[58]This is the rule in all jurisdictions: *Rios* v. *Enterprise Association Steamfitters Local 638 of U.A.,* 860 F.2d 1168 (2nd Cir. 1988); *EEOC* v. *Tortilleria "La Mejor,"* 758 F.Supp. 585 (ED. Cal. 1991).

To avoid violation, the employer should verify all applicants, and also if any of the present employees are suspect, the employer must have complete documentation or a showing of good faith effort to determine the employee's status. There has to be a statement from the CEO to all management personnel that the statute will be complied with. The law does not require retention of verification records unless counsel says it is necessary. The penalties for violation are severe fines, rather than reinstatement with back pay as under Title VII.

The fears that foreign-looking applicants and those with accents will not be hired are real when you consider that there has been very little national origin enforcement since Title VII was passed.[59]

To avoid national origin lawsuits under IRCA the employer should do the following:

1. Review the recruiting and selection procedures. The emphasis in the past has been on other forms of discrimination, and nationality has often been overlooked.

2. Audit supervisors' practices to be assured that they are not treating one ethnic group differently from another. Many individuals have subjective prejudices against an ethnic group that are often based on past experience.

3. Tolerate an accent unless it interferes with the job. Sometimes an accent will cause prejudices that result in discrimination charges.

4. Have a broad harassment policy that includes all members in the protected class, not just related to sex.

5. Require employees to speak English only when necessary.

6. Be sure height and weight requirements are necessary for the job.

7. Treat lawful aliens who are in process to become U.S. citizens the same as U.S. citizens.

8. Permit nationality discrimination allegations in your complaint procedure. If it is properly established, an employee will use the procedure rather than a regulatory agency if he or she believes it is fair.

The IRCA is not to be confused with the Immigration Act of 1991, which deals with U.S. immigration policy as to skilled workers. Experience has shown that this is not effective.

THE SELECTION AUDIT

The threshold issues originate with the recruitment and hiring procedures. Like other employment decisions, the recruitment and hiring procedures used by employers can result in numerous legal claims. In order to avoid exposure to lawsuits or a lengthy administrative hearing before a regulatory agency, it is advisable to conduct an internal yearly analysis of the total selection process.

If there is no disparate impact in the selection process the audit can be very brief. It is only when there is a disparate impact that a step-by-step analysis is necessary. The analysis would start with the recruiting efforts to find qualified candidates, followed by the various stages of the selection process. Then a determination should be made of whether the entire procedure results in a disparate impact on members of the protected class. The selection audit should also include the IRCA. The audit would determine whether the regulations were being followed.

Recruiting Practices

The most important element in a recruiting audit is to make sure that more than one source is used. There are a variety of methods used to inform the market that a vacancy exists. The source contact and the referrals must include recruitment in the labor market that the protected classes normally use. Information on the race and sex composite of these sources can be obtained from governmental agencies.

"Help wanted" advertisements should be reviewed to determine whether the wording would exclude members of the protected class. The use of different advertising channels for different job

---

[59]Under Justice rules 28 CFR Section 44.200(a), intent and knowledge are required for discrimination. In this respect IRCA differs from Title VII. The rule will have to be challenged in the courts to establish a true difference between IRCA and Title VII.

classifications is good evidence that a sincere effort is being made to notify the entire labor market of the job openings. The factor in determining whether recruiting methods are effective is the applicant flow, which should be reviewed with labor market population statistics on minorities, sex, age, and disabilities.

Application Review

The next step in the selection audit is to analyze the application form. The most important element is whether a conditional offer has been made after it was determined that the applicant has the skills necessary to perform all the functions of the job. The applicant should be requested not to answer questions that are not job related. The form cannot in any way indicate that the information would be used for discriminatory purposes. If there has been any change in policy since the last audit, such as to include an employment-at-will statement or a release to obtain medical information, the audit would verify that it was properly worded on the application form.

The important element in the audit of the application form is to determine for what purpose each question is being asked and how the information will be used. If there is a discriminatory purpose for any question, then business necessity must be shown.

Interviewing and Selection

The two main items to audit in the interview process are whether there is some degree of standardization in the questions asked by each interviewer and whether the criteria established for the job are being uniformly applied.

Another practice to audit would be to determine whether previous rejects were reconsidered in the event the criteria were later changed. It would also

be important to investigate whether the criteria for a higher job were being used for a lower-level job. There must be a possibility that the applicant would progress to the higher job in the foreseeable future.

The interview policy may be clear, but often it is not followed, especially at the second and third interview level. The entire selection process should be reviewed to determine whether there are any "disqualifiers," such as arrest records, tests, or being handicapped. As we saw in *Connecticut* v. *Teal*,[60] the law requires an equal opportunity to be employed. If there are disqualifiers, business necessity must be shown.

The audit should determine whether members of the protected class apply for vacancies. Sometimes there exists an element in the employer's policy that has a chilling effect on certain applicants. If this is the case, then an investigation is necessary to determine the cause.

The audit need not be as detailed as the one we have outlined, but it must be sufficient to determine whether a disparate impact exists. If one is found, a step-by-step investigation is necessary to correct it.

The employer's selection policy after almost 20 years of case law on Title VII should have little exposure to lawsuits. The greatest error the employer can make is to select applicants who are not qualified because of a false belief that such action constitutes compliance with the law. In the area of selection it is well-settled law that the employer can hire the best-qualified applicant available without the law interfering.[61]

---

[60]*Connecticut* v. *Teal*, 102 S.Ct. 2525 (1982).

[61]For review of effectiveness of selection procedures see K. Buckner, H. Feild, and H. W. Holley, Jr., "The Relationship of Legal Case Characteristics with the Outcomes of Personnel Selection Court Cases," *Labor Law Journal*, 41, no. 11 (January 1990), 31.

6

ACCOMMODATION FOR RELIGION AND PHYSICAL HANDICAPS

What Is a Disabled Person?
Accommodation for Physical Handicaps
What Is a Disability under ADA
Accommodation for Religious Beliefs
Habitual (or Controllable) Handicaps
Drug and Alcohol Problems
Dealing with AIDS in the Workplace

Antidiscrimination statutes require the employer not to take race, sex, national origin, color, age, or disability into account when making an employment decision. The goal is to achieve a work environment where discrimination is not present. The requirement of Title VII is that all individuals in the protected class are to be treated alike. In the handicap and religious section, the law requires equal employment opportunity plus giving special treatment to an employee with a disability or religious belief by requiring accommodation.

The issue in most handicap and religious discrimination situations is whether, and to what extent, the employer can accommodate an employee's disability or religious belief. It is in this respect that disability and religious discrimination differ from other antidiscrimination statutes. The existence of a disability or religious belief causes or is perceived to have caused an interference with work performance.

WHAT IS A DISABLED PERSON?

This is up to the courts to define. However, it appears that the EEOC has adopted the definition in the Rehabilitation Act of 1973. In their compliance manual for investigators, the definition is about the same.

Compliance Manual section 903 provides guidance and instructions for determining whether an individual has a "disability" as defined by the Americans with Disabilities Act of 1990 (ADA or Act). It has been issued for use by EEOC investigators when investigating charges of discrimination under the ADA.[1]

The definition of "disability" under the ADA reflects congressional intent to prohibit the

---

[1]For a good discussion see M. Zablocki, et al., "Americans with Disabilities Act Update," *Whitman Law Review,* 15 (1994), 127.

specific forms of discrimination that people with disabilities face.[2] Because the definition is tailored to the purpose of eliminating discrimination prohibited by the ADA, it may differ from the definition of "disability" under other statutes. A determination of whether a charging party has a "disability" turns on whether he or she meets the ADA definition of that term.

A charging party has a "disability" for purposes of the ADA if she or he (1) has a physical or mental impairment that substantially limits a major life activity, (2) has a record of such an impairment, or (3) is regarded as having such an impairment. A charging party must satisfy at least one of these three parts of the definition to be considered an individual with a "disability."

The law recognizes that the existence of these conditions may sometimes interfere with performance, and yet these impairments or religious beliefs require accommodation in the workplace. Legislatures, Congress, and the courts have also recognized that there are limits to the measures that employers have to take if such conditions interfere with performance. The law terms this *undue hardship* and will not require the employer to make adjustments. It is because of the conflict between disability or religious beliefs and the legitimate requirements of the employers that the courts have developed the concept of *reasonable accommodation.*

The discussion in this chapter will be different from chapters where other antidiscrimination laws are discussed. In this chapter we recognize that the religious and handicapped employee must be treated differently; the only issue is to what extent. Accommodation is required for both religious beliefs and disability, but the degree of the duty to accommodate may be different. In religious beliefs the employee can subjectively choose whether or not his or her beliefs should take precedence over conflicting employment requirements, where the disabled employee does not have that

choice.[3] As we shall see in the sections of this chapter on accommodations for the religious and the handicapped, the courts recognize the similarity but take choice into account when considering the degree of accommodation that is required.

ACCOMMODATION FOR PHYSICAL HANDICAPS

The two federal statutes that prevent discrimination because of a handicap are the Americans with Disabilities Act (ADA)[4] and the Rehabilitation Act of 1973.[5]

The Americans with Disabilities Act of 1990 (42 U.S.C. 12101–12213) prohibits discrimination against a qualified person in all employment practices.[6] Titles I–IV deal with discrimination against disabled persons in the private and public sectors. Title V prohibits retaliation or coercion in response to enforcement. It is enforced by EEOC. The act gives a clear and comprehensive mandate to everyone in interstate commerce to eliminate discrimination.[7]

On October 10, 1994, the EEOC issued final guidelines for preemployment disability related questions and medical examinations. The final

---

[3]See A. Mayerson, "The Americans with Disabilities Act of 1990—An Historic Overview," *The Labor Lawyer* (Winter 1991), 1; E. J. Kemp and C. G. Bell, "A Labor Lawyer's Guide to Americans with Disabilities Act," *Nova Law Review,* 15 (1991), 31–65.

[4]For a comprehensive overview of ADA, see Eileen P. Kelley and Robert Halberts, "Americans with Disabilities Act: Undue Hardship for Private Sector Employers," *Labor Law Journal,* 41, no. 10 (October 1990), 675; also R. Lee Creasman, Jr., and Patricia Greene Butler, "Will the Americans with Disabilities Act Disable Employers?" *Labor Law Journal,* 42, no. 1 (January 1991), 52; John D. Thompson, "The Time Has Come: The Americans with Disabilities Act," *The Bench and Bar of Minnesota,* April 1992, 18.

[5]P. Karlan, G. Rutherglen. "Disabilities and Reasonable Accommodation," *Duke Law Review,* 46 (1996) 1-41.

[6]A qualified individual is a person who can perform all the essential functions of the job with or without reasonable accommodation. The employer makes the assessment of which job functions are essential.

[7]Includes constructive discharge. Intent must be shown, *Johnson v. Shalala,* 998 F.2d 121 (4th Cir. 1993).

---

[2]Congress wants religion and disability to separate.

guidance makes several changes to the May 19 guidelines. The final guidance clarifies that an employer may ask certain questions about reasonable accommodation at the pre-offer stage, if it reasonably believes that the applicant will need accommodation because of an obvious or voluntarily disclosed disability, or where the applicant has disclosed a need for accommodation. The final guidance also makes clear that an employer may ask about an applicant's ability to perform specific job functions at the pre-offer stage, and about nonmedical qualifications, such as education and work history. Applicants may also be asked at the pre-offer stage to describe or demonstrate how they would perform job-related tasks.

For employers the heart of the ADA is the requirement that they make reasonable accommodation, without undue hardship, for any qualified person who can perform the essential functions of a job.[8]

Undue hardship is a defense, but examples given in ADA indicate that it must be greater than de minimis, which is specifically rejected. The degree of hardship required for a defense is greater than under the Rehabilitation Act, but it is not yet clear how much greater.

The literature is full of what to do and what not to do under the act. The EEOC has issued a technical manual.[9] This manual is useful to know the department's position and their interpretation of the law. The best policy is to do what the employer thinks is best on a case-by-case basis and wait for ADA interpretation by the courts and regulatory agencies.[10] If an informal approach is desired, a nonspecific policy will allow management to settle individual disputes on a case-by-case basis.[11]

WHAT IS A DISABILITY UNDER ADA

The employer is likely to violate the ADA when requiring an applicant to take a preemployment physical or inquiring about the nature or severity of the applicant's disability. However, the employer may inquire about the applicant's ability to perform job-related functions after a job offer.[12]

The most essential act of the employer is first to ask disabled applicants or present employees what jobs they think they can perform after a conditional job offer. The jobs they say they cannot perform would then be eliminated. Normally a person will not attempt to perform a job that the disability prevents him or her from doing.

Jobs that people think they can do but that the supervisor thinks they cannot do are the ones that create a problem. There are also facility requirements that the employer must consider. The employer can take certain steps to comply. Legal scholars feel that the exposure under ADA is minimized if the following steps could be taken:

1. Make facilities more accessible; this is especially important where the public is involved. (Title III covers this topic.)

2. Review job descriptions to make certain all the essential functions of the job are included. This should be done by an outsider or an industrial engineer. See Exhibit 6-1.

3. Eliminate all pre-offer medical examinations. As discussed in other chapters, all job offers should be conditional upon meeting certain criteria.

4. Always attempt to accommodate a disabled person. If there is one thing we can be certain about, it is that the act will require more accommodation than under

---

[8]Mary F. Cook, "Compliance with the Employment Provisions of the Americans with Disabilities Act (ADA)," *The Human Resources Yearbook, 1992/93* (Engelwood Cliffs, NJ: Prentice Hall), p. 437.

[9]This compliance manual (and other ADA information) can be obtained by writing to EEOC Office of Communications and Legislative Affairs, 1801 L Street NW, Washington, DC 20507.

[10]Three baseball umpires were talking. One said, "Some are balls and some are strikes, and I call them as I see them." The second said, "Some are balls and some are strikes, and I call them as they are." The third umpire said, "Some are balls and some are strikes, but they ain't nothing until I call them."

[11]However, there is no individual liability under ADA. *EEOC v. AIO Security Investigations*, 55 F.3d 1276 (7th Cir. 1995).

[12]See S. 933, Sect. 102 (b)[1–7] of Title I for full text of prohibitions.

EXHIBIT 6-1 *A Job-Description Listing of the Physical Demands of a Job*

Example: Wood Grinder Operator: Standing, 50%
Walking, 35%
Stooping, 70%
Reaching, 75%
Twisting, 70%
Hearing, seeing, 100%
Kneeling, 5%
Crawling, 10%
Using Hands, 100%

This is an example of a wood-grinding machine operator's physical demands when working 8 hours. A wood-grinder operator's job is heavy-duty work that involves moving levers, straightening wood in the hopper to prevent jams, and cleaning the work area. It is a classified job in a pulp mill.

previous laws.[13] Undue hardship will be decided on a case-by-case basis, but not before an attempt has been made. It is the failure to attempt to accommodate that will cause exposure to litigation.

5. Appoint an ADA person to become knowledgeable in compliance with ADA, and have that person report to the CEO or some other top management executive.[14]

Hostile environment is recognized under ADA.[15] Case law on the ADA will be plentiful, but a long time coming.[16] The act did not become effective until July 1992 for employers of 25 or more employees. For others it is effective in July 1994.[17] In 1994 the EEOC received over 15,000 ADA complaints. Four went to court. The number is expected to grow in 1995 and 1996.

Most legal scholars believe that the best guidance is case law under the Rehabilitation Act of 1973. The EEOC has issued final rules (28 CFR Part 1630, July 26, 1991). The EEOC has also issued a technical manual on Title I (29 CFR Sect. 1630).[18] It is always useful to know the department's position on the law. However, this is not necessarily the position of the courts. The Department of Justice has also issued rules as to the obligations under Title III (28 CFR Part 36, July 26, 1991). These rules give some guidance to the employer to prevent exposure to litigation. Over 41 states have antidiscrimination laws for the handicapped. State laws will be preempted only where the state law violates the federal law. State laws should always be checked.[19]

Rehabilitation Act of 1973 and ADA

The Rehabilitation Act of 1973 became more important with the passage of the ADA. The Rehabilitation Act of 1973 will be followed as to the definition of a handicapped worker. Case law

---

[13]Some suggestions on what constitutes a reasonable accommodation are making existing facilities accessible, restructuring jobs or schedules, and adopting new procedures.

[14]G. T. Holtzman, Kyle L. Jennings, and David J. Schenck, "Reasonable Accommodation of the Disabled Worker—A Job for the Man or a Man for the Job," *Baylor Law Review,* 44 (1992), 279.

[15]*Gongales v. Mert Systems Protection Board, 132 F.3d 53 (1996).*

[16]First jury verdict under ADA, *EEOC v. AIC Security Investigations,* 55 F.3d 1276 (7th Cir. 1995).

[17]For a good discussion on existing employees under ADA see M. F. Baker, "The ADA's Effect on Existing Employees," *Personnel Journal,* 71, no. 4 (April 1992), 16.

[18]This manual can be obtained from the EEOC Office of Communications and Legislative Affairs, 1801 L Street NW, Washington, DC 20507 or by calling 1-800-669-(EEOC).

[19]To determine whether a particular state has a handicap law, see R. Geen, William Carmell, and F. Goldberg (Eds.), *1993 State by State Guide to Human Resources Law* (New York: Pane Publishers, 1993).

under that act will also be given great weight by the EEOC when interpreting the ADA. The strict requirements for accommodation,[20] as well as other requirements under the ADA, are carried over by courts and required under the Rehabilitation Act. Most attorneys believe that employers can no longer depend upon some of the past broad interpretations of the Rehabilitation Act. They believe that employers under the Rehabilitation Act will be held to the same strict guidance as under ADA.

There are many gray areas under the ADA that will increase litigation for many years.[21] The astute employer will learn as much as possible about the act and then make reasonable business decisions on a case-by-case basis until case law interprets the act.[22]

Rehabilitation Act of 1973

The Rehabilitation Act of 1973 (87 Stat. 355, 29 U.S.C. Sect. 701–94) requires federal contractors to take affirmative action to hire or promote qualified handicapped individuals (Congress may change this).[23] The affirmative action required of government contractors and employers receiving federal assistance is similar to that required under Executive Order 11246 (discussed in chapter 9) with one exception. By definition a handicapped worker is not as qualified as a nonhandicapped worker for all job assignments. Therefore, there is a duty of the employer to accommodate the handicapped worker by making an effort to place the applicant or employee in a job that the person is qualified to perform with the same competency as a nonhandicapped worker.

The Rehabilitation Act of 1973, Section 503, requires any business that has a contract of $2,500 or more under the act and provides services or personal property to any agency of the federal government to take affirmative action to employ handicapped workers. This requirement also applies to subcontractors. This means that virtually every employer that sells or provides services directly or indirectly to the federal government, or all public sector employers, are covered under the act.[24] If the employer has government contracts that exceed $50,000, a written affirmative action program must be developed.

Definition of a Handicapped Person

The statute defines a handicapped person as "any person who has a physical or mental impairment which substantially limits one or more of such person's major life activities and has a record of such an impairment, or is regarded as having such an impairment.[25] The court has held that under Section 504 if any injury makes a person unable to perform the job that person is not qualified.[26]

Many of the issues that courts have to decide under the act concern the definition of a handicapped person. The statute provides that "no otherwise qualified handicapped individual shall, solely by reason of his handicap, be discriminated against." Any allegation of discrimination immediately raises the issue of whether the person is in fact handicapped.[27] The law in this area is developing on a case-by-case basis with only general guidance from the courts.

---

[20]Undue hardship is a defense, but examples given in the act indicate that it must be greater that de minimis, which is specifically rejected.

[21]*Dingess* v. *SuperFresh Food Markets,* 93 BNA Reports 1995.

[22]See Postol and Kadue, "Employer's Guide to the Americans with Disabilities Act"; also Wayne E. Barlow, "Act to Accommodate the Disabled," *Personnel Journal,* 70, no. 11 (November 1991), 119.

[23]A qualified individual under the act is a person who can perform all the essential functions of the job with or without reasonable accommodation. The employer states which job functions are essential.

[24]If not covered by this act, employers will be covered by ADA after 1994 if they have more than three employees.

[25]This was amended by Civil Rights Act of 1987 to make a contagious disease a handicap if not a threat to others.

[26]*Chiari* v. *City of League City,* 920 F.2d 311 (5th Cir. 1991).

[27]ADA uses the term *perceived to be handicapped.* Individuals who are not known to be disabled cannot claim discrimination under ADA. Basically the ADA definition and the Rehabilitation Act of 1973 definition of a disabled person are the same.

Judicial Definition of a Handicapped Employee

The definition of a handicapped employee is found in *Southeastern Community College* v. *Davis*, 442 U.S. 397 (1979). The plaintiff in *Davis* was a deaf applicant to a nursing school. She could not understand speech without lip reading. The school refused to admit her on the grounds that her hearing disability would make it unsafe for her to be a nurse. The court said that under Section 504 of the Rehabilitation Act of 1973, an "otherwise qualified person means one who is able to meet all of the program's requirements in spite of the handicap."[28]

The courts have stated that although certain physical conditions like height, weight, and strength may render the employee incapable of performing the duties of the job, they are not impairments that substantially limit one or more major life activities. An applicant who was denied employment because of morbid obesity may be able to prove discrimination under Section 504 of the Rehabilitation Act.[29] The key question is whether she can perform the job in spite of morbid obesity.[30]

Many states do not consider a medical condition a handicap, while others, such as New York and California, do. Most state courts are following the federal courts in interpreting their handicapped laws by deciding on a case-by-case basis. It is worth repeating that the best policy is to determine treatment on a case-by-case basis and wait for ADA interpretation of each factual situation. We do know that the handicapped individual has more rights since the passage of ADA and that these will probably carry over to the Rehabilitation Act.[31]

Accommodation for Handicapped Persons

The extent to which a covered employer must accommodate a handicapped worker depends upon the applicable section of the law. Section 504 deals with recipients of federal financial assistance. The employer is obligated to treat handicapped and nonhandicapped individuals equally.[32] Under Sections 501 and 503, federal employers and contractors may be obligated to take affirmative action to employ and promote in employment qualified handicapped individuals (California law notwithstanding). Regardless of whether an employer is covered by Section 501 or 504 or by a state law, there still exists a duty to make reasonable accommodation.[33]

The courts have struggled with the requirement of reasonable accommodation for many years. Employers have different degrees of obligations depending upon what section of law they are under or whether they have state law. The ADA also has an influence on these obligations.

In order for a court to have an issue of reasonable accommodation, there must be a job available. The Rehabilitation Act of 1973 is not a "make work" public employment statute but is an attempt to prohibit the discriminatory placement for existing positions.

The court guidelines for reasonable accommodation is found in *Southeastern Community College* v. *Davis*, 442 U.S. 397 (1979). The plaintiff, being deaf, could not meet all of the requirements of the program unless the standards were substantially lowered, and Section 504 does

---

[28]Discrimination because a person cannot meet requirement but supervisor doesn't think so.

[29]Morbid obesity is defined as 100 pounds overweight for the height.

[30]Also May Fiorson and K. Krummer, "Discrimination in the Workplace Under ADA and Rehabilitation Act," *California Western Law Review* (1994), 41.

[31]See "Rehab Act Provides Guidance for ADA Compliance," Employee Relations and Human Resources Bulletin Report No. 1754, February 21, 1992 (National Foremen's Institute, 42 Rope Ferry Rd., Waterford, CT 06386), p. 5.

[32]Employer would suffer undue hardship if required to change hours of work to accommodate under the Rehabilitation Act, for failure to get to work on time due to an illness: *Guice Mills* v. *Derwinski*, 967 F.2d 794 (2nd Cir. 1992).

[33]Wayne E. Barlow, "Act to Accommodate the Disabled," *Personnel Journal,* 70, no. 11 (November 1991), 119.

not impose this obligation upon an educational institution.

In *Stutts* v. *Freeman,* 694 F.2d 666 (11th Cir. 1983), the applicant could perform all the duties of the job but could not pass the aptitude test. It was not necessary to pass the test to perform the essential functions of the job (probably still good law). The court held that refusal to try the plaintiff on the job was a failure to accommodate.

Some courts have liberally interpreted the *Stutts* decision in favor of the handicapped person and required the employer to make some modifications.[34] Other courts consider the *Davis* decision as not requiring any modifications in the program. This is the majority rule in the circuit courts under the Rehabilitation Act, but not ADA.

BFOQ as Applied to Accommodation

One factual situation that often arises is where the employer feels that although the person can perform the essential functions of the job, he or she would not be able to perform it safely. This would be a Bona Fide Occupational Qualification (BFOQ) exception. The standard for BFOQ was established in *Weeks* v. *Southern Bell Telephone and Telegraph Co.,* 408 F.2d 228 (5th Cir. 1959), and followed in most state and federal jurisdictions. The court in *Weeks* said that in order to establish a BFOQ for sex discrimination, the employer "must show that all or substantially all members of the class would not be able to perform safely and efficiently the duties of the job." This is often difficult to show.

Although cases turning upon the question of reasonable accommodation are decided upon a case-by-case basis, one common thread running through all the decisions is that the employer must make a bona fide attempt to accommodate.[35] The problem that the personnel practitioner or manager often has is that supervision has a subjective notion that the handicapped worker cannot perform the job and refuses to give him or her a chance. The reason often given is the risk of future injury. Unless there are objective facts to substantiate the reason, it will not stand judicial scrutiny.

Bona Fide Effort to Accommodate

To avoid liability for discrimination for the handicap, the employer must make a good faith effort to accommodate. Often supervisors will give a subjective reason for not making an attempt. The courts in any area of discrimination will no longer tolerate management perception. The statutory duty to accommodate does not require the employer to prejudice the safety of the individual or co-worker. The law does not interfere with business objectives, change methods of doing business, or in any way intentionally increase costs.[36] What the courts and Congress are telling the employer is that he or she must make a bona fide attempt to accommodate. When making this attempt, failure to accommodate is not the issue as long as the effort was made in good faith without intent to discriminate. The court will seldom say that the reason it cannot be done is not a good business practice or that it is uncommon in business. They leave the determination of good business reasons up to management as long as they are nondiscriminatory.

Any reasonable offer of accommodation satisfies the statute. The Supreme Court made it clear that the employee does not choose the accommodation.[37] She or he must take what the employer offers as long as it is reasonable. From the case law it is safe to say that it is better to be wrong than not to attempt to accommodate and make no offer at all.

Accommodation Under Rehabilitation Act Relating to AIDS

Normally a person with AIDS is "otherwise qualified." Until the employee is in the advanced stages of disease caused by the HIV virus, the

---

[34]*Arneson* v. *Heckler,* 946 F.2d 90 (8th Cir. 1991).

[35]"Discrimination of Religious Harassment Under Title VII," *Labor Law Journal,* (Dec. 1995), 732.

[36]Unpaid leave not a reasonable effort to accommodate under ADA, *Meyer* v. *U.S.,* 50 F.2d (3rd Cir. Cal. 1995).

[37]*Ansonia Board of Education* v. *Philbrook,* 107 S.Ct. 376 (1986).

person can still perform the duties of the job. It is therefore very difficult to remove the employee under the Rehabilitation Act.[38] Under the ADA a person with AIDS is handicapped. When such a person is discharged for AIDS, ADA would be violated, unless the condition was such that the person could not perform all the duties of the job or had excessive absenteeism.[39]

ACCOMMODATION FOR RELIGIOUS BELIEFS

Title VII states that it is unlawful to discriminate because of religion.[40] The statute does not require complete religious freedom in an employment situation; in many situations this would interfere with the normal conduct of the business.[41] A nonprofit religious organization can discriminate on the basis of religion when making an employment decision. What Title VII does require of other employers or labor unions is to make reasonable efforts to accommodate the religious beliefs of the employees or applicants.[42] This duty to accommodate includes religious observance as well as religious beliefs.[43] Teaching a Bible class at night, being a lay preacher, or going to summer Bible camp would be some of the activities that would require an attempt to accommodate. However, the religious observance is not

unlimited.[44] ADA specially permits religious organizations to require applicants and employees to conform to their beliefs. Where employee belief conflicts with the church, the employer's belief controls.

The Concept of Accommodation

The concept of accommodation is rooted in the case law on religious discrimination as a violation of Title VII and the Constitution. Title VII allows the employer to discriminate on the basis of religious beliefs if "it is unable to reasonably accommodate to an employee's religious observance or practice without undue hardship on the conduct of the employer's business."[45]

The extent to which the employer must disrupt the business to accommodate for religious observance was decided by the Supreme Court in the leading case of *Hardison* v. *TWA*, 432 U.S. 63 (1977). The court required the employer to show reasonable efforts to accommodate.[46] If rescheduling work assignments caused seniority to be violated, co-worker rights to be infringed upon, or other changes in normal operations that would cause increased costs in order to accommodate, it would not be religious discrimination to refuse to do so. Under *Hardison* the Court said that the employer had to bear only de minimis cost to accommodate;[47] otherwise it would be discriminating against other employees for whom no similar expenses are made to allow them time off from work. But if the employer failed to show that

---

[38]*Severino* v. *North Fort Myers Fire Control*, 935 F.2d 1179 (11th Cir. 1991); *Leckelt* v. *Board of Commissioners of Hospital Dist. No. 1*, 909 F.2d 820 (5th Cir. 1990).

[39]The AIDS problem discussed later in this chapter.

[40]For complete reference on religious discrimination, see James G. Frierson, "Religion in the Workplace," *Personnel Journal,* (July 1988), 61.

[41]*Corp. of Presiding Bishops* v. *Amos,* 107 S.Ct. 2862 (1987). Applies to all religious beliefs, even though the religious order approves: *Frazee* v. *Illinois Dept. of Employment and Security,* 109 S.Ct. 1514 (1989).

[42]All religious beliefs must be accommodated. Where one belief was accommodated, attendance at a religious festival, but seven-day requirement to attend was not. The court said the employer must attempt to accommodate all beliefs: *EEOC* v. *Universal Mfg. Corp.,* 914 F.2d 71 (5th Cir. 1990).

[43]*Brown v. Polk County,* 61 F.3d 650 (8th Cir. 1995).

[44]In *Little* v. *Wuerl,* 929 F.2d 944 (3rd Cir. 1991), it was held to be no violation of Title VII when a Roman Catholic school refused a contract for a teacher whose remarriage was not sanctioned by the church. Also *United States* v. *Board of Education for School District of Philadelphia,* F.2d 882 (2nd Cir. 1990).

[45]For a good discussion on accommodation, see Thomas D. Brierton, "Religious Discrimination in the Workplace: Who's Accommodating Who," *Labor Law Journal,* (May 1988), 299. Also see Douglas Massengill and Donald J. Peterson, "Job Requirements and Religious Practices: Conflict and Accommodation," *Labor Law Journal,* (July 1988), 402.

[46]*Lee* v. *ABF Freight System, Inc.,* 22 F.3d 1019 (10th Cir. 1994).

[47]The ADA specifically changed this requirement as related to physical handicaps. Could be carried over to religious discrimination under Title VII. Need more case law.

rescheduling Saturday work was an additional cost and further evidence revealed that other employees volunteered to work, accommodation would not be undue hardship.

Duty to Make Reasonable Effort to Accommodate

If accommodation will reasonably preserve the employee's job (that is, compensation, terms and conditions of employment, and no adverse consequences to the employer) then the employer should accommodate.[48] Where the employer would have to either excuse the employee for Saturday work, permit make-up, or get volunteers, this would be a burdensome administrative task and could increase costs and undue hardship under the act.[49] This reasonable accommodation may extend to more than allowing the worker to trade shifts. Where the court held that inasmuch as the employee had religious objections to asking others to work for him on Sunday, reasonable accommodation required the employer to do so.[50]

Although only de minimis accommodation is required, a good effort is still the rule. In *Proctor* v. *Consolidated Freightways Corp. of Delaware,* 795 F.2d 1472 (9th Cir. 1986), the employee was told at the time of hiring that she would be required to work on Saturdays, but this did not relieve the employer of the duty to make a reasonable effort elsewhere to accommodate.

If the employer has a workable system for employees who are absent on Saturdays, it would not be unreasonable to give assurance that the nature of the position was such that being absent on Saturdays did not affect the employer's interests.[51] This duty to accommodate would extend to the situation where the employee after working for a period of time joined a church that

prohibited working on Saturdays or where Sunday was voluntary but was against the employee's religion, although this is a minority view.[52]

Alternative Accommodations

Although in almost every situation the employer has a duty to make a good-faith effort to accommodate, once this effort has been made the requirements of the statute are satisfied.[53] In *Ansonia Board of Education* v. *Philbrook,* 107 S.Ct. 376 (1986), the employee, after six years of being employed as a schoolteacher, joined a church that prohibited members from working on certain holy days, a practice that caused him to miss six school days a year. The board policy was to grant three days for sick leave and three days for personal business leave. The employee wanted to take the six days in this manner (three and three) and the school board offered leave without pay and several other alternatives to accommodate, but it rejected the employee's request that he be permitted to use personal business leave for religious purposes. The Court held that where there are several possible alternatives the employer need not grant the one the employee prefers and the employer does not have to show that each of the employee's alternative accommodations would result in undue hardship. All the employer has to do is offer a reasonable accommodation, and an unpaid leave is reasonable unless a personal business leave is allowed for other employees. If other employees are allowed paid leave for any purpose this could be discrimination.

Accommodation for Union Dues

One of the most common situations under religious discrimination is where under the labor agreement all employees must pay dues to the labor union, and an employee, because of religious beliefs, refuses to do so. The union demands termination under the terms of the labor

---

[48]*American Postal Workers Union* v. *Postmaster General,* 781 F.2d 772 (9th Cir. 1986).

[49]*Wisner* v. *Saunder Leasing Systems,* 784 F.2d 1571 (11th Cir. 1986).

[50]See "Religious Harassment Under Title VII", *West Virginia Law Review,* 20 (1995), 1181.

[51]*Protos* v. *Volkswagen of America,* 797 F.2d 129 (3rd Cir. 1986).

[52]*EEOC* v. *Ithaca Industries, Inc.,* 847 F.2d 116 (8th Cir. 1988).

[53]*Wilson* v. *US West Communications,* 58 F.3d 1337 (8th Cir. 1995).

agreement; the employer refuses. Courts that have considered this question have held that if the employee tenders the amount of the dues to charity, this is reasonable accommodation of the employee's religious beliefs by both the union and the employer.[54]

Employees' or applicants' religious observance and beliefs should not be a problem to the employer since the *Hardison* case. When an applicant is hired and there is some indication that religious beliefs will interfere with the employment situation, the employer should not refuse to hire the applicant, because that would be discrimination because of religion. The applicant, however, should be informed that an attempt will be made to accommodate; if that is not always possible, the applicant must decide whether to accept the job or from time to time be unable to observe religious beliefs.

Legally it is extremely important for the employer to attempt to accommodate when requested to do so because of religious beliefs. Failure to make a reasonable attempt will invariably result in violation even though it can be shown in retrospect that accommodation was not possible.

HABITUAL (OR CONTROLLABLE) HANDICAPS

Smoking Problems in the Workplace

Smoking in the workplace is a twofold problem for the employer.[55] Studies show that there is a marked difference in costs of keeping a smoker and a nonsmoker on the payroll.

The second problem is the contention of co-workers that passive smoke creates an unhealthy environment.[56] They argue that the employer is not providing a safe place to work or they are handicapped because they cannot tolerate passive smoke.[57]

To solve this problem the employers have formulated various policies from smoking in designated areas only (sometimes these areas are selected to discourage smoking) to a complete ban even during nonwork hours. (United States Gypsum announced such a policy in January 1986 and started enforcing it later that year and made it stick.)[58] Subsequent case law indicates this is enforceable if job related.[59] The problem has also entered the political arena, and states are passing statutes with increasing frequency restricting smoking both in public and in the workplace.[60] These statutes vary as to the degree of restrictions. Most of them require separation of the smokers and nonsmokers by requiring designated areas. They are carefully worded to protect the rights of both the smokers and the nonsmokers. Generally arbitrators will hold that smoking is a condition of employment and a bargainable issue.[61]

Legal Rights of Smokers and Nonsmokers

There have been relatively few legal battles between smokers and nonsmokers. One reason is that the state enforcement agencies first attempt voluntary compliance and have been very careful

[54]*Tooley* v. *Martin Marietta Corp.*, 648 F.2d 1239 (9th Cir. 1981); *Nottelson* v. *Smith Steel Workers*, 643 F.2d 445 (7th Cir. 1981). However, in *Wilson* v. *NLRB*, 920 F.2d 1282 (6th Cir. 1990), the court took an opposite view, ruling this accommodation unconstitutional to force payment to charity when contrary to religious beliefs, but the employee must belong to a religious order and not have an individual belief (minority rule).

[55]For a good overview on smoking see Mollie H. Bowers, "What Labor and Management Need to Know about Workplace Smoking Cases," *Labor Law Journal*, 43 (January 1992), 40–49; S. Marley, "Employers Pay When Workers Smoke," *Business Insurance*, 26 (February 1992), 3; "Accident Rates Are High for Smokers," *Safe Health*, 145 (April 1992), 71.

[56]See "Health Effects of Passive Smoking: Assessment of Lung Cancer in Adults and Respiratory Disorders in Children," EPA Report, 1990; also C. Naidoff, "Do You Mind If I Smoke," *Management Review*, 80 (Spring 1991), 38–41.

[57]Smoking restrictions remain legal under ADA.

[58]Company Prohibits Smoking at Work and at Home," *American Medical News*, F(ebruary 1987), 12; also T. L. Leap, "When Can You Fire for Off-Duty Conduct?" *Harvard Business Review*, 66 (January-February 1988), 28–30.

[59]*Grusendorf* v. *Oklahoma City*, 816 F.2d 539 (10th Cir. 1987).

[60]David Ezra, "Get off Your Butts: The Employer's Right to Regulate Smoking," *Tennessee Law Review*, 960 (1993), 905.

[61]For an arbitrator's position on smoking rules see Bowers, "What Labor and Management Need to Know," p. 40.

not to push expensive and difficult enforcement and risk the chance of bad case law. As a result the statutes have been effective and where resisted the agency has not pursued them unless the smoker or nonsmoker files a complaint. As one lower court put it as dictum, "the desire of employees who wish to smoke cannot be disregarded, but where people must work with a smoker there is a rational basis for prohibiting smoking."[62]

Nonsmokers often cite the landmark case of *Shimp* v. *New Jersey Bell Telephone Co.,* 368 A.2d 408 (N.J. S.Ct. 1976), to show they have some rights. In this case the employee, while working as a secretary, had for several years suffered from other employees' smoking. She had occasional nosebleeds as well as severe throat irritation. The court held that smoke was an unnecessary toxic in the workplace. The employer had failed to provide a safe place to work. The court was particularly concerned about the company ban on smoking around certain machinery in order to prevent damage but not around employees who may be damaged permanently.[63]

This case has been frequently cited for the rule that nonsmokers can win in the courts, but the nonsmoker has not prevailed in other cases.[64] The case law affirms the common law right to a safe workplace. Courts demand evidence of adverse physical condition from passive smoke. As more medical evidence becomes available, the passive smoke problem will become more troublesome. The exposure to lawsuits is created by the belief that passive smoke is harmful.[65] Litigants will search and find medical evidence to support this belief, regardless of case law or any other evidence. They will also be supported by such

organizations as the Association for Non-Smoker Rights and the American Society of Addiction Medicine. Some courts will allow the claimant to collect unemployment compensation when leaving the job because of passive smoke where hypersensitivity is shown.[66]

As evidence on the harmfulness of passive smoke grows, many employees with desks near smoking areas are complaining. If the employer doesn't act on a complaint of smoke in the workplace, there is exposure to a lawsuit.

Some employees are alleging that they are handicapped because they are sensitive to passive smoke. They seek protection under the Rehabilitation Act of 1973 or ADA. The case most often cited is *Vickers* v. *Veterans Administration,* 549 F.Supp. 85 (D.C. Wash. 1982), where the employee was supersensitive to passive cigarette smoke and the court took the minority view and held that she was a handicapped person under the Rehabilitation Act of 1973, but reasonable accommodation was made. This theory was also supported in *Parodic* v. *Merit System Protection Board,* 690 F.2d 731 (9th Cir. 1982), where the employee was able to show that smoke caused chest pains, congestion, and breathing trouble when she was transferred into a room where employees smoked. When removed from the areas where employees smoked, her condition improved. The court held that the employer had to either transfer her to a smoke-free area or make disability payments. Courts before ADA had not found that persons sensitive to passive smoke were handicapped under either federal or state law unless they had a severe physical reaction.[67] However, the *Parodic* case comes close.

One nonsmoker alleged that the employer breached the employment contract when he failed to provide a smoke-free environment, when he knew that she quit her former job because of the smoking in the office. The court held that there was no obligation to provide a smoke-free

---

[62]See *Smoking and Health: A National Status Report—A Report to Congress,* 2d ed. (Rockville, MD: U.S. Department of Health and Human Services, 1988).

[63]The *Journal of the American Medical Association* reports that as many as 3,000 lung cancer deaths per year can be linked to passive smoke; also National Academy of Sciences and U.S. Health Service, 1986 and *Billman* v. *Sunrall,* 464 So.2d 382 (La. App. 1985).

[64]*Smith* v. *Western Electric Corp.,* 643 S.W.2d 10 (Mo. App. 1982); *Gordon* v. *Raven System Research Corp.,* 462 A.2d 10 (D.C. App. 1983).

[65]Center for Communicative Disease Report (1991) says passive smoke can cause cancer.

[66]Most courts hold that the employee must show serious physical reaction from passive smoke before the employer is liable. As more studies show that passive smoke is harmful, the courts are changing their position.

[67]See *Pagan v. NY NEX Pension Plan,* 52 F.2d 178 (D.C.S. NY 1994).

environment based on knowledge that the employee quit her former job because of smoking. Such a provision would have to be expressly stated in an employment agreement or promise made at the time of hiring. The court also rejected the argument that there was a duty to protect employees by providing a smoke-free environment.[68]

Employers that continue to allow smoking in the workplace, even under the most restrictive circumstances, may be more vulnerable than ever to litigation by nonsmokers.

A recent Environmental Protection Agency (EPA) report labels environmental tobacco smoke a human carcinogen. People have sued their employers over ill-health effects they have suffered allegedly from secondhand smoke they were exposed to in the workplace. The employer's defense is that the person voluntarily chooses to smoke.

Even employers that have severely restricted smoking are not safe from litigation. In one recent case, a jury was convinced that enough second-hand smoke from a first-floor teacher's lounge wafted into a second-floor classroom, causing respiratory problems. The judgment was nearly $40,000.

Tobacco can drift even through the finest ventilation systems. Any employer that permits unrestricted smoking is asking for it, just as if particles of asbestos were leaking from the ceiling.

Some smokers have been successful in collecting workers' compensation when their physical condition is the result of their smoking both on and off the job. An employee was a smoker since age 15 and worked for the employer 33 years, during which time he suffered from bronchitis and allergic asthma. Over a period of time he was told by his doctor to quit smoking, but he didn't. He was medically determined to be totally disabled as the result of bronchitis. He filed for workers' compensation and the court held that even though his bronchitis was caused by smoking, job conditions aggravated the preexisting condition, and the employer was liable. However, this was a minority before ADA.

The *Arnold* case is illustrative of the exposure the employer has, whether it is from smokers or nonsmokers. The nonsmokers are saying, "We are exposed to passive smoke and this creates an unhealthy environment under which we have to work." The smokers are saying, "We were able to smoke when we were hired, there is no law against smoking in the workplace, and therefore we have the same rights as the nonsmokers." The employer has exposure to employee relations problems and lawsuits because of smoking unless nonsmokers are hired and a smoke-free environment is maintained.[69] Some statutes prevent smoking while others permit it.

Recommendations for a Smoking Policy

In the interest of reducing health care costs and exposure to lawsuits, the employer should control smoking at the workplace. Legal costs and the conflict between smokers and nonsmokers can become major personnel problems. There are several ways to control smoking:

1. The employer should consider the implications of recruiting if a policy were initiated to hire non-smokers only. This is legal in most states, because nonsmokers are not a protected class.

2. Prohibiting smoking in the workplace is certainly a possibility where there is a union that consents. If there is no union and ample notice is given, there may be a slight exposure to a lawsuit but more of an exposure to "political suicide" if the CEO or other top management personnel smoke. A complete ban on smoking is becoming more popular among adventurous employers. A ban on all smoking, both at home and at the workplace, is worth considering in certain industries.

3. Establishing designated areas is a compromise solution in the conflict between nonsmokers and smokers. This is the less exposure method to restrict smoking at the workplace but not necessarily the best. This is what most state and local statutes require and is a political solution.

---

[68]*Arnold* v. *Firestone Tire & Rubber Co.,* 686 S.W.2d 65 (Tenn. 1984).

[69]This is the position many employers are taking. It is legal and the best solution to the smoking problem. See W. Rissy, "Employers and Smokers Rights," *Supervision,* 53 (April 1992), 17–18.

4. When a smoker and a nonsmoker are located in the same area, it becomes a personnel problem to decide which one should be relocated. If the employees can't agree, some companies relocate the smoker while an equal number relocate the nonsmoker. Case law dictates that the nonsmoker must be relocated, if the employer is to provide a safe place to work or accommodate for the handicapped.
5. Incentive plans to encourage smokers to quit have been successful in large companies. Whatever works should be continued. To increase wages for employees who quit smoking appears to be rewarding the wrong people. A better plan would be to pay less to those who do smoke. It is well established that smokers are the more expensive employees; therefore, lower wages or other benefits should offset the higher costs.
6. Employers should provide treatment programs for smokers in the same manner they do for alcoholics.[70]
7. Until a completely smoke-free environment is achieved (all state airlines are smoke-free), smoking should be allowed only in those areas that do not physically affect other employees (unless the employer is required by statute to designate areas). To voluntarily designate areas for smoking does not create a smoke-free environment and only increases hidden costs. Enforcement is a constant problem both in keeping nonsmokers out and in making smokers take time out from their duties to idly smoke. The smoking breaks are comparable to coffee breaks in cafeterias, which have always caused an enforcement problem.

The employer should have a long-term objective of a smoke-free workplace. This can be achieved by one of several methods, but all have their faults. At present it is more of a personnel problem than a legal one. Apart from any personnel problems, which only the employer can assess, for a smoke-free environment in the workplace it is recommended that the employer

1. Hire only nonsmokers (not permitted in some states)
2. Offer treatment to smokers currently on the payroll
3. Give some extra benefits to nonsmokers
4. Set a realistic date for achieving a smoke-free workplace, not to exceed one year or when the CEO who smokes retires
5. If an informal approach is desired, have a nonspecific policy to allow management to settle individual disputes on a case-by-case basis.

DRUG AND ALCOHOL PROBLEMS

Virtually every employer that has one or more employees will have a drug abuse problem.[71] The problem is serious because of the high cost in workers' compensation, absenteeism, health care, loss of production, and poor work quality. Many companies are realizing the extent of their problem and are doing something about it.[72]

The most often used approach to the solution of the problem is to test applicants. More than 80 percent of the large firms test all applicants. Testing is expensive; the average cost in 1996 was over $16,000. For companies that do random testing the average annual cost is $33,159. Most companies feel that testing is cost effective. Very few eliminate the test because of the cost. As the courts resolve the privacy issue, there will be a continual increase of the companies who test for drugs. Drug testing, if handled properly, is an excellent detection measure and a deterrent to drug abuse.[73]

Many states have a statute that permits drug testing. The Drug Free Workplace Act of 1988 (P.L. 100–690, Sect. 5151 et seq., 102 Stat. 4305) applies to all federal employees and private

---

[70]There is a treatment center in almost every state—for example, Step Away from Smoking, a weekend retreat at Camp Mack in Milford, Indiana, and Smoking Treatment Center in Palm Desert, California.

[71]Edward J. Miller, "Investing in a Drug-Free Workplace," *The Human Resources Yearbook, 1992/93* (Englewood Cliffs, NJ: Prentice Hall), p. 8.10.

[72]American Management Association, "The Sixth Annual Survey on Workplace Drug Testing and Drug Abuse Policies," April 1992 (135 West 50th St., New York, NY 10020; 212-039-8052).

[73]See Rob Brookler, "Industry Standards in Workplace Drug Testing," *Personnel Journal*, 71 (April 1992), 128; *Human Resources Reporter,* Issue 104, "Business and Legal Reports," Spring 1986.

employers doing business with the government ($25,000 or more).[74]

Need for a Drug-Testing Policy

No matter how large or how small the company, a drug-testing policy should be written. If a drug abuse condition does not exist, it probably will in the future.[75] The possibility of having a problem is strong. The policy should be in place before there is a drug abuse problem.

The existence of a policy with the proper communication may prevent a substance abuse condition from developing in the workplace. Another reason for having a policy is that some states by statute require a written policy before any testing can be performed, and then a great deal of freedom is given for testing.[76]

The existence of a policy will prevent exposure to a claim of invasion of privacy. The employee is forewarned that the policy will be enforced. A violation of it will result in severe disciplinary action up to and including discharge. If the employee objects to the policy, he or she will have an opportunity to find another job. For this reason all policies should have a time period before they become effective. Some courts will hold that continued employment after the policy has been announced is implied consent to its terms, and therefore the policy is not an invasion of privacy.[77]

Essential Elements of a Policy

The purpose of the policy should be clearly stated in order to discourage the use of drugs.

Discharge should be the last resort for the violation of the policy.

The policy is not one that some other company has adopted but fits the needs and environment of the company where it will be enforced. The policy for the public sector would be different from the policy for private sector employees. The public sector employee has the protection of the Fourth Amendment of the Constitution. The policy usually applies to present employees and preemployment procedures. The type of industry may also warrant different procedures. There would be more latitude for enforcement in jobs involving significant risks of injury to co-workers, the public, or those who have security responsibility.

The policy should define a substance abuser, a definition that may not always agree with that of the state or federal statute. It can be different, but not violate a statute. The Rehabilitation Act of 1973 [Sect. 706(7)(b)] states that drug abuse is under the act if the substance use threatens the safety of others or interferes with job performance. The act is silent on whether a person in treatment is a handicapped person. A drug abuser is not considered a disabled person, but a person who has participated in a drug treatment program is protected under ADA. Although there may be some question under a state or federal statute as to whether a particular condition constitutes a handicap,[78] there should be no question under the policy if the term is properly defined. Using his or her own definition, the employer can always make a policy more strict or more clear than a statute. It would be enforced as a policy rather than relying upon a statute.

Surveillance for Presence of Drugs

In any surveillance issue, the law considers the balance between the employee's privacy rights and the employer's need to protect property and the safety of others (which usually prevails).

---

[74]This act does not require testing, but it would be difficult to comply if the employer did not do testing. However, Omnibus Transportation Employee Testing (P.L. 102–143, 1991) requires testing of all transportation employees.

[75]Over 13 percent of applicants and over 12 percent of current employees test positive. *The National Report on Substance Abuse.*

[76]See Minnesota Statutes, 181.94–181.97.

[77]For discussion on developing policy see Jeffrey J. Olsen, "Legal and Practical Considerations in Developing a Substance Program," *Hofstra Labor Law Journal,* 8, no. 1 (1990), 24.

[78]How the use of drugs affects the work must be considered: *Teahan* v. *Metro North Commuter R.R. Co.,* 951 F.2d 511 (2nd Cir. 1991).

The most reliable surveillance for drug abuse is observation on the job. The policy could be written to require any person who observes the use or possession of drugs in the workplace to report it to management or be subject to discipline for failure to do so. There are many warnings of drug abuse in the workplace that management can detect. Absenteeism, difficulty in concentration, spasmodic work patterns, generally lower job efficiency, relationship with co-workers, deterioration of personal appearance, frequent use of breath purifiers, and so on are all indications to management that make the employee a suspect, and the condition should be further investigated to determine the cause.

Often observance on the job comes in the advanced stages of drug use, however. The employer may want to correct the problem sooner. For this reason testing has become the most popular method of surveillance.[79] A surveillance method should not be used unless there is some reason to believe that the employee may be using drugs. The reason can be somewhat subjective, but it should be objective enough to show that it is not random. The Supreme Court has held that random testing or investigative testing is permissible where public safety is involved or it is job related.[80] Most state statutes also permit it where safety considerations or certain other conditions are present (the state may also have a statute on drug testing).

Testing Procedure for Drug Abuse

1. Prior to testing, the employee should be given a chance to list any drugs taken in the last month and under what circumstances.
2. When requested to take a test, the employee will be informed why the test is necessary, and if there is any other way to get the facts the company will use it first.

3. If the first test is positive, the employee will be suspended. Further testing by a licensed laboratory will be required before any further action is taken or the results released.
4. Test results will be disclosed only to those persons who have a need to know for job-related decisions. Any further disclosure must be with the employee's consent.
5. Upon receipt of final test results, if positive, the employer will give the employee an opportunity to explain or challenge the results before taking disciplinary action.

Other methods of surveillance that could be used, depending upon the state law, would be television surveillance and the use of electronic eavesdropping devices (about half of the states prohibit these). Undercover investigation is also permitted in many states. When any method of surveillance is used, it should be stated in the policy that the employer will from time to time use a test or other methods of surveillance when it is necessary to get the facts. If a polygraph test is used, considerable care should be taken in its administration, because this could be found to be an invasion of privacy or a violation of federal and state statutes. It should be administered by a professional, and before seeing the results the employee should sign a statement that the questions asked were job related and reasonable. If she or he refuses to answer questions she or he should be asked the reason.[81]

Regulation of Off-Duty Drug Abuse Activity

A positive drug test may be the result of off-duty use. To take action on the use of drugs away from the workplace, the employer must show that off-duty conduct affects the job or the employer's business. If an employee is arrested or convicted

---

[79]Drug and alcohol testing are mandatory subjects of bargaining under NLRB guidelines (Memorandum GC87-5, September 1987).

[80]*Skinner* v. *Railway Labor Executive Association,* 109 S.Ct. 1402 (1989), and *National Treasury Employees Union* v. *Von Raab,* 109 S.Ct. 1384 (1989).

[81]In *O'Brien* v. *Papa Gino's of America,* 780 F.2d 1067 (1st Cir. 1986), the court held that the discharge was not wrongful when the polygraph test revealed that the employee was using drugs, but upheld a jury award of $400,000 for invasion of privacy because the administrator went beyond permissible bounds in questioning.

on a drug charge, the arrest or conviction must render the employee unable to perform his or her job satisfactorily or affect the employer's business before he or she is disciplined. It is best to suspend the employee in such cases, until facts are investigated.

Correction of Drug Abuse by Employer

When the employer is positive that the employee is a drug abuser, the matter can be handled internally without the help of law enforcement authorities. The policy should make it clear that discharge will be delayed if the employee will voluntarily enter into treatment.[82] If the employee has undergone treatment and reverts to drug use, then termination is the only alternative. The termination should be for violation of the policy for the use of drugs that affects performance or the safety of others, and no mention should be made of any illegal activity.[83] The employee should be given the option to take treatment or quit. Treatment becomes a condition of employment. To avoid an unemployment compensation claim it should be made clear that the employee can remain as an employee only if treatment is taken and is successful.

Policy on Alcohol Abuse

Although there is some similarity between drug and alcohol abuse, such as treatment, high costs to employer in health care, loss of production, and causes of death and disability from auto accidents, the problems should be treated differently.[84] The problem of alcohol is often more an employee relations problem than a legal one. Many states consider it an illness, while others consider it a handicap. The techniques used for detection in alcoholism are not as legally restrictive as in the case of drugs. The use of alcohol is a legal activity and the danger of defamation is not as great. Often a person using drugs is selling drugs illegally to acquire more money to satisfy the habit. An alcoholic can legally buy all the liquor she or he wants and does not inflict the habit upon others. For this reason there is more tolerance in treatment of an alcoholic than of a drug abuser. Other reasons for treating the two differently depend on job category or type of industry.

Surveillance for Alcohol Abuse

The method of surveillance for alcohol abuse is practically unrestricted. Observation and undercover methods are the most effective and have as their objective to get the employee to seek help.[85] Undercover methods often involve the use of treated alcoholics to detect abuse among fellow workers and then an attempt to get the problem drinker to seek help.

Another effective method is the use of assessment centers located in most large cities. The assessment center will determine whether the problem is caused by alcohol and if so whether the person is addicted to it and needs treatment. Often the problem might be alcohol, but the person is not an alcoholic; he or she uses poor judgment in drinking too much at a particular time. This is common in driving-while-drunk situations.

The policy on alcoholism should not have as its objective to discourage the use of alcohol unless its use cannot be controlled. In this respect it differs from drug abuse. The employee must recognize that she or he has the problem and needs help. If the employee does not realize this and fails to seek help and the problem continues, then the only recourse for the employer is to terminate. The policy should therefore include a step-by-step procedure to correct the problem insofar as uncontrolled use of alcohol affects the work of the

---

[82]Fifth Special Report to Congress on Alcohol and Health, Washington DC, U.S. Dept. of Health and Human Services, 1983; also *Wilis* v. *Roche Biochem Laboratories, Inc.,* 21 F.3d 1768 (1994).

[83]Treatment is not required by ADA, but other federal statutes require it.

[84]Even ADA says there is a difference.

---

[85]Where an employee was excessively absent due to treatment for alcoholism and was discharged for absenteeism, the court held that the employee was not terminated because of a handicap under Section 504 of the Rehabilitation Act. See *Teahan* v. *Metro North Commutor R.R. Co.,* 951 F.2d 511 (2nd Cir. 1991).

employee. A policy on alcoholism should state the following:

1. After the employee admits that he or she needs help, the employee should be referred to an assessment center. If the employee refuses and alcohol is suspected to be the cause of the work-related problem, then terminate. The policy should clearly state that the options are to take treatment and continue as an employee or quit.

2. Once the employee agrees to seek help, treatment should be offered and medical leave without pay granted. Most companies cover this under their health care and sick leave policy. (A few states require it.)

3. While in treatment the employee should maintain his or her employee status. The employer's policy should determine what benefits he or she should have; however, they should be the same as for other ill or handicapped persons.

4. Only after the employee refuses treatment or treatment fails should the employee be terminated, not for alcoholism but for the work-related problems caused by the use of alcohol. Termination should always be for the result, not for the cause. If it is for the cause, it is often difficult to correct.

It must be remembered that, unlike drug abuse, alcoholism does not usually affect the co-workers' performance. The alcohol abuser can be tolerated longer than the drug abuser. The effect normally is not as immediate or as devastating to the job and on the co-workers. The objective of a policy on alcohol is to eliminate the job-related problem, and the policy for drug abuse is to eliminate the use or possession of drugs. Whatever policy works should be used.

Preemployment Procedures in Substance Abuse

Any reasonable substance abuse program can be started in preemployment procedures to determine whether the applicant is an abuser. Preemployment tests, under certain conditions, have been permitted in almost every state. The employer can set about any nondiscriminatory criteria for rejecting or requiring treatment before

considering the applicant. However, in those states where substance abuse is considered a handicap, there have been some court decisions that require the offer of treatment at the applicant's expense before total rejection. The application must be reconsidered after the applicant has been successfully treated.

Policy Needed to Avoid Lawsuits

The problem of substance abuse is not going to disappear. The employer must educate management personnel to cope with it. A policy that is judicially sound and considers employee relations consequences in its enforcement must be communicated to management personnel and all employees. The purpose of the policy is to discourage substance abuse in the workplace. The employee must be informed of what action the employer will take when policy is violated. The policy should be sensitive to the employee's expectations of privacy, the rights of co-workers, and the employer's necessity to have an efficient operation. It should advise an alternative of treatment once it is determined that the applicant is an abuser. Reasonable means to determine facts, including testing, are judicially acceptable.[86]

The courts have never interfered with an employer to correct a problem that affects the business and safety of others.[87] In this respect the rights of the employer are greater than privacy rights of the employee. Substance abuse is no exception. There is no interference from the law, provided the employer has as an objective correction of substance abuse in the workplace and not correction for the good of society.

Employer Third Party Liability for Inebriated Employees

When employees become inebriated at company-sponsored events or are sent home after drinking at work, most courts hold that the

---

[86]Employers can use any means to obtain information as long it is job related: *Baggs* v. *Eagle-Picher Industries, Inc.*, 957 F.2d 268 (6th Cir. 1992).

[87]*Despear v. Milwaukee County*, 63 F.3d 635 (7th Cir. 1995).

company is not liable. In some states, even where negligence is shown the courts have held that the states' "Dram Shop" laws do not apply. In *Meany* v. *Newett,* 367 N.W.2d 472 (Minn. 1985), the court refused to apply the "Dram Shop" statute to the employer. It was shown that the employer was negligent in serving the inebriated employee at a company-sponsored event. He later injured another person in an accident when driving while drunk. Decisions from the highest courts of New York, Maine, and Kansas as well as Minnesota have held that employers should not be held liable to third parties for the actions of the employees who become intoxicated at company-sponsored events (outside scope of employment).

In *Meyers* v. *Grubaugh,* 750 P.2d 1031 (Kans. S.Ct. 1988), the employee drank beer before going off duty. While going home he was involved in an accident that caused injury to the plaintiff. The court held that the employer is not liable for off-duty conduct of the employees although the condition was caused while on duty. This is the majority rule, but courts in some states such as Texas and New Jersey would hold otherwise.

Because the employer has the protection of the law does not mean that the employer should let an employee become intoxicated. There is always an exposure to lawsuit, and to some extent there is a moral obligation to control employees at a company-sponsored event such as a Christmas party.[88]

The employer can avoid a possible lawsuit either by having a cash bar or by controlling the period of time that a free bar is open. One way to do this is to start serving the food after a short refreshment period. If an employee comes to the event intoxicated, she or he should be sent home so others can have a good time.

DEALING WITH AIDS IN THE WORKPLACE

In order to properly solve the problem of AIDS in the workplace, the employer should have a basic understanding of the nature of the disease, modes of transmission, testing and disclosure of results, and the nature of the disability that results from the disease.[89] A suggested strategy for the employer is to have a planned program on the "back burner" to be used when needed. In addition, the employee should be currently educated on all aspects of the disease. The purpose of this section on AIDS as distinguished from the section on drugs and alcohol is to prepare the employer to cope with the problem when it exists. AIDS is not a workplace issue.

Basic Understanding of the Disease

According to the U.S. Centers for Disease Control (CDC),[90] AIDS is reliably diagnosed as a disease that causes the human immune system to be incapable of fending off certain fatal illnesses. An HIV positive test result means that the person has the virus that could cause AIDS; however, not all HIV positives end up with AIDS. There is a difference between being HIV positive and having AIDS.

Managing AIDS in the workplace has become a business problem. Medical science does not expect a cure until the late 1990s. In 1991 more than 200,000 persons in the United States were diagnosed with AIDS, and more than 130,000 deaths were caused by AIDS. One in 200 Americans test HIV positive and the number is growing.

---

[88]The author was in charge of a Christmas party where everyone got drunk and wives complained about their husbands being drunk and with other females. The company got blamed for everything. I vowed that never again would I be involved in any party sponsored by a company where liquor was free, although there was no liability.

[89]See I. Corless, "AIDS Education Replaces Fear with Facts," *Safety Management,* 351(6) (National Foremen's Institute, Waterford CT 06386, 1992, 1–4; Robert S. Burger and Gregory Lewis, "AIDS and Employment: Judicial and Arbitral Responses," *Labor Law Journal,* 43 (May 1992), 259–80, N. Ever, "Trends for Managing AIDS in the Workplace," *Personnel Journal,* (June 1995). 125.

[90]*Morbidity and Mortality Weekly Report,* 34, no. 45 (1985) 682–94; see also no. 221 (1986) as to guidelines for health care workers.

The HIV virus infects persons in various stages:[91] ADA makes HIV a handicap, but management has to learn to live with this.

1. In the first stage a person is exposed to the virus but has no physical symptoms. Medical science is not sure whether persons in this category can transmit the disease or what percentage will develop AIDS.

2. In the next stage a person gets mild warnings such as weight loss, abnormal fatigue, and swollen lymph nodes. This stage is sometimes called "AIDS-Related Complex." At this stage the victim may have moderate illness that affects the job but for the most part is able to work. Approximately 25 percent of this group will develop AIDS.

3. In the next stage the person will develop AIDS from the previous stage. He or she will contract such rare diseases as Kaposi's sarcoma and certain types of rare pneumonia. This individual often will be able to work but will be absent due to illnesses more than normal.[92]

4. In the final stage of AIDS a person is in the advanced stage of an illness. She or he requires extended hospitalization and is most likely unable to work. It is at this stage that death will come.[93]

Transmission of the Disease

The chance of transmission of the disease for employees who work alongside each other is between one in 100,000 and one in a million, unless there is a direct exchange of blood or exchange of other body fluids such as saliva.[94] Most employees will not believe this.

Medical data are in agreement that AIDS can be transmitted only through intimate sexual contact, intermingling of blood or blood products, and perinatal transmission from an infected mother to her offspring. All epidemiological evidence indicates that only blood and semen are the proven media of transmission. Employees who claim that they can contract AIDS by sharing a restroom or a drinking fountain, washing in the same sink, sharing a desk or a chair, using the same telephone, eating at the same table, wearing the same protective clothing, or talking at a meeting need more education on transmission. AIDS is hard to get; in fact, you have to go out of your way to get it.

Statutory Protection of AIDS

Many employers are prohibited under federal, state, and local laws from discriminating against a handicapped person. For the employer to take any other position than that the AIDS patient is handicapped would result in exposure.

There are relatively few cases that deal with an employee infected with HIV. The two federal statutes that an employer should be concerned with are the Rehabilitation Act of 1973 and the Americans with Disabilities Act. Protection under the Rehab. Act may be overshadowed by the ADA, although the definition of disability is the same as the Rehab. Act. ADA prohibits the employer from discriminating on the basis of medical examination and inquiries (before job offer). It allows four defenses to discrimination against a disabled person: business necessity, safety or health of others, religion, and handling food with a contagious disease.[95]

The Rehabilitation Act protects only otherwise qualified employees. Some courts will hold that in certain jobs the infected person is not "otherwise qualified."[96]

---

[91]*Leckelt* v. *Board of Commissioners of Hospital Dist. No. 1,* 909 F.2d 820 (5th Cir. 1990). For a good discussion on HIV see "Impact of HIV," *Labor Law Journal,* (June 1994), 338.

[92]Estimates for health care costs for this stage range from $91,000 to $140,000.

[93]The courts will permit cutting insurance coverage for AIDS. Coverage was reduced from $1 million to $5,000 after employee told employer he had AIDS: *McGann* v. *H&H Music Co.,* 946 F.2d 401 (10th Cir. 1991), cert. denied 1992.

[94]*Morbidity and Mortality Weekly Report,* 34, no. 45 (1985), 682.

[95]The Defense Department can discharge homosexuals from the armed services to serve government interests related to morals and discipline: *Steffan* v. *Cheney,* 780 F. Supp. 1 (D.C. 1991).

[96]*Leckelt* v. *Board of Commissioners of Hospital Dist. No. 1,* 909, F.2d 820 (5th Cir. 1990).

Tests for AIDS

The courts generally will not permit testing for HIV in the absence of a state statute.[97] In view of the available medical information, the employer has no demonstrable interest that would justify testing applicants or employees for HIV, although a person with AIDS affects production. The reliability of the tests is questionable. If the test is positive the information is of little value to the employer, because the mere presence of HIV does not affect the job. A test has no job-related purpose, so there is no justification for testing either applicants or present employees. In the case of applicants, they would create more job risk as to turnover, absenteeism, and medical care costs than an applicant without AIDS, but under most state laws AIDS is not a reason for rejecting an applicant who is considered handicapped.[98]

Knowledge of the presence of HIV should be received only from the employee or when his or her physical condition interferes with the job relationship. AIDS may be the cause of absenteeism or poor performance, but the employment decision should be made on the job-related result and not on the cause. When considering testing, one question should be asked: Why do I want to know? If you do know, what use is the information, other than to extend confidentiality to those who do not have a need to know? An AIDS employee's cost in health care can be lessened by reducing the insurance coverage[99] according to case law.

Problems with Co-workers of AIDS Victims

Legally there is nothing an employer can do when a co-worker refuses to work with an AIDS patient except educate, educate, educate. The largest exposure comes from the employer's discharging or transferring the person with AIDS. If the employer wants to do something with the person who has AIDS, there are several good business reasons to take action. However, few of them will stand judicial review.[100] Such defenses as that AIDS can be transmitted by casual contact, that the cost is too high on health insurance premiums, that the disease is fatal so it is useless to train because training costs will be too high, and that any employee with AIDS is more accident prone may sound logical to the employer, but the court will seldom agree. The defense of customer or co-worker rejection has been rejected in other areas, such as sex and race discrimination.[101]

The only answer to the co-worker who objects to working with a person with AIDS is education at all levels of the organization.[102] It is advisable to have a doctor as well as a supervisor present the information. One thing that can be done when an employee objects to working with a person with AIDS is to transfer him or her if possible and if the objecting employee will agree.

This policy of education or transferring is easily stated, but often it is not the solution to an all-too-frequent employee relations problem. Suppose an employee is suspected of being a "gay" who has recently had an extended period of absences and while at work looks flushed and weak. A group of employees approach the supervisor and state that they represent the concerns of all the employees in the department, who believe this person has AIDS. They demand that the employer test the employee and put him or her on an extended leave of absence until the test results are known. They express fear for their own health and that of their families. (Schools sometimes experience this same problem when a student who is a known AIDS patient is attending

---

[97]*Glover* v. *Eastern Nebraska Community of Retardation*, 867 F.2d 461 (8th Cir. 1989), cert. denied; *Leckelt* v. *Board of Commissioners of Hospital Dist. No. 1*, 900 F.2d 820 (5th Cir. 1990).

[98]States such as California, Massachusetts, Iowa, and Texas prohibit testing for AIDS or HIV.

[99]*Greenberg* v. *HHH Music*, 946 F.2d 506 (5th Cir. 1992), Cert. Den. 1992.

[100]*Petri* v. *Bank of New York*, 582 N.Y.S. 2nd 68 (N.Y. S.Ct. 1992).

[101]*Sprogis* v. *United Airlines, Inc.*, 44 F.2d 1194, 1199 (7th Cir. 1971) cert. denied; *Diaz* v. *Pan American Airways, Inc.*, 442 F.2d 389 (5th Cir. 1970), cert. denied; *Wigginess* v. *Fruchtman*, 482 F.Supp. 681 (S.D. N.Y. 1979), cert. denied.

[102]See J. Segal, "Aids Education Is Necessary High-Risk Activity," *The Human Resources Yearbook, 1992/93* (Englewood Cliffs, NJ: Prentice Hall), p. 10.15.

class.) The employees threaten that the whole department will refuse to work unless their demands are met or the employer can prove that the suspected employee does not have AIDS.

This puts the employer "between a rock and a hard place." The employees under the National Labor Relations Act have the right to withhold their services because of adverse working conditions.[103] An employee who feels that a fellow employee endangers his or her health has certain rights under the Taft-Hartley Act and Occupational Safety and Health Act. The employee who is suspected also has certain rights under ADA and most state statutes. There is also an invasion of privacy issue. If a union is involved, the matter could go to arbitration. Transferring to another department would only create the problem with another group. Suppose the employee admits she or he has AIDS? This doesn't mean other employees can be affected unless through intimate sexual relations or contact with the affected blood, neither of which are job related. Legally the employer cannot do much about avoiding the exposure to a lawsuit.

The solution to this problem is not found in the literature or from legal counsel. The employer must probe for the solution.[104] The education program must be changed; more emphasis must be put on transmittal. Try to convince the employees that their reservations are without medical authority; talk to the suspected employee and get his or her reaction and ask for help. If several alternatives are explored and none of them offers a solution, then the employer must "take the bull by the horns" and decide what is best for the organization. Either tell the complaining employees "to walk" or quit and get replacements or deal with the suspected employee in the best possible way to prevent a lawsuit. The next time the problem comes up the solution may be entirely different, depending upon the employees involved.

Arbitrator' Position on Disabled Employees

A well-established principle in arbitration is that an employer may discharge an employee who cannot perform the duties of the job because of a physical impairment.[105] Some arbitrators will hold that under the labor agreement the disabled person must be placed in a job that the employee can perform even if it means displacing a junior worker.[106]

Recommendations for Dealing with AIDS

1. AIDS should be treated like any other disability that is covered by state or federal laws against discrimination (more than three quarters of the states have such laws).

2. Educate co-workers about AIDS before an actual case presents itself. How it is transmitted and why it is not a work-related condition should be stressed.

3. Maintain confidentiality of all medical records.

4. Do not in any way discriminate against a person with AIDS. Be able to document any discipline as nondiscriminatory.

5. Do not exclude AIDS patients from training or consideration for promotion. (Hard to sell, so find another reason.)

6. Accommodate or make a good effort to accommodate the AIDS patient by offering a transfer to a similar job or by any other reasonable action.

7. Don't test for AIDS, whether it be an applicant or a current employee.

8. Between 6 and 9 percent of HIV positive persons get AIDS.

8. Have a policy that communicates the company's position.

A person with HIV may be a contributor for many years with improved HIV medications.

---

[103]See Abrams and Nolan, "AIDS in Labor Arbitration," *University of San Francisco Law Review,* 25 (1990), 67, for a good overview of AIDS in arbitration.

[104]For a judicial and arbitral forum on employees infected with HIV see Robert S. Burger and Gregory Lewis, "AIDS and Employment: Judicial and Arbitral Responses," *Labor Law Journal,* 43, no. 5 (May 1992), 259.

---

[105]See *Bucklers, Inc.,* 90 Lab. Arb. (BNA) 937 (Braufman); *Nursing Home,* 88 Lab. Arb. (BNA) 681 (Sedwick).

[106]*International Paper Co.,* 94 Lab. Arb. (BNA) 1990 (Mathews).

Policy on Life-Threatening Diseases

The policy should not be on AIDS alone but on all life-threatening diseases. To single out one disease that may currently be a problem is a shortsighted policy that could cause exposure to litigation. It is difficult to make a policy that is flexible, but at least the company's position is communicated to the employees. That is the reason and objective of the policy. The following elements should be included in the policy:

1. The contagious nature of an employee's illness will be determined by medical examination.

2. As long as an employee has acceptable performance, he or she can continue to work unless by medical determination the condition is a threat to others.

3. If an employee's condition creates a problem to co-workers, reasonable accommodation will be made wherever possible. Also educate, educate, educate.

4. An employee's health condition is personal and confidential; it will be disclosed only to those who have a bona fide need to know.

5. When a life-threatening disease causes a problem, the legal rights of co-workers, management, and the person with the illness must be balanced on a case-by-case basis. Considerable weight will be given to science and medical knowledge; myths, speculation, and hysteria will be considered to a lesser degree.

6. Remember, as a person with AIDS is, other employees may be someday.

The main point to remember when dealing with AIDS patients is that this is a protected class that will require accommodation under ADA. What this means is a question that the courts have not yet decided.

When the employer discovers that an employee has AIDS (not just the HIV virus), sick leave can be offered as a solution to the problem. The employee may be entitled to disability benefits. This approach doesn't necessarily prevent a lawsuit, because the benefits are usually lower than full salary. To force sick leave would increase the exposure, especially on an HIV person, whom ADA considers handicapped. Whatever else works, *do it*, as long as the employee does it voluntarily and it decreases exposure to a lawsuit.

The AIDS problem is basically an employee relations problem; however, the economic factors often bring the employer into reality. For a good discussion of the economic side of the AIDS problem see Wayne R. Cohen, "An Economic Analysis of the Issues Surrounding AIDS in the Workplace: In the Long Run the Path of Truth and Reason Cannot Be Diverted," *American University Law Review,* 41 (1992), 199.

WORKING CONDITIONS BASED ON SEX

HISTORICAL DOMINANCE OF THE MALE IN THE WORKPLACE

One of the most difficult provisions of Title VII for some employers to accept is the requirement that persons of equal qualifications be given equal employment opportunities regardless of sex.[1] The social norm that a woman's role is that of a housekeeper and child rearer is often the controlling factor. The norm permits the female to enter the labor market only from economic necessity or when men are not available. During World War II women were encouraged to enter the labor market as a contribution to the war effort. When G.I. Joe returned to the labor market after the war, "Rosie the Riveter" simply did not have the physical strength, in the employer's opinion, to do a man's job.[2] This thinking that the woman's place is in the home and not in the workplace was accepted in the courts as well as in social institutions. In the often-quoted case of *Mueller* v. *State of Oregon,*[3] Supreme Court justice Bremer stated, "History disclosed the fact that woman has been dependent upon man. He established his control at the outset by superior physical strength and this control in various forms with diminishing intensity has continued to the present."[4]

This stereotyped thinking among males was still in the Congress when Title VII was passed.

---

[1]Nancy Austin, "Ethics:Personal v. Professional," *Working Women,* (September 1992), 28.

[2]Rosie the Riveter" was the working girl in World War II. The song was written to eulogize the part women were playing in replacing men in the war effort industries.

[3]208 U.S. 412 at 421 (1908). Also see "What Great Women," *McCalls,* (May 1995), 83.

[4]*Congressional Record*, Vol. 110, pp. 2577–84 (1964).

Congressman Howard Smith of Virginia, in opposition to the act, reasoned that if sex were included as an amendment to Title VII, it would not pass. Although this maneuver failed, members of Congress expressed their skepticism about women in the workplace by stating in Section 703(a)(e)(l) of Title VII that "where sex is a bona fide occupational qualification, reasonably necessary to the normal operation of the business, it would not be unlawful to discriminate on the basis of sex."

The enactment of Title VII did not suddenly change the patterns of sex discrimination that had been around for a hundred years. A start can be made by the law, but the remainder will have to be done by the courts, the economics of operating a business or enterprise, and a change in the reluctance on the part of women to bring a lawsuit.

Even though affirmative action programs (though some are being challenged) are in place and working, they cannot undo by law a practice that existed for over a hundred years. Behavior is derived more from social, traditional, cultural value than from legislation. Women in the workplace may be treated in a polite and proper way in the social context, but in the subconscious thinking of the male decision maker such treatment is inappropriate for good business.[5]

Many male managers still believe that it would be awkward to offer a single woman travel opportunities because a single woman should not be traveling alone or with a male co-worker. They believe family priorities take precedence over the job and therefore transfers should not be offered. These inherited biases often create unintentional discriminatory behavior.[6] This chapter highlights some of the employment problems under Title VII, the Civil Rights Act of 1991 (CRA91), and the Equal Pay Act that are particular to women. EEOC

vows more enforcement in the future, especially regarding hostile environment. Proposed new guidelines covering discrimination, 58 CFR 189 (1993), codified 24 CFR 166.

A woman being harassed by a male presents different problems for the employer in the administration of equal employment opportunity.

TITLE VII RESTRICTIONS ON SEX DISCRIMINATION

Title VII states that an employee cannot be treated differently because of sex unless sex is a bona fide occupational qualification (BFOQ).[7] Subjecting any employee to an activity aimed at gender is prohibited by Title VII.[8] However, it is not a violation to harass a homosexual under Title VII because the activity is based on sexual orientation and not gender.[9]

In some early cases the only issue before the courts was whether women were treated differently from men and, if so, was there a BFOQ that justified such treatment. When a company refused to hire women with preschool children but hired men with preschool children, women were treated differently. The Supreme Court declared such a policy unlawful and remanded the matter to the lower court to determine whether a BFOQ existed.[10] What the Court was really saying is that different treatment between males and females based solely on gender raises the issue of BFOQ.

An example of whether the discrimination is gender based is found in those cases where pregnancy disability payments are excluded from health insurance plans. Payments are not included for men who become ill or disabled. In one

---

[5]A 1992 study shows that attendees at the most prestigious management training programs are less than 10 percent women. That figure rose to about 20 percent in 1995, showing some improvement, but the "glass ceiling" has not been broken.

[6]Women are finding the "glass ceiling" difficult to pierce. Sections 201–208 of CRA91 provide for a study committee to help solve the problem, but this study failed to reveal the real problem.

[7]Although *bona fide occupational qualification* (BFOQ) is a statutory term defined in Title VII and *business necessity* was defined by the courts, the two items are often used simultaneously and are given the same strict interpretation.

[8]*Sender* v. *Lucky Stores,* Lexus 182 (N.D. Ca. 1993), also C. Herbert, "Sexual Harassment is Gender Harassment," *Kansas Law Review,* 429 (1995), 563.

[9]*Dillion* v. *Frank,* 752 F.2d 403 (6th Cir. 1992).

[10]*Phillips* v. *Martin Marietta Corp.,* 400 U.S. 542 (1971). See also *Texas Dept. of Community Affairs* v. *Durdine,* 450 U.S. 218 (1995).

situation the Supreme Court said that because men are not given disability for pregnancy, there is no benefit that men are given that women are not.[11] This case was decided under the Equal Protection Clause of the Fourteenth Amendment. The next question was: Would the same reasoning apply to a case under Title VII? The court said that it did. The court reasoned that there is no doubt that Congress did not intend to change the Constitution when Title VII was passed; in order to be in violation of Title VII, it must be gender based.[12]

Grooming and Dress Code as Preferential Treatment

Whenever a question of discrimination because of sex comes before the court, the issue is: "But for" the employee's sex would there have been different treatment? If management requires a dress code for women different from that for men, this would be discriminating unless a BFOQ could be shown.

A common, discriminatory dress code is one that requires women to wear provocative clothing but that does not require men to do so. This is most common in bars and restaurants where the employer often argues that this is necessary for business reasons. However, this BFOQ argument is seldom accepted by the courts. Under present case law this could have been argued under harassment, because the Supreme Court has held that dress can be evidence of a hostile environment.[13]

Dress and grooming codes can be a violation of the race and nationality section of Title VII. In these areas the courts are more apt to find BFOQ. To avoid exposure for sex discrimination the company requirement on grooming and dress must be stated as a job necessity and should not be adopted for the sake of appearance or

management's beliefs (see *EEOC* v. *Strouter's,* not yet settled).

BFOQ as a Defense in Sex Discrimination

Section 703(a)(e)(l) of Title VII specifically states that sex discrimination is not unlawful if BFOQ can be shown. In race, religion, color, and national groups such an exception is conspicuously absent in the statute (although the courts have allowed the BFOQ defense in cases concerning these protected classes). When BFOQ is used as a defense, the employer automatically admits sex discrimination but under the terms of the statute it is justified.

EEOC guidelines construe the exception narrowly, and the courts have followed. From the case law, it appears the BFOQ will be decided very narrowly on a case-by-case basis. There are few guidelines for BFOQ, the Supreme Court will decide. An exception under the guidelines is when the employer had objective factual basis to believe that substantially all women would be unable to perform safely and efficiently the assigned duties of the job. Sex discrimination in this case would be legal.

Often it is the employer's perception that females are not qualified for the job. In *United States* v. *Gregory,* 818 F.2d 1114 (4th Cir. 1987), the county sheriff refused to hire female correctional officers for an all-male county jail. He argued that this would infringe upon the privacy of inmates and guards because of the personal contact required by the job. The court ruled that the county failed to show that gender was a BFOQ for correctional officers. According to the court, the employer could not demonstrate "why it could not accommodate female corrections officers through reasonable modification of the facility and job functions." Plaintiff talked qualifications and implied accommodation.

This is an example of where the job title and the fact that it was an all-male jail would indicate that sex would be a BFOQ for correctional officers. However, the court looked into the job content and held that sex would not prevent women from performing the duties of the job. The court here talks qualifications.

---

[11]*Geduldig* v. *Aiello,* 417 U.S. 484 (1974).

[12]In *United Automobile, Aerospace and Agriculture Implement Workers* v. *Johnson Controls,* 111 S.Ct. 1196 (1991), the Court held that Title VII and the Pregnancy Disability Act forbid specific fetus protection policies, that such a policy is gender-based bias. *Stacks* v. *Southwestern Bell Yellow Pages,* 271 F.3d 31 (8th Cir. 1994).

[13]*Meritor Savings Bank, FSB* v. *Vinson,* 106 S.Ct. 2399 (1986).

As in other discrimination situations, there is no substitute (if at all feasible) for giving the employee an opportunity to perform before using BFOQ as a defense. Job assignment based on sex cannot be defended except in rare cases such as a safety or privacy consideration. Normally customer preference is not considered a BFOQ. When an employer stated that foreign customers are prejudiced against women, the court said that reason for discrimination is invalid as a matter of law.[14]

Discrimination Because of Marriage

The presence of the historical social norm that the workplace is not for women makes it appropriate that when women get married they should be encouraged to leave the labor market. Airlines for years had a no-marriage rule for cabin attendants. The federal postal services in 1913 decided that married women should not hold a classified position.[15] The Economy Act of 1932 (Section 213) stated that married women in the federal service would be retained only if they were more efficient than their husbands.[16]

Title VII declares a no-marriage rule unlawful when it does not apply to both sexes equally,[17] but it does allow the application of BFOQ as provided in Section 703(e). What this means to the struggling personnel practitioner is that if two employees get married, a rule could require that one must go but the rule could not state which one, unless on some basis other than sex. However, not all courts agree. The rule also means that if there was a superior-subordinate relationship, BFOQ could be a defense on a showing that the spouse relationship interfered with the efficient operation of the business. In *Ross* v. *Stouffer Hotel Co. (Hawaii Ltd.),* 816 F.2d 302 (Hawaii 1991), the court said a policy requiring one or the other to resign or transfer violates Title VII.[18]

One decision pertaining to a no-spouse rule was a case where there was statistical evidence that because of a no-spouse rule, a disparate impact in hiring females resulted (73 female applicants were rejected compared to 3 males).[19] The court found what most managers know; problems between married employees lead to grief for employers, and BFOQ permits the no-spouse rule. The court also said that married couples working together could cause emotional problems that would affect their work performance.

The rule has been extended to unmarried couples living together. Some courts will not make a distinction and hold that an employer is not in violation for refusing to hire or continue to employ a person living with another employee. This may violate equal protection clause of federal statute, *Racher* v. *Lemon,* 11 N.W. 892 (Mich. Sup.Ct. 1993). However, some states include marriage as a protected class in their discrimination laws,[20] and in those states it would be a violation to discriminate against employees who are not married. In *State by Johnson* v. *Porter Farms, Inc.,* 382 N.W.2d 543 (Minn. App. 1986), the court held that termination of an unmarried employee for living with a person of the opposite sex violated the provision on marital status,[21] because married persons live together. These courts take the position that any restriction on marriage (or no marriage) is discrimination under the state statute.

In states that have statutes protecting the marital status discrimination for hiring and promotion, the employer is permitted to prevent a superior-subordinate relationship between spouses

---

[14]*Fernandez* v. *Wynn Oil Co.,* 653 F.2d 1275 (9th Cir. 1981).

[15]U.S. Civil Service Commission, *Women in the Federal Service,* 2nd ed. (Washington, DC: Government Printing Office, 1938).

[16]U.S. Civil Service Commission, *Women,* 1938.

[17]42 U.S.C. Sect. 2000(d) et al.

[18]See Kingsley Browne, *Sex Harassment in a Modern Society, Arizona Law Review,* 37 (1996), 121.

[19]*Yuhas* v. *Libbey-Owens-Ford Co.,* 562 F.2d 496 (7th Cir. 1977), cert. denied.

[20]Michigan, Minnesota, Montana, Rhode Island, and Washington, to name a few.

[21]See also *Slohoda* v. *United Parcel Serv., Inc.,* 475 A.2d 618 (N.J. Super. A.D. 1984) where an employee was discharged for having sexual intercourse out of wedlock when he was married. The court allowed a cause of action because the policy did not prevent an unmarried person from having sexual intercourse.

by transfers or in the hiring process. The employer usually can show BFOQ in this situation.[22]

Sex Discrimination in Work Assignments

It is a well-established principle in antidiscrimination law that one cannot determine categorically that all females are incapable of performing certain tasks. Stereotyped or antifemale language can be used to determine sex discrimination even though it is said unconsciously.[23]

When considering qualifications for promotion under a labor agreement, labor relations practitioners discovered early in their careers that unless the applicant is given an opportunity to perform, it is difficult to win in arbitration.

In work assignments for females it is advisable to permit performance before rejection, examining objective evidence whether they can do the job or might affect the safety of others.

Courts that have considered the issue of female work assignments have held that the employer cannot determine employment opportunities on the basis of physical capabilities and endurance of women as a group.

In a heavy-object-lifting case the employer rejected a female because it was alleged that she did not have the physical ability to perform the job. The court said that the applicant must be given a reasonable opportunity to demonstrate her ability to perform the duties. The same rule would apply when a job was refused because of race. The employer who categorically denies work assignments to females because of alleged limitations of females needs to be reminded of the song about Rosie the Riveter.

HARASSMENT—DEFINITION AND CONTROL

Harassment in the workplace is a violation of Title VII when a member of the protected group is treated differently from other persons. The act does not have a specific provision prohibiting harassment as such, but the courts[24] and later the EEOC have so interpreted the statute.

Racial harassment would be found in a case in which a black is subject to racial slurs and pranks or other bigoted acts of employees or supervisors.[25]

A nationality harassment situation involved a supervisor who, in order to communicate a no-smoking rule to a single violator (who was German), posted a no-smoking sign in German. Harassment was admitted, but the employee did not subsequently violate the no-smoking rule. (The relief requested was removal of the sign.)

Sexual Harassment in the Workplace

Most harassment situations involve sexual harassment or sexual relations.. Although it isn't necessary for conduct to be sexual in nature, it is difficult to determine what came first in the workplace: sexual relations or sexual harassment.

Until recently, management did not have to contend with the sexual relations between employees either within or outside the working relationship as long as they did not interfere with work performance or did not occur on company time.[26]

If management were aware of sexual advances, it would ignore them as a normal result of the attraction between the sexes and something that would be worked out between the parties involved. If in extreme cases correction were needed, the matter was handled on a confidential and individual basis. The typical manager reasoned (and many still do) that because of the personal nature of sexual harassment, dealing with

---

[22]For further information on marital discrimination, see Leonard Bierman and Cynthia D. Fisher, "Anti-Nepotism Rules Applied to Spouses; Business and Legal Viewpoints," *Labor Law Journal*, 35, no. 10 (October 1984), 634.

[23]*Price Waterhouse* v. *Hopkins*, 109 S.Ct. 1775 (1989).

[24]Harassment received its first formal judicial recognition in *Williams* v. *Saxbe*, 413 F.Supp. 654 (D.C. 1976), where the court held that Title VII's prohibition on sex discrimination includes a prohibition on sexual harassment.

[25]For the EEOC position on sexual harassment, see "Policy Guidance of Sexual Harassment," Equal Opportunity Commission, 1801 L Street NW Washington, DC 20507.

[26]Rules about no sexual relations at the workplace are difficult to enforce because they are a rarity to witness.

it openly would sometimes create more problems than it would solve.

Another reason for management's reluctance is that sexual advances are often difficult to define. Acquiescence and encouragement are always possibilities. Also, female employees are frequently reluctant to bring the matter to the attention of the employer for fear of embarrassment or because of creating an adverse condition with the supervisor or co-worker. There is uncertainty about what action management will take.[27]

Several surveys have been made to determine whether sexual harassment in the workplace is common. In general, these surveys found that unwanted sexual harassment existed;[28] 1 to 2 percent reported being coerced into sexual relations, which is the most extreme form of sexual harassment. The number may not seem large, but if accurate, based on the number of women employed, more than 400,000 working women a year have unwanted sexual relations, which could be called employment rape.[29]

These surveys may not be entirely reliable because there is no legal definition of sexual harassment. It means different things to different employees.[30] However, sexual harassment charges filed with EEOC are rapidly increasing.

Legal Basis for Sexual Harassment

Sexual harassment is a form of sex discrimination, but it is distinguishable in that the conduct involves sexual favors or the creation of an environment that tolerates unwelcome sexual advances or language. Where discrimination because of an employee's sex involves an adverse employment decision, this violates Title VII.[31] Also sex discrimination and sexual harassment can be distinguished in that sex discrimination is usually a single act, while sexual harassment usually involves continual conduct.[32]

The EEOC guidelines were issued in 1980 and codified the court decisions of the previous years. Most of these guidelines (29 CFR Sect. 1604.11) have judicial acceptance.

The reason sexual harassment is unlawful is that Title VII prevents one sex from being favored over another; where a male favors a female and not other males, there is a violation.[33] By the same principle a male could be sexually harassed by a female, and the courts have so held. A male sexually harassing a male is unlawful because females are not given the same attention;[34] however, a bisexual cannot be guilty of harassment because no favors are shown to either sex.

Using the same reasoning, a transsexual would not be protected by Title VII because it is yet to be determined medically which sex is being favored.[35] Where a transsexual was denied use of female restroom facilities, claiming to be a female at the time of applying for a job, and the employer discharged for misrepresentation because the plaintiff was a male in the employer's opinion, the court said discharge was not a violation of Title

---

[27]See Pollack, "Sexual Harassment: Until Then It Didn't Have a Name, It Just Happened," *Women,* 41 no. 11 (1991).

[28]J. Attanasio, "Sexual Harassment: View from the Top," *Redbook,* July 1976, 46–51; *Working Women,* December 1988.

[29]"Sexual Harassment in Federal Government—An Update," U.S. Merit Systems Protection Board, Washington, DC, July 1988.

[30]For the private sector, see Paul S. Greenkaw and John P. Kohl, "Proving Title VII Sexual Harassment: The Court's View," *Labor Law Journal,* 43, no. 3 (March 1992), 164.

[31]See "Policy Guideline on Current Issue of Sexual Harassment," EEOC Policy Statement No. 915.035 (October 1988).

[32]In *Shore* v. *Federal Express,* 777 F.2d 1155 (6th Cir. 1985), a female employee was involved in an intimate relationship with a male. The male was promoted to an executive position and, as a supervisor, terminated the female because the relationship interfered with office operations. This was sex discrimination but not harassment, because the conduct did not involve favors and was not continual, and because an unpleasant, sexually unacceptable working environment was not created. Also see *De Cintio* v. *Westchester County Medical Center,* 807 F.2d 304 (2nd Cir. 1986).

[33]Over 10 percent of male workers are harassed by females. It is considered rare when a female harasses a male.

[34]*Wright* v. *Methodist Youth Services,* 511 F.Supp. 307 (Ill. 1981); *Joyner* v. *AAA Cooper Transportation,* 597 F.Supp. 537 (Ala. 1983). Some courts do not agree.

[35]A transsexual is described as an individual who is mentally of one sex but physically of another. 63 ALR3d 1199 (1975).

VII; the act is not intended to cover transsexualism.[36] Supreme Court said action of the same sex is a violation.

If the harassment would not have occurred "but for" the employee's sex, it is harassment because it constitutes an unequal condition of employment.[37] However, the conduct must be sufficiently persuasive to alter the conditions of employment. In deciding whether there has been sexual harassment, the EEOC and the courts will look at the facts as a whole and the totality of the circumstances.[38] Some courts will consider evidence of the complainant's sex life to determine whether the conduct constitutes sexual harassment.[39]

Reverse Sexual Harassment

The EEOC guidelines [29CFR Sect. 1604.11] also deal with what might be called sexual harassment in reverse. In this type of case an employee climbs the corporate ladder, at the expense of other qualified persons, by giving sexual favors to the decision maker. The qualified employees passed over have a claim for sexual discrimination.[40] The employer may avoid litigation from the person promoted but then has an exposure from those who were passed over.

Third Party Actions

Third parties who have been affected by sexual harassment normally cannot sue,[41] although some courts will find a way, especially in hostile environment cases. In *Broderick* v. *Ruder,* 685 F.Supp. 1269 (D.C. 1988), the female attorney was allowed to sue although little of the harassment was directed at her. Several federal courts find strict liability if a top management person creates the hostile environment, although they are third parties,[42] while other courts limit strict liability to quid pro quo cases.[43] As the case law indicates, third party suits are a gray area in the law.

Effect of CRA91 on Sexual Harassment

The Civil Rights Act of 1991 may have changed the common law grounds for a tort action. The act amended Title VII to provide for compensatory and punitive damages as well as jury trial. In addition, the plaintiffs can now recover expert witness fees. The combination of jury trial and punitive damages could place the parties in a different settlement posture. The damages are expressly limited by statute and may conflict with a state statute, but federal statutes will prevail.

When the employer has knowledge and fails to do anything about it, the courts in almost every case have held the employer liable under Title VII. However, if they find a blatant example of inaction they will allow a negligence action before a jury and allow them to find punitive damages.[44]

---

[36]*Sommers* v. *Budget Marketing, Inc.,* 667 F.2d 748 (8th cir. 1982).

[37]*McKinney* v. *Dole,* 765 F.2d 1129 (D.C. Cir. 1985).

[38]Totality of circumstances can determine different results. An insurance defense attorney demanded a yes or no answer from a witness. After several appeals to the judge, the judge let the witness from the farm tell this story: "I was going down the road at 5:30 A.M. one morning with my dog Pal on the front seat and my cow Bessie in the back of the pickup. I came to an intersection and this car crossed and hit me real hard. My dog and I flew into the ditch. My cow also ended up in the ditch. The sheriff came along and saw the dog, pulled out his gun and shot him; saw the cow, pulled out the gun and shot it. He then came to me and asked how I felt."

[39]*Burns* v. *McGregor Electric Industries, Inc.,* 955 F.2d 559 (8th Cir. 1992).

[40]See *DeCinito* v. *Westchester Medical Center,* 807 F.2d 304 (2d. Cir. 1986), cert. denied (1987), and *Broderick* v. *Ruder,* 685 F.Supp 1269 (D.C. 1988), for different views.

[41]*Blaw-Knox Foundry and Mill* v. *NLRB,* 646 F.2d 113 (4th Cir. 1981).

[42]*Katz* v. *Dole,* 790 F.2d 251, 255 (4th Cir. 1983).

[43]*Steel* v. *Offshore Shipbuilding, Inc.,* 867 F.2d 1311, 1316 (11th Cir. 1989). See also William L. Kandell, "Mixed Motives: Sexual Harassment and CRA91," *Employee Relations Law Journal,* 17 (Spring 1992).

[44]This is still good law, but the CRA91 limitations will apply, unless a different statute is used.

The *Meritor* Case

Many questions about what is or is not sexual harassment were cleared up in the first case on the subject to come before the Supreme Court. In the landmark case of *Meritor Savings Bank, FSB* v. *Vinson* (hereinafter called *Meritor),* 106 S.Ct. 2399 (1986),[45] Ms. Vinson alleged that Taylor, who was a vice president of the bank, had asked for sexual relations with her. At first she refused, but later yielded out of fear of losing her job. She testified that she had sexual relations with the manager from 40 to 50 times in the previous four years both during and after business hours. She never reported her action to any of the manager's supervisors, nor did she attempt to use the complaint procedure that the employer had established. She also alleged that Taylor fondled her in front of other employees and followed her into the women's restroom when she went there alone, exposed himself to her, and even on occasion forcibly raped her. These activities ceased after she got a boyfriend. About a year later she took sick leave for an indefinite period. Three months later the employer fired her for excessive sick leave.

She brought suit alleging sexual harassment during the four years of employment. The district court held that she was not subjected to sexual harassment but merely was involved in a broken love affair. The appellate court reversed the decision, holding that the action was a violation of Title VII even though no job opportunities were involved. The court imputed notice to the employer because the manager obviously knew about the harassment. The manager was the representative of the employer; therefore, the employer knew or should have known.

The Supreme Court in a unanimous decision held that a violation of Title VII is predicated on two types of harassment:

1. Those involving economic benefits (quid pro quo)
2. Those where a hostile environment is created

The provocative dress and speech of the alleged victim and voluntary participation in sexual affairs do not preclude a finding that the episodes were unwanted and therefore unlawful.[46] The Court said that the employer is not relieved of liability in all situations where there is an announced policy against sexual harassment or by the failure of the victim to utilize existing grievance procedure. (In this specific case the grievance procedure required the employee to complain to her immediate supervisor—the person she wanted to complain about.)

The Court majority was not willing to impute knowledge in all cases in which a supervisor was involved, as had been ruled by the appellate court and the EEOC guidelines.[47] It stated that the facts and circumstances in each case should determine whether the employer had notice, but that the absence of notice did not necessarily insulate the employer from liability. Many state courts impute knowledge under the common law doctrine of respondeat superior.[48]

This decision summarizes all previous appellate court decisions on sexual harassment and clearly defines sexual harassment as unwelcome. It goes further in saying that voluntary participation does not necessarily mean that the activity is welcome. The Court invalidated the EEOC guidelines that state that you can impute knowledge where the supervisor is involved at least where no job opportunities are related to the activity. The Court thus reversed several appellate court decisions that have upheld the guidelines as to knowledge. The employer can be liable by imputing knowledge. Established grievance procedure was not used, but it depends upon the facts of each case. Knowledge is not automatic because the supervisor is involved, as stated in

---

[45]This case attracted considerable attention from the media and scholars. See "Employer Liability under Title VII for Sexual Harassment after Vinson," *Columbia Law Review,* 87 (1987), 1258; J. Sweeney, "Meritor Slaps at Competition," *Bankers Monthly,* 105 (July 1988); M. Morlacci, "Sexual Harassment and Impact of Vinson," *Employee Relations Law Journal* (Winter 1987–1988), 501.

[46]Appeal courts hold that such evidence can be used to determine that the activity was unwelcomed. Also see *Burne* v. *McGregor Electronics, Inc.,* 989 F.2d 959 (8th Cir. 1989).

[47]*Vinson* v. *Taylor,* 753 F.2d 141 (D.C. 1985). (Same case as *Meritor.)*

[48]See *Heaser* v. *Lerch, Bates & Associates,* 467 N.W.2d 833 (Minn. App. 1991).

EEOC guidelines. This case is quoted in subsequent decisions.

This landmark decision stated that in order to find sexual harassment there must be three elements:

1. It must be unwelcomed.
2. The employer must have knowledge, either actual or imputed.
3. Either job opportunities must be involved or a hostile environment created.

The *Meritor* decision cleared up many conflicting standards previously developed by the appellate courts. *Meritor* defined sexual harassment, but left many issues undecided or unclear, namely: employer liability, agency, the severity of the harassment and the severity from whose point of view, the meaning of such terms as "unwelcome," and matters of proof, such as the admissibility of evidence regarding a plaintiff's provocative speech and dress. The decision must be read in detail to aid the employer in policy development.[49]

Unwelcomed Harassment

The court recognized that a person may be the victim of sexual harassment even though she participated in or condoned acts of a sexual nature.[50] It is difficult for an employer to know whether an intimate relationship is "unwelcomed" or at what point it will be welcomed.[51] It appears the only way the employer will know is for the employee to say that advances are presently unwelcomed. The ruling on admissibility of evidence concerning the complainant's sexual behavior will help, because the employer can argue that because of the behavior a reasonable woman would believe that the conditions were not entirely unwelcomed.[52]

The more evidence that there is a personal relationship between the plaintiff and alleged harasser, the more difficulty the plaintiff will have in showing that it was unwelcomed. The Supreme Court in *Harris* v. *Forklift System, Inc.,* 114 S.Ct. 367 63 FEP 225 (1993) used a "reasonable person" test now found in a majority of courts.

Job Opportunities or Hostile Environment

There are two types of sexual harassment: quid pro quo harassment and hostile environment. Quid pro quo is defined as being forced to choose between acquiescence to a superior's sexual demands and forfeiting an employment benefit (for example, promotion, wage increase, leave of absence, or continued employment). Because quid pro quo is easily identified by its objectivity, there is little problem with it.

Hostile environment[53] claims are more difficult to prove. They are more subjective in that they do not involve a specific employment benefit and can involve a co-worker. Hostile environment is defined by the EEOC guidelines as an interference with the employee's work behavior or a creation of an offensive work environment.[54] The *Meritor* case merely reaffirmed the appellate court's position that hostile environment is a violation of Title VII and that provocative dress requirements and verbal statements could constitute hostile environment. It did not specifically define hostile environment.

The Supreme Court in *Harris* v. *Forklift System, Inc.,* 114 S.Ct. 367 63 FEP 225 (1993) said that a "reasonable person" standard should be used. This resolved a conflict among the circuits

---

[49]*Meritor Savings Bank, FSB* v. *Vinson*, 106 S.Ct. 2399, 477 U.S. 57 (1986).

[50]*Henson* v. *City of Dundee*, 682 F.2d 897 (11th Cir. 1982).

[51]*Staton* v. *Maries County*, 868 F.2d 996 (8th Cir. 1989); *Moylan* v. *Maries County*, 792 F.2d. 746 (8th Cir. 1986).

[52]*Ellison* v. *Brady*, 924 F.2d 872 (9th Cir. 1991); *Andrews* v. *City of Philadelphia*, 895 F.2d 1469, 1482 (3rd Cir. 1990); *Spencer* v. *General Electric Co.,* 894 F.2d 651 (4th Cir. 1990). Other cases in the 6th, 8th, and 11th circuits.

[53]For discussion of hostile environment see C. M. Keon, "Sexual Harassment: Criteria for Defining Hostile Environment," *Employee Responsibilities and Rights Journal*, December 1989; also L. Reinders, Comment, "A Reasonable Woman Approach to Hostile Environment Sexual Harassment," *Washington University Journal of Urban and Contemporary Law,* 41 (1992), 227; Arthur Silbergeld, "Reasonable Victim Test for Judging Hostile Environment–Sexual Harassment Cases," *Employment Relations Today,* Summer 1991; William L. Woerner and Sharon Oswald, "Sexual Harassment in the Workplace: A View through the Eyes of the Courts," *Labor Law Journal*, 41, no. 11 (November 1990), 86.

[54]29 CFR 16.011 (A).

where both the "reasonable person" and "reasonable woman" standard were used to find hostile environment. The employer, to be safe, uses the "reasonable woman" standard.[55] If the employer's knowledge of the condition being unwelcomed is required, it appears that the "reasonable woman" standard would be used. A hostile environment can be found as one that a "reasonable woman" would find unwelcome.

The court further held that it is not necessary that the plaintiff show a tangible psychological injury. Some courts such as the one in *Rabidue* said it was.[55a] So again the circuits were split and the Supreme Court cleared it up. It said, beginning at 63 FEP Cases 227:

Conduct that is not severe or pervasive enough to create an objectively hostile or abusive work environment—an environment that a reasonable person would find hostile or abusive—is beyond Title VII's purview. Likewise, if the victim does not subjectively perceive the environment to be abusive, the conduct has not actually altered the conditions of the victim's employment, and there is no Title VII violation.

But Title VII comes into play before the harassing conduct leads to a nervous breakdown ... so long as the environment would reasonably be perceived,[56] and is perceived, as hostile or abusive.

The Court took a middle ground between what the circuits had been saying. It reaffirmed its earlier holding in the *Meritor* case and did not reverse any case. However, it took an 8th Circuit case six weeks later to clear up what the plaintiff must show. In *Kopp* v. *Samaritan Health Systems,* 13 F.3d 264 at 269, the court outlined the five elements required for the plaintiff to show:

1. she belongs to a protected group;
2. she was subject to unwelcome sexual harassment;
3. the harassment was based on sex;
4. the harassment affected a term, condition, or privilege of employment;

5. [the employer] knew or should have known of the harassment and failed to take proper remedial action.

The plaintiff in *Meritor* was not specifically required or asked to give sexual favors as a condition of promotion. From the testimony, her promotions were based upon merit; the employer liability was therefore based on hostile environment and not quid pro quo harassment. The court held in this situation that the manager's behavior of exposure, fondling, and having sex relations on and off the job 40 to 50 times in four years constituted a hostile environment.[57]

Hostile Environment—A Definition

The court, in considering whether there is a hostile environment, must evaluate the conditions existing before the plaintiff was hired,[58] the background and experience of the plaintiff, her co-workers and supervisors, and the totality of the physical environment. However, if antifemale animus is found, the court will usually find hostile environment.[59]

Whether a hostile environment exists must be evaluated on a case-by-case basis. The court in *Rabidue* noted that in some work environments sexual jokes and vulgarity are extremely common and that Title VII was not meant to bring about "a transformation in the social mores of American workers." The remarks may be annoying, but if they are not so offensive as to have seriously affected the plaintiff there is no hostile environment. In *Davis* v. *Monsanto Chemical Co.,* 858 F.2d 345 (6th Cir. 1988), the court rejected *Rabidue* by stating that there are only two

---

[55]Before *Harris,* Michigan adopted "reasonable person" standard.

[55a]*Rabidue* v. *Osceola Refining Co., 107 S.Ct. (1983).*

[56]*Radtke* v. *Everett,* 471 N.W.2d 666 (Mich. 1991).

[57]See Ronald Turner, "Title VII and Hostile Environment, Sexual Harassment: Setting the Standard of Employer Liability," *University of Detroit Marcy Law Review,* 71 (1994) 817 .

[58]In *Burns* v. *McGregor Electric,* 989 F.2d 939 (8th Cir. 1993) the court said, "This is not a case where Burns posed in provocative and suggestive ways at work. Her private life, regardless of how reprehensible the trier of fact might find to be, did not provide lawful acquiescence to unwanted sexual advances at her work place by her employer."

[59]*Price Waterhouse* v. *Hopkins,* 490 U.S. 228 (1989); *Andrews* v. *City of Philadelphia,* 895 F.2d 1469 (3rd Cir. 1990).

requirements for hostile environment: repeated activity and management tolerance. The *Harris* case agreed. No interference with work performance was shown. Some courts hold that sexy posters create a hostile environment, while others disagree.[60]

There is no clear-cut definition of hostile environment.[61] The necessary elements of the definition are that the employee declare the environment hostile and unwelcome and that the employer have knowledge. If the condition is not important, why let it continue? The employer can always be relieved of liability by doing something about it. If the employer feels there is no hostile environment and lets it continue, it is a business decision whether the exposure is worth it.

Knowledge Imputed to Employer— State of the Law

Imputed knowledge is one of the cloudiest areas of the *Meritor* decision. Surveys show that only a small percentage of employees who are being harassed will report it to the employer. The EEOC-proposed guidelines[62] explicitly state that employers are responsible for all acts of sexual harassment in the workplace where the supervisor is involved, unless it can be shown that the employer took immediate action to correct. The Supreme Court was widely split on whether they should adopt the EEOC guidelines,[63] but the majority held in *Meritor* that employers are not strictly liable for act of supervisors. Most appellate courts that have considered the issue state that knowledge is imputed to the employer where the supervisor is involved and when such harassment is quid pro quo.[64] In *Meritor* the Court had no trouble in finding that knowledge was imputed,

because the grievance procedure required the plaintiff to go to the person involved. The employee was not encouraged to complain; the Court imputed knowledge.[65] From the dictum in the case, the Court indicates that if there was a different grievance procedure and a policy, knowledge would not be imputed unless it is reported or the employer should have known, but we cannot be sure.

The *Meritor* case cleared up many issues, such as that hostile environment is a violation under Title VII; that sexual harassment must be unwelcomed and acquiescence does not always mean that it is welcome; and that unless the employee can report to some other member of management other than the person involved, knowledge will be imputed. However, whether there is a hostile environment without specific proof that work performance is affected and whether proof is required that the employee is actually offended by the environment are still open questions decided by the totality of circumstances and on a case-by-case basis.[66]

Control of Harassment

Although the *Meritor* case did not specifically define what is unwelcome, when knowledge is imputed, or what is meant by hostile environment, the employer can define these elements with an enforceable policy. The employer can recognize that there are some gray areas and by policy can go further than the law and still not be contrary, which would prevent exposure and still not interrupt business operation. It is then the policy that is violated rather than an uncertain area in the law.[67]

The law recognizes that the employer may from time to time have difficulty in eradicating sexual harassment because it is difficult to define, but what the court will not recognize is the failure to

---

[60]See *Robinson* v. *Jacksonville Shipyards*, 760 F.2d 1486 (11th Cir. 1991).

[61]See S. Burns, "Evidence of Sexually Hostile Workplace," *New York University Law Review*, 21 (1994-95) 357-431.

[62]CFR Sect. 1604.11(d).

[63]The *Meritor* court was unanimous on all other issues but split 5-4 on this issue.

[64]*Steele* v. *Off-shore Shipbuilding, Inc.*, 867 F.2d 1311 (11th Cir. 1989); *Spencer* v. *General Electric Co.*, 894 F.2d 651 (4th Cir. 1990).

[65]A good analysis of the respondent-superior and negligence standard and imputed knowledge is in *Hirschfeld* v. *New Mexico Corrections Dept.*, 916 F.2d 572 (10th Cir. 1990).

[66]*Saxton* v. *American Telephone & Telegraph Co.*, 10 F.3d 526 (7th Cir. 1993).

[67]L. Ruban, , R. Riok, R. Allen B., "Unresolved Issues in Hostile Environment Claims of Sexual Harassment," *Labor Law Journal*, 45 (1994) 110-114.

do something about it after the employer has actual or imputed knowledge.[68]

Investigation of a Complaint

If the employee complains about being harassed, do not call your lawyer but investigate immediately. Prompt investigation and a written warning relieves the employer of liability. The employer can take steps to remedy the charge and that is adequate.[69]

If the employee has a bona fide belief that she or he is being harassed, this should be recognized by the employer regardless of whether the initial thought is that it is meritless. Through separate interviews with both the person involved and the complainant, the employer can determine how to relieve the situation and eliminate exposure to a lawsuit. At this point it is an employee relations problem and not a legal question. Whether the facts come within the *Meritor* case or whether there is a gray area is immaterial for policy enforcement. The legal issue does not arise until a complaint is filed and an adverse relationship is created. However, immediately doing something about the complaint will usually avoid litigation and the legal costs that follow.[70]

Need for Immediate Investigation

Whether or not an investigation is immediate is determined on a case-by-case basis. Some of the considerations are

1. What is the harassment complained of? (Sexual favors for job opportunities would demand quicker investigation than a hostile environment.)
2. What is the size of the company? (In a large company with a bureaucracy of management it would take longer to start an investigation than in a small company where everybody reports to the CEO.)
3. How well does the company know the employees involved, or how much investigation is needed to get both sides of the facts before the complaint can be evaluated?

When making a decision as to whether harassment exists, it is essential not to falsely accuse an employee of harassment, because a false charge is just as serious as not doing anything with an employee who is guilty of harassment. Some employers have an outside source do the investigation; the procedure makes it more impartial.

Steps in an Investigation

1. Interview both parties.
2. Interview other workers not being harassed.
3. Have more than one person weigh the evidence.
4. Take action depending upon the facts. (No action; monitoring without admission of guilt; transfer; warning; severe disciplinary action; discharge; etc.)

Necessary Ingredients for Policy

In the *Meritor* case the Supreme Court said that in order to bring an action for sexual harassment it must be shown that it is unwelcome, the employer has knowledge or there is reason to impute knowledge, there are job opportunities involved, or there is hostile environment. How the courts subsequently define these elements is not important if the employer drafts the proper policy. This policy must be internally enforced, and each of the ingredients is defined.[71] This is extremely important where, under a collective bargaining agreement, the employee has a right to arbitrate a discharge for harassment and the arbitrator cannot reinstate when the policy is violated.

---

[68]*Baker* v. *Weyerhaeuser Co.,* 903 F.2d 1342 (9th Cir. 1991). Also *Spicer* v. *Virginia,* 66 F.2d 705 (4th Cir. 1995).

[69]*Guess* v. *Bethlehem Steel,* 913 F.2d 463 (7th Cir. 1990). However, the remedial action has to be effective. See *Waltman* v. *International Paper Co.,* 875 F.2d 468 (5th Cir. 1989), also *Intlekofer* v. *Turnage,* 973 F.2d 773 (9th Cir. 1992). *Shoffield* v. *Hilton Sand & Gravel,* 896 F.Supp. 108 (Va. 1995).

[70]Burtch, "Risks in Interviewing the Sexual Harassment Client," *American Journal of Trial Advocacy,* 17 (1996), 56.

---

[71]V. E. Hauck and T. Pearce, "Sexual Harassment and Arbitration," *Labor Law Journal,* 43 (January 1992), 31, discusses arbitration in sexual harassment cases.

1. The policy should prohibit both quid pro quo and environmental harassment, and it should state that the employer will correct any valid sexual complaint.
2. As to knowledge, the policy should require the employee to report any unwelcome event or condition. A failure to report will indicate a welcome relationship.
3. The hostile environment should be defined as containing sexual advances, innuendos, or vulgar statements that the employee considers hostile or objects to. Although the law may not always consider isolated instances as a hostile environment, the employer can do so for investigation purposes.[72]
4. The policy should warn the employee that once it is established beyond a doubt that the policy (not necessarily the law) has been violated, swift and severe action will be taken.
5. If substantial facts cannot be established, it should be explained to the complaining party that the relationship will be monitored for a period of time.
6. There shall be no retaliation for reporting a complaint. This is an enforceable promise from the CEO. The policy should state that an unwelcome relationship exists as soon as the employee says so. This eliminates any confusion that the parties may have when harassment exists. The policy will further state that any unwelcome advance will be investigated as soon as possible after the employer knows or should have known of the incident.

Reporting Procedure for Policy Violation

An environment is hostile for purposes of investigation and action when the employee says so or the management, using the "reasonable-man" test, considers it hostile. As in other necessary elements for sexual harassment, the policy puts the responsibility on the employee to define harassment; the law steps in only after the employer does nothing about it. Inasmuch as the policy stresses reporting, a procedure should be included in the policy or otherwise communicated to supervisors and employees. The essential elements of a reporting procedure are these:

1. State that a complaint of harassment conduct can be reported to any member of management. The name of the person (or persons) involved must be disclosed.
2. State the method of investigation and the appropriate time limits. (Time limits should be very short.)
3. State that the employer will correct any valid sexual harassment complaint that is reported.
4. Give assurance that the information will be confidential and there will be no retaliation whatsoever. Say so a second time.
5. Clearly state the company's position on failure to report: that in this case it means that it is a welcome relationship and the employee does not consider the incident or condition unwelcome. State that fear of loss of a job is not a reason for not reporting to some member of management.

The existence of a policy does not relieve the employer of liability unless it requires reporting. In *Yates* v. *Avco Corp.,* 819 F.2d 630 (6th Cir. 1987), the court stated that although a policy existed it was not effective in encouraging the employee to report; therefore knowledge was imputed and the employer was held liable.[73] Some courts state that the employer has a duty to prevent reasonable anticipated harassment.

Training to Prevent Liability

Although more than 80 percent of employers surveyed have policies, less than 45 percent offer supervisory training for women.[74]

Employees with overall responsibility, all line managers or lead persons at any level, those designated to receive complaints, and workers who are being monitored should be required to attend training courses.

Training may be conducted by outside persons or can be a part of a regular training session. Usually about 10 minutes at every training session is all that is needed to remind the participants of the problem.

---

[72]*Radtke* v. *Everett,* 471 N.W.2d 666 (Mich. 1991); also *Kay* v. *Peter Motor Co.,* 483 N.W.2d 481 (Minn. App. 1992).

[73]See also *EEOC* v. *Mt. Vernon Mills,* 58 FEP Cases 73(BNA) [D. Ga. 1992], otherwise reported only in Westlaw.

[74]*Paroline* v. *Unisys Corp.,* 879 F.2d 100 (11th Cir. 1989); "Workforce 2000," Hudson Institute and Tower-Perrin Report (1990).

EXHIBIT 7-1 *Harassment Notice*

Date _____

For many years the management of this company has by policy and to the public stated that it is an equal opportunity employer. All management employees have, without exception, been instructed to strictly adhere to this policy. There are, however, rare instances of unwelcomed harassment of minorities, nationalities, and persons because of their sex, age, disability, or religion. Any type of discriminatory action or harassment of one employee against another because of race, age, religion, sex, or national origin that may interfere with good working conditions or job opportunities is a violation of company policy, and employees responsible will be subject to severe disciplinary action. Our commitment as an equal opportunity employer applies to all employees including members of management, and we intend to enforce it by immediately investigating all known incidents or complaints of employees and taking necessary disciplinary action where incidents are found to be in violation of company policy. Employees who are subjected to harassment of any type are required to report to any member of management any violations of the above policy. The report will be confidential, given to only those persons who have a need to know. Failure to report any type of harassment, including but not limited to sexual harassment, will be considered by management to indicate an acceptable relationship or that the incidents do not create unreasonable working conditions. You can be assured there will be no retaliation for reporting. The company also recognizes that false accusation of harassment can have serious effects upon the accused. Therefore, false accusations will result in severe disciplinary action.

The contents should always include a statement from top management on enforcement, as well as the policy's definition of quid pro quo and hostile-environment harassment. Some examples of conduct or speech that has been unwelcomed in the past could be given.

The legal definition, names of employees, and promises about how the violators will be treated should be left out. The training should be as informal as possible.

Other training activities can include

1. Periodically reprinting the policy.
2. Providing periodic training sessions on sexual harassment to managers.
3. Repeating from time to time that the company will act on all complaints.
4. Repeatedly assuring the employees that there will be no retaliation.
5. Requiring managers to discuss sexual harassment at department meetings, focusing on its meaning and on the consequences for violation.

Exhibit 7-1 will help the employer get started on a policy to control sexual harassment in the workplace.

This recommended policy goes further than most companies are willing to go.[75] However, in view of the appellate courts' imputing knowledge when supervision is involved and the 5-4 split in the Supreme Court, the employer must find some way to have the matter reported. Considering it welcome if not reported appears to be the only solution.[76]

Sexual harassment conduct is not any different from any other undesirable conduct with which the employer must cope in the workplace. Enforcement of house rules is always a problem; prohibition of sexual harassment is just another

---

[75]K. Abrams, "Gender Discrimination and Transformation of Workplace Norms," *Vanderbilt Law Review,* 42 (1989), 1183.

[76]Sometimes a welcome relationship becomes unwelcome. Or what might be welcome to one person is unwelcome to another.

rule that must be enforced, but it is more difficult to control.

Sexual harassment in the workplace will not go away. History reveals that sexual behavior has caused persons to give up kingdoms, ruined political and religious careers, and caused business careers to fail. This will not change because a policy exists. Employees, supervisors, and managers will continue to risk their jobs, reputation, and family structure for sexual activity.

Employers often think that the problem will go away or will not become one of the major consequences. They realize their mistake after they have paid large monetary sums in damages or have adverse public and employee reaction. To require a policy to eliminate sexual harassment's existence is unrealistic.

An effective policy and procedure may cause the activity to go underground, but the employer will be relieved of liability if the policy is effective.[77] The key to control of sexual harassment is to have employees report it, which forces the person involved to define it as unwelcome, and the employer must investigate. There is an increasing number of women entering the workforce and no controlling case law in some areas. Sexual harassment creates a great exposure for the employer.

WHEN OFF-DUTY CONDUCT COMES INTO THE OFFICE

Off-duty conduct begs the question of where the employee's right to privacy ends and the employer's right to interfere begins.[78] The personnel practitioner has a frustrating problem where the male-female relationship enters the workplace.[79] The problem is not new. The increase

of women in the workforce, the advent of Title VII, the CRA91 amendments, and the assertion of women's rights require a new discipline for the personnel management function.[80] In 1988, 7 of every 10 women were working (*Monthly Labor Review,* U.S. Department of Labor, March 1988). The number is now much greater. There is no reason to believe the number of women in the workforce will not continue to increase.

It is rare when a social relationship does not become work related, because there is a "built-in" connection. Unintentional promotions, pay increases, job assignments, giving time off, and excusing tardiness because of sexual favors are often the result of an off-duty relationship that at the outset is none of the employer's business.

Control of Social Relationships

When the off-duty relationship ceases or one of the persons involved terminates or is promoted, the problem is created and it is very difficult to defend any employer's decision. In *Hunt* v. *Mid-American Employees Credit Union,* 384 N.W.2d 853 (Minn. 1986), there existed an intimate relationship between a secretary and a sales manager. The two went on a business trip and upon their return the employer discharged the secretary.[81] She immediately filed a sex discrimination charge. The sales manager objected strenuously that there was a question of his loyalty, so he was also discharged. He filed a wrongful discharge suit based on the handbook. The employer successfully defended both charges but lost two good employees and incurred large legal costs as the result of off-duty conduct that originally was none of the employer's business.

Social relationships should be discouraged at the very beginning, but care should be taken not to interfere with privacy rights. The employees

---

[77]Approximately 80 percent of employers have sexual harassment policies. See also *Weaver* v. *Minnesota Valley Laboratories, Inc.,* 470 N.W.2nd 131 (Minn. App. 1991).

[78]See Hallman, "Invasion of Privacy in Protection Against Sexual Harassment: Co-Employee Dating and Employer Liability," *Columbia Journal of Law and Social Problems, 20 (1993), 425.*

[79]According to a 1991 Gallup poll, 50 percent of employed workers think dating at the workplace is acceptable.

[80]Margo Murray, *Beyond the Myths and Magic of Mentoring: How to Facilitate an Effective Mentoring Program* (San Francisco: Jossey-Bass, 1991), chapter 14, p. 73.

[81]In a graduate school course, the professor gave his class what was later realized to be the best advice this author has ever received in college: "Never have an affair with your secretary." That advice is more appropriate now than it was 40 years ago.

should be informed of the hazard both to themselves and to the company. Education and the hard sell is the best approach. The relationship should not be discouraged, only the problem created when the two people are working for the same employer.

If the education and hard-sell approach does not work, the employer may want to consider stopping the relationship, as was the case in *Patton* v. *J.C. Penney,* 719 P.2d 854 (Ore. 1986), where the employee refused to stop dating a co-worker and was discharged. The court held, in stating that the employer's interest outweighs the employee's right of privacy, that this was not a violation of public policy or an invasion of privacy.

In *McCluskey* v. *Clark Oil Refining Co.,* 498 N.E.2d 559 (Ill. App. 1986), the court upheld a discharge for marrying a co-worker, ruling that it was not a violation of public policy. Generally the prohibition against nepotism has been upheld.[82]

Discipline for Off-Duty Conduct

When considering whether off-duty conduct can be just cause for discipline,[83] the courts and arbitrators are influenced by the following factors:

1. The damage to the employer's business or reputation

2. The effect on co-workers of off-duty relationships or conduct

3. The effect the off-duty relationship or conduct may have on the employee's on-duty performance and on an efficient workforce

4. In criminal cases, the possibility of suspension prior to judicial determination if strong facts show that the employer's business is adversely affected.[84]

In all these factors the main element is that there must be a connection between off-duty activity and a detriment to the work relationship.[85] One

way to avoid exposure to litigation is to communicate by policy or rules at the outset that the company will not permit an off-duty social relationship between male and female. (This could also include a relationship between two males or two females.) At least the relationship should be discouraged, even to the extent of prohibiting it.

AN OVERVIEW OF THE EQUAL PAY ACT

The first interference by the federal government in the payment of wages was in 1938, when the Fair Labor Standards Act was passed and employers were told that they had to pay a minimum wage and overtime premium to their employees. For the next 25 years there was no further interference with employers' right to determine wages of their employees. By 1962 the percentage of women in the workforce increased from 25 percent to about 35 percent; earnings of women average 60 percent to 70 percent those of men for year-round full-time work.[86]

Congress considered this a social problem of the same type as minimum wage legislation. In 1963 it amended Section 6 of the Fair Labor Standards Act, and called the amendment the Equal Pay Act (EPA).[87] EPA simply states that no employer shall discriminate in the payment of wages within a facility on the basis of sex for equal work. Jobs that require equal skill, equal effort, and equal responsibility and are performed under similar working conditions should have

---

[82]*Platner* v. *Cash and Thomas Construction Co.,* 908 F.2d 902 (11th Cir. 1990).

[83]See Hallman, K.M., "Invasion of Privacy."

[84]For a good reference on criminal conduct outside the workplace, see Steve Bergsman, "Employee Conduct Outside the Workplace," *The Human Resources Yearbook, 1992–1993* (Englewood Cliffs, NJ: Prentice Hall, p. 8.13). Also *Hall* v. *Gas Cons. Pr. Co.,* 842 F.2d 101 (8th Cir. 1988).

[85]C. Woolsey, "Off-Duty Conduct None of Employer's Business," *Business Insurance,* 26 (February 17, 1992), 10–11; M. Finneran, "We're from the Government, We're Here to Help You," *Business Communication Review,* 22 (January 1992), 74–75; Also, R. Massingill and D. Petersen, "Legal Challenges to No Fraternization Dates," *Labor Law Journal,* 46 (July, 1995) 429-435.

[86]The percentage of women in the work force in 1993 was over 45 percent, and their wages were 68 percent of the men's: *Monthly Labor Review,* U.S. Department of Labor, January 1993.

[87]29 U.S.C. 206 et seq.

equal pay. If the differential is based on seniority,[88] a merit system, an incentive pay system, or any factor other than sex, then there is no violation.

The EPA statute is easily defined but can cause problems in wage and salary systems. Many employers have depended on loopholes and other defensive provisions for the survival of their wage and salary systems.

Sections 201–208 of Title II, CRA91 (the Glass Ceiling Act of 1991),[89] establish a study commission to solve the national problem of underrepresentation and artificial barriers to women and minorities in management and in decision-making positions. One of the barriers, according to the Department of Labor, is lack of management perception in determining compensation. The report of the commission helped but didn't break the glass ceiling.[90]

Definition of Equal Work

Management often believes that there is a difference in skills, responsibility, and effort and that is the reason for the difference in wages. This is usually a misconception and is the reason for the exposure under the EPA.

The first opportunity that the courts had to answer these questions was in *Shultz* v. *Wheaton Glass Co.,* where male selector packers were receiving $.21 per hour more than female selector packers.[91] They performed substantially the same work, which was inspection work, except that approximately 18 percent of the time the male selectors did materials handling tasks.[92] Females were not permitted to perform these tasks because

they were restricted from lifting anything over 35 pounds. The court, in a landmark opinion on the interpretation of EPA, established a legal principle in finding a violation of EPA; it has been followed by other courts in many decisions. In view of the refusal of the Supreme Court to review the decision, these principles can be considered as controlling. These principles are sometimes called the "equal work standard."

1. The equal work standard requires only that the jobs be substantially equal and not identical. Small differences will not make them unequal.[93]
2. When a wage differential exists between men and women doing substantially equal work, the burden is on the employer to show that the differential is for some reason other than sex.
3. Where some but not all members of one sex performed extra duties in their jobs, these extra duties do not justify giving all members of that sex extra pay.
4. That men can perform extra duties does not justify extra pay unless women are also offered the opportunity to perform these duties.
5. Job titles and job descriptions are not material in showing that work is unequal unless they accurately reflect actual job content.

What is a substantially different job is decided on a case-by-case basis.[94] Where there is a substantial difference in effort, skill, or responsibility, the courts permit a pay differential between the sexes. The principle that job content, not job titles or job descriptions, is what determines whether jobs are equal is followed in the 8th Circuit.[95]

Another justification for a wage differential between men and women on which the employer relied was shift work. Where all men worked the night shift and women the day shift, it was argued by employers that the differential was justified because they were not similar working conditions.

---

[88]Interpretative regulations were issued by EEOC. They give the EEOC position on all of these factors (29 CFR Part 1620). Case law is in accord.

[89]See U.S. Glass Ceiling Comm., (Robert B. Reich, Chair). *A Solid Investment: Making Use of the Nation's Human Capital.* Washington, D.C.: approved November 21, 1995.

[90]Ibid.

[91]21 F.2d 259 (3rd Cir. 1970), cert. denied, 398 U.S. 905 (1970).

[92]Right after the enactment of EPA, the first loophole that employers conceived in EPA was to change the job content to include tasks that women did not normally perform. The author in 1965 spent a great deal of time writing "compliance job descriptions."

[93]Meryl Gordon, "Discrimination at the Top," *Working Women,* (September 1992), p. 8.

[94]In *Glenn* v. *General Motors,* 841 F.2d 1567 (11th Cir. 1988), the court said that the difference in skills and duties must be substantial to justify a pay differential.

[95]*Katz* v. *School Dist. of Clayton Missouri,* 557 F.2d 153 (8th Cir. 1977).

In one of the few EPA cases to reach the Supreme Court, it was held that working conditions as used in EPA do not refer to the time of day when work is performed and different shifts do not justify a pay differential.[96]

This case also established the rule that equal pay violations could be remedied only by raising the women's wages, not reducing the men's, but left open the question of whether changes in job content could remedy the violation. Often employers attempted to justify pay differentials between men and women by arguing that working conditions were not similar, that the jobs performed by males were more hazardous tasks than ones performed by females. There are situations where this might be a defense. However, such a defense should be used with extreme caution. Statistics show that 70 percent to 85 percent of all industrial accidents are not caused by physical conditions but by unsafe acts of the employee. Under these statistics, hazardous working conditions would not justify the differential if accidents are caused by the employee and not the hazardous conditions.

Measurement of Equal Skills

When considering skills, such factors as experience, training, education, and ability are taken into account. Any one of these factors can justify a differential.[97] Possessing a skill is not enough; the person must also use that skill on the job.[98] Calling one employee a cleaner and another a custodian does not justify a wage differential. It is job content and not job title that the courts follow.[99]

A common "equal skill" situation that courts have struck down is where the employer trains men for promotional purposes but does not offer to train women, who for some reason are not considered in the promotion plans; when the jobs are compared, the trained men have more skills than women.

Where male tellers were paid more than female tellers, the employer argued that the males were being trained in all aspects of banking to replace senior officers; because they were in a bona fide training program, the differential was justified. The court said that mere recognition by management of the ability to be promoted does not constitute a bona fide job-training program. Subjective evaluation of potential for promotion standing alone cannot justify pay differentials under EPA.[100]

In order to justify pay differentials under EPA through a bona fide training program (1) it must be open to both sexes, (2) employees must be notified of the training opportunities, (3) there must be a defined beginning and ending of the training program, and (4) a definite course of study and advancement opportunities upon completion are essential. It is also advisable to put the program in writing.

Job Responsibility to Justify a Differential

The defense of a difference in responsibility to justify unequal pay occurs mostly in administrative, professional, and executive jobs, where before the 1972 amendment these employees were excluded from coverage under EPA.

One of the first cases under the responsibility defense was where the employer claimed that men had to make decisions that women did not have to make. The court found that although men did make decisions that women did not, such decisions were subject to review by supervisors. Therefore, the differential was not justified under the responsibility defense.[101]

Often the employer justifies a pay differential between sexes in the same job categories by claiming that one type of work is more difficult than another. Where the employer claimed that

---

[96]*Corning Glass Works* v. *Brennan,* 417 U.S. 188 (1974).

[97]In *EEOC* v. *McCarthy,* 768 F.2d 1 (1st Cir. 1985) the court held ability to be more important.

[98]*Fowler* v. *Land Management Group, Inc.,* 978 F.2d 158 (4th Cir. 1992).

[99]*Aldrich* v. *Randolph Central School District,* 963 F.2d 520 (2nd Cir. 1991).

[100]*Marshall* v. *Security Band & Trust Co.,* 572 F.2d 276 (10th Cir. 1978).

[101]*Hodgson* v. *Fairmont Supply Co.,* 454 F.2d 490 (4th Cir. 1972).

management of soft-line departments such as clothing, usually managed by women, had less responsibility than hard-line departments such as sporting goods, usually managed by men, the court held that there is no substantial difference to justify less pay for women than for men.[102] In *EEOC* v. *Madison Community Unit School District No. 12,* 816 F.2d 577 (7th Cir. 1987), the court held that paying female coaches of girls' track and tennis teams less than male coaches of male track and tennis teams is a violation of the Equal Pay Act; however, this is a minority view. An important point in the case was the fact that the school district discouraged women from applying for positions of coaching boys' teams. In all Equal Pay cases whether or not females had an opportunity to do or train for the work of the males is a very important factor.

Misuse of Term *Merit Pay*

One of the factors that will justify differentials is where a properly communicated bona fide merit system is applied without regard to sex. All too often the term *merit pay* is used to include cost-of-living increases, longevity increases, and, general across-the-board increases that have no relationship to meritorious performance.[103] The purpose of a merit pay plan is to motivate performance, not to justify pay increases. Merit increases that will survive judicial review under EPA are individual increases in pay related to the job performance of that individual. A bona fide merit policy is a pat on the back with dollar bills in the palm of the hand.

Determining a wage level on some factor other than performance is the major fault with merit pay plans and why they do not stand judicial scrutiny. In an inflationary period the employer wants to keep earnings in line with the labor market conditions, yet does not want to set a precedent by implying that pay increases are automatic or based

on labor market conditions. Rationalizations set in and any believable reason is given. In *Brock* v. *Georgia S.W. College,* 765 F.2d 1026 (11th Cir. 1985), the employer argued that the wage difference was due to a merit system. The court found that the ratings were based on subjective personal judgment, that they were ad hoc, and that in many cases the raters were ill informed.

In order for a compensation plan to be based truly on merit, it should be given at a time when some significant performance has been completed. For administrative purposes, that could be done in future periods, provided that the waiting period is not too long to chill the motivation. In production incentive plans for factory workers, the previous three-month period should be the maximum waiting period, and the merit pay should be given separately within two weeks after the end of the merit rating period.

Necessary Elements for a Bona Fide Merit Plan

In order for a merit pay plan to be bona fide under the various statutes, it must be in writing and contain all or most of the following elements:[104]

1. The employee must believe that good performance will result in additional compensation.

2. There should be a direct correlation between the amount of pay and the exceptional performance, without any upper limits. Upper limits tend to dampen the motivation of certain workers.

3. The employee should understand the merit plan before it is adopted so that there are no surprises at evaluation time. (The author can recall working with the most motivated incentive worker he has ever known. She was asked at 10:30 A.M. how much incentive pay she had earned so far that day and she knew. This employee understood the incentive plan.)

---

[102]*Brennan* v. *T. M. Fields, Inc.,* 488 F.2d 443 (5th Cir. 1973).

[103]J. Kanin-Lovers and R. Bevan, "Don't Evaluate Performance—Manage It," *Compensation Benefits,* 1 (March-April 1992), 51–53; D. Guns II, "Merit Pay—An Unbalanced Approach to Pay for Performance," *Personnel Journal,* 71 (April 1992), 16.

[104]This usually happens when the employer does not want to set a precedent of granting cost-of-living increases or longevity increases; thus it is called merit. The misuse of the term becomes evident in EEO cases where a merit increase is given one month and an employee is discharged the next month for poor performance. Often merit raise surveys are made, but they are in reality market surveys.

4. The performance should be accurately measured either by objective performance appraisals or by standards of performance with which the employee agrees. If agreement cannot be accomplished, the employer should be sure that it is right and adopt it. Sometimes employees have to work with the plan before they are convinced they can earn additional money.

5. The base pay should not be reduced because an employee is on a merit system. Merit pay should be given when performance is above the average worker's base pay.

6. The merit system must be updated periodically. Job content affects the performance; if not current, either the company or employee is unfairly affected.

7. Managers must believe in the system and be trained to properly administer it.

8. Follow-up procedures are necessary to prevent bias and leniency. Nothing can defeat a merit plan faster than leniency or bias.[105]

Factors Other Than Sex to Justify a Differential

Wage and salary plans based on seniority are not in violation of EPA if there is a direct correlation between seniority and pay levels and it is otherwise a bona fide seniority plan.

Another factor, other than sex, is the area of employee fringe benefits.[106] In order to justify a pay differential under the Equal Pay Act, the reason for the difference in benefits must be based on a factor other than sex. The employer argued that requiring a greater pension contribution for females than for males because women live longer was a factor other than sex. The Supreme Court adopted the lower court's position that actuarial distinctions based entirely on sex could not qualify as an exception.[107] In another case women received less benefits than men for the same contributions because of sex-segregated actuarial tables. The insured deferred compensation plan was optional as to contributions and method of receiving benefits. The Court said that longevity of life would not justify a differential under the Equal Pay Act.[108]

Examples of valid factors other than sex are (1) temporary or permanent assignments made to a lower-rated job with the employee retaining the rate of the old job (sometimes called a red circle rate), which is greater than for the female doing the same work; (2) a bona fide training program as discussed in this chapter; and (3) part-time work. The government takes the position that part-time employment (under 20 hours per week) is a factor other than sex to justify a pay differential – not logical, but codified.

EEOC Regulations Interpreting Equal Pay Act

In August of 1986 the EEOC issued new regulations interpreting the EPA (29 CFR Part 1620; 51 CFR 24716), which made some modifications to their position on certain issues. The regulations for the most part adopted the former Department of Labor regulations and court interpretations. Certain aspects of the changed regulations are worth noting.

The meaning of the term *establishment* was expanded to include two or more distinct physical portions of the business as one establishment as long as they are located in the same physical place of business.

There was some change in fringe benefits, but for the most part they adopted judicial interpretations. That is, employers must make the same benefits available to females as they do to males without regard to cost or actuarial studies.

Probably the biggest change was in the definition of "equal work."[109] The EEOC takes the

---

[105]R. Selwitz, "Blueprint for Performance Pay," *ABA Bank Journal,* 82 (May 1990), 18; J.A. Parmele, "Five Reasons Why Pay Must Be Based on Performance," *Supervision,* 52 (Fall 1991), 6–8; J. Feldman, "Another Day, Another Dollar, Needs Another Look," *Personnel,* 68 (January 1991), 9–11.

[106]*Braatz* v. *Labor Industry Review Comm.,* 496 N.W.2d 597 (U.S. Sup.Ct. 1993).

[107]*City of Los Angeles* v. *Manhart,* 435 U.S. 702 (U.S. S.Ct. 1978).

[108]*Arizona Governing Committee for Tax Deferred Annuity and Deferred Compensation Plans, Etc., et al.* v. *Nathalie Norris, Etc.,* 103 S.Ct. 3492 (1983).

[109]Must include all major factors to compare differential. *Smith* v. *Virginia Commonwealth University,* 68 FEP Cases (8th Cir. 1993).

position that if employers pay a higher rate to a new male employee than they do to a former or a present female employee, that is a violation. This definition assumes that the higher rate was based on sex and doesn't consider market conditions. Another significant change in the new regulations is that EEOC is going to consider any violation as a continuing violation.

The "regs" will disallow two of the former defenses and closely scrutinize two others. They will not allow a wage difference between one group of one sex and that of the opposite sex as a group. This is contrary to the majority of court decisions that state that market conditions must be considered. They also state that they will not allow unequal rates established by a collective bargaining agreement. This was formerly allowed under 29 CFR Section 1620.23, when the Department of Labor was enforcing the statute.

The EEOC said they will closely scrutinize any situation where additional duties are added to justify unequal pay. They will determine if it is bona fide. The former position of the Department of Labor that head of household will justify a difference will also be watched with a questionable eye.

The old defenses of merit, seniority, quantity, quality, and any other factor, other than sex, were left untouched by the regulations. However, the EEOC will not depend on job evaluations systems to justify the difference. Some changes in compensation are in order if the employer is to get along with the EEOC. Of course, the EEOC position can be challenged in the courts.

Failure of EPA to Correct Differentials between Sexes

From the outset EPA did not correct wage differences that existed before the act.[110] The employer took the position that existing wage and salary systems did give equal pay for equal work; that there was no need to change the policy of determining wages by job evaluation, market conditions, profitability, or competitive practices.

The determination of wages by market conditions and job evaluation were believed to have built-in sex bias.[111]

Starting salaries in job categories that are predominantly female are traditionally lower and will stay that way, as long as the supply of labor is adequate. Over the years study after study has confirmed that the average compensation of women is from 60 to 70 percent of men.[112]

If starting salaries for the same work are different between the sexes, the differential continues as salary increases are granted. The justification usually given by employers is that the jobs are not the same.

The law permits pay discrimination as long as the employers give legally acceptable reasons. If these reasons are not challenged by the employee or by the enforcement agency, it is never determined whether they are legally acceptable.

Where violations are found under EPA, the correction is made only within the specific job categories. The basic wage and salary procedures are not considered by the courts, nor will the courts require the employers to change them. Due to changes in job assignments, the violations recur and remain that way unless another complaint is filed.

This section has shown why employers' present wage and salary procedures have failed to eliminate wage differentials between the sexes. It would be presumptuous to assume that the factors that determined wages and salaries in the past will be abandoned by employers.

Such considerations as employee qualifications, job content, union membership, labor market conditions, employee work behavior, local practices, profitability, and competition will continue to determine the compensation level unless the courts or Congress intervenes. As long

---

[110]E.M. Bowen, "Closing the Female Pay Gap: Redefining the Equal Pay Act's Affirmative Defense," *Columbia Journal of Social Problems,* 27 (1994), 225.

[111]J. Quinn, "Visibility and Value: The Rule of Job Evaluation in Assuring Equal Pay for Women," *Journal of International Business,* 25 (1994), 1403.

[112]G. Koretz, "Women Earn Less but They've Come a Long Way," *Business Week, (*December 24, 1990), 14; "Recent Gains in Women's Earnings: Better Pay or Longer Hours," *Monthly Labor Review,* 113 (July 1990), 11–17.

as these factors determine compensation, there will be continual exposure to violations of EPA.[113]

Audit of EPA Compliance

Most employers are in violation of the Equal Pay Act, and when an employer is challenged, a lengthy and expensive lawsuit results. The factors mentioned previously, although valid, offer very little defense. For this reason it is good insurance to audit your compensation plan to determine the extent of noncompliance. Where it is found that there are serious compliance problems, the corrections can be made gradually and often without anyone knowing a violation ever existed. This is much better than an equal pay complaint by the EEOC where the employer is being accused of taking compensation from the employees in violation of the law. Necessary procedures for EPA audit are as follows:

1. Determine the distribution of pay percentages within each job category and whether there is any relationship with performance.
2. Calculate the average pay level within each job category by race and sex.
3. Determine the average pay increase given by each supervisor within each job category.
4. Examine pay differentials among all jobs involving equal skill, effort, responsibility, and working conditions. If you find an instance where a pay differential may be based on sex, eliminate the inequity by bringing the pay of the lower-paid employee to the level of the higher paid.
5. Be consistent in the application of your hiring, promotion, and pay increase practices and criteria, to avoid any inference of sex discrimination.
6. Document your reasons for pay actions that may later be questioned, and be certain your reasons are legally defensible.

This is not an exhaustive checklist; the basic premise—equal pay for equal work (not necessarily *identical* work)—must be kept in mind and acted on to avoid creating inequities and to rectify inequities created in the past.

---

[113]Seminars, employment law literature; EEOC do not give EPA a very high priority. This may change in the future.

These various procedures are necessary to determine whether there is any logic to the company's compensation system. If there is some logic to the compensation system, it is much easier to defend when an equal pay charge is made by the EEOC.

In summary, management should do three things:

1. Have a rational reason for its compensation levels.
2. Explain to the employees how their wages are determined.
3. As much as possible, correct wage differentials between sexes, rather than trying to justify them.

The failure of employers to abandon traditional methods of determining pay levels and pressures of the labor market conditions make compliance with EPA difficult. That does not mean that the statute should be ignored. Programs and procedures that show good faith efforts to eliminate differences between sexes will minimize exposure to litigation. They are an effective defense in the event a lawsuit is started.

COMPARABLE PAY
FOR COMPARABLE WORTH

Comparable worth is a theory of determining wages by requiring equal pay for employees whose work is of comparable worth even if the job content is totally different. The proponents of the theory state that the Equal Pay Act, Title VII, and Executive Order 11246 require its application. The concept was first developed by the Classification Act of 1923, which required equal pay for equal work in the executive branch of the federal government. Later the National War Labor Board issued General Order No. 16 (November 1942), which allowed adjustment between male and female rates based on comparable quality and quantity of work. This was a wage and price controlled economy. As the increase of women in the workforce continued, the pressure to do something about the difference in earnings increased. Because the Equal Pay Act failed in other respects there was hope that the revival of the theory would be legally supported by new interpretation of the Equal Pay Act or Title VII. The concept was called the "women's issue of the 1980s" and became a very controversial equal employment issue.[114] The issue went before the Supreme Court, who stated in *County of Washington* v. *Gunther,* 101 S.Ct. 2242 (1981), that the four defenses under the EPA applied when there was an issue of whether Title VII or EPA could be used. The Bennett Amendment required the EPA defenses to be used when there was conflict between EPA and Title VII. Therefore, the plaintiffs could not apply the "equal work" standard under Title VII. However, the Court stated that this didn't preclude the plaintiffs from starting an action under Title VII alleging disparate treatment and sex discrimination.

Legal Death of Comparable Worth Theory

Although several circuits had previously held that it is not up to the courts to determine the worth of an employee,[115] the issue was settled in *State of Washington* v. *Am. Federal, State and County and Municipal Employees,* 770 F.2d 1401 (9th Cir. 1985), where the court held that Congress did not intend Title VII to interfere with the law of supply and demand or prevent employees from competing in the labor market.

The theory judicially died as quickly as it was born. There is no feasible method to apply the theory unless you start from zero for all classifications and then agree upon criteria to set the differentials. This is politically and economically infeasible.

There is no practical way to solve the wage inequity problem through the comparable worth theory. However, the comparable worth theory as an academic concept was an attempt to correct the wage differences between sexes. It has had a value in that it is telling the employer that the social problem of unequal pay for equal work must be solved.

No one sweeping method or theory will achieve this goal, but this fact doesn't relieve the employer from trying. The market conditions must be considered, but the laws of supply and demand can be influenced by management policy. Litigation under the Equal Pay Act on a case-by-case basis will continue unless employers integrate jobs.

---

[114]J. Hersch, "The Impact of Nonmarket Work on Market Wages," *American Economic Review,* 81 (May 1991), 157; P. F. Orazem, "Comparable Worth and Factor Point Pay in State Government," *Industrial Relations,* 31 (Winter 1992), 135–215.

[116]*Lemons* v. *City and County of Denver,* 620 F.2d 228 (10th Cir. 1980), cert. denied, 449 U.S. 888 (1980); *Christenson* v. *Iowa,* 563 F.2d 353 (8th Cir. 1977); *Spaulding* v. *University of Washington,* 740 F.2d 686 (9th Cir. 1984), cert. denied, 105 S.Ct. 511 (1984).

8

PROTECTION AGAINST AGE DISCRIMINATION IN EMPLOYMENT

An Overview of ADEA
Age as a Factor in Making a Decision
Early Retirement Programs
ERISA Does Not Prohibit Use of Early Retirement Pension Waivers
Punitive Damages under ADEA
Avoiding Litigation

The problem of what to do with the older worker has haunted employers for many years. There seemed to be no easy solution to the problem of the marginal worker who has been with the company for 30 years and has substandard performance for 25 of the 30 years. Like many other personnel problems, the solution was an arbitrary one: compulsory retirement at age 65 for all employees, except the board of directors and chief executive officer. This solution was destined to meet with social and political opposition for two reasons. First, many employees were still productive at age 65;[1] physical and mental ability and attitude toward retirement are an individual matter, not one that can be categorized. Second, there is no medical or other authority for age 65 as the time when most employees cease to be productive.[2]

The compulsory retirement at 65 became almost universal in American business as well as in other organizations. Most companies had compulsory retirement, typically at age 65. The usual reason given was to create job opportunities for younger persons. When almost all employers have a policy with social and economic implications, political forces will usually step in to

---

[1]By the year 2000 it is estimated that persons 35 or older will increase by 70 million. By 2030, 35 percent of the workforce will be 55 or older, and there will be 55 million in the workforce over 65. D. Ruegger, "A Twenty-Year History and Review of ADEA," *Labor Law Journal*, 40, no. 1 (January 1989), 34–35.

[2]The basis that a 65-year-old worker was so old as to warrant compulsory retirement came from German Chancellor Otto von Bismarck in 1887 as the age when the German social security system should start. Life expectancy is greater than it was in 1887. Further, Bismarck was neither a doctor nor an entrepreneur but an army general.

correct it.[3] As members of Congress have so often said about employer practices, "You correct it yourself or we will do it for you" (when it becomes politically advisable). Compulsory retirement, demotion, or discharge to make room for a younger person was an easy solution until Congress stopped it in 1978. Ten years later more than 15,000 cases involving age discrimination were filed with the EEOC.

AN OVERVIEW OF ADEA

The purpose of the Age Discrimination in Employment Act (ADEA) is to promote employment of older persons based on their ability to perform and to prohibit compulsory retirement (29 U.S.C. 621 et seq.). This Act is over 25 years old. Most employers know the provisions. Age discrimination is more of a concern to employers than when the act was first passed.[4]

The act and its amendments contain the following basic provisions:

1. It forbids employers with 20 or more employees, including public employers, employment agencies, and labor organizations (with 25 or more members), to make employment decisions based on a person's age when that person is over 40. This is interpreted to mean that preference cannot be shown within the protected group. An employer could not express preference for a 45- to 55-year-old person as this would discriminate because of age.

2. The act invalidates compulsory retirement in pension plans in the private and public sectors. If inability to perform the job can be shown, or if an executive in a policy-making position is involved, or if the person has a pension above $44,000 without Social Security, the employee could be subjected to compulsory retirement.

3. The act authorizes jury trial of any issue of fact.

4. The act expressly authorizes employers to discriminate against older employees under certain circumstances.

Exemptions under ADEA

The employee is subject to compulsory retirement if he or she is an executive in a policy-making position or has a pension over $44,000, or if unsatisfactory performance can be shown. The ADEA provides that if an employee has been employed for two years preceding the retirement date in a "high policy-making position" this employee would be exempt from the compulsory retirement restrictions of the ADEA. The issue in all these cases is what constitutes a policy-making decision. The cases decided state that the person must perform policy-making duties for at least two years before termination. Level of salary is not the determining factor. The court looks at the duties that the employee performs.[5]

When considering whether or not an executive can be retired at age 65, the employer must consider the job content, the reporting relationship, and whether or not the employee participated in policy-making decisions and had discretionary powers. Also, ADA doesn't cover the total employee relationship.[6]

Problems in Defending Employment Decisions

Because ADEA is concerned with workers who are over 40, many unique problems are created that are not found in other antidiscrimination laws. With the baby boom generation coming under the act in the late 1980s and early 1990s, employees over 40 will be the largest protected class under antidiscrimination laws.

---

[3]See C. Solman, "Unlock the Potential of the Older Worker," *Personnel Journal*, (Oct. 1995), 56.

[4]As an amendment to the Fair Labor Standards Act, ADEA covers public employees: *Davidson v. Board of Governors of State Colleges and Universities for Western Ill.*, 920 F.2d 441 (7th Cir. 1990).

[5]*Stillman's* v. *State of Iowa*, 843 F.2d 276 (8th Cir. 1988).

[6]Some courts view poor work performance as a pretext where poor performance was tolerated for a period of time: *Hagelthorn* v. *Kennecott Corp.*, 716 F.2d 76 (2nd Cir. 1983).

ADEA is the only antidiscrimination law that allows jury trial as such.[7] Because the average age of people selected to serve on a jury is over 40 and almost all jurors are now or were at one time employees, there isn't much sympathy for the employer. It is also "human" for a judge to sympathize with the older worker because his or her age is usually over 40.

The employer has another "built-in head wind" when dealing with the older worker. Due to the length of service, the worker's salary is usually higher than the market price for the same skills, and these skills are believed to decrease with age.[8] When the labor costs have to be reduced, the older worker can be replaced by a younger person (who is probably as well qualified) at less cost. ADEA inhibits management's desire to perpetuate the company by training and promoting younger workers. At one time the older worker could be retired at 70 so at least there was some room to move up the younger worker, but with the age 70 limitation removed, management must now prove poor performance before the older worker can be replaced. This is often difficult to do with a worker of 30 years of service. Some companies are still using personality traits to measure performance. It is not surprising that age discrimination lawsuits are second largest of all antidiscrimination lawsuits filed with EEOC.

Bringing in "new blood" is considered a violation of ADEA where it is accompanied by age-related comments. In *Wilson* v. *Monarch Paper Co.,* 939 F.2d 1138 (5th Cir. 1991), it was considered constructive discharge. The court upheld a jury award for punitive damages.

AGE AS A FACTOR IN MAKING A DECISION

The ADEA affects every employment decision where the employee involved is over 40.[9] Under CRA91 it is believed that age need be only one factor to find a violation. To establish a prima facie case under ADEA the employee must show that the job was performed satisfactorily and that the employee was dismissed and replaced by a younger person (not necessarily under 40).[10] The employer must show that age was not a contributing factor.[11]

A unanimous U.S. Supreme Court decision held that an employer does not violate the Age Discrimination in Employment Act (ADEA) by firing an older employee to avoid pension benefits that would have vested by virtue of the employee's years of service.

The plaintiff had been employed by Hazen Paper since 1977 as its technical director. In 1986, at the age of 62, and a few weeks before his pension would have been vested, plaintiff was terminated for doing business with competitors of Hazen Paper. The plaintiff sued Hazen Paper for violating the ADEA, and the Employee Retirement Income Security Act of 1974 (ERISA). On his ADEA claim, plaintiff claimed that age had been a determinative factor in the decision to fire him. A jury rendered a verdict in favor of plaintiff on his ADEA claim, and specifically found that the company had acted "willfully" so as to be liable for liquidated damages under 29 U.S.C. § 626(b).

The district court, however, granted the company's motion for judgment notwithstanding the verdict as to the finding of willfulness. In upholding ADEA liability, the appeals court considered evidence that Hazen paper had fired plaintiff in order to prevent his pension benefits from vesting. The appeals court also reversed the

---

[7]Under CRA91 certain conditions must be met before jury trial is permitted. National average jury awards exceed the CRA91 limit of $300,000. More case law is needed to determine the effect of CRA91 on ADEA.

[8]In *Bay* v. *Times Mirror Magazines,* 936 F.2d 112 (2nd Cir. 1991), it is not a violation to replace an older worker with a younger one if the reasons are economic. However, there still is an exposure.

[9]Most state laws prohibit age discrimination. State employees are covered under federal law if not under state law: *Davidson* v. *Board of Governors of State Colleges and Universities for Western Ill.,* 920 F.2d 441 (7th Cir. 1990).

[10]*Kristoffel* v. *Hangman Ford Service Co.,* 985 F.2d 364 (7th Cir. 1993); *Visser* v. *Packer Engineering Assoc., Inc.,* 924 F.2d 655 (7th Cir. 1991).

[11]*Flynn* v. *Shoneys, Inc.,* 850 S.W.2d 488 (Tenn. App. 1992) affirmed (6th Cir. 1993)

district court's judgment with respect to willfulness, finding sufficient evidence to establish that the company knew that its action violated the ADEA or showed reckless disregard for the matter.

The U.S. Supreme Court held that an employer does not violate the ADEA by interfering with an older employee's pension benefits that would have vested by virtue of the employee's years of service. The court reasoned that the employer's decision was wholly motivated by factors other than age.

Factors other than age may include discharge for just cause. Where a 56-year-old repeatedly ignored specific directions of his supervisors, the court held that discharge was not because of age but for insubordination.

The inability to satisfactorily perform the particular job and incompetence are factors other than age[12] that could justify a discharge or transfer. Performance and incompetency determinations are often subjective when age is involved. Therefore, the burden of proof is greater than in traditional misconduct situations where objective facts are more easily obtainable.[13] It is advisable for incompetency situations to have objective measurements of unsatisfactory performance before a decision is made involving an older worker's performance. When an employee is not performing satisfactorily, the company has to either transfer or terminate. It is difficult for the older employee to admit poor performance. If there is protection under ADEA, very often the employee will allege that if it were not for his or her age, the decision would not have been made.

In *Wilson* v. *Monarch Paper Co.*, 939 F.2d 1138 (5th Cir. 1991), the jury awarded the plaintiff more than $3 million (no limits then), mostly for pain and intentional infliction of emotional distress for age discrimination. The company reduced the job of a vice president and assistant to the president to janitor. This steep downhill push was to humiliate the plaintiff. The court noted that age-related comments ("bring in new blood") made about the plaintiff by the defendant's officials and absence of criticism of the work performance caused them to affirm the age discrimination verdict.

Where the employer can show that the decision to terminate was not based on age, it can be defended.[14] Employer actions do not always create an inference of age discrimination. Assignment of work to younger employees, hiring a younger person to replace an older person, and comments about age by persons in a non-decision-making position are not per se a violation.[15] Evidence that there were attempts to improve performance and that the plaintiff was warned about unsatisfactory performance is a strong defense to rebut the employee's contention that the decision was based on age. In *Bohrer* v. *Hanes Corp.*, 715 F.2d 213 (5th Cir. 1985), the plaintiff had been a salesman for 20 years. He was moderately successful in meeting his sales quotas but according to the company was deficient in other aspects of his job. Performance, not age, was the reason. The company gave subjective evidence that he did not institute merchandising techniques with his customers and would not follow management policy or instructions. The evidence showed that supervision had several meetings with the employee in order to correct the problem. The employee acknowledged the criticisms and expressly resolved to do better, but he didn't. This evidence gave the subjective evaluation credibility. He was terminated and replaced with a 28-year-old person. The jury awarded the plaintiff $167,320; the employer moved for a judgment notwithstanding the verdict. The lower court granted it and the circuit court in affirming stated that there was substantial evidence of poor performance so that if allowed to stand the jury verdict would be a miscarriage of justice. The U.S. Supreme Court denied review. This is a good example of a case in which there was evidence of trying to correct the poor performance, age could not have been a factor in terminating, and the jury

---

[12]See *Shell* v. *Metropolitan Life Insurance*, 391 S.E. 174 (1993); also *Holmberg* v. *Boyter Health Care*, 901 F.2d 1287 (7th Cir. 1990).

[13]*Hazen Paper Co.* v. *Biggins*, 113 S.Ct. 1701 (1993).

[14]*Fowle* v. *C &C Cola*, 868 F.2d 59 (3rd. Cir. 1989).

[15]*Frieze* v. *Boatmen's Bank of Beiton*, 950 F.2d 538 (8th Cir. 1991); *Goetz* v. *Farm Credit Services*, 927 F.2d 398 (8th Cir. 1991). Circuit courts are split on this issue.

had no basis for the award, but legal fees were expensive for the employer.

Sometimes an employer will argue that an older worker was replaced by a younger worker to reduce costs.[16] The courts will recognize this as a factor other than age if there would be severe economic consequences by retaining the older worker.[17]

EARLY RETIREMENT PROGRAMS

It is not a violation of ADEA if the employee voluntarily retires.[18] Most companies offer early retirement incentives to employees over 55 years and with a specified length of service (10 years or more being the most popular). Early retirement programs avoid layoffs or involuntary terminations. For this reason, they were offered more frequently during a recession than during high economic activity. In 1982, in the midst of a recession, 27 percent of the companies surveyed had made early retirement offers to their employees. However, in subsequent years when there was no recession more than 75 percent of the employers offered retirement programs, which indicates that these programs are becoming popular as a personnel technique without a recession.[19] While early retirement plans are gaining wide acceptance among employers, employees also like them. Most employers underestimate the number of employees who will accept the incentive and take early retirement.[20] However, voluntary retirement programs are not without problems, as illustrated in the case history in this chapter.[21]

In making early retirement offers the employer often faces the loss of skills and management know-how that cannot quickly be replaced.[22] One way to bridge the gap between training new employees and losing the old is to make a consulting agreement with the early retirees. Consulting agreements are very popular, not only to bridge the gap but also to provide the retiree with additional income while the adjustment is being made from full salary to retirement income.

Employers try to cap exposure to ADEA lawsuits by the use of waivers and releases.[23] It is hoped that the Older Workers Benefit Protection Act of 1990 (OWBPA) will put to rest the judicial confusion over waivers and releases.[24]

Almost all early retirement programs require the employee to sign a waiver or a release.[25] The legal result is not the same. In waiver, the employee waives all rights. In a release, the employer is relieved of liability, but no rights are given up. A waiver under ADEA is enforceable in the courts if there is no showing of coercion. It is uncertain in the case of a release; it depends upon what it does.[26]

ERISA DOES NOT PROHIBIT USE OF EARLY RETIREMENT PENSION WAIVERS

Waiver Requirements under OWBPA

The following requirements apply to waivers under the OWBPA:

[16]See *O'Connor* v. *Consolidated Coin Caterers Group,* 116 Sup.Ct. 1307 (1996) where court held that older person does not have to be replaced by a person outside the protected class.

[17]The courts are more reluctant to consider over-qualification a factor other than age: *Taggert* v. *Time, Inc.,* 924 F.2d 43 (2nd Cir. 1991).

[18]29 CFR Sect. 1625.9(f).

[19]B. Singleton-Green, "The Future of Retirement: Work Longer, Die Later," *Accountancy,* 109 (March 1992), 29.

[20]In some companies is it as high as 80 percent.

[21]If a labor union is involved and incentives are offered, the amount of incentives is a negotiable issue: *Toledo Typographical Local 63* v. *NLRB,* 907 F.2d 1220 (D.C. Cir. 1990).

[22]See C.A. Cerami, "Special Incentives May Appeal to Valued Employees—A Supplement to Their Retirement Plan," *HR Focus,* 68 (November 1991), 17.

[23]For a discussion of waivers before CRA91 see Ronald Turner, "Release and Waiver of Age Discrimination in Employment Act Rights and Claims," *The Labor Lawyer,* 5, no. 4 (Fall 1989), 739; also B. Alsher, "Validity of Waiver in Discrimination Cases," *Labor Law Journal,* 42 (February 1991), 81.

[24]*Oshea* v. *Commerce Credit Corp.,* 930 F.2d 358 (4th Cir. 1991).

[25]For increased use of waivers, see "Use of Waivers by Large Companies Offering Exit Incentives to Employees," U.S. General Accounting Office Study (1989).

[26]*Lockheed Corp.* v. *Spink,* 116 S.Ct. 1783 (1996).

1. The agreement must be in clear concise language, signed by the employee.
2. The agreement must clearly state that the employee is waiving all rights under ADEA.
3. The employee has 21 days to decide whether to accept and one week to rescind after signing.
4. The waiver must state that the employee has consulted an attorney.
5. The employee can waive rights or claims only in exchange for something he doesn't already have.
6. Although not required, there should be evidence of negotiations as to the benefits for retiring.

The OWBPA provides that no waiver agreement may affect the EEOC's rights and responsibilities to enforce ADEA.[27] These requirements are designed to assure the EEOC that the early retirement was "knowingly voluntary." Signing a waiver does not prevent the employee from filing a charge, although his or her right to recover any damages may have been waived. When signing a release, the employee is prevented from recovering damages.

The employee usually has the opportunity to allege coercion after the retirement plan is accepted. The employer must be cautious not to imply any form of coercion when the early retirement plan is accepted by the employee.[28] In one case the employee stated that he would not have signed the agreement had he thought the waiver was enforceable. The court considered the testimony creditable, but enforced the waiver because the employee had consulted an attorney.

Any evidence that age was a factor and retirement was not voluntary would result in an exposure to a lawsuit. An option of early retirement or termination for whatever reason would be construed as a discharge if not voluntary. One court held that the employer was required to pay severance pay to employees who elected early retirement because it was paid to employees discharged as a result of reduction in force. It would be a violation of ADA to give a smaller amount to those who retire at 65 than if they retired early, but not a violation of ADEA if the same amount is given to early retirees.[29]

An employer who is convinced that a release or waiver will eliminate all exposure to employment litigation needs a good lawyer. Sometimes a release is more costly to defend than the employment decision at issue.

Elements of an Early Retirement Option

In order for a person to sue based upon acceptance of voluntary retirement incentives, the person must allege that he was coerced into accepting the early retirement incentives. In other words, the person must claim that the "voluntary" retirement incentives were not, in fact, voluntary.

Because of the exposure in early retirement plans, certain facts should be present and well documented.

1. Give ample inducement for the employee to retire. Some of the most popular early retirement incentives include early vesting of pension benefits, continuation of health care insurance, severance pay above the normal amount, maintaining an employee on a consulting basis, and retraining for a retirement vocation.
2. Explain what benefits the employee would receive if he or she continued working and retired at a later date. Some negotiation is helpful.[30]
3. Get a signed statement that the early retirement option was absolutely voluntary. This is the key to avoid exposure.

Early retirement can be a useful tool in avoiding age discrimination charges, but it also can cause litigation if not properly administered.[31]

---

[27]For a good article on waivers see Bennet Alsher, "Validity of Waivers in Discrimination Cases," *Labor Law Journal*, 42, no. 2 (February 1991), 81.

[28]*Wamsley v. Champlin Refining and Checmicals, Inc.* 37 F.3d 634 (5th Cir. 1994).

[29]*Harvey Karlener v. College of Chicago,* 837 F.2d 314 (7th Cir. 1986).

[30]N. E. Cutter, "Employee Benefits and the Retirement Decision," *Journal of American Society of CLU &CHFC,* 46 (January 1992), 26–28.

[31]For additional reading see Rebecca S. Stith and William A. Kohlburn, "Early Retirement Incentive Plans after the Passage of Older Workers Protection Act," *St. Louis University Public Law Review,* 11 (1992).

*A Voluntary Retirement That Was Not Voluntary—
A Case History*

---

*The following case history is an illustration
of a typical problem of the aging worker.*

John Doe, age 64, was for 40 years a marginally qualified administrative manager for a
250-employee manufacturing facility. As
most of his work was being computerized,
John realized that either he had to learn
computer procedures or retire. He went to
his supervisor of 20 years and requested
special projects for the next year, after which
he would retire, at age 65. His supervisor
orally agreed. They shook hands and everybody was happy.

During the succeeding year, John trained
his replacement to the limit of his ability and
performed useful special project assignments
with a high level of competency. In his
retirement plans, John had not done
sufficient financial planning to allow for
inflation. Also, during the year his wife died,
and working became much more interesting
than a lonely retirement. John saw his supervisor and told him that he had changed his
mind and wanted his old job or a similar job,
and he was willing to learn the new computer procedures and considered himself

more qualified than applicants being
considered for a vacancy in another facility.
The supervisor called the personnel director
and requested advice. The personnel director
consulted the legal department. The legal
counsel advised that because John had a
satisfactory work performance for the past 40
years, it would be difficult to convince a jury
in an age discrimination suit that he was not
qualified until he was given an opportunity
on the new job and his performance
objectively measured.

This case is a classic example of an employer making an employment decision that
was considered fair to both parties without
anticipating what could happen in the
ensuing year. It is possible that the employer
could have argued that there was an oral
agreement and that the employee had to
retire as agreed. However, lengthy litigation,
exposure to punitive damages, employee
relations consequence of an employee with
40 years of employment suing the employer,
and a jury trial warranted a business decision
to make retirement attractive to John.
Therefore, an agreement was drafted.

Reduction in Force (RIF)

One of the areas that has been given particular
attention under ADEA is termination as a result of
a reduction in force (RIF).[32] There are several
reasons for this. Often the older worker's
performance has not been objectively evaluated
for a long period of time, yet she or he continues
to be employed and receives periodic wage
increases. However, when it comes to RIF the
employer considers the advantages in having a
younger workforce and looks for reasons to reduce

the force by terminating the older workers. This
practice runs head-on into ADEA. In any RIF
program care must be taken to be sure that age is
not a factor in selecting the employees to be
reduced.[33]

Discrimination claims arising from RIF can be
premised on either disparate treatment or disparate
impact theories. The premise of a disparate
treatment claim is that the reduction in force was
simply a subterfuge or pretext for the employer's
actual objective to rid itself of certain employees,

---

[32]The RIF could also be a result of a merger when there are
two persons for the same job.

[33]If as a result of RIF there is a disparate impact, it is very
difficult to defend: *Uffelman* v. *Lonestar Steel Co.*, 863 F.2d
404 (5th Cir. 1989). Also *Barnes* v. *Gen Corp. Inc.*, 896 F.2d
1457 (6th Cir. 1990) and *Rose* v. *Wells Fargo & Co.*, 902 F.2d
841 (9th Cir. 1991).

such as older workers, members of a minority group, women, and so on. The premise of a disparate impact claim is that the RIF, while having a bona fide business rationale and facially neutral criteria for job elimination, resulted in a disproportionately adverse impact on protected categories of employees. Common to both arguments is the claim that the employees were terminated "because" they were members of a group protected from employment discrimination by state or federal law.

A legitimate RIF is motivated by business considerations. Because these justifications are the employer's best defense in the event terminated workers claim discrimination, it is absolutely essential for the employer to understand why it is downsizing, reorganizing, and eliminating jobs. The business rationale should be explicit and well defined. The courts have emphasized that in most reduction in force cases the evidence demonstrates that the company had some kind of plan to reduce expenses by eliminating jobs. These plans generally include objective criteria by which to determine which jobs will be eliminated and often include objective evidence of a business decline.[34]

In the absence of a "smoking gun" or foolish admissions by corporate managers, the statistics are frequently the most powerful, and in some instances the only, evidence supporting the plaintiff's claim of discrimination.

One of the biggest legal hot spots in reductions in force is the statistical picture.[35] No matter what method a company uses and what review is done of line manager decisions, an analysis that shows the reductions had a discriminatory effect can expose the company to age discrimination collective actions or race and sex class actions.

Selection of Employees for RIF

The employer can reduce the exposure associated with selecting employees for RIF by

1. Adopting an objective business criterion
2. Providing supervisory training in the use of that criterion
3. Eliminating any words, such as a code, that might suggest age is factor
4. Analyzing statistical data of the employees selected for RIF and having ave more than one person rate without knowing the employee's age[36]
5. Providing any employee with assistance in job transition
6. Being sensitive, but not apologetic, when informing employees selected for RIF

The selection of the person to be terminated cannot be subjective. There must be an objective business method of selecting the most-qualified person that leaves no doubt that the protected class was not a factor in the selection process.[37] The courts are clear that ADEA is not a guarantee of employment beyond age 40, but "shabby employment practices" would indicate that age might be a factor.[38] Where the employer used a supervisor peer committee and a number of rating systems, which were sent to the personnel department and objectively reviewed, and some of the senior older workers were terminated, the court held that the employer had proved the nondiscriminatory basis for its decision.[39]

Severance Pay as an Exposure

The principle behind severance pay is that the employee is economically supported until he or she finds another job. When employers implement this theory on older workers, it is often interpreted

---

[34]*Hillebrand* v. *M-Tron Industries, Inc.*, 827 F.2d 363 (8th Cir. 1987), cert. denied 488 U.S. 1004 (1989).

[35]*King* v. *General Electric*, 906 F.2d 107 (7th Cir. 1992). Also *Bozemore* v. *Friday*, 106 S.Ct. 3000 (1986).

[36]Wage levels should not be used as a basis for RIF: *Tolan* v. *Levi Strauss & Co.*, 867 F.2d 467 (8th Cir. 1989).

[37]The use of the term *overqualified* creates an exposure to a lawsuit: *Taggart* v. *Time, Inc.*, 924 F.2d 43 (2nd Cir. 1991). However, an employer can refuse to place an overqualified person on the grounds it may have a negative effect on performance: *Bay* v. *Times Mirror Magazines*, 936 F.2d 112 (2nd Cir. 1991).

[38]If there is a labor union, the employer is not required to bargain over RIF but generally is required to bargain over the effects of the RIF decision: *NLRB* v. *Emsing's Supermarket, Inc.*, 872 F.2d 1279 (7th Cir. 1989).

[39]See *Gaworski* v. *ITT Commercial Finance Corp.*, 17 F.3d 1104 (8th Cir. 1994).

as discrimination against older workers. So when a company denied severance pay to all those who were eligible for early retirement, the court said this was a "heartless corporate policy." Any time decisions are made that will have a disproportionate impact upon a protected class of employees, there is an exposure to a lawsuit.

PUNITIVE DAMAGES UNDER ADEA

Originally the courts were reluctant to allow punitive damages under ADEA. The CRA91 amendment to the ADEA allows punitive damages under certain conditions, but imposes a cap of $300,000. More case law is needed before we can be certain of the effect of the cap.[40]

ADEA incorporates the enforcement powers of the Fair Labor Standards Act. In punitive damages requests, the plaintiff is required to prove the violation to be a willful violation. In *Trans World Airlines, Inc.* v. *Thurston,* 105 S.Ct. 613 (1985), the Court stated that under ADEA, it was willful if the employer either knew or showed reckless disregard for the statute on whether its conduct was prohibited by the ADEA. If the employer did not know that the act was being violated or did not recklessly disregard the ADEA, the action could not be willful.[41]

Punitive damages are going to be difficult to obtain apart from CRA91 if the *Foley* v. *Interactive Data,* 765 P.2d 373 (Cal. S.Ct. 1988), case is followed in other jurisdictions. In *Foley,* the court reversed all previous California decisions and held that in discharge cases damages are limited to contract damages where a breach is shown. Several state statutes are being passed to limit damages in discharge cases where ADEA is violated. If CRA91 applies, this will end the punitive damages issue in ADEA cases. When the jury or the court does not like the way the employer discharges, it will award large punitive damages for the abuse. If CRA91 applies, there

will be a cap of $300,000 on punitive damages. If CRA91 doesn't apply, then punitive damages are unlimited. The *Foley* case limits punitive damages in discharge cases (at least in California).

AVOIDING LITIGATION

Age discrimination will be a problem for the employer in the late 1990s as race discrimination was in the 1960s. The older worker is becoming a powerful force, which the employer must recognize if costly litigation and high damage awards are to be avoided. Charges to the EEOC under ADEA have been on the increase for several years, and the employer must develop positive programs to stop the trend. Failure to do so will result in ADEA being the most costly and disruptive of all antidiscrimination laws.

One of the most popular methods to prevent litigation is the early retirement program. As discussed elsewhere in this chapter, the key to these programs is to obtain a voluntary decision to retire under OWBPA. Because it is very easy to get into court and allege coercion, the signing must be absolutely voluntary.

The employer must show that an analysis was made of selection in a reduction of force or that performance was measured objectively and that factors other than age were used in making a decision. Then litigation can be avoided. If the employer is not certain that a factor other than age can be defended, an individual agreement to voluntarily retire or a general early retirement program should be considered. If nothing else works, make a deal with the employee. It may not work, but it is worth a try.[42] Employer procedures can aid in encouraging retirement. These procedures should be designed to mitigate the impact of retiring and prevent adversity when the employee is faced with a retirement decision.

Procedures to Avoid Litigation

The following recommended procedures will aid in preventing exposure to litigation:

---

[40]*Post Retirement Plan* v. *Trustees of Purdue University,* 5 F.3d 279 (8th Cir. 1992).

[41]See *McLaughlin* v. *Richland Shoe Co.,* 108 S.Ct. 1677 (1988); also *Biggins* v. *Hazen Paper Co.,* 953 F.2d 1405 (1st Cir. 1992).

[42]See case history on in this chapter.

1. First and foremost, management must develop and enforce objective standards of performance for employees in all job categories. The essential functions of the job must be clearly defined.

2. Employment decisions must be based on performance and competence. Some practitioners will claim that performance cannot be measured in certain jobs. Any human endeavor can be measured, some more easily than others.

3. Termination policies or practices must make it clear that failure to meet the standards of performance is just cause for discharge (and applies to all marginal employees).

   Before legislation of employee rights, many employers tolerated less-than-acceptable work performance from older workers who were near retirement age. When they reached retirement age, they could be forced to retire. This option is now cut off.

   Under ADEA the older worker must meet the same performance standards as any other worker. The employer cannot afford the luxury of a marginal worker with no option to terminate.[43]

4. Mobility among employees must be encouraged.

   The assistant counsel who will not become general counsel must be encouraged to keep up broad legal training to be ready to join a small law firm when conditions change if there is a reduction in staff or the management becomes dissatisfied. Transfers within the organization must be the first consideration.

   The practice of supporting only job-related training programs backfires when early retirement is encouraged. Educational programs must be expanded in order to provide related skills for the second career or a transfer to other jobs in the organization.[44]

Retirement Counseling

Preretirement counseling should be designed to fit the individuals' needs and not be structured to what the management thinks that they need.[45] The employer should not first tell the employees what their problems will be in retirement and then offer a solution. The program should start with each employee stating what problems are anticipated and requesting aid in solution.

Flexible retirement arrangements should be developed with employees as much as possible. Policies should be developed on an individual basis.[46] Phased retirement may fit some individuals (company allows employee to work three days a week and then two or one before retirement). With others, financial security is most important. For others, maintaining prestige is most important. Some employees want to work part-time; others want to be occupied or challenged, if not in their present job, in some other endeavor. Some employees fear domestic problems of being home every day. As one employee put it, "My wife said that she married me for better or worse but not for lunch." Preretirement counseling must be meaningful to the employee, and this can be accomplished only on an individual basis.

Litigation caused by ADEA can be reduced if the employer does not use age as a factor in making an employment decision.[47] Releases, waivers, and early retirement programs are not the complete answer, but will help especially after OWBPA and CRA91. Age in the workforce will remain a problem, but exposure to litigation can be greatly reduced by recognition that age does not always affect work performance.

Section 7(e) of ADEA was amended by CRA91. The effect of the amendment (Section 115

---

[43]*Hagelthorn* v. *Kennecott Corp.*, 716 F.2d 76 (2nd Cir. 1983), held that poor work performance was tolerated for a period of time, so it could be viewed as a pretext for age discrimination when the employer discharged.

[44]It is common to give educational financial assistance to employees only for those subjects directly related to their job. If other subjects are desired, the employee does not receive aid for tuition, and so on. This should be changed to include broader subjects in the job area.

[45]H. M. Cohen, "Retire the Way You Want To," *Finance Executive*, 18 (March-April 1992), 51–53.

[46]Some employees ready to retire cannot anticipate their problems in retirement. Counseling should be available after retirement.

[47]"Joe is not too old, but too slow," is a way to say it with less exposure.

of CRA91) is to extend the period for filing a charge under ADEA to 90 days after the notice of dismissal under ADEA. This amendment is of little concern to the personnel practitioner. However, it could be a meal ticket for legal counsel who believe the litigation should be continued. Counsel could use all the provisions of CRA91 including jury trial. It is difficult to predict what the courts will do.[48]

---

[48]Like the story of two baseball fans who thought it would be nice to give one day of their season tickets to the local nuns who were also baseball fans. They could only watch the games on TV, because they couldn't politically buy tickets. While watching the game they overheard two fans in back, who couldn't see because of the hoods. One said, "I am going to Utah; I hear there are no Catholics there." The other said,"I am going to Colorado; there are no Catholics there." One nun turned around and said, "Why don't you both go to hell; there are no Catholics there."

CHAPTER 9

AFFIRMATIVE ACTION AND PERFORMANCE APPRAISALS

Scope and Purpose of Affirmative Action
Reverse Discrimination and Affirmative Action
Seniority and Antidiscrimination Laws
Exposure of Performance Appraisal Plans

SCOPE AND PURPOSE OF AFFIRMATIVE ACTION

The basic theory of all affirmative action executive orders relating to the private sector is that if you are to receive government funds or do business with the government, certain conditions can be imposed.[1] One of these conditions is that you must adopt an affirmative action (AA) program to employ and promote members of the protected class.[2]

Affirmative action means different things to different people. Some believe that, within reason, a preference should be given to those members of the protected class who have in the past been discriminated against.[3] They believe that it is not important that members within the class have not been victims of discrimination. This group argues that there should be a set-aside goal or preference quotas to correct the past discrimination.

Others believe that affirmative action should not favor one class over another. In doing so, you are granting benefits to groups who may not be as well qualified. The opponents argue that the effort will fail to improve the economic position of the very groups that the executive order was designed to protect. This school of thought believes that affirmative action should not be used to remedy the effects of either actual or historical discrimination that benefits the nonvictims to the detriment of the nonprotected classes. They argue that only

---

[1] M. D. Esposito, "Update Your Affirmative Action Plan," *The Human Resources Yearbook, 1992/1993* (Englewood Cliffs, NJ: Prentice Hall), p. 9.5. Also, L. Mead and J. Kleiner, "What New Rights Law Means to Organizations," *Labor Law Journal,* (Oct. 1995), 627.

[2] This is the basis for set-aside programs in the public sector. *Metro Broadcasting, Inc.* v. *Federal Communications Commission,* 110 S.Ct. 2297 (1990).

[3] See Buddy Robert S. Silverman, "A Litmus Test for EEOC Philosophies," *Personnel Journal ,* (May 1987), 143.

those who have actually been discriminated against should be given a remedy through affirmative action preference.[4]

The Supreme Court has had this issue before it several times and has failed to set a clear and concise policy to follow. A close study of Supreme Court decisions will confuse the lay employer. The only thing constant in the decisions is change. One cannot be certain that a particular affirmative action program will stand judicial scrutiny. A review of Supreme Court decisions indicates that in the private sector affirmative action programs must be remedial and cannot increase participation at the expense of others.[5] Affirmative action that is remedial requests labor unions, employers, and employment agencies to take action to correct past discrimination. The positive steps to be taken are voluntary and intended to improve the working conditions of minorities, females, handicapped disabled workers, and Vietnam veterans. Under this theory the assumption is that there has been past discrimination and the employer's action is to correct this without discrimination against others.

In the public sector (involving public employees), Supreme Court decisions appear to allow AAP to increase participation without proof of past discrimination. However, the action cannot contravene the expectation of competing persons.[6] The compelling interest must be shown.

The Difference between Affirmative Action and Diversity

Affirmative action is quite different from diversity. Affirmative action is legally driven and is about trying to achieve equality of opportunity by focusing on specific groups. Diversity efforts focus on managing and handling the workforce you already have.

The Value of an Affirmative Plan

Over 80 percent of the workforce is covered under Title VII, the Americans with Disabilities Act (ADA), the Age Discrimination in Employment Act, and the Equal Pay Act.[7] State and federal equal employment opportunity legislation extends to all but the smallest employer. The employer who has 1 or 100 employees cannot afford to disregard the national, state, or local policy that every person shall have a right to employment without regard to race, color, religion, sex, national origin, disability, or age. It is good personnel policy to have an affirmative action program (except in California). Whether it is voluntary or forced on the employer by the government should not be a factor in adopting a policy. If the employer is to select and train the best-qualified applicants available, over 80 percent of the labor force cannot be ignored. It is difficult for the personnel administrator to explain to the sales manager why a government contract was lost because of the failure to adopt an affirmative action program; a program is neither a cost consideration nor impossible to institute. If the employer chooses not to have a program, the government may choose not to do business with that employer.[8]

The lack of affirmative action policies for minorities, females, and handicapped also has legal and moral implications when a discrimination charge is filed.

The regulatory agency discovers that the employer did not have an affirmative action program. The employer's defense to a discrimination charge is badly shattered when the absence of an affirmative action program is discovered at some point in the proceedings. Usually the plaintiff's attorney will do so when cross-

---

[4]This was the position of the Reagan and Bush administrations; also *City of Richmond* v. *J. A. Croson Co.,* 109 S.Ct. 706 (1989).

[5]*City of Richmond* v. *J. A. Cronson Co.,* 109 S.Ct. 706 (1989).

[6]*Metro Broadcasting, Inc.* v. *Federal Communication Commission,* 110 S.Ct. 2997 (1990).

[7]*Employment and Earnings,* 39, no. 5 (Washington, DC: Bureau of Labor Statistics, May 1992). This publication reports a total civilian labor force of 117 million in 1992, of which over 90 million are in the protected classes. This figure was compiled from employment status tables by sex, age, race, and disability.

[8]Thomas E. Hanson, Jr. "Note. Rising Above the Past: Affirmative Action as a Necessary Means of Raising the Black Standard of Living as Well as Self-esteem." *Boston College Third World Law Journal,* 16 (1996), 107.

examining the employer's witness, but often the agency will discover it. No bona fide effort, no AA program.

The scope of affirmative action is as broad as making the first sale and hiring the first person.[9] The law does not prevent the Office of Federal Contract Compliance (OFCC) from reporting violations to the EEOC or Justice Department for enforcement of Title VII or any other antidiscrimination statute. Executive Order 11246 and appropriate statutes do not require the employer to hire an applicant who is not the best qualified. The courts require the employer to make a good faith effort to find and hire qualified applicants who are members of the protected class.

The objective of affirmative action programs in the private sector has been accomplished if there is a measurable improvement in hiring, training, and promoting minorities or females in those job categories that show underutilization of the protected class.

Basic Elements of an Affirmative Action Plan

An affirmative action plan has six basic elements:

1. An Equal Employment Opportunity Policy Statement [41 CFR §§ 60–2.13(a) and 60–2.20]. This is usually a statement from the CEO.

2. Procedures for internal and external dissemination of the policy [41 CFR § 60–2.13(b) and 60–2.21]. Include the union, if any, large customers, and employee groups, as well as all employees.

3. Specific allocation of responsibilities for implementation of the plan. See 41 CFR § 60–2.13(c) for details. It is advisable to include a job description of the person assigned.

4. A workforce analysis of all job titles [41 CFR § 60–2.11(a)]. This is a most important element. It determines what is needed to correct past discrimination.

5. Plan of action [41 CFR § 60–2.13(f) and 60–2.24]. An action program should be developed to eliminate any identified problem areas or to show improvement.

6. Internal audit and reporting system [41 CFR § 60–2.13(g) and 60–2.25]. This should be a record of what you have accomplished.

Implementation of the Plan

If AA programs are realistic, honest, and current, compliance should not be a problem. The first step in determining whether one can improve employment opportunities is to determine whether there will be any employment or promotion opportunities in a given period. The next step is to determine whether there has been a denial of job opportunities for the protected class. Why are there no members of the protected class in that job category? If there is a possibility to improve a job category as to employment or promotion of a member of the protected class, then it is considered an underutilized job category that can be improved on. Affirmative action does not demand that underutilization be corrected immediately, but that a good faith effort be made to improve the number of the protected class in the underutilized job category.

It has been judicially determined that a labor market is defined for purposes of compliance to Title VII as an area where the employer has been recruiting.[10] However, new areas should be considered in affirmative action recruiting if the old method is not bringing results.

The implementation of an affirmative action program to increase job opportunities meets the requirements of Title VII in the recruitment and selection process. A good affirmative action program will be a good defense when a charge is filed for discrimination in hiring.[11]

---

[9]Terpstra, D., "Affirmative Action: A Focus on Issues," *Labor Law Journal*, May 1995.

[10]*Hazelwood School District* v. *United States,* 433 U.S. 299 (1977).

[11]The distinction between enforcement of Title VII and Executive Order 11246 is that Title VII deals with individual or affected class complaints alleging that discrimination has taken place. Order 11246 is concerned with programs to correct past or future discrimination without reference to any specific complaint by an individual.

Because the law is confused on AA programs doesn't mean the employer should not have one. In recent years AA programs have come under attack. The reason is that they promote hiring a lesser qualified person to do the job. The employer in the past has not been willing to take a stand on this issue. Those employers who had a policy that only the qualified person would be hired regardless of past discrimination have nothing to be concerned about. The pressure from the EEOC and other organizations is now "coming home to roost." To do away with AA programs is a mistake. To hire or promote only the qualified is not a mistake.

The AA program should motivate the employer to find qualified minorities. If they cannot be found—keep trying. Don't lose any sleep over it and tell the EEOC that you will keep trying, but do not eliminate the program. The idea is not wrong, but the implementation is bad. The EEOC Compliance Officer and the law told the employer to hire unqualified applicants to comply with the AA program. AA is in trouble because they tried to correct past discrimination by unqualified persons. It is not the program, but how it handled applicants, that has caused the confusion.

REVERSE DISCRIMINATION AND AFFIRMATIVE ACTION

The exposure to reverse discrimination charges is created when the employer wishes to reduce the workforce, make temporary layoffs, or promote, and still comply with the affirmative action plan that was previously agreed to and communicated.[12]

The Supreme Court justices over the years have had difficulty in agreeing how this should be done. In most of the decisions relating to the problem of reverse discrimination and correcting past discrimination by affirmative action, the Court has been widely split.[13]

Affirmative Action in Selection

Where admissions favored blacks over whites, the Court held that this program violated Title VII and the equal protection clause of the 14th Amendment as it favored one class over another. The Court didn't agree with the school's position that it should increase participation of the protected class in the medical school. The Court considered the students in the private sector.

One year later, again by a 5-4 majority, the Court approved a program that reserved 50 percent of all openings in a maintenance department for black applicants. The minority applicants might have less seniority, but would be selected over the white applicants. The Court said this did not violate Title VII.[14] This decision followed the philosophy that it is not a violation to increase participation of the protected class in the private sector if it is temporary. The Court reasoned that because it was agreed upon by the employees (union in this case), it was temporary until racial balance was achieved. The whites were given the same opportunity as the blacks to compete for 50 percent of the job openings. Therefore, the program was not in violation. The courts in subsequent cases allowed past discrimination to be corrected by affirmative action if the conditions in *Weber* were present; otherwise they would revert and find reverse discrimination.[15]

Affirmative Action when Reducing Workforce

The issue again came before the Court in *Firefighters Local Union No. 1784* v. *Stotts*, 467 U.S. 561 (1984). In this case the municipality laid off according to a court-approved voluntary affirmative action plan. It was the result of a discrimination charge. The charge alleged that the department was discriminating against blacks. The layoff violated the seniority provisions of the collective bargaining agreement but maintained the balance of the court-approved affirmative

---

[12]N. Kaufman, R. Robinson, et al., "Affirmative Action and White Males in America," *Labor Law Journal*, (Nov. 1995).

[13]*Astroline Communications Co.* v. *Sherberg Broadcasting* (consolidated opinion), 110 S.Ct. 997 (1990). Set-aside programs are no longer legal, unless there is a compelling interest to do so.

[14]*Kaiser Aluminum and Chemical Corporation* v. *Weber,* 443 U.S. 193 (1979).

[15]*Regents of the University of California* v. *Bakke,* 438 U.S. 265 (1978).

action program. The Court approved the settlement. (Fifty-one cities had similar programs.) The Court held that the seniority provisions of the collective bargaining agreement couldn't be ignored. (The Court will usually protect seniority regardless of how it affects discrimination.) The decision also stated that the plan was inconsistent with the spirit and the letter of the antidiscrimination laws unless a lower court first ruled that discrimination existed. In *Stotts,* the lower court, without a trial, had determined that discrimination was practiced, but didn't provide a remedy because a voluntary agreement had been reached, although white persons and the union did not participate.

In the similar case of *Wygant* v. *Jackson Board of Education,* 106 S.Ct. 1842 (1986), the Court majority found that past discrimination alone is insufficient cause to justify racial preference. It held that in order for a layoff procedure under an affirmative action plan to favor one race over another, there must be convincing evidence of prior discrimination as determined by a court.[16]

The *Wygant* decision was very narrow, as the Court in *Sheetmetal Workers Local No. 93* v. *City of Cleveland,* 106 S.Ct. 3063 (1986), said an employer may develop an affirmative action plan for hiring and promotion in the settlement of an employment discrimination charge. Here the employer and union had violated the statute and entered into a court-approved settlement agreement to remedy the violation. The union also violated the settlement agreement. The Court said the agreement was identical to a private out-of-court settlement. However, in another case the Court held that those employees who were not directly affected could receive race-conscious relief.[17]

Case law holds that unless there was judicial determination that past discrimination existed and the court ordered a remedy, the plan could not favor one class over another. Courts strike down affirmative action plans that favor one class over another in hiring, layoff, and promotion as being a violation of the 14th Amendment and Title VII unless a federal government program is involved. An exception would be if the conditions existed as found in *Weber.*[18] (This is stated in most recent 1995 Supreme Court decisions.)

Affirmative Action in Promotion

The proper determination of whom to promote is a primary consideration in the successful management of any organization. It is a commonly accepted personnel doctrine that one determines promotion on the basis of ability to perform the job. No other criteria should be used, with the exception of seniority. This usually supersedes minority interests or any affirmative action plan. (Seniority is a determining factor only after candidates are in every other respect equally qualified to perform the job.)

In 1972 a lower court found the state of Alabama guilty of systematically excluding blacks from state trooper jobs. They were ordered to follow a quota for hiring and promotion. By 1979 no black had been promoted to the upper ranks.

The court then approved a program whereby the state would develop a program within one year for promotion of blacks to the rank of corporal. The lower court found contempt and the Supreme Court affirmed EEOC guidelines in all other respects. Two more years passed and no black had been promoted. The department then agreed to develop a test, which proved to have an adverse impact on minorities. The court ordered that 50 percent of promotions to the rank of corporal go to blacks if a vacancy existed, under the theory that an AA program can be designed to increase participation of blacks as state troopers. The state challenged that order in the Supreme Court.

---

[16]In *City of Richmond* v. *J. A. Croson Co.,* 109 S.Ct. 706 (1989), the Court struck down a city minority set-aside award plan for public contracts, because it favored one race over another although there was a racial imbalance. This case has been followed in layoffs, promotion, and hiring, except for federal government programs. However, the Supreme Court reversed this in *Adarand Constructors Inc.* v. *Pena,* 115 S.Ct. 2097 (1995).

[17]*Local 28 of Sheetmetal Workers* v. *EEOC,* 106 S.Ct. 301 (1986); also *Cunico* v. *Pueblo School District No. 60,* 917 F.2d 431 (10th Cir. 1990).

[18]Congress by statute can constitutionally favor one race over another: *Fullilove* v. *Klutznick,* 444 U.S. 448 (1980). Otherwise a compelling interest has to be shown.

The Supreme Court in *United States* v. *Paradise et al.,* 107 S.Ct. 1063 (1987), by a 5-4 vote affirmed the lower court's order, stating that the court had wide discretion in ordering remedies where discrimination had been found. The plan was temporary and whites had an equal chance to be promoted. The Court to some extent followed *Weber, City of Cleveland,* and *Fullilove* in affirming that racial preference can be given under certain conditions.

The real uncertainty of affirmative action programs that result in reverse discrimination was created by *Johnson* v. *Transportation Agency, Santa Clara County,* 107 S.Ct. 1442 (1987). The facts of the case lacked the requirements of previous decisions that upheld racial preference to correct past discrimination in affirmative action plans. There is some doubt if this is law because AA is under attack. There was no previous court determination of discrimination; there was no record of past discrimination against women, although an imbalance existed. The Court said taking a woman over a man for a nondiscriminatory reason is okay where there is an imbalance. The plan was permanent, and the plan did not have the approval of the employees or any employee representative. The plan expressly authorized that race and sex were factors when evaluating qualified candidates in areas where these groups were not proportionally represented.

In *Johnson* both a male and a female had been rated as qualified, although the male was two points higher in the interview evaluation. The male was the unanimous choice of the evaluators among nine candidates and the most qualified. Of the 238 employees in the department, none was a woman; the female was selected by the agency director to correct an imbalance. Sex was one of numerous factors taken into account, and the facts indicate that it was the major factor (in a labor market that was 36 percent women).

The court in a 6-3 decision held that Title VII permits the employer to voluntarily rectify a manifest imbalance in the workforce by an affirmative action program. The Court didn't overrule the previous cases of *Bakke, Wygant,* or *Stotts* but relied heavily upon *Weber.* According to the Court, the facts were similar to *Weber* (except *Weber* was in the private sector).

The plan was permanent and allowed excusion of whites who were better qualified. The holding in the case is that a bona fide affirmative action plan can use race, sex, or ethnic background as a factor in hiring or promotion. How much of a factor is uncertain.[19]

One thing certain is that this case will not avoid further litigation. Reverse discrimination has been dealt a serious blow that will not be allowed to stand. Employers cannot live with promoting people who are not qualified and later being challenged when they are removed from the job because of poor performance. However, most courts will put qualifications first where there is a big difference between the two candidates. (In *Johnson* the candidates were almost equal.)[20]

In promotions there is some certainty about affirmative action plans upholding that use reverse discrimination to correct an imbalance, as indicated in the *Johnson* case. However, because of the confusion in previous cases, the employer cannot be absolutely safe from exposure.

To be safe, an employer would be wise to have a procedure whereby all employees would be informed of a vacancy and be given consideration if they had an interest. Although supervision may object to this policy, it not only would eliminate some exposure but also would be a good personnel practice. Exhibit 9-1 is a suggested form that could be used when promoting a qualified person and attempting to correct a past discrimination.

Recommendations for an Acceptable Plan

This chapter states that every employer should have an affirmative action program as defense for discrimination charges. The case law review has not changed this; in fact, it appears from the *Johnson* case that affirmative action plans can be used as defense for reverse discrimination. To what extent these defenses can be used is an uncertainty. It also appears from the *Johnson* case

---

[19]This is difficult to reconcile with *Bakke* (1979), where the Court said you cannot correct discrimination by affirmative action.

[20]Here the Court permitted increased participation, but refused to do so in *Bakke.*

EXHIBIT 9-1 *Position Opportunities Announcement*

	DATE OF ANNOUNCEMENT REMOVE DATE
JOB TITLE	DIVISION/DEPARTMENT
SUPERVISOR	SALARY CLASSIFICATION
REQUIREMENTS	
DUTIES	
IF YOU WISH TO BE CONSIDERED FOR THIS POSITION, PLEASE CONTACT	
WE ARE AN EQUAL OPPORTUNITY EMPLOYER	

that an employer now has less exposure than previously to reverse discrimination charges. It must be remembered that reverse discrimination charges had a degree of certainty under *Bakke* in 1978, lost it under *Weber* in 1979, regained it under *Stotts* and *Wygant* in 1986, but lost it again in 1987 under *Johnson.*

In order to avoid exposure to litigation, the employer should do the following:

1. Step up a recruiting plan that encourages qualified employees in the protected class to go into positions not commonly held by protected groups.

2. Continue to hire or promote the most-qualified person for the position based on criteria established by the employer. To do otherwise will only postpone litigation to when the employer has to terminate the marginal worker.

3. Change affirmative action plans only if they are not achieving the desired results. If after a long period of time there still remains a statistical imbalance in certain jobs, a documented nondiscriminatory reason is essential to the survival of the plan.

4. Adopt an affirmative action plan that promotes the objective of the business. If such a plan causes an exposure to litigation, then the employer must decide whether to change the plan or risk exposure to reverse discrimination. Any plan that excludes members of the protected class from consideration will cause an exposure.

5. State specifically in the plan that one class will not be favored over another in achieving a balanced workforce but an imbalanced workforce will be a consideration when promoting.

6. Post all job vacancies. Exhibit 9-1 is a suggested example of a notice.

The Supreme Court decided more than 10 AA cases, mostly by a 5-4 vote, and never reversed itself.[21] If there is any consistency in these cases it is that programs in the private sector are valid if they correct judicially determined past discrimination; otherwise, there is a serious exposure to reverse discrimination. In the public sector there is less of an exposure to reverse discrimination when the AA program increases participation to correct an imbalance even though there is no past discrimination. In *Adarand Construction Co. v. Pena* the Supreme Court resolved two important issues. Both must have a compelling governmental interest and must be narrowly construed. It remains to be seen whether the courts will follow the narrow construction as in business necessity or BFOQ.

Employer Posture in a Compliance Review

If the employer is a government prime contractor of $10,000 or more, it is likely that a compliance review will be conducted. The compliance review will determine adequacy and implementation of an affirmative action policy. If in the opinion of the compliance officer the program is not effective, then recommendations are made to change it. The employer can refuse the changes, and the compliance review officer can recommend cancellation of an existing contract or bar future contracts. The final decision is made by the OFCC, subject to judicial review. As prejudice and discrimination are less damaging when inflicted by a member of one's own ethnic or social group, intraracial discrimination must be recognized as an extant and impermissible form of workplace discrimination that must not be hidden by nor lost under the protective cloak of so-called solidarity.

To avoid a dispute over the affirmative action program, the employer, after receiving notice from the review agency, should make preparation for compliance reviews. Proper preparation will enable the review officer to obtain all the pertinent

facts about the program in the shortest possible time.[22] It will also show an attitude of cooperation. Records such as applicant flow data, hiring records, and EEO-1 report and number of vacancies, promotions, and demotions should be readily available.[23] Employees are often interviewed, so it is advisable to have some names in mind if asked by the compliance officer what employees that employer would like to be interviewed.

The employer should be prepared to give a business reason for underutilized categories and other implications of discrimination or lack of good faith effort. Cooperation with the compliance officer is advisable, but it should not extend to those areas where the employer feels the compliance officer is on a fishing expedition. It may be an unreasonable burden to keep or supply irrelevant records.

SENIORITY AND ANTIDISCRIMINATION LAWS

The original method to eliminate subjectivity was to make decisions based on seniority. For many years seniority has been used to eliminate prejudice or subjective decisions in labor agreements, in the judicial system, and in many other social institutions. In the federal court system the chief judge of a district or appellate court is usually the senior judge. The U.S. Supreme Court and the legislative branch of the government rely heavily on seniority in many of their administrative procedures and customs.

Seniority Systems That Perpetuate Discrimination

Seniority systems that discriminated against minorities and females were common before the antidiscrimination laws. Unions had segregated

---

[21]One sure way to get a court challenge is not to notify of job openings, not to give tests, and not to have an interview: *Lindahl* v. *Air France*, 930 F.2d 1434 (9th Cir. 1991).

[22]A good policy is to obtain a copy of the EEOC compliance manual and have it visible at the time of the review. Also the combined poster "EEOC Is the Law" should be posted.

[23]The Standard Compliance Review Report requires the company to complete an adverse-impact analysis of all promotions and terminations. A compelling interest has to be shown.

locals, employers had separate seniority lists for males and females and for blacks and whites, and many companies had segregated facilities.

Because discriminatory seniority systems were established many years before antidiscrimination laws, they would accordingly perpetuate discrimination toward minority or female workers. The Supreme Court held that as long as the system was neutral on its face, the seniority system did not violate Title VII although it perpetuated discrimination.[24]

Seniority as a Defense

The Supreme Court made it clear in a later case that if there were any evidence of intentional discrimination, such a system would be invalid.[25]

From these cases a legal principle has emerged that unless intent to discriminate can be shown, a seniority system that has an adverse impact and perpetuates discrimination is valid. The courts said in effect that seniority is a compelling interest over antidiscrimination laws and AA programs. Under CRA91, Section 112, any employee affected by seniority can challenge the plan any time, regardless of when the employee was affected or when the plan was formed.

EXPOSURE OF PERFORMANCE APPRAISAL PLANS

Personnel literature is abundant on what is a legally effective performance appraisal plan to improve employee effectiveness. We are told that appraisals should motivate employees to perform at their highest levels.[26] Various methods and goals to achieve these results often evaluate work behaviors, while others focus on personality traits. Some academic writers and practitioners tell what

management is doing wrong to cause performance appraisals to be ineffective. Others take a positive approach and tell how to make them effective.[27]

This section will be concerned with the legal aspects of performance appraisals as a personnel technique. Performance appraisal can be effective as a training device in improving performance. However, if a system is used to make an employment decision on a member of the protected class, it must be a valid system or it will be challenged in the courts. A familiar statement on termination records is "Employee had poor performance appraisals"—a performance appraisal that was never validated. All too often management fails to realize that evaluating performance is subject to external audit in the same manner as any other employment program.

In some organizations the performance appraisal systems are seldom audited as to their usefulness. Criteria for employee performance were originally developed around the personality characteristics of white males. Very few female or minority employees were (and still are) at organizational levels that merited performance reviews. With the advent of discrimination laws, this reliance on obsolete standards and practices is particularly dangerous, especially if the results are used in selecting candidates for promotion and in granting wage increases.

Under present court decisions a rating system that depends upon subjective criteria and measures personality traits rather than behavior or results is worse than having none at all. When allegations are made that a rating system is discriminatory and therefore violates Title VII, the employer must defend the methods used.[28] If they prove to be subjective, the defense becomes difficult.

---

[24]*International Brotherhood of Teamsters* v. *United States,* 431 U.S. 324 (1977). Even a seniority system instituted after Title VII is still valid: *American Tobacco Co.* v. *Patterson,* 102 S.Ct. 1534 (1982).

[25]*Pullman Standard* v. *Swint,* 102 S.Ct. 1781 (1982); also in *Cunico* v. *Pueblo School District No. 60,* 917 F.2d 431 (10th Cir. 1990).

[26]Surveys show that performance appraisals fail to accomplish this. *Personnel Journal* (June 1995), 31.

[27]G. R. Ferris and T. P. King, "Politics in Human Resources Decisions," *Organizational Dynamics,* 20 (Autumn 1991), 59–71; J. M. George, "Extrinsic and Intrinsic Origins of Perceived Social Loafing," *Academy Management Journal,* 35 (March 1992), 191; "The Smell of Success" (editorial), *Training,* 28 (November 1991), 10; R. A. O'Hare and M. P. O'Hare, "Feedback: The Key to Error-Free Performance," *Supervision Management,* 35 (January 1990), 5.

[28]A. Scheele, "Making the Most of Your Performance Review," *Working Women,* (August 1992), 30.

An example of what can happen when subjective appraisals are used is the case of a black engineer at General Motors. He filed a class action lawsuit alleging that GM was using a discriminatory performance appraisal system. As a result there existed an adverse impact in selecting candidates for promotion.[29] The court decisions emphasize the point that failure to correct the faults in a subjective system invites litigation, legal costs, and possible penalties.

Many practitioners believe that certain jobs cannot be measured. Any human endeavor can be measured, some better than others. If the human endeavor cannot be measured, that fact may be a good signal that the position is not needed.

Reasons for Failure of Appraisal Systems

Most appraisal systems fail because the rater is trained to rate not behavior but personal characteristics. Often raters will use their own prejudices or those of the management as paramount. The rater

1. Rates all performance on one impressive performance on a job
2. Has a dislike for one particular trait
3. Stays away from extreme ratings, never excellent or unacceptable
4. Relies on recent events instead of performance for the whole period
5. Avoids conflict or justification by giving a good appraisal[30]
6. Compares ratee with self and how performance affected his or her own situation
7. Does not inform ratee what part of performance is being appraised and how it will be measured[31]
8. Does not rate results or behavior but uses subjective measurements

9. Fails to give proper feedback
10. Accepts management influence to obtain certain results[32]

The rater doesn't have all of these, but use of any one of them causes the procedure to be invalid.

Judicial Review of Performance Appraisals

It took judicial action to force management to review performance appraisals and question whether they accurately measured performance on the job. For years the courts have considered performance appraisals a legitimate management right and function. With the advent of the antidiscrimination laws, the courts were forced to review the function. They found subjective appraisals. Any resemblance between actual performance on the job and what the appraisal said was coincidental.

One of the first appellate courts to scrutinize performance appraisals was the 5th Circuit in New Orleans. The employer's appraisal methods did not relate to performance on the job but to trait characteristics. The court said that where the appraisal is used to make an employment decision or an adverse impact is shown, the appraisal methods must be validated with performance.[33] In this case, promotions were dependent almost entirely on favorable recommendation of the immediate supervisor, who used subjective evaluations of job performance as a basis for promotion. Subjective evaluations permitted the supervisor to exercise race discrimination in the promotion process.

It was clear that evaluations are based on best judgments and opinions, with no evidence of identifiable criteria of job performance.

The courts are quick to reject appraisal systems that are subjective and not related to job performance. A subjective appraisal by its nature

---

[29]This case was settled out of court for a large sum in back pay and an agreement by GM to revise the performance appraisal system.

[30] F. Buhalo, "You Sign My Report and I Will Sign Yours," *Personnel Journal,* (May 1991).

[31]G. Heill & Associates, "Implanting a Leadership Feedback and Development Process," (1992).

[32]The management had a prejudice against truckers and told the author to rate them all low. He changed the job title to material handlers and gave them valid ratings.

[33]*Rowe* v. *General Motors,* 457 F.2d 348 (5th Cir. 1972).

uses different criteria for different job categories and for different persons and therefore gets the attention of the courts, just as other subjective decisions do.

In one case the court said that unless there are written guidelines for the raters and they are otherwise trained in the standardized method of appraisal, the process is invalid.[34]

There is little disagreement among the courts that subjective appraisal methods are in violation of Title VII;[35] however, an appraisal method is bound to have some subjectivity and this is recognized by the courts. The courts have approved subjective methods in hiring if they include objective standards. A subjective oral interview was given to applicants for an electrician's job. There was a requirement that the applicant meet certain tests or have eight years experience as a journeyman. The court said that the subjective oral interview is not discriminatory as long as objective criteria of certain skill tests or experiences are also used.[36] It would appear from the rationale of this case that if an objective standard for performance were established and subjective reasons were stated why that performance standard was not met, the appraisal method would be valid.

Need to Change Performance Appraisals

Many progressive employers have changed their performance appraisal methods and have adopted the use of management by objectives (or some other objective system). Where performance appraisal uses MBO, it must be an ongoing procedure between the supervisor and the subordinate. A meeting every six months during which only the most recent data are used is not a valid system. Those who have been successful with an MBO approach have insisted on the classical form of quantitative and measurable objectives rather than the more subjective type used by some companies.

If the employer does not validate performance appraisals, the courts will on a case-by-case basis. In *Allen* v. *City of Mobile,* 466 F.2d 1245 (5th Cir. 1972), cert. denied, 411 U.S. 909 (1973),[37] the court said that the performance rating system was discriminatory and prescribed another performance rating system. There is no assurance that the judicially prescribed method of appraisal has any more validity or would serve a more useful purpose for promotion than the employer's system.[38]

Another court followed the *Allen* case and ordered a rating system that would ensure that minorities and nonminorities would be equally graded. The federal district court prescribed the performance appraisal as an alternative to the one that it struck down. However, it was not a validation method that could be applied to other factual situations.

The problem of performance appraisal systems as related to court decisions was studied by Feild and Holley of Auburn University. These investigators found that the courts consistently rejected appraisal systems as invalid when no specific instructions were given to the raters, appraisals were trait oriented rather than behavior oriented, and job analysis was not used in developing the content of the rating form.[39]

The need for validation of performance appraisal systems cannot be overemphasized. If the organization does not review its system, the courts may on a case-by-case basis. The court-prescribed system may not be any better than the one struck down, but its use will be required to free the employer from liability.

---

[34]In *Bohrer* v. *Hanes Corp.,* 715 F.2d 213 (5th Cir. 1985), the court found objective standards and dismissed an age discrimination charge.

[35]If there is no rating system, creditable supervisor testimony is acceptable. See *Cova* v. *Coca-Cola Bottling of St. Louis,* 574 F.2d 576 (6th Cir. 1978).

[36]*Hamilton* v. *General Motors Corp.,* 606 F.2d 576 (5th Cir. 1979).

[37]J.E. Davidson, "The Temptation of Performance Appraisal Abuse," *Louisiana Law Review,* 81 (1995), 603.

[38]"Ongoing Employee Evaluations, Making Worklife Easier" *Supervisors Bulletin,* Sept. 15, 1994.

[39]See also D. Rosen, "Appraisals Can Make—or Break—Your Court Case," *Personnel Journal,* 71, no. 11 (November 1992), 113.

Recommendations for Validating Appraisal Plans

The first step in the validation of a performance appraisal procedure is to eliminate—as far as possible—all criteria based on personality traits. The next step is to determine whether any relationship exists between what the appraisal procedure measures and job performance. If the correlation is not good, institute a new procedure. The next thing to do is to develop a system that utilizes some of the court decisions in discrimination cases.

At this point it may be a good idea to reevaluate the purpose of the rating procedure. Is the purpose to improve performance (a training function)? Do you want a basis for wage and salary determinations or for promotion decisions? If you decide that the main use is for training, then the procedure—minus the subjective elements—must meet the validation requirements of the courts. If the purpose is to determine wage and salary levels or to establish eligibility for promotion, it is imperative that the method relate clearly to job performance. Key considerations in your validation review should include

1. The level of performance expected of the employee expressed in quantitative terms to the extent possible and clearly communicated to the employee
2. Criteria that will determine whether the employee met the expectations of the job
3. An audit of the effectiveness of training of those doing the rating
4. The use of standardized rating methods

Removing Subjectivity from Appraisal Results

The courts are saying that unless performance appraisals are objective and measure performance,[40] they cannot be used to make employment decisions when members of the protected class are involved.[41] A performance appraisal program is objective if it contains the following elements:

1. The rater states what is expected of the employee in the form of job standards based on assigned responsibilities. The employee must understand what part of the job is being appraised.
2. The rater evaluates and discusses the performance informally during the appraisal period. The employee must be told how she or he is doing and not be surprised at appraisal time.
3. Written ratings are supported by specific examples or observations of behavior related to the job. These observations should be made by the rater and be continual.[42]
4. Where the rater cannot observe continually, the opinion of others who use the employee's services can be used.
5. The rater appraises results, not effort or personal characteristics. The only proper subject for performance appraisal is productive behavior that produces results.[43]

Suggestion for a Judicially Acceptable Appraisal Plan

What type of form the rater is required to use depends upon the job category and the purpose for which the rating is to be used. Exhibit 9-2 is a suggested procedure that considers all the decisions of the courts and at the same time would serve to evaluate performance and improve the

---

[40]The evaluation criteria must relate to the specific jobs being rated. See *EEOC* v. *Mississippi State Tax Commission,* 873 F.2d 97, 99 (5th Cir. 1989).

[41]Appraisals that do not measure objectively are also poor personnel administration.

[42]For a small company, observation is probably better than a formal rating system. However, the observation must be communicated to the ratee.

[43]A consultant was once asked by a client to speak to the client organization and "motivate them to communicate." "What aren't they doing?" asked the consultant. " They aren't getting their reports in on time," replied the client. "Well, I have a suggestion for you," said the consultant. "Call them together and tell them 'Get your reports in on time or you are likely to be fired.' You will get your reports." It is sometimes helpful to remember that your system should concentrate on measuring what you want employees to do, not on what you want them to be.

EXHIBIT 9-2 *Valid Performance Appraisal Procedure*

Steps in Developing a Valid Procedure

1. Rater meets with ratee to discuss
   a. Job responsibilities.
   b. Improvements to be achieved during the rating period.
   c. A work plan to achieve those improvements, which concentrates on results and behavior.
   d. The method used to evaluate performance under the work plan (see Exhibit 9-3).
   e. The standardized form to be used in the evaluation process.
   f. How the evaluation results will be used (salary review, for promotion or for training only, and so on).
2. Ratee makes a self-assessment of strengths and weaknesses and what he or she feels is needed to achieve the improvements. (This is not communicated to anyone except that it was done.) This is important, but not essential.
3. Rater does periodic monitoring of the progress during the review period, communicating to ratee unacceptable performance, praising superior performance, and modifying the work plan if necessary. This is an ongoing procedure that communicates to the ratee the progress toward achieving results.
4. Rater states the reason for conclusions on the form and analyzes the ratee performance as to why the expected improvements were exceeded or not met. Rater prepares for meeting with ratee.
5. Rater meets with ratee and discusses his or her evaluation of the ratee's performance and develops a plan for improvement through formal training or on-the-job exposure if appropriate. (The evaluation should be no surprise to ratee if progress reports were made.)
6. Rater explains to ratee how the results are going to be used according to what was discussed in the initial meeting at beginning of review period.
7. Rater has the next level of supervision review the process; this eliminates the charge of bias, fixes responsibility for compliance, and ensures that rating will be done.

effectiveness of the ratee.[44] Exhibit 9-3 gives the steps sometimes used in drafting an appraisal plan.

Self-assessment is not a requirement of the court for a valid plan. It is advisable for the employer to provide an opportunity for the employee to make a self-assessment of his or her strengths and weaknesses. It will help achieve the expectations of the job. This self-analysis may then be used for comparison with the rater's report. Self-assessment not only is a training exercise but also may eliminate serious differences between the rater and the person being rated. Of considerable importance is the fact that the procedure is less likely to be challenged in the courts.

Performance appraisals have enjoyed extensive application in both public and private employment, but the decisions of the courts placed the system in a precarious position. Basically, the objection to them is that they do not measure actual job performance (workers say the same thing). The courts are in complete agreement that—where a member of a protected class is involved—a subjective, unstandardized system cannot be used as a nondiscriminatory reason for

---

[44]For a good discussion on how to develop a plan see D. Seaton, "Performance Management: Steps for Legal Compliance, Risk Reduction and Effective Direction of Personnel," *Employment Law Handbook*, vol. 1 (St. Paul: Minnesota Bar Association, 1991), no. 14.

EXHIBIT 9-3

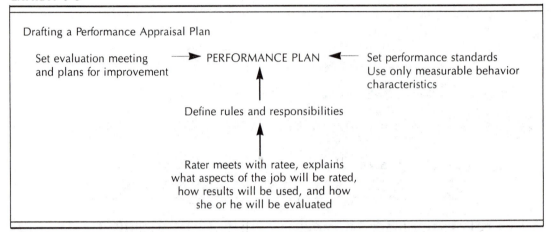

Drafting a Performance Appraisal Plan

Set evaluation meeting and plans for improvement → PERFORMANCE PLAN ← Set performance standards / Use only measurable behavior characteristics

Define rules and responsibilities

Rater meets with ratee, explains what aspects of the job will be rated, how results will be used, and how she or he will be evaluated

treating one person differently from another.[45] Faulty appraisals contribute to liability where there is an allegation that an antidiscrimination statute is violated.[46] An appraisal that is defective (usually subjective, among other faults) also contributes to liability in any lawsuit where it is used as basis for an employment decision.[47]

---

[45]Some courts hold that subjective ratings are not illegal per se. Subjective criteria can survive a pretext claim. However, the use of them will cause an exposure. See *Fowle v. C & C Cola*, 868 F.2d 59 (3rd Cir. 1989).

[46]*Norris* v. *Hartmax Specialty Stores, Inc.*, 913 F.2d 253 (9th Cir. 1990).

[47]*Sivel* v. *Reader's Digest, Inc.*, 677 F.Supp. 183 (S.D. N.Y. 1988).

10

REGULATION OF BENEFIT PLANS AND EFFECTIVE USE OF EMPLOYEE AGREEMENTS

Family and Medical Leave Act of 1993
Worker Adjustment and Retraining Notification Act (WARN)
Regulation of Pregnancy Disability Benefits
Reemployment Rights after Military Service
Effect of Statutes on Unpaid Leave of Absence Policy
Restrictions on Vacation Policy
Regulation of Health Care Benefits and Pensions
Effective Use of Employment Agreements

An employee benefit (as used in this chapter) is something of a monetary value that is not related to work performed and that is paid for either in whole or in part by the employer. Health insurance, life insurance, and pensions are employee benefits when the employer is the purchaser of the plans for the benefit of the employee. Normally this type of benefit is granted by a policy decision of the employer or in collective bargaining, is not taxable, and ceases when employment terminates.[1]

Another type of benefit discussed in this chapter is payment for time not worked, such as holiday pay, vacation pay, disability leave, parental leave, and in some cases leaves of absence for reasons other than medical. Usually these benefits are defined in a benefit policy statement and vested in all employees when hired or shortly thereafter.

These benefits have averaged about 35 percent of payroll in annual surveys made by the U.S. Chamber of Commerce. In certain circumstances the employer does not want to treat all employees alike when it comes to terms and conditions of employment. To separate some employees from others, an employment agreement is necessary. The chapter describes how statutes have regulated

---

[1]Section 132 of the Internal Revenue Code requires that benefits meet certain conditions before they are nontaxable. Also, under statute, insurance doesn't necessarily terminate when employment ceases. This topic will be discussed later in this chapter.

employee benefits even though they were granted voluntarily by the employer.[2]

FAMILY AND MEDICAL LEAVE ACT OF 1993

The Family and Medical Leave Act of 1993 (FMLA). PL 103-3 requires employers to provide up to 12 weeks of unpaid leave during any 12-month period.

FMLA regulations require the posting of a notice regarding FMLA. It is similar in form to the notices that must be posted concerning minimum wage, OSHA, immigration, and so on.

Second, employees who request FMLA leave must be given a written statement regarding the employer's policy.

Third, if the employer uses a policy manual or has a union contract, the leave of absence provisions of the manual or the contract must be amended to be brought into compliance with FMLA.

Fourth, forms should be developed to be given to the employee by the employer when the employer requests medical certification when leave is requested because of medical necessity.

The leave must be for the purpose of caring for children and parents of eligible employees. Where both husband and wife work for the same employer, the 12 weeks leave is an aggregate amount for either a parental leave or leave to care for the parent of either employee.

One stated purpose of the act is to "balance the demands of the workplace with the needs of families, to promote the stability and economic security of families, and to promote the national interests in preserving family integrity." Another purpose of the act is to "entitle employees to take reasonable leave for medical reasons, for the birth or adoption of a child, and for the care of a child, spouse, or parent who has a serious health condition."

FMLA covers employers who have 50 or more employees within a 75-mile radius. It covers Federal Civil Service employees. To be eligible an employee must have worked 1,250 hours in the previous 12-month period.[3] It is enforced by the secretary of labor, who must prescribe necessary regulations for enforcement. FMLA does not supersede more generous laws; however, other laws cannot be contrary or more restrictive than FMLA. More litigation is likely.

This is billed as a major piece of legislation. What effect it will have on employers' operations is an open question. It is expected that many employees will not use the act unless they have to, as the leave is unpaid.

As a result of the leave, the employer must not deny benefits, but is not required to credit the employee with seniority or accrual benefits. After the leave the employee must be reinstated to the same or equivalant position. This is a major change from the way many employers operate.

The act has many uncertainties, exemptions, and special provisions. The secretary of labor issued rules in January of 1995 that will clear up some of the problems.[4]

Although it is predicted that few employees will take advantage of FMLA, the human resources manager should be familiar with the act and its regulations for the following reasons:

1. The employer must be able to distinguish between an FMLA leave and a non-FMLA leave. The employee has more rights under FMLA. The employee knows this and so should the human resources manager.
2. The final regulations, effective April 6, 1995, require a detailed procedure for the employer. A mistake has severe consequences for the employer.
3. The regulations allow employers certain safeguards against abuse of the FMLA leave. (The author foresees very little abuse.)
4. An important provision of FMLA has certain interfaces with workers' compensation and other disabilities, and time off with pay (vacations, and so on) which can be taken concurrently under certain conditions.

---

[2]For a comprehensive source of statistics related to benefit plans, see *Databook of Employee Benefits,* 2nd ed. (Washington, DC: Employee Benefit Research Institute, 1992).

[3]The individual can be personally liable.

[4]Lisa J. Gitnik, Note. Will the Interaction of the Family and Medical Leave Act and the Americans with Disabilities Act Leave employees with an 'Undue Hardship?' *Washington University Law Quarterly,* 74 (1996).

WORKER ADJUSTMENT AND RETRAINING NOTIFICATION ACT (WARN)

This legislation comes in response to congressional acceptance of research that indicates that worker dislocations occurring as a result of plant closings and mass layoffs are a problem of national concern. It has been shown that millions of American families, affected by these closings and layoffs, suffer great losses financially as well as in terms of their mental and physical health.

The act became effective on February 4, 1989, and is enforced by the secretary of labor. Employers are prohibited from ordering a plant closing or mass layoff until the end of a 60-day period after providing written notice to each employee of the closing or layoff. Rather than notify every affected employee, an employer may serve notice to each "employee representative" within the meaning of the National Labor Relations Act or the Railway Labor Act. State dislocated worker units, created or designated under Title III of the Job Partnership Training Act, must also be given notice of the closing or layoff. The chief elected official of the unit of local government within which the closing or layoff is to occur must also be notified. Where there is more than one unit of local government, an employer must notify the chief elected official representing the local governmental unit to which the employer paid the highest taxes in the preceding year. No notice is required if the shutdown is not foreseeable.

Reduction of Notification Period

Under the legislation, there are several types of scenarios that permit an employer to give less than 60 days notice of a plant closing or mass layoff. An employer may order the shutdown of a single site of employment[5] if at the time that notice would have been required the employer is actively seeking capital or business which, if obtained, would allow the employer to avoid or postpone the shutdown.[6] This provision applies only if the employer has a reasonable good faith belief that giving the notice will prevent the employer from obtaining the needed capital or business.

A plant closing or mass layoff may be ordered before the conclusion of the 60-day notice period if caused by business reasons not reasonably foreseeable at the time notice should have been given. No notice is required if the closing or layoff is due to any form of natural disaster. The act specifically mentions the drought of 1988 as an example of such a natural disaster, in addition to floods and earthquakes. Because of these loopholes, employers were not opposed when the act was passed. However, there has been considerable litigation over the law.[7]

Virtually since the first litigation cropped up under the statute, the applicable statute of limitations has been an issue on which reasonable minds have differed. The various federal appeals courts certainly have, making the Supreme Court's pronouncement on the matter a particularly welcome one. In its first opinion construing the 1988 statute, the court unanimously held that civil actions to enforce the WARN Act are subject to the most analogous state statute of limitations.

REGULATION OF PREGNANCY DISABILITY BENEFITS

In 1978 Congress amended Title VII (Sect. 701), which corrected a Supreme Court decision that denied women pregnancy-related disabilities because they were not offered to men.[8] The amendment required the employers to include disability for pregnancy if they had an existing temporary disability sick leave or health insurance benefits program. The only exception is in the case of abortion, which could be excluded unless the life of the mother would be endangered if the fetus were carried to term.

---

[5]In *Alcorn v. Keller Industries, Inc.* 27 F.3d 386 (9th Cir. 1994) short notice of job loss does not violate the act.

[6]Does not apply to job security of employee.

[7]Union can sue under the act.

[8]*General Electric Co.* v. *Gilbert,* 429 U.S. 125 (1976). This case also established a legal principle used in all discrimination cases that in order for an employer's action to be sexually discriminatory it must be gender based.

Where medical complications result from an abortion, it is considered an illness and must be covered. The amendment, however, does not prevent abortion coverage on a voluntary basis. Abortion is very controversial.

The amendment expands the definition of sex discrimination in employment to include all employment practices where there is discriminatory treatment due to pregnancy.[9] The refusal to hire, promote, or transfer because of pregnancy is discriminatory and is considered a violation of the act.

The congressional intent of the amendment is clear. In all employment practices, pregnancy must be treated like any other illness.[10] The disability period begins when the employee medically can no longer perform her duties satisfactorily and ends when she is medically able to return to work. The amendment does not require the employer to grant any more benefits for pregnancy than for any other type of disability, but they must be equal.[11] However, the state by statute may change this.

State Laws Concerning Pregnancy Disability

Most states have passed laws specially prohibiting discrimination based on pregnancy or interpreting their fair employment practice laws, state constitutions, or other laws to prohibit treating pregnancy differently from any other illness.

Because Title VII covers only employers in interstate commerce with 15 or more employees, there is no conflict with the federal law for this group of employers. Where there is dual coverage and the state law conflicts with the federal law, the same rule applies as in all other Title VII provisions; that is, the state statute can be more restrictive but not conflict with federal law or the Constitution. This conflict sometimes comes up in

the abortion section of the pregnancy disability amendment where state laws are different. They can run afoul of the constitutional right to terminate a pregnancy.[12] The practitioner should be familiar with state law before drafting a policy on pregnancy disability.[13]

Generally, state laws on pregnancy disability grant more benefits than the federal law does. In addition to granting benefits for pregnancy disability, some states are giving leave to the father as well as the mother, not only for childbirth but also for adoption. This is commonly called parental leave.[14] Minnesota Statute 181.940–944 as amended is a good example.

Difference between Pregnancy and Other Illnesses

The problem with treating pregnancy like any other illness is that pregnancy is not like any other illness. The employee has notice of the forthcoming event. After the birth there is a natural tendency of the mother to want to be with the baby after she is physically able to return to work. In some cases it could be argued that she may not be mentally able to return to work if forced to leave the baby too soon after birth.

Another problem occurs when the mother is physically able to return to work, but chooses to stay home to nurse the baby. Another difference is that after any other illness the employee usually returns to work; this is less likely in the case of pregnancy leave. Because these differences inherently exist, the courts have had difficulty in

---

[9]*Toupe* v. *May Department Stores,* 20 F.3d 73 (7th Cir. 1994)

[10]*Byrd* v. *Lakeshore Hospital,* 30 F.3d 1380 (8th Cir. 1994).

[11]Pregnancy leave is based on a disability; granting a leave beyond disability (one year) for females and not to males violates Title VII:*Schafer* v. *Board of Education of Pittsburgh School Dist.,* 903 F.2d 243 (3rd Cir. 1990).

[12]*Roe* v. *Wade,* 410 U.S. 113 (1973).

[13]In *California Federal Savings and Loan Assn.* v. *Guerra,* 107 S.Ct. 683 (1987), the Court upheld a statute that requires the employer to grant four weeks of unpaid leave and job protection. Five other states and Puerto Rico have similar statutes. In *Wimberly* v. *Labor and Industrial Relations Commission,* 107 S.Ct. 821 (1987), the Court found no bar of Title VII to a Missouri statute denying unemployment compensation to a worker who leaves work because of pregnancy.

[14]W. E. Even, "Determinants of Parental Leave Policies," *Applied Economics,* 24 (January 1992); R. J. Nobile, "How to Cope with Family Leave Laws," *Personnel,* 68 (July 1991), 11. See also Federal FMLA in this chapter.

interpreting the law according to the congressional intent of the act.

Many practitioners have difficulty in treating pregnancy like any other illness in keeping the job open until the employee returns.[15] There is a tendency to make the policy different for pregnancy because of the large number of female employees who do not return to work after delivery. The employer has no knowledge of this unless the employee advises before the leave that she will not return to work.

At the time of leaving for pregnancy disability, the employee really doesn't know whether she will return. Individuals differ and so do facts. If the baby has "colic," maybe she will return the next week. Often the worker becomes attached to the baby and wants to remain home for a long period of time, even if she is medically able to return. In this case, she may request an unpaid leave of absence. A personnel practitioner should not accept a commitment before the baby is born. Consider the situation uncertain until after the birth and until there is some indication from the employee when she intends to return to work.

Case Law on Pregnancy Disability

The first problem for the courts was the period of illness. It is obvious from the language of the statute that the period of disability cannot be arbitrary as was the practice before the act.[16] The court in one situation stated that a forced-leave pregnancy policy violated the act if leave were required when first learning of the pregnancy. It did not violate the act when it applied to flight attendants in their second and third trimesters of pregnancy. The court reasoned that in the later stages of pregnancy BFOQ is a defense. The court said that evidence showed that in the second stage or trimester (13 to 28 weeks) it is a medical question and after 28 weeks (third stage) there is a substantial growth of passenger safety risks to warrant the policy.

A plan made no distinction between male and female employees, but imposed a $500 deductible on the spouse of male employees for maternity benefits in the absence of complications. The male employees complained to EEOC that they were being discriminated against because their spouses were not covered in the same manner as female employees.[17] The Supreme Court agreed, reasoning that the statute makes it discriminatory to give married male employees a benefit package for their dependents that is less than that provided to married female employees.[18] The Court reasoned that difference between men is not gender-based although men cannot have babies. All sex discrimination cases must be gender-based after this case.

REEMPLOYMENT RIGHTS AFTER MILITARY SERVICE

The Uniformed Services Employment and Reemployment Rights Act of 1994 (USERRA) clarified and expanded the rights of persons returning from uniformed services leave to reemployment and retraining rights, as well as to employee benefits offered by their employers. USERRA completely overhauled the former Veterans' Reemployment Rights Act, which had been in effect for 54 years This statute restricts termination, promotion, probationary periods, payment of wages, leaves of absence, and vacation policies. The purpose of the statute is to maintain the same rights as if the employee were working, although he or she was in the service instead.[19] The exception to this principle is when there is an hours-worked requirement in order to receive a

---

[15]Diane Harris, "You're Pregnant—You're Out," *Working Women,* 9 (August 1992), 48.

[16]Common practice was to force unpaid leave of absence after five months of pregnancy and require return to work within three months after birth of child.

[17]According to U.S. Bureau of Census (1990), women make up about half of the workforce, and 80 to 90 percent of them will bear children while employed.

[18]*Newport News Shipbuilding and Dry Dock Co.* v. *EEOC,* 103 S.Ct. 2622 (1983).

[19]Where the employee was serving in a two-week training camp, it was not necessary to actually work the day before or the day after a holiday in order to receive holiday pay. *Walter Myer* v. *Aluminum Co. of America,* 804 F.2d 821 (3rd Cir. 1986).

benefit or when contribution to a profit-sharing plan is based on work effort.[20]

The courts take the position that the act doesn't require preferential treatment, but the employee should not lose benefits because of military service.[21]

Probationary Period for Returning Veteran

USERRA applies to persons who are honorably discharged from service in the uniformed services. Service in the uniformed services is defined as the performance of duty on a voluntary or involuntary basis in a uniformed service, including active duty, active duty for training, initial active duty for training, inactive duty training, full-time National Guard duty, and a period of absence for an examination to determine the person's fitness for such duty. USERRA prohibits an employer from discriminating against a person in initial employment, reemployment, retention in employment, promotion, or benefit of employment on the basis of the person's service in the uniformed services.

Employment and Reemployment Rights

A person who is absent from a position of employment due to uniformed services leave is entitled to reemployment rights if the person gives advance notice of the service, the cumulative length of all uniformed services leave does not exceed five years, and the person reports to or applies for work with the employer. The specific reporting or application requirements vary depending upon the length of the absence.

An employer is not required to reemploy a person if the employer's changed circumstances have made reemployment impossible or un-

reasonable, employment would impose an undue hardship on the employer, or the position that the person left was temporary and there was no reasonable expectation that employment would continue for a significant period. Factors to review in determining whether reemployment is an "undue hardship" include the difficulty and expense of reemployment in light of the overall financial resources of the employer, the number of employees, the number, type, and location of the employer's facilities, and the composition of the employer's workforce. According to the legislative history of the act, an employer will not be excused from reemployment obligations merely because the employer has hired another employee to fill the position or because no opening exists at the time of reapplication. Thus, an employer may be in a position of terminating a current employee to accommodate a person returning from uniformed services leave.

If the period of uniformed services leave was for less than 91 days, the employer must reemploy the person in the position that person would have been in if employment had not been interrupted by uniformed services leave. If the person is not qualified for that position and cannot be qualified after retraining, the employer must reemploy the person in the position the person held at the commencement of the service. If the period of uniformed services leave was for more than 90 days, the same requirements exist, but the employer may reemploy the person in a position of like seniority, status, and pay rather than in the same position.

General Pay Increases While in the Service

Returning veterans are entitled to certain types of pay increases granted while in the military service. These increases must be of a general type, such as group increases, cost-of-living increases, or longevity increases. Individual merit increases are excluded. A loose compensation policy that does not define the real reason for an increase can be troublesome, especially if the employer denies the increase to the veteran because it was a merit increase and in fact it was a cost-of-living increase. As mentioned in chapter 5, all too often

---

[20]In *Raypole* v. *Chemi-trol Chemical Co.,* 754 F.2d 169 (6th Cir. 1985), the court held a contribution to profit sharing was not required while an employee was in service, because the employee made no work contribution.

[21]Military service is defined as any period of active service under the act: *Moe* v. *Eastern Airlines,* 246 F.2d 215 (5th Cir. 1957). The U.S. Court of Veterans Appeal takes the position that they can issue writs to lower courts to enforce the act.

the reason given for a wage increase is merit but everybody is granted one, without any reference to meritorious performance. Such an increase would not come under the exclusion in the *Hatton* case. One thing is certain under USERRA—the employee has more rights.

Accommodation for Reserve Duty

The USERRA requires that veterans must be given a leave of absence when going into military service. This also applies when the reservist is called into active service, the annual two- or four-week training period, or active duty for an emergency. All such leaves of absence are unpaid unless the employer's policy states otherwise. But time off for reserve duty weekly training is treated a little differently.

One problem an employer sometimes faces is a reservist's request for an extended leave of absence (6 to 12 months) to enroll in an advanced school for additional training necessary to be promoted as a reservist. Because the leave for an extended period puts the employer at an inconvenience and the enrollment is voluntary, the normal interpretation is that the act does not require the employer to grant the leave. Leave of absence for military service must be for a reasonable period of time. In *Gulf States Paper Corp.* v. *Ingram,* 811 F.2d 1464 (11th Cir. 1987), the court said that a one-year leave for a reservist to attend a practical nursing training course was not an unreasonable burden for the employer. A replacement could be easily obtained. In *King* v. *Vincent's Hospital,* 112 S.Ct. 570 (1991), the Court held that leave of absence under the act has no limits. The appellate court said three years was unreasonable, but the Supreme Court reversed. We cannot be sure what is unreasonable.

EFFECT OF STATUTES ON UNPAID LEAVE OF ABSENCE POLICY

In granting unpaid leaves of absence, most employers determine cases individually. The decision depends on the reason for the leave and on whether an employee is needed or can be replaced during the leave of absence period. In many cases it depends on the whims of the supervisor. Often one department within a facility would have a different rule from another. Most labor agreements provide for granting an unpaid leave for specific reasons such as medical or extended leave for union business. Beyond these specific reasons there is broad language in the labor agreement, which usually leaves it up to the employer when to grant an unpaid leave of absence, subject to challenge by the union.

With the requirements of the various anti-discrimination statutes that all employees should be treated alike, the unilateral right to grant unpaid leaves of absence is rapidly diminishing.

For example, where an employee wants a leave to see a dying mother in Sweden, a leave of absence is granted by extending the vacation period. Another employee wants to see a dying mother in California; another employee has a 22nd cousin who is dying in Florida (the only relative known); another wants to go to a religious summer camp for four months; another wants to work for passage of the Equal Rights Amendment for one year or the right-to-work law for six months. If the employer does not have some policy that is uniformly applied to all these situations, there is exposure to a violation of some statute and retaliation charges.

The court will not question the conditions under which a leave is granted but will question whether the determination of who should be allowed a leave was discriminatory. Sexual harassment and religious discrimination are retaliation charges that are often alleged by a member of the protected class and often have to be defended. The employer, in view of exposure to litigation, should review the leave of absence policy and if needed set a few broad guidelines for supervisors. Decisions to grant leaves of absence should not be left entirely to the whims of the supervisor. The granting should be uniformly applied as much as possible throughout the organization. The court usually holds for the veteran.

RESTRICTIONS ON VACATION POLICY

Granting Vacation Pay in Lieu of Time Off

In the beginning, when the employer granted vacation benefits, it was considered time off with pay. The purpose of granting vacations was to grant a period of relaxation from day-to-day activities. When returning to work the employee would be a better employee. As vacations became longer, employers began to make vacation payments in lieu of time off for two reasons. First, a replacement for a long period of time was difficult to train and costly in quality and quantity of work performed by the replacement. Second, some employees could not afford a four-week vacation trip but could afford two weeks. The employer would give four weeks' vacation pay, and the employee would take a two-week trip and work the other two weeks. Everybody was happy.

The granting of vacation pay in lieu of time off was extended to where an employee terminated and was paid unused vacation time if certain conditions were met at the time of termination. This caused the thinking that vacation benefits were not necessarily time off but wages for nonworking time.[22]

Enforcement of Vacation Pay as Wages

Most states have nonpayment wage statutes that permit a state agency to be used for collection of wages. Some of the states have held that because payment is made in lieu of time off, vacation benefits are wages and therefore take jurisdiction over payment of vacation benefits.[23]

In one situation, an employee was terminated due to loss of customers. She demanded her vacation pay and sued her former employer for it.

One year later the employer paid the vacation pay, but not her accumulated attorney's fees. The court ruled that vacation pay is wages and attorney's fees are due under the Nonwage Payment Statute even though the statute makes no mention of the vacation pay or attorney fees.[24]

Where employees went on strike, the NLRB held that they were entitled to vacation pay accrued before the strike because the employer paid one employee vacation pay in lieu of vacation time off.[25]

New Mexico is one of the states that consider vacation benefits wages. (California, Iowa, Montana, Connecticut, and Kansas as well as others concur.) An employee in a New Mexico bank in April told the employer that she would take her vacation in September. She quit in July and requested vacation pay in lieu of her scheduled vacation. The New Mexico State Labor Commission agreed with her. The court disagreed; the employer's vacation policy said that vacations must be actually taken and also stated that no compensation could be paid in lieu of vacation.[26] If the Deming Bank had a history of paying compensation in lieu of vacation time off and did not have an expressed policy prohibiting it, the result might have been different.

The practice of granting vacation pay in lieu of time off is an employee relations decision. The employer should be aware that it can be considered wages. Unless the policy is properly written, some courts call it wages. If wages, the employer loses discretion in how and when it is paid.[27]

One technique to avoid having vacation pay interpreted as wages is to make a distinction

---

[22]Vacation pay as wages is being claimed as back pay in discrimination cases. Some states call vacation pay wages for purposes of meeting the wage requirement for unemployment compensation benefits. In *Gray* v. *Empire Gas Co.,* 679 P.2d 610 (Colo. App. 1984), the court called a discretionary bonus wages.

[23]ERISA does not preempt a state nonpayment wage statute when applied to vacation benefits: *Massachusetts* v. *Morash,* 109 S.Ct. 1668 (1989).

[24]*Becnel* v. *Answer Inc., et al.,* 428 So.2d 539 (La. App. 1983).

[25]*Thorwin Mfg. Co.,* 243 NLRB No. 118 (1979).

[26]*New Mexico State Labor and Industrial Commission* v. *Deming National Bank,* 634 F.2d 695 (N.M. 1981).

[27]It is costly practice because vacation for many office job categories is not a cost item. The employee works to get caught up before leaving on vacation and works twice as hard when returning as no replacement is made. If pay is given, it is a straight-cost item.

between the last day worked and termination date. If vacation pay is granted upon termination, the period between the last day worked and termination date is vacation time off.[28]

The California court takes the position that an employee has a "vested right to vacation pay which accrues from the time of hire." The company had the usual requirement of earning vacation time during the previous year; however, the employee had to work one full year before vacation time was due. The employee was terminated after six months, into the vacation period. The court in a unanimous decision held the rule invalid and granted a prorated vacation plus 30 paid working days if denial of vacation pay was found to be willful.[29]

The *Suastez* decision was challenged on the basis that the Employment Retirement Income Security Act (ERISA) preempted the state nonpayment wage statute. This challenge failed.[30] The U.S. Department of Labor takes the position that ERISA does not preempt vacation plans that are paid out of general funds.[31]

Effect of "Use It or Lose It" Policy

Vacation policies that give vacation pay in lieu of time off are in effect admitting that vacation pay is wages. The right of the employee to recover wages is often defined by a state statute that removes from the employer the right to determine under what conditions vacation benefits will be paid. To avoid vacation time being considered as wages, the employer can have a policy of "use it or lose it" and then make a distinction between last day worked and termination date. Through such a

policy the employer can pay for unused vacation time at termination and still not have vacation time count as wages. The cost of the continuation of an employee on the payroll for a short period of time (usually 30 days), in which health insurance benefits and some pension credits are continued, is minimal compared to the exposure of paying vacation pay in lieu of time off.

The California court takes a different view in both the *Suastez* and *Boothby* cases. In Boothby the appellate court made it clear that a use-it-or-lose-it policy is a violation of the state statute. Vacation time vests as the employee works. But the court did a little double-talk and said that the employer could limit the amount of vested vacation time that is unused. This would seem to imply that the employer has a limited right to determine when to grant or pay for vested vacation time.

REGULATION OF HEALTH CARE BENEFITS AND PENSIONS

Pensions and health plans are regulated by state and federal statute.[32] Compliance with these statutes is complicated and usually requires professional assistance.[33] No statute requires the employer to grant employee benefits. Once granted, they restrict the employer and grant the employee additional enforcement rights that were not present before the benefits were granted.[34]

Sex Differences in Benefits

A preceding section considered sex discrimination in pregnancy disability plans, but in other benefit plans sex differences may also occur. For example, sex differences appear in pension plans because of greater life expectancy of women. Benefits are greater for females for the

---

[28]In *Teamsters Local No. 688* v. *John Meir,* 718 F.2d 286 (8th Cir. 1983), the court called vacation benefits wages but did not require payment to strikers because the company had prorated benefits to terminees from the last day worked.

[29]*Suastez* v. *Plastic Press-up Co.,* 647 P.2d 122 (Cal. Sup.Ct. 1982); also *Boothby* v. *Atlas Mechanical, Inc.,* 8 Cal. Rptr. 600 (Prelim.) 1992 Cal. App. LEXIS 726 (Cal. 3rd Dist. 1992).

[30]*California Hospital Assn.* v. *Henning,* 770 F.2d 856 (9th Cir. 1985).

[31]This received judicial approval in *Massachusetts* v. *Morash,* 109 S.Ct. 1668 (1989).

[32]See J. Castagnera and D. Littell, *Federal Regulation of Employee Benefits* (New York: John Wiley & Sons, 1991).

[33]The legal principles developed when there is a collective bargaining agreement often control benefits litigation. See C. Nelson, "Providing Welfare Benefits and Enforcing Claims for Benefits in Collective Bargaining Context," *Benefits Law Journal,* 1, no. 5 (Autumn 1988).

same cost, or the cost of the plans are more than for males, if the same benefit level is to be maintained. Where the employer required women to make greater contributions than men to the pension fund in order to receive an equal benefit on retirement, the Supreme Court held that this policy violated Title VII.[35] The Court stated that the basic policy of Title VII is "fairness to individuals rather than fairness to classes." Although women as a class may live longer than men, some do not; for those individuals who do not, the policy would be discriminatory according to the Court.

In a related situation, where the employer's plan allowed equal contributions but provided lesser benefits (based on greater life expectancy), the Court reached the same result as in the *City of Los Angeles* case. In subsequent discrimination cases the Supreme Court has been consistent in considering the effect on individuals rather than a class or group of employees.[36] The position of the Court was reaffirmed when they had to decide whether an annuity plan that was voluntary violated Title VII. The amount of contributions was optional with the employee. The plan had three options (lump-sum, periodic payments for a fixed period, or an insured annuity plan).[37] The women received greater annuity payments than the men for the same amount of contributions; however, if the other two options were selected the pay-out would be the same. The annuity option had a greater payment for women than men because of the use of sex-segregated actuarial tables. The Court held this violated Title VII. The effect of the decision is that the use of sex-segregated actuarial tables is illegal regardless of the type of plan.

Older Workers Benefit Protection Act (OWBPA) of 1990

Title I of the Older Workers Benefit Protection Act prohibits discrimination against older workers in employee benefit plans.[38] It amends ADEA and reverses *Public Employees Retirement System of Ohio* v. *Betts*, 109 S.Ct. 2854 (1989).

The OWBPA also regulates voluntary early retirement practices. Severance pay cannot be denied because the employee is eligible for retirement benefits. However, there can be an offset in limited situations if the offset is not related to the employee's age. (An example would be a plant shutdown.)

Employers may provide lesser benefits to older workers than to younger workers if the following conditions are met:

1. The benefit reduction is essential to observe the terms of a bona fide employee benefit plan.
2. The benefit plan or any provision cannot be a subterfuge to evade the purposes of the ADEA.

ERISA does not prevent an older job applicant from waiving the right to participate in a pension plan as long as it is voluntary and knowingly made.[39] It would be wise to follow OWBPA requirements to make sure it is voluntary.[40]

Requirement of Alternative Health Care Plan (HMO)

The Health Maintenance Organization Act of 1976, as amended, requires employers to include in any health plan offered to its employees the

---

[34]Most interests in benefit plans (including pensions) are exempted by ERISA from being considered assets in a bankruptcy estate: *Patterson* v. *Shumate*, 1992 U.S. LEXIS 3546 (1992).

[35]*City of Los Angeles* v. *Manhart*, 435 U.S. 702 (1978).

[36]In *Connecticut* v. *Teal*, 102 S.Ct. 2525 (1982), they said that discrimination is an individual matter and that the fact that other employees were not discriminated against is irrelevant if the plaintiff is discriminated against.

[37]*Arizona Governing Committee for Tax Deferred Annuity and Deferred Compensation Plans, Etc., et al.,* v. *Nathalie Norris, Etc.,* 103 S.Ct. 3492 (1983).

---

[38]Because in most organizations the executives of an advanced age are the decision makers, it is unlikely that the older worker will be treated differently on benefits.

[39]*Laniok* v. *Advisory Committee of Brainerd Mfg. Co. Pension Plan*, 935 F.2d 1360 (2nd Cir. 1991).

[40]A doctor was examining a patient: "For a 55-year-old you are in fine shape. How old was your father when he died?" "Who said he was dead?" "Then how old was your grandfather when he died?" "Who said he was dead?" "You mean your grandfather is still living?" "He sure is and is getting married next week." "At his age why would he want to get married?" "Who said he wanted to?"

option of membership in a qualified health maintenance organization (HMO). An employer that refuses or fails to comply with the act may be subjected to a civil penalty of up to $10,000 for an initial violation and a like amount for each additional month of noncompliance.

It covers all employers who have 25 employees or more. Once the employer is contacted by a qualified HMO, the employer must offer the option either to the union that can speak for the employees or to individual employees. The HMO option cannot increase the employer's cost. The employee must be willing to make up the difference if the cost is higher than the company plan. The plan is very popular.

The HMO has given the personnel practitioner little or no problems except occasionally in the communication area. Often when the employer attempts to communicate, there is a tendency to favor either its plan or the HMO. For this reason it is advisable to let the HMO organization communicate its own plan, and the employer-sponsored plan be communicated by the insurance carrier or, if self-insured, by someone other than the one responsible for administration of the plan. Many states have their own HMO laws; the state regulations and laws must be reviewed when an HMO problem occurs to determine whether state or federal law applies.

Consolidated Omnibus Budget Reconciliation Act (COBRA)

COBRA (29 U.S.C. Sect. 601–608 of ERISA)[41] provides for continued health care coverage to terminated and qualified beneficiaries. The benefits must be identical to those benefits offered to employees who have not been laid off or terminated.The purpose of the act is to prevent immediate termination of employer-sponsored group health insurance.[42]

It is an amendment to ERISA and Section 4980 of the Internal Revenue Code of 1986. It is enforced by disqualifying a violator for tax deductions of health care costs. The act applies to all employers with 20 or more employees who have group health care plans.[43]

Certain events (called qualifying events) require continued coverage if the employee or his or her dependents or divorced spouse elects to be covered with a 60-day period of the occurrence of a disqualifying event. The employer should cover if the employee has a claim in a 60-day period but before electing coverage.[44]

When giving notice that the plan has been triggered, it is best to include a copy of the plan summary and the 60-day limitation for deciding to be covered. In *Branch* v. *G. Bernd Co., et al.*, 955 F.2d. 574 (11th Cir. 1992), the employee was not instructed to fill out the election form. The court said that the 60-day limitation was a floor. The employee gets longer to decide under certain facts. In this situation the employee was not put on notice that the law required a decision in 60 days. Further, the employee did not receive a good summary and description of the plan.[45]

The plan administrator and employer is liable for an improper notice to the employee.[46] For this reason the continuation notices given out when the employee is terminated should be carefully written. The employee charged with counseling on COBRA rights should receive adequate training on COBRA laws.[47]

---

[41]A rule change was made in 1988, 1989 and 1990.

[42]The act does not cover continuation of life insurance, but a few state statutes do.

[43]See H. Morgan, "Who Is an Employee and When Does It Matter?" 10th Annual Employee Benefits and Executive Compensation Institute (Minnesota State Bar Assoc., 1987); see also *Nationwide Mutual Ins. Co.* v. *Darden*, 112 S.Ct. 1344 (1992).

[44]*Meadows* v. *Cagle's*, 954 F.2d 686 (11th Cir. 1992). Also *Truschler* v. *Pacific Holding Co.*, 778 F.Supp 97 D.R.C. 1991.

[45]*Meadows* v. *Cagle's*, 954 F.2d 686 (11th Cir. 1992).

[46]*Bruno* v. *United Steelworkers of America*, 784 F.Supp. 1286 (D. Ohio 1992); *Truesdale* v. *Pacific Holding Co., Hays Adam Div.*, 778 F.Supp. 77 (D.C. of D.C. 1991).

[47]See *National Companies Health Benefit Plan* v. *St. Joseph's Hospital*, 929 F.2d 1558 (11th Cir. 1991).

Dependent children who no longer qualify because of age under the employer's plan must also be offered coverage.[48]

A qualifying event is termination (unless for misconduct) or reduction of the employee's hours so there is no coverage under the employer's plan.[49] In the case of the employee, coverage must be continued for 18 months; for all others who qualify it must be continued from 29 to 36 months (P.L. 101–239).

Coverage can be terminated (1) when the employee or dependents stop paying the premiums (which can be as high as 102 percent of the cost; 150 percent if disabled),[50] (2) the employer ceases to provide a group plan to all active employees, (3) a dependent gets married to a person who is covered by another plan, or (4) the employee or dependents are covered under another group plan, including Medicare.[51] Under the Revenue Reconciliation amendment of 1989, if the beneficiary is covered under another group plan that has an exclusion for a preexisting condition, continuation under the old plan is not terminated provided that the beneficiary elected to be covered and pay for the continuation coverage [ERISA, Sect. 602(D)(i); see also IRC Sect. 4980B (f)(2)(B)(iv)1].

The plan administrator can be personally liable up to $100 per day from date of failure to give notice for continued coverage (or any other relief that the court may deem proper). This is an unusual provision because under the common law persons acting for the corporation are not normally held personally liable.

COBRA permits state plans (over half of the states have similar plans) to be more strict; if not as strict they are preempted by COBRA. The Department of Labor, the Internal Revenue Service, and the Department of Health and Human Services are authorized to issue interpretive regulations. The Department of Labor has issued Technical Release No. 86–2, which is a guideline and has a model statement to notify employees of continued coverage.

Gross Misconduct

Gross misconduct is an exception to a COBRA qualified event. Neither IRC Section 4980(B)(f)(3)(B) or Treasury Regulation Section 1.162–26 Q7A 18(b) gives any definition of gross misconduct. Because it is unclear what Congress meant by gross misconduct, the courts usually will hold in favor of the employee.[52] Until more case law and regulatory interpretation is developed, the employer should define and communicate gross misconduct in a policy statement or handbook.[53]

Health Care Insurance for Retirees

More than 60 percent of all firms with more than 100 employees offer retiree health care coverage of some sort, even after 65. The issue is whether management has a right to cut benefits in the same manner as for active employees. Where this has been attempted, the courts have held that once an employee satisfied the requirements for retirement his or her benefits are vested; however, it depends upon language of the plan.[54] The courts have extended the principle to a situation where the employer was bankrupt. The court held that the rights of the retirees were vested and coverage must be continued; however, if the plant reserves the right to change or rescind, the employer may do so in some states.[55]

---

[48]If the employee moves out of the service area of the employer's insurance, as long as coverage is offered, the COBRA obligation is satisfied: *Coble* v. *Bonita House, Inc.,* 789 F.Supp 320 (N.D. Cal. 1992).

[49]A strike is considered a qualifying event.

[50]ERISA preempts state law as to the employee requirement to pay 102 percent of premium; the employer cannot require a higher premium.

[51]If employer accepts premium and coverage was offered, this cannot be changed although not eligible under COBRA: *National Companies Health Benefit Plan* v. *St. Joseph's Hospital of Atlanta,* 929 F.2d 1558 (11th Cir. 1991).

---

[52]*Paris* v. *F. Korbel & Bros.,* 751 F.Supp. 834 (N.D. Cal. 1990).

[53]An example of a misconduct statement is given in chapter 11.

[54]See *Hoefel* v. *Atlas Tack Corp.,* 581 F.2d 1 (1st Cir. 1978); *Autoworkers* v. *Yard-Man, Inc.,* 716 F.2d 1476 (6th Cir. 1983). However, the Medicare Catastrophic Coverage Act (PL 100–360) (1988) may allow employers to change their plans. This problem is again in the courts.

[55]*Patterson* v. *Shumate,* 1992 U.S. LEXIS 3546 (1992).

Cost containment health care under court decisions must begin with active employees, although this may be inharmonious with good employee relations. It appears it is too late after they retire. However, the employer may limit retirees to be the same as active employees if the plan is properly worded.

Employee Retirement Income Security Act (ERISA)

The Employee Retirement Income Security Act of 1974 (29 USC 1001 et seq.; ERISA) as amended is a difficult statute to understand, and even more difficult to stay in compliance with. If the employer wants assurance that benefit plans are in compliance with ERISA, it is necessary either to seek outside professional advice or to employ a full-time specialist. Anything less results in unnecessary risks. The personnel practitioner should have a general knowledge of the law and its regulations, but time can be better spent in other problems than to attempt to become an expert on ERISA.[56] For these reasons this section only gives an overview of the law and leaves the details to ERISA specialists.[57]

Although the administration of ERISA is by the Department of Labor, the compliance to ERISA is through the Internal Revenue Service (IRS). All plans must be qualified plans in order to receive tax credits when contributions are made to the trust funds or payment of premiums if an insured plan. If the plan does not meet the requirements of IRS, it is not a qualified plan and does not receive the tax deductions. Not many other enforcement procedures are necessary.

ERISA is a comprehensive statute that regulates virtually all aspects of private sector employee benefit plans and their administration.[58]

It is essential for the personnel practitioner to have some knowledge of the reporting and disclosure obligations as well as a limited number of other rules.[59]

Purposes of ERISA

ERISA was passed by Congress to solve the social problems created by private pension plans and other benefit plans.[60] Congress, through ERISA, attempted to correct these problems by the following provisions:

1. Requiring a minimum level of funding for past service credits to better protect benefits if the company went out of business.
2. Requiring termination insurance so that if a company went out of business, the pension credits already earned would be protected until retirement. The goverment insurance was almost broke.

Problem Areas under ERISA

ERISA regulates not only pension plans but also all types of benefit plans, such as all types of health care benefits, death benefits, unemployment insurance benefits, holiday and vacation pay, apprenticeship or other training programs, daycare centers, scholarship funds, prepaid legal services, and certain types of severance pay plans.[61] Communication of the benefit plan is a problem for the practitioner. Sections 1002(a) and (b) and 1024(b)(1) of ERISA require that participants be furnished with a clear, timely explanation of disqualifications, ineligibility, denial, or loss of benefits.[62] Where the administrator failed to mail an amendment to the pension

---

[56]*Anderson* v. *Operative Plasters' Cement Masons Local #12 Pension Welfare Plans,* 91 F.2d 353 (7th Cir. 1993).

[57]An exposure can be created when employees argue that ERISA allows jury trial and punitive damages: *Lytle* v. *Household Mfg., Inc.,* 494 U.S. 545 (1990); *Petrilli* v. *Drechsel,* 910 F.2d 1441 @ 1449 (7th Cir. 1990).

[58]For a guide on ERISA, see "What You Should Know about the Pension and Welfare Law" (Washington, DC: U.S. Department of Labor, 1978); also *Confer* v. *Custom Engineering Co.,* 952 F.2d 41 (3rd Cir. 1991).

[59]"What ERISA Really Means," *Futures,* 21 (April 1992), 57; L. Perham, "Circle the Wagons, Here Comes DOL's Crackdown," *Pension World,* 26 (July 1990), 8.

[60]Can waive participation in pension plan if voluntary and does not violate ADEA: *Lanick* v. *Advisory Committee of Brainard Mfg. Co. Pension Plan,* 935 F.2d 1360 (2nd Cir. 1991).

[61]*Ingersoll-Rand Co.* v. *McClendon,* 111 S.Ct. 478 (1990).

[62]"Use of a Bulletin Board to Announce a Plan Reduction Is an Improper Notice," *Employee Benefit Plan Review,* 44 (April 1990), 98–99. Also *Farr* v. *US West Communications,* 58 F.3d 1361 (9th Circ. 1995).

participants, but stated the information was in the union hiring hall, the court said this was a violation of Sections 1022 and 1024 of the act. Even if the distribution had been adequate, the content of the notice was insufficient because it failed to explain how the amendment related to other provisions of the plan.[63] Most employers do not know the provisions for ERISA.

ERISA and Employee Rights

Under Section 510 it is a violation to discriminate against any participant or beneficiary for exercising any right for a benefit that is given under any benefit plan (a retaliation provision).[64] This would be extended to rights provided for under the plan but not yet earned.[65] ERISA in effect guarantees that no employee will be terminated where the purpose of the discharge is interference with any benefit right. In *Fleming* v. *Ayers & Associates,* 948 F.2d 993 (6th Cir. 1991), the court found that the employer, in order to avoid paying for future medical costs of the employee's sick child, violated Section 510 even though the discharge was between her date of hire and first day of work. In order to have any rights under Section 510 of ERISA the plaintiff must in fact be a participant or a beneficiary.[66]

If the employee is denied profit sharing and pension service credits after age 65, this is a violation of ADEA and ERISA.[67] This would be especially true where it is shown that such denial was to discourage working after 65.

Section 502 of 29 USC Section 1132 (a)(3) permits a private right of action to redress violations or enforce the terms of the plan or statute.[68] When an employer is considering the discharge of an employee with 9 years and 11 months of employment and that employee would be vested in pension rights in 1 month, a good and valid reason should be established before the termination action is taken. This will prevent a pretext from being alleged. The enforcement would be by the Department of Labor if the employee files a complaint.

Preemption over State Laws

The regulation of benefit plans raises the question of whether state benefit plans are preempted by ERISA.[69] The Supreme Court on several occasions has considered the issue. It has held that if state law prohibits reduction of pension benefits while workers' compensation is being paid such a law is invalid. In a leading case a state law required the employer to pay disability benefits to all employees. This was contested by employers who argued that the law was unenforceable because ERISA preempted the state law. The Court held that ERISA preempts state laws if they prohibit practices that are lawful under ERISA.[70] The disability plan in question was not prohibited by ERISA and therefore was enforceable.

The issue of whether ERISA preempts other state laws is in almost continual litigation.[71] In *Metropolitan Life Insurance* v. *Commonwealth of Massachusetts,* 105 S.Ct. 2890 (1985), the Court held that where state laws required mandated health care benefits they are not preempted by ERISA because they are insurance regulations. ERISA does not preempt state-regulated severance pay plans. The preemption issue was pretty well

---

[63]*Chambless* v. *Master, Mates & Pilots Pension Plan,* 772 F.2d 1032 (2nd Cir. 1985), cert. denied (1986).

[64]*McLendon* v. *Continental Can Co.,* 908 F.2d 1171 (3rd Cir. 1990); also *Ingersoll Rand Co.* v. *McClendon,* 111 S. Ct. 4780 (1990), Court said state plan is preempted by ERISA.

[65]*Conkwright* v. *Westinghouse Electric Co.,* 933 F.2d 231 (4th Cir. 1991).

[66]*McKinnon* v. *Blue Cross & Blue Shield of Alabama,* 935 F.2d 1187 (11th Cir. 1991).

[67]*AARP* v. *Farmers Group, Inc.,* 943 F.2d 996 (9th Cir. 1991), cert. denied (1992).

[68]*Gridley* v. *Cleveland Pneumatic Co.,* 924 F.2d 1310 (3rd Cir. 1991).

[69]Section 514(a) of ERISA states that ERISA shall supersede "any and all state laws insofar as they may now or hereafter relate to any employee benefit plan." The purpose of this section was to ensure employers that they would not face conflicting or inconsistent state and local regulation of employee benefit plans.

[70]*Shaw* v. *Delta Airlines, Inc.,* 103 S.Ct. 2890 (1983).

[71]*FMC Corp.* v. *Holliday,* 111 S.Ct. 403 (1990); *Metropolitan Life Insurance* v. *Taylor,* 481 U.S. 58 (1987); *Alday* v. *Container Corp. of America,* 906 F.2d 660 (11th Cir. 1990), to name a few.

settled by *Pilot Life Insurance Co.* v. *Dedeaux,* 481 U.S. 41 (1987).

EFFECTIVE USE OF EMPLOYMENT AGREEMENTS

An employment agreement is any agreement, whether written or oral, between an employer and an employee concerning the conditions of employment. Its purpose is to specifically state certain rights and obligations of the employer and employee, as opposed to unwritten general employment terms.

This chapter considers only the written agreement; the oral agreement has legal problems of proof that would be inappropriate to consider here. The written employment agreement sets out selected specific conditions of employment. These conditions do not eliminate all other conditions normally granted to employees who do not have an agreement.

Many practitioners use model contracts or related materials as a policy or as a contract that will apply in their operations. However, they still are subject to review.

Need for Employment Agreements

Employers often fail to consider the employment agreement as a useful tool in administering a personnel policy. Many practitioners have the misconception that employment agreements are suited only to determine the duration of employment or job duties. In reality employment agreements are practical for any situation where the employer wants to set out certain conditions for one or more employees apart from other employees.

Suppose that the employer wants to hire a qualified manager and one of the demands of the applicant (often it is more a demand of his family) is that the four-week vacation granted by the former employer be continued. Because the employer's vacation policy is that four weeks' vacation is not granted until after 12 years of service, the policy must be violated or the applicant not hired. An employment agreement could grant the four weeks as an exception to the vacation program. Other benefits would come under the regular benefit plan. Sometimes applicants don't want to lose higher life insurance benefits when changing jobs. An exception can be made by purchasing an insurance policy different from what other employees have. Some practitioners feel that agreements of this type may set a precedent that makes it difficult to deny others the same benefit. This has not been the author's experience, nor can the author find any case law that supports this feeling.

Use of Employment Agreements

An employment agreement should not be used unless it changes the working conditions for the employee from what other employees have without an agreement. Here are some situations where employment agreements should be considered:

1. Where it is necessary to define specially the rights, responsibilities, and terms of employment, including duration of those special conditions.
2. To deter acts of unfair competition while employed or after being terminated (very common).
3. Where job content exposes the employee to trade secrets or to patentable inventions.
4. To define duration of employment because of the nature of the job (athletic coaches and players, executives hired away from competitor, and so on).
5. Where employees are on commission and salary draws or have selling expenses as part of their commission (a must for this type of job).
6. To deal with routine matters that are often overlooked at the time of termination, such as travel advances and return of keys, records, and other company property.

Provisions in a Typical Employment Agreement

Usual clauses in an employment agreement are terms of employment, which state the beginning and end of the agreement, but not necessarily the end of the employment relationship. A general outline of the job duties should not be too specific. Compensation, which may include special benefits, secret information restrictions and no-compete restrictions, after termination are examples of this type of clause. Restrictive covenants must be reasonable.

Confidentiality and Covenants Not to Compete

Although the employee owes a certain loyalty to the employer not to perform any acts that will adversely affect the business, it is essential that where the job content creates unusual exposure to trade secrets, the employee is contractually bound not to expose the trade secrets. Enforcement of this provision is usually against the employee and the person or corporation to whom the trade secret is revealed.[72]

Some employment agreements have covenants not to compete with the employer for a certain period after termination. These covenants are generally enforceable.[73]

In suits concerning the validity of noncompetition covenants, courts generally consider four factors: (1) Is the restriction reasonably necessary for the protection of the employer's business? (2) Does the employee have certain rights to the trade secrets? (3) Is it prejudicial to the public interest? (4) Is the employee being denied the right to make a living?[74]

Courts have refused to enforce covenants that are overly broad or unnecessary to protect the employer's legitimate interests. In *National Settlement Associates* v. *Creel*, 349 S.E.2d 177 (Ga. 1986), the court found that a provision that prohibited a former employee from being

employed "in any capacity" was overly broad.[75]

The noncompetition covenant would be valid if it prohibited the employee from using skills acquired while employed, provided they were used within the time and territorial limits of the agreement.

Courts have held that restrictions must be reasonable in duration and geographic scope. Generally a noncompete geographic area of 50 to 100 miles from the employer's base of operation is considered reasonable. Although the courts are split on whether the time and space limitations must be defined, it is advisable to define them to avoid the issue. A three-year limitation is usually enforceable unless special conditions exist.[76]

Customers and customer lists are considered trade secrets or proprietary information sufficient to support enforcement of a restrictive covenant.[77]

Conflict-of-Interest Clauses

Some employee agreements have special provisions that do not exist in a normal employee-employer relationship. These special provisions would not be enforceable in the absence of a formal contract. One example of a special provision is a conflict-of-interest clause. This type of clause prevents the employee from engaging in any activity that would interfere with decision making or in making a judgment in performing duties on behalf of his or her employer.

Employers are often concerned about an employee who has two jobs, which interferes with job duties and performance. This is commonly called "moonlighting." If there is an overall corporate policy against moonlighting that applies to all employees, it is not necessary to put the restriction on moonlighting in an employment agreement. An exception would be against certain individuals.

---

[72]Whitmore, "A Statistical Analysis of Noncompete Clauses in Employment Contracts," *Journal of Corporation Law,* 15, no. 483 (Spring 1990); McKinney, "Noncompetition Clauses in Executive Employment and Severance Agreements," *Employee Relations Law Journal,* 16, no. 29 (Summer 1990).

[73]John W. Bowers, Stacey L. Katz and Charles W. Backs. "Covenants not to compete: their use and enforcement in Indiana." *Valparaiso University Law Review,* 31 (1996), 65.

[74]*Lamp* v. *American Prosthetics, Inc.,* 379 N.W.2d 909 (Iowa 1986).

[75]See also *Baxter International, Inc.* v. *Morris,* 976 F.2d 1189 (10th Cir. 1992).

[76]*Mathieu* v. *Old Town Flower Shops, Inc.,* 585 So.2d 1160 (Fla. 4th DCA 1991). Five years would be difficult to defend.

[77]See E. M. Schulman, "Economic Analysis of Employee Noncompetition Agreements," *Denver University Law Review,* 69 (1992), 97.

Enforcement of Employment Agreements

Employment agreements are generally enforceable in the courts if they meet the three basic requirements of a contract: (1) offer, (2) acceptance, and (3) consideration. The offer is the conditions of employment set out by the employer. Acceptance is the employee agreeing to those conditions. Continued employment has been stated by the courts to be an adequate consideration.[78] The offer and acceptance requirement of a legally binding contract is self-serving when the applicant starts work or continues to work after an agreement is executed.[79]

Most employees will accept the obligations of the agreement if clearly defined and if the agreement is entered under amiable conditions. Accordingly, enforcement during the term of employment is seldom a problem.

The starting of a new business by a manager on the employer's time and with the employer's records and equipment is not uncommon. Without an employment agreement the employer has few remedies to stop it unless disloyalty can be shown.[80]

Some jurisdictions are reluctant to enforce covenants not to compete, but the agreement not to disclose trade secrets is almost always enforceable; therefore, both clauses should be in an employment agreement.

Some employers do not like to use employment agreements because they feel that this limits their right to discharge for poor performance or some other legitimate reason. An employment agreement does not protect a poor performance or violation of company policies but usually

describes what is expected of the employee. Where a salesperson worked harder than anyone else but did not sell anything, the court said that working hard is not enough and discharge for ineffective performance was held not to be a breach of the employment agreement.[81]

Arbitration of Employment Agreements

Some employment agreements provide for final and binding arbitration when there is a dispute over their terms. If arbitration is not specifically provided for in an agreement, the parties may still arbitrate the dispute by entering a mutual agreement to do so when the dispute occurs. In this situation the parties must decide whether arbitration is desirable. If the dispute is arbitrated, it does not have the legal exposure as in a judicial review; arbitration awards are seldom appealable.

One consideration when determining whether a disputed employment agreement should be arbitrated is that some courts have awarded punitive damages, which are rarely awarded in arbitration awards.

Arbitration serves a purpose in disputes involving small amounts of monetary damages. When large sums are involved, it is better to have the matter decided under legal procedures. An acceptable clause is one that limits arbitration to small claims such as $25,000, with court determination thereafter.

Alternative Dispute Resolution

One alternative to full-scale litigation or arbitration is Alternative Dispute Resolution (ADR). This is a method used to resolve disputes between the parties without final and binding arbitration or going to court. The parties must agree to enter into ADR. They can use mediation, fact-finding, arbitration, minitrial, and so on,[82] or a combination of processes to resolve the dispute.

The process often results in narrowing the issues where no settlement is reached. It allows a

[73]John W. Bowers, Stacey L. Katz and Charles W. Backs. "Covenants not to compete: their use and enforcement in Indiana." *Valparaiso University Law Review*, 31 (1996), 65.

[74]*Lamp* v. *American Prosthetics, Inc.*, 379 N.W.2d 909 (Iowa 1986).

[75]See also *Baxter International, Inc.* v. *Morris*, 976 F.2d 1189 (10th Cir. 1992).

[76]*Mathieu* v. *Old Town Flower Shops, Inc.*, 585 So.2d 1160 (Fla. 4th DCA 1991). Five years would be difficult to defend.

[77]See E. M. Schulman, "Economic Analysis of Employee Noncompetition Agreements," *Denver University Law Review*, 69 (1992), 97.

[78]Some states hold that where an agreement is signed after employment, continued employment is not adequate consideration: *Rollins* v. *American State Bank*, 487 N.E.2d 842

Lawsuit with an Employment Agency—A Case History

The agency called the sales manager to inquire whether there was a vacancy for a salesperson. The manager stated that he was always looking for good salespersons but there was no specific vacancy at that time. On persuasion by the agency he agreed to interview an applicant. The agency orally stated that its fee was 10 percent of annual compensation if the applicant was hired. The applicant was not hired because his qualifications were not exceptional enough to hire him when there was no vacancy.

Four months later the applicant stopped to see the sales manager. There happened to be a vacancy and he was hired.

The employment agency alleged that the hire was feeable because the initial interview was through its referral; the fee was explained, and the employee hired. A fee of $4,500 was payable. The legal basis for the suit was an implied contract because the employer interviewed the applicant four months before the second interview, after which he was hired. The employer argued that there was no referral and too much time had elapsed. The case was settled out of court for the cost of litigation. An agreement containing time limits on referrals would have prevented this lawsuit.

---

face-to-face meeting and in many situations will avoid final and binding arbitration or litigation.[83]

The advantages of ADR are causing the process to become increasingly popular in complex employment matters.

ADR is not for every situation. There are conditions that make it appropriate:

1. Parties to the dispute can be easily identified.
2. Parties have a good relationship that litigation could change. Litigation often becomes bitter.
3. Each party must have some power or leverage over the other.
4. The outcome of litigation is very questionable.
5. Resolving the dispute is more important than the legal principles involved or getting your name on a case.
6. The parties have an incentive to settle the dispute due to the cost of litigation, management, time, and the interference with productivity as well as many other problems if the dispute goes to court.
7. The parties want to keep the solution confidential.
8. Mediating parties involved must have authority to settle.

Employees in our litigation-happy society are increasingly willing to take their disputes to regulatory agencies. They have more rights and should use them. Employers are interested in finding alternatives to litigation in order to prevent these disputes from becoming lawsuits. ADR is one alternative. It is frequently less expensive and less time-consuming, and settlement is quicker than going to litigation. ADR gives the employer and employee a forum to reach a solution without third-party intervention.

The litigation process is becoming too expensive and is a burden upon the courts. Society must provide mechanisms that can produce an acceptable result in the shortest possible time, with the least possible expense and minimum of stress to the parties. That is what justice is all about. ADR is a good solution to this judicial and social problem.

Use of Agreements with Employment Agencies

When the HR manager needs to fill a vacancy in the skilled or managerial job category, the use of an employment agency is one way to find a

---

[83]For a more detailed analysis of this subject see T. Olsen, "Alternative Dispute Resolution," *The Human Resources Yearbook, 1992/1993* (Englewood Cliffs, NJ: Prentice Hall), pp. 16.60–16.71.

[84]*Pegues* v. *Mississippi State Employment Serv.*, 699 F.2d 760 (7th Cir. 1983).

qualified applicant. Relationships with an employment agency can result in legal consequences that often the personnel practitioner is not aware of. Problems and misunderstandings concerning fees, pro rata refunds when the employee is discharged or resigns, and the right to deal with the applicant privately without being "feeable" are all exposures to lawsuits when using an employment agency, as is shown in the case history.

Another exposure is the liability incurred when the employment agency, either knowingly or otherwise, commits a wrongful act. If the agency is acting as an agent of the employer it may be liable for the act.[84]

Most of these problems can be avoided by an initial agreement between the employer and the agency that anticipates these problems and provides for their solution. A contract between the applicant and the agency often does not affect relationships between the employer and agency. There is no federal law that regulates employment agencies; some states have laws that regulate through licensing the relationship with the applicant. Usually the employer is not a party.[85]

Guidelines in Drafting an Employment Agency Agreement

Where an employment agency is requested to find applicants for the high salary level jobs, an agreement should be executed (maybe a simple letter that both parties sign). The agreement should contain clauses to cover the following:

1. Fees, the amount of payment, payment dates. If a year-end bonus is paid, is that included in the annual salary for fee purposes?
2. Refunds if the employee does not work out, apart from agreement between applicant and agency. This

is often detailed in the applicant's contract with the agency. Usually the employer that agrees to pay the fee has no contractual relationship with the agency as to refunds except through applicant's contract.

3. Time limits on referrals. The time between referral and hiring should be agreed upon. Once the applicant is interviewed and not hired and reapplies later, should it be feeable? If so, how long?
4. A situation where the applicant is hired for a different job. The referral applicant is not qualified for the job vacancy placed with the agency but is hired for another job later. In the absence of an agreement, some courts say that it is feeable. A contract prevents litigation in this area.
5. An indemnity from liability for violations of certain laws by the agency, such as antidiscrimination laws, drug testing, and various state laws.
6. Requirements for the agency to follow all laws and monitor their procedure to determine if it is being done. Such laws as the Immigration Reform and Control Act make the employer liable for the employment agent's acts or omission.
7. A clause that the employer is to be held harmless in the event that the agency violates the law. This may require drafting by an attorney and the cost may be too great.
8. Steps that the agency should take to verify skills or qualifications.
9. A refund should be given if the applicant is employed and the fee paid, but applicant quits or is discharged after a given period of time.
10. A refund should be given if the agency is negligent and the employee leaves.[86]

Specific language should be drafted to fit the employer's operations and the personality of the organization. If an agreement contains most of these provisions, costly litigation can be avoided.

---

[85]See Gerard Panaro, "How to Structure a Contract with Your Employment Agency," *Personnel Practices and Ideas,* 5, no. 12 (Warren, Gorman and Lamont, Inc., 1340 Braddock Place, Alexandria, VA 22314, August 1990), p. 2.

[86]For specific language see Panaro, "How to Structure a Contract," p. 2. (See p. 146, footnote 90.)

11
THE AT-WILL DOCTRINE

DEFINITION AND HISTORY OF EMPLOYMENT-AT-WILL DOCTRINE

The employment-at-will doctrine states that an employee can be terminated without legal liability for good cause, bad cause, or no cause at all. The at-will doctrine is not applicable where there is an express statutory prohibition or formal contract. A union contract would remove an employee from the at-will status. This general rule of the common law is stated in the American Law Reports (ALR) as follows:

Despite its sometimes harsh operation and the obvious opportunities for abuse it affords an unscrupulous employer, few legal principles would seem to be better settled than the broad generality that an employment for an indefinite term is regarded as an employment at will which

may be terminated at any time by either party for any reason or for no reason at all.[1]

Under a century-old common rule, an employment relationship can be terminated at the whim of either party. As one court put it, an employee can be dismissed "for good cause, for no cause or even for a cause morally wrong. . . ."[2] This is the common law doctrine of employment at will. The doctrine had its origin in the English law. Horace Gray Wood *(Treatise on Master and Servant)* made an analysis of employment in the United States that contained the at-will rule, and

---

[1]62 ALR 3rd 271 (1975, 1992 suppl).
[2]*Payne* v. *Western and Atlantic R.R. Co.,* 81 Tenn. 507, at 519–520 (1884).

the courts were influenced.[3] The unquestionable acceptance of the at-will rule is illustrated in the extreme case where an employee was discharged because his wife refused to sleep with his supervisor. He challenged the employer's right to discharge for this reason, but the court rejected his suit because the employment-at-will doctrine empowered his employer to discharge him at any time, even if the reason was immoral.[4] Within a short time Wood's precept was accepted by the Supreme Court in *Adair* v. *United States,* 208 U.S. 161 (1908), when the court declared a statute unconstitutional that prohibited the discharge of a railroad employee because of his union membership. The Court said because the duration of the employment was not specified, both the employer and the employee had equal rights to terminate for any reason.

Harshness of the Rule

With the mass migration of labor from farms to assembly lines, it became a social problem when a person's survival depended on the whims of the employer. There is little doubt that the employer-employee relationship is one of the most important relationships in life. It affects the material well-being of every person. The jobs of more than 60 percent of American workers depend almost entirely on the continued good will of their employers.[5] The employer's right to terminate without a legal risk came under attack by social, economic, and legal scholars. Another concept that became popular in the employer-employee relationship was that a person had a property right in a job. It was a social requirement that an employee should expect job security.[6]

Property Right in a Job

On occasions the courts have held that an employee has a property right in a job. The job is necessary to maintain himself and his family, and therefore she or he should receive the protection of the government. The Supreme Court took this view in *Perry* v. *Sindermann,* 408 U.S. 593 (1972), when a school board failed to renew a teacher's contract and did not give an official statement as to the reason or allow an opportunity for a hearing. The teacher alleged that this denied him due process required by the Fourth Amendment. (Private sector employees do not have protection of this amendment). The Supreme Court held that job security, whether it was expressed or implied, was a property right that could not be abridged without a procedural due process.[7] The property right in a job has been established only in the public sector. However, there is an indication that courts are influenced by the property-right-in-job theory when making exceptions to the at-will rule. The influence can also come from legal theorists who argue that state and federal government should intervene in the

---

[3]For further reading on the history of the at-will doctrine, see Brian Hershizer, "The New Common Law of Employment: Changes in the Concept of Employment at Will: *Labor Law Journal,* 36, no. 95 (February 1985); Kenneth T. Lopatka, "The Emerging Law of Wrongful Discharge—A Quadrennial Assessment of the Labor Law Issue of the 80s" *Business Lawyer,* 40 (November 1984), 1–32; the opinion of the Supreme Court of Alabama in *Comerford* v. *International Harvester Co.,* 178 So.2d 894 (Ala. 1932); a bibliography published by the Bar Association of the City of New York called "Selected Materials of Employment at Will"; "Discharge at Will," *The Record,* 40, no. 3 (April 1985); Jay Feinman, "The Development of the Employment-at-Will Rule Revisited,"*Arizona State Law Journal,* 23 (1991), 733.

[4]*Comerford* v. *International Harvester Co.,* 178 So.2d 894 (Ala. 1932). See also *Tomkins* v. *Public Service Electric & Gas Co.,* 568 F.2d 1044 (3rd Cir. 1977), where there was discharge over refusal to have sexual relations with the supervisor.

---

[5]Information is based on a study of government statistics issued monthly. U.S. Department of Labor (Monthly Labor Review).

[6]See D. Hamermesh and A. Rees, *The Economics of Work and Pay,* 3rd ed. (New York: Harper & Row, 1984), pp. 172–74; W. Delmendo, "Determine Just Cause: An Equitable Solution for the Workplace" (comment), *Washington Law Review,* 66 (1991), 831.

[7]There should be an objective criterion when educational institutions grant tenure: *Franklin* v. *Marshall College,* 775 F.2d 110 (3rd Cir. 1985), cert. den. 1986; see also *University of Pennsylvania* v. *EEOC,* 850 F.2d 969 (3rd Cir. 1988), aff'd 110 S. Ct. 577 (1990).

employment relationship because the employee should receive constitutional protection.[8]

Based on the history of other social problems, one would think this would be an acceptable field for political activity. However, this hasn't happened and there are very few statutes that protect job security (except as a due process action). When legislation fails to correct a social problem, courts relate to the problem on a case-by-case basis.[9]

Judicial Application of At-Will Doctrine

Few legal doctrines have been more firmly established than the at-will doctrine. Under this doctrine the employer can do no wrong. An employee was discharged for trading in a certain store that the railroad decided to put out of business. The court said that the employer had a right to discharge even if it is morally wrong and "the law cannot compel them (employers) to employ workers, nor to keep them employed."[10] As late as 1949 a court held that an employer could discharge for no reason at all.[11] Some states have passed laws asking the employer to give a reason.

With legislation concerning employees' rights, such as the Labor Management Relations Act as amended,[12] and Title VII of the Civil Rights Act of 1964 as amended,[13] the courts started to take a look at this unblemished common law doctrine.

Some argued that their employment was for a fixed period either expressed or implied. Other discharged workers argued that the employer had an obligation to evaluate job performance in good faith and therefore could terminate only on just cause.[14] Some employees relied more on the traditional reasons to justify their claims for relief, such as lack of due process, contrary to fair and good faith dealing, or malicious action by the employer.

In a climate of employee rights created by Congress in other areas the courts began to favorably receive the wrongfully discharged employees' arguments. They searched for an exception to the common law doctrine. Almost all these cases involve either a breach of contract or statute. They are tried in state courts and accordingly there is a variation of law among the states.

The early 1980s was a period of the beginning of the erosion of the common law doctrine of employment at will. As one court stated, "It represents an area of the law undergoing dynamic development."[15] As a result, employees and lawyers are more willing to pursue discharge cases that they rejected in the past. Another important fact is that the reporting of court settlements by the news media has resulted in more exposure of the employer to litigation related to discharges than at any other time in history.

The proponents of eliminating the at-will doctrine are quick to point out that the United States is the only industrialized country that does not provide employees with some form of comprehensive protection against wrongful discharge.[16] The just-cause provisions of labor agreements cover some employees, but union membership has failed to keep pace with the growing workforce. More than 80 percent of the workforce are not covered by labor agreements.

The employer should not be deceived into believing that the at-will doctrine has been suddenly abolished by the courts[17] or into believing that it must show just cause in all cases of discharge. But the employer must become

---

[8]See C. Peck, "Unjust Discharges from Employment: A Necessary Change in the Law," *Ohio State Law Journal*, 40, no. 1 (1979), pp. 25–35; "The Employment-at-Will Doctrine: Time to Collapse Another Citadel," *University of Dayton Law Review*, 2, no. 2 (1985), p. 399.

[9]Laureen B. Edelman, Steven Abraham, and Howard S. Erlanger, "Professional Construction of the Law: The Inflated Threat of Wrongful Discharge," *Law and Society Review*, 26 (1992), 47.

[10]*Payne* v. *Western and Atlantic R.R. Co.*, 81 Tenn. 507 (1884).

[11]*Lewis* v. *Minnesota Mutual Life Insurance Co.*, 37 N.W.2d 316 (Iowa 1949).

[12]29 U.S.C. Sect. 158 et seq.

[13]42 U.S.C. Sect. 2000 et seq.

[14]Studies show that an estimated 150,000 to 200,000 discharged workers could assert legitimate claims under a just cause standard.

[15]*Savodnik* v. *Korvettes, Inc.*, 488 F. Supp. 822 (E.D. N.Y. 1980), p. 824.

[16]Spain has mandatory severance pay for a discharged worker: Spain Public Act 9 (1980). Japan also gives protection.

[17]*Adzick* v. *AGS Computers*, 554 N.Y.S.2d 182 (1990).

aware of the changes in this area of personnel law. The employer cannot discharge without an exposure.

STATUTES THAT VOID AT-WILL DOCTRINE

The first statutory restriction of the at-will doctrine was the National Labor Relations Act. This act protects any union employee from discharge when engaged in concerted activities for the purpose of mutual aid and protection of working conditions. Protection from discharge because of concerted activity extends to verbal complaints about working conditions as well as dissatisfaction because of wages. Most unions when bargaining for the employee have been able to get the employer to contractually agree that an employee will not be discharged except for "just cause." This goes beyond any statutory protection. The contract terms remove the employee from the at-will status.[18]

Major Federal Statutes That Limit Employment-at-Will Doctrine

1. National Labor Relations Act § 8(a)(1), (3), (4), 29 U.S.C. § 158(a)(1), (3), 4 (1975) (prohibits discharge for union activity, protected concerted activity, or filing charges or giving testimony under the Act).
2. Fair Labor Standards Act, 29 U.S.C. §§ 215(a)(3), 216(b) (1975 and Supp. 1982) (prohibits discharge for exercising rights guaranteed by minimum wage and overtime provisions of the Act).
3. Occupational Safety and Health Act of 1970, 29 U.S.C. § 660(c) (1975) (prohibits discharge of employees in reprisal for exercising rights under the Act).
4. Title VII, Civil Rights Act of 1964, 42 U.S.C. §§ 2000e-2, 2000e-3(a) (1981) (prohibits discharge based on race, color, religion, sex, or national origin and reprisal for exercising Title VII rights).
5. Age Discrimination in Employment Act of 1967, 29 U.S.C. §§ 623, 631, 633(a) (1975 U Supp. 1982) (prohibits age-based discharge by private employers

and federal government of persons between ages of 40 and 70 and reprisals for exercising statutory rights).
6. Rehabilitation Act of 1973, 29 U.S.C. §§ 793, 794 (1975) (prohibits federal contractors or any program or activity receiving federal financial assistance from discriminating against handicapped persons).
7. Employee Retirement Income Security Act of 1974, 29 U.S.C. §§ 1140, 1141 (1975) (prohibits discharge of employees in order to prevent them from attaining vested pension rights).
8. Consumer Credit Protection Act, 15 U.S.C. § 1674(a) (1982) (prohibits discharge of employees because of garnishment of wages for any one indebtedness).
9. Civil Service Reform Act of 1978, 5 U.S.C. § 7513(a) (1980) (permits removal of federal civil service employees "only for such cause as will promote the efficiency of the service").
10. Judiciary and Judicial Procedure Act, 28 U.S.C. § 1875 (Supp. 1982) (prohibits discharge of employees for service on grand or petit jury).
11. Americans with Disabilities Act, 42 U.S.C. § 12112 (1992) (prohibits discharge of individuals based on disabilities).
12. Family and Medical Leave Act, Pub. L. No. 1033 (107 § 6) (1993) (prohibits discharge based upon exercise of statutory leave for family or medical reasons).
13. Federal Worker Adjustment and Retraining Notification Act, 29 U.S.C. § 2101 (1988) (prohibits discharge of employees in connection with plant closings without specified notice and/or severance pay).

This list is not exhaustive. For a complete listing see *Federal Labor Law,* 16th Ed., (West Publishing Co.), St. Paul, MN, 1996.

Retaliation in an Antidiscrimination Statute

In the preceding chapters we have discussed the various antidiscrimination statutes that protect the employee from being discharged because of race, color, sex, religion, nationality, age, disability, or pregnancy. Many states also add substance abuse and marital status to this list.[19]

---

[18]Researchers estimate that more than 150,000 unjust dismissals each year in the private sector are unprotected by collective agreements or by statute.

[19]See Ronald M. Green, A. Carmell, and Jerrold F. Goldberg, *1993 State by State Guide to Human Resources Law* (New York: Panel, 1993).

Retaliation

In addition to protection because of discrimination, the statutes grant protection to the employee for retaliation.

The employer is often not aware of the retaliation provision. It believes the alleged discharge for discrimination is without merit and no consideration is given to the retaliation restriction. In order to have retaliation the discrimination section of the statute does not have to be violated.[20] Of all the antidiscrimination statutes, the protection most often used is Title VII (sexual harassment), with ADA second. However, retaliation is the most often overlooked employee protection.

Mixed Reasons for Discharge

An employee who is involved in a wage dispute, as well as in many other adverse situations involving the employer, has the protection of various statutes. The first thing the employer wants to do when there is a dispute is terminate the employee without checking the law.

Mixed Discharge

If an employee violates a policy or has poor performance but also engages in a protected activity when discharged, it is called a mixed discharge. Whether the employee was discharged for the rule violation or the protected activity is always the issue before the courts. The NLRB adopted the rule that the burden of proof is on the employer to show that the discharge was not the result of a protected activity. This rule was enforced in *NLRB* v. *Wright Lines,* 662 F.2d 899 (1st Cir. 1981). However, not all courts agreed with the *Wright Lines* case, and the Supreme Court had to settle the issue. The Court held that the board's position was reasonable.[21]

The issue came before the court again in *Price Waterhouse* v. *Hopkins,* 490 U.S. 228 (1989).

Although disparate treatment was part of the case, the plurality opinion concluded that the plaintiff must prove that the impermissible factor was part of the employment decision (109 S.Ct. 1775).

CRA91 affirmed this position and stated that discrimation is established where the plaintiff demonstrates an impermissible element was part of the decision, even though other permissible factors may have motivated the decision. If the employer shows that the plaintiff suffered no actual damages as a result of the illegal bias, then the plaintiff can recover only attorney's fees, but cannot receive an individual gain [Sect. 505 42 U.S.C. Sect. 2000e–2(m)].

It is difficult for the employer to prove that discharge was for legitimate reasons once the plaintiff shows that impermissible reasons existed. Under *Price Waterhouse,* the employer could prove that a legitimate reason substantially motivated the decision, and there was no recovery. This part of *Price Waterhouse* was changed by Section 107 of CRA91 to allow the plaintiff to recover in part if any impermissible element was present.

Several areas of potential litigation were created by CRA91. It is difficult to determine what Congress really meant. An exposure exists in almost every mixed discharge case until there is more case law.

State Whistle-Blower Statutes

A continuation of granting employee rights in the workplace can be found in the enactment by state legislatures of "whistle-blower" statutes. Although the first state whistle-blower statute was not adopted until 1981, the majority of the states have adopted a statute. These statutes apply to the private sector as well as the public sector (almost all public employees are protected by whistle-blower statutes). The various statutes have some degree of uniformity, but beyond the basics they have a wide diversity.[22] The intended objective of all state statutes is to provide protection for an

---

[20]In *Sherman* v. *Burke Contracting,* 891 F.2d 1527 (11th Cir. 1990), plaintiff used tape to prove retaliation.

[21]*NLRB* v. *Transportation Management Corp.,* 103 S.Ct. 2469 (1983).

[22]For a more complete review of whistle-blower statutes, see R. Boyle, "Review of Whistle-Blower Protections and Suggestions for a Change," *Labor Law Journal,* 41, no.12 (December 1990), 821.

employee who for the public good discloses a violation of the law.[23] However, the statutes also give protection to the employer in preventing false or unwarranted disclosures.

Most statutes provide a very broad protection to the employee and prohibit retaliatory action against the employee who testifies or provides information to a public body. In some states there must be an objective belief that the employer violated the law, while in others the employee must make an attempt to verify the accuracy of the information.

There is a wide variation in the statutes concerning to whom the disclosure must be made. Some require disclosure to any local, federal, or state agency, while other states permit it to be made internally to the attorney general of that state. Various forms of notice provisions also appear in the statutes. Some require that the employer be put on notice before the disclosure, while others do not.

The remedies providing for a violation also vary from making the employee whole to punitive damages. Some even provide for a criminal as well as a civil penalty.

The employer's defense against whistle-blower statutes is to establish procedures and policies that require the employee to report to the company any belief of company misconduct. This allows time to correct any wrongdoing or to explain to the employee why the company takes such action.

State Statutes That Require Just Cause

The first state statute to regulate discharge was passed in Montana in 1987. The act does not eradicate the at-will doctrine but restricts wrongful discharge suits and the amount of damages.

The Conference of Commissioners of Uniform State Laws, composed of representatives from the AFL-CIO, American Trial Lawyers Association, NAM, ABA, and U.S. Chamber of Commerce, worked for more than 5 years on developing a model termination act for the states to consider. This model act extinguishes all common law rights of termination. The suggested act requires a

good cause for termination. It allows for individual agreements or severance pay. It permits specific employment contracts with a built-in termination of employment without cause. (In this respect it partly retains the at-will doctrine.) Many actions connected with termination would be abolished including, but not limited to, defamation, infliction of emotional distress, malicious prosecution, false imprisonment, and assault.

The majority of the states have adopted parts of the recommendation. The U.S. Congress has not been able to enact a statute.[24] The conference encourages the states to get started. (Montana acted before the conference made its proposals public.)

Not all scholars agree that the model employment act is fair and equitable. For a critique of the act, see the proceedings of the Industrial Relations Research Association Spring Meeting as reported in the August 1992 issue of the *Labor Law Journal* (vol. 43, no. 8, pp. 495–507). Theodore J. St. Antoine and Paul Tobias discuss the pros and cons of this new model act.

Leonard Bierman and Stuart A. Youngblood have made an preliminary analysis of the Montana statute.[25] Indications are that wrongful discharge lawsuits will be controlled by some sort of state statute by the year 2000. It appears that most of these statutes will have a limit on liability for wrongful discharge.

PUBLIC POLICY EXCEPTION TO AT-WILL DOCTRINE

The public policy exception has been adopted by the majority of state courts. It states that the employer should not be permitted to discipline or discharge an employee for reasons that are violative of public policy. Public policy is a broad term used by the courts as a reason for an

---

[23]See Sect. 181.93 Minnesota Statutes as amended.

[24]There is some control by Congress under antidiscrimination and other statutes that prohibit discharge except for just cause.

[25]Leonard Bierman and Stuart A. Youngblood, "Interpreting Montana's Pathbreaking Wrongful Discharge for Employment Act: A Preliminary Analysis," *Montana Law Review,* 53 (1992), 599.

exception to an otherwise well-accepted principle of law. Under this exception, the employee's cause of action is based on the harm that society suffers as a result of the employer's conduct. The employee is not alleging that there is an injury to himself or herself in the tort sense but to society.[26]

Some law textbooks define public policy as a private dealing that is restricted by law for the good of the community. Another definition is "whatever contravenes good morals or established interests of society." Public policy is decided on a case-by-case basis and often is not defined by the court until violated. For example, the courts have said that a gambling contract, although it complies with all necessary elements of a contract, will not be enforced because it is not for the benefit or for the convenience of the public to do so. Other exceptions to principles of law are not as widely accepted as the enforcement of gambling contracts. The common law exception of public policy to employment at will is one of them.

Where a discharge has been held to be a violation of a public policy, the reason for the discharge is probably also against a good employee relations practice. Three distinctly different reasons for discharge have been held to be contrary to public policy: first, exercising a right under a statute; second, refusing to disobey a law when requested to do so by the employer; third, disclosing the employer to authorities when the law is being violated, commonly called the whistle-blower cases.[27]

In all these situations the employee alleges that a public policy exists. When the employer refused to follow public policy, the employee was discharged in retaliation for following the policy.

The basis for the public policy violation concept is founded in tort law. Tort law as applied to this concept is based on the premise that each member of society owes an obligation to every other member to be treated fairly. If public policy has been violated, the employee, under this exception, has not been treated fairly.[28]

Exercise of Employee Right under a Statute

A violation of an explicit provision in a statute is not considered an exception to employment at will but simply a violation of the statute. The remedy is provided for in the statute. This straightforward situation does not warrant further consideration in this chapter.

One of the statutory rights that employers sometimes object to is the employee's right to file for and receive workers' compensation benefits. Central Indiana Gas Company discharged an employee without a reason after she obtained a settlement on a workers compensation claim.[29] In this landmark case the court explained the reasoning behind other situations when an employee exercises a right under the statute when it said (at 427):

> If employers are permitted to penalize employees for filing workmens compensation claims, a most important public policy will be undermined. The fear of being discharged would have a deleterious effect on the exercise of a statutory right. Employees will not file claims for justly deserved compensation—opting, instead, to continue their employment without incident. The end result, of course, is that the employer is effectively relieved of his obligation.

Discharge is an employers' most common retaliation for employees' filing workers compensation claims or exercising other rights based on various statutes. The issue in all of these cases is whether the discharge is for filing a workers' compensation claim or for a policy violation. The interpretation of CRA91 as to mixed discharges is important in this kind of case.

---

[26]See James A. Bryant and Michael Giallourakis, "Employment at Will: Where Is It Going and What Can Be Done?" *SAM Advanced Management Journal,* Autumn (1984), 12–21.

[27]*Smith* v. *Calgon Carbon Corp.,* 917 F.2d 1338 (1990); *Adzick* v. *AGS Computers,* 554 N.Y.S.2d 182 (1990).

[28]For further explanation of public policy exception see "Employment-At-Will: Defining the Parameters," *Cumberland Law Review,* 16, no. 2 (1985–1986).

[29]*Frampton* v. *Central Indiana Gas Co.,* 297 N.E.2d 425 (Ind. 1973).

Refusal to Disobey a Law

When an employee refuses to break the law and is discharged, most courts say it is contrary to public policy to force an employee to choose between violating the law and keeping a job. Making continued employment contingent upon the commission of a felony is a tortious violation of public policy and an exception to the at-will doctrine.

Other public policy exceptions to common law employment-at-will doctrine are discharge for performing jury duty, reporting to authorities any violation of the law by the employer, malice and bad faith when discharging, reporting a health hazard, and any treatment of the discharged employee that the court or jury thinks should not happen.

Discharge for Whistle-Blowing

One of the most common public policy exceptions is where an employee complains to public officials about an employer's practice or acts that are in violation of a statute.[30]

Many employers believe that if an employee cannot be loyal to the employer,[31] the person should be either demoted or terminated. When this occurs, there is a possibility that the employer could become involved in a whistle-blower public policy exception to the employment-at-will doctrine. Loyalty, according to court rationale, is openly expressed where the employee tries to persuade the employer to comply with the law and the employer refuses.

Many states have the public policy exception to employment at will, but still pass whistle-blower protection statutes.[32]

Malice and Bad Faith

A few courts have protected at-will employees when discharged for reason of malice and bad

faith.[33] These jurisdictions hold that an employee must be protected from the unrestricted discretion to be discharged. Where the courts find malice and bad faith, the action must be severe, and they are telling the employer that they do not like the discharge procedure. State courts allow malice and bad faith as cause for action but seldom find the activity severe enough for plaintiff to collect.

Choosing a state court for damages rather than seeking a remedy under arbitration has been approved by the Supreme Court in *Lingle* v. *Norge Div. of Magic Chef, Inc.,* 108 S.Ct. 1877 (1988), where the Court held that union-represented employees can sue the employer in state court over a dismissal, even when the contract provides a grievance procedure and arbitration.[34]

THE EMPLOYMENT RELATIONSHIP AS A CONTRACT

Most courts will find a contract in the employment relationship. Under contract law there must be an offer, an acceptance, and consideration. The courts will say that the offer of employment is an offer under contract law. The acceptance is coming to work at a certain time. The consideration is the wages paid for services.

There is nothing in writing in most employment relationships. The courts say that the statute of frauds[35] does not apply because the contract of

---

[30]For more on job protection for whistle-blowing, see M. W. Aron, "Whistleblowers, Insubordination and Federal Law Protecting Whistleblowers," *Labor Law Journal,* 43 (April 1992), 211–20.

[31]M. H. Malin, "Protecting the Whistleblower from Retaliatory Discharge," *University of Michigan Journal of Law Reform,* 16, (1983), 277–318.

[32]T. Barnett, "Overview of State Whistleblower Protection Statutes," *Labor Law Journal* 43, no. 7 (July 1992), 440.

[33]Alaska, Arizona, California, Connecticut, Massachusetts, Minnesota, and Montana are a few states where this occurred.

[34]If the labor agreement did not provide for arbitration, the union can still sue under Section 301 of NLRA to enforce the agreement. It is not necessary to strike to enforce a labor agreement: *Groves* v. *Ring Screw Workers, Ferndale Fastener Div.,* 111 S.Ct. 498 (1990).

[35]The statute of frauds is a state law, however, all states have passed a statute of frauds in some form. They are patterned after the English statute (29 Car. II, c.3) that was passed in 1677. These statutes state that no suit or action shall be maintained on certain classes of contracts or engagements unless there is a note or memorandum in writing signed by the party to be charged, or by an authorized person. If the contract can be performed within one year that statute doesn't apply. Some states put this in the statute, while others leave it to court interpretation, but the result is the same: Employment relationships do not come under the statute.

employment can be performed within one year. The employee can quit or the employer can discharge within one year.

IMPLIED CONTRACT THAT MODIFIES AT-WILL DOCTRINE

The human relations manager who takes pride in good employee relations would consider the foregoing public policy exceptions as something that could not happen in his or her organization. In companies that have positive personnel policies, the common law exception of public policy, whistle-blowing, and malice and bad faith is academic, but this assumption would not be necessarily so with the implied contract exception. Positive personnel administration could increase the exposure to the implied contract exception. Aggressive recruiting and promotion that result in promises being made at the time of hiring, handbooks to sell the company as a place of continuous employment, and salaries quoted as annual salaries, which may imply a contract of employment for one year, are all positive programs that could result in an implied contract.[36]

Implied Contract

The personnel administrator is the most vulnerable where in the interest of selling the company or promoting good employee relations a certain promise is made. In determining whether such a promise is an implied contract of continuous employment, the courts look at the surrounding circumstances at the time of hiring to determine whether a promise was in fact made.[37]

Where a promise is considered an implied contract, the employee must show some reliance on the promise. One example would be a long-distance move where the employee left a secure job with a competitor and at a later date was discharged without cause or where there was a reliance on a promise of a better opportunity, that never materialized. Promises of this kind are not uncommon when an aggressive employment manager is operating in a tight labor market. The reason that the job does not materialize or the employee is laid off may be legitimate, but the employee is still emotionally and financially harmed. In this situation the courts often allow punitive damages.

One of the more definitive statements from a court that adopted the implied contract approach is found in *Pugh* v. *See's Candies, Inc.,* 116 Cal. App. 3rd 311 (1981), where a vice president of employee relations of 32 years of service was terminated. When he asked why, he was told, "Look deep within yourself." The jury determined that length of service, a series of promotions and commendations, the lack of direct criticism of his work, and the assurance by his superior that if he did a good job his future would be secure established an implied contract.[38] The company violated the contract by the discharge.

Quoting an Annual Salary

A common practice that can result in an exposure is quoting an annual salary in a job offer. This is a good selling point but often backfires. An annual salary figure impresses the applicant because it looks much larger than a weekly or a monthly figure. The practice has caused unnecessary litigation. The courts consider how the statement reacts upon the employee rather than the intent of the person who orginated it.

In *Berand* v. *IMI Systems, Inc.,* 8 IER Cases 325 (BNA 1993), the court, in reversing a long-established precedent, said that an employee expects to be employed at will when hired and an annual salary quote does not mean a 1-year contract. The few state courts that have had the issue before them are split on whether a 1-year contract is formed by quoting an annual salary.

---

[36]M. R. Wallace, "Employee Manuals as Implied Contracts: The Guidelines That Bind" (comment), *Tulsa Law Journal,* 27 (1991), 263.

[37]*Rognlien* v. *Carter,* 443 N.W.2d 217 (Minn. App. 1989).

[38]F. Vickory, "The Erosion of the Employment-at-Will Doctrine and the Statute of Frauds: Time to Amend the Statute," *American Business Law Journal,* 30 (May 1992), 97–122; also Axel R. Granholm, *Handbook of Employee Termination* (New York: John Wiley & Sons, 1991), 19.

South Dakota has a statute that states that when you quote an annual salary, it results in a contract for 1 year [S.D. Codified Laws Sec. 60(1)(3)].[39] This concept—that you created a contract by quoting a salary for a fixed period of time—is not the law in all jurisdictions. Only very few state courts have had the issue come before them.

The problem in the use of annual salary is that it creates exposure to a lawsuit win or lose.[40] Although only a few courts have held that quoting an annual salary forms a contract for 1 year, why use it if you can communicate by some other language? Quoting a monthly salary does not create the same exposure, and the applicant can multiply. *Annual salary* is another term that should be blocked out in the practitioner's vocabulary.

Hiring Strike Replacements

The use of strike replacements will be discussed in Chapter 19, so it will only be mentioned in this section as related to implied contract. When a strike replacement is recruited and is promised that the job will be permanent (which means that it will continue when the strike is over), this becomes a contract under the implied contract theory.[41] If the person is replaced after the strike is over, she or he could sue in a state court for breach of contract. It would depend upon the state whether the court would find a breach of contract.

Applicants are often promised permanent jobs in order to recruit under strike conditions. When the strike is settled, the company, unless it wants to face a breach of contract suit, could not bargain away their jobs. This chills the union's desire to go on strike, because their jobs are at stake when permanent replacements are hired.

Handbooks and Policy Manuals[42]

Certain statements made in an employee handbook or a policy manual have been held to be an implied contract. The Michigan court, in a leading case, held that guidelines and the supervisor's manual were an expressed contract.[43] The clauses that were especially troublesome were where the supervisor's manual stated that an employee could be discharged only for just cause and "could work until 65 as long as he did his job."

In a companion case the employee testified that he was promised at the time of hiring he could work for the company "as long as I did my job." The court said that was a contract that changed the at-will doctrine, although it was an oral promise.[44]

In one situation the handbook stated that an employee would be discharged only for just cause. When hired, the employee signed the application form, which stated that employment would be subject to the *Handbook on Personnel Policy.* Eight years later he was discharged. The court held that it was a contract; just cause had to be shown, as stated in the handbook. However, to reach this conclusion the court held that this was an expressed contract.[45] (New York is a state where an employment contract is not an implied contract.)

One of the well-quoted cases after *Toussaint* on a handbook being an implied contract involved a loan officer in a bank who was in default on his personal loan and had approved 56 out of 57 loans in violation of the loan policy. The discharge was held to be a breach of contract because the employer failed to follow the discharge procedure outlined in the handbook, although there was a legitimate reason to discharge.[46]

---

[42]Only the law as to whether or not a handbook is a contract will be discussed here. The writing of a proper handbook is given in detail in chapter 12.

[43]*Toussaint* v. *Blue Cross and Blue Shield of Michigan,* 292 N.W.2d 880 (Mich. 1980); also *Bullock* v. *Auto Club of Michigan,* 444 N.W.2d 114 (Mich. S.Ct. 1989). Michigan is an employee-at-will state.

[44]*Ebling* v. *Masco Corp.,* 292 N.W.2d 801 (Mich. 1980).

[45]*Weiner* v. *McGraw-Hill,* 443 N.E.2d 441 (N.Y. 1982). However, in *LeNeave* v. *North American Life Assurance Co.,* 854 F.2d 317 (8th Cir. 1988), the court held that the same language did not always imply a contract.

[46]*Pine River State Bank* v. *Richard F. Mettille Sr.,* 333 N.W.2d 622 (Minn. 1983).

---

[39]In *Goodwyn* v. *Sencore, Inc.,* 389 F.Supp. 824 (D.S.D. 1975), the court held that an annual salary formed a 1-year contract. This was before the statute was adopted.

[40]In *Tipton* v. *Canadian Imperial Bank of Commerce,* 872 F.2d 149 (11th Cir. 1989), the court rejected the concept. Some courts will reject but hold that annual salary is an inducement to accept the job.

[41]*Belknap, Inc.* v. *Hale,* 103 S.Ct. 3172 (1983).

The two Michigan cases and *Pine River* were subsequently accepted by several other jurisdictions and caused an alarm to be sounded in personnel law. Many practitioners became "gunshy" and discarded their handbooks. As more and more states adopted the *Pine River* case, personnel literature became abundant. You could get advice on handbooks for any position that management wants to take.[47]

By 1985 the vast majority of the states held that a handbook was a contract, although some industrial states such as New York, Illinois, and Indiana still required the written contract before the at-will status could be changed.[48] (A policy manual for the purpose of this discussion is the same as a handbook.) Practitioners became aware of another past practice that would not stand judicial scrutiny. The language in the handbook often was designed to provide flexibility when applying it to certain individuals. This had to be changed to become less flexible to stand a court test.

Changing the Implied Contract

One of the reservations in changing a handbook was whether it could be changed if it is an employment contract. Employment documents can be changed. However, to be sure to avoid exposure, the effective date of the change should be set for some reasonable time in the future. When working conditions are changed, the employee should be able to have a reasonable time to find another job if he or she does not like the change.

Use of Term *Probationary Period* in a Handbook

The dictionary defines *probation* as the term used for one who is being tested—a trial or

evaluation period—and this is the way it has been used in personnel documents for many years. The courts never really accepted this definition. Under the USERRA, when a probationary employee went into military service and returned, the probationary period is considered to have been served even though the employee may have been tested or observed for only two weeks.

Some courts are saying that the term means more than a trial period. When used in a handbook or policy manual it indicates that once the trial period has passed, the employee has a permanent job, and just cause has to be shown before he or she can be discharged. The term under this interpretation changes the employment-at-will status to a contractual relationship. How far this concept has gone was shown in a 1986 unpublished survey in Nebraska and Iowa. The majority of employees contacted stated that they expected permanent employment after serving a reasonable probationary period.

It can be seen from the case law that the use of the term *probationary* offers no security to the employer in discharging without cause, in acting with bad faith, or in breaching the covenant of fair dealing. It can create an employment contract that will cancel the at-will doctrine. In some cases the employer would have had a better case if no reason for the discharge had been given. The employer can rely upon the at-will doctrine in most states. The use of the term *probationary period* often gives the employer a false sense of security that it unfortunately relied upon in defense.

If an employee is an at-will employee before the use of the term, some courts will hold that the use of the term will not change the status. Other courts will hold that this does create a contract of job permanency. It only takes a few courts to agree with the employee to create an exposure to litigation. An attorney is more likely to take the case on a contingency basis if some authority can be cited to justify the employee's position.

Risks in Use of a Probationary Period

In the vast majority of jurisdictions, the at-will doctrine is upheld when the employer does not create a condition that enables the courts to find an

---

[47]See John D. Combe, "Employee Handbooks: Asset or Liability?" *Employee Relations Law Journal*, 12, no. 1 (Summer 1986), 4–17.

[48]*Enis* v. *Continental Ill. Nat. Bank & Trust*, 582 F.Supp. 876 (N.D. Ill. E.D. 1984); *Mead Johnson and Co.* v. *Openheimer*, 458 N.E.2d 668 (Ind. App. 1 Dist. 1984). See *Fleming* v. *Kids and Kin Head Start*, 693 P.2d 1363 (Ore. App. 1965) for majority rule.

exception. The use of the probationary period creates such an opportunity. Courts have always upheld the right of the employer to discharge for poor performance. In this sense the employee is always on probation. Why limit to a specific time period?

The use of the term is an invitation to litigation. Why use it at all? There are other ways to communicate to the employee that the standard of performance and benefits are less during the first few months of employment than after a longer time. The standard of discipline, however, should be the same regardless of the length of employment—always assuming that the employee has been properly informed of the consequences of certain actions. *Probationary period,* except as the term is used in labor agreements, is another term that personnel practitioners should consider eliminating from their vocabulary.

A labor agreement is an enforceable contract, and until the employee serves the probationary period just cause does not have to be shown. For this reason it should be kept in the agreement. The labor agreement provision is one reason why the courts associate just cause with the probationary period in a nonunion situation.

CONSTRUCTIVE DISCHARGE

In the simplest terms, constructive discharge may be taken to mean that when an employee apparently quits, he or she has actually been fired. However, the law applies a special—and much more complex—meaning to the term. Black's Law Dictionary defines constructive discharge as "that which occurs when an employer deliberately makes employee's working conditions so intolerable that the employee is forced into voluntary resignation."[49] Although this legal definition has been followed by most courts, it is not generally understood by the first-line supervisor. For this reason, a termination is often recorded as a voluntary quit when in effect it is a constructive discharge and the employee has the

same remedies under the law as if she or he had been discharged.[50]

Definition of Intolerable Conditions

The courts follow a general guideline on constructive discharge. If the employer creates working conditions that are so intolerable that a reasonable person is forced to quit voluntarily, the termination is not voluntary, but a discharge. The employee would then have the same remedies under the law as if he or she had been discharged.[51]

Constructive Discharge under the NLRA

The original concept of constructive discharge usually involved a situation where the employer wanted to discharge an employee but was concerned about the possible legal repercussions. By making life on the job so miserable as to force a quit, the employer expected to avoid the need to discharge. Among the first cases to reach the courts were those based on charges of unfair labor practices where the employer would have "evil intent or motive" because of union activity and would set up a program to get the employee to quit.

An early case involved an employer who learned that an employee was supporting a union drive and became hostile toward her. In retaliation the employer altered the employee's method of pay—putting her on incentive rates when she was not even earning the minimum wage. She protested, but nothing was done and she quit. The court ruled that she had been fired for union activity in violation of Section 8 (a)(3) of the National Labor Relations Act. The evidence in this case showed an intent or programmed action to force the employee to quit.[52]

---

[49]*Black's Law Dictionary,* 6th ed. (St. Paul, MN: West, 1990), p. 863.

[50]For further reading, see Ralph H. Baxter and John M. Farrell, "Constructive Discharge—When Quitting Means Getting Fired," *Employee Relations Journal,* (Winter 1978), 346.

[51]*Kass* v. *Brown Boveri Corp.,* 488 A.2d 242 (N.J. Super. 1985).

[52]*J. P. Stevens & Co.* v. *NLRB,* 461 F.2d 490 (4th Cir. 1972).

Intolerable Working Conditions as Determined by Courts

The courts consistently apply the general rule that conditions must be so intolerable that a reasonable person is forced to quit. This rule is applied on a case-by-case basis. The court determinations as to what are unreasonable actions is less each day.

Probably the best example of constructive discharge without specific intent involves a plaintiff who was hired as a teller. At the time of hire she was told that all employees were required to go to a staff meeting. At the first staff meeting she discovered that the agenda included a religious talk and prayer, both delivered by a Baptist minister. Being an atheist, she refused to go to the meetings. The employer countered that she must attend staff meetings and that if she objected to the devotions she could "close her ears." She still refused and the employer asked for a letter of resignation stating that she was not being fired. She charged that she was constructively discharged for reasons of religious discrimination. The court held that mandatory attendance at company prayer meetings imposed intolerable working conditions because attendance would have forced the employee to sacrifice her fundamental religious beliefs.[53]

After the enactment of antidiscrimination laws, the courts had to consider whether a violation of an antidiscrimination law created an unreasonable atmosphere sufficient to warrant a finding of constructive discharge. One of the most common situations where intolerable conditions are alleged involves inadequate or discriminatory salary increases. The charge of intolerable salary derives its legal basis from Title VII of the sex discrimination section.

What Are Intolerable Conditions?

One employee argued that she was contructively discharged because of intolerable conditions of sex discrimination. She had come to work for a company as a secretary and had worked her way up to the position of buyer. After 90 days as a buyer, she was given a requested increase but she was still making $130 per month less than the male person she replaced. Because of her disappointment she quit and filed a charge of sex discrimination alleging that she was doing the same work as males but was paid $130 less per month. The court cited the general rule that if the employer deliberately made conditions so intolerable that the employee was forced to quit, the employer was guilty of constructive discharge. The employer was liable for any illegal conduct involved just as it would have been if it had formally discharged the employee. The court found further that the pay arrangement did show sex discrimination but that in taking the promotion the employee had agreed to work for less money. Under these conditions the court found that a reasonable person would not have quit because of unequal pay.[54]

Other courts have followed the *Bourque* precedent in holding that there is no constructive discharge even though the condition that causes the resignation is found to be unlawful. The plaintiff must prove more. He or she must show that the unlawful condition created by the employer is so offensive that the reasonable person would have found it intolerable. Failing in this proof, the employee must continue working while seeking to remedy the allegedly unlawful practice.

The employee is not required to show the employer's intent in order to prove constructive discharge, only that the employer knowingly permitted the condition to exist.[55]

The courts are consistent in finding that the conditions created by the employer must be more than disagreeable.[56] If the conditions are severe enough for whatever reason, the court will find constructive discharge and will usually find that, because of the intolerable conditions, intent can be assumed.[57]

---

[54]*Bourque* v. *Powell Electrical Manufacturing Co.,* 617 F.2d 61 (5th Cir. 1980).

[55]*Goss* v. *Exxon Office Systems Co.,* 747 F.2d 885 (3rd Cir. 1984).

[56]*Fraze* v. *KFC National Management Co.,* 492 F.Supp. 1099 (M.D. Ca. 1989).

[57]See *Cockrell* v. *Boise Cascade,* (10th Cir. 1986).

---

[53]*Young* v. *Southwestern Savings & Loan Association,* 509 F.2d 140 (5th Cir. 1975).

In deciding whether an intolerable working condition exists, the court determines whether a "reasonable person in the employee's position and circumstances would have felt compelled to resign." This was the rule in the *Bourque* case, and it is followed in most jurisdictions. The issue in all these cases is not whether a particular employee feels that the job is objectionable, but whether a reasonable person in the employee's shoes would have been compelled to resign. An employee's own subjective assessment of what is tolerable is not sufficient to lead to a finding of constructive discharge.

Demotion or Transfer

An action by an employer that could lead to a claim of constructive discharge is transferring or demoting an employee.[58] In such a claim the transfer or demotion itself is alleged to be the intolerable condition. The reason for the action is alleged to be the unlawful act. Discrimination is often claimed at the same time. The reason is that if constructive discharge is found, discrimination provides a statutory basis for claiming a wrongdoing. Although antidiscrimination statutes may be violated, courts will not find constructive discharge if the condition created by the transfer or demotion is not severe enough.

In determining the severity, the court will compare the job offered with the job the employee had. The comparison will consider differences in pay and benefits, day-to-day job conditions, increased travel requirements, and similar considerations. The courts will also consider the negative effect on the employee's prestige—this must be more severe than ordinary—and whether the employee was embarrassed by the employer's action. In evaluating embarrassment claims, courts seek to find out whether the embarrassment would be daily and unavoidable and whether there was a radical change in job responsibilities to warrant embarrassment.

Discrimination

In constructive discharge cases age discrimination is often the alleged legal basis for action. Lawyers prefer this choice because age cases are tried before a jury, and the chances that conditions will be found intolerable are better than before a judge. In one such case the employee, a supervisor, was not performing her job up to standard and the employer gave her a choice between being retired or being transferred to a nonsupervisory position in the department that she formerly supervised. She chose retirement but then brought an age discrimination suit stating that she was encouraged to retire. The jury agreed. The court said that there was enough evidence to allow the jury to find that the employee was constructively discharged.[59] The employer might have anticipated that when someone is transferred to a nonsupervisory position in a department that she formerly supervised very well, she would be forced to work with her former subordinates and that this would create an unreasonable condition.

A transfer sometimes can result in a breach of an employment contract. An employer entered into a written agreement with an electrical engineer specifying that he would be employed as a manager of a department. The contract permitted discharge for "just cause." After a period of time the supervisor of the employee attempted to reclassify him to the position of sales engineer. The engineer quit and sued for breach of contract. The court held the action of the supervisor to be a breach of contract.[60]

Alternative of Resigning or Discharge

The clearest form of constructive discharge occurs when an employer tells an employee that she or he has an opportunity to resign, but that if the employee does not do so she or he will be

---

[58]*Alicia Rosado* v. *Garcia Santiago*, 562 F.2d 1143 (1st Cir. 1988).

[59]*Cazzola* v. *Codman & Shurtleff, Inc.*, 751 F.2d 53 (1st Cir. 1984).

[60]*Kass* v. *Brown Boveri Corp.*, 488 A.2d 242 (N.J. Super. 1985).

discharged (also called a smoking gun threat).[61] This is a common practice of employers, and the reason it is used is probably to promote good employee relations by making a terminated employee more employable.[62] Whatever its effect on morale, the approach does open the door to possible litigation and sometimes to liability greater than would have been incurred if the employee had been discharged outright. This type of case is difficult to defend as the courts often feel that the employer has threatened the employee even though the employer may have the right to discharge.

Mr. Knee had a written contract, but the school board asked for his resignation. He resigned and then brought action for breach of contract (*Knee* v. *School District No. 139 in Canyon City,* 676 P.2d 727 [Idaho App. 1984]). The court held that the mere request to resign is not enough to justify a finding of constructive discharge. Discharge must be stated as the alternative. The fact that he had a contract would lead one to believe that he could not be discharged.

A different outcome resulted when an employee was told that she had the option of resigning or being discharged. She resigned and filed a claim for violation of handbook provisions, which in that state was considered a contract. The court not only found constructive discharge but also allowed punitive damages. The court said that the employer stands to gain from a resignation rather than a discharge because it will insulate itself from a wrongful discharge claim.[63]

An employer can be guilty of constructive discharge in encouraging early retirement. An employee who could either have taken early retirement or have been transferred under a reorganization program was told that it would be a waste of time to transfer if he preferred early retirement. He took early retirement and filed suit alleging that he was coerced into this action. The court held that in order to be considered coercion in violation of ADEA, the alternative to early retirement had to be so intolerable that a reasonable person who wanted to continue work would have refused it.[64]

Prevention of Constructive Discharge Claims

Employers should not assume that constructive discharge cases are the exception rather than the rule. Employees—particularly in white-collar occupations—generally want to continue working and will resist being separated from their jobs. Exposure to charges of constructive discharge exist in every transfer, demotion, promotion, or termination, especially if the employee is approaching retirement age. Successful constructive discharge cases are on the increase as the courts require less to find unreasonableness. Once intolerable conditions or an unreasonable alternative have been established, the courts do not expect the employee to continue working and will consider a voluntary quit as a discharge.

An employer can take several steps to reduce exposure to constructive discharge claims.

1. Educate the supervisors. This is probably the most important defense; the supervisor is frequently the one who seeks a way to make the employee quit.
2. Encourage the employee to accept the demotion or transfer rather than to resign. Make sure that he or she understands that the action is not intended to result in termination.
3. If you do intend to discharge the employee, be honest and open with him or her and go through with the discharge rather than give the option to resign. The employee is less likely to feel that he or she was treated unfairly, and the judge or jury will be less suspicious if the matter does end up in court.
4. Beware of resignations; always ask for a reason. This prevents the employee from later raising allegations of constructive discharge. Courts give little weight to this technique.

---

[61]In *Staggs* v. *Blue Cross of Maryland,* 486 A.2d 798 (Md. App. 1985), two salespersons were permitted to resign rather than be discharged. The court held this was constructive discharge per se. Also *Cockrell* v. *Boise Cascade,* (10th Cir. 1986).

[62]*Gates* v. *Life Montana Ins. Co.,* 668 P.2d 213 (Mont. 1983).

[63]*Gates* v. *Life of Montana Ins. Co.,* 668 P.2d 213 (Mont. 1983).

[64]*Toussaint* v. *Ford Motor Co.,* 581 F.2d 812 (10th Cir. 1978).

CHAPTER
12
PREVENT WRONGFUL DISCHARGE LITIGATION

Preventing Wrongful Discharge Exposure
Writing a Handbook or a Policy Manual
The Discharge Process
The Use of Waivers or Releases

In recent years the practitioner has been given a steady diet of the exceptions to the employment-at-will doctrine. The state courts have eroded the traditional termination authority of management to terminate at will for any reason or no reason to the point where the employer believes that the right to discharge is lost. Management fears are well founded. Studies show that more than 25 percent of employers are sued for wrongful discharge. Most suits are filed by professional, managerial, technical, and clerical employees who are usually not protected by an existing collective bargaining agreement. (Most agreements require "just cause" for discharge. Less than 20 percent of the workforce is under a collective bargaining agreement.) It is estimated that more than 20 percent of the workforce has no contractual or statutory protection from discharge. Present employees are knowledgeable of their legal rights and are not reluctant to sue their employers when they feel that their discharge was unfair and their reputation was damaged. They read about the high awards won by other employees and are encouraged by legal advertising to have their cases assessed. It is no wonder that employers are "gun-shy" about discharging an employee.[1]

Most managers and practitioners have been exposed to the reams of literature on how the at-will doctrine has been eroded.[2] Discharge is still a management right, but it has to be done differently from the way it has been in the past.

---

[1] Laureen B. Edelman, Steven Abraham, and Howard S. Erlanger, "Professional Construction of the Law: The Inflated Threat of Wrongful Discharge," *Law and Society Review,* 26 (1992), 47.

[2] Sami M. Abbasi, Kenneth W. Hollman, and Joe H. Murray, "The Erosion of the Employment-at-Will Doctrine: Recent Developments," *Labor Law Journal, (*Feb., 1994). *Labor Law Journal,* 38, no. 1 (January 1987), 21; Daniel J. Koys, Steven Briggs, and Jay E. Grenig, "The Employment-at-Will Doctrine: A Proposal," *Loyola Law Journal,* 17 (Winter 1986); William J. Holloway and Michael J. Leech, "Employment Termination—Rights and Remedies" (Washington, DC: Bureau of National Affairs, 1985); Henry H. Berritt, *Employee Dismissal and Practice* (New York: John Wiley, 1984) (1985 Supp.).

EXHIBIT 12-1

> The employment relationship between the employee and the employer is at-will and may be terminated at any time by either party with or without cause, unless specifically changed in writing by an authorized company representative. I understand that false statements on my application will result in discharge. This statement supersedes all prior statements, either written or oral, as to terms and conditions of employment.

If a discharge is decided on by the supervisor, the personnel practitioner must take action and defend it with all available evidence to establish a legitimate reason. One can rely on an abundance of authority to defend a position provided that the proper precautions are taken before the discharge. If a manager decides to discharge, the manager will do so. The task of the personnel practitioner is to advise that it be done in a way that will result in the least exposure to litigation; therefore, the personnel practitioner must be notified well in advance of the discharge date.[3]

At-will employees still exist, and the doctrine should be considered when other reasons are judicially weak, but fewer and fewer courts are adhering to the old common law doctrine.

PREVENTING WRONGFUL DISCHARGE EXPOSURE

A policy to prevent discharge exposure must start out with the audit of the application form. The wording in the form is drafted in such a way that it does not create an expressed contract unless that is what is intended. Some employers want their application form to say that it is an expressed contract and the applicant is expected to abide by its terms. Exhibit 12-1 is an example of a statement of this type.

The At-Will Clause

Because employment at this point is still in the prospective, the applicant will usually not refuse to sign the form.[4] Those employers who have the disclaimer in the application form state that it does not have a chilling effect on the applicant flow or obtaining good, qualified applicants.[5] Others feel that it puts the company in a negative position at the start of the employment period.

The courts will enforce an at-will clause in the applicant form and will usually hold that it is an expressed contract at the time of hiring. Exhibit 12-1 is acceptable language.[6] Where a handbook stated that discharge will be for just cause only, and the employee was discharged after eight years, the court held that just cause had to be shown.[7] New York is a strong at-will state, but the court held that the clause in the application form was an expressed contract and removed the employee from the at-will status.

In addition to legal and employee relations considerations when making a decision whether or not to include an at-will clause in the application form, it must also be considered whether or not it prevents subsequent charges. Some courts hold that although the application form clearly states one thing, a later statement in the handbook or a posted memo can modify the original statement.[8] A decision to include expressed contract language

---

[3]How do you discharge? Very carefully.

[4]The experience of the employment manager is that an applicant will sign anything and remember nothing at the time of hiring.

[5]R. Hilgert, "Employers Protected by At-Will Statements," *The Human Resources Yearbook, 1992/93* (Englewood Cliffs, NJ: Prentice Hall), p. 818. See also *McKennon* v. *Nashville Banner,* 66 FEP 1192 (1995).

[6]However, many courts require that it be duplicated in other employment documents.

[7]*Weiner* v. *McGraw-Hill,* 443 N.E. 2d 441 (N.Y. 1982).

[8]*Thompson* v. *Kings Entertainment Co.,* 653 F.Supp. 871 (E.D. Va. 1987). For an opposite view, see *Leathem Research Foundation of CUNY,* 658 F.Supp. 651 (S.D. N.Y. 1987).

EXHIBIT 12-2

This job offer contains the entire understanding between _____ and _____ with respect to the conditions of employment. No other promises, agreements, or understandings, written or oral, not mentioned above shall be binding. No changes, additions, or modifications of this letter shall be binding unless they are in writing and signed by the parties to this letter.

must consider future circumstances that may be troublesome. Sometimes it is better to say nothing.

Audit of the Interviewing process

A promise made at the time of hiring can result in establishing a contractual relationship and removing the applicant, once employed, from an at-will status to an enforceable obligation under contract. However, not every utterance of the employer is binding.[9] Secondary interviews can result in forming a contract; accordingly they are structured so promises are not made that are relied upon, because often the employee will later allege that they were broken. When the plaintiff can show that the promise was relied upon and he or she suffered damages when it was broken, there is a serious exposure to litigation.[10] Although the employer may have checklists and guidelines for interviewing, there is no assurance that they will be followed. The audit can only assure the management that such instructions exist. The instructions to the interviewers should not be specific. It is sufficient if they are told that any promises made at the time of hiring will create an exposure to a lawsuit in the future in the event that those promises are not kept. Apart from the legal consequences, there is an employee relations problem of working for an employer who does not keep promises.

The Job Offer Letter

Any offer of employment above a certain level should be in writing. There are two reasons for this. The first is to avoid any misunderstanding of the conditions of employment, and the second is that in the event a promise was implied or otherwise understood to be a promise, it can be voided in the job offer letter.

The audit notes that an annual salary is not quoted either orally or in a job offer letter. The job offer letter should also contain a "zipper clause." Zip up tight any promises that may have been made at the time of the interview so it is clear that such promises were not relied upon when accepting the position.

Exhibit 12-2 is suggested language to be inserted in the job letter. The language should be as nonlegal as possible but have the necessary elements for enforcement. After the terms of employment are stated (who pays for new curtains, connecting the washer and dryer, etc.), the language in Exhibit 12-2 could be inserted. This is the last paragraph of the letter, and when the employee reports to work, some written or at least oral assurance should be given that the letter was understood.

Effectiveness of a Complaint Procedure

The complaint procedure is one of the most important elements in the prevention of exposure to lawsuits in discharge cases. An effective complaint procedure will eliminate more than 70 percent of the exposure to wrongful discharge cases. The audit makes certain that it is used the way it was intended. Often the restrictions in the procedure chill its use; if this is the case they should be changed. The less formal it is, with liberal time limits and no restriction on what

---

[9]*Dumas* v. *Kessler & Maguire Funeral Home*, 380 N.W. 2d 544 (Minn. App. 1986).

[10]*Bower* v. *AT&T Technologies*, 852 F.2d 361 (8th Cir. 1988).

member of management the employee can express a complaint to, the more it will be used. (In *Meritor Savings Bank, FSB* v. *Vinson,* 106 S.Ct. 2399 [1986]), the employer was found guilty of sexual harassment. The complaint procedure was useless because the employee was required to report to the person involved.) Also if a peer review or an impartial arbitrator is not provided for (assuming a nonunion facility) and the complaint procedure is not being used by the employee, serious consideration should be given to changing it.

Audit of Performance Appraisals

Although an objective performance appraisal based on behavioral characteristics may appear on paper, the audit should determine how it is being used. It is much easier for a manager to be subjective than to have to verify objective data. So after a good procedure is adopted, often there is a tendency to let it fall back into subjectivity. The audit determines whether or not the ratee has been communicated with during the appraisal period, whether the ratee understood what performance was expected, and the consequences if the standard of performance communicated was not met. This would serve as a warning to the employee of what the consequences would be for poor performance. Courts are particularly sympathetic to an employee's cause where there is documented evidence that the employee had previously received subjective favorable performance ratings and a short time later was discharged for poor performance.[11]

Audit of Just-Cause Policy

The audit of a just-cause policy assumes that one has been established. A study of wrongful discharge cases indicates that the employer's policy must be carefully considered when

discharge occurs.[12] The development of legal doctrines that make an exception to the common law employment-at-will doctrine encourages employees to file previously unthinkable claims for relief. The vague definition of public policy by the courts gives the employee free access to the courts and discourages the employer from discharging anyone except in extreme cases. Employees will file lawsuits in almost any discharge case where just cause is not clearly evident. The first question that the court will ask is the reason for the discharge. If none can be shown, the reason alleged by the employee could be an exception to the at-will doctrine.

Seldom will a wrongful discharge suit succeed when the employer adopts a just-cause termination policy. Employer communicates to the employee the exact conditions that will cause severe disciplinary action or discharge. Where just cause is shown, the courts have supported the discharge rather than rely on the common law exceptions.

What is just cause is decided on a case-by-case basis by arbitrators whose task is to interpret the labor agreement. However, in a nonunion facility just cause must relate more to employee relations problems than a legal context.

Fortunately we have two court decisions that give a logical definition of "just cause." In *Danzer* v. *Professional Insurers, Inc.,* 679 P.2d 1276 (N.M. 1984), the Supreme Court of New Mexico stated, "Termination for good cause is shown . . . i.e., some causes inherent in and related to qualifications of the employee or a failure to properly perform some essential aspect of the employee's job function." The author accepts this as one half of the definition of just cause. However, another court completed the definition when in *Staton* v. *Amax Coal Co., Div. of Amax, Inc.,* 461 N.E.2d 612 (Ill., App. 3 Dist. 1984), the court, after reviewing the decisions[13] on just cause involving arbitration under labor agreements,

---

[11]Some courts hold that failure to evaluate performance accurately is proof of discrimination: *Vaughan* v. *Edel,* 918 F.2d 517 (8th Cir. 1990) (minority opinion).

[12]See W. Delemendo, "Determining Just Cause: An Equitable Solution for the Workplace" (comment), *Washington Law Review,* 66 (1991), 831.

[13]For case law on successful and unsuccessful defense of just cause, see the most recent monthly *Employment-at-Will Reporter,* New England Legal Publishers, P.O. Box 48, Boston, MA02101.

found that "just cause includes only that conduct that an employee knows or should know is subject to discipline." In addition the court found that statutes protecting public employees from discharge have defined "cause" as a situation where the employee's continuance in his or her position is in some way detrimental to the efficiency of the operation. The law and sound public policy recognize that there is good cause for no longer employing the person. Not all courts have adopted the definition of the above two courts.[14]

If a court is presented with the fact that the employee was adequately informed, it is quite certain to find "just cause." In *Conner* v. *Fort Gordon Bus Co.,* 761 F.2d 1493 (11th Cir. 1985), the employee argued that the just cause was only a pretext for discrimination. The court said it was just cause as long as the standard or policy violation was the basis for the discharge and the standard or policy was communicated[15] to the employee before the violation. On previous occasions the employer had only issued reprimands for violations. The fact that the employer did not issue the reprimand but discharged instead doesn't mean the discharge was wrongful. The just-cause audit accordingly should determine the following when an employee was discharged: Was there a rule violation or poor performance? Was the employee knowledgeable before committing the act? In the case of poor performance was there an opportunity to correct? In cases where the employer has been successful in defending just-cause discharges, the employee often unsuccessfully alleges that she or he failed to

understand the consequences of committing the act.

WRITING A HANDBOOK OR A POLICY MANUAL

In the early 1950s communication was one of the most popular subjects in management literature. Management associations, publications, and seminar leaders discussed at length the problem of upward and downward communication. While opinions varied, the consensus of the majority of management decision makers was that the problem of downward communication could best be solved through the use of employee policy manuals or handbooks. The solution to the problem of upward communication was never quite as certain. Some managers relied on employee committees, while others depended on attitude surveys.

A rather large group of employers did nothing about the communication problem until they were threatened with union organization; then it was too late. Even then the usual response was to have the president write a letter to the employees. This usually was not effective, because the only time employees received a letter was when they threatened to join a union. When this tactic failed and the facility was organized, the union leadership became the vehicle for communication to the employees.

In time, managements came to recognize that this too was an unsatisfactory and ineffective approach to the problem. Once again the use of the handbook and employee manual became more popular. The CEO had an opportunity to write a "welcome aboard" letter to the employees. The personnel practitioner found the manual a method for informing employees of organizational rules and procedures. To the supervisor the document was a way to justify a position already taken, or if she or he disagreed with its provisions it was ignored.

The typical handbook was loosely written with the intent of satisfying everyone. Unfortunately, it often contained language that was confusing to both management and employees. With the advent of employee rights legislation—quickly followed

---

[14]Rebecca M. Guerra, "Comment. Oral Contracts to Fire for Good Cause Only. Courts Putting the Cart Before the Horse." *Baylor Law Review,* 47 (1995).

[15]Communication in this context is best described by a situation where an employer had to get 100 percent participation in order to have a group life insurance program. One employee would not sign; the supervisor talked to him, but could not convince him; the plant manager tried without success. They reported to the president that they could not put the program in. The president talked to the employee and said, "Sign up or you are fired." The employee signed. The supervisor and plant manager were bewildered. They asked the employee why he signed when the president talked to him but refused when they tried to get him to do so. The employee's reply was, "Nobody explained it to me before."

by lawyers' looking for material for litigation—the handbook became a fertile source of ideas both for employees and for the legal profession. The wording frequently was designed to mean everything to everybody, so it was inevitable that the interpretation would ultimately be left to the courts.[16]

Need for a Handbook

The first decision to be made when writing a handbook is to decide whether one is needed. For a company of 25 employees or less it is doubtful whether it is. Communications in a small organization are often more effective by dealing with the employees directly than by trying to fit each one into a written policy. Items that must be put in writing can be done by a memo or a letter to the employees.

For a larger organization a well-drafted handbook has several useful purposes:

1. It gives an opportunity for a welcome page.
2. It establishes the fact that it applies to all levels of employees.
3. It may clearly state that a handbook is not a contract.
4. It is an important element in the employer's defense against equal employment opportunity charges by ensuring consistency. When the company's policies are stated in writing, agencies investigating charges give more credibility to the company's position.
5. The handbook is useful in training supervisors how to carry out the policies and ensuring some consistency in their application. This is often difficult because of the difference in philosophy of the supervisors who have wide discretion in administering policies.
6. Oral promises as well as practices by members of management are often held by the courts to be binding. This can be avoided by eliminating them in a handbook. Those employers who feel that a written handbook is a contract forget that oral statements or practices can also be enforced as a contract.
7. A handbook can be extremely helpful in the event of organization attempts by the union. It affords ahead

---

[16]For consideration of all elements in a handbook, see William Hartsfield, *How to Write an Employee Handbook* (Madison, CT:Business and Legal Reports, 1989, 1991).

of time the opportunity to set forth the policies and advantages of a union-free environment. It avoids any misunderstanding or false statements of policies or benefits.

Problem Areas in a Handbook

The aforementioned advantages can be offset if the handbook is not properly drafted. It removes flexibility. When employee handbooks were originally written, the legal implications of certain statements were often not even considered. The language in handbooks is intended to provide a degree of flexibility to management in dealing with specific situations. This approach may have its advantages, but it may also be dangerous. A statement that "it is important that all accidents or injuries are promptly reported to your supervisor" may appear to give the supervisor some freedom of action, but it also may incur enforcement that was not intended, because it is not forceful enough.

There is no substitute for a definitive choice of words that accurately reflects what is meant. If you don't mean it, don't write it. If there is no intention of implying permanency of employment, the use of *probationary period* should be avoided. Many handbooks have such terms as

1. "We reserve the right to . . ."
2. "Exceptions may be made for . . ."
3. "You have permanent employment.'
4. "There is job security here."
5. "Fair treatment and the opportunity for promotion from within the company according to high moral standards . . ."
6. "Employees are classified as permanent, part-time, and temporary."
7. "We request" or "We encourage you to use this complaint procedure."
8. "These rules are guidelines," or, "You are encouraged to follow them."
9. "We pay fair wages."

These are all "canned" terms that have conveyed one meaning to the employees and another to management personnel. They are also often interpreted by the plaintiff's bar differently from what management intended. The problems arise when the courts listen to arguments by the employees and award large amounts for breach of contract. It is ironic that the courts take the position that the employee is considered to have no legal knowledge but that the employer is aware of the legal consequences of every statement. Under these circumstances the employer must consider every clause in the employee handbook not only for its communication value but also for the legal consequences if interpreted differently. There is no substitute for personal distribution following an explanation meeting.

Contents of a Well-Written Handbook

The main problem with most handbooks is that they tell the employees what the company is going to do for them. President John Kennedy's statement in his inaugural address in 1961 should be remembered when writing a handbook:"Ask not what your country can do for you—ask what you can do for your country." In writing a handbook, the employer should tell the employee what is expected of him or her and not what the employee should expect from the company. Not "we encourage" but "you shall" or "you are required." If this theme is carried out, it is beneficial if the handbook is interpreted as a contract. It would be an enforceable document against the employee. It is often better to do things for the employee and not write them, because this affords more flexibility. A well-written handbook contains:

1. Conduct that causes various degrees of disciplinary action, including "sudden death" discharge offenses. These are immediate discharge offenses where the employee has been forewarned before committing the act (call it "sudden dealth" offenses). The listed causes should be as specific as possible as to the conduct, but a clause should be inserted that states that discharge will not be limited to the offenses, but other offenses would require a warning unless added to the "sudden death" list.

2. Rules of conduct, including absenteeism, tardiness, leaving the work site, adherence to coffee break time, work schedules, overtime, and so on.

3. Certain safety rules and the requirement that they be followed.

4. A policy on harassment of all types, including but not limited to sexual harassment, should also be stated in a personal communication.

5. A policy on searches that involve company and employee property. This should also be stated in a separate communication as well as in the handbook.

6. A policy on drug testing and alcohol abuse.

7. A complaint procedure that will be used.

8. A detailed discharge procedure.

Some companies include performance requirements in the handbook, while others feel this is operational and it is better to do this by department or according to job title. Whether performance requirements should be included depends upon the size of the company and upon the job category. It may be necessary to list some general rules particular to the operation so the employees are informed what conduct is expected.

The handbook should contain a clause that defines misconduct that will aid unemployment compensation appeals and also other statutes, such as COBRA. Exhibit 12-3 defines misconduct and discharge policy for a handbook.

The handbook should inform the employee that from time to time management may have to change it. Exhibit 12-4 is suggested language to cover this contingency.

The employer should be assured that the employee not only has read the handbook but also understands it. Sometimes the employee will state that she or he understood it when it was presented, but later actual practice was different. An employee then might be able to allege that he or she didn't know which one to follow. To eliminate this argument, the handbook should contain a statement that the employee should ask questions at any time the handbook is not understood. Exhibit 12-5 is a suggested statement that should be given to the employee at the time the handbook is distributed; after it is signed,[17] it should be put in the employee's personnel file. The statement

---

[17]*Crain Industries, Inc.,* v. *Cass,* 810 S.W.2d 910 (Ark. S.Ct. 1991).

EXHIBIT 12-3

> Whenever the employee willfully, wantonly, and adversely affects the employer's or other employee's interests, it will be considered a gross misconduct that will result in immediate discharge once the facts are ascertained. The following violations will be considered gross misconduct. [List the violations—no more than 15; 10 is better.]
>
> The employee will be warned either verbally or in writing for violation of all other offenses not listed above (excluding those that have been added to the above list after due notice). It is considered a gross misconduct to repeat a violation after being warned in writing or being disciplined and where both parties understand that another violation will result in discharge for gross misconduct.

EXHIBIT 12-4

> From time to time as conditions change, it will be necessary to change or add rules and procedures governing employees. Such changes will be posted well in advance of their effective date, after which time they will become a part of this handbook.

should make it clear the responsibility is on the employee to clear up any misunderstanding.

Disclaimer Clauses in a Handbook

Many lawyers feel that the solution to the problem of having enforceable rights created by the handbook is to include a disclaimer stating that the handbook is not a contract and can be changed at any time at the discretion of the company. Exhibit 12-6 is an example of a typical disclaimer.

If disclaimers are desired, they have a better chance of being enforced if the language is highlighted so it is conspicuous and clear.[18]

1. The handbook is not nor is it intended to be a contract of employment.

2. The handbook is not to be interpreted by the employee as a contract of employment.

3. The employer retains the right to terminate its employees at any time for any reason not prohibited by law, and employee can terminate at will. (Or, some other at-will clause that does not raise a "red flag" may be used.)

4. The employer retains the sole discretion to modify any or all provisions of the handbook at any time for any reason. (This is often used but legally is not necessary. The employer has this right, so why say so?)

In addition to the proper language, other factors are necessary to close loopholes to prevent a disclaimer from being challenged.

1. The language must be clear, conspicuous, and easily understood (keep the legal jargon out).

2. The at-will language must appear in other documents, such as application forms and job offer letters.

3. There must be unambiguous evidence that the employee has received the disclaimer, has read it, understands it, and is required to ask questions if it is not understood.

4. Subsequent employer action and communications with the employee must establish that the employee is treated as an at-will employee.

Whether a disclaimer is legally enforceable often depends on the court. In *Castiglione* v. *Johns Hopkins Hospital*, 517 F.2d 786 (Md. App. 1986), the court said that a disclaimer makes the handbook only a statement of the intent of the employer. This is the position of at least 26 states, as long as intent is clearly shown. However, a

---

[18]*McDonald* v. *Mobil Coal Producing, Inc.*, 820 P.2d 986 (Wyo. 1991).

EXHIBIT 12-5

I, _____ (Social Security number), have read, understand, and have in my possession the company's policies and procedures. I agree as a condition of employment to follow the policies in the handbook, and if there is at any time something that I do not understand, I agree to ask a company representative. I further understand that this signed statement will be a permanent record in my personnel file.

EXHIBIT 12-6

This handbook [or manual] is designed to familiarize you with the conditions of employment which the company expects you to follow. The conditions stated herein are not intended to be and do not constitute a contract of employment.

or

This manual [or handbook] is not intended to and does not constitute a contract between the company and its employees.

sizable minority of the courts take a different view (the list is growing). Sometimes the courts are concerned with the superior bargaining power of the employer and will not enforce the contract without evidence of the employee's interpretation of the clause. In *Helle* v. *Landmark, Inc.,* 742 N.E.2d 765 (Ohio 1984), the court held that a disclaimer would be disregarded if oral promises were made later. Sometimes a disclaimer will not be enforced where it has the effect of giving up statutory rights, such as workers' compensation or discrimination claims.

As we can see from the foregoing cases, the disclaimers are not an absolute assurance that there will not be exposure to a lawsuit. Less exposure would result from eliminating the disclaimer and writing the handbook in such a manner that its provisions were enforceable against the employee. In this case it would not be damaging if the employee attempted to enforce the handbook. If the language itself doesn't grant the employee any rights but is enforceable against the employee, it is difficult to see where there is reason to have a disclaimer and risk the exposure and false security.[19]

There is also an employee relations problem with disclaimers. It certainly strains the company's stature at the orientation program to go over the provisions of the handbook and at the end state that it is discretionary with the company to follow but employees are expected to follow it. Also it may expose the company to union organization, because the employee may feel that she or he has little protection in company policies when they can be changed at will. This could not happen if there were a union and a labor agreement.

A disclaimer clause in a handbook from a personnel practitioner's point of view does not seem advisable but from an attorney's point of view it is the method to avoid liability for a poorly written handbook.

Audit of a Handbook

Any handbook should be reviewed at least once a year. If it has not been revised for the last three years, major changes are very likely to be in order. The review of the handbook should be made regardless of whether the state considers the

---

[19]See "The Use of Disclaimers to Avoid Employer Liability under Employee Handbook Provisions," *Journal of* *Corporation Law,* 12 (Fall 1986), 105. For the opposite view, see "Unjust Dismissal of Employees at Will—Are Disclaimers a Final Solution?" *Fordham Urban Law Journal,* 15 (1987), 533–65.

handbook a legal contract. The legal principles followed in states that do consider a handbook as a contract are also good personnel principles for those states that do not consider the handbook a communications tool. You have a procedure in a contract; the law says that you must follow it. Where the law will not enforce the procedure, it is poor employee relations to promise or agree to do one thing and then do something else.

The basic principle to be followed in reviewing the handbook is to tell the employees what the organization expects of them and not what the organization is going to do for them. Any procedure in the handbook that is not being followed or is not likely to be followed should be eliminated. These procedures should be guidelines for the supervisors to follow but should not be communicated to the employees as an enforceable right.

Language of the Handbook

Most handbooks say too much. A handbook states the rules and regulations that the employees must follow and the consequences if they are not followed. Progressive discipline clauses have legal difficulties. Serious violations should be "sudden death" violations. This information is communicated to the employees in a way that will make certain that they know that there will be no warning or progressive discipline, just discharge. These "sudden death" violations are limited to very serious offenses. If ten of them were listed in the handbook, it would be enough.

Management can do many things without stating them in the handbook. A policy on absenteeism can be a guideline for management personnel to follow without being detailed in the handbook. By spelling it out in detail you lose the flexibility to deal with special situations. A promotion policy can be instituted without mention in the handbook.

The handbook should not deal with benefits, such as health insurance, vacations, and holidays, that are controlled by federal or state laws. Certain detailed communications that are required are out of place in the handbook.[20] It would cause an exposure when the courts apply the handbook language to statutes that require certain benefit language.

Another reason for keeping the benefits separate is that you can make the benefits subject to change without destroying the employee relations value of the handbook. Benefits usually are expected to change from time to time. Because they have always increased in the past, statements such as "these benefits effective from January 1, 19___, will remain in effect until further notice" would have little employee relations consequences as compared to "this handbook is not a contract and the organization reserves the right to alter or change the provisions at its discretion." Management has the right anyway, so why make the statement? Doing so only raises a red flag. It causes employee dissatisfaction, and it diminishes the stature of the handbook.

A good handbook may not win any prizes in legal or personnel literature, but it will tell the employees in unambiguous terms what is expected of them and what will happen if they take—or fail to take—certain actions.

The handbook still can be useful as a communication tool, but it must have a different objective than in the past and more care must be used in its language. For organizations in those states that still do consider a handbook merely a statement of organization policy, it can be a better communication tool if it is written as if it were a contract. A sincere and direct approach is better from an employee relations point of view. From a legal point of view, it offers less encouragement to sue by some members of our "litigation-happy" society.

THE DISCHARGE PROCESS

Employers give a great deal of consideration to whether or not they should terminate an employee,

---

[20]Section 1022(b) of ERISA requires detailed information: *Hicks* v. *Fleming Companies, Inc.,* 961 F.2d 537 (5th Cir. 1992).

but when the decision is finally made they give little thought to the procedure. Even in a "litigation-happy" society most terminations are never challenged in court.[21] There is still a slight stigma to suing your former employer. As this stigma diminishes, there will be an increase in wrongful discharge suits unless the employer does something about it.

Generally, a discharged employee's decision to sue is not an easy one. Litigation poses fear of the unknown and the embarrassing prospect of airing a private misfortune in public. Most people have never started a lawsuit and fear starting one. However, legal advertising and use of contingent fees are helping to alleviate this condition. Presumably the plaintiff's lawyer will assess the case before deciding to handle it. If the employee is angry enough, he or she can find a lawyer who will handle almost any claim. It isn't that the employee knows the law but rather that the employee is angry and his or her only relief is to find a lawyer and try to establish some grounds for suing.

Exposure to Lawsuits Is Expensive

Throughout this chapter we have been talking about exposure to lawsuits, because once the employee files a lawsuit, the employer usually loses, regardless of whether she or he prevails on the merits. There is adverse publicity, lost time, and the distraction associated with having to defend a wrongful discharge. The lawyer must take a great deal of the employer's time in preparing for the case, because the employer is the only one who has all the facts that the lawyer must depend upon to defend the case. This hidden management cost is in addition to the huge legal fees associated with a lawsuit. If the employer loses, usually it pays the fees for both sides. However, if the employer wins, it usually pays its own fees. Exposure to lawsuits can be minimized if the procedure recognizes that the less provocation generated, the less likelihood there is for a lawsuit.

Proper Discharge Procedure

There are certain elements that a discharge procedure should have. The first essential element is that the discharge responsibility should be centralized in one or two persons. It should not be solely in the hands of the first-line supervision. Discharge is no longer a simple task of telling Joe he is fired. The matter should be in the hands of a person or persons who can handle the case impartially and with due regard to the rights and feelings of both the supervisor and the employee. First-line supervisors are normally charged with getting the job out and usually have little concern for the niceties of human relations when the operation is shorthanded because it was necessary to discharge a worker.

The second necessary element is that the procedure should be fair, firm, and friendly. For the employer it means writing off an investment, and for the employee it is the end of a source of income. This often generates a sense of insecurity. The discharge procedure must consider the impact upon the parties involved.

The third element is that the reason must be logical from the employee's point of view. An employer would not discharge somebody because of failure to say "hello" when spoken to, because that would not be a logical reason for termination. The termination must be for something that a normal employer would do and must be understandable to a reasonable person.

The fourth important element in the discharge process is that a proper investigation must be made to determine the facts. An investigation should be made even when the employer is sure of the facts. There is nothing that convinces the employee more of fairness and receives more weight from a court than a thorough investigation of the facts.[22]

Causes of Provocation

One of the first things to avoid is provocation. The act of discharging is inherently provocative, so to avoid exposure to lawsuits management must do something to mitigate it. More often than not,

---

[21]It is estimated that there are more than 100,000 discharges for which damages could be collected if the employee sued.

[22]See William E. Hartsfield, "Suggestions for Investigating Employee Misconduct," *The Practical Lawyer,* (March 1, 1985), 11.

the merits are not as important as the way the employee was discharged. The judge or the jury may "tune out" the facts of the discharge and hear only how it was done. Some of the causes of provocation are:

1. Indecisiveness, when the company behaves in a way that indicates it doesn't know whether or not to discharge. The employee is tormented.

2. Humiliation. Every employee has some worth or value to the company and at some time made a contribution. These assets should be stated as well as faults that caused the discharge.

3. Misrepresentation, which fans the flame of anger more than any other factor, especially when the employee knows that the statement is not accurate. The most common misrepresentation is a charge of poor performance after a wage increase was given a month before. Misrepresentation also indicates vulnerability, which in turn encourages aggressiveness to see a lawyer.

4. A rejected feeling. The employee has lost a job and has no place to go. If there is no union the law office is a good place for condolence. One of the biggest barriers to litigation is fear of what will happen if she or he sues. The employee needs help, not a lawyer.

How to Prevent Provocation

1. Develop a concise reason for discharge. It is important for the employee to logically understand why she or he was discharged. Obscure reasons "to soften the blow" will backfire.

2. Decide upon all the severance details. There should be no ambiguities to negotiate.

3. Tell the employee who the decision makers are. If possible the decision makers should participate in the discharge process.

4. Be brief and to the point. Lengthy dissertations usually sound weak and defensive and prolong the employee discomfort.[23] One can be sensitive and still not be defensive.

---

[23]This is advisable in communicating other misfortunes. Sometimes the reaction isn't what is expected. The author once told a spouse in a brief and to-the-point statement that her husband was killed in a work-related accident an hour before. Her reply was, "How much do I get?"

5. Thank the employee for his or her contributions. This may not always be appropriate, but if this is possible the employee is less likely to be upset to the point of seeing a lawyer.

6. Offer some counseling service about finding another job. Outplacement service or advice on where the employee can sell his or her skills would be helpful to give the employee a sense of security other than seeing a lawyer.[24]

Timing and Place of Discharge

Although there is never a good time to discharge, some times are worse than others. Some employers believe that Friday afternoon is a good time because the employee can leave without much embarrassment or undue interruption. That is the most common time to discharge.

Why on Friday?

In many respects Friday afternoon is the worst time to discharge because it makes the employee angry; the weekend is spoiled—mother-in-law is coming over; there are plans to go to the beach with the children; it's your turn to have the bridge club. By Saturday morning the employee has talked to so many people justifying the ego that she or he is ready to see a lawyer.

Why not do it on Monday morning when the children are in school, the lawyer is in court, and several employment offices are taking applications? The discharged employee can fill out a few applications and tell the family that night that she or he was discharged but already has several prospects for another job. The whole family relaxes and watches "Monday Night Football."

The exit interview should be held in a place where there will not be any interruption and where the manager can conclude the meeting by leaving. The place of the meeting should be apart from co-workers. The discharged employee should be able to leave the plant without contact with a co-worker. It should be as private as possible. Only those who have a need to know should be told of the discharge.

---

[24]The outplacement services industry grosses more than $5 million annually.

Final Steps in Discharging

A discharge is an adversity and therefore is an exposure to a lawsuit. The employer should assume that the employee will challenge it. The preceding predischarge preparation affords less chance that it will be challenged. The final steps in the process will supplement this preparation.

Step One. The first step is to suspend and allow time for investigation. This shows the employee and the court that the employer gave some consideration to the act. Suspension should be used even if it is a "sudden death" offense. There may be some question as to whether the act was committed, but even if the employer is sure of the facts suspension is a good defensive move. The suspension should be of short duration. The employee should not be left in the dark any longer than necessary. One of the virtues of the suspension technique is that it forces management to investigate immediately. In the event the employee is exonerated, the period of the suspension should be paid for by the employer; this is another reason why the suspension period should be short.

Step Two. The next step is the investigation of all the facts that will establish a just cause for the discharge. Another purpose of the investigation is to consider any legal problems of the discharge. The investigation should be well documented. Performance appraisals should be reviewed, and the selection procedure should be checked to determine whether there were any promises made at the time of hiring. The handbook or the policy manual should be examined to determine whether there was any language in it that might establish a contract of employment or denote permanency of employment. After the investigation is completed, a second person who is not familiar with the case should review the file to determine if the reason makes sense.

A Second Fresh Look

It is preferable that this audit be conducted by some person who has not yet participated in the discharge decision. However, in a small organiza-

tion this is not practical, so there may be some overlapping between the investigation and the audit to the extent that the same person does it. The person who is responsible for reviewing the discharge procedure should carefully evaluate and review the following:

1. Any evidence that the person was terminated for a reason that might be held to be contrary to public policy, such as refusing to commit perjury, whistle-blowing, refusing to be excused from jury duty, filing a workers' compensation claim, refusing to violate a professional code of ethics, or any other act that may be construed to have the public policy protection.

2. The company's handbook or policy manual to determine whether there are any statements that indicate permanency status or if there is a permanent employee classification. Does the document provide for a discharge procedure, and was it followed? Any statement in the handbook or policy manual that is not followed results in serious exposure in most states.

3. The performance appraisals to determine whether there are any inconsistencies between the performance appraisals and the reason given for the discharge.

4. The recruitment and selection procedures to determine whether there have been any promises made as to job security, promotions, or termination only for just cause.

5. Is there any evidence that a statute has been violated?

6. Was an exit interview conducted in which more than one person participated? Were the reasons for discharge established and clearly communicated to the employee, and if so, have they been consistent when communicated to other members of management and for use on the unemployment compensation claims? The reasons should somewhat correlate with the facts revealed in the investigation.

The Exit Interview

The predischarge information should be reviewed and applied at the exit interview. The purpose of the exit interview is to establish the reason for the discharge that will be used by all members of management and when an unemployment compensation claim is filed.[25] The important point is that the employee is told what the reason is. Some attorneys advise not to give a reason. This is acceptable in most states under the at-will doctrine. However, if the employee files an unemployment compensation claim, a reason will have to be given. If one isn't given at the exit interview, the employee's version will be given to the unemployment claims representative and the employer will immediately be put on the defensive. The ambiguity can later be used in a wrongful discharge action to the detriment of the employer.

The exit interview should be structured so the employee leaves with dignity and without being emotionally upset. Two persons should participate in the meeting. Having a person just as a witness causes the meeting to be too legalistic. If both participate, then there is a built-in witness. At the exit interview the employee should be told what the employer's reply will be to reference inquiries, what position will be taken on unemployment compensation claims, and why.

Employment Agreements at Time of Hiring

At-will agreements are often written in the application form and are signed at the same time that the entire form is signed. This type of clause has been used by several companies for many years and reads as follows:

In consideration of my employment, I agree to conform to the rules and regulations of XYZ Company, and my employment and compensation can be terminated, with or without cause, and with or without notice, at any time, at the option of either the company or myself. I understand that no manager or representative of XYZ Company has any authority to enter into any agreement

for employment for any specified period of time, or make any agreement contrary to statement.[26]

This clause has been enforced in most courts that have had the issue before them.[27]

Some surveys show that this type of clause chills applicants against accepting a job offer, especially when they have more than one to choose from.[28] Like disclaimers in a handbook, a signed piece of paper is seldom a substitute for positive personnel administration. The presence of this clause could also be "fodder" for a union organizer.

When the law moved into the personnel function, the employer had a tendency to overreact; an at-will statement may not be necessary and could create certain risks.[29] Most arbitrators do not consider the clause necessary as long as the labor agreement has a "just-cause" provision.[30]

THE USE OF WAIVERS OR RELEASES

Some companies feel that the way to stop all claims after discharge is to have the employee sign a release. This would certainly discourage a

---

[25]Many discharge unemployment compensation appeals have been lost because several members of management give different reasons for the discharge. See also *Flanigan* v. *Prudential Federal Savings &Loan Association,* 720 P.2d 257 (Mont. 1986), where three managers all testified to different reasons for the termination in a wrongful discharge case.

[26]*Eliel* v. *Sears, Roebuck and Co.,* 387 N.W. 2d 842 (Mich. App. 1985).

[27]See *Reid* v. *Sears, Roebuck and Co.,* 790 F.2d 453 (6th Cir. 1986), *Batchelor* v. *Sears, Roebuck and Co.,* 574 F.Supp. 1480 (E.D. Mich. 1983), as well as several other Sears, Roebuck and Co. earlier cases; *Crain* v. *Burroughs Corp.,* 560 F.Supp. 849 (D.C. Cal. 1983); *Whittaker* v. *Care-more, Inc.,* 621 S.W. 2d 395 (Tenn. 1981). However, in the *Reid* case the court said that because the application was signed 17 years before her employment was terminated, these facts couldn't be completely ignored.

[28]See Raymond L. Hilgert, "How At-Will Statements Hurt Employers," *Personnel Journal,* (February 1988), 75.

[29]See "The Hazards of Firing-at-Will," *Wall Street Journal,* (March 9, 1987), 16; Raymond L. Hilgert, "Discipline and Discharge from an Arbitrator's Point of View," Proceedings of the 1986 meeting of the Midwest Society of Human Resources and Industrial Relations, Terre Haute, IN: Indiana State University School of Business.

[30]See Frank Elkouri and Edna Asper Elkouri, *How Arbitration Works,* 4th ed. (Washington, DC: Bureau of National Affairs, 1985), pp. 650–707; also 1987 supplement, pp. 131–48.

lawyer from taking a case where a release was signed, provided it was tightly worded and properly drafted.

Furthermore, signed releases do not necessarily prevent litigation.[31] They are often challenged as not being completely voluntary or not understood or because the employer has taken advantage of its superior bargaining position. They must be carefully drafted, and precautions must be taken to be sure that the employee fully understands what she or he is signing and that the language covers all claims that the employee might have, both present and future. The Older Workers Benefit Protection Act (OWBPA) requires that an employee be given 21 days before deciding to sign a release and 7 days to rescind after signing.

Some states require a period of time to rescind the release after it has been executed.[32] Whether it be an agreement signed separately or a release at the time of termination, there is still an exposure if the employee feels that he or she was forced into it or is angry with the employer for how he or she was discharged. To be sure that it is voluntary the provisions of OWBPA must be followed.

Purpose of Discharge Procedure

This chapter may leave the impression that the discharge process is so complex that it is better not to start it but to live with the problem. The purpose of this detailed analysis is to prevent exposure to lawsuits, not to stop discharges. Anyone can start a lawsuit, but most people are not predisposed to do so. Although winning in court can be satisfying, in the real sense "the horse is already out of the barn" when a claim is filed with a court or an agency. With careful, creative, sensitive procedures, objective performance appraisals, and proper discipline, most claims arising out of a discharge can be prevented. The courts and juries are telling the employer that they will not interfere with the discharge process unless they do not like the way employees are being discharged. Juries tend to overreact when the discharge is not done in a humane way using the "reasonable person" standard.

The employer that believes that employment at will is a management right is challenging the discharged employee to test the doctrine and is exposed to litigation. The employer who modifies the discharge policy and procedures to protect against some exceptions to common law employment-at-will doctrine has considerably less exposure. A policy should not be such as to prevent the employer from discharging an employee or from taking advantage of what is left of the at-will doctrine. Just-cause policies along with other procedures should not be ignored.[33] The law makes one thing clear: The day has passed when a supervisor or a manager in an emotional state can walk up to an employee and say, "You are fired," and not be exposed to litigation.

Checklist to Prevent Exposure to Wrongful Discharge Litigation (Some Are Judgment Factors)

1. Is employee covered by any type of written agreement (including a collective bargaining agreement)?
2. Have written or oral representations been made to form a contract?
3. Is a defamation claim likely?
4. Is there a possible discrimination allegation?
5. Is there any workers' compensation involvement?
6. Have reasonable rules and regulations been communicated and enforced?
7. Has employee been given an opportunity to explain any rule violation or to correct poor performance?
8. Have all monies been paid within 24 hours after separation?
9. Has employee been advised of his or her rights under COBRA?
10. Has employee been advised of what the employer will tell a prospective employer in response to a reference inquiry?

---

[31]See *Pratt* v. *Brown Machine Company,* 855 F.2d 1225 (6th Cir. 1988).

[32]Minnesota Statutes Section 363.031 allows 15 days to rescind after the agreement has been signed by both parties.

[33]Michael D. Fabiano, "The Meaning of Just Cause for Termination When an Employer Alleges Misconduct and the Employee Denies It" (Note). *Hastings Law Journal,* 399 (1993).

CHAPTER 13

BALANCING EMPLOYEE PRIVACY RIGHTS AND EMPLOYER'S RIGHT TO KNOW

Use of Personnel Records and Requirements to Retain
Overview of Privacy Rights in Employer-Employee Relationship
Use of Polygraph Tests
Employer Right of Search and Seizure
Common Law on Disclosure of Employee Information
Negligent Hiring and Retention
Exposure for Defamation
Recommendations That Consider Employee's Privacy
and Employer's Need to Know

USE OF PERSONNEL RECORDS AND REQUIREMENTS TO RETAIN

Definition and Purpose of Personnel Records

It is common practice for employers to keep individual records on each employee. These records are commonly called employee records or individual personnel files. Employee records are defined as records that contain initial application forms, results of physical examinations, interviewer's notations, test scores, periodic appraisals, transfers and promotions, disciplinary actions, releases and rehirings, wages, salaries, taxes paid, contributions, and similar items.[1] It is highly

important that everything about the employee go into the employee's individual file. Some attorneys believe that the personnel file is the first line of defense in litigation.

The purpose of personnel records is to record information about an employee obtained during the course of employment. The fact that records are kept puts the employee on notice that there is documentation of his or her activities while employed. It also permits an audit of whether addresses are up to date, whether beneficiaries are current, and other necessary personal employee data.

Documentation for purposes of discrimination charges, unemployment compensation determination, and arbitration is an essential element of a case. When considering whether to record or retain a fact, always ask the question, For what

---

[1]Dale Yoder, *Personnel Management in Industrial Relations,* 6th ed. (Englewood Cliffs, NJ: Prentice Hall, 1970).

purpose was the fact recorded, and is it necessary to retain it?

All too often important arbitration, EEOC cases, unemployment compensation, or court decisions are lost because the employer fails to produce the proper evidence to substantiate a fact. Some practitioners believe that separate personnel files according to subject matter should be kept for each employee. They suggest a general file, job performance file, medical file, I-9 forms, and closed file where all letters of references, records of investigations, or other matters that employees should not see are filed. The justification often given for the separation of files is that sensitive information would not be given to outsiders and information will not be disclosed inadvertently. Further, the person reviewing the file would not be able to consider irrelevant material that may be damaging in litigation or in other employee relations problems.

The reason given by proponents for keeping everything in one file is that, when segregated, relevant information is often missed; further, an employee problem is seldom categorized according to the way the data are filed. Data in one file may not offer a solution to a particular problem unless all the files are reviewed. The author's experience favors the one-file concept as the most reliable method to keep employee records, except possibly certain medical records. Most access statutes do not permit employees to review the entire file.

Statutory Requirements to Retain Certain Records

There are certain statutory requirements stating that an employer must keep records on an individual employee. These requirements often change, so regulations must be periodically reviewed. The antidiscrimination laws, OSHA, the Fair Labor Standards Act (FLSA), the Equal Pay Act, CRA91, ADEA, and ADA require that relevant information be available for investigation purposes and to ensure the proper administration of the laws.

The Immigration Reform and Control Act of 1986 (IRCA) requires employment records to be kept for three years or one year after termination,

whichever is later. IRCA imposes a fine up to $1,000 for failure to keep the necessary records. The unique part of the requirement is that the person responsible for keeping the records can be personally liable.[2]

Record retention requirements are also indirectly found in the Consolidated Omnibus Budget Reconciliation Act (COBRA). Under this amendment to ERISA, the plan administrator can be personally liable up to $100 per day for failure to give notice of the right to be covered, or the court can grant such other relief as it may deem proper. This result is considerable personal liability for the plan administrator.

Under Employee Retirement Income Security Act (ERISA), records must be kept for not less than six years after the filing date of the documents. When the documents are changed the six years start all over again. Under ERISA it would be advisable to keep all current records and their respective changes.

Regulations promulgated by the agencies responsible for enforcing the antidiscrimination statutes have established record-keeping retention policies. The employer should comply because the records may become the proof that an employment decision was legally made.

Under Title VII, job applications, resumes, payroll records, and employee personnel files must be kept for a minimum of six months or until disposition of a pending legal action.[3] Employers of 100 or more employees are required to file the EEO-1 report annually; this gives an inventory of employees by race, ethnic group, disability, sex, job category, and salary. Unions with 100 or more members must file an EEO-3 report, and records must be kept for one year after the report. Private employment agencies have not been subject to the Title VII record-keeping or reporting requirement except in their capacity as employers.

Government contractors under Executive Order 11246 do not have a specific record-keeping requirement except to make all their records

---

[2]See H. Frye and H. Klasko, *Immigration Compliance Guide* (1991), Bureau of Immigration and Naturalization, 425 I St. N.W., Washington DC 20536.

[3]*Capellopo* v. *FMC Corp.*, 50 FEP Cases (BNA) 11 57.

available for compliance review. Under the Rehabilitation Act of 1973 and CRA91 contractors and subcontractors must retain complaints or action taken for one year. The same rule applies for contractors under the Vietnam Era Veterans Readjustment Act of 1974.

The Equal Pay Act of 1963[4] requires that employees' records concerning wages, hours of work, and other terms of employment (including exempt-status employees) be kept for two years. Records supporting employment decisions under the act must also be kept for two years.

The Age Discrimination in Employment Act of 1967 rules require that employment records including the employee's personnel file must be kept for one year. However, payroll information and information relating to name, address, birth date, and job category must be kept for three years. Under the Fair Labor Standards Act records must be kept for three years. If a lawsuit is commenced, all revelant records must be retained for the duration of the lawsuit. For further record retention requirements, see "Guide to Record Retention Requirements" in 1988 Code of Federal Regulations, U.S. Government Printing Office, Supt. of Documents, Washington, DC 20402; also W. Hancock, "Guide to Records Retention," also published periodically by the Federal Register as a guide to record retention..

Record Retention as a Personnel Policy

Proper personnel practice in the areas of discipline, performance appraisals, skills inventories, and so forth, requires the personnel practitioner to go beyond what the law requires in the area of personnel record keeping.

What records the employer should maintain is a policy as well as a legal question (except that the employer must keep all records pertaining to a charge or a complaint from the date it is filed). The employer should have records to show that company policy and procedures are complying with the law.

On the other hand, too many records can be damaging in the event of a lawsuit. If the employer

does not have certain information, it cannot be disclosed and a decision by the regulatory agency must be made only on the information available. This at times can be advantageous to the employer.

The employer should audit personnel records at least every three years and destroy irrelevant, immaterial, or damaging records if not required to keep them. It is also advisable to separate certain records that you are required to keep and note a destroy date. This policy will give stature to the records you retain and at the same time not subject damaging records to the subpoena process in the event of a lawsuit.[5]

Attorneys usually advocate keeping too few records for sound personnel administration. The attorney reasons that if the plaintiff wants more information, he or she can use the discovery process. Positive personnel administration and space limitations dictate that only those records that are useful should be kept. If you look at all records with a critical eye, you are likely to find that you are keeping more than are really necessary.

Statutory Requirements of Disclosure

Records are the property of the employer, but certain statutes require the employer to disclose specific information for certain reasons.[6] These reasons are usually to enable a government regulatory agency to carry out its function of enforcing the law.

Under most statutes the statutorily required disclosure must be made upon request. The burden is upon the party who requests to show that they are entitled to the information. Often the disclosure of employee information causes an employee relations problem, so the employer may take the position that it is better to be ordered to disclose than to do it voluntarily.

Under NLRB the employer is required to give certain information. Often a certified labor

---

[4]29 U.S.C. 206 et al.

[5]See *Ramsey* v. *American Filter Co.,* 772 F.2d 1303 (7th Cir. 1985), where damaging notations on the applicant form cost the employer $92,500.

[6]Under *University of Pennsylvania* v. *EEOC,* 850 F.2d 969 (3rd Cir. 1988), regulatory agencies have broad subpoena powers.

organization will request information on an employee or group of employees. The information requested must be relevant to the collective bargaining agreement. It must be needed for the union to represent the employee properly. The information requested must concern wages and working conditions and protect the collective bargaining relationship. The NLRB and the courts have given a liberal interpretation to this general principle. However, if the information requested relates to matters not within union jurisdiction or is of individual concern, it will be denied.[7]

Another statutory requirement to release limited employee information comes from a regulation promulgated under the authority of OSHA. This statute states that an employer must give access of the records to employees or their representatives and to other employees who are exposed to toxic and hazardous substances when requested.[8] The person requesting the records must show a need and have professional qualifications to interpret the information requested. The regulation requires that the medical records on exposure to toxic substances be kept for 30 years. The employee must be informed at the time of hiring and each year thereafter that such records are available.

This regulation has been judicially accepted.[9] In both cases the court required that the National Institute for Occupational Safety and Health (NIOSH) be given the information. However, the court said that the employee's privacy is a factor to be considered in the use of that information by the governmental agency.

As in other areas under antidiscrimination laws, if employee information has a disparate impact on the categories of individuals being protected, it is unlawful. The information cannot be used for making an employment decision unless a business necessity can be shown. This does not mean that background investigations are prohibited, but it does mean there must be a nondiscriminatory use and purpose for such information.

When a charge is broad and includes several allegations, information must be furnished for all the allegations. If the charge is properly worded, the agency has considerable latitude in seeking information. In this type of charge the employer has less opportunity to refuse information, and the defense of relevancy must be used with discretion.

Disclosure Rights of Public Employees

Federal employees are protected by the Privacy Act of 1974.[10] The act requires federal agencies to permit employees to examine, copy, correct, or amend employee information in their file. If there is a dispute on the accuracy of the information or what is to be included, an appeal procedure is provided. The act prohibits, with certain exceptions, the disclosure of information to outsiders without written consent of the employee to whom the information pertains. The agency has no obligation to inform the employee that the information exists except to publish it annually in the *Federal Register.*

Almost all states have enacted comprehensive privacy acts for the public sector. Other state legislatures have not gone quite as far as a comprehensive plan but have imposed certain restrictions on disclosing employee information in the public sector.

Although the Federal Fair Credit Reporting Act[11] regulates the activities of consumer reporting agencies, it does affect the disclosure of information by the employer where the employer engages a consumer agency to make an investigation.

The employer, when using a consumer agency, must inform the employee that an investigation is being made as to character, general reputation, personal characteristics, and mode of hiring. If the employee so requests, the employer must provide a complete disclosure of the nature and scope of the investigation.

---

[7]*NLRB* v. *Holyduke Water Power Co.,* 788 F.2d 49 (1st Cir. 1985).

[8]29 CFR Part 1910.20 and 29 CFR Part 1913.10.

[9]*United States* v. *Westinghouse,* 638 F.2d 570 (3rd Cir. 1980); *E.I. duPont de Nemours and Co.* v. *Finklea,* 422 F.Supp. 821 (S.D. W.Va. 1977).

[10]U.S.C. Sect. 552(a), 5 CFR 297.101.

[11]15 U.S.C. Sect. 1681 et seq.

The Freedom of Information Act (FOIA) states that where a federal agency maintains a system of records, on request any individual or representative may gain access to that record if the proper authorization is shown by the representative.[12] The FOIA further provides that an individual or representative may request amendment to the record; if refused, adversary proceedings to determine the facts are triggered. Such proceedings are subject to judicial review.

FOIA's stated purpose is to require the information to be released and to inform the public; it is not for the purpose of benefiting the litigants in a lawsuit. The rules and regulations in compliance with this purpose are promulgated with emphasis on disclosing information to the public.

There are exceptions under the access act. The federal agency may promulgate challengeable rules where revealing personnel records will obstruct the agency's enforcement function. If the right of disclosure is doubtful, the courts normally rule in favor of disclosure. Medical records are exempted under FOIA, but under certain conditions they can be revealed under Section 552(a) of the act.

OVERVIEW OF PRIVACY RIGHTS IN EMPLOYER-EMPLOYEE RELATIONSHIP

The protection of a person's privacy is a common law right that has been protected by the courts for many years.[13] The Restatement (Second) of Torts Section 652b states:

One who intentionally intrudes, physically or otherwise, upon the solitude or seclusion of another or his private concerns is subject to liability to the other for invasion of his privacy, if the intrusion would be highly offensive to a reasonable person.

This principle has been used in a wide variety of situations.[14] On the issue of abortion the court has held that a state statute prohibiting it is an invasion of privacy.[15] In police investigations the officer must be careful not to invade the privacy of the accused. The Supreme Court held in *Eisenstadt, Sheriff* v. *Baird,* 405 U.S. 438 (1972), that it is an invasion of privacy to question another person about marriage and sex life, because these are fundamental rights entitled to privacy protection.

Various state laws that require safety measures (wearing of helmets by motorcycle operators) have on a case-by-case basis been held to be an invasion of privacy. In many situations, the plaintiff claims emotional distress is caused by invasion of privacy.

An uninvited intrusion into a person's solitude or seclusion may also provide for an invasion of privacy claim.[16] This is a common argument in drug and alcohol testing as well as other areas.

As illustrated above, invasion of privacy claims are found in all walks of life.[17] However, this chapter will be concerned only with the invasion of privacy in the employer-employee relationship.

Technology and Training

We take technology as a part of our daily lives. A person can hardly move in our society without using technology. It is the very fiber of our society. We get up in the morning and turn on the television set for the news. From that time on we are dependent upon technology to run our lives.

In the job market technology has caused many persons to be retrained. Training has been developed to run information systems. Training in technology is the most popular subject in corporate training programs. This training has more to offer toward the success of the organization than ever before. The workers are not only expected to know their craft, but expected to apply it technically. We have no doubt that we have gone

---

[12]5 U.S.C. Sect. 552(a)(1) (FOIA).

[13]Prosser and Keeton, *Law of Torts,* 5th ed. (1984).

[14]See D. Warren and Louis Brandeis, "The Right to Privacy," *Harvard Law Review,* 4 (1990), 193.

[15]*Roe* v. *Wade,* 410 U.S. 113 (1973).

[16]See "Snoops Put a Strain on Employee Loyalty" (editorial), *Business Week,* January 15, 1990, p. 91; Also J. Rothfeder and M. Galen, "Is Your Boss Spying on You," *Business Week,* January 15, 1990, pp. 74–75.

[17]R. Machsun, and J. Monteleone, "Insurance Coverage for Wrongful Employment Practice Claim Under Various Liability Policies," *Business Law,* 49 (1994), 68.

from an industrial era to a knowledge era. (The weekday edition of the *New York Times* contains more information than the average person was likely to come across in a lifetime during the 17th century.) As a child we thought "Buck Rogers" was a fancy, that the moon was romantic (not an objective in technology), that radio had its limitations, space was for the astrologer, not for the lay person. Our forefathers never dreamed that one could travel faster than sound or even measure it.

Technology has created a whole new vocabulary with such words as Internet, bits, programmers, word processing, steel collar. The computer operator has replaced the comptometer operator, hardware and software now have new meanings, hi-tech consulting is now a profession. All are now a part of our new vocabulary.

Technology has created obsolescence in the human rights field. The average human relations manager knows little about technology, unless that person has gone through extensive training. A good manager can operate a company via computer. Absentee management is no longer a myth but is here to stay. Unless the manager knows at least some technology he or she can become obsolete in a very short time.

Technology and Privacy

Electronic mail, voice mail, and other technical devices have caused a legal confrontation in the common law doctrine of the invasion of privacy.[18] In a lawsuit in federal court, a manager sued McDonald's Corporation for monitoring and taping his voice mail messages. According to the lawsuit, the messages contained intimate exchanges with a co-employee with whom the manager was having an affair. The manager alleged that his employer secretly recorded the messages and played them to his wife, possibly violating federal and state wiretapping laws and the Electronic Communications Privacy Act. The manager argued that he had an expectation of

privacy in the communications because he accessed his voice mail with a confidential code.

This case helps define the contours of appropriate employer monitoring of electronic communications such as e-mail and voice mail systems. As technology becomes increasingly common in the workplace, further challenges to employer monitoring are certain to arise.[19]

William Prosser (author of *Restatement of Torts* that calls the invasion of privacy a tort) would turn over in his grave if he knew what technology has done to the right of the individual "to enjoy solitude and seclusion." With the proper information system one person can find out anything about another person. The lawsuits of the future will involve the invasion of privacy and the use of technology.[20]

In summary, the employer can ask personal questions about personal matters as long as they are business related and reasonably executed.

Statutory, common law, technology, and constitutional privacy protection has been accelerated by social legislation in discrimination and employee rights. The availability of attorneys to pursue any and all possible indications of a violation has also helped.[21] There is also pressure on state and federal levels of the government to pass legislation to protect various privacy rights of the employee.

Protection by statute is necessary, because under the common law, the employee in the employer-employee relationship has fewer rights than as a citizen. As the court said in *United States* v. *Blok,* 186 F.2d 1019 (D.C. Cir. 1951), it was a violation of privacy under the Fourth Amendment for the police to search the employee's desk, but it would have been proper for the supervisor to do so.

Many believe that the legal scales are weighted too heavily for the employer. The greatest exposure to litigation on privacy rights of the

---

[18]Michael Levy, "The Electronic Monitoring of Workers: Privacy in the Age of the Electronic Sweatshop. *Legal Reference Service Quarterly,* 14 (1995), 5.

[19]See D. McCartney, "Electronic Surveillance the and Resulting Loss of Privacy in the Workplace," *University of Missouri-Kansas City Law Review,* 62 (1994), 859.

[20]See L. Ganft, "An Affront to Human Dignity: Electronic Mail Monitoring in the Workplace," *Harvard Journal of Law and Technology,* 8 (1995), 345.

[21]Michael Levy, "The Electronic Monitoring of Workers: Privacy in the Age of the Electronic Sweatshop. *Legal Reference Service Quarterly,* 14 (1995), 5.

employee is in the areas of drug and alcohol testing, record keeping, psychological and honesty testing, and communication on discipline. All forms of technology will be next.

Employer Invasion of Privacy

Under the common law, employer invasion of privacy usually occurs when the employer commits some act that damages the employee's right to enjoy a good reputation. Public disclosure of facts could be an invasion of privacy.[22] An example is disclosure by the employer of information about an employee's drinking habits or failing a drug or an AIDS test. The plaintiff must prove that these facts are highly offensive and are not of legitimate concern to the public in order to recover under tort law.[23]

The public not only includes persons unrelated to the employment situation but also includes supervisors and others closely related to the employment situation who do not have a reason to know.

A flight attendant directed her private physician to supply the employer with information concerning her medical condition. Based on this information the employer's medical examiner waived weight limits imposed for appearance regulations and applicable to her job. The information supplied included details of contemplated gynecological surgery. The employer's medical examiner disclosed this information to her male supervisor and to her husband. She sued the employer for invasion of privacy. The court found that it was an invasion of privacy to disclose the information to her supervisor and her husband. The supervisor had no authority to act on the data disclosed, and her husband "faced no problem involving his own well-being or emergency care for his spouse"; therefore, neither recipient had a need to know.[24] The court allowed compensatory damages but

denied punitive damages because there was no evidence of malice. Unless malice can be shown in privacy cases the court will not allow punitive damages.[25] In a related case the court held that a consultation between the company physician and the employee's personal physician concerning the employee's illness did not constitute an invasion of privacy. Employer conduct was motivated by concern for the employee when the information related to a requested leave of absence.

Rights in Public Sector

Employees in the public sector have more rights than those in the private sector, because they are protected by the Fourth Amendment of the Constitution. Where a police officer was discharged for living with a married woman, the court found invasion of privacy. However, if the private life of the employee affects the job, the court will find that the job requirements will override the privacy right.[26] In *Potter* v. *Murray City,* 760 F.2d 1065 (10th Cir. 1985), cert. denied (1985), the discharge of a Utah policeman was upheld when he was practicing plural marriage in violation of a Utah statute.

The courts, with increasing frequency, are finding that certain types of sexual harassment (as discussed in chapter 7) are an invasion of privacy. To avoid liability under privacy law, the court must find that the plaintiff had a reasonable expectation that the employer's action would cause damage to one's reputation.

USE OF POLYGRAPH TESTS

A major cause of property losses is employee theft related to the expanding use of drugs and alcohol. The use of polygraph tests and other forms of lie detectors is one way to stop or decrease these

---

[22]Where a city ordinance requires employee to sign an affidavit the court held to be invalid.

[23]*Restatement (2d) of Torts* Sect. 652E., M. "Privacy in the Workplace: Balancing Title VII Mandates with Privacy," *Columbia Law Review,* 123 (1995), 62.

[24]*Lewis* v. *United Airlines,* 500 N.E.2d 370 (Ohio App. 1985).

[25]This is important, because if punitive damages can be shown, a jury trial is allowed under the CRA91 amendment to Title VII.

[26]*Soraka* v. *Dayton-Hudson Corp.,* 1 Cal.Repr. 2d 77 (Cal. App. 1st Dist.).

losses.[27] This may or may not be an effective way to control losses, but it involves a certain degree of exposure.

One of the personnel practitioner's most important tasks is to determine the facts when a job applicant is alleged to be dishonest. Applicants often do not seek jobs for wages, but for the opportunity to embezzle, steal, sell company secrets to competitors, or commit other dishonest acts. This type of person is often difficult to detect. When the actions of one dishonest employee are not discovered, the example becomes a challenge to others. As a result, pilferage and dishonesty become more widespread.

The obvious solution to the problem is not to hire the person in the first place or to discharge him or her when the acts are detected, but this is not always practical

For many years the use of a lie detector test has been an available—but controversial—method of detecting dishonesty. The most common technique involves the use of the polygraph machine. Other methods have also been used, such as an intravenous injection of sodium pentothal ("truth serum"), which like the polygraph measures bodily changes that indicate whether the subject is telling the truth when responding to certain questions.

Employee Polygraph Protection Act

The Employee Polygraph Protection Act of 1988[28] was passed by the Congress "to prevent the denial of employment opportunities by prohibiting the use of lie detectors by employers involved in or affecting interstate commerce." The act prohibits the use of mechanical or electrical devices. It is illegal to use the results for the purposes of rendering a diagnostic opinion regarding the honesty or dishonesty of an employee.[29] For those employers who are now using any mechanical or electrical means to obtain facts, or who may consider doing so in the future, this act will be limiting.

The employer is prohibited from requiring, requesting, or even suggesting that any employee or prospective employee take any type of lie detector test. The act further prevents the employer from using or threatening to use any of the results of a lie detector test in making an employment decision. The act is enforced by the secretary of labor, who has promulgated rules and regulations under the act. The secretary has also prepared a summary of the act to be posted by each employer in conspicuous places on its premises where employee and applicant notices are normally placed. (This is usually in the employment office or where employees normally come with problems, such as the personnel office.)

If an employee is discriminated against for refusing to take a test or for testifying that another employee or prospective employee was discriminated against, the act will protect such an employee from any employer adverse action.

The secretary of labor has investigative powers, can conduct a hearing, and usually finds a loophole. Violation of the act has a civil penalty of not more than $10,000. The amount is determined by the secretary of labor, who can go to court to collect the fine or have an employee reinstated. An employee can also go to court within three years after the alleged violation. The act provides for attorney fees for the prevailing party. Waiver of employee rights and procedures under the act is specifically prohibited.

Sections 7 and 8 of the act provide for very broad exemptions that are important to note.[30] Under Section 7, all employers in the public sector are exempt, including consultants, experts, or contractors employed by the federal government when performing any counterintelligence function.

---

[27]Elliot Lasson, "How Good Are Integrity Tests?" *Personnel Journal*, 71 (April 1992), 35; also Office of Technology Assessment, "The Use of Integrity Tests for Preemployment Screening" (1990), p. 8.

[28]Public Law, 100–347, 102 Stat. 646 et seq. 29 U.S.C. 2001 et seq., CFR Part 801 1991 is a revision.

[29]Pencil-and-paper dishonesty tests (sometimes called employee theft proneness tests) are permitted. The real purpose of these tests is to get the facts on a theft.

[30]Testing for drugs is exempt. *O'Brien* v. *Papa Gino's of America*, 780 F.2d 1067 (1st Cir. 1986), is still good law.

Under Section 8 of the act, certain employers in the private sector are also exempt. If there is an ongoing investigation involving an economic loss or injury, the test can be used. (Why would any employer otherwise use it?) It also has a specific exemption for investigation of drugs. When the polygraph test is used under Section 7 or 8, the results must be used only as supportive evidence. It could be argued that most present uses of the polygraph test are exempted under these sections,[31] except preemployment testing.[32]

The act also has several restrictions for examiners.[33] Only certain questions can be asked, and the examinee can terminate the test at any time (which makes it strictly voluntary). The act restricts disclosure of the results to the examinee, the employer who requested the test, or any court or governmental agency. The examinee, in writing, may permit disclosure to any other person.

The special preemption provision of the act (Section 10) provides that no state or local law or collective bargaining agreement will be preempted if it is more restrictive than the act. As a practical matter, most state laws are less restrictive, so the result of the act will be to preempt them, except under the exemptions, which will need extensive court interpretation.[34] The act has not been as troublesome to employers as they first thought. One reason could be that the exemptions allow the employers to do what they have been doing for years.

The act is silent on the situation where the employee offers to take the test without a request from the employer, which is a common occurrence and for which a great deal of case law has been developed.[35] The employer has a choice of not using a polygraph test at all or being exposed to

litigation. Suppose the examinee terminates the test. Must there be a good reason?

For the employer who still feels it is important to use the test, a policy or procedure should be developed to conform with federal and state law as much as possible and then wait for court interpretation. However, have a lawyer review the policy or procedure as a showing of a good faith attempt to comply.

Recommended Policies for Polygraph Testing

When it becomes necessary to obtain evidence about the suspected dishonesty of an employee, the first consideration must be what techniques are allowed by federal and state law. Some states restrict the use of electronic devices in varying degrees while others have no restrictions. Both the polygraph test and search are means of obtaining evidence to determine guilt or innocence. If it is permitted by state and federal law, there is no reason why the polygraph test cannot be used. Not only is it a method of obtaining evidence, but also exposure of employees to the test may have a chilling effect on employee dishonesty. The personnel practitioner should always consider the possible effects of the use of the polygraph on employee relations. An atmosphere of un-warranted suspicion may cause more harm than the test results can cure; refusal is not an admission of guilt.

A policy or guideline regarding the use of the polygraph test might include the following provisions:

1. The polygraph test can be used in preemployment screening where the applicant is being considered for a position of trust or one that requires handling a large amount of cash from customers (bank teller, safekeeping department of a hospital, and so on) under the exemptions of the federal statute.

2. If used, it will not be the sole qualifying or disqualifying factor in a preemployment evaluation but be supportive of other information.

3. For present employees a rule should be established to require that a voluntary test be only supportive in determining the facts, that an employee be a suspect

---

[31]Firing of travel office employees by Clinton is an example.

[32]29 CFR Part 801 allows private employers to give polygraph tests in jobs where a large amount of cash is acquired from customers.

[33]Examiner is as liable as employer: *Rubin* v. *Tourneau, Inc.,* 797 F.Supp 247 (D.C. S.N.Y. 1992).

[34]For reference on state laws, see *State by State Guide to Human Resource Laws* (New York: Panel Publishers, 1993).

[35]*Kamrath* v. *Suburban National Bank,* 363 N.W.2d 108 (Minn. 1985).

before the test is given, and that there is no other way to determine the facts.

4. The polygraph test will always be used in combination with other techniques.

5. Passing or failing the polygraph test will not be considered by itself to be conclusive nor will the refusal to take the test, but in both situations the presumption of innocence or suspicion of guilt may be affected.

6. Results of the test will not be disclosed, except to those who have a right to know, or where a written release is given by the examinee.

EMPLOYER RIGHT OF SEARCH AND SEIZURE

The employer/employee relationship must be distinguished from the situation where a person might be committing a crime. The U.S. Supreme Court on numerous occasions has restricted search and seizure under the Fourth Amendment.[36] Surveillance by the police is restricted to what is observable—although the court allows various techniques to make evidence observable such as trained dogs, "beepers," flashlights, and the like. The law as it relates to search in the criminal sense is in place.[37]

In a police/citizen confrontation the search of lunch buckets would be a violation of Fourth Amendment rights. The employer/employee relationship is different because the employer has a legitimate interest in protecting its own property and that of other employees.

Fourth Amendment Protection in the Public Sector

Would it be proper for a supervisor of a public employer to search an employee's desk when the public employee has the protection of the Fourth Amendment? The court in *O'Connor* v. *Ortega,* 107 S.Ct. 1492 (1987), said a reasonable search is

permitted, but left it up to the trial court to determine what is reasonable. In *O'Connor* the employee had been placed on administrative leave from his hospital job pending investigation of a charge of work-related conduct. While on leave his office was searched, including his desk and files. Several items of personal effects were taken from his desk as well as work-related information, all of which were later used in adverse administrative hearing. The employee claimed that the purpose of the search was to obtain evidence for the hearing, while the employer argued it was designed to inventory state property. The employee sued the persons making the search.

The Court in a 5-4 decision said that public employers must be given wide latitude to enter offices and should not be subject to probable cause requirements as police officers are. The standard applied was the same as in the private sector, one of reasonableness. The Court said what is reasonable is decided on a case-by-case basis. Justice Scalia wrote a separate opinion and stated that any work-related search is reasonable regardless of how private or public the employee's office may be.

The significance of this decision is that even where the employee has the protection of the Fourth Amendment, his or her office may be searched. This decision gives both the public and the private employer considerable authority to make searches at the workplace.

Limitation of Searches by Labor Agreement

Privacy matters are seldom found in labor agreements because the parties choose to bargain about them on a one-by-one basis. The usual practice is that the company makes a rule, and if the union feels that it is unreasonable, they challenge it through the grievance procedure. If the matter is not settled, then it goes to arbitration.

Generally speaking, arbitrators have given management the right to search employees and their private property and have permitted disciplinary action when the employees refuse. The basis for this position is that employment can be conditioned upon compliance with reasonable rules. The employer also has a legitimate right to

---

[36]This is different from entrapment, which is not allowed: *Jacobson* v. *United States,* 112 S.Ct. 1535 (1992).

[37]*Smith* v. *Maryland,* 422 U.S. 735 (1979); *Texas* v. *Brown,* 103 S.Ct. 1535 (1993).

EXHIBIT 13-1 *Search Policy*

Effective _____ [at least two weeks] the company will implement procedures to improve security and to protect employees' property from theft and to obtain facts for accusations of theft of company property. All persons entering and leaving the company's premises will be subject to questions and a search as a condition of employment. The search may include lockers, parked vehicles, packages, purses, handbags, briefcases, lunch boxes, and all other possessions. Failure to cooperate will be considered a violation of this policy. Employees or others violating this policy will be treated accordingly.

prevent theft not only of property of the company but also of property of employees. As in any arbitration situation, there is always a minority view.[38]

While most arbitrators permit searches, they disagree widely on the treatment of evidence obtained in a search. Arbitrators also differ substantially on the right of the employee to refuse search. Generally, a showing of probable cause is enough to support discipline for refusing to permit a personal search. An organization must not act in an unreasonable fashion and must have a reasonable basis for the search of lockers of employees. Such a basis might be the fact that certain property of the organization is missing.[39] Some arbitrators require the organization to have a rule or a record of past practice before they will uphold a search. A company changed its policy to require employees to purchase their own locks for toolboxes and use them for company and personal use. The arbitrator held the company cannot search the toolboxes after the policy change. There was an indication that the company could have done so before the policy change.[40]

Most arbitrators consider a parking lot company property, especially if it is close to the work facility.[41] However, a rule to prohibit smoking in the parking lot is reasonable where there is evidence of injury to health or property. A company can prohibit smoking on company property only if non-union.

It appears from arbitration decisions and the absence of court cases on searches and seizures that if an employer has a probable cause to search the personal property of employees at the workplace—including the parking lot—the search will be permitted.[42] This conclusion is in line with other case law and with the common law that the employee cannot refuse to answer questions because of possible self-incrimination, has no right to see his or her own personal files (except by statute), and must reveal any information that was acquired during the course of employment.

Recommended Procedures for Searches

In order for the employer to exercise the rights granted by the common law, it is necessary to establish a policy on searches if exposure to invasion-of-privacy claims is to be avoided. Most courts will permit any reasonable search, especially if the employee is warned that it might happen. A policy on searches shown in Exhibit 13-1 is a must. Several courts take the position that continued employment after being warned that routine searches will be made is implied consent,

---

[38]*Higher Market, Inc.,* 97 LA 92 (Prasyzich 1991).

[39]*B.F. Goodrich Chemical Div.,* 709 LA 326 at 329 (Oppenheim 1978).

[40]*Kawner Co.,* 86 LA 297 (Alexander 1985).

[41]*Hess Oil Virgin Islands Corp.,* 93 LA 580 (Chandler 1989).

[42]For arbitration cases on searches, see Frank Elkouri and Edna A. Elkouri, *How Arbitration Works,* 4th ed. (Washington, DC: Bureau of National Affairs, Inc., 1985), pp. 790–91.

which would prevent any lawsuit for invasion of privacy.[43]

There should be guidelines for the supervisors to follow if exposure to privacy lawsuits is to be avoided. The guidelines should state the following:

1. The purpose of the policy is to protect company and employee interests.
2. Searches will be used only when there is legitimate reason to believe that pilferage is taking place. This includes employees' property as well as company property.
3. In all searches personal privacy will be respected but this consideration will not eliminate the search.
4. Searches, if possible, will be conducted away from other employees, on company time, and on company premises.

Search could be an invasion of privacy (which is defined as something highly offensive to a reasonable person) if not conducted for the purpose of obtaining facts. Often the person doing the search becomes abusive and acts with malice in the attempt to get the employee to admit the wrongdoing, and a suit for invasion of privacy results. In *K-Mart Corp. Store No. 7441* v. *Trotti*, 667 So.2d 6329 (Tex. App. 1984), the court held that it was an invasion of privacy to search lockers when there was no warning that lockers would from time to time be searched; also unreasonable methods were used.

Whether it be the use of a voluntary polygraph test or a search, the real purpose of the procedure is to prevent others from doing the same thing. The purpose of the policy should be made clear, that the objective is to prevent pilferage and not to find somebody guilty.

The law permits the employer to use all reasonable means to protect property,[44] whether it be the company's or that of the employee, and all

management has to do is exercise the rights that the law has given it.

Sometimes management takes the position that the way to prevent pilferage is to involve the law enforcement authorities. This, in the author's opinion, is a serious mistake. The major reason is that the law enforcement authorities need more proof of a violation than an employer does. All the employer needs is knowledge that the company policy was violated, but the police need substantial evidence that the employee committed the act and violated a law.

If the employer accuses and the authorities fail to prosecute or the employee is found not guilty, the employer has "egg on its face" and employee relations have been dealt a severe blow.

The second reason why the authorities should not be involved is that the employer's primary business is not improving society and removing all dishonest persons from the streets. The employer's concern must be work related, so the only penalty the employer should be concerned with is severe discipline or discharge.

Most employees will accept the truth but are quick to challenge any falsehood. In the past, it is not what the employer has been doing that has caused the lawsuits, but it is the way that it was done that resulted in large awards and caused many of the employers to become "gun-shy" in exercising their common law rights.

COMMON LAW ON DISCLOSURE OF EMPLOYEE INFORMATION

Disclosure of information about employees has been increasing; the subject is becoming more popular in professional literature and personnel textbooks.[45]

Under present legal doctrine, personnel records (defined as all information about employees kept

---

[43]*Faulkner* v. *Maryland*, 564 A.2d 785 (Md. 1989).

[44]A search is reasonable if the measures adopted are reasonably related to the objectives of the search and there is no excessive intrusion considering the nature of the misconduct being investigated: *O'Connor* v. *Ortega*, 107 S.Ct. 1492 at 1503 (1987).

[45]D. J. Duffy, "Privacy v. Disclosure: Balancing Employee-Employer Rights," *Employee Relations Law Journal* (1982), 594–609; Phillip Adler, Jr., Charles Parsons, and Scott B. Zolke, "Employee Privacy: Legal and Research Developments and Implications for Personnel Administration," *Sloan Management Review*, Winter (1985), 17; William Petrocelli, *Low Profile—How to Avoid the Privacy Invaders* (New York: McGraw-Hill, 1981), p. 112.

by an employer) are not confidential but are the property of the employer to be used at its discretion. The employee can do little to stop disclosure.[46]

Releasing information about employees is largely a consideration by the employer of who wants the information and for what purpose. The discretionary control of personnel records by the employer has often been considered by civil rights advocates, academics, and the general public as an unjust infringement on employee privacy.

With the advent of the antidiscrimination laws in the 1960s and 1970s, certain restrictions were imposed on the disclosure of information about employees. The upsurge in the interest of employee privacy and the recognition of the judicial system of individual rights have caused the employer to become aware of the employee privacy problem in the use of personnel records. The employee privacy problem has two distinct facets. On one side is the need of the employer for data on the employee for benefit packages, job placement, promotion, and compliance with government information requests. On the other hand, employees have an interest in preventing unwarranted intrusions into their private lives.

To avoid obsolescence, the personnel practitioner must become familiar with court decisions and statutes regarding disclosure of employee information. The use of a subpoena to obtain employee records is excluded from this discussion. It can be used only in legal proceedings and is not normally discretionary with the personnel practitioner.

Right of Employee to Review Own Records

It is a well-established principle of common law that information obtained by the employer about an employee relating to the employment relationship is the property of the employer. This also applies to the request of the employees to see their own records.[47]

Some states have passed laws requiring the employer to give access to the employee's own record.[48] Those states that require disclosure in the private sector usually permit the employer to remove certain information before disclosing the file to the employee. These statutes should not be confused with the Freedom of Information Act (5 U.S.C. Sect. 552), which requires federal agencies to disclose information about agency activities to the general public.

Over 250 employers, both large and small, have adopted policies allowing an employee restricted access to his or her own records (apart from any statute). They argue that denying an employee access to such records is not good employee relations. Many advocates of the employee privacy doctrine state that if the employers continue to deny employees access to their own records, Congress will do something about it, especially in view of advancing technology.

Those companies allowing employees to see information from their own files have a policy that the employer can remove certain information that it chooses not to disclose. Normally the policy does not define the information that may be removed. Determinations are made on a case-by-case basis. Information that probably would be withheld from the employee might include consideration for promotion, the fact that an employee is suspected of violating a rule and therefore must be watched, and the scheduled elimination of the job or that of the supervisor.

It is also common to "sanitize" investigatory reports of all types, supervisors' notes, and recommendations about future salary increases.

---

[46]*Cort* v. *Bristol-Meyers,* 431 N.E.2d 908 (Mass. 1983).

[47]G. A. Abramson and E. J. Lyons, "Protection of Employer's Records from Disclosure to Employees, Government Agencies, and Third Parties," *Labor Law Journal,* 41 (June 1990), 353–363; A. Hartstein, "Rules of the Road in Dealing with Personnel Records," *Employee Relations Journal,* 17 (Spring 1992), 673–692.

[48]At least 15 states have passed such laws, including but not restricted to California, Pennsylvania, Illinois, Delaware, Michigan, Minnesota, New Hampshire, North Carolina, Oregon, Tennessee, Utah, Wisconsin, and Vermont.

Exposure to Liability in Reference Requests

The employer has no obligation to grant requests for disclosure of personnel records to anyone unless required by statute. At the same time almost nothing can prevent voluntary disclosure by the employer. If the employer wants to cooperate with the local law enforcement agencies or with the Federal Bureau of Investigation (FBI), it may do so. If the employer chooses not to do so, the law enforcement agency must either decide on the facts that it has or start court action and obtain the information by subpoena.

Where the employer decides to reveal information in the personnel file that is detrimental to the employee, the employee may sue for damages under certain conditions. This kind of suit usually occurs when facts that invade privacy under the common law are revealed to the public. The public is interpreted by the courts to mean a small group of people. If it is revealed to only one person, regardless of the seriousness of the injury, the employee has no tort action.[49]

Defamation Defined

Defamation can best be described as follows: (1) One person knows it (no injury to one's reputation); (2) two persons know it (only a slight injury, no tort); (3) three persons know it (wrong); (4) 111 now know it (enough know it to damage the reputation).

Under the common law of privacy, public disclosure of embarrassing private facts about a person is an invasion of the individual's interest in acquiring, retaining, and enjoying a good reputation. The violation of this interest is called defamation, which includes libel and slander.[50]

Common law invasions of privacy occur where the employer discloses information such as medical condition or drug abuse to someone who has no business need to know, as in *Bratt* v. *IBM*, 785 F.2d 352 (1st Cir. 1986).[51]

Liability for this tort usually arises when an employer communicates to a prospective employer or a credit agency information that is injurious to the reputation of an employee or former employee. Because nothing prevents an individual from filing a lawsuit, one might say that every time an employer discloses adverse information about an employee to a prospective employer, this is an exposure to a lawsuit.

Protection by the Qualified Privilege Doctrine

Exposure for a lawsuit is greatly diminished by the common law doctrine of a qualified privilege. This doctrine protects the employer when revealing information about former or present employees. The qualified privilege doctrine can protect from defamation liability, but often an innocent statement related to job performance can be a serious exposure. Where the employer told an executive search agency that a former employee was a homosexual, no malice was involved. The employer had no liability, but paid almost a million dollars in legal fees.[52] Privilege is defined in the *Restatement of Torts* as

. . . the modern term applied to those considerations which avoid liability where it might otherwise follow . . . in its more common usage, it signified that the defendant has acted to further an interest of such social importance that it is entitled to protection, even at the expense of damage to the plaintiff. He is allowed freedom of action because his own interests or those of the public require it, and social policy will best be served by permitting it.

This definition of privilege has been applied to employee records. The courts have taken the position that the public good is best served by a free exchange of information between the

---

[49]*Biderman's of Springfield, Inc.,* v. *Wright,* 322 S.W.2d 892 (Mo. 1959).

[50]*Prosser & Keeton on Torts,* 5th ed., Hornbook Series (St. Paul, MN: West, 1984), p. 771.

[51]See Suzanne Cook, "Invasion of Privacy—a 1984 Syndrome," *Industrial Management,* 29, no. 5 (September–October 1986), pp. 18–21.

[52]*Boehm* v. *American Bankers Insurance Group, Inc.,* 557 So.2d 91 (Fla. App. 3rd Dist. 1990).

prospective employer and former employer as to work habits and performance. Where an employee falsified production records and the employer told other employees about it, the court said that the employer was justified in that it would discourage other employees from committing the same act.[53] However, this immunity from liability when disclosing adverse injurious information is not without limitations; an employer must take certain precautions if liability is to be avoided.[54]

Requirements of the Privilege Doctrine

As a general rule the courts will allow an employer to give information about a former employee that may be defamatory if such information is in the interest of the requesting employer and the public. The giving of information must protect that interest.[55] This is called a privilege that the courts will protect, but it is not without conditions.

1. The information must be given in good faith. Where a supervisor accused an employee of starting a competitive company and repeated other office rumors that he failed to investigate, the court awarded $19,000 in punitive damages.[56] (Punitive damages are damages that compensate above actual loss and are punishment for evil behavior.)
2. The information given must be limited to the inquiry. Asking about work habits does not require facts on personal life or information on union activities.[57]
3. The statement must be given under the proper occasion and in the proper manner. If given at a cocktail party or while playing bridge, an otherwise

proper statement could be construed as invasion of privacy or libel.
4. The information must be communicated to the proper parties and not the general public. In one case an inquiry was made by an aunt, uncle, and spouse as to an employee's whereabouts. The reason given for the inquiry was that he was accused of misappropriating company funds. The court said that it was not privileged because relatives had no job-related interest in receiving the information.[58]
5. Information requested must be related to the requirements of the job.
6. Information revealed must be true, or a reasonable effort must be made to seek the truth.
7. Information must be revealed without malice and bad faith.[59]

Reference checks run afoul of antidiscrimination laws only where it can be shown that the reference check was for a discriminatory purpose or information received was used in a discriminatory manner. If conclusions drawn from reference reports are biased, the result will be considered discriminatory or malicious. A minority applicant may receive a poor reference report because of poor performance on the job for a former employer. This does not necessarily mean that the applicant is unqualified for a different position and different employer. The reasons for poor performance must be considered; poor performance cannot always be used as a reason for not hiring a member of the protected class. Often the prospective employer will ask if the former employee is eligible for rehire; if the answer is negative, the person will not be hired. Relying solely on this answer may indicate a discriminatory motive in refusal to hire, if the applicant is a member of a protected class.

[53]*Ponticelli* v. *Mine Safety Appliance Co.,* 247 A.2d 303 (R.I. 1968).

[54]For additional information on this privilege, see Jack Turner and Terry Esser, "Reference and Background Checks: Myth and Fact," *Human Resources Management Ideas and Trends,* no. 36 (Chicago: Commerce Clearing House, April, 1983); E. Dube, "Employment Reference and the Law," *Personnel Journal,* 65, no. 2 (February 1986), pp. 87–88.

[55]For good explanation see *Circus Circus Hotels* v. *Witherspoon,* 657 P.2d 101 (Nev. 1983). Also see *Humphrey* v. *National Semiconductor Corp.,* 18 Mass. App. 132 (1984).

[56]*Calero* v. *Del Chemical Corp.,* 228 N.W.2d 737 (Wisc. 1975).

[57]*Sindorf* v. *Jacron Sales,* 341 A.2d 856 (Md. 1975).

[58]*Stewart* v. *Nation-Wide Check Corp.,* 182 S.E.2d 410 (N.C. 1971).

[59]*Bolling* v. *Baker,* 671 S.W.2d 559 (Tex. App. 4 Dist. 1984). The employer stated that the discharged employee was a liar and not trustworthy. Although this was revealed only to other employees, the court found the privilege doctrine was violated by statements made with malice and reckless disregard for the truth.

When the Privilege Is Lost

The most common reason for losing the privilege is that the information is given out of malice. Whether it is malice is a factual question determined on a case-by-case basis. In most situations the person disclosing knows whether or not it is malice, because intent is usually present.

In one case the employee was discharged under a company policy of automatically terminating everyone working a shift during which a cash shortage occurred. The plaintiff could not get employment elsewhere as the result of the termination. The court held that a qualified privilege existed; therefore, the employer was not liable unless the plaintiff could prove that there was malice. In finding that there was insufficient evidence of malice, the court said "actual malice requires proof that the statement was made with malice in fact, ill-will or wrongful notice." Here there was no evidence from which a jury could infer any motive founded on ill will toward the plaintiff or a desire to harm her; it was merely an enforcement of a policy.[60]

Refusal to Disclose Reference Information

More than half of all employers have adopted a policy that information disclosed about former employees should be limited to verification of employment and the length of employment.[61] This policy may be considered the safest to avoid lawsuits. But from an employment point of view it could result in the hiring of many undesirable applicants. It would create ill will among former employees who are refused favorable references. An employer can reduce the risk of litigation to near zero, still maintain good recruiting practices, and maintain good employee relations by taking advantage of the qualified privilege doctrine.

The Legal Paradox

It is a legal paradox that the courts are granting immunity from prosecution by ruling that it is in the public interest to exchange information about employees to discourage hiring of undesirable applicants; at the same time many employers are unwilling to disclose because of the danger of being sued. Releasing information makes good personnel sense and will help convince the jury that the employer is dealing fairly with its employees.

It has been a common practice among employment managers to check the references of an applicant by calling the applicant's former employer and requesting specific information for preemployment purposes. Large jury awards have caused employers not to give reference information except for dates of employment and job titles. This policy is intended to avoid exposure to litigation,[62] but disregards the qualified privilege doctrine. If this practice continues, reference disclosures as a source of preemployment information will be as obsolete as the corner blacksmith shop.

Reliability of References

Whether refusal to disclose employee information will have a damaging effect on the hiring of qualified applicants depends on how valid reference information has been. It has probably been as valid as other subjective selection procedures that have been common in the past. Some personnel administrators feel that the abolition of reference checks concerning performance would have no effect on hiring qualified persons because reference checks are not a valid method of determining an applicant's acceptability as to performance. Reference requests regarding character are somewhat unreliable as to performance unless a personal confidential relationship exists between the person requesting the information and the person disclosing the information. If a personal

[60]*Haldeman* v. *Total Petroleum, Inc.*, 376 N.W.2d 98 (Iowa 1985).

[61]See Janet Swerdow, "Negligent Referral: A Potential Theory for Employer Liability" (note), *Southern California Law Review*, 64 (1991), 1645.

[62]Refusal to give information to avoid one kind of lawsuit often creates another kind of lawsuit.

relationship exists, exposure is not usually present.[63]

The only absolute protection against being sued is not to give any reference information to anybody. However, an employer that is interested in selecting qualified and stable applicants must obtain background information from some source. If no reference information is provided by employers concerning an applicant's qualifications or trait characteristics, then criminals and sex offenders will be hired. A subjective selection process is almost certain to run afoul of the antidiscrimination laws. The refusal of former employers to give background information may also result in selection of problem applicants.

NEGLIGENT HIRING AND RETENTION

A more serious exposure to litigation exists in a form of tort action called negligent hiring and negligent retention.[64] This action has been created in part by the legal paradox mentioned above. The courts are saying that an employer will not be liable for giving information about former employees and the employers are saying that they will be liable if they do. Is it any wonder that the courts have little sympathy for the employer when an action of negligent hiring is filed by an employee?

The tort action of negligent hiring and negligent retention is relatively new. Most of the cases have been filed in the last 15 years. It is now recognized as a cause of action in the majority of state courts.

Negligent hiring or retention is defined as a situation in which an employer is liable to third persons for injury and the employer knew or should have known of the employee's dangerous characteristics. The employer's negligence must be the proximate cause of the injury to those whom the employer could reasonably expect to come in contact with the employee. The injury does not have to be personal or physical.[65] In one case the employer was held liable for hiring a person who committed forgery and fraud.

To be liable the employer must have known or exercised ordinary care to know of the dangerous tendencies. Under tort law there is no liability, unless the employer's negligence caused a foreseeable injury.[66] Where the applicant had a clear record and nothing to indicate a bad record, there was no duty to check. However, where the employee had a free access to customers' homes the court held there was a duty to inquire into the applicant's background.[67]

Liability for Negligent Hiring

The employer's liability for negligent hiring will depend on the soundness of the preemployment investigation into the employee's background.[68] Important factors in the background check are the job responsibilities for which the applicant was hired and the applicant's record that indicated risk of harm to co-workers or injury to third parties.

In *Stephanie Ponticas et al.* v. *K.M.S. Investments,* 331 N.W.2d 907 (Minn. 1983), the employer hired a caretaker for an apartment building. The employee had been convicted of armed robbery, burglary, and auto theft. Using his passkey to enter an apartment, he raped one of the tenants. The court held that an employer has a duty to exercise reasonable care in hiring individuals who because of the nature of their employment may pose a threat to members of the public.

A truck driver was hired with a criminal record of violent sex crimes and aggravated sodomy of two teenaged hitchhikers while driving a truck for another employer. The defendant employer gave instructions not to pick up hitchhikers but the

---

[63]This is one advantage in being active in local professional associations.

[64]J. Fenton, Jr., "Negligent Hiring and Retention Doctrine Adds to Human Resource Woes," *Personnel Journal,* 69 (April 1990), 62–73; also *Garcia* v. *Duffy,* 492 So.2d 435 (Fla. App. 2nd Dist. 1986) for a good discussion of a negligent hiring cause of action.

[65]Negligent hiring and retention is a common law action. See *Restatement of Torts* Sect. 213 (1958).

[66]*HarveyFreeman & Sons* v. *Stanley,* 384 S.E2d. 682 (Ga. App. 1989).

[67]*Abbot* v. *Payne,* 457 So.2d 1156 (Fla. 1984).

[68]*Tallahassee Furniture Co.* v. *Harrison,* 582 So.2d 744 (Fla. App. 1st Dist. 1991).

driver did. In the sleeping compartment of the truck he raped and threatened to kill the plaintiff. The court found that it was the duty of the employer to hire competent drivers. The employer knew or should have known that entrusting a truck with a sleeping compartment to a person with a history of sex crimes was negligent hiring (employer didn't check).[69] However, where a background of an employee was not investigated the court held there was no duty to do so because there was denial at the time of hiring of any previous criminal convictions or episodes of violence.

Some courts will hold that if the act was employment related the employer is liable. In *Tolbert* v. *Martin Marietta Corp.,* 621 F.Supp. 1099 (Colo. 1985), the employee was sexually assaulted on the way to lunch, and the court held that it was employment related. The employer failed to make the premises safe for the employees.

Negligent Retention

In one situation there was evidence that the employee had a drinking problem, and while drinking he assaulted a guest. The court had little difficulty in finding negligent retention.[70] Because there is an exposure to negligent retention complaints, the employer who has knowledge of dangerous tendencies has a duty to other employees to do something about it. It is not uncommon for an employee in the heat of an argument to threaten a supervisor or another employee, and if the employer does nothing about it and later the threat is carried out on another employee, there is a good possibility that the employer will be liable for any resulting injury under negligent retention decisions.

The law is, therefore, well in place that an employer has a duty to investigate applicants for certain jobs. If the practice by employers of not supplying information becomes universal, a greater exposure will be created than disclosing

information about employees.[71] The court will protect under the qualified privilege doctrine but not negligent hiring. The policy of not disclosing information may eliminate a small exposure in one area but create a larger exposure in another area. Failure to disclose information on applicants to prospective employers might result in all kleptomaniacs on the labor market being hired. If an employer is not liable for negligent hiring he may be for negligent retention.

Thoroughness of the Investigation

Although there are no hard-and-fast rules on the adequacy of an investigation, there appears to be more duty imposed when jobs have a public relationship or expose the employee to opportunities to injure others. There is a greater duty to investigate for security guard or taxicab driver than for a bartender.[72] In certain jobs the risk is foreseeable, as in the case of Pinkerton's guards or a maintenance job in an apartment complex. The legal principle is that unless there is a strong reason not to do so, there exists a duty to investigate. As more criminal records become available, courts are requiring a duty to check with increasing frequency.[73]

Hiring a Person with a Known Criminal Record

Under a federal program to provide specific skills to the unemployed, including former

---

[69]*Slaton* v. *B&B Gulf Service Center,* 344 S.E.2d 512 (Ga. App. 1986).

[70]*Pittard* v. *Four Seasons Motor Inn,* 688 P.2d 333 (N.M. App. 1984).

[71]"Negligent Referral: A Potential Theory for Employer Liability," *Southern California Law Review,* 64 (1991), 1645; also A. Ryan and M. Lasek, "Negligent Hiring and Defamation," *Personnel Psychology,* 44 (Summer 1991), 293–391.

[72]In *Welch Mfg. Co.* v. *Pinkerton's,* 474 A.2d 436 (R.I. 1984), the court held that a police record and contacting two former employers was not enough. In *Burch* v. *A&G Associates,* 333 N.W.2d 140 (1983), the court said that a taxicab company has a higher duty to investigate than other employers. However, in *Evans* v. *Morsell,* 95 A.2d 480 (Md. 1978), the court said there was very little duty to check on a bartender. See also *Kassman* v. *Busfield Enterprise, Inc.,* 639 P.2d 353 (1981).

[73]For further reading, see R. Jacobs, "Defamation and Negligence in the Workplace," *Labor Law Review,* (September 1989), 52.

convicts, the employer hired on a work release status an applicant who had been convicted of second-degree murder and had a record of other crimes. The prisoner started his employment as a carpentry instructor. Later he was released from prison and allowed to live on the premises and act as security guard. While in this capacity, he sexually assaulted and murdered a 12-year-old boy. The plaintiffs conceded that there was no negligent hiring to perform the duties as a carpentry instructor. The court in *Henley* v. *Prince George's County,* 503 A.2d 133 (Md. 1986), agreed that there was no negligent hiring, but it was for the jury to determine whether or not it was negligent assignment of security duties. From this case as well as dicta in others, the courts will not find that hiring a criminal is negligent hiring, but it appears that there is some exposure to properly assigning the employee.

Case Law on Negligent Retention

Negligent retention is the breach of an employer's duty to be aware of an employee's propensity for malicious or violent behavior regardless of cause. The duty requires the employer to take corrective action through retraining, assignment, reassignment, or discharge. Once the employer knows or should have known of the employee's dangerous tendencies, it is wise to obtain a medical evaluation, even if the behavior takes place off duty.[74] In *Cherry* v. *Kelly Services, Inc.,* 319 S.E.2d 463 (Ga. App. 1984), the court held that where a defendant's driver injured the plaintiff there was no negligent retention because the employee did not have a bad driving record. However, the fact that the employee had one prior moving violation raised an issue of whether or not there was negligent hiring.[75]

Negligent Training

It is clear from the case law that where an employer fails to train adequately and an employee subsequently does harm to third parties, the court will find the employer liable. Increased training efforts are required to avoid liability. This is particularly true where the employer's business or service is publicly oriented. The 1990s are a litigious decade; the employer must take all steps necessary to avoid exposure. The following training is recommended:[76]

1. Confirm claims of skills and experience for all applicants.[77]
2. Abate the risks of harm by extensive training for employees who work with equipment, materials, or processes that are dangerous.
3. Include procedures to protect third parties' health and safety (including employees).
4. Evaluate the training activity to determine its effectiveness to reduce negligence risks.

EXPOSURE FOR DEFAMATION

The law has been extended since the last edition. This is good for adventurous attorneys, but not for the defense. In *Boton* v. *Dept. of Human Resources* (1995), the court held that you can communicate by action. In Boton the employee was escorted out of the building after being discharged. This may be a minority opinion, but it shows how far the court will go to find defamation.

A common law tort of defamation,[78] in the employment context, is most common after the employer gives a false oral or written statement as to why the employee was discharged. In order to

---

[74]For a good discussion on negligent hiring and retention, see W. J. Woska, "Negligent Employment Practices," *Labor Law Journal,* 42 (September 1991), 605; also *Hutchinson* v. *McDonald's Corp.,* 110 S.Ct. 57 (1989).

[75]D. Gregory, "Reducing Risk in Negligent Hiring," *Employee Relations Law Journal,* (September 1988), 34.

[76]A good discussion of negligent training to relieve exposure is J. Fenton, William Ruud, and J. Kimbell, "Negligent Training Suits: A Recent Entry into the Corporate Employment Negligence Arena," *Labor Law Journal,* 42 (June 1991), 351.

[77]R. L. Lansing, "Training New Employees," *Supervision Management,* (January 1989), 16–20.

[78]To prove defamation the statement must be false, unprivileged, and negligent on the part of the publisher. There must also be damages to the plaintiff.

make out a claim for defamation the plaintiff must prove that

1. A statement has been made about him or her to another person.
2. It is false or given to someone who has no need to know.
3. It harms the reputation of the plaintiff by lowering his or her esteem or stature in the community or with other persons.[79]

There are several defenses to defamation: (1) privilege; (2) no publication; (3) truth; (4) not capable of conveying a defamatory meaning; (5) opinion; and (6) plaintiff consent. The one most often used in employment law is privilege, whether absolute or qualified.

When the qualified privilege doctrine is violated, a defamation suit is the remedy. Once the court determines that the privilege doctrine applies, the burden is on the plaintiff to show that the doctrine was violated.

Defamation "Per Se"

Ordinarily, when a person brings a defamation suit, the person must show an impairment of his or her reputation, loss of standing in the community, or mental distress. With defamation "per se," whatever is said or written is presumed to be damaging, therefore no damages have to be proven.

In order for a statement to be defamatory it must be a personal attack upon the plaintiff. A hearty disagreement with the plaintiff's views or a statement about an overly sensitive person is not defamatory. Depending upon the circumstances, a plaintiff must have some "thickness of skin."

Disclosing Information to Co-workers Who Have a Need to Know

One of the conditions of the doctrine of qualified privilege is that information be given only to those persons who have a legitimate business right to receive it.[80] This requirement goes to the very roots of the doctrine. The courts say that information about the reasons for the discharge of an employee should be released to other employees who have a reason to know. By so doing the employer may prevent others from making the same mistake and also being discharged. Preventing acts that will result in discharge is in the public interest. The release of information about the reason for a discharge to employees who are not exposed to the opportunity to commit similar acts can be ruled to be defamatory.

The acquisition of one organization by another is commonplace in American business culture. Frequently such combinations leave the merged organization with two persons for only one job. Though both may be competent, one has to go. In a fairly typical case, one company acquired another with an effective date on a Friday. On Saturday, three top executives were discharged. Over the weekend all other officers and department heads were called and instructed not to go to the office on Monday morning but to attend a meeting at a nearby hotel at 8 o'clock on Monday. At the meeting, the officers and department heads were told why the three executives were fired. Only the top management was told. Other levels of management were excluded because they would not be directly affected and did not have the same need to know. By following this carefully thought out procedure, the organization substantially reduced the risk of litigation. If all levels of management had been invited to the meeting, the organization would have been exposed to charges of defamation.

In *Benassi* v. *Georgia-Pacific*, 662 P.2d 760 (Ore. App. 1983), a general manager was discharged for allegedly having a drinking problem and using a "loud voice and considerable

---

[79]*Stuempes* v. *Parke, Davis & Co.*, 297 N.W.2d 252 (Minn 1980). Also see W. Keeton, *Prosser and Keeton on Torts*, 5th ed., Sect. 111 (1984), p. 774; *Restatement of Torts*, Sect. 558 (1977).

[80]*Hutchinson* v. *McDonald's Corp.*, 110 S.Ct. 57 (1989).

profanity." The employer called in all the employees and stated at a meeting, "I gathered you here to tell you why Mr. Benassi is no longer with the company. The man was drunk and misbehaving in a bar. The man had a drinking problem. Georgia-Pacific looks unkindly on this kind of conduct. It was not the first time. He had been warned." Mr. Benassi sued on the basis of this statement. The court found that there was an abuse of the qualified privilege doctrine because there was no reason to communicate to all employees in order to protect the interests of the employer.

The level of employees to whom information should be communicated should be determined by the employer, taking into consideration the likelihood that the employee will benefit from the information. When an employee was discharged for falsifying company records, the employer told higher-level employees as well as employees on the same or lower levels. In the resulting defamation suit, the court laid down the rule that communication was proper to all who have a need to know as well as those employees who would be directly affected by the discharge.[81] In this case, the court said that all employees to whom the information was communicated had a "need to know."[82]

Statements That Impute Crime

Statements that impute crimes are susceptible to a defamatory meaning. *Karnes* v. *Milo Beauty and Barber Supply Co., Inc.* 441 N.W.2d 565, 568 (Minn. Ct. App. 1989). Store #190, was managed by plaintiff, who was stealing money from the cash register drawer. "How much more noncompliance must we tolerate from [plaintiff]?"

An employee sued for intentional infliction of emotional distress, alleging that employer initiated a drug investigation with a reckless disregard of whether or not he had committed the offense. Employer also communicated the information about the drug investigation to the narcotic unit of the police department. The court found that the initiation of a drug investigation without a reason was outrageous conduct. Although the information was privileged, it was defamatory because the narcotic unit of the police department did not have a business right to receive it. *Linebaugh* v. *Sheraton Michigan Corp.,* 497 N.W.2d 585, 587 (Mich. Ct. App. 1993). A cartoon drawn by a co-worker, whether captioned or uncaptioned, imputed lack of chastity to plaintiff, and was actionable as libel "per se."

Statements that impute crime are not always defamatory.[83] If properly made they come under the qualified privilege doctrine, as in the case where the employer, based on a polygraph test, had reason to believe that the plaintiff was involved in vandalism and the statement of this fact was only made to other employees who had a need to know. The statement was protected by the qualified privilege doctrine.[84]

Giving False Reasons for Discharge

Many organizations make a practice of "softening the record" in the case of discharges. This avoids an adverse reaction on the part of the employee being terminated. It will also make him or her more employable. For many years it was common to avoid giving the real reason for discharge. A relatively innocuous reason such as "personality difficulties"—or the more recent version, "a chemistry problem with the supervisors"—was entered into the record. If the statements are not damaging to the reputation of the employee, there is little exposure to charges of defamation.

Without Malice

If the false reason is damaging to the reputation of the employee, defamation is found. In *Lewis* v. *Equitable Life Assurance Society of the United*

---

[81]If the person can do something about the situation, he or she has a need to know, according to most courts.

[82]*Hodges* v. *Tomberlin*, 319 S.E.2d 11 (Ga. App. 1984).

[83]*Gillson* v. *State Department of Natural Resources,* 492 N.W.2d 835, 843 (Minn. Ct. App. 1992). The statement "the readers should ask themselves if they would want a female relative to spend the night with [the sexual harassment offender]" was not defamatory "per se."

[84]*Larson* v. *Homet Aluminum,* 449 N.W.2d 1172 (Ind. App. 3 Dist. 1983).

States, 389 N.W.2d 876 (Minn. 1986), the plaintiffs submitted an expense account after returning from a business trip. The employer considered it excessive and requested them to reduce the amount. The employees refused because it was legitimate. When they again refused they were discharged. The reason given was "gross insubordination." When they applied for employment the reason was repeated to prospective employers. They could not find employment, so they sued their former employer for defamation. The court ruled that the reason given was false and the employer should have known that the defamatory words would be repeated. Although the false reason was defamation, however, it was without malice and the privilege doctrine prevented damages from being awarded.

Defamation can result when a false reason for discharge is given through an interoffice communication. In one case the reason stated in an interoffice memo was "failure to increase business as a major Project Sales Representative," which was in fact untrue. Although the reason was communicated by memo only to the supervisor and CEO, the court held it was defamation, but without malice.[85]

It is a well-established principle that no liability results from releasing information about an employee or former employee to a prospective employer as long as care is taken to follow the doctrine of qualified privilege. Where exposure to liability is most likely to occur is in a situation where the information is released to persons who are not employers or who do not have a business need to know.

A vice president of engineering was discharged. He alleged that Title VII was violated and that he was discharged because of his color. In preparation for the EEOC hearing, the employer allegedly made statements to suppliers that the plaintiff was discharged because he was incompetent. The court said that such statements were not privileged and that an action for defamation could exist if the statements were false. The privilege doctrine does not extend to statements made to suppliers.[86]

Statements must be job related and without malice. Where a former employer told a prospective employer that the plaintiff married another employee, causing the man to have a mental breakdown, the court found this defamatory.[87] The court found that accusations of dishonesty or theft, even if indirect, were defamatory.

Guidelines to Prevent Exposure for Defamation

In all the cases where the court found defamation, the employer either made some assumptions without foundation or knowingly made malicious or false statements. There is a lot of difference between stating that you no longer have confidence in a person and calling her or him a liar. The fact that the qualified privilege doctrine has some restrictions does not mean that it cannot be used. The courts are telling the employer that it should be used and when used properly the employer is protected from any liability. The "bottom line" is whether the statement was intended to be damaging to the reputation of the employee or was factual with no purpose of being malicious. If the effect of it was damaging to the reputation of the employee, without malice there is no defamation. The term *poor performance* is often used as a matter of convenience and is troublesome if the employee does not in fact have poor performance.

In order to avoid exposure to defamation lawsuits the employer should

1. Have a well-defined termination policy that prevents managers and supervisors from discharging first and then looking for a reason.

2. State the facts without adjectives that may imply malice or bad faith.

---

[85]*Frankson* v. *Design Space International,* 394 N.W.2d 140 (Minn. 1986); also *Banas* v. *Matthews International Corp.,* 502 A.2d 637 (Pa. Super. 1985). The court in *Rouly* v. *Enserch Corp.,* 835 F.2d 1127 (5th Cir. 1988), took the opposite view.

[86]*Medina* v. *Spotnails, Inc.,* 591 F.Supp. 190 (E.D. N.D. Ill. 1984).

[87]*Marshall* v. *Brown,* 190 Cal. Rptr. 392 (Cal. App. 1983).

3. Train managers and supervisors in the use of the qualified privilege doctrine or instruct them to let somebody who is qualified make the statements.[88]

Often it is the attitude toward the person and not the truth of the statement that influences the court. For this reason the immediate supervisor or someone directly involved should not give the reference.

RECOMMENDATIONS THAT CONSIDER EMPLOYEE'S PRIVACY AND EMPLOYER'S NEED TO KNOW

In any policy on disclosure of employee information, consideration must be given to the employee's right to enjoy a good reputation as well as the employer's concern to employ qualified and desirable people. The employer must also be concerned with the welfare of other employees. The failure to discover that the person hired is a kleptomaniac or has a history of sex crimes is not in the best interest of the employer or employees. A policy, therefore, must not discourage reference information but must be drafted in a way that reflects a real concern for the employee's privacy and the employer's need to know.

The following provisions are designed to accomplish this goal:

1. Only certain designated and trained persons should be permitted to release information. These persons should be trained in the legal requirements of disclosing employee information. The practice of allowing the supervisor to disclose reference information over the telephone should be eliminated. This practice probably was started because many application forms ask the applicant, "Who was your immediate supervisor on your former job?" If the application form asks, "Who was the immediate supervisor?" the question should be eliminated.

2. Except for dates of employment, all requests for information should be in writing. Because information should be given only to persons who have a reason to receive it, this cannot be ascertained over the telephone. Sometimes former employees seek information under disguise of a prospective employer; requiring the request in writing will eliminate this problem.

3. The firm should give out only information that is requested and is job related. When the inquirer asks the time of day, don't tell how to build a watch. If there is any doubt as to its accuracy, one should not release the information.

4. The employee should be required to consent to the release of the information requested. Although the courts hold that this is not needed, it is convenient to have this consent when the employer is being sued by an employee who consented to its release. In one situation where the employee was a member of an association, the court said that he had consented to the written cause of his dismissal through his membership. The *Restatement of Torts* puts it this way: "Moreover, one who agrees to submit his conduct to investigation knowing that its results will be published, consents to the publication of the honest findings of the investigators."[89]

It is also good employee relations to get the employee's consent; the employee receives some satisfaction in exercising the right to determine whether certain information should be released. For example, the employee may not want disclosure of an address to a mother-in-law but may want full disclosure of all information to the promoter of an exclusive country club.

5. Information should be put in the employee's file only if it is truthful and there is a job-related or business need for it. Particular attention should be paid to records kept by persons outside the personnel office (for example, front-line supervisors or group leaders). Many problems are found in these records. Collecting irrelevant or inaccurate information adversely affects the quality of the relevant information as well as causing legal problems.

---

[88]A $250,000 award could have been avoided if one person had been designated and trained in qualified privilege doctrine: *Sigal Construction Corp.* v. *Stanbury,* 586 A.2d 1204 (D.C. App. 1991).

---

[89]*Restatement of Torts,* Sect. 583 (1938), p. 221.

6. Information should be collected from reliable sources. Hearsay and subjective evaluations should be avoided.

7. The employer should refrain from giving information about performance on a specific job. This is often subjective and is not predictive of how the applicant will perform on another job. Also always express any information on performance as an opinion with a reservation.

8. The employer should be wary of giving information for background or future reference. If the recipient is not a prospective employer, the qualified privilege doctrine may not apply. It is also difficult to predict how the information will be used. This is one method to get information for use of a union for organizing purposes, for a sales mailing list, or for a sales contact.

9. Employee personnel files should be released within the company only to those who have a job-related purpose to know it. Only that information in the file that is not challengeable as to its validity and pertains to the stated purpose of the inquiry should be released.

10. Employee access to the file should be permitted but the file should be sanitized or at least reviewed. Release of such information as comparative evaluations, mental problems, investigative interviews,

and physical conditions could do more harm than good to employee relations.

11. When an employee disagrees with the information in the file, the disputed statement should be put in the file without comment in the event it becomes material.

12. The procedure should detail what, to whom, by whom, and under what limitations the information should be disclosed.

13. Tell employee at the exit interview what reference you will give to a prospective employer when asked.

If a practice or procedure contains most of these provisions, the employer not only will be exchanging information for the public good but will also be able to select qualified and desirable applicants objectively while enjoying good employee relations. These provisions will also eliminate exposure to charges of negligent hiring and negligent retention.

The law does not restrict disclosure of employee information but encourages it. An employer policy or practice that respects the privacy of the employee but gives prospective employers certain accurate and nonmalicious facts will prevent unwanted litigation.

14

THE FAIR LABOR STANDARDS ACT AND INDEPENDENT CONTRACTORS

Coverage and Penalties
Definition of Compensable Time
Employees Working at Home
Exempt and Nonexempt Classification
Controlling Overtime Costs
Definition of Independent Contractor

The problem of the proper worth of a job is as old as the employment of one person by another. Judging the worth of a job raises questions involving philosophy, economics, and sociology. From a practical standpoint the important issue is what the employer is willing to pay and what the employees are willing to accept.

Until the enactment of the Fair Labor Standards Act of 1938 (FLSA),[1] the employer and the employee decided between themselves what compensation should be paid for services rendered. The employer developed compensation systems that attempted to reward the worker for output and for contribution to the organizational objectives. The supply and demand for a particular

skill in the marketplace had to be considered when setting a wage level.

The FLSA interfered with the employer-employee relationship in determining the amount of compensation to be paid an employee. It prohibited the employer from employing a person for more than a specified number of hours per week without paying time and one half of the regular rate. After the Fair Labor Standards Act, Congress passed several other statutes to control wages: Walsh-Healey Public Contracts Act,[2] Davis-Bacon Act,[3] Service Contract Act,[4] and Equal Pay Act,[5] to name a few.[6]

---

[1]29 U.S.C. Sect. 201 et seq. Congress amended the act in 1991. After the amendment the Department of Labor promulgated rules that increased penalties and set up procedures for appealing decisions of administrative law judges.

[2]41 U.S.C. Sects. 35–45.
[3]40 U.S.C. Sect. 276.
[4]41 U.S.C. Sects. 351–58.
[5]29 U.S.C. Sect. 206 et seq.
[6]See Stephen Light, "Interpreting the Fair Labor Standards Act," *Golden Gate Law Review,* 21, no. 1 (1991), 147.

The legal principles established under the FLSA by the administrator of the Wage and Hour Division (WH) of the Department of Labor (DOL) are used for other statutes that the department enforces. Therefore, these statutes are not considered here, because they have the same administrator and have limited application. This chapter is concerned with the situations that frequently arise under the FLSA and the problems involved in compliance. Minimum wage requirements under the act involve a relatively small percentage of the gainfully employed and have fewer compliance problems than other sections of the act. Therefore they are not discussed in this chapter.[7]

Cost control under FLSA is most effective in determining compensable hours, exempt and nonexempt classifications, whether a worker is an independent contractor, and pay for meal periods.[8] Managers often take the attitude that the law prevents them from instituting effective cost-control measures and that the statute must be accepted as a necessary cost of doing business.

The FLSA does restrict the freedom of the employer in the payment of wages. It does not prevent the establishment of policies and procedures to control costs.[9]

Violations under the FLSA can exist for a long time before anything happens. Often the employee is content with the violation either because it is not known to be a violation or because it is more convenient (such as coming to work early and working) to ignore the requirements of the act.[10] When "the honeymoon is over," the employers are caught with egg on their faces.

An investigation by the Wage and Hour Division of the Department of Labor for compliance can be caused by complaints from the employee, unions, or competitors. Most investigations occur through employee or union complaints. Seldom does the agency make spot checks unless it finds a flagrant violation in one company and wants to determine if it is a practice in the industry. Compliance with certain provisions of the act is not difficult, while in other situations it can be an employee relations problem. Often the employer, when a condition is questionable, is willing to take the risk of being determined in violation, such as in exempt and nonexempt classifications.

COVERAGE AND PENALTIES

The FLSA covers employers of any enterprise engaged in interstate commerce that has two or more employees[11] and produces goods and services exceeding $500,000. (If more than one facility, then the amount is $362,500.) This definition excludes several enterprises; however, most states have enacted little fair labor standards acts that cover employees not included in the federal act. For this reason whenever an employer-employee relationship exists, it is rare that employees are not covered.

Section 203 exempts enterprises such as religious organizations and and mom-and-pop businesses where only the family is employed. Nonprofit organizations not having a business purpose and seasonal recreational establishments are also exempted under the act. State and local governments are not exempt because of the Supreme Court decision in *Garcia* v. *San Antonio Metropolitan Transit Authority*, 105 S. Ct. 1005 (1985).

Exemptions are numerous under FLSA. The determination of when an employee comes under these exemptions is discussed in subsequent sections.

If a state law is more strict than the federal law, it will supersede the federal law; otherwise, the federal law controls. Also an agreement between the employer and the employee to waive coverage is illegal, void, and unenforceable, except under

---

[7]The 1989 amendment deals mostly with minimum wage and certain tips on training.

[8]See "Handy Reference Guide to the Fair Labor Standards Act," U.S. Dept of Labor, WH Publication 1282, April 1990.

[9]See *Labor Law Journal,* (August 1995), 46 no. 18, 469 and 486.

[10]The basic statutory limitation for liability is two years; three years for willful violations. As one manager told the author, "I have been doing it unintentionally for five years. I am already three years ahead if found wrong."

---

[11]*Employee* has been interpreted to mean any individual who is "dependent upon the business to which they render service"; *Bartels* v. *Birmingham*, 332 U.S. 126 (1947); *Weisel* v. *Singapore Joint Venture, Inc.*, 602 F.2d 1185 (5th Cir. 1979).

"Belo" conditions that will be treated later in this chapter.

Penalties for Violation

The FLSA is enforced by the Wage and Hour Division with the Department of Labor (DOL) and carries with it a criminal and civil penalty for willful violations. The penalty for willful violations includes fines up to $10,000 and imprisonment up to six months. In *Williams* v. *Tri-County Growers, Inc.*, 747 F.2d 121 (3rd Cir. 1984), the court said the fact that no complaints had been filed does not mean that the employer did not intend to violate the law.

The *Williams* case was one definition. Other courts were more liberal and stated that if the employer merely knew that the FLSA was a consideration during the time the act was being violated, it was willful.

The Supreme Court in *Trans World Airlines, Inc.*, v. *Thurston*, 105 S.Ct. 613 (1985), rejected this concept and defined *willful* as applied to the Age Discrimination in Employment Act (an amendment to FLSA) as where the "employer either knew or showed reckless disregard for the matter of whether its conduct was prohibited by the ADEA." If the employer didn't have knowledge, there was no reckless disregard for the statute.

The *Thurston* definition was adopted in *McLaughlin* v. *Richland Shoe Co.*, 108 S.Ct. 1677 (1988). The Court said that the employer acted willfully if it "knew or showed reckless disregard for the matter or whether its conduct was prohibited by the Fair Labor Standards Act."[12]

The employer would not be charged with a willful violation unless he or she knew or should have known that the action was violating a statute and made no attempt to comply.[13] This would make it very difficult to sustain a willful violation unless the employer wanted to violate the statute or totally disregarded it. Certainly advice of

counsel or serious consideration as to whether a statute was being violated would be sufficient to make any violation "nonwillful."

Where no willful violation is found, the penalty is restitutionary back pay. The 1989 amendment increased the ceiling on fines and generally made a civil violation more severe. The amount of back pay and liquidated damages awarded is discretionary with the court.

Often in determining the damages for failure to pay overtime, the amount of overtime worked is difficult to determine. The courts have stated that in the absence of employer records, the employee's recollections of the hours worked is sufficient if reasonable.[14]

In all situations under the act the plaintiff has a right of jury trial; the successful plaintiff may obtain attorney's fees and costs from the defendant.

Many answers to questions concerning enforcement and interpretation of the act by the DOL can be found in its interpretive bulletins. Such bulletins as "What Are Hours Worked," #785; "Records to Be Kept," #516; "Overtime Compensation," #778; "White Collar Workers," #541; and "Handy Reference Guide to FSLA" (1990) are useful in understanding the division's position on the interpretation of the act. For the most part these interpretations have had judicial acceptance but cannot be entirely relied upon as law.

DEFINITION OF COMPENSABLE TIME

The act does not limit the hours that an employee can work but requires that the employee be compensated for all the time worked. The Fair Labor Standards Act (FLSA) governs the procedural aspects of paying employees and establishes minimum standards. An employer was held to violate the FLSA when it paid wages to employees 14 to 15 days after payday.[15]

---

[12]The court in *Richland* virtually put to rest all appellate court conflicts over the definition of *willful* in all statutes relevent to FLSA, Equal Pay, Walsh-Healy, and so on.

[13]*McLaughlin* v. *Richland Shoe Co.*, 108 S.Ct. 1677 (1988).

[14]*Mumbower* v. *Callicott*, 526 F.2d 1183 at 1186 (8th Cir. 1975).

[15]*Biggs* v. *Wilson*, 1 F.3d 1537 (9th Cir. 1993), *cert. denied.*

In *Biggs,* the state of California paid state workers two weeks late because the Legislature had not approved and the governor had not signed the state budget. When the established payday was missed, William Biggs filed a class action lawsuit for highway maintenance workers.

The state argued that the FLSA only requires employers to pay a minimum wage and that it does not require that the wage be paid promptly. The court rejected this argument, stating that "'shall pay' plainly connotes shall make a payment." If a payday is missed, the employer has not met its obligation to pay.

It also provides that the employee must be compensated at time and one half for all hours over 40 in one work week. The act contains no definition of *work* and only a partial definition of *hours worked.*[16] A study of the countless court cases on the subject discloses that if the employee is serving the interests of the employer, it is considered time worked under the act.

It is immaterial whether the work was requested by the employer or authorized as long as it was performed or the employer had reason to believe that the work was being performed. If the work is performed, it is difficult for the employer to plead no knowledge. The work product is something the employer knows or should know about with reasonable effort. Where the employee works and the employer fails to pay for the work, there is an exposure to overtime back pay.

Sleep Time

Under the statute, an employee must receive at least five hours sleep in a 24-hour period. It need not be contiguous,[17] but it cannot be frequently interrupted or the entire period is compensable[18] [29 CFR 553.223(c)]. Firefighters and police officers usually have an expressed or implied agreement.

Meal Periods

The act does not require payment for meal periods when employees are serving their own interests [29 CFR 553.223(c)]. Mail carriers must remain in uniform during lunch hour and are often subjected to job-related questions by patrons. These occasional questions do not substantially interfere with their duties to warrant compensation for lunch hour.[19]

However, in many work situations employees are working on behalf of the employer.[20] A shipping clerk is not required but chooses to remain at the desk during meal periods eating a brown bag lunch and directing the unloading of a truck while chewing on a sandwich. A secretary knits at her desk; the supervisor asks for a file. A maintenance mechanic is called to repair a machine during lunch hour. In all these situations the employer often does not pay for meal periods. If the shipping clerk is acting on behalf of the employer a substantial part of the meal period, all meal periods are considered time worked.[21]

Where the duties performed during lunch hour were related to the work normally assigned, the work was compensable. If work during meal periods is voluntary, it is not compensable, but often there is a fine line between what is voluntary and what is not. Many assignments appear to be voluntary, but if they are refused, serious adverse consequences result, which makes them not truly voluntary.

These examples are common situations where the employer unknowingly has considerable exposure. An agreement to exclude sleep and meal time from compensable hours is not enforceable

---

[16]R. Doyle, "Management: A Process for Building the Work Productivity and Profitability Throughout Your Organization," *Am. Mgmt. Assn.* New York, 1992.

[17]Where employees were required to remain on the premises, employer had to pay for sleep time: *Agilar* v. *Association for Retarded Citizens,* 285 Cal. Reptr. 515 (Cal. App. 4th Dist. 1991).

[18]Sleep time is compensable if interrupted by patient care: *Hillgren* v. *County of Lancaster,* 913 F.2nd 498 (8th Cir. 1990).

[19]An occasional emergency interruption would not cause employer to pay for meal time.

[20]*Taylor-Callahan-Coleman Counties District Adult Probation Department* v. *Dole,* 948 F.2d 953 (5th Cir. 1991). Also, *Henson* v. *Pulaski County Sheriff Dept.,* 6 F.3d 531 (1993).

[21]A special arrangement could be made to allow a 45-minute lunch period, deducting 30 minutes per day for the meal period and paying for 15 minutes at an overtime rate.

where the agreement is extracted by the threat of termination.[22] If the employee is never relieved from serving the employer's interest, all inactive hours and active hours are compensable.

Voluntary Work

The employer argues that employees are not required to work. They work as a matter of convenience or to please the employer, and the time should not be counted as compensable work time. The agencies and the courts state it must be shown that the work performed is not benefiting the employer to be held noncompensable.

Rest or snack periods are usually paid for as a policy matter. Under the Department of Labor interpretations, (29 CFR Sect. 785.18), if less than 20 minutes they are compensable. However, this interpretation can be sucessfully challenged.

Some courts, because employees are serving their own interests, do not support the Wage and Hour Division's position that less than 20 minutes is compensable. In *Cole* v. *Farm Fresh Poultry, Inc.,* 824 F.2d 923 (11th Cir. 1987), the court stated that reliance upon a Labor Department interpretative bulletin that is vague with broad concepts will not relieve the employer from paying for overtime. The statement in the bulletin making breaks of more than one half-hour noncompensable was not a defense when the employees could not use the time for their own purposes. In all these situations, a bulletin or a guideline is only a position of the department and can be challenged, and often the courts will not validate what the bulletin says. It is when they go unchallenged that they are often treated as the law.

Other courts enforce the regulation on the presumption that rest periods promote efficiency, which is in the employer's interests. A safer approach, if the employer does not want to pay for rest periods or snack periods, would be to offset rest periods against other working time, so total hours worked do not exceed 40. This offset has been approved by at least two courts.[23] However,

this is not always possible, and employee relations problems could become prevalent. See the case history *The 10-Minute Meal Period.*

The leading cases on meal periods are *Mumbower* v. *Callicott* and *Marshall* v. *Valhalla,* 590 F.2d 306 (9th Cir. 1979). The general rule is that the employee does not have to be completely relieved from duty. But the time must be long enough to enable the employee to use the time for his or her own purpose.[24] This often comes up where waiting time is involved. If the waiting time is part of the job, it is compensable; if the employee is free to use the time for his or her own purpose, it is not considered waiting time.[25]

A distinction must be made between waiting to go to work and being engaged to wait to go to work. If it is the latter, then it is compensable. The employer required the workers to wait for customer flow before they were paid for working. The court held that waiting time was compensable. The employees were ready, willing, and able to work when they arrived at the work site. This is an example of being engaged to wait for work.[26]

Another problem often arises when the employee is required to be on call. The usual rule is that if the employee is not required to remain on the premises but is required to leave word with the company officials or at home where to be reached, it is not considered work time while on call. However, if the employee is required to remain on the employer's premises or so close to them that he or she cannot use the time effectively for his or her own purposes, it is working time on call. The controlling factor is whether they can use the time for their own purposes.

---

[22]*Johnson* v. *Columbia, S.C.,* 949 F.2d 127 (4th Cir. 1991).

[23]*Mitchell* v. *Greinetz,* 235 F.2d 621 (10th Cir. 1956); *Ballard* v. *Consolidated Steel Corp.,* 61 F.Supp. 996 (S.D. Cal. 1945).

[24]*Owens* v. *Local 169, Association of Western Pulp and Paper Workers,* 971 F.2d 347 (9th Cir. 1992).

[25]*Martin* v. *Ohio Turnpike Commission,* 968 F.2d 606 (6th Cir. 1992), cert. denied 1993.

[26]In *Bright* v. *Houston Northwest Medical Center Survivors, Inc.,* 934 F.2d 671 (5th Cir. 1991), the employee had to wear a "beeper," stay sober, and be at the work site 20 minutes after being called. The court said the employee still could use the time for own benefit, so call time was not compensable. Also *Smith* v. *City of Jackson, Miss.,* 954 F.2d 296 (5th Cir. 1992).

The 10-Minute Meal Period—A Case History

The employees made a deal with the manager that if they took a 10-minute lunch period they would be able to quit 20 minutes early and still work 8 hours per day. (They also had two rest periods.) After a 3-year period one employee evidently got indigestion or a nervous stomach and complained to the Wage and Hour Division.

The division took the position that under its regulations, CFR Sect. 785.18, this must be a paid period because it was less than 20 minutes. Investigation revealed that employees left their machines and went to the lunchroom for 10 minutes (one even stated that he went home for lunch). When the bell rang, they all returned to their machines. The Wage and Hour Division demanded two years' back pay (the statute permits only two years) because employees worked 40 hours and 50 minutes per week under their interpretation. This amounted to over $12,000 for about 60 employees. The employer took the position that because employees were serving their own interest for the 10-minute meal period, it was not work time, therefore not compensable, and refused to pay the back pay. After a period of threatening litigation, the Wage and Hour Division dropped the matter. Because employees were serving their own purposes for the 10-minute period, it was not work time.[27]

[27]Making change for vending machines during lunch was held to be on the employee's own time and not compensable, but answering phones was compensable. *Rector* v. *Laing Properties*, 26 W.H. Cases (BNA) 1365 (N.D. Ga. 1984).

Coming to Work Early

Another common exposure of an employer is where an employee comes to work well before the regular starting time. This happens when a spouse drops an employee off or with car pools, which causes the employee to get to the work site early. Being a good employee, the person performs duties before being clocked in. This is compensable work time that the employer neither stops nor approves but tolerates.

The work performed before starting time must be an integral part of the employee's duties. Preshift work is almost always held to be compensable. Where a butcher sharpened his knives outside shift hours, the Supreme Court held it compensable.[28]

A leading case involves employees who were required to fill out daily time and requisition sheets, assemble material to be used on the job, fuel the trucks, and pick up a daily work plan before starting work at 8:00 A.M. The court stated that the test in these cases is whether the activities are an "integral and indispensable" part of the performance of the regular work and in the ordinary course of the business.[29] Time spent is compensable if it was necessary in the performance of the job. For example, the electrician putting gas in a truck is not doing electrical work, but it is necessary to the business and benefits the employer. This definition has been supported in other jurisdictions.[30]

Employees may arrive at the work site 15 to 20 minutes early, and the employer may have no knowledge of whether they are working or not. The rule of thumb used by some courts is that if they arrive 15 or more minutes early, they are presumed to be working unless the employer can prove otherwise.

[28]*Mitchell* v. *King Packing Co.*, 350 U.S. 260 (1956).

[29]*Dunlop* v. *City Electric*, 527 F.2d 394 (5th Cir. 1976).
[30]*Marshall* v. *Gervill, Inc.*, 1195 F.Supp 744 (D.C. Md. 1980).

Coffee Time

A question often comes up whether requiring a nonexempt person to make coffee at the start of the day is compensable. The test is whether making coffee is an intregral part of the job. This is certainly an exposure to a complaint if the employee calls WH. The employer, to avoid exposure, should either require an exempt employee to make the coffee or have it done after the start of the shift. Making it strictly voluntary on the part of the employee would greatly reduce the exposure. Another alternative would be not to allow the employee to start coffee making until 10 minutes or less before the start of the day.

There would be a serious exposure if the employee was required to be at the work site 20 minutes before the start of the day to make coffee. If exempt and nonexempt personnel drank the coffee, the exposure would be even greater. Most WH offices make coffee. When they do it, and who drinks it, would influence the degree of exposure.[31]

Travel Time

Travel time and walking time are not compensable under the Portal to Portal Act,[32] unless there is a custom or practice that makes it compensable. In the building trades, most labor agreements have a clause that pays for portal-to-portal time. If travel time is integrated with work and does not involve merely getting to work, it is compensable. An example would be travel on company business by nonexempt field workers or repair personnel. If it is a routine assignment the pay doesn't start until reaching the work site. Under the Portal to Portal Act this would be going to and from work and not compensable. The change in the work site is a regular part of the job. If the same nonexempt employee had an occasional assignment in a distant city, travel time would be compensable.[33] This is not going to and from work as a regular part of the job.[34]

Travel time also must be considered on a weekly basis; the employer can avoid excessive overtime due to travel by giving compensatory time off in the same work week in which the overtime was earned.

Often travel time is spent for meetings and training programs. The usual rule is that if time spent in the training program is not compensable, then neither is travel time.

Training and Overtime[35]

The criterion to determine whether a nonexempt employee is to be paid for training programs is whether or not the employee is performing any significant amount of work that benefits the employer.[36]

Another important factor is whether or not the training is compulsory. (Related training in apprenticeship programs is excepted.) Being necessary for advancement or to prevent obsolescence doesn't imply that it is compulsory. Most courts will hold that it is compulsory when the employer tells the employee that she or he must take the training or be terminated. Another problem with formal training that the practitioner has to solve is whether or not a trainee must take a course to get a job. If so, overtime would be due for an employee while training. IRS withholding and state workers' compensation and unemployment insurance coverage would have to be paid if the trainee were an employee.

The Wage and Hour Division criteria for determining whether or not a trainee is an employee have been accepted by most state and

---

[31]A client once asked a woman in a law office to get him a cup of coffee. When she returned she asked him what she could do for him. Realizing he had mistaken his attorney for a secretary, he apologized. She said she didn't mind taking her time at $200 an hour. The cup of coffee cost him $50.

[32]29 U.S.C. Sects. 251–62, an amendment to the Fair Labor Standards Act.

[33]Usually hours worked begin when the employee is required to be on the premises and perform work that is an integral part of the employee's assignment.

[34]A management employee once asked the author if he could leave early to get ahead of the traffic. The author told him to leave when he did at 6:00 P.M.; there is no traffic then.

[35]The leading case is *Walling* v. *Portland Terminal Co.*, 330 U.S. 148 (1947).

[36]There must be a benefit to the employer to be counted as overtime: *Martin* v. *Parker Protection District*, 774 F.Suppl. (D. Colo. 1991).

federal courts. These guidelines state that a trainee is not an employee if

1. The training program is similar to that which would be offered in a vocational school although the employer facilities are being used.
2. The training is only for the benefit of the trainee.
3. The trainee does not displace regular employees.
4. There is no immediate benefit to the employer who provides the training, although the training or lack of it causes a disruption in the operations.
5. The trainees are not guaranteed a job at the end of their training period.
6. The trainees are informed that they will not be paid for the time spent in training.[37]

The question has been raised in the airline industry where flight attendants and reservation agents must take training before hiring. Most of these programs met the foregoing criteria and trainees are not considered employees.[38]

As for training programs for present employees,[39] the criteria are similar. The time is not compensable under Wage and Hour Division rules if

1. The session is held outside of working hours.
2. Attendance is, in fact, strictly voluntary.
3. The training session is not directly related to the employee's job.
4. The employee does not perform any productive work while attending the meeting or training session.

Change Time

This often comes up when the employer requires the shift going off to instruct the shift coming on as to what has happened during the preceding shift. By the court rules the instructions are for the benefit of the employer but I seldom find where it is compensable. The New York court so held in *Arcadi* v. *Nestle Food Corp.,* 38 F.3d 672 (2nd Cir. 1994). However, it must be remembered in this case the union wanted overtime but dropped it at the bargaining table. The *Nestle* case is the law of the second circuit and perhaps others will agree that FLSA excludes change or "lap time."

Employees of a New York food corporation participated in a voluntary uniform wearing program for almost 40 years. The parties then negotiated a collective bargaining agreement that made the use of work uniforms mandatory. Although the union bargained for employee compensation at overtime rates for changing time, this demand was dropped and the final collective bargaining agreement did not include pay for changing time. Local employees then filed a grievance over the issue, which was denied, and the employees filed a lawsuit against the employer in the U.S. District Court for the Northern District of New York, alleging violations of FLSA. The court granted the employer summary judgment, and the employees appealed to the U.S. Court of Appeals, Second Circuit.

The court of appeals determined that the FLSA excluded changing time from coverage unless expressly included in a collective bargaining agreement or where it was acknowledged by custom or practice. In this case, the collective bargaining agreement contained no express terms for changing time. Although the mandatory uniform policy was relatively new, it established a "practice" grounded upon the parties' collective bargaining negotiations. The parties to a collective bargaining agreement were deemed to have established a practice if they negotiated over an issue and came to an understanding that resolved it without including it in the final contract. Accordingly, the grievance had been properly denied and the court affirmed the district court's summary judgment order.

[37]On time spent on meeting, see William L. Richmond and Daniel L. Reynolds, "The Fair Labor Standards Act: A Potential Legal Constraint upon Quality Circles and Other Employee Participation Programs," *Labor Law Journal,* 37, no. 4 (April 1986), 244.

[38]See *Donovan* v. *American Airlines,* 686 F.2d 267 (5th Cir. 1982).

[39]Under 29 CFR part 516 and 778, 56 Fed. Reg. 61100 (1991), employees who lack a high school or an eighth grade education level are exempted from 10 hours per week overtime for training. The training time must be paid for at the regular rate and taken during working hours. This is called a remedial education exemption.

EMPLOYEES WORKING AT HOME

Many employers treat individuals who perform work at home as independent contractors not subject to the minimum wage and overtime provisions of FLSA. However, in almost every reported wage/hour case turning upon their status, such "homeworkers" have been found to be employees covered by the FLSA.

In deciding whether an individual is an "employee," the courts follow the directive of the U.S. Supreme Court that the "economic realities of the relationship govern,"[40] and the focal point is whether the individual is economically dependent on the business to which he renders service.

Travel Time

Normally, travel to and from the employer's place of business, that is, commuting time, is not compensable. See 29 CFR Sect. 785.35.

However, in the case of homeworkers, the Department of Labor's enforcement policy is that time spent traveling to and from the employer's premises to obtain materials or equipment and/or to deliver finished work is primarily for the employer's benefit and therefore is compensable work time. See, for example, Wage and Hour op. ltr No. 286 (Aug.. 25, 1964).

Record Keeping

Employers are required to keep certain records for homeworkers in addition to those required for all nonexempt employees. These required records are described in 28 CFR Sect. 516.31. With respect to each lot of work, the employer must record (1) the date on which work is given out to worker, or begun by worker, and amount of such work given out or begun; and (2) the date on which work is turned in by worker, and amount of such work.

EXEMPT AND NONEXEMPT CLASSIFICATIONS

In most companies the control of overtime costs hinges on the classification of employees into exempt and nonexempt classifications. Often two or three employees may appear to be wrongly classified. The Department of Labor (DOL) may take the position that certain exempt employees should be nonexempt but that compliance with regulations is a question of fact for the courts to decide. Frequently DOL will not pursue its position in the courts for one or two employees.

Further complicating decisions is the fact that employers often classify an employee exempt by job title. They may consider the employee will become part of management.

Changing the classification downward may become an employee relations problem even though the change may not be allowed by a strict interpretation of the regulations.

An employer exempted general assignment reporters, producers, directors, and assignment editors. The court said they are nonexempt because their primary duties are not supervising, training, disciplining, or evaluating employees, nor do they perform administrative acts, and they are not professionals. Being highly skilled workers does not make them exempt.[41]

The act specifically exempts professional, executive, and administrative employees.[42] In determining whether an employee is exempt, Interpretative Bulletin 541 is helpful. The bulletin lists several job titles that are usually exempt. The revised bulletin added computer-related jobs to the list (P.L. 101–583)[43] and in the future will add others. It is important to become acquainted with this list. The WH will seldom audit these job titles that are in 541.

A few basic principles and some case law may give some guidance in dealing with this troublesome problem. Each case is decided on its

---

[40]*Dole* v. *Snell,* 875 F.2d 802 (6th Cir. 1989). Also *Brock* v. *M.W. Fireworks, Inc.,* 871 F.2d 307 (8th Cir. 1989).

[41]*Dalheim* v. *KDFW TV,* 918 F.2d 1220 (5th Cir. 1990).

[42]Sect. 13(a)(1). Besides exemptions for white-collar employees, the act has several other exemptions, such as motor carriers, air carriers, and agriculture workers. Also see *Reich* v. *Gater Press, Inc.,* 13 F.3d 685 (3rd Cir. 1994).

[43]29 CFR Part 541, Fed. Reg. Nov. 9, 1992.

own merits. Each company must decide to what degree it is in compliance. Is the exposure to a possible violation great enough to justify the employee relations problems that may be caused by making the necessary changes? Some managements will take the position that in questionable areas the employee relations problem overrides the exposure. They will wait for the Wage and Hour Division or the courts to tell them that they are wrong.[44]

The Salary Test

The Wage and Hour Division uses a salary test to determine whether an employee is included under one of the exemptions. If an employee is paid more than a certain salary (this is regularly increased by the department), an employee can spend 20 percent of work time in nonexempt work and still be considered exempt. (This is called the short test.) An important requirement of the salary test is that an employee cannot be docked when working less than 40 hours per week.[45] In *Abshire v. County of Kern,* 908 F.2d 483 (9th Cir. 1990), the court said that docking for absences of less than a day is "completely antithetical to the concept of salaried employees."[46]

The salary test alone doesn't make an executive, professional, or administrative employee exempt. In *Donovan* v. *United Video, Inc.,* 725 F.2d 577 (10th Cir. 1984), the court said that although salary level was very important, it alone does not make the employee exempt.[47] The duties of the job must also be considered. The employee is not compensated for the time spent on the job, but for the value of services performed.

Salary level will often prevent an audit of those job classifications that are above the level for the particular category. Changing the salary or the job

title will not make the employee exempt. The key to whether an executive, professional, administrative, or outside salesperson is exempt is the type of work[48] that is being performed.

Outside Salespersons

Another exempt classification is outside salespersons. Under Section 213(a)(1) of the act they are exempted if they sell regularly or obtain orders for goods or services while off the employer's premises. Comparatively speaking, this classification is less troublesome than administrative, professional, or executive classifications because the activities can objectively be defined.[49]

Other Considerations in Determining Exemption

Most employees tend to stress the importance of their jobs. Often when interviewed by a compliance officer, they rate their jobs at a level higher than reality, which makes them exempt,[50] but in fact they are nonexempt (unless they are complainants who feel that they are denied overtime pay). From an employee relations standpoint, the personnel practitioner tends to classify an employee as exempt in questionable cases. Another reason the employees are often classified as exempt is that employers can control their overtime. One way to eliminate the problem is for the employer to make them exempt and hope that it can be defended in a wage-and-hour audit. There are many gray areas where exempt and nonexempt classifications are being interpreted for reasons other than payment of overtime. As a result, the employer is continually exposed to violations. A business decision is often necessary on whether to take the exposure for employee relations considerations or to strictly construe the FLSA in order to avoid the penalities of back pay.

---

[44]For further research on exempt classifications, see James A. Prozzi, "Overtime Payment in the Managerial Employee—Still a Twilight Zone of Uncertainty," *Labor Law Journal,* (March 1991), 18.

[45]See James A. Prozzi, "Docking Pay of Managerial Employees: The Wage and Hour Law's Trap for the Employer," *Labor Law Journal,* 42, no. 7 (July 1991), 444.

[46]Split in circuit courts.

[47]*McDonnel* v. *City of Omaha,* 999 F.2d 1293 (8th Cir. 1993), *cert. denied,* 1994.

[48]See K. Paco, "What It Doesn't Take to be a Salaried Employee: The Future of Docking," 215 LEXIS 49 (1993).

[49]*Rorch* v. *Newspapers of New England Daily, Labor Rev. No. 210* (NH 1993).

[50]Some states issue a bulletin on how to determine exempt status. See Minn. Rules Chapter 5224–0010 and 5224–0340 (1989).

Conclusions from Case Law as to Exemptions

1. The white-collar exemptions depend on the quality—not quantity—of work performance.
2. Compensation systems that focus on hours worked focus on the quantity of service rather than the substance of the job performed. These systems are basically antithetical to the concept underlying the exemptions. This looses the exemption.
3. Compensation systems for exempt employees must focus on the work achievement of the employee.
4. Salary (or fee for professionals) is the basic component.
5. Incentive compensation may be added based on factors that reward meeting job-related goals and not lose exemption.
6. Any compensation system that uses an hourly pay as a basis puts the exempt status of all employees in jeopardy.

Recommendations for Exempt Classification

The first step in an exemption policy is to assign one person the responsibility for handling exemptions. This person should be given the final authority in each case to determine whether an employee is exempt or nonexempt. Every supervisor or manager has a special interest in making an employee exempt or nonexempt; often it has nothing to do with job content.

Guidelines for all gray areas as to exempt and nonexempt classifications should be communicated to all supervisors.[51] Often the employer, for employee relations reasons, wants to take the risk of a violation. This should also be pointed out in the guidelines.

Job descriptions are developed for wage and hour compliance; they should include the distinctions in Bulletin 541. As a defensive measure, one should require employees to write

their own job descriptions. The job descriptions should be reviewed by the supervisor or personnel department to ensure that all the activities are included. In compliance reviews when the investigator interviews the employee, it is difficult to change a position during the interview when the employee wrote the job description originally.

There is often an incentive to change job content if the employee becomes aware of the amount of back pay.

Job Descriptons

Most job descriptions for wage and hour compliance either are too vague or merely follow the wording of the regulations. They are meaningless to determine exempt or nonexempt status. The best job descriptions for wage and hour compliance are those that list specific duties and their frequency of performance.

The job description should pinpoint those activities that answer whether the exempt or non-exempt requirements are met. The job description for wage and hour compliance is for the purpose of documenting the management position on the exempt or nonexempt classifications. It may not be applicable for other purposes for which job descriptions are used, such as hiring, disability, promotion, and compensation.

When determining exempt or nonexempt classifications there is no exposure to violations if an employee is wrongly classified as nonexempt and paid overtime. It is only when an employee is wrongly classified as exempt that the employer has liability for overtime pay. An employee can be misclassified as exempt for a considerable time and nothing happens until there are complaints and the WH investigates and takes a position. For this reason, in those gray areas it is advisable to keep a record of hours worked by questionable exempt employees, although it is not necessary under WH rules.

Partly Subjective Nature of Determination

One reason why exempt classifications are troublesome is that in the final analysis a part of the determination is subjective. The best example

---

[51]For a questionable exempt employee, it is advisable to have the employee make his or her own job description. The WH is more likely to accept it.

of this was where a fast-food chain had all its assistant managers classified as exempt supervisors and the WH claimed that they were nonexempt employees. The court gave the following rules to determine whether assistant managers were supervisors:[52]

1. They must recommend hiring and firing.
2. They must direct the work of two or more persons.
3. They have management duties.
4. They regularly and customarily exercise discretion.

Two of the four requirements are subjective; the gray areas were not eliminated. In any given situation subjective determination must be made whether management duties existed and discretion was customarily and regularly exercised.

In determining whether an employee has an exempt status, three elements are necessary:

1. Weight must be placed on job duties that are usually considered exempt and less weight placed on job title. In *Blackmon* v. *Brookshire Grocery Co.,* 835 F.2d 1135 (5th Cir. 1988), the court held that meat department managers were not supervisors when they spent two thirds of their time cutting meat.[53]
2. The exempt duties must actually be performed and not just assigned or expected of the employee.
3. The level of compensation should be above the minimum required for exempt classification in that category.

When in doubt about an employee's status, it may be advisable to check with the local WH office. The caller does not have to give an identification, but even if he or she does, the WH does not usually follow up these calls with an investigation. It takes an employee complaint to trigger an investigation. In addition to the interpretative bulletins mentioned elsewhere in this chapter, the *Wage and Hour Field Operations Handbook* and *Guidebook to Federal Wage-Hour Laws* are very instructive. These guidelines should be in the possession of the person who is responsible for administration of the FLSA. They can be obtained at a nominal cost from the Wage and Hour Division office or the Government Printing Office.

CONTROLLING OVERTIME COSTS

Often the employee's desire for overtime pay is stronger than any action the employer wants to take.[54] This makes overtime cost control difficult, but not impossible. A waste control clerk or sales service expeditor can always find a reason to work overtime when money is needed to buy a new boat.[55] The first step in the control of overtime is to remove from the employee as much as possible the decision of when overtime should be worked. This can be done by a communicated policy of requiring authorization before overtime can be worked.

The enforcement of the rule of requiring authorization must be by discipline; the mere promulgation of a rule is not enough. It is the duty of the employer to enforce it;[56] if the employee works the overtime, it must be paid for. The WH takes the position that unauthorized overtime still must be paid if known or tolerated; the courts sustain this position.[57]

The employer can adopt many different procedures to control the costs of overtime payments required by the FLSA. A complete approach to the problem requires consideration of individual steps to be taken in each area of exposure.

Compensatory Time Off

The law requires that overtime be paid only after 40 hours in one work week, but

---

[52]*Donovan* v. *Burger King,* 672 F.2d 221 (1st Cir. 1982).

[53]In *Brock* v. *Norman's Country Market, Inc.,* 825 F.2d 823 (11th Cir. 1988), the court said time is not the only factor in determining executive duties; whether they are discretionary supervisory functions must be considered.

[54]The average manufacturing employee worked 3.6 hours overtime in 1991 compared with 2.3 hours in 1982.

[55]The author once made a study of overtime for nonexempt group leaders and found that their overtime increased before they went on vacation and before Christmas.

[56]29 CFR Sects. 778.316 and 785.11 and 785.13. Also see *Lindow* v. *United States,* 738 F.2d 1057 (9th Cir. 1984).

[57]The author once discharged an employee on Christmas Day. The author knew that the employee was working overtime to keep up in his work without recording it but could never catch him. The employee never suspected somebody would be around on Christmas Day to find him working.

EXHIBIT 14-1

_____(Company Name)_____ hereby agrees to employ _____(Name of Employee)_____ as _____ at a regular hourly rate of pay of $_____ per hour for the first forty (40) hours in any work week and at the rate of at least time and one-half or $_____ per hour for all hours in excess of forty (40) in any work week, with the guarantee that _____(Name of Employee)_____ will receive in any work week in which he or she performs any work for the company the sum of $_____ as total compensation for all hours performed up to and including (insert the total hours agreed upon; however, hours agreed upon cannot exceed 60 hours per week) hours.

COMPANY NAME

By _____

Accepted:

_____(Employee's Signature)_____

compensatory time off can be given any time during the work week in order to avoid overtime.

Overtime hours worked in one week cannot be offset by granting compensatory time off in another week. However, in certain industries, such as health care, the Wage and Hour Division will grant an exception. Premium pay for time worked may offset overtime hours worked in that week. If an employer pays double time for not working a holiday and the employee works more than 40 hours that week, there is no overtime due. Under the act, overtime would not start until the employee actually worked more than 40 hours in the work week during which premium time for the holiday was paid. However, this policy may cause some employee relations problems. (Many collective bargaining agreements provide that holiday pay be considered time worked for purposes of overtime.)

The Belo Contract

The Belo contract is a guaranteed wage contract made with the nonexempt employee where hours vary widely from week to week. This plan is an effective method to control overtime where the employee can control hours of work. It is widely used for field repair service, customer service jobs, and other situations where the job requires work off the premises by nonexempt employees.

The conditions necessary to qualify for a Belo contract were stated by the Supreme Court in *Walling* v. *Belo Corp.,* 317 U.S. 706 (1941). The court listed five requirements:

1. The duties of the job covered by the Belo contract must require working hours that fluctuate above and below 40 hours per week.[58] This is the key requirement. The fluctuation must not be caused by economic conditions or employer control but by job duties of the employee.
2. The contract must pay the employee a regular hourly rate above the statutory minimum wage requirements.
3. The weekly guarantees must pay at least one and one-half times the regular rate for all hours over 40.
4. The contract cannot cover more than 60 hours a week.
5. The total hours to be worked and paid for weekly must be agreed upon.

Exhibit 14-1 is a Belo contract that complies with these requirements, except total hours agreed upon.

---

[58]This is enforceable, although an agreement to waive the provisions of the FLSA is not.

The total hours inserted in the last line must bear a "reasonable relationship to the hours an employee actually works." This is usually determined in the first contract by past overtime records. However, the actual hours worked before a Belo contract is usually greater than what is worked after the Belo contract. When the incentive to work overtime is removed by the Belo contract, the overtime hours usually decrease with no effect on job performance. To anticipate a decrease in hours by entering less than the previous average would not be in violation of the Belo requirements but may result in the employee not signing it. A better plan would be to review the contract in six months or a year and base the average hours on the experience under the Belo contract.

In the second contract term, the hours could be reduced if the average shows it. If the hours are reduced to the average, the employee is not being rewarded for efforts in doing the work in fewer hours. This is not advisable.

Compliance and Overtime Control

Supervisors should be made aware that if the employee is required or permitted to work for the employer's benefit, the employee must be paid. When a policy is adopted that all overtime must be authorized, it must be enforced. Like any other policy, if it is not enforced, it creates an environment of false security in the belief that unauthorized overtime is compensable.

For the employer to control overtime, two strong positions must be taken. One is enforcement of a strong overtime policy that as much as possible removes the control of hours from the employee. Second, where control of overtime hours cannot be removed from the employee and exempt status cannot be justified, the Belo contract or some other pay plan should be considered. If a Belo plan is not possible and there is an uncontrollable fluctuation in the hours worked, another plan should be submitted to the Wage and Hour Division for approval.

Compliance with any statute starts with knowing the requirements of that statute. The employee relations consequences must be integrated with any policy of compliance. The decision then becomes a business decision, with consideration given to the legal exposure.

DEFINITION OF INDEPENDENT CONTRACTOR

Employers are sometimes tempted to avoid the costs and responsibilities associated with the employer-employee relationship by claiming that those who perform certain services are independent contractors.[59] If an independent contractor relationship is in fact established, the employer has certain advantages.

Advantages to the Employer

1. The requirements of the Fair Labor Standards Act do not apply.
2. Unemployment compensation payroll taxes do not have to be paid.
3. Social Security taxes do not have to be paid.
4. City, state, and federal income taxes do not have to be withheld.
5. Compulsory workers' compensation coverage does not apply.

Advantages to the Worker

1. The worker has much greater flexibility with respect to the time, place, and manner of performance of services.
2. The independent contractor has enhanced flexibility with respect to the deduction of business-related expenses. For example, while employees may deduct only those business and miscellaneous expenses that exceed 2 percent of their adjusted gross income, independent contractors may deduct 100 percent of their expenses related to self-employment.
3. Independent contractors may establish individual pension and profit-sharing plans that may be more desirable than those offered by employers.

---

[59]A. Rocen, "Employee–Independent Contractor Issues," *Tax Advisor,* (April 1991), 226. Also R. Hubbard, "IRS Working on Revenue Ruling to Minimize Snags Surrounding Employee-Contractor Status," *Tax Notes,* (December 1, 1990), 1395.

Obviously, there is considerable economic advantage in avoiding the statutory requirements. There is strong incentive for establishing an independent contractor relationship wherever possible, but there are also certain risks in doing so.[60]

Risks in the Independent Contractor Relationship

Although the advantages are great, so are the risks if the court finds that an independent contractor is in fact an employee.[61] No statute defines the exact meaning of an independent contractor. The interpretation is left entirely to the courts, using agency principles. The principal liabilities when it is determined that an independent contractor is in fact an employee are

1. Failure to withhold under IRS regulations, and therefore the employer is liable for the amount of the employee's tax plus interest.
2. Overtime or minimum wages under the FLSA.
3. Right to join a union under the National Labor Relations Act.
4. Liability to the state for unemployment compensation insurance tax.
5. Failure to carry workers' compensation insurance, so the employer becomes liable under the common law for a work-related injury.
6. Failure to pay Social Security taxes; under IRS regulations the employer is liable for its share plus what is owed by the employee and interest on the entire amount.

To determine whether or not an independent contractor relationship exists, one must look to the common law,[62] the IRS code, the National Labor Relations Board cases, decisions under the FLSA, state agencies' positions on workers' compensation coverage, and liability for unemployment insurance.

Most of these agencies use either all or part of the common law definition, but some put more stress on certain factors than others. For example, the NLRB looks only at the control factor, while the IRS looks to see whether or not it was a businesslike operation.

For the purposes of this section the common law guidelines will be used, but the interpretation of the enforcement should be reviewed before creating an independent contractor.

Guidelines to Establish Independent Contractor Relationship

The courts have said on numerous occasions that no one element establishes an independent contractor relationship.[63] The historic base for determining whether such a relationship exists comes from the law of agency. An attempt to define the distinction between an employee and an independent contractor was made by the *Restatement of the Law of Agency* (2nd, Sect. 220), which stated,

While an employee acts under the direction and control of the employer, an independent contractor contracts to produce a certain result and has full control over the means and methods that shall be used in producing the result. He is usually said to carry on an independent business.

In *Nationwide Mutual Ins. Co.* v. *Darden,* 112 S.Ct 1344 (1992), the Court held that a person is an employee under ERISA unless Congress says otherwise. The Court used the common law agency principle in determining whether there was an independent contractor. Under ERISA, the Court in *Darden* listed the factors to be considered when determining whether there is an independent contractor or employee. The Court pointed out (at 1349) that no one factor is decisive.

The 5th Circuit, in *Reich v. Circle C Investments, Inc.,* 498 F.2d 824 (5th Circ. 1993),

---

[60]The IRS estimates that more than 3 million workers are misclassified as independent contractors and that $1.5 billion in taxes are lost each year.

[61]The IRS has a manual on how to identify an independent contractor. Most other agencies issue similar guidelines.

[62]M. Hulen, et al., "Independent Contractors, Classification Issues," *American Journal of Tax Policy* 11 (1994) 13.

[63]For discussion on totality of circumstances, see *Oestman* v. *National Farmers Union Insurance,* 958 F.2d 363 (10th Cir. 1992); also IRS Rule 87–41.

found one factor that would indicate that the topless dancers were independent contractors but on balance, four other factors made them employees. In this situation the dancers received no compensation from the club, only tips from customers, and at the end of each night the club received $20 from each dancer regardless of how much they made in tips from dancing on the tables. The club said this was rental. However, the club controlled the number of customers and tables.

The court focused on control, investments of the worker (costumes and a padlock), opportunity for profit (the club controlled the customer flow, where money could be made if the dancer was sexy enough), skill and initiative required to perform the job (no training was needed), permanency of the relationship (this was very short). This would indicate a nonemployee status, but the court found that others outweighed it and found they were employees. The main factor was control.

Control—manner and means

Skill required

Source of instruments and tools

Location of work

Duration of relationship

Method of payment

Regular business of hiring party

Hiring party role in the business and paying assessments

Employee benefits

Tax treatment

The Supreme Court requires two main conditions for finding that an independent contractor condition exists. First, there must be independent performance of the assigned job. Second, the initiative and decision-making authority must involve the performance of the work by the independent contractor.[64]

The major factor in the determination of independent contractor status is the degree of employer control. The more control, the more likely the worker will be found to be an employee.

A person who is required to comply with instructions about when, where, and how to work is ordinarily an employee. Some employees who are experienced or proficient in their work need little instruction; however, this does not put them in an independent contractor status. The control element is present if the employer retains the right to instruct.

For the purpose of determining an employer-employee relationship under the National Labor Relations Act, the board applies only the right of control test. If the person for whom services are performed retains the right of control of the end result and the manner and reasoning to be used in reaching that result, an employer-employee relationship exists.

The right to instruct a person who works for the employer eight hours a day in one job and cleans the office at night or mows the lawn on Saturday often makes a worker an employee. If an employer-employee relationship exists, overtime compensation is due for all hours worked over 40 unless a flat fee is greater than time-and-a-half for hours worked. There is an implied right to instruct a person who works for the employer eight hours a day on one job and does additional work in off hours. If it is an employee-employer relationship, overtime compensation is due. If the flat fee exceeds the overtime rate for the hours worked, then there is compliance.

If an employer assumes that an independent contractor relationship exists and in fact it does not, the exposure in other areas is far greater than the payment of overtime. Because of this exposure the employer should be cautious when treating the relationship as independent contractor status. Serious consideration should be given to requesting a determination from the appropiate regulatory agency. Most agencies will furnish a list of guidelines upon request. Such a request usually will not trigger an investigation.

---

[64]For a complete analysis of factors used by the Supreme Court in determining an independent contractor, see E. Delaney and R. Hollrah, "Independent Contractor vs. Employee," *Employer's Handbook* (Washington, DC: Thompson Publishing Group, 1992).

Examples of Employer-Employee Relationship

To prevent exposure to liability where an employer assumes an independent contractor relationship exists but an employer-employee relationship legally exists, some examples may be helpful. These are old cases, but controlling legal principles haven't changed.

Where a gasoline distributor leased stations to operators, the court found that not only was the lessee an employee, but those persons whom the lessee hired were also employees of the distributor. The evidence showed that the distributor controlled the hours of operation, prices of major items, and daily management of money and took the risk of profits and loss. The court reasoned that the employees of the lessee were an integral part of the operation; therefore, they were also employees of the distributors and the lessee.[65] Other cases where the court found an employee-employer relationship are where an agent who operated a retail cleaning outlet under a contract was held to be an employee of the owner[66] and where crew leaders for a builder registered under a state law as labor contractors but were in practice employees.[67] In the 5th Circuit a contract laborer who was a mechanic and supervisor was held to be an employee; however, the contract laborer was a concrete subcontractor of this employee who was held to be an independent contractor.[68] The test in these cases is whether the party for whom the service is being performed retains control over the general outcome.[69]

Essential Elements of an Independent Contractor Relationship

Because of the risks involved and the possibility of litigation, employers should have a very strong reason for attempting to establish an independent contractor relationship. If such a reason does exist, then it is advisable to state specifically in the agreement that

1. The only supervision will be related to result and not to method.
2. Inasmuch as possible, the individual will make the investment in equipment.
3. The independent contractor will be responsible for the profit or loss of the operation.
4. In all other respects the independent contractor will be performing as a separate business.
5. The employer does not give benefits, such as holiday or vacation pay.
6. The person is to be employed for a specified length of time.
7. The parties do not believe they are creating an employer-employee relationship.
8. The materials and equipment will be supplied by the contractor.
9. The parties enter into the relationship with a specific intent: to create an independent contractor relationship.
10. The work is either a distinct occupation or a business.

Use of Contracts to Establish an Independent Contractor Relationship

The "economic reality" of the relationship is the strongest element in establishing an independent contractor relationship that will stand the scrutiny of the courts and the regulatory bodies. If such a relationship is intended, it must be objectively established by a written agreement. The contract should be written with a careful eye toward common law and agency interpretation. The contract should emphasize the elements listed above.

Creating an independent contractor status is one way to control overtime. Extreme care should

---

[65]*Marshall* v. *Truman Arnold Distributing Co.,* 640 F.2d 906 (8th Cir. 1981).

[66]*Donovan* v. *Sureway Cleaners,* 656 F.2d 1368 (9th Cir. 1981).

[67]*Marshall* v. *Presidio Valley Farms, Inc.,* 512 F.Supp. 1195 (W.D. Tex. 1981).

[68]*Donovan* v. *Techo, Inc.,* 642 F.2d 141 (5th Cir. 1981).

[69]*Reich* v. *Circle C Investments, Inc.,* 498 F.2d 824 (5th Cir. 1993).

be taken to make certain that although an independent contractor status was intended, an actual employee-employer relationship does not exist. Liability for uninsured workers' compensation and payment of unemployment, Social Security, and withholding taxes often offsets the advantages of establishing a questionable independent contractor status. In any independent contractor status a written contract should be executed and contain the requirement of independent contractors outlined in this section.

When a firm wants to employ an individual as an independent contractor, the terms of that relationship should be put into an agreement.

The agreement should contain

1. Objectives of the relationship
2. The various factors that are necessary for an independent contractor relationship (the 20 elements stated in the *Darden* case)

Administrative agencies and the courts will give great weight to the agreement. However, they will also look to other factors that reflect the tasks of the individual, the terms and conditions of employment, and whether the parties are following the agreement. In questionable situations professional advice should also be considered. This shows a good faith effort to comply with the law.

15

SAFETY LAW

Safety as a Personnel Function
Management's Stake in the Safety Program
The Occupational Safety and Health Act (OSHA)
The General Duty Clause
Refusal to Work under Unsafe Conditions

The Occupational Safety and Health Act of 1970, 29 U.S.C. §651 et seq., (OSH Act), requires employers to provide a place of employment that is "free from recognized hazards that are causing or are likely to cause death or serious physical harm." Employers' duties are of two kinds: First is the general duty to provide a safe work environment, and second is the specific duty to conform to specific health and safety standards promulgated by the secretary of labor and the Occupational Safety and Health Administration (OSHA).

Purpose of the Law

Congress stated that personal injuries and illnesses were rising and that the stated purpose of the act is to provide for the general welfare, to assure, as far as possible, every working man and woman in the nation safe and healthful working conditions, and to preserve our human resources. It includes all companies in interstate commerce and gives the states power to legislate their own acts. Twenty-seven states have their own act, so the federal government does not make inspections. The government then remits the savings to the states. The State Review Boards have been successful in hearing the appeals faster than on the national level, which is sometimes two years behind. Congress said a workplace can be made safe by:

1. Encouraging employers and employees to reduce the number of accidents, instituting new programs and perfecting existing ones.
2. Giving employers and employees separate responsibilities and rights to achieve safe working conditions.
3. Authorizing the secretary of labor to set safety and health standards and granting power to enforce the same.
4. Providing for an increased number of inspectors for compliance and providing for the training of inspectors.

5. Encouraging labor-management safety committees to help create a safe place to work.

The intent of Congress from the stated purpose was to have a police action to enforce safety. In the early 1970s this police action had limited success. The matter became political and subsequent administrations turned their backs on the act unless the unions forced the matter. Creating a safe place to work is the objective of the act, but this does not happen overnight. Each new person in charge of OSHA would say the act would be enforced, and then proceed not to enforce the act. The new secretary of labor and OSHA supervisor (assistant secretary of labor) show some signs that police actions will be reinstituted. New life is put into the act by increased litigation, increased fines, and a new law awaiting congressional approval.

Appeal Procedure

Employees (or the employee representative) who do not like the citation received by the employer can appeal the matter to OSHA. A hearing is held before an administrative law judge who makes a recommendation to the Commission. The recommendation is usually accepted and made a final order. The Review Commission (OSHRC) can reverse OSHA. The case then goes to the court of appeals and the Supreme Court (if *certiorari* is granted). In practice, the labor organizations bring most of the cases. OSHA matters become legal and the parties usually have a lawyer represent them at hearings before OSHA administrative law judges and other steps in the appeal procedure.

The common law requires the employer to provide a safe place to work. State workers' compensation (WC) laws say that employers have to pay regardless of the cause. Otherwise, the law leaves the employer alone until there is a work-related accident that is under WC or until an Occupational Safety and Health Administration (OSHA) inspector knocks on the door.

Legal literature on work-related accidents was first concerned with problems after the accident

happens.[1] Since 1970 compliance with OSHA and how effective it is to prevent accidents has been controversial topic. Safety program literature talks about the effectiveness of posters, training programs, and safety committees. None are required by law. Little is written about how the law can be used to further a safety program. Also, we have more data than in 1995. See the Exhibits 15-1, 15-2, and 15-3.

This chapter will show how safety is a training function with a legal connection. OSHA compliance can be used to enhance a safety program. If the employer is to avoid exposure to expensive litigation, provide a safe place to work, and have an efficient operation, the merging of safety with OSHA is essential.

Safe workers are not born—they are made.[2] The operating and safety managers' functions are to develop safety-conscious employees. If the manager can show the employees that management cares, the employees will be more apt to develop an attitude that supports working safely. The company must establish safety policies and procedures and enforce them. If an employee violates a safety policy, the discipline should be no less severe than for violating a discrimination policy or punching somebody else's time card. (If an employee is injured, some believe that the injury is enough to get the message across. This is not true.)[3]

SAFETY AS A PERSONNEL FUNCTION

The personnel function of safety training can be performed by the operating manager or any other

---

[1]J. H. Wigmore, "Responsibility for Tortious Acts: Its History," *Harvard Law Review,* 7, 315; C. Beard, "The Industrial Revolution," U.S. Department of Labor Bulletin 20 (1927); *OSHA Handbook for Small Business,* U.S. Department of Labor, OSHA, No. 2209 (1990 Revised).

[2]See "Is Your Safety Attitude Showing," Bureau of Business Practice No. 2012, June 25, 1992.

[3]Richard Braden, "Can OSHA Survive in the New International Economic Order? New Constraints on the Promulgation of Permanent Health Standards." *In the Public Interest,* 14 (1994-1995), 121.

EXHIBIT 15-1 *Fiscal Year 1994 Most Cited Standards, National*

Standard	Description		Frequency
1910.1200	Hazard Communication		27,235
	Written program	10,254	
	Employee information	6,970	
	Labeling	5,136	
	Material Safety Data Sheets (MSDS)	4,875	
1926.59	Hazard Communication in Construction		13,843
	Written program	5,892	
	Material Safety Data Sheets (MSDS)	3,551	
	Training	3,262	
	Labeling	1,138	
1904.2(a)	OSHA 200 form - recordkeeping		4,321
1910.215(b)(9)	Safety guards on abrasive wheel machinery not adjustable or not adjusted for decreasing diameter		3,578
1910.147(c)(1)	No energy control (lockout/tagout) program		3,209
1910.212(a)(1)	Machine guarding – general requirements		3,143
1903.2(a)(1)	OSHA Poster		3,135
1910.147(c)(4)	Hazardous energy (lockout/tagout) procedures were not developed or were deficient		3,029
1910.305(g)(1)	Improper use of flexible electrical cords		2,704
1910.305(b)(1)	Conductors entering boxes, cabinets, or fittings not protected from abrasion and/or openings not effectively closed		2,617

EXHIBIT 15-2 *1994 Most Cited Standards, Overall*

Standard	Description		Frequency
MN Rules 5206.0700, et al	Employee Right-To-Know		663
	No program	440	
	Written program deficiencies	38	
	Multi-employer worksites	6	
	Records	29	
	Frequency of training	30	
	Training deficiencies	12	
	Lack of Material Safety Data Sheets (MSDS)	56	
	Labeling	52	
1910.134(a)(2)	Respiratory Protection Program		134
1926.100(a) and 1926.28(a)	Hard hats in construction		100
1910.151(c)	Emergency eyewash/shower facilities		99
1910.304(f)(5)(v)	Grounding of cord and plug connected equipment		97
1910.219(d)(1) and (e)(1)(i)	Machine guarding – belts and pulleys		96
1910.305(g)(1)	Improper use of flexible electrical cords		88

EXHIBIT 15-3 *Lost Work Days*

per 100 Full-Time Equivalent Workers per Year in the United States, 1988–1991 Average	
Construction	145.3
Transportation and public utilities	128.6
Agriculture, forestry, and fishing	105.8
Manufacturing	115.6
Mining	134.6
All private industry	81.3

per 100 Full-Time Equivalent Workers, Private Sector, 1980–1991	
1980	65.2
1981	61.7
1982	58.7
1983	58.5
1984	63.4
1985	64.9
1986	65.8
1987	69.9
1988	76.1
1989	78.7
1990	84.0
1991	86.5

Source: U.S. Bureau of Labor Statistics, annual survey of occupational injuries and illnesses.

member of management. If the safety director reported to personnel or to the human resources manager, there could be a communication gap, which would be eliminated if the function reported to the operating manager.[4]

If the safety function reports to the operating manager, back-to-work procedures are more realistic. The temptation of the safety director to protect the record can be restricted. Settlement of grievances and promotion of worker-management cooperation for a motive other than safety are always considerations. When the reporting relationship is to operations and indirectly to all divisions that are serviced, there is a better safety program.

The personnel or human resource function cannot create a safe place to work. This must be done by operating personnel and the workers. OSHA tends to increase employee participation. It causes safety and operating functions to move closer together. All elements of loss prevention—such as health and wellness programs, environment, medical security, and fire prevention—are training functions. The term *safety engineer* is not descriptive of the primary function in an accident prevention program.

MANAGEMENT'S STAKE IN THE SAFETY PROGRAM

Apart from the requirements of OSHA, top management must be committed to safety.[5] It not only reduces the cost of operations and fosters community reputation and customer relations, but it also attracts good workers. The commitment of top management is the most important element of

---

[4]R. W. Lack, "The Safety-HR Connection," *Personnel Journal,* (July 1992), 18.

[5]For a good review of safety programs, see M. Cook, "How to Run a Safety Incentive Program," *The Human Resources Yearbook, 1992/93* (Engelwood Cliffs, NJ: Prentice Hall), p. 12.1. Also see newsletters of state agencies.

a safety program. Once a commitment is made, everything else seems to fall in place.[6]

The supervisor has a stake in an effective safety program.[7] Safety and production cannot be separated. It is a question of what rung safety is going to have in the operations ladder. The same supervisory techniques used to prevent accidents are used to obtain good production.

The worker's stake in safety is more than financial. Workers' compensation benefits do not pay full wages[8] (although some states are getting close). The suffering that accompanies an accident cannot be measured in dollars. It is indeed a dreadful price to pay for a few seconds of inattention, yet it is paid every day.

All of these reasons to avoid an accident existed before OSHA. When OSHA was enacted, it told the employer, "If you don't follow the standards, the government will penalize you, so you will do so in future."[9] The law steps in to determine whether the workers and supervisors are following the standards. The standards do not prevent all the accidents, but the enforcement helps to convince management. It is not uncommon for a company to have a good accident-prevention program and be cited by OSHA for violations.[10] Although it is demoralizing to everyone involved, OSHA does not consider individual programs, but only whether the standards are followed. However, their consulting services can be used.[11]

A good safety program is accident-prevention awareness. It contains the following elements:

1. Management, supervisors, and workers should participate in identifying and analyzing existing hazards. All work-related hazards and unsafe acts must be communicated to affected employees repeatedly. Having a safety program does not guarantee compliance with OSHA, although it will help defend a citation.[12]

2. The key to success of a safety program is top management involvement.[13] Top management must make each person in the organization responsible for safety, like any other business function.

One of the major mistakes management makes is to depend upon one person to reduce accidents.[14] This is usually the safety director. As one manager wrongly put it, "We got a safety director; if accidents are not reduced we replace the safety director." Safety is everyone's business. The safety director cannot do it alone. Often it takes a couple of safety director replacements to find this out. The safety director is a resource person whose major function is to keep all members of management involved and establish liaison with the workers. When management delegates all the responsibility to the safety director, there is frustration.

3. Existing causes of accidents must be identified. The major cause of accidents is unsafe acts. Physical plant conditions cause about 15 percent of all accidents. They must not be overlooked. A safety work order should be given top priority by maintenance. The exposure still exists until it is corrected. (This kind of response also shows concern by management and reminds the employee to work safely.) To correct unsafe acts is a training function not without problems.[15] The company hires the whole person.[16] All the domestic problems and frustrations outside the workplace are brought to the work site.[17] Most unsafe acts in the workplace occur when the employee is thinking about something other than the job.

4. Communicate the safety program. Communication must be continual. Information from the National Safety Council and other organizations can be very

---

[6]As the sign on the CEO's desk said, "The buck stops here."

[7]In *Leich* v. *Hornsby*, 885 S.W.2d 34 (Tex. Appl. 1994) employer and officers were held liable for failure to provide safety equipment.

[8]For state maximum benefits, see Cook, "How to Run a Program," p. 12.19.

[9]See "All about OSHA," U.S. Department of Labor, OSHA 2056 (1991 Revised).

[10]*Pedraza* v. *Shell Oil Co.*, 942 F.2d 48 (1st Cir. 1991).

[11]*OSHA Handbook for Small Business.*

[12]S. G. Minter, "The One Rule Safety Program," *Occupational Hazards,* 53, no.7 (August 1991).

[13]When the author called a safety meeting, all the production executives were too busy. After the executive VP talked to them, they were all in attendance.

[14]See "Training Program Results Measured in a Unique Way," *Supervision,* 53 (1992), 18.

[15]Minter, "The One Rule Safety Program."

[16]See Peter F. Drucker, *The Practice of Management* (New York: Harper & Row, 1954), p. 262.

[17]When things got tough and one prophet in sinful Israel gave up, God sent in another team. God didn't give up on people, and management can't either.

helpful. Gimmicks, recognition, and contests are part of the act.[18] The company develops literature to sell a product. Literature to sell a safety and health program must be developed in the same way. Tailgate meetings at the start of the shift, frequent safety posters, and the like are all helpful in training the workers to work safely.

5. Investigate each accident. The author, as safety director, would audit safety programs in subsidiary plants. All he had to look at was the first report of injury (required in most states). If the correction said, "Be more careful," he knew that the safety program was bad. If management starts out with the belief that all accidents have a cause, then the investigation and remedy are on the right track.

A safety program that contains these basic procedures will cut workers' compensation costs, reduce absenteeism due to work-related injuries, and show that management cares.

THE OCCUPATIONAL SAFETY AND HEALTH ACT (OSHA)

Compliance with OSHA

The Occupational Safety and Health Act[19] does not define safe working conditions, but establishes two types of obligations.[20] The first obligation is a restatement of the common law. This requires the employer to provide a place of employment that is free from all recognized hazards that are causing or are likely to cause death or serious harm to the employees. This is called the "general duty clause" and in simple terms states that you, Employer, are responsible for any condition that is recognized or foreseeable as being unsafe or injurious to one's health. The obligation further requires the employer to take necessary steps to correct this condition, including the proper training, supervision, and discipline of employees, or get a citation.

The second obligation imposed upon the employer by the law is to comply with specific standards promulgated under the authority of the secretary of labor.[21] The violation of these standards subjects the employer to citations, civil and criminal penalties,[22] or litigation.[23]

Intent of OSHA

The original intent of OSHA was to reduce accidents in the workplace. It fixes the responsibility for accidents on the employer. The act has no enforcement teeth against the employee. Congress, in all its wisdom, felt that the employer is in a better position to prevent unsafe acts and correct unsafe conditions than for the law to force employees to comply.[24]

The National Labor Relations Board and the courts hold that safety is the responsibility of management. Employees have no right of enforcement. If a union is involved, safety is a bargainable subject. The employees can complain to OSHA about unsafe conditions, and under certain circumstances. They can refuse to work.[25]

Employees will sometimes use unsafe conditions as a means of harassment or as an expression of dissatisfaction in other areas of the employment relationship. When an employee (usually a union member) complains of an unsafe

---

[18]One of the best gimmicks, in the author's experience, is to post a safety slogan, call home to see if anyone knows it, make it so many dollars a call until you get a winner, and then give the pot.

[19]29 U.S.C. Sect. 553–651 et seq. It preempts most state laws: *Gade* v. *National Solid Waste Management Association*, 1992 LEXIS 3686 (1992).

[20]See "Safety, Law," Minnesota OSHA Dept. of Labor Industry (Fall, 1995).

[21]Enforced by OSHA, a division under the secretary of labor. Standards are subject to judicial review. See *AFL-CIO* v. *OSHA*, 965 F.2d 962 (11th Cir. 1992).

[22]Interest for penalties starts on date of penalty rather than date of final judgment, *Reich* v. *Sea Sprite Boat Co.,* 50 F.3d 418 (7th Cir. 1995).

[23]For good case law on standards, see M. Breger, "Recent Developments in OSHA Litigation," *Labor Law Journal,* 43, no. 11 (November 1992), 687–94.

[24]The secretary of Labor may not require workers to wear testing equipment for OSHA inspections or permit the employer to be present for an OSHA employee interview: *Martin* v. *Trinity Industries,* 959 F.2d 45 (5th Cir. 1992).

[25]*Whirlpool Corp.* v. *Marshall,* 445 U.S. 1 (1980).

condition, OSHA must inspect.[26] OSHA needs to give notice to the employer under the law before the inspection is made. This can be at the time of the inspection. Some regional directors will give an early notice, and this gives the employer time to determine whether it is harassment or an unsafe condition. The government states they cannot make a workplace safe alone, but in this area refuses to change the law from a police action.

Safety practitioners argue that the law does not get to the real cause of an accident. According to studies, unsafe acts of employees are the major cause of accidents.

THE GENERAL DUTY CLAUSE

Section 5 (a)(1) of OSHA (commonly referred to as the general duty clause) states: "Each employer shall furnish to each of his employees employment and a place of employment which are free from recognized hazards that are causing or likely to cause death or serious physical harm to his employees."[27] The clause is usually used by OSHA where there are no standards. (It is also used for ergonomics citations.) OSHA has to prove several elements to find a violation of the general duty clause.[28] Although some conditions may be recognized hazards, employer knowledge and feasibility of abatement methods are difficult to prove. The Emergency Temporary Standard [Section 6(c)] is too cumbersome to be used when there is an injury. An injury is not required to establish a hazard under the general duty clause, but specific abatement methods must exist.[29] When the general duty clause is used for a

violation, the employer should carefully consider contesting it.[30] Many OSHA inspectors believe that whenever there is an injury, the general duty clause has been violated. Case law does not support this view.[31]

Passing an OSHA Inspection

As with any regulatory agency, a little public relations will go a long way in reducing citations and penalties. In 1995, OSHA expects penalties to reach over $2 billion. This would be an increase of $30 million over 1990. This money comes right off the top of the profits of an organization. There are several steps the employer can take to minimize the impact of an inspection:

1. Have good records. Keep the employees informed of the number of injuries by posting the log at least once every six months.
2. The first report of injury should reflect the corrective steps taken—not "Be more careful." Give these records to the OSHA inspector before they are requested.
3. Have an active safety committee that keeps good minutes. Have these minutes available for the inspector.
4. Keep good records of the safety activities and have them available for the inspector. (The ADA may affect back-to-work procedures.)
5. The person assigned to accompany the inspector should be well trained. Make sure all members of management know whom to notify when the inspector arrives.
6. Try to determine the reason for the inspection. Sometimes inspectors will not tell, and they have to be asked. Occasionally they will not give the real reason. The law says they have to give some reason.
7. Insist upon a closing conference before the inspector leaves the facility.
8. Treat the inspector like a professional even though some members of management think he or she is not.

---

[26]An employee complaint can establish probable cause for a search warrant: *Martin* v. *International Matex Tank,* 928 F.2d 614 (3rd Cir. 1991). The employer must comply: *Justice* v. *Martin,* F.2d 121 (7th Cir. 1991), cert. denied.

[27]Sect. 5 (a)(1) 29 U.S.C. 654.

[28]See Edwin G. Faulke, Jr., and Thomas M. Beck, "The General Duty Clause of the Occupational Safety and Health Act of 1970," *Labor Law Journal,* 44 (March 1993), 131.

[29]For a more detailed discussion of the general duty clause, see M. Rothstein, *Occupational Safety and Health Law,* 3rd ed., West Publishing Co., Hornbook Series (St. Paul, MN: West, 1990, with updates); S. A. Bokat and H. Thompson III, "Occupational Safety and Health Law," BNA (1988) p. 114.

[30]*Ed Taylor Construction Co.* v. *OSHRC,* 938 F.2d 1265 (11th Cir. 1991).

[31]M. F. Cook, *The Human Resources Yearbook, 1992/93* (Englewood Cliffs, NJ: Prentice Hall), pp. 12.7–12.15.

9. Do not agree to an abatement period. This admits the violation of the standard cited.

10. Agree to nothing that is questionable, but do not create an adverse relationship.

OSHA budget limitations permit only a certain number of inspections.[32] There are about 1,000 inspectors to inspect 6 million workplaces and they usually run out of money to travel. The company should make periodic internal inspections as if the OSHA inspector were present. The internal inspection is preparation for the inspector's arrival. The company never knows when an OSHA inspector is going to appear, so they should be prepared to explain why certain conditions exist. (The inspector will not accept an economic reason.)

An Ergonomics Program

Ergonomics (from Greek words *ergon,* "work," and *nomos,* "law") is the science of adapting the mechanics of a job to fit an employee's movement. In short, ergonomics involves the study of the relationship between the workers and their jobs. OSHA defines an ergonomist as an individual who possesses a recognized degree or professional credentials in ergonomics or a closely allied field, who has demonstrated the ability to identify and recommend effective means of correction for ergonomic hazards in the workplace.[33]

Repetitive motion injuries from video display terminals, chronic eye fatigue, and carpal tunnel syndrome[34] are examples of conditions that can be corrected by ergonomics.[35] Many employers have concluded that certain repetitive movements are the cause of cumulative trauma disorders.[36] These conditions are prevalent in the meat-packing industry, and studies have shown that there is much work to be done in other industries.[37]

Discipline for Safety Violations

An employee who is a union steward, member of a safety committee, female, or minority does not have the right to violate a safety rule. The law is quite clear that the employer can do whatever is necessary to enforce safety rules. The discipline may be challenged because there is a protective clause under the act, but this protection cannot be used by an employee to defend the violation of a safety rule. The act specifically states that the purpose is to assure employees of a safe place to work, and not allow injury to self or co-workers. Prevention is the employer's obligation.

One problem with discharging for a safety rule violation is top management's belief that the facility is a safe place to work. However, OSHA and most state safety codes say otherwise.[38] Safety codes state that it is the employer's responsibility to prevent accidents. It is no defense that is was "an act of God," or that the accident was caused by an unsafe act or a physical condition that could not be prevented, or that the employee was informed

---

[32]The author once knew a management person who refused to change any condition until there was an OSHA citation. He believed that the facility was safe, and he didn't need the law to force him to change. The only reason he would make a change was to avoid a penalty.

[33]*Ergonomics Program Management Guidelines for Meat-packing Plants* (Washington DC: U.S. Department of Labor, OSHA, 1991), p. 21; also R. Weltmann, "A Work-place Designed to Be Efficient Can Save Money—E=MC," *Workers Compensation Cost Control* (Boston: Northeast), July 1992, p. 3.

[34]*Schlup* v. *Auburn Needleworks, Inc.,* 479 N.W.2d. 440 (Neb. 1992).

[35]In February 1993, OSHA issued ergonomic safety and health guidelines that cover most industries. NIOSH estimates that more than 20 percent of Americans will risk developing carpal tunnel syndrome by the year 2000.

[36]Data from the Bureau of Labor Statistics state that over 50 percent of all occupational illnesses are due to repetitive motion. Repetitive motion injuries accounted for 40 percent in 1990. This compares with 21 percent in 1982. Also see "Office Ergonomics Erases Back and Wrist Complaints," *Safety Management* (Waterford, CT: National Foremen's Institute), no. 350 (1992), p. 1.

[37]See C. M. Gross, "Reduce Musculoskeletal Injuries with Corporate Ergonomics Program," *Occupational Health and Safety,* 1 (1990), pp. 28–33. Also *Employee Benefit News,* 14 (April 1992), 15; H. J. Reske, "Repetitive Stress Suits Consolidated," *ABA Journal,* 78 (September 1992), 21.

[38]The state cannot impose safety rules without the federal government's approval: *Gade* v. *National Solid Waste Management Association,* 1992 LEXIS 3686 (1992).

of the rule but didn't follow it.[39] Management must see that it is enforced.

Another reason for the reluctance that employers have for not giving discipline for a safety violation is employee protection from the various statutes, such as whistle-blowing, workers' compensation, and OSHA. If the reason for the discipline is a violation of a safety rule, no statute will prevent it. OSHA and most state statutes give employers enforcement power; all they have to do is use it.[40] OSHA will cite the employer when a rule is not enforced. However, there is an exposure if the discipline is not well founded.

REFUSAL TO WORK
UNDER UNSAFE CONDITIONS

The right of an employee to refuse to work in unsafe conditions is protected by two different statutes: Sections 7 and 502 of the Labor Management Relations Act of 1957 (LMRA)[41] and Section 11(c)(1) of the Occupational Safety and Health Act.[42]

Rights under LRMA

In the interpretation of Section 502 of the LRMA the courts have stated that a refusal to work is protected by the act. In the field of employee safety, injury, and disability, almost every aspect of the employer-employee relationship—from preventing workplace injuries to providing leave to injured employees, removing barriers to employment of injured/disabled workers, and finally to compensating injured workers—is governed by the OSH Act, FMLA, the ADA, and the state laws. Sometimes, these laws pull employers in four seemingly divergent directions at once. But employers can comply with all four with proper attention and guidance. There must be good faith belief with objective evidence that the working conditions are abnormally dangerous. Also the workers must be competent to testify as to the physical conditions.

The protection under Sections 7 and 502 of LRMA is exclusive. A no-strike clause in the labor agreement or an arbitration clause does not affect the employees' rights, although the arbitration is permitted if the labor representatives want to seek that remedy under the labor agreement.

In order to receive NLRA protection in a dispute over unsafe conditions, there must be concerted activity. That is, the employee must have talked to co-workers or have acted specifically under their authority.

Where the employee acted unilaterally in refusing to drive a truck that he contended was unsafe, the Supreme Court stated that as long as it was an enforcement of the labor agreement it was protected.[43]

Rights under OSHA

The right under OSHA of the employee to refuse to work under unsafe conditions is found in the Secretary of Labor's interpretation of what constitutes discrimination under Section 11(c)(1) of OSHA. The secretary's directive interpreting this section stated that an employee can refuse to work if (a) the employee's fears were objectively reasonable, (b) the employee attempted to get the employer to correct, and (c) there was not time to use the normal enforcement procedures under

---

[39]An employee cannot be sanctioned for the employer's criminal violation of OSHA: *U.S.* v. *Doig,* 950 F.2d 411 (7th Cir. 1991). However, the employer can: *People* v. *Magnetic Wire,* 534 N.E.2d 962 (Ill. App. 1989).

[40]See *CCH Employment Safety and Health Guide* (Commerce Clearing House, 4025 W. Peterson Ave., Chicago, IL 60646; 1971 and 1973) for procedural aspects of OSHA.

[41]LMRA Section 502 states: ". . . nor shall the quitting of labor by an employee or employees in good faith because of abnormally dangerous conditions for work at the place of employment of such employee or employees be deemed a strike under this Act." Section 7 of the act gives the employees the right to strike.

[42]OSHA Section 11(c)(1) states: "No person shall discharge or in any manner discriminate against any employee because such employee has filed any complaint or instituted or caused to be instituted any proceeding under or related to this Act or has testified or is about to testify in any such proceeding or because of the exercise by such employee on behalf of himself or others of any right afforded by this Act."

[43]*NLRB* v. *City Disposal Systems, Inc.,* 104 S.Ct. 1505 (1984).

OSHA (or any other statute) so the danger could be eliminated.

This interpretation was considered in *Whirlpool Corp.* v. *Marshall,* 445 U.S. 1 (1980). The Supreme Court held that in order to have a violation of 11(c)(1) of OSHA two conditions must exist: (1) reasonable belief that the employees will be placed in jeopardy of injury or death and (2) reasonable belief that there was no other alternative but to disobey the employer's order (no opportunity to go to an OSHA office or seek redress from another level of management).

The Court further held that this may be termed a strike and although the employees would be protected, they would not receive pay for not working. The Court also reaffirmed the rule established under Section 502 of LRMA that if a hazardous condition were found not to exist or employees were acting in bad faith, they could be discharged for insubordination.

In cases subsequent to *Whirlpool,* the courts will often cite *Whirlpool* as their authority but will not require the conditions stated in *Whirlpool.* Where a foreman refused to work when he believed the condition to be unsafe, the court ordered his reinstatement, citing *Whirlpool* as authority.[44] This is an example of the court following Whirlpool although the conditions listed by the court were not present.

If an employee has objective evidence of the unsafe condition, it would appear that she or he could refuse to work under the NLRA, regardless of whether the conditions under *Whirlpool* were met.

Safety is a Joint Effort

Representative William A. Steiger (R. Wis.), co-author of OSHA, said shortly after the act was passed that both employers and employees would benefit from reduced accidents. It is essential, if the act is going to work, that there be voluntary compliance through safety committees and self-inspections.[45] The record is clear: You cannot legislate safety. If must be conceived in management's womb. Babies will be born when the employer makes it happen. The employee must want to work safely or be made to work safely.

All too often the employer gets concerned with compliance with the standards promulgated by OSHA, forgetting that the objective of these standards is to prevent accidents. Compliance doesn't relieve the employer of liability.[46] When employee cooperation fails, enforcement through discipline is necessary. Be nice but carry a big stick in the closet.

Congress realized that employee compliance is required, but left it up to the employer. Under the common law the employer must provide a safe place to work. OSHA supplemented the common law in putting the emphasis on physical conditions. It supplemented the unsafe act. The employer must train the employee to comply.

---

[44]*Donovan* v. *Hahner, Foreman, Harness, Inc.,* 736 F.2d 1421 (10th Cir. 1984).

[45]See William A. Steiger, "OSHA: Four Years Later," *Labor Law Journal,* 25 (December 1974), 723; also M. Berger, "Recent Developments in OSHA Litigation," *Labor Law Journal,* 43, no. 11 (November 1992), 694–98.

[46]Compliance with OSHA doesn't prevent a state tort action: *Pedrazo* v. *Shell Oil Co.,* 942 F.2d 48 (1st Cir. 1991).

16
CONTROL OF WORKERS' COMPENSATION COSTS

History of Workers' Compensation in the United States
Basic Concepts of Workers' Compensation State Laws
Living with the System
Definition of Work-Related Injuries
Employee Back Problems
Recommendations for Control of Costs

Workers' compensation (WC) is not a new concept. The purpose and intent can be traced as far back as the time of Henry I (about the 12th century). These laws provided that if a person is on a mission for another and death occurs in the course of the mission, the sender or creator of the mission is responsible for the death. Likewise, an early German law held masters liable for the death of their servants. A money payment had to be made for an injury or death.

The present WC system had its origin in German law. In 1838 the German state of Prussia passed a law making the railroads liable for injuries to their employees and passengers, unless caused by acts of God or negligence on the part of the injured employee.

The first modern WC law was adopted in Germany in 1884. This law required compulsory insurance for industrial accidents. The reason for pressure to pass such a law was a socialist movement supporting it. The Iron Chancellor, Otto von Bismarck, wanted to head off the socialist movement and pushed the law through the Reichstag.

The German approach to WC was a compulsory system. The common law defenses of the assumption of risk, contributory negligence, and fellow-servant doctrine were too harsh for the social thinking of the late 19th century. The impetus was to treat workers' compensation as a part of a broad social insurance system.[1]

---

[1]For a more complete discussion of workers' compensation in Europe, see Ralph H. Blanchard, *Liability and Compensation Insurance* (East Norwalk, CT: Appleton-Century-Crofts, 1917) *Ives* v. *South Buffalo Railway Co.,* 94 N.E.2d 431 (N.Y. App. 1911).

HISTORY OF WORKERS' COMPENSATION IN THE UNITED STATES

The movement to take care of the injured started in the United States at the turn of the century. It was founded on the belief that misfortunes, disability, and accidents of individuals are a social matter—that the state has a duty to take care of the injured, regardless of any other facts. In 1902, Maryland passed an act providing for a cooperative accident insurance fund. This was the first legislation embodying any degree of the compensation principle. This and later laws in Massachusetts and Montana were declared unconstitutional as a denial of due process. The first real workers' compensation law was passed in New York in 1910, but like the others it was declared unconstitutional.[2] This decision was met with an explosion of opposition; Teddy Roosevelt was so angry that he openly advocated changing the judicial system. Following this decision, states became more liberal toward the injured worker, and in 1911 Wisconsin passed the first WC law that stood the constitutional test.[3] By 1925, 24 states had passed laws. The last state (Mississippi) passed the law in 1948[4]

Space prevents this chapter from describing the current law of each jurisdiction. The law differs in each state as to benefits levels, administration, eligibility, and premium costs. This chapter will give an overview of the law in most of the states. Knowledge of the law in the state where the employee works is essential for effective cost control.

BASIC CONCEPTS OF WORKERS' COMPENSATION STATE LAWS

All workers are covered now, including maritime workers, other than seamen, who have never been covered by state laws. Political conditions have caused an increase in benefits and the scope of the laws.[5] Basic concepts have not changed. All the state laws have six basic concepts:

1. To provide benefits regardless of fault or financial condition of the employer.[6]

2. To reduce delays caused by litigation and controversy over responsibility for the injury, thereby reducing attorney's fees.[7]

3. To relieve public charities of the financial drain caused by occupational injuries or diseases. The legislative bodies reason that the employer is in a better position to pay for the social ills caused by occupational injury by passing the cost to the consumer than the government is through taxation (an astute political decision).

4. To encourage employer interest in reducing accidents by making the employer liable for all costs.[8]

5. To generate maximum employer interest in safety and rehabilitation through an appropriate experience-rating mechanism.

6. To promote frank study of causes of accidents (rather than concealment of fault)—reducing preventable accidents and human suffering.

There is a wide difference of opinion on whether these objectives have been achieved.

---

[2]*Ives* v. *South Buffalo Railway Co.,* 94 N.E.2d 431 (N.Y. App. 1911).

[3]By 1920 nearly half of the workers were covered by some sort of workers' compensation and the court rejected the employer's arguments of due process: *White* v. *New York Central Railroad,* 343 U.S. 188 (1917).

[4]The leading legal treatise is Arthur Larson, *Workers Compensation Law* (New York: Matthew Bender & Co., 1982). This is in ten volumes, but a two-volume desk edition is available. It has annual revisions. Other references include *Analysis of Worker's Compensation Laws,* U.S. Chamber of Commerce, revised annually.

[5]As benefit levels increase so does utilization. See the 1992 report of the Workers Compensation Research Institute.

[6]Also see "An Employer's Guide to Employment Law Issues," *Small Business Office,* Vol. II (1994), 65. 432 E. Seventh St., St. Paul, MN.

[7]Statutes in most of the states not only fail to reduce litigation, but make litigation necessary to resolve the issues.

[8]The cost must be excessive in relation to other costs before the employer's interest is aroused beyond moral consideration. Minnesota, Massachusetts, and several other states have changed their laws to increase the incentive to return to work. They have cut costs in most areas, but have made some change in the benefit levels. This area is subjected to considerable lobbying pressure in each legislative session.

However, the National Commission on State Workers' Compensation Laws states that reform is needed, but the workers' compensation system is fundamentally sound. It is a valued institution in our industrial economy. The National Commission on State Worker's Compensation Laws and a task force in the Department of Labor have both rejected proposals to replace the various state systems with one federal program. But they conclude there is a need to change the state laws and make them more effective within the social insurance system.

LIVING WITH THE SYSTEM

The administrator of a WC system considers that the most important element in administration is to make the employer financially responsible for benefits.

The second most important element is to supply the employer with all the necessary data to control the cost.

However, the biggest problem the state administrator of WC has is the lack of data for effective cost control. The employer must depend upon its own program for effective cost control. This program basically establishes a relationship with the employee and outside sources who have a substantial influence on the employer's costs. Once the employer learns how to establish the proper relationship with other related sources, policies or practices can be instituted that will reduce the costs. These policies and practices will be recommended in the last section of this chapter after many of the problems related to the system have been discussed.[9]

Treatment of the Seriously Injured

When an employee is seriously injured, it is a traumatic experience. Employees react to the injury differently. Sometimes they are angry with the employer, sometimes with another employee;

others are not angry with anybody but are concerned about their finances. Sometimes they are worried about their ability to work again or pursue a favored hobby. Whatever the concern, the employer immediately should find out and relieve the injured of the worry as much as possible. Maybe the employee wants to be left alone; then direct contact after initial approach is not advisable. By working through others the same results can be accomplished. The employer should be certain that the best possible medical care is being provided;[10] if financial assistance is necessary, it should be obtained. The employee should have assurance that if he or she is not able to return to the old job, the employer will try to accommodate by finding other jobs or provide rehabilitation training for other vocations. This is the law.[11]

For the seriously injured employee, some suggested employer practices are as follows:

1. Visit the hospital immediately and assess how or through whom the employee can best be relieved of any worry.

2. Contact the family; if the injured wants to be left alone, offer help indirectly through someone else if such help is needed.

3. Keep in touch with the employee, to show interest in the recovery progress, and to assure the employee of returning to the job. Accommodation, rehabilitation, possible job vacancies, and so on should be discussed.

4. Avoid any implication that it will be necessary to obtain legal counsel at the early stage of recovery. Explain the workers' compensation law and company employee benefits. If a lawyer becomes involved, establish a relationship with the employee's lawyer. Inform the attorney that the company is aware of the

---

[9]For control of abuses under workers' compensation, see Bruce S. Vanner, "Cut beneath Abuse of Workers Compensation," *Personnel Journal,* 67, no. 4 (April 1988), 30.

[10]To reduce costs, the Massachusetts legislature in 1992 established a fraud bureau for WC cases, and set up procedures for managed care. In 1995, Minnesota objectives were to reduce costs.

[11]This concern should not imply a guilt complex on the part of the employer because this would have a chilling effect on anything that the employer does for the benefit of the employee. Avoiding a guilt complex is especially important when informing the next of kin of an occupational death, if emotional and legal consequences are to be avoided.

law and will keep the matter as nonlegal as possible.[12]

Relationship with Doctor

To reduce costs successfully, the employer must have the cooperation of the doctor or doctors involved. This is sometimes difficult due to the conflict of interest with the patient-doctor relationship. The doctor often aids the employee in continuing to be paid for not working when physically able to do so. Instances of no-work slips without seeing the doctor, diagnosis of a condition over the telephone, or light-work slips that do not define light work are not uncommon. These problems could be eliminated by an employer-doctor relationship. To establish the employer-doctor relationship, the following program is suggested:

1. The employer should inform the doctor of the physical requirements of certain job categories. This can be done on the doctor's visit to the plant site. If this is not possible, send an accurate job description listing the physical requirements of the job. Often bad medical opinions are caused by the doctor not being informed.

2. If a medical opinion is suspect, the employer should challenge it by sending the employee to another doctor. If the employee refuses, inform the employee that you are stopping the benefits unless the employee returns to work.

3. The employer should establish sound back-to-work procedures that are based on the physical condition of the employee.

A double standard for occupational and for nonoccupational injuries confuses the doctor. The return-to-work policy must not exclude any make-work to protect a safety record. The job the employee returns to must exist, and if the injured worker doesn't do it some other worker must. The

employer should inform the doctor about the employee's activities off the job after the injury. If the employer cannot get an accurate medical opinion, the employer should consider finding the right doctor. Without an accurate medical opinion about the employee's physical condition, back-to-work programs are useless.

Relationship with Insurance Carrier

The proper relationship with the insurance carrier is extremely important, especially for small companies who do not have large legal staffs, personnel practitioners, and a security department to investigate doubtful claims.[13] If the insurance carrier does the proper job, it can make a real contribution in controlling costs.

Many times the insurance carrier, when trying to get a new account, will stress the effectiveness of its cost control department (safety engineering). An employer considering the selection of an insurance carrier should question how effective the carrier's claim control department is. All too often the insurance carrier's play-dead attitude in claim abuse is what the employee is seeking.

The evening paper reports that the softball team the employee was playing for won the city championship Sunday afternoon. However, there were three injuries during the game, but the names were not given. A Monday morning injury is reported to the insurance investigator. The investigator tells the safety director that the injury probably happened while playing ball. However, in view of the social welfare attitude of the courts the case would be difficult to win. It would be wise not to contest it. Everybody is satisfied. The employee is paid compensation for a back that was injured playing ball. The insurance company is satisfied because it saves investigation and litigation costs that have already been included in the premium rate. The safety director is satisfied because it is not a reflection on the company's safety record but is an uncontrollable accident.

---

[12]Sometimes a lawyer becomes involved in a probable third-party product liability lawsuit against the manufacturer of the machine that caused the injury. The employer should not aid in such a lawsuit until the workers' compensation case is closed. Often cooperation in the third-party suit can adversely affect the employer's workers' compensation case.

---

[13]If the employer is self-insured, *insurance carrier* as used herein should be interpreted to mean the consulting organization or whoever is responsible for claim control.

To develop an effective relationship with the insurance carrier for claim control it is suggested that

1. When injuries are first reported to a state commission and insurance company, the employer should "flag" all doubtful claims and demand that they be thoroughly investigated. In almost yearly surveys by the National Institute for Occupational Safety and Health it is reported that nationally less than 10 percent of workers' compensation claims are contested. Considerably more than 10 percent of the claims should be investigated.

   When investigating a doubtful claim, the employer's representative should take an active part in the investigation. All pertinent facts must be given to the insurance carrier. The carrier must then make a thorough investigation.

2. Approximately 10 percent of all contested claims should be disputed beyond the investigation stage. The employer should stay with the case to judge the quality of legal service[14] being provided and avoid complacency on the part of the insurance carrier.[15]

3. Contested claims should not be settled by the insurance carrier unless the employer approves. Settlements often have employee relations consequences. Sometimes it may be advisable to litigate although economically the case should be settled. Many lawsuits are tried on other than an economic basis.

The chances of winning might be slim, but forcing a disputed claim to hearing and having the employee testify to something different from what is known to be a fact by co-workers has a sobering effect on other employees.

Many insurance carriers have no real interest in premium cost control. Experience-rated premiums usually have a percentage of add-on costs for administration. As premium costs increase, so do profits through administration charges.

DEFINITION OF WORK-RELATED INJURIES

A major objection to common law that preceded WC was that too much time and money was being spent on litigation. Questions concerning the injured worker's right to benefits and the amount she or he should receive were common. It was expected that WC laws would avoid these issues and, accordingly, litigation would be avoided.

In order for an injured worker to receive compensation benefits, there must be a showing that he or she was an employee of a covered employer—that an accidental injury occurred in the course of employment. All of this is subject to interpretation. In addition, the employee must give timely notice to the employer or give some legal excuse for not doing so. The wage basis upon which his or her compensation is paid must be agreed upon, the duration of the disability must be determined, and if it is a permanent disability the degree of disability must be medically established. It is no wonder that the goal of reducing the cost of litigation is still far off.

Mental Condition

Early interpretations of an injury were limited to a traumatic physical injury. The courts, in keeping with the socialist intent of the law, have expanded this definition to mean various nontraumatic events.

Some courts take the position that in order for a disabling mental condition or a nervous disorder to be compensable there has to be a traumatic incident. Other courts (in over 18 states) require only a mental stimulus, such as shock, to make a condition compensable.[16]

---

[14]T. Thomson, "Are Attorneys Paid What They're Worth? Contingent Fees and the Settlement Process," *Journal of Legal Studies*, 20, no. 1 (January 1991), 187–223.

[15]The author once had an insurance company attorney drop in at 11 A.M. to prepare for a case that was to be argued at 1:30 that day. It is needless to ask who won.

[16]See *Kinney* v. *State Industrial Commission*, 423 P.2d 186 (Ore. 1967) for a view of not requiring a physical trauma and *Sibley* v. *City of Iberia*, 813 P.2d 69 (Ore. 1991), for requiring a physical trauma. See also Derek R. Girdwood, "Can I Collect Workers Compensation Benefits If My Job Drives Me Crazy?" (comment), *Detroit Civil Law Review*, (1992), 591.

Accidental Injury

All but six states require that an injury be accidental before it can be compensable. The basic element of an accident is that some part of the incident must be unexpected. Most states require that the injury be traceable to a reasonably definite time, place, and occasion or cause. This comes up often in heart, back, or other conditions that could happen off the job. Most courts require that the exertion has to be in some way unusual for the injured worker although it may not be for other workers.

The accident requirement is also important for infectious diseases that result from unusual or unexpected events or exposure. If the disease follows the accident, it is usually considered an accident and there is little litigation over this. Some states make a disease compensable by statute without the requirement of an accident. Without a statute, the courts in other states have held that an unexpected contraction of an infectious disease is an injury by accident. Some courts reason that the invasion of the body by microbes is in itself the injury.[17]

Injury Must Arise Out of Employment

The requirement that the injury must arise out of employment is the leading cause of litigation. It is the most common problem to the practitioner. Generally speaking, the injury must be work related and in the course of employment.[18] However, there are so many variations of this requirement that the reader is advised to consult Arthur Larson, *Workers Compensation Law,* Vol. 1, Sect. 13 (New York: Matthew Bender Co., 1982), and current monthly issues of *Worker's Compensation Law Bulletin* (Quinlan Publishing Co., Boston) where subjects are indexed for a particular problem. Space permits only a limited treatment of the subject.

One consideration is whether the job involves a risk. If the risk is personal, then it is not compensable. It was considered a risk associated with the job when an employee was mugged while dropping off the mail on the way home from work.[19]

Some courts will hold that if the risk is increased by the job assignment, it is compensable. If the employee was injured by an "act of God" (for example, lightning or an earthquake), the large majority of the courts would hold that such an injury arose out of employment. Working conditions increased the probability of injury.

Sometimes the injury is related to the personal condition of the worker. The general rule is that this is compensable if the employment in any way contributed to the final disability. If the injury was caused by placing the person in a position where the condition was aggravated or was weakened by strain or trauma it is compensable. Thus if a person had a heart attack or an epileptic seizure and fell to the floor, this would probably be held to be personal and not compensable. However, if while in a high place a worker fell due to an epileptic seizure, the employment would have contributed to the final injury. Some states hold that a heart attack while having sexual intercourse is compensable if the employee was placed in a position by the employer where such activity might be expected. An overseas assignment or a game warden working in the woods at night would be good examples. [20]

The majority of the courts also hold that where the original injury was in the course of employment, every natural consequence that results from the injury is also compensable. However, there may be an intervening cause attributable to the employee's own intentional conduct. For example, if a driver runs over a child while driving in the course of employment and

---

[17]HIV has been found to be within the definition of occupational disease if acquired during the course of employment: *Hansen* v. *Gordon,* 602 A.2d 560 (Conn. S.Ct. 1992).

[18]A company picnic can be in the course of employment, *Ludwinski* v. *National Carrier,* 873 S.W.2d 890 (Mo. App. E.D. 1994).

[19]*Wayne Adams Buick, Inc.* v. *Ference,* 421 N.E.2d 733 (Ind. 1981).

[20]In *Signorelli* v. *GKN Automotive Components, Inc.* (Mich. Comp. Appeals 1982), an administrative law judge held that where an employee died while having intercourse with his secretary it was compensable, because you can't expect an employee on an overseas assignment to "stare at the walls of his hotel room."

subsequently gets a divorce and has a nervous breakdown, it would be a question of fact. Did the incident of employment cause the condition? Was the divorce caused by the incident? Did either one cause the mental disorder? This is a situation where it would be difficult to avoid litigation unless employer wants to settle.

Definition of Course of Employment

The course of employment requirement is concerned primarily with the time and place of the injury, also the activity of the employee when the injury occurred. The hard-and-fast rule would be that only an injury received during working hours would be compensable. However, in line with the socialist concepts of WC, this has not been followed in all cases. Much has to do with the type of work being performed and whether there is a causal relationship between the work and the injury.

Where a salesperson was returning home from a call after normal hours, the court held that this was not compensable because there is nothing unusual about a salesperson returning home after normal hours. However, if this had been a person who normally quits at 4:30 and for some reason had to work overtime, the result might have been different.

The Work Site Makes a Difference

It also makes a difference whether the person is an outside worker, is an inside worker, or is living on the premises. If the person is an inside worker, the course of employment starts the minute she or he steps on the premises. For an outside worker (such as a salesperson), the usual interpretation of course of employment is that when he or she leaves home the work period starts and is covered until returning.

If the employee is living on the premises, most state courts will call everything course of employment except eating, bathing, sleeping, and dressing.

Outside Scope of Employment

Because a worker is injured on the premises doesn't always mean the injury is compensable. If the injury is caused by an activity that substantially departs from the usual employment duties, some courts will consider this outside the scope of employment.[21] Other courts will hold that this is still the scope of employment.[22] If an employee disobeys orders and is injured, it can be argued that this is outside of scope of employment and not compensable. Employers must integrate WC coverage with the Americans with Disabilities Act (ADA). In the hiring procedures they cannot ask about WC claims until a conditional job offer has been made.[23] They must know the essential functions of the job to prevent injuries and provide for reasonable accommodation to the disabled. There is a serious exposure to a discrimination charge if the entire situation is not properly handled. This is where the advice of an attorney may be needed.

Retaliation Under Workers' Compensation Laws

Another problem is retaliation when the employee files a WC claim. The ADA and state statutes will increase the frequency of retaliation charges. Employer will claim it is a disability, employee will say it was because a WC claim was filed.

Drug-related accidents are probably compensable when the injury occurs during the course of employment. If the employer enforces a strong policy of no use, possession, or sale of drugs, it appears that a good argument could be made for a discharge if the policy is violated. However, it is doubtful whether the employer would be relieved of paying WC benefits. This is all the more reason why drug abuse should be detected before an injury occurs to the person or a co-worker.

---

[21] For a discussion in which horseplay was considered to be the course of employment, see G. Caruso and M. Alberty, "Worker's Disability Compensation," *Wayne Law Review*, 38 (1992), 1292.

[22] See *Hoyle* v. *Isenhour Brick & Tile Co.*, 293 S.E.2d 196 (N.C. 1982), where the employee was killed while driving a forklift truck in violation of rules and the court held it was compensable because he was acting in behalf of the employer.

[23] Some states deny WC benefits if the applicant lied on an application form about a disability.

Off-duty use of drugs should not be permitted if the employee comes to work under the influence. (Thus a testing policy is needed.) The employer could make a strong case that there is too much danger of injury to self or co-workers and that such injury would be compensable.

EMPLOYEE BACK PROBLEMS

The employer who has not experienced a back problem is either new or very rare.[24] A back condition as referred to in this chapter is an alleged injury that occurred on or off the job or is no injury at all.

Weak backs can be found in all levels of management. Many times the employee tolerates the bad back. The work doesn't require extensive use of the back. This is true in many nonphysical jobs.

Employees who do work that requires the use of the bad back attempt to seek redress through statutes or lack of employer policies.

To eliminate the back problem, employers in their preemployment physical x-ray backs. If it medically appears that the back condition will interfere with job performance, the person isn't hired. This practice has created a pool of unemployables because of a back condition.

Applicants then allege they are handicapped and seek redress under a state law or ADA. (Over 45 states now prohibit discrimination because of a physical condition; some include the bad back as a handicap.)

The employee with a recurring disability creates a complex problem in the workplace for which there is no single solution. That is probably why the problem has been around for a long time.

To seek a solution to the problem, it is necessary to put employees in two categories: first, those who have a desire to work with their back condition; second, those who use the

condition as a pretext for not working in order to collect benefits.[25]

The severity of the back condition is medically difficult to determine. The questionable employee and/or his or her attorney will allege the back condition more often than any other disability. Tendinitis (a condition caused by a repetitive action) is probably the next most often alleged disability that is hard to prove. These employees are often called the "plant lawyers." They become knowledgeable on how to use the law to their advantage. Their constant appearances at hearings and as witnesses often make them better lawyers in this area than the company counsel. Every employer has had or will have in the future at least one "plant lawyer." The solution is not hopeless, because there are only a few. Something can be done about them through injury reduction programs and back-to-work procedures.[26]

Discharging Employees with an Injury

An employee who is discharged and has a work-related injury often alleges that the discharge is wrongful. The employee seeks damages beyond the state workers' compensation statute under a wrongful discharge claim. It is usually alleged that the discharge is contrary to public policy because the employee was exercising a right under the statute. Often the employer takes longer to discharge a back case than for other injuries. For this reason the issue of excessive absenteeism often is raised by the employer.

In most states it is contrary to public policy to discharge for exercising a right under a statute. In these cases the court must determine whether the discharge was for excessive absenteeism or for filing a claim under the statute. The employer should make sure that the discharge was for a valid reason other than filing a workers' compensation claim. Under *Price Waterhouse* the filing of a claim would be one.

---

[24]More than 25 percent of lost workdays per year are due to back injuries: OSHA Fact Sheet No. 87–09.

[25]See Neil G. DeClercq and John Lund, "Back Injuries, OSHA General Duty Clause Citiations, and the NIOSH Lifting Guidelines," *Labor Law Journal,* 42, no. 12 (December 1991), 807.

[26]Tested workers could stay in if it screws up numbers.

A nurse technician injured her back while helping a patient into bed. She was ordered by her doctor not to work for three months. She returned to work after a month and her condition recurred seven months later. She was off for another long period. The next year she was absent 128 days, 29 days the following year, and 34 days the first five months of the third year. She was then discharged. The reason for discharge was excessive absenteeism. After her discharge she filed a workers' compensation claim and sued. The statute prohibits discharge for filing a complaint under WC. The court held that her discharge was for excessive absenteeism that was caused in part by the work-related injury. The court noted that the statute protects the employee if the reason for discharge was for exercising a right under the statute. The real reason in this case was excessive absenteeism.[27] If there is a collective bargaining agreement, the court will normally hold that the grievance procedure must be used.

The plaintiff sustained a series of work-related back injuries. After the second injury he was asked by the personnel manager to return to light duty for a short period and to delay filing a workers' compensation claim, because in 10 days the company would receive a six-month award for no lost time because of an accident.[28] After a week of light duty, he returned to his old job of forklift operator. About a month later the plaintiff became ill at work and slipped and fell while descending stairs (a common case when the injury is not work related and the employee claims it is). Six months later the employee had back surgery, after which the doctor advised him to return to work. He was restricted to lifting less than 75 pounds. The personnel manager disputed the validity of the last injury as being work related. Rather than let him return to work, he sent him to the company doctor. The company doctor sent the employee back to work, but restricted him to lifting to 50 to 60 pounds. After working for a short period of time, the employee was discharged. Reason: "He was physically unable to perform his job without

causing a safety hazard to himself and fellow employees." (The employer was obviously trying to avoid another injury.) The employee alleged the discharge was in retaliation for filing a WC claim. The jury awarded $50,000 in actual damages and $75,000 in punitive damages. The court held that the jury could reasonably find malice and intentional infliction of emotional distress.

The verdict was especially damaging to the employer. The plant manager became angry when the employee reported the condition for the second time. He questioned the validity of the injury as being work related. The court was displeased with the employer's action in disputing the claim for disability payments.

The difference in the outcome of these cases is that in the one case the company didn't question the validity of the claim. The employee may have been using the back as a pretext to be off work, but the employer just waited until there was enough absenteeism to discharge. It is easily predictable with this type of employee. In the other case the company first wanted to protect its safety record and asked the employee to cooperate. This fits the game plan of a "plant lawyer." The company is creating a job and not making a back-to-work decision based on medical opinion. It is never wise to question the validity of a back case. Just act as if it is valid and take steps to eliminate the employee's game plan (once you are certain that there is a plan). Some employers use a technique that says to the employee, "You and I know that you are not going back to work for some reason other than your back." This may be acceptable for a doctor, but not for an employer.

It often becomes a question of how far the employer has to go in accommodating the handicapped employee to avoid violation under ADA or a state law. Whether or not the injury is job related doesn't affect the duty to accommodate; however, as a practical matter the court may be more sympathetic to a job-related injury.

In *Carr* v. *General Motors Corp.*, 389 N.W.2d 686 (Mich. 1986), the employee was operated on for a ruptured disk. After the operation he was medically restricted to lifting 50 pounds or less. He requested a promotion to a job that required lifting more than 50 pounds. He was refused the promotion because of the lifting restrictions. He

---

[27]Majority opinion upholds discharge because of absenteeism due to work-related injury: *Johnson* v. *St. Francis Hospital*, 759 S.W.2d 925 (Tenn. App. 1988).

[28]*Malik* v. *Apex Intern. Alloys, Inc.*, 762 F.2d 77 (10th Cir. 1985).

contended that the job required lifting only a small percentage of the time. Other workers in the department could lift for him. He argued that the employer could accommodate without undue hardship. The court held that in the majority of the states the employee must perform all the essential functions of the job.

The duty to accommodate is relevant only when the employee can perform the job. A claim for discrimination under ADA is not valid unless the person is qualified to perform all functions of the job.

A Latent Back Condition

The situation becomes more complicated if the employee has a latent back defect. The condition doesn't prevent the employee from presently performing the job but may in the future. This becomes a potential WC liability. In one case the plaintiffs, both experienced over-the-road truck drivers, failed the preemployment physical.[29] They were told about the failure one week before their probationary period was up under the labor agreement. The X-rays had revealed that one plaintiff had a spur on his spine and the other had a condition known as spondylitis. On this basis alone, they were terminated. The company believed that their back conditions created a substantial likelihood of a disability. Heavy lifting is sometimes required of a truck driver. They sued under the state handicap law, stating they were terminated because of a handicap. The Human Rights Commission ordered reinstatement, back pay, and payment of the plaintiffs' attorneys' fees. The court[30] found that according to the medical evidence the condition was not of any value to predict a risk of back injury or disability from heavy lifting. Their condition had nothing to do with the safe operation of the truck. The court found physical handicaps that entitled them to protection of the handicap law. They could perform the duties of the job. Even if the employer could show a present likelihood of lower back injury, it would not be sufficient to prove that in the future the employees would injure their backs.

Under case law a latent back defect is normally not a handicap. Very strong evidence is needed to show that injury to the employee or co-workers is medically predictable.

Identification of the Pretext Physical Condition

When the employer has notice of a back condition, it must be treated like any other physical condition. It must be assumed that the employee is willing to return to work as soon as it is medically possible. A bona fide effort on the part of the employer and the employee will be beneficial to both.

If the effort is unsuccessful in returning the employee to work, the employer's posture may change. The employer should investigate whether the employee is developing a nonmedical reason not to return to the job. The employer must always be aware that there are a few employees who are not motivated to return to work. They use their physical condition as a pretext to collect benefits for not working. This type of employee becomes an educated professional litigator and should be handled differently from an employee with a bona fide injury.

The employer must be certain that the employee is falsely using the disability as a reason not to return to work. To treat a situation as a pretext when in fact it is a bona fide condition can be disastrous, especially if the condition is caused by a work-related accident.[31] The employer should treat all physical conditions as legitimate. If substantial facts indicate that the physical condition alleged by the employee is not work related, the employer should treat the employee accordingly.

There is a certain pattern of events that this type of employee follows.

1. The injury alleged is in the back or is a condition that is equally difficult to determine medically.

2. The exact date of the injury is not certain, but usually it occurs on Monday morning.

---

[29]Passing the physical was a condition of employment.

[30]*Rozanski* v. *A-P-A Transport, Inc.*, 521 A.2d 335 (Me. 1986).

[31]See "Hiring the Handicapped: Overcoming Physical and Psychological Barriers in the Job Market," *Journal of American Insurance,* (3rd Quarter 1986), 13–14.

3. There were no employees present when the injury occurred. The incident is usually a fall or slipping in a remote place—the steps to the locker room, the parking lot, and so on. If a back injury, it could be from lifting as a regular part of the job. It is seldom the usual work-related incident that can be identified.

4. It was reported to the supervisor several days or even weeks after it happened. The employee usually states that at first the injury didn't seem to be severe enough to report.

5. The supervisor to whom it was reported is one known to forget things.

6. The employee never commits a major rule violation but does just enough to harass the supervisor (not wearing safety glasses, filing many grievances, taking long coffee breaks, going to the rest room often, and so on).

7. The employee's statements are not logically true but could be true, so that an investigation is required before action can be taken.

When the incident has these elements, there is at least a suspicion that it is not work related. Often the employee plans the absence from work. If the employee is brought back, there is a series of recurring injuries according to plan. You have now discovered the "plant lawyer."

When there is a suspect, several steps should be taken to validate your suspicion.

1. Investigate the employee's record. Determine whether there is a previous pattern either with other employers or in different jobs with the same employer.

2. When in doubt, get more than one medical opinion. Usually the employee's activity will not correlate with the medically determined physical condition. The second or third opinion should be from a well-known specialist who makes a medical determination without being influenced by the employee. Based on a medical analysis, the doctor should be able to detect the pretext.

3. Make every effort to accommodate even where you believe that the condition is a pretext. Avoid adversity, give the employee the benefit of the doubt, but be suspicious. (Trust, but verify.) Sometimes a back heals rapidly when the employee is offered a job that is for lower wages, or the conditions are not as good as a job he can do but doesn't want to. A bona

fide job offer is a very effective way to heal a back condition that is medically questionable. If a good faith job offer is refused, the employer should immediately take steps to stop the benefits. Sometimes the insurance carrier will resist this but it is the only way the employer can determine whether the condition is a pretext for not returning to work.

4. Give medical leave or terminate where the employee has a recurring condition (on or off the job) after a bona fide attempt to return the employee to work. Under ADA and most state statutes, the employer would have to make an attempt in accommodate before termination.

The courts have constantly held that under WC there is no obligation to treat the employee any differently from other employees. If the employee is excessively absent due to a work-related injury, he or she can be terminated like any other employee.

Sometimes the employer is reluctant to discharge an employee for absenteeism when on WC. There is a fear of an allegation that the discharge is in retaliation for filing a WC claim. In *Pierce* v. *Franklin Electric Co.*, 737 P.2d 921 (Okla. 1987), the court said that "an employer who terminates an at-will employee for the sole reason that he is physically unable to perform his job duties does not commit a retaliatory discharge." The overwhelming majority of the courts in other jurisdictions hold that an injured employee can be terminated for absenteeism. In order to hold a retaliatory discharge, the court must find that one of the reasons for the discharge was filing a WC claim. This is very difficult when there is excessive absenteeism or some other valid reason for the discharge. Not being physically able to perform the duties of the job would be a valid reason to terminate after an unsuccessful attempt to accommodate under ADA. Employers have been successful in arguing that a neutral absenteeism policy or failure to perform the duties of the job provides a valid, nonpretextual reason for the discharge. Many employers still do not use this method to correct a condition that cannot legally be corrected by another method. The case law is in place; all the employers have to do is use it.

Some states have statutes that prohibit discharge while the employee is on WC. In this case medical leave would be the answer. The courts say that the employer is not expected to show different treatment because of a work-related injury. If the employee is not physically able to work, the remedy is benefits under WC and not special treatment at the workplace.

5. Investigate all doubtful claims of disability. Often the employee is at home doing physical work that medically he couldn't do when on the job. If another medical examination allows the employee to return to work, he or she should be terminated if she or he fails to do so. The termination record should state it is a voluntary quit for failure to report to work.

In these doubtful situations termination should be the last resort.

Physical therapy should be attempted. If accommodation is not possible or physical therapy fails, then a medical leave without pay is the best solution.

A policy or labor agreement may permit termination because of the length of the absence or failure to return to work when medically authorized.

Employees who use their backs as a pretext ("plant lawyers") will not disappear. The number found in each plant will depend on how individual cases are dealt with. With proper attention and action, but always being concerned for good employee relations, the "plant lawyer" will appear less often. The Mary Hogan case is a good example of the problems occurring in a typical back case. Many personnel problems are created in back cases. The WC attorney often influences the employee's actions.

In reading this case it should be noted that legal counsel was available to the operating management at all times. After the charge was filed with the city, legal counsel was involved, except for one action—when Mary was terminated for insubordination.

The Mary Hogan case has an abundance of practical facts that involve many phases of antidiscrimination law, personnel practices, and supervisor techniques.

WC was not the issue with Mary Hogan, because the employer had accepted that the back condition was work related. However, the back condition was the source of all other problems. Her condition also made her WC attorney available at little or no cost. The extent of recovery would be of special interest. This case illustrates that a WC claim is accompanied by many side personnel problems, and the attorney involved often influences the employee's action.

Company Mistakes in Dealing with Mary Hogan

The company's major mistake was to permit her to continue as an employee. In the interest of good employee relations, the supervisor or personnel practitioner will often give the employee the benefit of the doubt and not apply a strict construction to the rules. This policy will backfire with the Mary Hogans. When the labor

---

Mary Hogan's Back—A Case History

Paul Smith,[32] department superintendent of Acme Bag Company for the past 14 years, noticed that the conveyor belt was jammed with paper bags. He told Mary Hogan, a polypropylene (PE) inserter on the machine, to get a pallet and remove the bags from the belt.

Mary replied, "I am not able to because my back is bothering me." Paul replied, "Get one that you are able to handle." Mary replied, "I will not do it." Paul said, "I think you can do it." Mary said, "No." Paul said, "You are terminated; clock out and leave the plant." Mary Hogan did just that.

Mary Hogan was employed by Acme as an unskilled worker; she worked in various unskilled positions throughout the plant during her employment.

Eighteen months after employment, Mary filed a charge with the Mill City Civil Rights Commission under the city ordinance alleging that the company discriminated because of her sex. She was given a two-day suspension for refusing to mop the floor. She alleged males and minorities

---

[32]All names and places are fictitious. Only the facts bear resemblance to an actual case.

Mary Hogan's Back—A Case History (continued)

were not required to do so. Mary did not file a grievance under the labor agreement over the suspension. A similar charge was filed with EEOC under Title VII; EEOC referred it to the Minnesota Civil Rights Commission, a Section 706 referral agency. The charge was investigated by the city. Before the investigation under the EEOC charge, Mary amended the charge alleging that Acme had refused to allow her to return to light duty of lifting 10 pounds or less. She alleged that this was a violation of Title VII and state law. Acme had not received any medical report of Ms. Hogan's condition for 11 months. This ·amended complaint was based on the fact that Ms. Hogan was not given the opportunity to work for the 11-month period. The state civil rights specialist discovered that Ms. Hogan had not worked for 11 months and inquired about the absence. She was told by Acme that Ms. Hogan was on a medical leave. Acme stated they would be glad to have her return to work if the company doctor approved it. Acme further stated, when questioned, that the reason Ms. Hogan had not returned to work was that she had not contacted Acme stating that she was physically able to perform the job in the plant that she had previously selected or that she could perform any other job.

Acme received a medical report from the company doctor stating that Ms. Hogan was able to lift only 5 to 20 pounds. Eleven months before her stated condition, Ms. Hogan had signed a statement that she would perform only the job as bottom feeder and table loader, jobs that required lifting 20 to 35 pounds and 60 to 75 pounds respectively. This is the reason Acme gave her medical leave.

Ms. Hogan had applied for unemployment insurance, which Acme originally contested on the grounds that the claimant was on medical leave. It was ruled that Ms. Hogan was available for work, and

she received unemployment compensation. The notice to allow unemployment benefits was not received by the Acme plant. It was sent to the parent company's office, which failed to forward it. Acme plant management would have appealed the decision.

No medical leave was applied for by Ms. Hogan under the terms of the labor agreement. However, Ms. Hogan's status was considered a voluntary medical leave during the period she was off work. Premiums for her health insurance were paid by Acme rather than terminating her as permitted by the labor agreement. During the 11-month period Ms. Hogan was considered by Acme as not available for work but was never contacted to determine her status.

When Ms. Hogan was called to return to work after being contacted by the civil rights specialist, she stated that she was still under a doctor's care. After two weeks she inquired when she could see a company doctor. On advice of corporate counsel, the personnel coordinator arranged an appointment. The company doctor stated that she could return to light work, but lifting 40 to 50 pounds repetitively would cause back symptoms. Ms. Hogan was notified of her physical condition, which permitted her to return to work a week later. She agreed to return to her old job of bottom feeder (requiring the lifting of 25 to 40 pounds).

The next day she alleged that she hurt her back. A meeting was called to determine what job Ms. Hogan could do. With the union present, she was asked what she wanted to do. She selected the table loader job and was returned to that job for the remainder of the day. (This required the lifting of 40 to 50 pounds, which was contrary to the doctor's advice.) On the following day, her husband called and stated that she hurt her back on the previous day and wanted

Mary Hogan's Back—A Case History (continued)

an appointment to see another doctor. It was assumed by Ms. Hogan that this other doctor would be somebody other than the company doctor. She was told she could see any doctor whom she wanted. She requested the company doctor. An appointment was made with the company doctor the following day.

Nothing was heard from Ms. Hogan after her physical examination until her husband called five days later. He wanted to know what the doctor had found, stating that the doctor never told her the results of the recent examination. When told that nothing was wrong with her, she stated that she wanted to see another doctor. She went to see another doctor. Ten days after her most recent physical examination she was ordered to return to work in the next three days. Rather than return to work, she saw another doctor who authorized her to return to work.

However, rather than return to work, she saw another doctor who authorized her to return the next day but no heavy lifting. She reported to work the next day. She told her supervisor that she could not load tables (a job that she said she could do her last day worked).

As a result of her statement, a meeting was held on the same day with the union and management. Ms. Hogan requested that she be taken off the table loader job and be assigned to PE inserting. It was explained to her that this job requires lifting 50 to 70 pounds. It was stated to Ms. Hogan and the union that she would be used on a temporary basis in other departments. Ms. Hogan performed the job of PE inserting until she was discharged for refusing to get a pallet. The pallet weighted 30.1 pounds and required her only to slide it to carry out the order of her supervisor, Paul Smith. The complaint to the state civil rights commission was again amended, stating that her discharge was due to retaliation for filing the original complaint. As a result of the discharge, a grievance was filed under the labor agreement and the dispute was arbitrated. The arbitrator found insubordination as the cause for the discharge.

The state civil rights commission, after an investigation, determined two years after the incident that there was no reasonable cause to the sex discrimination charges regarding the suspension for refusing to mop the floor. The commission had reasonable cause to believe that Ms. Hogan was discriminated against for not returning to work for 11 months and that the discharge was a retaliation for filing a complaint. The civil rights commission in its conciliation proposal demanded $9,000 in back pay and and reinstatement. The corporate EEOC investigator was told by the local manager that he didn't discriminate and any settlement would look like guilt. The parties were requested to attend a conciliation meeting. If this failed, the matter would go before the state civil rights commission hearing examiner; an appeal from that decision would be to the district court.

Management has to make a decision to settle or fight. What would you do?

agreement says termination after three months, then she should be terminated. If the medical report states that she cannot do a particular job, she should not be allowed to do it, but a good faith effort should be made to accommodate for other jobs. If none are available, she should not be permitted to return to work until one is available.

In Mary Hogan's case, when there were no jobs that she could do, she should have been terminated and health insurance should not have been paid. When she hurt her back, she should have been taken off the job and not permitted to do other work until medically authorized.

It was not a mistake to permit her to go to several doctors, as this is permitted under most state laws. The mistake was made when one doctor said that she could do only certain jobs and she was permitted to do jobs that doctors said she could not medically do. When medical advice is conflicting, the company can take action on any one of the conflicting medical statements. If the company acted on wrong medical advice, under most court decisions, and statutes there is no additional liability.

The other mistake was discharging Mary. Sending her home as being physically unfit to work would have been a better solution. The EEOC charge of retaliation is much easier for Mary to sustain than failure to accommodate. Discharge is exactly what Mary wanted. She had successfully irritated her supervisor so that his patience ran out and he discharged her, which set the company up for a retaliation charge.

Why did the company act the way it did in Mary Hogan's case? First, it thought that if it were lenient, Mary would not have a good reason to complain. Second, because Mary had been successful in irritating everybody who became involved in her case, the less adverse decisions, the less misery. The pressure increased so that the only way the supervisor could relieve the emotional pressure was to discharge her. The company's mistakes could have been avoided if it had bitten the bullet at the early stages by termination and let Mary exercise whatever remedies were available to her.

Return-to-Work Procedures

One of the most important elements of any back-to-work procedure is development of the proper atmosphere. The employer must be interested in the welfare of the injured employee and that of the family. The employer must immediately show some concern about the employee's misfortune.[33]

One of several ways to do this is to explain the benefits the injured is entitled to under WC and how to start receiving those benefits. There is nothing that will impede a back-to-work program more than creating an adverse situation.

One of the most important aspects of recovery from any physical condition is the attitude of the worker. Nothing can happen until she or he wants to return to work.

The next step is to make sure the doctor understands the physical requirements of the job the employee was performing before the injury or the job you want him or her to return to.

No back-to-work procedure should be considered without a valid medical opinion. Often more than one opinion is needed to be assured it is medically sound and not influenced by the employee.[34] To bring an employee back to work to protect a safety record is a short-term way of creating more costs. This creates an exposure to legal proceedings when up to that point the whole matter was nonlegal.

The next step is a good faith job offer, but the employer should be certain it is a job the employee can do. There are some basic rules that should be followed when making a job offer.

1. There must be a job available. One should not be created, nor should somebody be "bumped" unless a voluntary transfer is possible.

2. The job the employee returns to should have adequate supervision. More supervision is required, at least at first, of an injured person returning to work than of other employees.

3. The employee must be able to perform all the aspects of the job in spite of the physical condition. It does nothing for the employee's morale if the employer does not require the same standard of performance, after a training period, as for a person who was not injured. Doing favors for one employee creates legal problems with others.

4. The employer must be certain that employees feel ready to return to work. Back-to-work efforts will fail unless the employee is mentally and physically ready.

---

[33]Most states stress early employer response after an accident and good back-to-work procedures. See "Controlling Workers' Compensation Costs," Minnesota Department of Labor and Industry, Research and Education Unit, July 1991; also J. Gardner, "Return to Work Incentives," Workers Compensation Research Institute, April 1989, p. 1.

[34]R. A. Deyo, A. K. Diehl, and M. Rosenthal, "How Many Days of Bed Rest for Acute Low Back Pain?" *New England Journal of Medicine*, 315, no. 17 (October 1986), 1064–70.

5. If a light-duty assignment is considered, it still must be within the employee's physical restrictions. It is difficult to keep the employee from doing work that exceeds the physical restrictions. The employee often violates the restrictions when exposed to a task that will violate them. Often a co-worker will ask for help that goes beyond the restrictions.

The job offer should be made even though the compensation is not the same or there is a belief that the employee will not accept. In most states there is mitigation of damages if a suitable job offer is made. It doesn't have to be accepted. For purposes of mitigation of damages, most states define a suitable job as one that the employee can perform according to the employer's standards. It must also be within the employee's medical restrictions. It must restore the employee as close as possible to the economic status he or she had before the injury.

Successful back-to-work procedures restore morale in an injured employee. They reduce WC or health care costs and exposure to invalid claims.

RECOMMENDATIONS FOR CONTROL OF COSTS

Often the employer gets so discouraged with the socialist WC interpretation of the law that he or she gives up trying to do something about it.[35] This "play-dead" attitude will not solve the problem.

It is only when the employer decides to do something about it that costs can be controlled. There are many things the employer can do. Space will permit discussing only those cost-control procedures that are considered to be the most effective.[36]

The Delayed Recovery Syndrome

Delayed recovery is the situation where the employer becomes the most discouraged. The employee has a work-related back injury and has been off work for three months. His doctor says he can come back to work. The employee says he has a terrible pain and insists that he cannot work. A management person meets him on the golf course, where he just made a hole in one. He is jumping up and down all the way back to the clubhouse, where he buys everybody drinks and is shaking hands from the top of a table.

The first impression is that he is malingering, and maybe he is, but to treat it as malingering only causes adversity and litigation. It is difficult to get this person back to work unless steps are taken to create a desire to do so. The employee is getting some kind of gain from the injury that outweighs the benefits of getting well and going back to work. Researchers call this a "delayed recovery syndrome," not malingering.[37] They claim (the author's experience confirms this) that many serious accidents are caused by internal conflicts of a personal nature, such as divorce or separation, drug or alcohol abuse, sex problems, or pending litigation. These factors may delay recovery. The most important thing to remember, according to research, is that delayed recovery is an emotional problem. Although it is unconscious, it is real. The golfer honestly believes that he cannot return to work but can play golf.[38]

Stopping Malingering

There is about 1 to 2 percent of the compensation population who manage to convince their doctors, employers, and insurance carrier that they are unable to function on the job. These people—better known as malingerers—start to develop the attitude that they'd rather stay home and collect $350 to $500 per week. Some go even further in

[35]"Worker's Compensation Costs Can Be Controlled by Managed Care," *Employment Alert* (Warren Gorham Lamont, Boston), 9, no. 22 (October 22, 1992), p. 5.

[36]D. Fitzpatrick, "Civil RICO and Anti-Trust Law: The Uneven Playing Field of the Workers Compensation Fraud," *Pacific Law Journal*, 25 (1994), 311.

[37]E. Yehn, "The Myth of Malingering: Why Individuals Withdraw from Work in the Presence of Illness," *Milbank Quarterly*, 64 (1986), 622.

[38]A 10-year study reported in 1991 made on 3020 Boeing Company employees reveals that 60 to 65 percent of back problems are due to psychological factors.

their attempts to violate the system and collect unemployment benefits at the same time as workers' compensation.

Unlike the delayed recovery syndrome, true malingering is conscious avoidance of responsibility, and according to the researchers it is rare.[39] (In the author's experience malingering is found in more than 10 percent of all cases.) Malingering is difficult to prove.[40] Even if you feel certain about it the wrong thing to do is to confront the employee with your suspicion. The best way is to treat her or him as an injured employee with your tongue in your cheek. These steps should be tried before getting tough and terminating, although some discharges may still result in an exposure to litigation.

1. Offer a suitable job that the person can medically do. This is required by ADA and most state statutes. Work closely with the doctor, because the employee will often resist. Even work with a rehabilitation consultant if a good one is available.

2. Get the person active to regain strength and psychological well-being. Most back injuries medically require only a few days of bed rest. If the employee resists, get a medical directive.

3. Limit the narcotics to only what is needed. Doctors will often be pressured into more. Most doctors recommend the use of drugs be limited to two weeks at the most.

4. Offer relaxation training; stress and other psychological factors can aggravate back and neck conditions. Deep breathing and other techniques can relieve this. Get the doctor involved to force the employee to do something to help in recovery.

Steps to Reduce Costs

As an employer, let the employee know that you need her or him back on the job. Call or visit the employee during recovery. Strongly encourage treatment programs. Carry a stick in the closet; if nothing works, then terminate for being absent from work or not following medical directives. Some type of litigation will likely follow, so be prepared for it.

Other Steps to Reduce Costs[41]

1. Monitor early, especially in the case of a serious injury. Give the employee information before he or she seeks outside help. It is too late if the employee has to see a lawyer for necessary information. Keep in touch after the first contact.

2. Get a medical assessment as soon as possible. One way to do this without being defensive is to make a sympathetic inquiry about the employee's financial condition.

3. Give a job offer as soon as medically possible. This should not be a make-up job but one that is contributing and useful. Consider light-duty work, but only where there is not an exposure to doing other work that the employee is not physically capable of. In sports medicine, when an athlete is injured he or she must keep up with normal practice that is within the person's capacity, although unable to play.

4. Get a rehabilitation assessment where necessary. It is possible that the injured may not be able to return to the old job but can do something else. It should be done within 30 days after the injury to be successful. This is an effective technique for the delayed recovery syndrome and complies with ADA.

5. Monitor the medical aspects; this is extremely important. Medical opinion and directives are given great weight in hearings and by the courts.

If the foregoing steps do not work and you cannot think of anything else, then terminate. Studies in all states have disclosed that litigation is second only to permanent and temporary disability costs in WC cases. Many researchers believe that

---

[39]About 1 to 2 percent of the compensation claims.

[40]For discussion of this problem, see S. Miura, "Halting Abuse of Workers' Compensation System," *Worker's Compensation Control* (Northeast Publishing Group, Boston), June 1992, pp. 1–2. Also V.E. Densford, "Workers' Compensation Program Seek to Heal Emotional Disorders from Worksite Accidents," *Employee Benefits*, (Jan 1995), 25.

[41]Many of the following steps the author has practiced and found successful, eliminating the unsuccessful. They are also confirmed by studies made by various state departments charged with administration of workers' compensation. See "Controlling Workers Compensation Costs: A Guide for Employers," Minnesota Department of Labor and Industry, 444 Lafayette Road, St. Paul, MN 55101 (1985).

the biggest contributing factor to WC costs is employer complacency.[42]

Employers are Becoming Concerned

Employers have been concerned for the last two years about controlling medical care costs under workers' compensation. These costs have been growing at an annual rate of almost 16 percent, compared with a general medical care inflation rate of around 10 percent. The Robert Wood Johnson Foundation, Princeton, N.J., has announced that it will award $6 million in grants over the next four years for demonstration and evaluation projects that will look for innovative ways to control costs and to improve the quality of medical care under workers' compensation.

The total cost of workers' compensation coverage (medical and disability benefits) grew from $2.1 billion in 1960 to $60 billion in 1992. Medical costs rose more than tenfold from 1970 through 1990. Treatment of workplace injuries under workers' compensation cost $28 billion in 1993. A study by the National Council on Compensation Insurance found that medical claims under workers' compensation from 1988 through 1991 were 140 percent to 309 percent higher than costs for similar group health insurance claims.

As one employer put it, "this is worth going after." If employer's would sit down and put a pencil to the figures they could realize the truth in the above statement.

---

[42]There was a job to do for four persons named Everybody, Somebody, Anybody, and Nobody. Everybody thought it would be done, Somebody would do it, Anybody could do it, but Nobody did it.

CHAPTER 17

HOW TO REDUCE UNEMPLOYMENT COMPENSATION COSTS

Historical Basis for Unemployment Compensation
Constitutional Restrictions
Provisions of State Laws
The Use of Appeal Proceedings
Policies and Practices to Reduce Costs

The stated purpose of unemployment compensation laws (UC) is to provide benefits for persons who are unemployed through no fault of their own. For more than 50 years, unemployment compensation insurance has been considered one of the most successful social insurance programs.[1] Unemployment compensation insurance had a welfare origin. The drafters of this legislation wanted the benefits to partially replace wages during periods of limited unemployment. Because wages were being replaced, workers would not have to meet the "needs test" of traditional welfare programs. The U.S. Congress usually extends the benefit period during an economic downturn. Congress believes that getting money into the economy at a time when it is most needed speeds up recovery.

HISTORICAL BASIS FOR UNEMPLOYMENT COMPENSATION

UC insurance is not a new idea. By 1800, trade unions were providing economic aid for members forced into temporary idleness. After 1850, supplemental UC benefits were provided in such European countries as Germany, Austria, Belgium, and most of Scandinavia. The first public UC insurance law was passed in 1898. The city of Ghent passed a local ordinance that supplemented trade union benefits. In 1911, England established the first compulsory UC system.

In the United States, as in European countries, the beginnings of UC are found in trade union benefit plans. The first plan was established by a New York printers' local in 1831. From this period

---

[1]For an overview of the law, see P. Wall, "A Survey of Unemployment Security Law: Determining Unemployment Compensation Benefits," *Labor Law Journal,* 42, no. 3 (March 1991), 179.

to 1932, UC was provided either by trade unions or by joint plans arising from agreement between employers and unions. Private voluntary plans established by individual employers were not as common as in trade unions plans.

At the beginning of the 20th century there was a movement to establish a public compulsory unemployment compensation plan. In 1916 a limited UC was passed by the Massachusetts legislature. More than 20 other states followed. Some states hesitated to pass unemployment compensation legislation because it would put them at a competitive disadvantage over other states that would not pass it.

This competitive concern of the various states caused pressure for legislation on the federal level. The argument whether the states or the federal government should do it delayed action by both federal and state legislative bodies. By 1935 the federal concept had won the battle. UC was included in the Social Security Act.

Taxation by Federal Government

The legislation is a perfect example of the federal government's ability to use its taxing power to encourage states to adopt certain policies. The Social Security Act of 1935 provided that all employers who were not exempted had to pay a federal tax on wages. The federal government would return over 90 percent of the tax if the state adopted an approved program.

The UC section of the act provides that the federal government would set certain minimum standards. It leaves it to the states to decide which type of plan best suits their needs. However, if a state had no plan or if the state law was not in compliance with the federal law, the employers would still be taxed but the tax would not be returned to the states. Needless to say, all 50 states passed laws.

These historical developments continue up to the present time. They have influenced legislative bodies and the courts to consider UC an established employee welfare benefit. The laws in the various states are given a liberal interpretation by administrative agencies and the courts.

It is not the purpose of this chapter to present the law in any particular jurisdiction. The chapter will give only an overview of the law. The administrative procedures are common to most jurisdictions. However, the law differs from state to state as to the payment of benefits and level of state taxes. Knowledge of both the federal and state law is essential for effective cost control.

Excluded Workers

Excluded workers under the federal law include employees who are paid less than $1,500 in wages during a three-month period; domestic workers; farm workers; state, county, and city workers (with some exceptions); employees of the federal government (if covered by another program); and employees of certain nonprofit organizations (religious, charitable, or educational organizations).

Financing Benefits

The system is financed by two taxes. The state tax finances the benefits, and the federal tax finances state and federal administrative costs. The federal government taxes 6.2 percent of the first $7,000 in wages paid to each employee. A credit of 5.4 percent is returned. This leaves 0.8 percent to be used to finance state and federal administrative costs. The tax is also used to maintain a loan fund for the states to borrow from when they exhaust their funds available to pay benefits. Benefits are always paid.

All states have adopted an experience rating system to encourage employers to maintain stable employment. These systems excuse employers with stable employment from paying all or part of the state unemployment tax, and grant a credit against the federal tax.

State taxes are usually based on a "flexible" taxable wage base; increases in the wage base automatically follow increases in statewide wage levels. The taxable wage base ranges from $15,000 to $29,700. In all states, only the employer is taxed for unemployment compensation benefits.[2]

---

[2]See "Highlights of State Unemployment Compensation Laws" (Washington, DC: National Foundation for Unemployment Compensation and Workers Compensation, January 1995).

FISCAL YEAR 1994 MOST CITED STANDARDS, NATIONAL

Standard	Description		Frequency
1910.1200	Hazard Communication		27,235
	Written program	10,254	
	Employee information	6,970	
	Labeling	5,136	
	Material Safety Data Sheets (MSDS)	4,875	
1926.59	Hazard Communication in Construction		13,843
	Written program	5,892	
	Material Safety Data Sheets (MSDS)	3,551	
	Training	3,262	
	Labeling	1,138	
1904.2(a)	OSHA 200 form - recordkeeping		4,321
1910.215(b)(9)	Safety guards on abrasive wheel machinery not adjustable or not adjusted for decreasing diameter		3,578
1910.147(c)(1)	No energy control (lockout/tagout) program		3,209
1910.212(a)(1)	Machine guarding – general requirements		3,143
1903.2(a)(1)	OSHA Poster		3,135
1910.147(c)(4)	Hazardous energy (lockout/tagout) procedures were not developed or were deficient		3,029
1910.305(g)(1)	Improper use of flexible electrical cords		2,704
1910.305(b)(1)	Conductors entering boxes, cabinets, or fittings not protected from abrasion and/or openings not effectively closed		2,617

1994 MOST CITED STANDARDS, OVERALL

Standard	Description		Frequency
MN Rules 5206.0700, et al	Employee Right-To-Know		663
	No program	440	
	Written program deficiencies	38	
	Multi-employer worksites	6	
	Records	29	
	Frequency of training	30	
	Training deficiencies	12	
	Lack of Material Safety Data Sheets (MSDS)	56	
	Labeling	52	
1910.134(a)(2)	Respiratory Protection Program		134
1926.100(a) and 1926.28(a)	Hard hats in construction		100
1910.151(c)	Emergency eyewash/shower facilities	99	
1910.304(f)(5)(v)	Grounding of cord and plug connected equipment	97	
1910.219(d)(1) and (e)(1)(i)	Machine guarding – belts and pulleys	96	
1910.305(g)(1)	Improper use of flexible electrical cords	88	

Although the states are free to develop their own plan, most states follow the model plan recommended by the federal government. Also, through funding regulations the federal government retains a degree of control and forces some standardization among the various states.

CONSTITUTIONAL RESTRICTIONS

State unemployment compensation statutes are limited by the U.S. Constitution. One state denied benefits when an employee voluntarily quit for religious reasons. The Supreme Court held that this was a violation of the First Amendment.[3]

The Supreme Court also struck down a Utah statute that denied benefits to pregnant women without regard to physical capacity to continue working. The Court found this a violation of the Fourteenth Amendment.[4]

However, the employee could continue to work after the baby was born. The court allowed the state of Missouri to deny benefits if the employee leaves the job for pregnancy and there are no openings when she is able to return. The Court in *Wimberly* v. *Labor and Industrial Relations Commission,* 107 S.Ct. 821 (1987), stated that pregnancy is not a job-related illness, and as long as pregnancy leaves are not treated differently from other illnesses it is legal to deny benefits.

Courts generally hold that a state cannot deny benefits when the employee is protected by an antidiscrimination law. An employee joined a church two and a half years after being employed. Her new religion prohibited working on Saturdays. She was discharged when she refused to work on Friday nights and Saturdays. The court held that denial of benefits would violate the First Amendment, although she had worked Saturdays until Saturday became her Sabbath. Whether or not she could be discharged was not an issue.[5]

States can deny benefits when an employee is discharged for religious use of drugs. The drug use was a violation of a state statute, although it was off-duty conduct. The denial of benefits was not a First Amendment violation.[6]

A state can deny benefits to claimants who are attending school, but not if they are attending night school because they would be available for work.[7]

When New York gave unemployment compensation benefits to strikers, the court held that it was not a violation of any clause in the Constitution and it was within the authority of the state to do so.[8] In *Brown* v. *A.J. Gerard Mfg. Co.,* 695 F.2d 1290 (11th Cir. 1983), the circuit court held that unemployment compensation could not be deducted from a Title VII back pay award.[9] If a NLRB remedy, same result: see NLRB v. *Illinios Department of Employment and Security* 988 F.2d 735 (7th Cir. 1993).

PROVISIONS OF STATE LAWS

The federal government requires certain conformity provisions before the employer as taxpayer is granted tax credits. However, the states have considerable flexibility to design their own program. To ensure that the UC payments are in keeping with the intent of the federal law, it is necessary for the states to establish eligibility requirements. The state must also establish benefit amounts and reasons why an unemployed individual should be denied benefits or be disqualified from receiving further benefits.

In developing rules to determine the right to receive benefits, states have generally followed the principle that UC is intended to provide temporary financial assistance to persons who are

---

[3]*Thomas* v. *Review Board of Indiana Employment Security Div.,* 101 S.Ct. 1425 (1981); see also *Frazee* v. *Illinois Dept. of Employment and Security,* 109 S.Ct. 1514 (1989).

[4]*Turner* v. *Department of Employment and Security of Utah,* 423 U.S. 44 (1975).

[5]*Hobbie* v. *Unemployment Appeals Commission of Florida,* 107 S.Ct. 1046 (1987).

[6]*Department of Human Resources of Oregon* v. *Alfred L. Smith,* 110 S.Ct. 1595 (1990). Usually drug use must be job related, but here the Supreme Court said that use didn't have to affect performance.

[7]In *Idaho Dept. of Employment* v. *Smith,* 434 U.S. 100 (1977).

[8]*New York Telephone Co.* v. *New York State Department of Labor,* 440 U.S. 519 (1979).

[9]This is well-settled law: *EEOC* v. *Enterprise Assn. Steamfitters Local 638,* 542 F.2d 579 (2nd Cir. 1979).

out of work through no fault of their own.[10] In order to carry out the main intent of the act, state laws require eligible claimants to remain available for work and to be seeking work actively or face the loss of benefits. This requirement is loosely administered in many states.

Variation of Benefit Levels

One way to instill an incentive to seek to work is to establish benefit levels that pay only a portion of the wages that an employee would have received if fully employed.

On the other side of the problem, the states want the benefit level high enough to cover the claimant's nondeferrable expenses. Usually, this is a weekly benefit equal to about 50 percent of the claimant's normal weekly wage. Some states use the claimant's average weekly wage as a guideline for determining benefits.[11]

Most states have the absolute minimum and maximum based on the employee's weekly earnings. Others determine the minimum and maximum on the average statewide annual wage. The minimum benefit requires a certain level of earnings; if an employee earns below a certain level, no benefits are paid. The amount of benefits is usually a fixed sum, but in a few states it depends upon the number of dependents.

More than 14 states provide for the payment of dependents' allowances. Although there is some variation, generally a dependent must be wholly or mainly supported by the claimant.

In almost all states, the waiting period to receive benefits is one week, although a few states pay benefits on the first day of unemployment. All states have a maximum period for benefits. This varies from 26 to 36 weeks.[12] Congress usually extends the period during an economic downturn.

Disqualifications for Benefits

The laws of various states follow the intent of the act by establishing disqualification provisions. Each state has certain procedures to be followed for obtaining facts involved in a disputed claim. The state agency responsible for payment of compensation claims makes a determination whether the claimant is disqualified.[13] The employer or claimant may appeal and request a hearing. The decision of the hearing referee as to disqualification may be appealed to a higher reviewing authority within the department. Subsequent appeals then may be carried to the state courts. If a constitutional question is involved, the U.S. Supreme Court has jurisdiction. Some states merely disqualify the claimant for a period of time. Other states deny the benefits for the entire period of unemployment if certain facts exist.

Reporting Termination Information

Before information is reported to the agency, the reason for separation should be well established. The reason given by the employee for an involuntary quit is often quite different from that stated after the employee decides to file a claim. When an employee is discharged, a documented statement should be given to the employee stating the reason for the discharge. Nothing weakens a case more than a showing that one party changed the statement of the reason for the discharge after the claim was filed. The reason given to the employee should be the same as will later be reported to the agency.

When a claim is filed, the agency will request separation information. The person responding to this request should first make sure that the facts stated coincide with the material available in the personnel records. When reporting separation information, give facts. Do not give conclusions. Avoid subjective terms such as *not cooperative, unsatisfactory,* and *poor worker.* They mean

[10]K. Matheny, "Labor Dispute Disqualification for Unemployment Compensation Benefits," *West Virginia Law Review,* 95 (1993), 791.

[11]Benefit levels continually increase, although in some states tax rate schedules have decreased.

[12]Unemployment Compensation Act of 1992 (P. L. 102–318).

[13]For further information on disqualification, see "Highlights of State Unemployment Compensation Laws," National Foundation for Unemployment Compensation and Worker's Compensation (January 1992), pp. 63–86.

nothing to the person making the determination. It is also advisable to expand the reason given. For example, when reporting a voluntary quit, the reason for the quit might be

- To resume home duties
- To seek other employment
- To get married
- Dissatisfaction with the job
- Failed to report after _____ days contrary to policy

These are all reasons to disqualify the claimant. If the facts exist, it is wise to give a definitive reason that the agency has previously held to be disqualifying.

In discharge cases, the separation information should establish that the action was willful or detrimental to the employer's interest. If the employee had been previously warned, give the date and a report of what was said. Stay away from vague or undocumented recollections when reporting the information. If you do not have good documentation, do not make the statement. Rely instead upon creditable supervisor testimony in the event that you have to go to a hearing.

Saying that the employee was unable to perform the job is always damaging.[14] It is better to say that employment rules were violated and then specify the rules that were violated, introducing evidence that the employee was aware of the violation when committing the act. Say when or how it was communicated, and show that the employee was previously warned—if such was the case.

Saying that the employee was rude to customers has very little meaning unless you can cite specific incidents. If the employee was guilty of excessive absenteeism, give the dates of warnings and state the number of times absent. Show that the number is excessive in comparison with the records of other employees.

When answering an agency request for information, remember that separation information aids in getting the proper determination from the agency. This eliminates the number of appeals. Often the person supplying the information limits the statement of information to the space provided in the form. Usually this space is not enough. When it is not, attach another sheet and use all the space necessary. The information provided in response to the initial request guides the agency in making a determination whether the claimant is disqualified. It also is the basic information that is used in the event of an appeal.

The appeal process seeks to obtain facts that verify the original position of the employer. For this reason more time should be spent in supplying complete information in the first step than in all the others. Time spent in supplying the original information will reduce the number of appeals.[15]

If the person supplying the information has some doubts about what should be said at the initial stage, he or she should get expert help. Often so much damaging information has been reported in the first response that no one can save the case.

Qualifications for Benefits

Whenever the claimant is receiving any type of income, the employer should question it. Such income is often disqualifying. Income such as holiday, vacation, and back pay may be disqualifying in some states. Even though the statute may not be specific as to kinds of income, any income should be considered.

The state laws require that the claimant be unemployed and available for work. The receipt of any income from a physical disability would raise a question as to whether the claimant is available for work. Pension payments indicate retirement from the labor market, and therefore the claimant is not available for work.

The federal law requires the state to reduce the weekly benefit payments by the amount received per week from any source. States may reduce the benefits on less than a dollar-for-dollar basis in order to take into account any contributions that

---

[14]Most state case law holds that discharge for incompetence is not misconduct, and benefits are paid: *Larson* v. *Employment Appeal Board*, 474 N.W.2d 570 (Iowa 1991).

[15]Martin H. Malin, "Unemployment Compensation in a Time of Increasing Work-Family Conflicts." *University of Michigan Journal of Law Reform*, 29 (1996).

the worker must make to an employer deferment or retirement plan.

Voluntary Quit without Good Cause

Benefits are paid to persons who are out of work through no fault of their own. It would therefore follow that a voluntary quit would automatically disqualify. Every state disqualifies from benefits individuals who bring about or perpetuate their own unemployment. If they quit their job without good cause, commit work-related misconduct, or refuse suitable work, they have caused their own unemployment. Most states disqualify until claimant meets earning requirements for a new base period.[16] However, some states just reduce benefits.

The issue of whether the voluntary quit is without a cause attributable to the employer is important. If it is found that the quit was no fault of the employer, benefits may still be paid to the claimant, but in some states the employer's experience rating will not be charged. Most employers do not recognize this. They attempt to justify the discharge by misconduct that is often difficult to prove. If they argued that it wasn't a cause attributable to the employer they would have better employee relations.

The employee would get the benefits, but the employer's account would not be charged, so the experience rating would not be affected. The benefits come out of the general fund in some states. The referee takes a dim view of an employer who is trying to deny benefits when his or her experience rating will not be charged.

Quitting must be work related; otherwise good cause cannot be established. Sometimes a quit can be considered a constructive discharge. To find constructive discharge the claimant must show that a prudent person would have quit under similar working conditions. (Sexual harassment is a good example.) Whether the claimant attempted to remedy the situation prior to quitting is highly revelant.

Some reasons for quitting that disqualify are to accept other work, to join or accompany a spouse or companion (some states will not disqualify), to go to day school, to retire, or to become self-employed.

Often there is a fine line between a voluntary quit and a discharge. In most states a quit is defined when the employee exercises directly or indirectly a free-will choice to terminate the employment relationship.[17] Wherever possible, the employer should call a separation a voluntary quit, such as where the employee fails to report for work after a certain number of days. A discharge is usually defined as an employer action that indicates to the employee that his or her services are no longer wanted.

A supervisor had a heated argument with an employee, the employee walked away toward the door, and the supervisor said, "Keep on walking"; this was a discharge. If the supervisor had let him walk through the door, however, it would probably have been a voluntary quit.[18] Quitting to avoid being discharged is usually held to be a quit. Also, a good personal reason is not usually considered enough of a justification to leave a job, and the claimant is disqualified unless discrimination is involved.

Disqualification for Misconduct

Misconduct is the most common issue in disqualification proceedings. Misconduct that results in disqualification is defined as "conduct resulting in such willful or wanton substantial disregard of the employer's interests." Misconduct was first defined in *Boynton Cab Co.* v. *Newbeck*, 296 N.W.2d 636 (Wis. 1941). It is one of those rare decisions that have been adopted by all the states. Often the employer confuses willful misconduct with inability or negligence.[19] If a school bus driver has three accidents in 30 days,

---

[16]A common disqualification is not earning sufficient wages during the base period.

[17]See *Bongiovanni* v. *Vanlor Investments*, 370 N.W.2d 828 (Minn. App. 1985), for a discussion of a quit.

[18]*Brown* v. *Port of Sunnyside Club, Inc.*, 304 N.W.2d 877 (Minn. 1981).

[19]*Richers* v. *Iowa Dept. of Job Service*, 479 N.W.2d 308 (Iowa 1991); the court said that inability or incapacity is not intentional; it cannot be misconduct.

this may not be misconduct but only negligence, which is not disqualifying. If an employee throws paper, swears, and insults the boss, this may be misconduct, but it would have to be shown that the incident was a substantial disregard for the employer's interests.

Misconduct Schemes

In misconduct cases the employer must have acted reasonably to control or prevent the employee's behavior. There must be no question that the employee was aware of the work rule violated. In determining what constitutes misconduct, the employer's condoning of similar behavior is relevant. This question often comes up where alleged discrimination has not been properly investigated.

Misconduct usually means something different to the employer from what it means to the agency or appeal referee, as illustrated in the following example.

This example explains better the difference between what the employer feels is the reason for the discharge and the guidelines used by the agency.

In discharge cases, the burden is on the employer to show that insubordination is misconduct. In the employer's mind, insubordination was the direct refusal to follow an order that did not involve the employee's personal safety. Under this definition refusal to conduct a training program that the employee had conducted before—and with performance that the employer considered satisfactory—was insubordination in the employer's mind, but not in division's mind.

There was a serious question whether the action was misconduct under the definition used by the agency. Under case law followed in every jurisdiction, misconduct is "wanton, willful, and substantial disregard for the employer's interest." The employee was insecure about conducting the program. Did the failure to do so show a "substantial disregard for the employer's interest"? Does failure to conduct a training program result in direct economic loss to the employer?

Under these facts the discharge could not be for willful misconduct. The employee was insecure in doing the training. Did this failure to train substantially affect the employer's interest? This would be difficult to show because somebody else could do the training or failure to train would not cause a definable economic hardship.

An employer should never let the possibility of UC benefits interfere with the decision to discharge. Once that decision has been made, the method used in the discharge will sometimes determine whether the employee will receive benefits. In this example, it is difficult to show that the reason for discharge was misconduct. It would be a mistake to argue that the employee should be denied benefits because of misconduct. It could be argued that it was a cause not attributable to the employer.

In misconduct cases the employer must show that

1. An existing rule was violated.
2. The rule was communicated to the employee prior to the violation.
3. A direct causal relationship existed between the offenses committed and the discharge.[20]

It is important to remember that the longer the interval between the offense and the discharge, the less chance there is for sustaining before an appeal referee. Normally, an act is considered misconduct when

1. It is not an isolated incident (unless gross misconduct such as a felony is involved).
2. It is detrimental to the employer's best interests (usually a monetary consideration).
3. It takes place during working hours on the employer's premises.
4. The employee's act disregards job duties that were previously defined and communicated by the employer.

If the action meets this definition and is well documented, it will usually be considered misconduct.

---

[20]Some states hold that the loss of a driver's license necessary for performance of job duties is misconduct. In other states it would be exposure to litigation: *Markel* v. *City of Circle Pines,* 479 N.W.2d 382 (Minn. S.Ct. 1992).

Gross Misconduct

Some states identify two levels of misconduct—gross misconduct and simple misconduct. In gross misconduct the employer has no duty to warn or to show that the employee was aware of the work rule violated. Stealing from the employer, willful destruction of property, sabotage, and unprovoked insubordination, for example, would be in this category.

Drug Testing

Employee drug testing has opened up a whole new set of problems in unemployment compensation law.[21] The issue in most of these cases is whether the refusal to take a drug test is misconduct so benefits can be denied. Different states have decided differently.[22]

The employer can avoid this exposure by having a policy that an employee's refusal to take a drug test is a voluntary quit. The employee has a choice of quitting or taking the test under a policy. Refusal to take a drug test can hardly be a willful or wanton substantial disregard for the employer's interest (misconduct definition). The employee claim that it is an invasion of off-duty privacy is not listened to by more courts.[23] If the employer's records show that employee refuses to take the test, contrary to a communicated policy, a quit is much better than using misconduct as the reason. However it must be made clear that the employee has an option to continue working if the test is taken.

If misconduct evidence is not strong, the employer should argue that the cause of the separation was not attributable to the employer.

The burden is then on the claimant to show that he or she did not cause the separation.

In controlling UC insurance costs, there is no substitute for a clearly communicated policy. The communication should be in such a manner that there is no doubt that, if a violator is caught, disciplinary action will be taken.

THE USE OF APPEAL PROCEEDINGS

If the claimant or the employer objects to a determination made by the agency, either party has the right to appeal. The most common type of appeal concerns rights to benefits. Issues such as ability to work, unavailability for work, or failure to accept suitable work may arise after benefits have been received, and the question of whether the employee is eligible for benefits must be considered periodically during the benefit period.

The appeal must be filed within a specified time, which varies from state to state. In all states the time limit allows no exceptions. The agency loses jurisdiction if the appeal is not made within the time limits. The right to appeal is lost forever. Failure to file an appeal within the specified time limits is one of the most common reasons that employers lose appeals. Often the determination notice from the agency goes to the employer's tax or finance department. It gets put aside or the person responsible is away on vacation or sick. As a result all chances of appeal are lost. When the person regularly responsible for appeals is not available, provision should be made for a substitute.

No Waiver or Agreement

The employer and claimant may decide to make an agreement or employee draft a waiver. The employer may agree to pay the benefits if the claimant agrees not to do certain things; or the employer may want to be nice and agree to pay benefits. This type of agreement is not valid. Only the agency decides when benefits are to be paid. The only way to assure that benefits are not paid is for the employer to report to the agency that the separation was due to a layoff. Any other statement runs the risk that the agency will not refuse benefits.

---

[21]Some states hold that refusal to take a drug test is misconduct: *Fowler* v. *Unemployment Compensation Appeals,* 537 So.2d 162 (Fla. 5th DCA 1989); also *Schwamb* v. *Administrator, Division of Employment Security,* 577 So.2d 343 (La. 1991).

[22]Gary Coffey, "Ruling Backs Work-Related Drug Testing," *Nashville Business Journal,* (October 15–19), 1990, 1–24.

[23]A state did not violate the First Amendment when it denied benefits where an employee was discharged for religious drug use on his own time. The drug use was a violation of a state statute.

Hearsay evidence is inadmissible in judicial proceedings. In an unemployment hearing the referee can admit hearsay evidence but cannot use it as the sole basis for a decision. As a practical matter, the referee treats hearsay evidence any way he or she wants to.

Preparations for an Appeal

In preparing for an appeal hearing, it is important to determine what the issue is. To prepare for the presentation before the appeals referee, the first step is to examine the statement that the claimant made to the agency in comparison with the one you made. If an inconsistency is apparent—as is usually the case— you must seek facts to prove the validity of your statement.

Witnesses are often required. If they are, they should be prepared before the hearing. Some referees question the claimant before you have a chance to do so. You should anticipate this possibility in preparing your case. The proceeding is mostly fact finding and is nonlegal. Formal rules of evidence usually are not observed. Seldom is any evidence excluded. When in doubt, put it in.

You can object to the remarks or evidence admitted, but it is advisable to do so in a nonlegal way. Usually objections are overruled, so why do it? Have as many exhibits as possible. There is no substitute for having the person who made the statement come to the hearing and testify.

When it is difficult to get operating people to document their actions, the best way to ensure documentation in the future is to have the supervisor testify. Frequently the testimony will induce the claimant to deny previous statements. The importance of the document becomes obvious. You also will have fewer problems in getting documentation when the claimant denies the supervisor's statements under oath.

If you think that there are some legal arguments, it is best to present them in writing. Seek help in preparing the memorandum. If your theory is unusual, you may want to provide a short memorandum citing similar case law. You should also take advantage of the opportunity to make a summary—called a closing statement in legal proceedings. It is not necessary to quote a lot of authority, but it is useful to the referee for you to summarize your position. The state agency other than a referee on the case will usually give help in this area.

After the hearing, the referee will take the case under advisement and render a decision. The proceedings are recorded either by tape or by court reporters. In most states, however, a transcript is seldom made unless the case is appealed to the commissioner level.

You should always consider an appeal to the commissioner level when you receive an adverse decision that you feel is not sound. Sometimes certain witnesses were not available at the time of the hearing or certain evidence was overlooked. At the commissioner level it may be proper to ask for a remand so that other evidence can be considered.

If a key person is in Florida for the winter and it is not possible to get the hearing postponed, you might have had to go ahead with the best effort you can make. If you get an adverse decision, the testimony of the person in Florida might have changed the position of the referee. A request for a remand is in order and would probably be granted.

The hearing at the commissioner level follows the same nonlegal format as the first hearing. It is advisable to prepare a memorandum before the hearing. State your position and the reasons for the appeal. This statement should not introduce any new evidence, but simply point out that based on the evidence presented, the determination of the referee was in error. If new evidence not previously available is to be introduced, the memorandum should request a remand. It is important to give a summary in writing at the close of the hearing. This makes certain that the commissioner's representative will consider the important points.

Use of Attorneys in the Appeal Process

In the preceding paragraphs it has been shown that the appeal procedure is a nonlegal process, yet many employers feel more secure if an attorney represents them. The increased complexity of the appeals process has led to more of a need for representation than in the past. However, getting too legal in a process that is basically nonlegal is often fatal. As in other areas of personnel law, we must get a little more legal than in the past, but not to the extent of transferring an administrative hearing into a court setting.[24] Michigan and New Jersey have joined the vast majority of the states that permit nonattorneys to appear before the Employment Security Commission's referee hearing as representatives of employers. Even the courts recognize that nonattorneys can represent the parties before referees.

Sometimes one party is represented by an attorney, and the other party is not. In this situation it is the duty of the referee to see that the unrepresented party can fairly present the case. Sometimes the impartial referee is not able to do this.

There are situations where if the other party had known that the opponent had a lawyer, she or he would have been represented by counsel. Usually the referee does not know until the hearing who is going to be represented, and this makes it even more difficult to determine whether representation is needed.

A better procedure is to call the opposing party and ask if he or she is going to be represented. The other party can then decide what to do about representation.

The best role of an attorney in UC hearings is to help the client prepare the case and not be present at the hearing. Representation at a fact-finding hearing often makes the proceeding too legal, which is a disadvantage.

Reasons for Unsuccessful Appeals

Research by the author with hearing referees has revealed that most cases are not lost on the merits, but on the way they were presented. All too often, the people directly involved in the case do not testify. Witnesses are not properly instructed on what the case is all about or they don't take the task seriously.[25]

Most appeals proceedings are lost for the following reasons:

1. Witnesses do not have actual knowledge of the facts.

---

2. Proper documentation of facts is not available at the hearing.
3. The employer fails to give a clear reason for termination.

The employer must determine the reason for termination on objective facts, eliminating all subjectivity.

POLICIES AND PRACTICES TO REDUCE COSTS

Unemployment compensation disputes all start with the termination process. Although many states have laws that disqualify the claimants from receiving benefits if they quit voluntarily, many types of terminations can result in benefits being paid. Employers often invite this result by giving an ambiguous or wrong reason for the termination. An employee is disqualified from benefits if the termination results from one of the following:

- General job dissatisfaction because of
  —lack of advancement
  —low wages, or
  —too much travel
- Failure to request or return from a leave of absence
- Failure to attempt to remedy a work situation first with the employer (this is particularly damaging to the claim for benefits)
- Marital or domestic situations

The following reasons for quits are considered a good basis for benefits, a cause not attributed to the employer, but may not be charged to employer's experience rating in some states:

- Health reasons
- The employer moves to a location outside the commuting area
- Forced or requested resignation (opportunity to quit before being discharged)
- Quitting because of smoking ban at the workplace.

One of the most difficult and important problems is being sure that the proper procedure is followed in the discharge. Supervisors often do

---

[24]For a complete discussion on the use of counsel in unemployment proceedings, see *The Labor Lawyer,* 4, no. 1 (Winter 1988), 69.

[25]In the opinion of one commissioner's representative, the worst witnesses are accountants, the next worst witnesses are personnel directors, and the third worst witness is the CEO.

not think about the unemployment compensation consequences when they decide to discharge. This oversight is damaging. Sometimes a slight change in what the employer does when discharging can make a big difference.

The Audit of Charges

One of the areas most often overlooked in the control of unemployment compensation insurance costs is the audit of the quarterly statement where all the charges to the employer's account are listed. Even with advanced technology, many errors can creep into this statement. Because state tax rates are experience rated, finding these errors can be an important step in cost control.

Because the finance department usually pays the taxes, some employers leave the audit of the charges to them. This is a mistake; the finance department usually does not have the facts necessary to make the audit. Some of the errors to look for in an audit are the following:

1. In the extreme case, a charge may be made for an individual who was not even employed by the organization.

2. If an employee has not earned enough wages during the base period, no charge should be made even though he or she may otherwise be qualified to receive the benefits (common error).

3. Sometimes a charge to the employer's account is made when the employee has already been disqualified. If the finance department does not receive all the decisions promptly after the appeal process is over, it has no way of knowing whether the charge is proper.

4. The appeal may be pending, in which case the account should not be charged, according to the law in most states.

5. Situations occur where the employee may be suspended for a period of time, such as after being arrested and awaiting trial. Benefits should not be paid for this period unless a determination has been made.

6. Cases have occurred where benefits have been charged for a period when wages or severance pay has been paid for the same period.

7. Some states have a disqualification waiting period. An audit may show that benefits were charged for this period.

The appeal procedure for wrong charges is very simple. Usually all you have to do is to point out the mistake, and the agency immediately makes the correction. A hearing is rarely held over wrong charges. The law and regulations are clear on the conditions under which charges should be made.

Seldom is it discovered that an account was undercharged, as this is the responsibility of the agency. If an undercharge is found in an audit, the employer has a moral duty to call it to the attention of the agency. In some states, the law goes beyond the moral duty.[26]

So many mistakes occur in the charges that people have been known to make a good income by auditing reports for various organizations. They charge a percentage of the amount saved. Organizations that have a high experience rating that puts them at or near the maximum tax sometimes do not bother to audit the report. Wrong charges will not materially affect the tax rate, but this practice is shortsighted. If the tax rate does come down for the next rating period and the practice of auditing the charges has not been established, a great deal of money may be lost. Auditing the quarterly reports should be as routine and automatic as auditing the accounts receivable or checking material received at the shipping dock.

Claim Control Programs

It becomes extremely advantageous to keep the benefits charged to the account to the lowest possible amount. This will not happen without some affirmative action through claim control programs and personnel policies. Some suggested policies and programs are as follows:

1. Plan manpower needs to avoid layoffs. Often overtime is cheaper than hiring additional employees when one considers the cost of hiring and training a new employee plus fringe benefit costs (approximately 35 percent of wages) as well as unemployment compensation costs.

---

[26]An employee's wages were overpaid one week and two weeks later were underpaid. He complained to the paymaster for being underpaid. The paymaster asked why he didn't complain when overpaid. The reply was that he could tolerate one mistake, but not two.

2. Where possible, train or hire employees who have several skills. This allows lateral or upward transfers that not only save unemployment costs but also give flexibility in work assignments.

3. Have one person responsible for the entire program, who by practice and training becomes knowledgeable in unemployment compensation rules and appeal procedures. Some employers have one person responsible for the employee's work relationship, another for the taxes, and a third for accounting procedures. This is a mistake.

4. Have the person responsible for the program audit all charges to the account such as quarterly reports. Often wrong charges to the account are found. They can be corrected by a mere protest by the employer representative who is familiar with the employees and their activities.

5. When in doubt about a determination as to whether the claimant is entitled to benefits—*appeal it.* Over half of all initial benefit determinations appealed by the employer are reversed by the appeal procedure. It is important that a determination is appealed in the event of a wrongful discharge claim. The failure to appeal weakens the employer's position in the wrongful discharge case, because it indicates that the discharge was not proper.

6. Hold exit interviews for all terminations where possible. Attempt a mutual agreement on the reason for termination. In unemployment compensation matters, employees often have a short memory between termination and the interview with the unemployment compensation representative who determines whether benefits are to be paid.

It is in the parties' best interests to provide information concerning separations, to protest adverse claims, to document files, to attend appeal hearings with appropriate witnesses, and to have a basic understanding of the appeal process.[27]

Becoming familiar with the unemployment compensation procedure does not require extensive training, and the financial rewards are great. This is one area where the personnel department or other staff departments can show big savings with a little effort.[28] Once one has experience with a few cases and is exposed to various situations, knowing what to do becomes easier. In rare cases the practitioner should seek help. Paying more attention to this area is long overdue in most organizations.

The legal structure to pay unemployment compensation benefits only where employees are out of work through no fault of their own is available to the employer. All the practitioner must do is use it properly.

---

[27]"Employers May Reap Savings from Improved Unemployment Comp. Benefits Administration," *Employment Benefit News,* (1992), 87.

[28]For several years the author had an undisclosed personal goal to save his employer four times his annual salary. Savings in workers' compensation and unemployment compensation were two areas that greatly contributed to achieving this goal. Undisclosed goals of this nature afford job satisfaction when one attains them and do little harm if one fails.

CHAPTER
18
NONUNION EMPLOYEES UNDER THE NATIONAL LABOR RELATIONS ACT

Distinction Between Rights of Nonunion and Union Employees
Function of the National Labor Relations Board
Definition of Concerted Activity
Use of Employee Committees
An Effective Complaint Procedure
Selection of a Bargaining Representative

The subject of personnel law deals with the rights of the employee and the employer. These rights are granted by statute, court decisions, and under the common law. Rights that employers are often unaware of are those granted to the nonunion employee under the National Labor Relations Act (NLRA) and its subsequent amendments, known as the Taft-Hartley Act of 1947 and the Landrum-Griffin Act of 1959. These three acts can be found in 29 U.S.C. Sect. 151 et seq.

Managers and immediate supervisors are often unaware of the nonunion employee's rights under the NLRA. They often act defensively by discipline or discharge for a protected activity. Cases of this nature are not unique.[1] The number of unfair labor practice cases filed by nonunion employees with the National Labor Relations Board (NLRB) has exceeded 16,000 each year. As the nonunion segment of the workforce continues to grow,[2] employees will rely more and more upon the NLRB for enforcement of their rights.

The law is clear that the employee does not have to be a member of a union, a certified union does not have to be involved, and there does not have to be an organizing drive in existence for the employee to have protection under the NLRA. Section 7 of the act guarantees all employees the right "to engage in concerted activities for the purpose of collective bargaining or for other mutual aid or protection." Section 7 refers to "all employees." If the employee chooses to act through a bargaining representative (commonly called a union), the right to do so is also protected by the act. But under the act employees can

---

[1]In a seminar conducted by the author, over 80 percent of the managers and supervisors in attendance were unaware that nonunion employees have a right to strike.

[2]Fifteen percent of the civilian workforce belong to unions: "Union Members in 1997," (Washington, DC: Bureau of Labor Statistics, U.S. Department of Labor, 1997).

represent their own interests by collective action without a union.

Section 8(a)(1) of the act prevents the employer from interfering with these protected rights. It is an unfair labor practice to "interfere with, restrain or coerce employees in the exercise of the rights guaranteed in Section 7." If the employer violates the act, the NLRB (1) can take remedial action to make the affected employees whole or (2) can order the employer to cease and desist from the unfair labor practice.

The NLRA is the oldest statute in personnel law. The interpretation of this statute is mature as compared to other personnel laws. The case law was developed many years ago, some dating back to the early 1950s.

DISTINCTION BETWEEN RIGHTS OF NONUNION AND UNION EMPLOYEES

The union represents the employee and bargains collectively in behalf of the employee. The terms and conditions agreed upon become a contract between the union (as representatives of the employees) and the company. Most labor agreements grant additional rights not granted by the law or to nonunion employees. Such rights as seniority and restrictions on promotions, layoffs, and recalls are common in a labor agreement. Also, the agreement almost always provides for a grievance and arbitration procedure, and discharge can be only for just cause. A nonunion employee seldom has these rights. This is probably the reason the discharge rate in a nonunion plant is double that in a union plant.[3] The covered employees can sue both the employer and the union to enforce the provisions in an labor agreement.

In a nonunion setting there is no written agreement between the parties as to rights and obligations. However, policy manuals and handbooks have been held in some states to be enforceable contracts but usually are not as easily enforced as a labor agreement, where there is more mutuality.

Differences in Wages and Employment Practices

In a union plant, wages and benefits are determined by collective action. Often there is no logical basis for a wage level except the economic power of the union as pitted against the company's ability to take a strike. The wage levels cannot be changed up or down except as provided for in the labor agreement or with union approval.

In a nonunion operation, wages are determined unilaterally by the employer. The market conditions as well as other factors, such as job evaluation, merit pay plans, and job analysis, determine the wage level. If the wages are not satisfactory to the nonunion employee she or he will quit. If the union is involved, the employees attempt to raise the wage level through collective action by a threat to collectively withhold their services. Another major difference as to wages is that they are not standardized in a nonunion operation. Different wage rates are usually not permitted by the union. This is politically inadvisable for the union leadership.

FUNCTION OF THE NATIONAL LABOR RELATIONS BOARD

The NLRB is the administering agency of the NLRA.[4] It has two main functions: (1) determine of appropriate collective bargaining representatives for employees and (2) deciding unfair labor practice charges and, if found, providing a remedy.

This chapter and the next cite several cases that will be board orders with which the employer complied without appeal. These will be cited as Volume number NLRB No.——(in board cases only one party is involved).[5] If the employer refuses to comply with board orders, the board is forced to seek enforcement in the circuit court of

---

[3]A national committee has recommended a Model Termination Act and encourages the states to adopt it.

[4]The board consists of five members appointed by the president with the consent of the Senate for five-year terms. They cannot be removed during their term.

[5]Some NLRB cases are cited_____ NLRB No_____ as reported in the services such as BNA or CCH, which means that the case was yet to be placed in the official NLRB reports. After being placed in an official volume the case number is omitted; the same case will appear as_____ NLRB_____.

appeals. Such a case will be cited as any other circuit court case would be.

Procedure for Unfair Labor Practice Charge

If an employee or his or her representative feels that an unfair labor practice has been committed, a charge may be filed with the board. The charge is then investigated. If merit to the unfair labor practice charge is found, an informal settlement is attempted. This settlement can be made without union consent [*NLRB* v. *United Food and Commercial Workers Union,* 108 S.Ct. 413 (1988)]. If the parties fail to settle, a formal complaint is filed as in any other legal proceeding. A hearing is held before an administrative law judge (ALJ), who gives a finding of facts and conclusions of law. The ALJ recommends to the board what action they should take. Either party can contest this recommendation and ask the board for discretionary review of the judge's recommendation. The board may grant the review or follow the recommendation of the ALJ. The board has no power to enforce its orders; it tries to convince employee/employer or the courts to do so.

If either party does not agree with the order, they do nothing and the board then must go to the circuit court of appeals for enforcement. The board order is argued as to whether it is proper under the law. The court either enforces or denies enforcement of the order. Appeal from the circuit court decision goes to the U.S. Supreme Court, which decides as in any other appeal, whether to hear it or let the decision stand and become law of the circuit. The board does not publish guidelines or interpretative opinions like other agencies. Board law is decided on a case-by-case basis. It does, however, issue procedural rules and regulations for the conduct of hearings in the NLRB *Case-Handling Manual.* Where facts are similar, the board will establish a precedent for a certain group of subjects. However, the board sometimes changes the precedent when members are changed by the political party in the White House.

DEFINITION OF CONCERTED ACTIVITY

Board statistics show that there is a continual increase of cases where nonunion employees are contesting the employer's denial of their right of concerted activity. This concerted activity is common in wage demands, safety matters, working conditions, and employee walkouts over failure to settle dissatisfactions. The employee's statutory right to engage in concerted activity is not often recognized by the employer. Violations result in an exposure to a lawsuit that may force the employer to make the employee whole for the wrongdoing.

Three conditions must exist before concerted activity is protected by the act. One, the activity must be for mutual aid or other protection for a group of employees. Two, employee activity must involve wages, hours, or other conditions of employment defined in the act.[6] Three, it must be an activity where the employee has a specific authority to act on behalf of other workers.

If there is a group of employees involved, the board has little problem in finding concerted activity. Where four employees asked to leave work early and were refused but left anyway, the board held that this was a one-day strike and a protected activity.[7] The result would be the same if only two employees were involved.

The courts and the board give a broad interpretation on what working conditions are. Because disputes are determined on a case-by-case basis, some examples would be appropriate. Complaints over discriminatory hiring practices; filing complaints with government agents; circulation of petitions that express a desire for a wage increase or additional overtime; aiding other employees in processing complaints with respect to work assignments, vacation policies, and holiday pay practices have all been held by the board to be working conditions.

---

[6]See E. Stephens and J. Clay, "Concerted Activity under NLRA: Current Interpretation of Its Definition," *Labor Law Journal,* 42 (September 1991), 640.

[7]Daniel International Corp., 277 NLRB No. 81 (1985).

Some of the activities that are not considered working conditions include abusive or insulting language, threatening fellow employees with violence, or other activities that are for the sole benefit of the protesters.

Examples of Group Activity

The leading case for concerted activity occurred when a group of nonunion employees left their jobs over the cold working conditions in the plant.[8] The walkout took place after repeated complaints about the lack of heat at the work site. The employees were discharged for walking out and stopping production. The board held that their discharge violated Section 8(a)(1) of the act and ordered reinstatement with back pay. The employees were engaged in a protected activity to improve working conditions. On appeal the Supreme Court held that the board's order was proper. The employer interfered with concerted activity as guaranteed by Section 7 of the act, and the employees' request was neither unlawful nor indefensible. The act protects concerted activity, regardless of whether it comes from a small group or from a nationally recognized union.

Where a group of employees would consider a union only if the employer would change working conditions, it was an indication that they were considering concerted activity.[9] Employees left their jobs to protest the discharge of two employees for falsifying their time cards; the court held it was a protected activity although the employer had good cause to discharge the two employees.[10]

Activity by Individual Employee

Usually, concerted activity involves two or more employees; however, it is possible that only one employee can be engaged in concerted activity.[11] This is especially true if an individual is enforcing a collective bargaining agreement.

Where the employee complaint was directly related to working conditions and was the concern of several employees, it was held to be concerted activity.[12]

Individual action is not is not always concerted activity when there are others involved. A thorough investigation is necessary to avoid exposure to litigation.

The employer may have to make a business decision whether stopping a possible protected activity by discipline is more important than the exposure to an unfair labor practice.

If disloyalty or insubordination can be shown, it will lose protection of the act. The landmark case for employee disloyalty involved employees of a television station. They were distributing handbills criticizing the station's quality of programs. The Supreme Court, in holding that the employer had just cause for discharging the employees, said, "There is no more elemental cause for discharge of an employee than disloyalty to his employer."[13] (The handbills being distributed made no reference to a labor dispute or improvement of working conditions.)

When an employer refused to recall an employee from layoff because he filed an unemployment compensation claim, the board held that there was no violation. The employee was ruled to be acting in his own behalf.[14]

The board made a precedent-changing decision in Meyers Industries, 268 NLRB No. 73 (1984). The board stated that in order to be concerted activity when an individual acts alone, the employee must be engaged with or acting under the authority of others or must have at least discussed the action with others. This drastically changed the definition of concerted activity. The *Meyers* rule was reconsidered by the D.C. Circuit, which agreed

---

[8]*NLRB* v. *Washington Aluminum Co.,* 370 U.S. 9 (1962); also Alameda Technical College, 303 NLRB No. 56 (1991).

[9]*Squeer Distributing* v. *Teamsters Local 7,* 801 F.2d 238 (3rd Cir. 1986). In *D & D Distributing Co.* v. *NLRB,* 801 F.2d 636 (3rd Cir. 1986), there were similar facts and the same result.

[10]*United Merchants Mfg., Inc.* v. *NLRB,* 554 F.2d 1276 (4th Cir. 1977).

[11]*NLRB* v. *Oakes Machine Corp.,* 897 F.2d 814 (2nd Cir. 1990).

[12]*NLRB* v. *P.I.E. Nationwide,* 923 F.2d 566 (7th Cir. 1991).

[13]*NLRB* v. *Local Union 1229, IBEW (Jefferson Standard Broadcasting Co.),* 346 U.S. 464 at 472 (1953). Note the Court now would probably allow handbills or pickets and not call it disloyalty.

[14]Bearden Company, Inc. dba Collins Refractories, 272 NLRB No. 113 (1984).

to enforce the rule in *Prill* v. *NLRB* (on remand), 835 F.2d 148 (D.C. Cir. 1987). Other courts followed, so now the rule has judicial approval.[15]

An employer cannot be charged with an unfair labor practice for disciplinary action unless there is knowledge of the activity and its concerted nature. The requirement of the *Meyers* rule is difficult to administer. The employer would seldom know whether the employee discussed the complaint with others or was acting under their authority.

The Supreme Court limited the rule when it held that an individual employee may act in behalf of others without discussing it when enforcing a collective bargaining agreement.[16] In the *City Disposal Systems* case the employee refused to drive a company truck that in his good faith belief had faulty brakes. He did not discuss it with others, nor was he acting under their authority as is required in the *Meyers* rule (must be discussed with co-workers). The Court held that as long as there was a provision in the collective bargaining agreement that provided for a procedure over safety matters and the company didn't follow it, seeking to enforce the provision was acting in behalf of the entire bargaining unit. Therefore, it was a concerted activity.[17]

Recommendations for Dealing with Concerted Activity

A nonunion employer's concern should be greater when employees complain about working conditions than if they walk off the job. Although both may be concerted activities, if workers walk off the job, the employer can hire replacements.

If it is group action involving a complaint about working conditions, the employer should do this:

1. Require that it be done on nonworking time; if it is during work time the employee could be disciplined. (It would be a rule violation, which would take precedence over concerted activity.)
2. Require that employees use a complaint procedure, if there is one.

3. Do not retaliate because of the employee's activity.
4. Do not take any adverse action, which would be an unfair labor practice. In group conduct it is almost always concerted activity unless it does not concern working conditions.

Recommendations When Employees Go on Strike

1. The employer must first determine whether the walkout (strike) is a protected activity.
2. If it is over working conditions, wages, or hours or for any other lawful purpose, then it is an economic strike and a protected activity. However, the employer would have the right to hire replacements and not hire the strikers until they reoffer their services and a vacancy exists. (It is advisable that a formal request to return to work be required.)
3. If the walkout is caused by an employer's activity that under the law would be considered an unfair labor practice (defined in Section 7, 29 U.S.C. 158 et seq.), such as interfering with union membership, discharge for concerted activity, or retaliation of any kind, then the employee has reinstatement rights over any replacements hired.
4. A partial strike such as a slowdown or refusal to work overtime or perform certain reasonable tasks is not a protected activity under the act.
5. If there is any doubt whether it is a protected activity, seek legal advice before acting, because the consequences are severe.
6. If management disciplines for concerted activity, it is good organizational technique for the union to file an unfair labor practice charge, whether they win or lose.

Recommendations When Activity Is by an Individual

1. The key is whether the individual discussed the activity with other workers. The employee must also act under the specific authority of co-workers.
2. Because it is often difficult to determine whether it is a protected activity, it is advisable to suspend the employee while investigating.
3. Explain before suspending that she or he may have a legal right to act, but you first have to determine whether the employee's actions are legal. If not, there may be discipline.

---

[15]Followed in *Ewing* v. *NLRB*, 861 F.2d 353 (2nd Cir. 1988).

[16]*NLRB* v. *City Disposal Systems*, 104 S.Ct. 1505 (1984).

[17]*NLRB* v. *P.I.E. Nationwide*, 923 F.2d 506 (7th Cir. 1991).

4. If the individual refuses to work, it is usually considered a strike and he or she can be replaced. If it is not a protected activity, the employee can be disciplined for leaving the job.
5. When the employee leaves the job, either discipline or replacement is the employer's legal remedy. If possible this should be explained to the employee before he or she leaves the job.

The only legal exposure that the employer has in concerted activity is if the employer does not consider it a protected activity when in fact it is. The right of nonunion employees to engage in concerted activity without retaliation is a well-established law. The employer, when faced with the problem, need only act reasonably. Listen to the problem, investigate, and, if necessary, correct it. Don't try to eliminate the problem by retaliation against the employee who calls it to management's attention.

USE OF EMPLOYEE COMMITTEES

Restrictions Under NLRA

Employee discontent is often based on the lack of communications. Many labor relations experts agree that the cause of employees joining a union can be traced to a lack of communications.

Some employers believe that the solution to these problems is the formation of an employee committee. The committee would provide a two-way management-employee communication system. It is often an effective substitute for employee representation by a union. However, if not properly constituted it can run afoul of the National Labor Relations Act, Section 15.2(5), which states:

The term "labor organization" means any organization of any kind, or any agency or employee representation committee or plan, in which employees participate and which exists for the purpose, in whole or in part, of dealing with employers concerning grievances, labor disputes, wages, rates of pay, hours of employment, or conditions of work.

Section 158(a)(2) of the NLRA provides:

It shall be an unfair labor practice for an employer to dominate or interfere with the formation or administration of any labor organization or contribute financial or other support to it: Provided, that subject to rules and regulations made and published by the Board pursuant to section 6, an employer shall not be prohibited from permitting employees to confer with him during working hours without loss of time or pay.

It is evident from the language of these two sections of the act that interpretation is needed. The board must determine whether in a given case an employee committee is in violation of the act.

If an employee communication committee functions the same as a union, the board will find it is a company-dominated union and order that it be discontinued.

In the leading case on employee committees, the evidence showed that the committee had bylaws that were prepared by the company. The employee representatives on the committee established a procedure for handling grievances in nonunion plants. They also made proposals to management as to seniority, job classifications, job bidding, holiday pay, and vacation pay in the same manner as a union negotiating committee. The Supreme Court held that this was clearly a labor organization under the act and was company dominated.[18]

The Court had the most concern over the fact that the committee handled employee complaints. Although Section 9(a) of the act permits nonunion employees to present their own complaints to the employer, they cannot do so on behalf of other employees (unless through concerted activity). This would be a representation situation and come within the definition of a labor organization.

The real test of whether an employee committee violates the act is whether the employer actually coerced or restrained the committee from representing the interests of the employees.[19]

---

[18]*NLRB* v. *Cabot Carbon Co.,* 360 U.S. 203 (1959).

[19]In *Airstream, Inc.* v. *NLRB,* 877 F.2d 1291 (6th Cir. 1989), the court refused to enforce a board order. The committee was not prevented from representing the interests of the employees. The key is that employees on the committee must be selected by the employees: Electromation, Inc., 309 NLRB No. 163 (1992).

NLRB Determination of Committee Status

Some of the facts that the board considers when determining whether there is a violation of the act are these:

1. Did the company choose the committee members? If so, it would be a strong indication of a company union.[20]
2. How much staff assistance was given, as distinguished from control? The more control, the more likely it was a violation.[21]
3. Were committee members rotated? This is helpful because it stresses communications objectives.[22]
4. Was the committee organized after a notice that the union was organizing? This is evidence of a company-dominated union.
5. Was a committee formed to discuss supervision, production, or quality circles? This would be legal because they are not subjects that unions are concerned with.[23]
6. How were members selected?

Objectives of Employee Committees

Objectives of the committee should be stated in writing.

1. The declared purpose of the committee should be for communications from management and from employees communicating voluntarily to management.
2. Individual problems should not be discussed, but a separate complaint system should be instituted.
3. The broad problems should be in the form of the employee communicating dissatisfactions and the employer explaining its position on employee problems.
4. Changes in working conditions such as lunch hour or wage and salary programs should be in the form of

two-way communication of employees asking why and management explaining its position, but not necessarily changing it.
5. If employees express a general dissatisfaction, management should consider the problem and correct it or give a rational reason for not doing so.

Although there is exposure to a violation of the act (the remedy for which is to cease and desist, in other words, discontinue the committee), this does not mean that it should not be used. If properly structured, employee committees can be a useful tool in an employee communication program. It can be instrumental in keeping the employees nonunion.[24]

Guidelines for Forming a Committee

1. The committee should be initiated by the employees or jointly by employees and management. (Encouragement by management is acceptable if it doesn't go too far.)
2. Committee membership should be voluntary, and employees should select the members.
3. Committee members should be rotated often (every six months is preferable).
4. The purpose of the committee should be stated in writing at the first meeting. The purpose should state that
   (1) It is a method of obtaining employee suggestions and ideas for improving operations.
   (2) It is a means for better communications between management and employees.
5. The committee should agree not to discuss any antiunion animosity or in any way substitute for the functions performed by a labor union.
6. Officers should be rotated between employees and management representatives and all minutes be prepared and approved by employees and management representatives.
7. Wage and salary policies can be discussed so employees understand them, but no individual wages, grievances, or working conditions should be discussed.

---

[20]*Irving Chute Co.* v. *NLRB,* 350 F.2d 176 (2nd Cir. 1965).

[21]Ripley Industries dba Missouri Heel Co., 209 NLRB No. 79 (1974).

[22]In *NLRB* v. *Scott Fetzer,* 691 F.2d 288 (6th Cir. 1982), the court said that continuous rotation of committee members was management speaking directly to its employees.

[23]In *Airstream, Inc.* v. *NLRB,* 877 F.2d 1291 (6th Cir. 1989), a committee discussed pay, working rules, sick leave, and other working conditions. The court said it was not a violation (not a majority rule).

[24]See Dennis J. Franiecki, Ralph F. Catalanello, and Curtiss K. Behrens, "Employee Committees: What Effect Are They Having?" *Personnel,* (July-August 1984), 67.

8. The broad problems should generally be in the form of communicating dissatisfaction and the employer explaining its position on employee problems.

9. Management should take all ideas and suggestions under consideration no matter how silly they seem.

10. The committee should meet periodically off company premises and off company time. (Often a quarterly dinner meeting at a local hotel sets up the right environment.)

11. Always have a graceful way to discontinue if necessary.

Exhibit 18-1 illustrates that the committee should not have elaborate bylaws and procedures. Formal written guidelines should be only what is necessary to permit the committee to function under broad informal procedures.

The committee structure in Exhibit 18-1 of five management representatives and seven employee representatives is designed to make the committee a more effective communications device. Usually management representatives can easily communicate subjects as the information comes from one or two sources. The employee representatives have a less homogeneous group to represent; therefore, their communication problem is more difficult. There is more of a tendency to discuss wages and working conditions, which may result in the board declaring it a company-dominated union if there are only a few employee representatives.

EXHIBIT 18-1 *Employee-Management Communications Committee*

The general purpose of this committee, consisting of employee and management representatives, is to promote better communications between the company and its employees.

The purpose of employee representatives shall be to communicate to management the acceptability of management policies and practices, to make suggestions for improving management-employee relationships, and to communicate generally their problems and dissatisfactions.

The purpose of management representatives shall be to communicate business conditions, customer relations, employee benefits, wage and salary policies, community and governmental problems, management policies and practices, and new developments and to represent management's position concerning general employee problems and dissatisfactions.

Selection of Committee

The committee shall consist of management representatives from production, administration, and general management, except that the plant manager or employee relations representative shall not sit on the committee. Employee representatives shall be selected by the employees whom they represent; representation from different departments is desirable but not essential. There shall be a maximum of seven employee representatives and a maximum of five management representatives. Each member of the committee shall serve for no more than one year and shall not be eligible for reappointment (a questionable provision). Vacancies shall be filled in the same manner as they were appointed.

Committee Organization

The committee shall meet at least once every three months until discontinued on request of either party. They shall elect a chair and a secretary. The chair shall be alternated from year to year between an employee and management representative. Minutes of the meeting shall be kept and distributed to all employees. The committee shall adopt such other rules and procedures as necessary to carry out its function.

With an unbalanced committee, the thought is conveyed that this is not a voting situation where the majority vote rules. Management's being underrepresented clearly communicates this to the employees.

Pitfalls of Employee Committees

There are risks involved in employee committees, apart from the legal exposure of committing an unfair labor practice. If there is irresponsible leadership on the committee, a whole host of employee relations problems could be created.

Success of a committee is largely dependent on the trust that management can develop with the employee representatives. How well the employee representatives communicate to the entire employee body often depends upon how well they believe management. If distortions occur that are damaging to the business, then the committee should be diplomatically discontinued.

The committee should be carefully formed before there is a threat of a union organization. If a large number of issues remain unsolved, or are settled by an arbitrary position of management, a tailor-made organization is handed to the union organizer.

Management can avoid these pitfalls by continual audit of the effectiveness of the committee. If there is not a harmonious relationship, it can diplomatically discontinue the committee. The advantages of an employee committee outweigh the disadvantages. Positive personnel administration should seriously consider employee communication committees in spite of the solvable problems that they create.

AN EFFECTIVE
COMPLAINT PROCEDURE

Need for a Complaint Outlet

A common cause of employees' concerted activity over working conditions is the failure of the employer to have an effective complaint procedure. There must be a place for employees to go to let the steam off. After attempts to do so fail with the employees' supervisor (who often is the source of the problem), concerted activity results. Such activity usually would not be protected if a complaint procedure were available. For example, if a complaint procedure were available when co-workers protested discharge of a fellow employee, as in the *United Merchants* case,[25] a work stoppage would not be justified. There are other means available to adjudicate the dissatisfaction.[26]

Nothing in the act prevents any employer from establishing an informal or formal complaint procedure. There are two reasons why complaint procedures avoid concerted activity. First, if the employee is offered a forum for the solution of the problem, concerted action is less likely or it would be restricted to a complaint procedure. Second, the employer is forced to take a position that is documented, and this often satisfies the employee. Sometimes a forum to discuss the dissatisfaction is all that is needed to satisfy the employee.[27]

Elements of Effective
Complaint Procedure

There are many types of complaint procedures in union and nonunion organizations. What is effective for one organization may be ineffective for another. However, all procedures should be designed to contain the following elements:

1. The procedure should be designed so that it encourages the employee to use it. If the employee at the first instance is required to discuss the complaint with the immediate supervisor, who probably caused the problem, the procedure will not provide an outlet for the complaint. In *Meritor Savings Bank, FSB* v. *Vinson,* 106 S.Ct. 2399 (1986), the complaint procedure was ineffective because it required the employee to complain to the immediate supervisor. The Court said, at 2409,

---

[25]*United Merchants Mfg. Inc.* v. *NLRB*, 554 F.2d 1276 (4th Cir. 1977).

[26]The author purposely has avoided the use of the term *grievance.* A grievance is defined as an employer action in violation of a labor agreement. A dissatisfaction or complaint is any employee concern over wages and working conditions.

[27]Many dissatisfactions or grievances are settled by permitting the employee (union or nonunion) to talk while the employer just listens. Often employees talk themselves out of the dissatisfaction.

"Moreover, the bank's grievance procedure apparently required an employee to complain first to her supervisor, in this case Taylor. Since Taylor was the alleged perpetrator, it is not altogether surprising that respondent failed to invoke the procedure and report her grievance to him. Petitioner's contention that respondent's failure should insulate it from liability might be substantially stronger if its procedures were better calculated to encourage victims of harrassment to come forward."

2. The solution of the complaint is the most important part, not who gets it first. Investigation can start at any level.
3. A staff person should be indirectly involved in the solution of the problem; leaving it solely up to operating management causes inconsistency.
4. The objective of settling complaints should be what is right, not who's right.
5. All complaints are real to the employee and should never be considered ridiculous, although they may be to management.

Need for Impartial Final Step

Unless a complaint procedure has a final impartial resting place, the employee will not have complete faith in its impartiality. The most valuable benefit of a union contract is the final and binding arbitration procedure of a grievance. It is something that is only found where the union represents the employees. This is often used by the union in their organizing efforts. "If you had a union, management couldn't get away with it" is a common argument used by the organizer.

The three impartial methods used in a nonunion setting are arbitration,[28] similar to that under a union contract, peer review, and mediation (ADR). Peer review had its genetic origin in the jury system. None of these methods is easy to sell to management because they involve giving up a traditional managerial prerogative. Mediation is a voluntary procedure where management keeps control. It is difficult to understand why management would resist a complaint procedure. One of the first clauses management agrees to in a new labor agreement is a complaint procedure. The labor agreement gives away many management prerogatives under bargaining pressure. One way to eliminate the union organizer's best selling point is to have an appeal procedure in a nonunion setting.[29]

Arbitration in Nonunion Setting. In the nonunion setting, arbitration takes many forms. Protesting employees may represent themselves or may bring friends, fellow workers, or attorneys. Some companies appoint a personnel staff person to represent the employee or have an ombudsman who, among other duties, represents the employee.

The arbitrator is selected either by the company or by a professional association such as the American Arbitration Association or a governmental agency. Sometimes there is a panel of arbitrators, for which the employee and management each select one and the two select the third. This often helps to correct the problem of lack of knowledge of the operation by a single arbitrator.

Another problem is the question of who pays the arbitrator. If the company pays, it is difficult for the employee to understand the impartiality of the decision. If the employee is liable for one half the fee (as the union is under most labor agreements), the arbitrator, in discharge cases, is tempted to reinstate the employee so her or his fees can be paid. One approach would be to have the employee pay one half if he or she wins and to have the employer pay it all if the employee loses. This may be a good solution in some cases, but not in others.

The greatest difficulty in nonunion arbitration is the lack of a definite document to provide a basis for the decision. Under a union arbitration the arbitrator is restricted to the language of the labor agreement. In a nonunion setting a rule or policy is often vague, or it is a loosely worded oral promise. This often makes it difficult for the arbitrator to find an objective basis for a final and binding decision that would render justice to both sides.

---

[28]A. Rutkowski, "Mandatory Arbitration: A Panacea or Simply Two Bites of the Same Apple."

[29]There are various methods to deal with employee complaints. Whatever works the company should do. See D. Phillips, J. Cooke, and A. Anderson, "A Surefire Resolution to Workplace Conflicts," *Personnel Journal,* 71, no. 5 (May 1992), 111.

As the concept of employment at will continues to be eroded, employers will resort to arbitration, at least in discharge cases. This is a welcome alternative to costly court proceedings. However, some of the problems inherent in nonunion arbitration need to be worked out.

The use of a panel instead of a single arbitrator would solve some of the problems. A panel would make it easier to settle before the hearing. Management and employee representatives on the panel make a settlement more just. Management rights would not be eroded, and the employee's position would be better represented.

The problems of who pays and the lack of a definitive document as a basis for a decision will have to be solved before arbitration in a nonunion setting will become popular.

Peer Review in Nonunion Setting. Many companies, dissatisfied with the little-used "open door" grievance policies, are instituting peer review boards as the final step in a complaint procedure.[30] Most of these boards consist of two management representatives and three employees. The unbalanced board with the employee representatives in the majority has resulted in management's position being upheld in over 60 percent of the cases. Evidence shows that employees are more strict with their peers than are their supervisors. Also there can be little criticism that the procedure is biased toward the company.

The peer review has been used by more than 100 companies for nonunion employees, including such large organizations as Federal Express Corporation, General Electric Company (in nonunion facilities), Citicorp, Borg-Warner Corporation, Adolph Coors Company, and Control Data. In most of the companies the employee is not permitted to use an outside representative. The company provides staff to help prepare the case for the employee if it is requested. This keeps the procedure informal and puts the employee in a more relaxed and a more nearly equal position to management.

The peer review has many advantages over arbitration in that it can be handled internally.[31] This approach enables the dispute to be settled more quickly than if an outsider is involved. Many managers want to avoid reversal by their peers. They are more careful when disciplining an employee to make sure that the procedures are followed. They are more fair and open about the matter, and give better feedback to the employee and other subordinates.

In the author's view, the peer review method or some process in ADR will gain in popularity as the best final step in a nonunion complaint procedure.[32]

Exhibit 18-2 is an example of a final and binding step in a complaint procedure. It is a substitute for the type found in a union agreement. This type of procedure will avoid protected concerted activity and will promote good employee relations.

In summary, the complaint procedure is an area in which personnel law has very few restrictions except to avoid retaliation liability and protect concerted activity. Complaint procedure is an important part of effective personnel administration and is an effective method to prevent litigation. Management should spend considerable time and effort in developing a procedure that will work for their particular operation.[33]

SELECTION OF A BARGAINING REPRESENTATIVE

Right to Select Bargaining Representative

The basic authority for the right of employees to select bargaining representatives is Section 7 of the NLRA. This section provides that employees "shall have the right to self-organization to form,

---

[30]B. Thompson, "An Early Review of Peer Review," *Training,* (July 1, 1991), 42–46.

[31]For further reading on peer review, see D. Hoffman and N. Kulver, "How Peer Group Resolution Works at Northern States Power Co.," *Employment Relations Today,* 19 (Spring 1992), 25–30; H. S. Caras, "Measuring the Success of Peer Review," *Employee Relations Today,* 18 (1991), 103–108.

[32]Peer review materials are available to EEOC if subpoena powers are used: *University of Pennsylvania* v. *EEOC,* 110 S.Ct. 577 (1990).

[33]See P. M. Panken, "What Every Company Should Have: Formal Employee Complaint Procedure," *Management Review,* 73, no. 1 (January 1984), 42–45; T. J. Condon, "Use Union Methods in Handling Grievances," *Personnel Journal,* 64, no. 1 (January 1985), 72–75.

EXHIBIT 18-2 *Suggested Complaint Procedure for Employees Not Represented by a Union*

When an employee becomes dissatisfied with the working relationship or some other problem for which a solution is desired, the employee may discuss this dissatisfaction with the immediate supervisor or with the supervisor's supervisor. If a satisfactory solution is not received at these levels, the dissatisfaction or problem shall be put in writing and submitted to the employee relations representative.

The employee relations representative shall investigate the matter and make a recommendation in writing to the manager of the department. The manager shall, after due consideration and consultation, make a determination and so inform the employee in a person-to-person meeting, by presenting a copy of the decision to the employee and sending a copy to the employee relations representative and the employee's immediate supervisor.

If the employee is dissatisfied with the manager's decision, the employee may refer it to an employee-management committee consisting of two management representatives and three employee representatives, whose majority decision shall be final and binding on both the company and the employee. This procedure shall be communicated to all employees affected; employees must be made to feel, beyond any reasonable doubt, that they will not be in any way penalized for using this procedure.

The employee-management committee shall be discontinued on 30 days' notice of either party to discontinue. Such discontinuance date shall not be effective until all pending employees' problems or dissatisfactions have been resolved.

join, or assist labor organizations to bargain collectively through representatives of their own choosing and to engage in other concerted activities for the purpose of collective bargaining or other mutual aids or protection."

Section 7 was amended by the Taft-Hartley Act to state specifically that an individual shall have the right to refrain from any or all union activities. This was a loophole in the original act.

The interpretation of Section 7 by the board and the courts is very complex and voluminous. It is only possible here to give a brief overview of the law. Important decisions concerning union-employer posture and remedies for violations are covered only briefly.

In *NLRB* v. *Town & Country,* 116 S.Ct. 450 (1995), an electrical contractor refused to grant employment interviews to 10 job applicants who were union members. The only union applicant accepted for employment was fired after a few days on the job. The union members filed a complaint against the contractor with the National Labor Relations Board (NLRB), asserting that the contractor had failed to hire or retain them because of their union affiliation in violation of the

National Labor Relations Act (NLRA). An administrative law judge held for the union members and a panel of the NLRB affirmed the decision. The U.S. Court of Appeals, 8th Circuit, reversed the NLRB's decision, finding that the job applicants were not "employees" for the purposes of the NLRA because they were being paid by the union to organize the company. They were therefore not protected from antiunion discrimination. The U.S. Supreme Court agreed to review the case.

The Court stated that the NLRB's broad, literal interpretation of the statutory term *employee* was consistent with NLRA purposes, one of which was to protect the right of workers to organize for mutual aid without employer interference. The contractor argued that common law agency principles prohibited this interpretation, and that the applicants were paid union organizers who could only serve the union's interest. The Court noted that common law agency principles did not prohibit workers from accepting employment from more than one employer. Union organizing was equivalent to performing work for another employer during nonwork hours, which no employer had a legal right to prevent. The Court held that the NLRB's interpretation of the term *employee* was correct.[34]

When an employer is faced with a union organizational drive, a general knowledge of the law prevents mistakes in the initial stage of organization of the drive. Professional advice by a person thoroughly versed in this area is advisable immediately after knowledge of an organizational attempt exists and after the first meeting with the employees.

Steps in Selection of Bargaining Representative

If a company becomes aware of an organizational effort at its inception, it will probably be through supervisors, by loyal or ambitious employees ("apple polishers"), or by observation of some kind of solicitation.[35] Sometimes, organizational efforts are kept secret. The employer is not aware of the effort until a letter or telegram demanding recognition is received from the union. If this happens, the initial stages of the organizational campaign have passed.

The company's position should be clear as soon as it has notice of any kind of organizational attempts. A special employee meeting can be called for that purpose without seeking professional advice. After the initial meeting nothing more should be done until after professional advice has been obtained. However, to state that one does not want a union is always safe.[36]

The initial organization objective of a union is to obtain a sufficient number of authorization cards or authority (some unions use a list similar to a petition) to represent the signatory employees for collective bargaining purposes.

There are two types of cards. On one, the union is authorized to represent the undersigned employees for collective bargaining purposes. On the second type, the union is designated as the exclusive bargaining representative of the signatories and requests the NLRB to hold an election.

Various meetings; coffee parties; beer sessions; calls at the employee's home, sales parties for cosmetics, at which an organizer is present; telephone surveys by students for a term paper, whose real purpose is to discover prounion employees; and hard sell from other employees are all part of the procedure to get employees to sign authorization for representation.

The union needs at least 30 percent of the eligible voters in the appropriate bargaining unit to sign authorization cards. The board, under their procedural rules, will not honor a petition for an election unless 30 percent sign. As a practical matter, to ensure winning an election, most unions will not petition the board for an election unless they have 60 percent or more signed authorizations from those eligible to vote.[37]

Request to Bargain without an Election

Before the union petitions the board for an election, it sometimes requests orally or in writing that the employer bargain without an election. The union tells the employer that they represent the majority of the employees and would like to be recognized as a bargaining representative. They usually suggest a date for the first meeting.

Sometimes the union presents the authorization forms to prove its claim of majority status. It then requests recognition and a collective bargaining meeting. Unless the employer decides to recognize the union without an election, the authorization cards should never be reviewed. If the employer has any knowledge whatsoever of any employee's signature on a card, the employer cannot later demand an election or question the majority status of the union. This is the position that the board

---

[34]D. Payne, S. Crow, and S. Hartman, "Fate of Full-Time Union Organizer: As Employees, What Next for the Supreme Court?" *Labor Law Journal,* (June 1995).

[35]In *Lechmere, Inc.* v. *NLRB,* 112 S.Ct. 841 (1992), the Court held that outside union organizers had no right to be in the parking lot distributing literature. The parking lot is owned by the developer and store owner. Also, Davis Supermarkets, Inc., and United Food and Commercial Workers Local 23, 306 NLRB 86 (1992). Also *NLRB v. Adco Electric, Inc.,* 6 F.3d 1110 (5th Cir. 1993).

[36]Even if the employer wants a union to get an affirmative vote, sometimes it is better to say you don't want it.

[37]In 1992 unions won a little less than half of the elections. In 1995 they were almost even.

takes and the courts will enforce.[38] The employer should always demand an election unless there are rare circumstances that dictate otherwise.

Signed authorizations are not always predictive of how the employee will vote.[39] Sometimes an employee signs cards for reasons other than union representation. A person may have signed a card to get rid of the union organizer or changed after hearing all the issues. The beer party may have lasted too long, and the employee did not reflect on his or her true feelings.[40] Once an employee signs a card, the board will not accept any testimony on why the person signed the card.[41] However, persuasion to withdraw authorization is not in itself illegal.[42]

Another reason for demanding an election is that there may be more than one union involved.[43] Often the employer will have knowledge of only one but there are two unions involved. If one union is recognized without an election there could be a charge of an unfair labor practice by the second union involved.[44]

If the employer denies recognition and requests the board to hold an election, the board must do so in the absence of an unfair labor practice.[45]

When the board orders the election, the time and place are determined as well as the eligible list of voters. If the employer and the union agree with all the conditions, a consent election petition is signed. If they do not agree, a hearing is held. The regional director makes a determination of the issues and then orders the election. This order is appealable to the circuit court. After the election is ordered, the campaign to influence the employees on how to vote starts.

One of the frequent issues is determination of who is eligible to vote.[46] Often there is a dispute over confidential employees. They must be directly involved in labor relations policy to be confidential.[47] Another area of dispute often is close relatives of the owner or the manager. These employees are not allowed to vote under board policy that was upheld by the Supreme Court.[48]

When an issue of eligibility or any other issue arises, the board will order the election and permit those issues in dispute to be challenged by either party. If the challenged ballots would change the outcome of the election, a hearing is held. The board makes a determination on the challenged ballots that is appealable to the circuit court.[49]

Preelection Conduct

Section 8(a)(1) makes it a violation to interfere with, restrain, or coerce employees in exercising their rights to join or not to join a labor organization.

Violation by the employer usually takes the form of threatening the loss of jobs or benefits, questioning employees about their union activities or membership, spying on union gatherings, or granting wage increases deliberately timed to discourage employees from joining or voting for the union.[50] This should be distinguished from false and misleading statements, which are permissible unless documents are forged or otherwise deceptive.[51]

The statements made during a campaign cannot be defamatory, but a suit can be brought in a state court apart from the organizational environment.[52]

---

[38]*Retail Clerks Union* v. *NLRB (John L. Serpa Inc.)*, 376 F.2d 186 (9th Cir. 1967).

[39]The author as state agency representative once held an election where all voters were dues-paying members of the union but they all voted not to have the union represent them.

[40]Cards signed after drinking 26 bottles of beer were held to be valid: American Art, 170 NLRB No. 70 (1968).

[41]Midstate Beverages, 153 NLRB No. 14 (1965).

[42]*NLRB* v. *Monroe Tube Co.*, 545 F.2d 1320 (2nd Cir. 1976).

[43]See *NLRB* v. *Fremond*, 927 F.2d 109 (2nd Cir. 1991).

[44]*Hadden House Food Prods., Inc.* v. *NLRB*, 764 F.2d 182 (3rd Cir. 1985).

[45]*Linden Lumber Div. & Summer Co.* v. *NLRB*, 419 U.S. 301 (1974). Even if an employer wants a union, it is safer to have an election.

[46]*Wilcf Transportation, Inc.* v. *NLRB*, 949 F.2d 1308 (7th Cir. 1991).

[47]*NLRB* v. *Hendricks County Rural Electric Membership Corp.*, 450 U.S. 964 (1981).

[48]*NLRB* v. *Action Automotive, Inc.*, 105 S.Ct. 984 (1985).

[49]Election procedures are found in the most recent NLRB *Case Handling Manual.*

[50]*Gold Tex, Inc.* v. *NLRB*, 14 F.3d 1008 (7th Cir. 1993).

[51]*NLRB* v. *Affiliated Midwest Hospital*, 789 F.2d 524 (7th Cir. 1986).

[52]*Bill Johnson's Restaurants, Inc.* v. *NLRB*, 103 S.Ct. 2161 (1983); *MECO Corp.* v. *NLRB*, 986 F.2d 1430 (10th Cir. 1993).

It is usually held to be unfair labor practice where the employer is guilty of coercion, promises, threats, and seeking information about employees' attitude toward the union. However, the conduct must be recent. Where eight months old, the court held it was ineffective.

One of the common violations is where the employer solicits dissatisfaction or grievances in order to determine why employees joined the union. He then corrects or promises to correct the conditions before the election. This is almost always held to be an unfair labor practice. Soliciting complaints is permissible, but promises to remedy them are unlawful.[53]

Other employer conduct held to be unlawful is a statement that a plant shutdown is a possibility because the union would make it impossible to survive.[54] The company might try to grant an unusual number of employee loans a week before the election.[55]

Some permissible common conduct includes

- Granting benefits and wage increases—a past practice[56]
- Withholding from paychecks and paying separately sums equivalent to union dues[57]
- Holding a raffle for groceries, stating that their value was equal to the amount of union dues for one year
- Using strong persuasion to get employees to withdraw their authorization card

Unions are also held to the same standard of conduct as employers under the law. However, it is often difficult to get evidence of union conduct because of the reluctance of employees to testify against each other. Where a union waived initiation fees for those who signed authorization cards before the election, the Supreme Court held this to be unfair labor practice.[58] However, the union was within its right to give a free turkey to all employees attending a union meeting.[59] There

has been developed a large body of law on what the union and employers can say and what they cannot say. This also involves the constitutional right of the freedom of speech.

Solicitation Rules During a Campaign. One problem often comes up when a union is attempting to organize a solicitation. What degree of solicitation by pro-union employees must be permitted by the employer? The Supreme Court has held that prohibition of union activities during nonwork time interferes with the employee's right to organize. However, this is valid if necessary to maintain discipline or production.[60] The problem for the employer is what degree of solicitation by pro-union employees must be permitted. The Supreme Court decision makes it clear that it is permitted only during nonwork time. Often there is a fine line between work and nonwork time.

There is picketing to organize the store on the parking lot owned by the land developer. The union must prove there is no other way to communicate to the employees. The burden to establish inaccessibility is a heavy burden for the union. Under *Lechmere, Inc.* v. *NLRB,* 112 S.Ct. 841 (1992), it takes more than undue hardship or showing that the alternative is cumbersome or less than ideal.[61]

A rule that requires permission from management for any kind of solicitation is usually held to be too broad because it could include nonwork time.[62] Another rule was struck down where all talking during work time was prohibited. The court said that such a rule was unreasonable.[63]

The Supreme Court put some restrictions on solicitation during nonwork time in hospitals and health care institutions. Such activity would interefere with visitors and patient care, such as in patients' rooms and corridors. However, the court stated that solicitation in a cafeteria would not interfere with patient care or visitors.[64]

---

[53]Montgomery Ward & Co., 225 NLRB 112 (1976).

[54]W. A. Kruger Co., 224 NLRB No. 148 (1976).

[55]*Bradley Lumber Co.* v. *NLRB,* 128 F.2d 768 (8th Cir. 1942).

[56]*NLRB* v. *Otis Hospital,* 545 F.2d 252 (1st Cir. 1976).

[57]Geyer Mfg. Co., 120 NLRB 208 (1958).

[58]*NLRB* v. *Savair Mfg. Co.,* 414 U.S. 270 (1973).

[59]Jacqueline Cochran, Inc., 177 NLRB No. 39 (1969).

[60]*Republic Aviation Corp.* v. *NLRB,* 324 U.S. 793 (1945).

[61]For discussion of this issue see K. Boroff, "Shopping for Access After Lechmen," *Labor Law Journal,* 14 (June 1995) 281.

[62]*Birmingham Ornamental Co.* v. *NLRB,* 615 F.2d 66 (5th Cir. 1980).

[63]*NLRB* v. *Chem Fab Corp.,* 691 F.2d 1252 (8th Cir. 1982).

[64]*Beth Israel Hospital* v. *NLRB,* 437 U.S. 483 (1978); also *NLRB* v. *Baptist Hospital,* 422 U.S. 773 (1979).

The situation that most often confronts employers is where, as a matter of good employee relations, the employer has permitted conversation or solicitation of the other subjects during work time. Then, when a union campaign takes place, the employer prevents conversation or activity for union organization as well as other subjects.

The employer that permits selling Girl Scout cookies during work time but prohibits union solicitation after a petition has been filed is exposed to an unfair labor practice charge.[65] If the union activity were far more excessive than what had been permitted, restriction of union subjects would probably not be in violation.

The employer who had a past practice of permitting non-work-related conversation and civic projects during work time must be cautious when establishing a rule prohibiting solicitation for union activity. Social solicitations are difficult to control, and for good employee relations it is better not to control them. The courts recognize that it would not be practical to prohibit all conversations of all non-work-related subjects.

The court held that six instances of ad hoc nonunion solicitation during work time was not enough. A facially valid no-solicitation rule against union solicitation did not show disparate treatment while tolerating social solicitation during work time.[66]

As in other situations concerning employer conduct in representation elections, the employer should receive professional advice before too much is said.[67]

Remedy for Violations During Campaign. When the board finds that the union or employer has committed an unfair labor practice, it will order a new election. If the offense is severe enough, it will order certification without an election (called the *Gissel* rule). In order to certify a union without an election, there must be substantial proof that the company committed a serious unfair labor practice. The Court said that the employer's action must have a marked impact on employee sentiment that is expressed on the authorization forms and the election results. The employer's action, under the *Gissel* doctrine, must undermine the majority status of the union.[68]

The board takes the position that the union must make a showing that the majority of the bargaining unit has authorized the union to represent them. Without a showing of a majority status, it would not be possible for the employer to affect the outcome of the election by committing an unfair labor practice.[69]

Supervisor Conduct in Support of Union Activity

In combating union organization efforts, the most important management representative is the front-line supervisor. Supervisors' rapport with the employees gives them the greatest exposure to unfair labor practices.

For this reason they must be briefed on their legal rights in representing management. Most managements assume that the supervisor will support their position, but what happens with the supervisor who supports union activity? Is there any restriction on discharging a supervisor who supports union activity? Supervisor support of union activity is not uncommon. Dissatisfied supervisors will often reason that if a union represents the employees and their wages or benefits are increased, the supervisors' will also be increased.

Sections 2(3), 2(11), and 14(a) of the Taft-Hartley amendments to the act specifically exempt supervisors from the protection under the act. The question arises that if a supervisor is discharged for supporting union activity, is this in any way interfering with the employee's right to join a union?

Section 7 of the National Labor Relations Act does afford the supervisor some protection where the employer discharges the supervisor for

---

[65]*Restaurant Corp. of America* v. *NLRB*, 801 F.2d 1390 (D.C. Cir. 1986).

[66]*PACECO Co., Div. of Fruehauf Corp.* v. *NLRB*, 601 F.2d 180 (5th Cir. 1979).

[67]For additional reference, see Steven C. Kahn, Barbara A. Brown, and Brent G. Zepke, *Personnel Director's Legal Guide* (Boston: Warren, Gorham & Lamont, 1984–1986 Supp.) pp. 11-2–11-52; 12-45–12-59.

[68]*NLRB* v. *Gissel Packaging Co.*, 395 U.S. 575 (1960).
[69]Gourmet Foods, Inc., 270 NLRB No. 113 (1984).

1. Refusal to commit an unfair labor practice
2. Refusal to testify on behalf of management in a board hearing involving union activity
3. Giving adverse testimony in a board hearing
4. Failure to prevent a union from organizing employees

Section 2(11) of the act states that the supervisors are not employees, but the board and the courts have held that it is a violation of employee Section 7 rights if a supervisor is discharged for any of the foregoing reasons.[70] The court in *Talladega* was quick to point out that it is not extending the act to nonemployees. It is giving protection to nonemployees where their action adversely affects employees' rights as defined by the act.

The supervisor can be discharged for sympathizing with the union. There is no protection from the employer's action. This must be distinguished from where the employer tells the supervisor that if a union gets in he or she will be discharged. The board holds that this is an unfair labor practice, and the supervisor is protected.

In *Automobile Salesmen's Union* v. *NLRB,* 711 F.2d 383 (D.C. Cir. 1983), the supervisors attended a union meeting and generally sympathized with the employees' organizational activities. The board refused to extend protection of the act to the supervisors upon discharge. It stated that it was within the prerogative of management to discipline its supervisors for sympathizing with the employees' desire to join a union. The court affirmed the board's position. It held that in order to receive protection under Section 7, the supervisor's activity must directly interfere with employee rights to organize.

The act does not prevent the supervisor from taking a vigorous role in the management campaign to prevent a union. A supervisor who refuses to commit an unfair labor practice and is discharged is protected by the act. The discharge for the refusal is the crux of the protection.[71] If the supervisor actually commits an unfair labor practice, this is not protected because the action would be a violation under the act. An employer would be enforcing the law by the discharge. When the employer discharges a supervisor for activity that has direct impact on the employee's rights under the NLRA the discharge is protected.[72]

Reason for Seeking Representation

Could I do this if I had a union? If the answer is no, then the planned activity should be undertaken very carefully or there will be a union to deal with some day.

Employees do not request the union to represent them because they want to but because they feel that management is not listening to their problems. This is one way to get them to do so. *Management organizes employees into a union.*[73] All the professional organizer does is wait for management to make enough mistakes to cause the employees to seek representation. A knowledge of the rights of nonunion employees will keep employers from making these mistakes, and at the same time promote good employee relations.

---

[70]*NLRB* v. *Talladega Cotton Factory, Inc.,* 213 F.2d 209 (5th Cir. 1954).

[71]*NLRB* v. *Miami Coca-Cola Bottling Co.,* 341 F.2d 524 (5th Cir. 1965).

[72]*Howard Johnson Co.* v. *NLRB,* 702 F.2d 1 (1st Cir. 1983).

[73]The author once asked a union organizer why he didn't organize a certain plant. His answer was, "Management has not made enough mistakes yet." Later management did, and he organized the plant.

CHAPTER
19
BARGAINING UNDER THE NATIONAL LABOR RELATIONS ACT

Differences Between Union and Nonunion Employers
Employer Duty to Bargain
Enforcement of a Collective Bargaining Agreement
Restraints on the Right to Strike
Use of Arbitration in Dispute Resolution
Problem-Solving Bargaining
Alternative Dispute Resolution

When the personnel practitioner looks at the title of this chapter, the thought may occur that because one does not have a union or expect to have one in the foreseeable future, this would be one chapter to skip. This would be a mistake. Employer action in a nonunion setting should always consider whether such action could be taken if a union represented the employees.

For example, a nonunion employer in an effort to get workers to work the graveyard shift (12:00 P.M. to 8:00 A.M.) decided to pay all workers an extra four hours' pay for the graveyard shift. When economic conditions changed and jobs became more plentiful, it was decided to change this expensive policy and pay only for time worked. In a union setting policy could not be changed without employee consent.

How can one change the policy to have the least impact on the workers' attitude? It must be done very carefully. If workers were organized, it could not be done without union acceptance,

which would be unlikely. Without a union the policy change must be well communicated to the employees, or the employer will have a union.

Nonunion employers and employees should know the rights of union employees and what restrictions labor agreements contain. They must make decisions that will have the least impact. The union should not be given the opportunity to say, "If you were represented by a union, the employer could not do this."

DIFFERENCES BETWEEN UNION AND NONUNION EMPLOYEES

Chapter 18 stated that a nonunion employee has the same rights under the National Labor Relations Act (NLRA) as a union employee. What differences does it make whether an employee belongs to a union? Why is there such effort by employers to keep out unions? The major difference is in the procedures. Employees represented by a union cannot individually discuss with the employer the wages and working conditions but must do so through an elected representative, the union. The second difference is that in a union setting a labor agreement exists that may restrict the employer in making certain employment decisions.[1]

To select a representative for the purpose of discussing wages or other conditions of employment is a right granted to the employee by Section 7 of the act. When the National Labor Relations Board (NLRB) holds an election and the majority of those voting select a union to represent them for bargaining purposes, the employees can no longer individually represent themselves. The law requires the union to represent all the employees, if the majority of those voting chose the union. All employees (members and nonmembers) in the bargaining unit must go through the union for any problems concerning working conditions and wages.

From the employer's point of view, a third party has come between the employee and the employer. The employer can no longer change working conditions without agreement by the employee representative.

Once a union is certified by the NLRB, the employer, under the law, must make a good faith effort to reach an agreement as to the terms and conditions of employment.[2] Once an agreement has been reached, both the union and the employer must follow it. The employee may force the union and the employer to do so through the NLRB. Whatever rights are granted in the labor agreement are additional rights that a nonunion employee may not have, such as grievance procedures, seniority, and posting of vacancies.

This chapter describes the procedures under the law that force the employer to deal with the union as representative of the employee. It also reviews the additional rights that an employer has granted to an employee in the collective bargaining agreement.

Most of the law is mature in this area. The subject is well covered in the literature and court decisions, and only an informational summary will be given here.

EMPLOYER DUTY TO BARGAIN

The union is certified by the NLRB as the bargaining representative of the employees. The first real contact that the employer has with the union is the request to meet for the purpose of bargaining over wages and working conditions. The usual procedure is for the union to make several proposals to be put into a written agreement between the union and the company.[3] Under the act, the company must meet with the union for the purpose of collective bargaining, but they do not have to agree to the laundry list the union presents. Section 8(d) of the act requires only that both parties bargain in good faith and have a sincere purpose to reach an agreement.[4]

Bad Faith Bargaining

Where there is evidence that the employer has no intention of reaching any agreement, the union can file an unfair labor practice charge. If it is found that the employer or union was not bargaining in bad faith, the board can issue a cease-and-desist order to require the parties to bargain in good faith.

Bad faith bargaining is most likely to occur when the initial contract is being negotiated. Often the employer, who is still trying to recover from

---

[1]There are other differences. In a union facility, the discharge rate is lower (0.9 percent of total employment in a union facility and 1.8 percent in a nonunion facility), and the absentee rate is higher (4.2 percent for nonunion and 4.5 percent for union firms). For other nonwage effects of unions, see Lloyd G. Reynolds, Stanley H. Masters, and Colletta H. Moser, *Labor Economics and Labor Relations,* 9th ed. (Englewood Cliffs, NJ: Prentice Hall, 1986), p. 590.

[2]For research on collective bargaining and labor relations, see John A. Fossum, *Labor Relations, Development, Structure, Process,* 3rd ed. (Plano, TX: Business Publications, Inc., 1985).

[3]At these initial bargaining sessions most union proposals are the promises that the union made during the campaign of what it would force the employer to do if the employees voted for it.

[4]*Air Line Pilots Association* v. *O'Neil,* 111 S.Ct. 1127 (1991). Also see S. Estreicher, "Collective Bargaining v. Collective Begging," *Michigan Law Review,* 93 (1994), 511.

the shock of loss of the representation election, will be reluctant to increase conditions.

The employer goes to the bargaining table with the objective of giving as little as possible. Management hopes that employees will realize how little the union can do for them and vote the union out the following year.[5] The employees may stop paying dues (if the new labor agreement permits it). They may realize that the dues they have to pay are not worth what they get.

It takes a skillful negotiator to give nothing or very little and not be charged with bad faith bargaining (this is sometimes called surface bargaining). Often there is a fine line between bad faith bargaining and saying no. There is no legal definition of bad faith bargaining, because the board relies on a case-by-case basis for its decisions.[6] What the board looks at is the total conduct of the parties at the bargaining table. This requires a subjective evaluation by the board or the courts of the parties' attitude toward intent to reach an agreement. It is difficult to sustain a surface bargaining charge. One party must be totally arbitrary for the court to find surface bargaining.

Unilateral Action as Bad Faith Bargaining. Where a union is certified by the board, the employer is required by law to deal exclusively with that union as a bargaining agent for the employees. Sometimes an employer would like to give a superior employee an extra bonus or wages above the contract rate. If this is done without the union's consent, it is bad faith bargaining. The rule in plain language is "no side deals" with union-represented employees.

Other conduct that supports a strong inference of bad faith bargaining is failing to give management representatives sufficient authority to bind the employer, refusal to sign an agreement already reached, withdrawal of concessions previously granted, and delaying tactics. (These are difficult to stop or prove.) One of the problems of the board in bad faith bargaining cases is that

the only remedy for the unfair labor practice is a cease-and-desist order. That is not much liability if the employer is found guilty of bad faith bargaining. The board tried to remedy this in a situation where the employer engaged in flagrant bad faith bargaining. One of the union's demands was a union shop.[7] The board in an attempt to remedy the violation ordered the company to include a union shop provision in the agreement. The Supreme Court said that such action was going beyond the intent and scope of the act. Congress never intended to give the board power to compel a union or the employer to agree on any contract provision.[8]

Bad faith or surface bargaining complaints usually come before the board when the employees do not want to strike but the company will not accede to their demands.[9] The union hopes that they will be in a better position after the company is found guilty of an unfair labor practice.[10] The union leadership reasons that the employees might be willing to strike or the employer will accede to a few more demands after being found guilty.[11]

Regulation of the Bargaining Process

The refusal to bargain, by either party, over certain subjects is one of the most common reasons for bad-faith-bargaining charges. Usually the union files the charges—the more bargainable subjects, the more gains for the union. If the employer refuses to bargain and it is a non-

---

[5]Under board rules, an election to decertify the union cannot be held until one year after the first election.

[6]In *Air Line Pilots Association* v. *O'Neil,* 111 S.Ct. 1127 (1991), the union was charged with bad faith bargaining, and the Court upheld it. This was also a fair representation case.

[7]Union shop is a contract provision that requires all new employees to become members of the union within a certain period after hiring, usually 30 days. It also requires all present employees to become and remain members of the union.

[8]*H. K. Porter Co.* v. *NLRB,* 397 U.S. 99 (1970).

[9]Employer's bargaining position was not bad faith bargaining: *Cincinnati Newspaper Guild* v. *NLRB,* 938 F.2d 284 (D.C. Cir. 1991).

[10]When the employer is found guilty of an unfair labor practice, the board requires that a notice be put on the bulletin board that the employer has been found guilty to reassure the employees that in the future the firm will follow the law.

[11]This situation reaffirms what the employer should have told the employees before the election: The union can make all the promises that it wants, but the employer has to agree before any benefits are granted.

bargainable issue, the union does not have the right to strike over it.

The NLRA names certain subjects as mandatory subjects of bargaining, such as wages and working conditions.[12] Refusal to bargain over these subjects is a per se violation.[13] Where mandatory subjects of bargaining are involved, the court does not consider the attitude of the parties. The parties are required by statute to bargain over these subjects.

Questionable Mandatory Bargaining Topics

Other bargaining topics are not so clear-cut under Section 8(d). The NLRB or the courts must decide whether a particular subject at issue is a working condition or a management right.

The board has established certain guidelines in questionable areas. If the action taken by the company results in an economic impact on the employees involved, it is a bargainable subject. This topic comes up regularly in a situation where the company wants to contract work out to a third party rather than have the employees do it. The labor agreement is usually silent on this right.

A company contracted maintenance work out to another company and laid off employees in the maintenance department. The Court held that contracting out was a subject that the firm had to discuss with the union.[14] If the contracting out had not resulted in the layoff of employees, the results would have been different.

The economic impact rule is not always followed where certain subjects are traditionally management prerogatives. Where a company for economic reasons closed part of its operation, the court held that the employer was required to bargain about the effect of the decision on the employees but not the decision itself.[15] The court

reasoned that the economic burden placed on the employer in continuing the operation outweighed a benefit gained over labor management relations by the bargaining process. It would be a violation of the WARN Act. Under the Worker Adjustment and Retraining Act (WARN; 29 U.S.C. Sect. 2101 et seq.) the employer must give 60 days notice to employees and governmental agencies before closing the plant and laying off employees.

The board extended the balancing test analysis to a situation where the employer would transfer or relocate bargaining unit work to a nonunion facility during the term of the contract. The board held that this was not unlawful if the employer satisfied the obligation to bargain under the contract (the contract was silent on the issue). If the parties were bargaining over the relocation, the only requirement before relocating was that the parties had to be at an impasse in bargaining before the employer could relocate.

But, where a company subsidized in-plant food services by an independent caterer, the Court held the company must bargain over prices. The Court affirmed the board's position that food services are "terms and conditions of employment" under Section 8(d) of the act. If the employer had not subsidized the food services, it would probably not have had to bargain over prices. A subsidy is a benefit to the employees and price affects the amount of the subsidy; therefore, it is a working condition.[16]

Another frequent issue is in the benefit area, such as Christmas bonuses or turkeys at Christmastime. This situation arises where the company has a profitable year; it gives a Christmas present to the employees (turkey, ham, fruit). Next year profits are down so the firm decides not to do it. The general rule in this case is that if the benefits are intermittently given with no consistency, they are considered gifts. If they are unilaterally skipped after consistently being given, regardless of conditions, the courts reason that they are compensation that must be bargained over.[17] Where turkeys and hams were discontinued without bargaining with the union, the board held

---

[12]Section 8(d).

[13]*Per se* as used in legal context means taken by itself, it constitutes a violation (*Black's Dictionary of Law*, 6th ed., 1990).

[14]*Fibreboard Paper Products Corp.* v. *NLRB*, 379 U.S. 203 (1964).

[15]The employer may relocate the whole plant if certain conditions exist: Dubuque Packing Co., 303 NLRB 386 No. 66 (1991).

[16]*Ford Motor Co.* v. *NLRB*, 441 U.S. 488 (1979).

[17]*NLRB* v. *Wonder State Mfg. Co.*, 344 F.2d 210 (8th Cir. 1965).

that they were too minimal to be considered wages. In other cases benefits may not be, depending upon their monetary value.[18]

Whether a particular subject is bargainable or not is important to the parties. For this reason the board and the courts hear a reasonable number of these cases. The company does not have to agree that a subject is bargainable, but the union can legally strike over a bargainable demand.

Once the employer consistently grants a benefit like a Christmas bonus, it may not be able to stop the benefit. Although this additional compensation was not bargained for by the union, the union can bargain over taking it away.[19]

Union Security Clauses in Collective Bargaining Agreements. After a union has been certified as the collective bargaining representative, one of the first bargaining demands of the union is a security clause. These clauses, according to the union, are necessary to support the cost of the bargaining and otherwise representing the employees. It is a form of compulsory unionism or financial support that the employer must agree to before the collective bargaining agreement can be enforced. There are primarily six types of union security clauses:

1. Closed Shop. This requires union membership as a precondition of employment and to continue membership as a condition of maintaining employment. The NLRA as amended by the Taft-Hartley Act no longer permits the closed shop [29 U.S.C. Sect. 158(a)(3)], except in a hiring hall situation.

2. Union Shop. This clause requires all new employees to become members of the union within a certain period of time (usually 30 days after hire, except in the construction industry, where it is 7 days after hire). They must remain members until the expiration of the labor contract. Under a union shop agreement,

an employee may be omitted only when membership is available under the same conditions as other employees. Under this clause an employee can refuse to become a member of the union for religious reasons. If the union expels her or him or refuses membership, the employee cannot be discharged as long as dues are tendered. As nonmembers, such employees cannot be discriminated against, but are not permitted to vote on ratification of the labor agreement to which they will be bound. The state can prohibit unionship; this is called a right to work state.

3. Modified Union Shop. Those who are employees at the time of agreement do not have to become members, but all new employees do. Also, under Section 14(b) of the NLRA, states are permitted by statute to prohibit union shop clauses. More than 20 states have such statutes.

4. Maintenance of Membership. This requires all members of the bargaining unit who are members at a specified time to remain members. If they later become members, they must maintain their membership for the duration of the contract. Those employees who are members of the union at the time of the certification have an escape period (usually from 15 to 30 days after the agreement takes effect) to resign.

5. Agency Shop. An agency shop agreement requires all employees in the bargaining unit to pay regular dues and initiation fees, but they do not have to become members of the union.

6. Hiring Hall. Section 8(f) of the NLRA permits the use of a hiring hall agreement in building and construction trades. Union control over employment referral requires union membership as a precondition to being referred. This is tantamount to a closed shop, but lawful only in the construction industry.

ENFORCEMENT OF A COLLECTIVE BARGAINING AGREEMENT

Some employers believe that they have the sole discretion in making a decision except where restricted by the labor agreement.[20] The employer's belief is based on the theory that the firm may

---

[18]Benchmark Industries, 270 NLRB 22 (1984).

[19]For further references and details on the employer's duty to bargain, see Leonard E. Cohen, "The Duty to Bargain over Plant Relocations and Other Corporate Changes: Otis Elevator v. NLRB," *The Labor Lawyer,* 1 no. 3 (Summer 1985); "Proceedings of the Industrial Relations Research Association, Spring 1985 Meeting," *Labor Law Journal,* 36, no. 8 (August 1985); Brian K. Brittain and Brian P. Heshizer, "Management Decision Bargaining: The Interplay of Law and Politics," *Labor Law Journal,* 38, no. 4 (April 1987), 220.

[20]W.M. Green, "Negotiating the Future: The NLRA Paradigm and the Prospects for Law Reform," *Ohio Northern University Law Review,* 21 (1994), 417.

retain everything that it did not specifically give away in the bargaining process. If the agreement is silent about a particular subject or practice, under this theory, management has the right to act without interference from the union.

In 1960 three cases, called the Steelworkers Trilogy, went to the Supreme Court.[21] In all three cases the issue was whether the company had to arbitrate an issue not covered in the labor agreement. The Supreme Court said a labor agreement cannot cover every situation. The employee has certain rights not specifically stated in the labor agreement by virtue of the employer-employee relationship. This became known as the common-law-of-the-shop theory. This was expanded by arbitrators into the past practice rule of labor agreements. This rule usually applies in arbitration cases where a clause is ambiguous or the agreement is silent on a particular practice. The rule as followed by most arbitrators is that a past practice is a part of the contract unless the contract clearly states otherwise.[22]

The courts have continued to follow the Steelworkers Trilogy cases and have said that a past practice is an integral part of the contract.[23] The past practice concept has been followed into nonunion situations. In discrimination cases the court or agency looks to past practice to determine whether members of the protected class are treated differently.

Changing a Past Practice

If a union employer were to change a past practice, it would be a bargainable issue. If the practice is contrary in clear language to the labor agreement, the agreement controls. If the appropriate clause in the labor agreement is

ambiguous, then a past practice controls until changed by bargaining.

Sometimes a nonunion employer will have an immediate problem caused by a previous practice. If the practice is followed, a serious economic or employee relations problem will result. It is a mistake for the employer to change the practice when confronted with a problem. If the employee involved is a member of the protected class, the change may result in an exposure to a lawsuit. It also may invite union organization.

The nonunion employer is well advised not to apply the past practice to the situation at hand and bite the bullet but give notice effective on a certain date that the practice will no longer be followed.

Duty of Union to Represent Employees

One right that a union employee has that a nonunion employee does not have is to enforce the collective bargaining agreement. The Supreme Court has interpreted Section 301 of the act to mean that the individual rights of an employee under a collective bargaining agreement can be enforced in the courts and even union bylaws can be enforced. Suits can be brought by the union on behalf of the employees or by individual employees against the union or the employer. The employer can also sue the union.[24]

Employees can sue their union when the union does not enforce the contract against the employer. These are called fair representation cases.[25]

In a leading case, several over-the-road drivers were discharged for falsifying their expense account. Their grievance was denied before a joint labor-management arbitration committee. The employees as individuals sued the union and the employer. The basis of their suit was that the charges of dishonesty were false and that the union made no effort to investigate to determine the real facts. The court held that this was a breach of the

---

[21]*United Steelworkers of America* v. *Warrior and Gulf Navigation Co.*, 363 U.S. 574; *United Steelworkers of America* v. *Enterprise Wheel and Car Corp.*, 363 U.S. 593; *United Steelworkers of America* v. *American Mfg. Co.*, 363 U.S. 564 (1960).

[22]For discussion of past practice in arbitration, see Frank Elkouri and Edna Elkouri, *How Arbitration Works,* 4th ed. and 1985–1987 supplement. (Washington, DC: Bureau of National Affairs, 1985), chap. 12.

[23]*Norfolk Ship Building Corp.* v. *Local 684,* 671 F.2d 797 (4th Cir. 1982).

[24]In *W. R. Grace* v. *Rubber Works Local 759,* 103 S.Ct. 2177 (1983), the Court held the contract could be enforced through arbitration even though management and the EEOC had made a settlement to the contrary. The issue was over seniority.

[25]Right does not expand to arbitration. *Garcia* v. *Zenith Electronic Corp.*, 149 LRRM 2746.

union's duty to represent the employees adequately under the collective bargaining agreement.[26] If it can be shown that the union's failure to process a grievance was unlawful, the union would be liable to the employees for any resulting loss.

The union owes a duty to represent the employees. This duty has been relaxed by the *O'Neil* case.[27] How much it has been relaxed is settled on a case-by-case basis. Unions are taking fewer cases to arbitration. There has been less fear of an unfair representation charge from a member since the *O'Neil* case. Also the courts say that unions cannot withhold information in a litigation hearing.[28]

Employee Rights Under the *Weingarten* Doctrine

The court in *NLRB* v. *J. Weingarten, Inc.*, 420 U.S. 251 (1975), expanded the rights of employees as provided by Section 7 of the NLRA. The Court reasoned that the employee who reasonably believes an investigatory interview will result in disciplinary action is seeking "aid and protection" against a perceived threat to his or her employment security. According to the Supreme Court, four conditions must exist:

1. The employee must request a representative. Employee silence is a waiver.[29]

2. The employee's right to request representation as a condition of participation in an interview is limited to where the employee reasonably believes the investigation will result in some kind of disciplinary action. (This would include a mere warning.)

3. The exercise of the right may not interfere with legitimate employer prerogatives. This means that management's investigative process can't be interfered with. Management determines the rules of the interview process but must permit a representative to be present.[30]

4. The employer has no duty to bargain with the representative who is attending the interview. However, the representative has the right to participate in the interview. The employee may consult with his or her representative prior to and during the meeting.[31]

Litigation over whether the doctrine applies is a useless exercise. The same result can be obtained by other investigative means. The employer can cancel the interview at any time and make a decision on the available facts or continue to investigate by other methods. There has been considerable litigation as to the remedy when a violation is found. The majority rule is that reinstatement is allowed only when a prima facie case for reinstatement can be established. If concerted activities are not present, there can be no reinstatement. If these reinstatement requirements do not exist, then a cease-and-desist order is the proper remedy for a violation. If the employee would have been discharged for just cause, there can be no reinstatement, even though the doctrine was violated.[32] This makes a *Weingarten* case less important. The violation of the doctrine does not have serious consequences. Under the labor agreement there would be more serious problems than violation of the doctrine if the employee was not discharged for just cause.

---

[26]*Hines* v. *Anchor Motor Freight, Inc.*, 424 U.S. 554 (1976); also *Bowen* v. *U.S. Postal Service*, 103 S.Ct. 588 (1983). The author had a related experience. He found 25 maintenance employees drinking in the local bar. He recommended discharging five of the least productive workers. The union objected, because there were others in the bar. The author told the union that if they would disclose the names, he would discharge them too. This was the end of the grievance because the union did not want to investigate further. In this situation the *Hines* case would apply for the five workers discharged.

[27]In *Air Line Pilots Association* v. *O'Neil*, 111 S.Ct. 1127 (1991), the Court said that the union must be totally emotional and arbitrary to be in violation of a duty of fair representation.

Under this ruling it is not certain whether the *Hines* case is still law.

[28]*Achilli* v. *John J. Nissen Baking Co.* 989 F.2d 561 (D.C. Cir. 1993).

[29]*Prudential Insurance Co.* v. *NLRB*, 661 F.2d 398 (5th Cir. 1981).

[30]Manville Forest Products Corp., 269 NLRB No. 72 (1984).

[31]For the role of union representatives in employee disciplinary interviews, see *N.J. Bell Telephone* v. *Local 827 IBEW*, 308 NLRB 32 (1992).

[32]This was first decided by the board in Taracorp Industries, 273 NLRB No. 54 (1984) and reaffirmed in *Communication Workers of America* v. *NLRB*, 784 F.2d 847 (7th Cir. 1986).

Extension of Doctrine to Nonunion Employees. The board originally took the position that the doctrine does apply to nonunion employees. The board states that this would be contrary to the exclusivity principles of the NLRA. In other nonunion situations the exclusivity principle is not applied. The court in *Slaughter* v. *NLRB,* 876 F.2d 11 (3rd. Cir. 1989), agreed with the board and enforced the board's order.

The employer who refuses representation to a nonunion employee could have considerable exposure to litigation. The best policy would be to allow the representation under the conditions of the *Weingarten* doctrine or not have the interview at all. To trigger litigation over a matter that can be resolved by some other means would seem not to be the most advisable approach.

RESTRAINTS ON THE RIGHT TO STRIKE

None of the parties to a labor dispute likes a strike. The consequences fall most heavily upon the union members and the company. For this reason there is a built-in incentive for the negotiators to avoid strikes. Management does not like the loss of revenues, customers, market share of their products, or community goodwill that results from a strike. Likewise, unions and workers do not take lightly the loss of wages and benefits, the family problems, and the poor public image that may result from the strike.

Because of the consequences of a strike, it is the threat of a strike that forces concessions and compromise in the negotiation process. Often more is gained by the threat than by engaging in the strike. The right to strike under the NLRA, as opposed to the threat, is used very sparingly. From 1971 to 1980, 2.6 percent of the workers in the United States were involved in a strike. In 1991 the number of strikes involving 1,000 or more workers was only 69 in 1994.[33] The state of the

economy is not the only factor affecting the frequency of strikes; economic strength and tactics by either side to force a compromise or an agreement also play a leading role.

Use of Strike Replacements

The law permits the employer to operate during a strike by the use of replacements.[34] The replaced strikers are placed upon the preferential hiring list.[35] After they have communicated an unconditional request for reinstatement, they are entitled to receive their jobs back or substantially equivalent work as a vacancy occurs. The employer must recall all qualified strikers on the preferential hiring list before hiring new employees to fill vacancies.[36] Subsequent to the *Mackay Radio* case, the main issue at the bargaining table was what to do with the replacements after the strike was settled. A condition of the union for a settlement was to terminate the "scabs." Often the employer would agree,[37] reinstate the strikers, and terminate the replacements.

Belknap v. *Hale*

In the leading case of *Belknap, Inc.* v. *Hale,* 463 U.S. 491 (1983), the Supreme Court allowed the terminated replacements to bring a cause of action in a state court if they were promised permanent jobs when hired as strike replacements.

This ruling opened the door for the employer to offer permanent jobs during the strike that could not be changed through bargaining. *Belknap* applies only where the replacements have been clearly offered permanent jobs. This gave the

---

[33]See *Monthly Labor Review,* U.S. Department of Labor, Bureau of Labor Statistics. See current issue for years after 1991.

[34]*NLRB* v. *Mackay Radio & Tel. Co.,* 304 U.S. 333 (1938). Also see L. Bierman, and R. Gely, "Striker Replacement Law, Economics and Negotiation Approval," *California Law Review,* 685 (1995), 363.

[35]The right does not deny the employees their jobs if they haven't been replaced. This would take away their jobs because they went on strike: *American Linen Supply Co.* v. *NLRB,* 945 F.2d 1428 (8th Cir. 1991).

[36]*NLRB* v. *Fleetwood Trailer Co.,* 389 U.S. 375 (1967); Laidlaw Corp., 171 NLRB 1366 (1968) enf'd 414 F.2d 99 (7th Cir. 1969), cert. denied, 397 U.S. 920 (1970).

[37]M. LeRoy, "Employer Treatment of Permanent Replacements," *Yale Law and Policy Review,* 13 (1995).

employer a strong bargaining position before the strike. The union would threaten a strike and the employer would say, "Go ahead and we will hire permanent replacements." The threat of replacements to sue for breach of contract is assigned great weight by union negotiators. Union members, knowing they may not get their jobs back, are reluctant to strike.

The use of replacements has for years been seen by the employer as not being effective. The *Belknap* decision is now used as a threat in bargaining that can be carried out. Business is also discovering that an increasing number of employees will cross the picket line rather than lose their jobs to replacements.[38] Further, the employer is discovering that replacements can be trained in a short time for skilled jobs.

To further strengthen the employer's bargaining position, one court has held that replacements can be used for a legal lockout.[39] The lockout itself was not antiunion and it was not destructive of employee rights as long as no antiunion action was taken. Strikers on a preferential hiring list do not retain their seniority when they return to work. They cannot be placed above the employees who refused to strike.[40] The use of replacements does not mean that the union has lost its majority status.[41] The board has reaffirmed its position that when in doubt about the union's majority status, the employer can take a poll to find out. This poll can be taken even when the employer has no objective evidence to justify withdrawal of recognition.[42]

Often when union members return to work during the strike, the union will invoke provisions of the union constitution and fine the members. To avoid this, members crossing the picket line give notice to the union that they wish to be "financial core" members. The board in Carpenters Local

470, 277 NLRB No. 20 (1985), held that this was lawful as long as the dues were tendered. They could return to work without being fined.[43] A union member has the right to resign, although a strike has begun and a collective bargaining agreement doesn't provide for it.

The use of replacements will be a continuing employer response to the strike threat. When a strike occurs, the permanent replacements will be effective in bringing striking workers back to the job. As one replacement said to a picket, "If you don't want your job, I do." This means that the use of a strike to force economic demands has diminishing effectiveness.

The effectiveness of a strike has diminished and the right to appeal to the public has also diminished.

Restrictions on Strikers' Conduct

The right to picket during a strike is protected by the act, although the act does not expressly say so. It is inferred from the right to engage in concerted activities or other mutual aid and protection under Section 7. This right is conditional. The strike must be lawful and picketing must be peaceful.[44]

Picketing in an unlawful strike will result in the strikers losing their employment status. They will not have the right of recall when the strike is over. An unlawful strike would be picketing for a closed shop, a secondary boycott, or for the purpose of inducing the employer to enter into a "feather-bedding" arrangement.

Violence can also result in denial of reinstatement rights. Violence during a strike can take several forms other than physical contact. Insulting language directed at the employer (a threat like "I am going to kill you") has been held to be violence and a reason to deny reinstatement.[45] Verbal threats to a nonstriker that his

[38]The McDonnell Douglas and Hormel strikes and strikes in the airline industry are good examples.

[39]In *Local 825 Operating Engineers* v. *NLRB,* 829 F.2d 458 (3rd Cir. 1987).

[40]*Trans World Airlines* v. *Independent Federation of Flight Attendants,* 109 S.Ct. 1225 (1989).

[41]*NLRB* v. *Cortin-Matheson Scientific,* 110 S.Ct. 1542 (1990).

[42]Texas Petrochemicals Corp., 296 NLRB 136 (1989), rem. and mod. 923 F.2d 398 (5th Cir. 1991).

[43]*NLRB* v. *Local 54 Hotel and Restaurant Employees,* 887 F.2d 28 (3rd Cir. 1989).

[44]In *General Indust. Empl. Union Local 422* v. *NLRB,* 951 F.2d 1308 (D.C. Cir. 1991), an unlawful strike was converted into an economic strike.

[45]Clear Pine Mouldings, Inc., 268 NLRB No. 173 (1984).

family will be harmed are sufficient to deny reinstatement.[46]

It is not necessary to be an employee of the facility being picketed. Section 2(9) of the act defines a labor dispute to include "any controversy regardless of whether the person stands in proximate relation of employer and employee." This means that a union can hire professional pickets if it so desires. As a practical matter usually the pickets are either employees or members of the union employed elsewhere.

Enforcement of a No-Strike Clause

The law permits the employee to enforce the labor agreement against the union and the employer.[47]

It also permits the union to sue the employer or the employer to sue to enforce the labor agreement.

Enforcement of Labor Agreement

The employer's enforcement of a labor agreement against a union is most common, where the union authorizes a strike in violation of a no-strike clause. Labor unions can enforce an agreement against the employer by starting a lawsuit in federal court. Previous to *Groves* v. *Ring Screw Works, Ferndale Fastener Div.,* 111 S.Ct. 498 (1990), the only way the union could enforce a labor agreement was to go on strike. Under the Norris-La Guardia Act of 1932, the courts are prohibited from granting injunctions for strike activity. But where there is a no-strike clause, the question is whether it can be enforced in view of the Norris-La Guardia Act. Until 1970 no-strike clauses could not be enforced because the Supreme Court held that the Norris-La Guardia Act superseded the contractual no-strike clause.

However, in certain situations the court partially reversed itself; it held that a no-strike clause can be enforced provided the labor agreement contains a mandatory grievance adjustment or arbitration clause. The court

reasoned that a no-strike clause is a trade-off for an arbitration clause; therefore, the union must arbitrate rather than go on strike.[48] In subsequent cases the court has made it clear that the presence of an arbitration clause is a prerequisite to issuing an injunction to enforce a no-strike clause.

Where employees went on strike in sympathy with other employees from another company, the court held that such a strike could not be enjoined. The strike was not over a dispute of the employer in the labor agreement but in support of others not subject to arbitration.[49] This case reaffirms the court's position in the *Boys Market* case that the decision is narrow. The Norris-La Guardia Act is by no means dead.

USE OF ARBITRATION IN DISPUTE RESOLUTION

The courts and Congress have stated that arbitration is a preferred method to settle disputes under a labor agreement. It is a federal policy to encourage the inclusion of grievance and arbitration clauses in the collective bargaining agreements.[50] The judicial policy of favoring arbitration in the resolution of labor disputes was first outlined in the three landmark decisions of the Supreme Court previously cited. They are frequently referred to as the Steelworkers Trilogy. In one case the court compelled arbitration where the arbitration clause in the contract did not relate to the particular grievance.[51] In the second case the court held that the NLRA made arbitration awards enforceable in the courts.[52] In the third case the court compelled arbitration of a dispute although

---

[46]*Newport News Shipbuilding and Dry Dock Co.* v. *NLRB,* 738 F.2d 1404 (4th Cir. 1984).

[47]*Sinclair Refining Co.* v. *Atkinson,* 370 U.S. 195 (1962).

[48]*Boys Market* v. *Retail Clerks Union,* 398 U.S. 235 (1970).

[49]*Buffalo Forge Co.* v. *United Steelworkers of America,* 428 U.S. 397 (1976). This was a 5-4 decision.

[50]Ninety-five percent of all labor agreements contain arbitration clauses. Over 50 percent of arbitration cases are related to discharge.

[51]*United Steelworkers of America* v. *Warrior and Gulf Navigation Co.,* 363 U.S. 574 (1960).

[52]*United Steelworkers of America* v. *Enterprise Wheel and Car Corp.,* 363 U.S. 593 (1960).

there was no arbitration clause in the collective bargaining agreement.[53]

The *Collyer* Doctrine of Referral to Arbitration

The right to arbitrate a dispute arises only from an agreement between the employee representative and the employer.[54] The board takes the position that whenever possible it will refer to arbitration, providing the parties agree to arbitrate and the interpretation of the contract is the basis of the dispute. This is commonly known as the *Collyer* doctrine from the board decision in Collyer Insulated Wire, 192 NLRB No. 150 (1971). The board later took the position that it would defer all cases to arbitration that could be settled under the labor agreement. The board cannot defer all disputes to arbitration under the *Collyer* doctrine. The issue must pertain to the interpretation of the labor agreement and cannot involve an unfair labor practice.[55]

Whenever possible, the employer should assert the *Collyer* doctrine. Arbitration is faster than going to court and much more economical. By referring it to arbitration, often the dispute is resolved without any arbitration, because one or the other party may feel it is better to settle than to arbitrate. It is doubtful that the union will file with the board unless they cannot resolve the dispute by some other means.

Determination of Arbitrability of a Dispute

Sometimes the dispute is over whether the contract requires the issue to be arbitrated.[56] The logical solution is to let the arbitrator decide the arbitrability of the dispute. The Supreme Court, relying upon the Steelworkers Trilogy cases, said that it was up to the courts, not the arbitrator, to determine whether an issue should be arbitrated.[57] The court stated that it is a judicial question whether the parties have ever agreed to arbitrate the issue.[58] Most agreements state that "all issues over the interpretation of this agreement must be submitted to arbitration." This statement makes it advisable for the parties to be more specific in the collective bargaining agreement on what is and what is not subject to arbitration. Under the *AT&T* case failure to do so will only result in litigation.

Enforcement of Arbitration Awards

Arbitration is not judicial process. There are no standard rules of evidence or procedure, and one arbitrator is not bound by another's decision. Most arbitrators ignore previous decisions of others except to justify a position they have already taken. Reliance on prior decisions could reflect on the arbitrator's ability to decide the case on its merits.

Arbitration awards have no bearing on the employee's right to sue under a statute. The court takes the position that an arbitrator's specialized competence pertains primarily to the "law of the shop and not the law of the land."[59]

The law enters into arbitration only when the award is challenged in the courts.[60] Arbitration awards are challenged by either party because of:

1. Fraud, misconduct, or gross unfairness by the arbitrator (rare)

---

[53] *United Steelworkers of America* v. *American Mfg. Co.,* 363 U.S. 564 (1960).

[54] If the contract has expired, the dispute must arise out of the expired contract to arbitrate: *Litton Financial Printing Division* v. *NLRB,* 111 S.Ct. 2215 (1991). See also R. Schupp, "When Is a Contract Not a Contract?" *Labor Law Journal,* 43, no. 4 (April 1992), 239.

[55] *Hammon Tree* v. *NLRB,* 925 F.2d 1488 (D.C. Cir. 1991).

[56] If an arbitrator acts as mediator after arbitration fails, there must be an agreement beforehand. See N. Nelson and M. Uddin, "Arbitrators as Mediators," *Labor Law Journal* (April 1993).

[57] *AT&T Technologies, Inc.* v. *Communication Workers of America et al.,* 106 S.Ct. 1415 (1986).

[58] In *Bender* v. *A.G. Edwards & Sons,* 971 F.2d 698 (11th Cir. 1992), the court held that Title VII claims are subject to compulsory arbitration under the Federal Arbitration Act. Also see *First Options of Chicago, Inc.* v. *Manual Caplan,* 72 F.3d 1920 (7th Cir. 1995).

[59] *Alexander* v. *Gardner-Denver,* 94 S.Ct. 1101 (1974). Also Frank Elkouri and Edna Elkouri, *How Arbitration Works,* 4th ed. (Washington, DC: Bureau of National Affairs, 1985); also 1991 supplement.

[60] P. Fecille, Micheal Le Ray, and Timony Chandler, "Judicial Review in Arbitration Awards," *Labor Law Journal,* 41 no. 8 (August 1990), 477.

2. Fraud by one of the parties affecting the result (very rare)
3. Failure of the arbitrator to stay within the contract (or arbitrator exceeds his or her authority)
4. Violation of public policy of the award (used quite often)

Normally the courts are reluctant to reverse arbitration awards. Arbitration is a nationally recognized method to settle labor disputes. The parties have agreed that the award will be final and binding.

The three most compelling reasons to overturn an award are (1) the arbitrator exceeds his or her authority under the labor agreement,[61] (2) the award is contrary to the clear language of the contract, and (3) contrary to public policy.

Overturning of Awards by Courts

The Supreme Court, referring to the arbitrator, stated in *United Steelworkers* v. *Enterprise Wheel,* 363 U.S. 593 (1960), "He may, of course, look for guidance from many sources, yet his award is legitimate only so long as it draws its essence from the collective bargaining agreement."[62]

The Court said there was no authority in the contract that permits rehiring of workers with unsatisfactory work records. The Court further stated that the arbitrator exceeded his authority under the agreement, "although the interpretation of the contract is none of our business." [63]

Another reason for overturning an arbitration award is the arbitrator's substituting his judgment for that of the parties to the contract. This often happens when the contract limits the right to challenge a disciplinary action after the facts are determined. In *Riceland Foods* v. *Carpenters Local 2381,* 737 F.2d 758 (8th Cir. 1984), the arbitrator unlawfully mitigated the discipline for a rule violation. The contract said that the arbitrator

was limited to determining if the rule had been violated and not if the discipline was proper.[64]

Violation of public policy is another reason the courts will not enforce an arbitration award. In *W.R. Grace and Co.* v. *Rubber Workers Local 759,* 103 S.Ct. 2177 (1983),[65] the Supreme Court stated that the courts may not enforce any collective bargaining agreement that is contrary to public policy. Because public policy is a vague term, it is often difficult to determine what is contrary to public policy. Awards have been vacated as being contrary to public policy where a truck driver was reinstated despite the fact that his discharge had been for drinking on the job.[66] The award was held to be contrary to public policy where an employee was found guilty of graft. The arbitrator held that discharge was not for just cause because he agreed to pay money back.[67] In another case the award was contrary to the principles of labor law.[68]

In *United Paper Workers* v. *Misco,* 108 S.Ct. 363 (1987), the Court agreed with the arbitrator that there were insufficient facts to warrant a discharge. The arbitrator should not be second-guessed by the courts. To find a public policy reason for setting aside the award, it must be shown that a clear and explicit public policy exists. A generalized notion of a public interest is not a reason for vacating an award.[69] In many situations it is difficult to show that a clear and explicit public policy exists. One court said, "we will tell you it is a violation when it is violated." From the subsequent case law it appears that the Supreme Court will look favorably on challenges to arbitration awards where a clear and explicit public policy exists. In *Newsday* v. *Long Island*

---

[61]*APP Parts Co.* v. *Auto Workers,* 923 F.2d 486 (7th Cir. 1991).

[62]More than 74 percent of the appeals involve claims that the arbitrator erred under the agreement.

[63]*Miller Brewing Co.* v. *Brewery Workers,* 739 F.2d 1159 (7th Cir. 1984).

[64]See also *Devine* v. *Pastre,* 732 F.2d 213 (D.C. Cir. 1984); *Morgan Services* v. *Local 323 of Amalgamated Clothing Textile Workers,* 724 F.2d 1217 (6th Cir. 1984).

[65]Also *First Options of Chicago, Inc.* v. *Caplan,* (6th Cir. 1994).

[66]*Meatcutters Local 540* v. *Great Western Food Co.,* 712 F.2d 122 (5th Cir. 1983).

[67]*U.S. Postal Service* v. *Postal Workers,* 736 F.2d 822 (1st Cir. 1984).

[68]*Carpenters Local 1478* v. *Stevens,* 743 F.2d 1271 (9th Cir. 1984).

[69]In *Stead Motors of Walnut Creek* v. *Automobile Machinist Lodge No. 1173,* 886 F.2d 200 (9th Cir. 1989), the court held there was not a clear public policy for failure to tighten bolts on front wheels, although a state statute was violated.

EXHIBIT 19-1 *Suggested Clause to Limit Arbitrator's Authority in Discharge*

The following offenses are deemed sufficient cause for discharge, and are subject to arbitration only to determine the facts of whether the offense was committed. Once facts are established the discharge can be invoked. [List "sudden death" offenses, such as possession of firearms and drugs, sleeping, and violation of certain safety rules.]

Typographical Union No. 95, 915 F.2d 840 (2nd Cir. 1990), the court held it was contrary to public policy to reinstate an employee guilty of sexual harassment.[70] There must be little doubt that a public policy exists, before the arbitrator as the trier of fact will be interfered with.

After *Misco,* some legal scholars believed that arbitrators' decisions would no longer be overturned for public policy reasons. In many situations it is difficult to show that a clear public policy exists. Over the years court decisions in other areas have been very vague in defining public policy.

Discharge Arbitration

The most common issue in arbitration under the contract is discharge.[71] It is in discharge cases that the arbitrator often goes beyond the labor agreement. This is especially true where those agreements allow the arbitrator only to determine the facts and not determine whether the penalty justifies the offense.

It is desirable for both parties to include in the contract a clause to prevent arbitrators who do not believe in "capital punishment" from exceeding their authority in reinstating the employee.[72] The parties to a labor agreement can put in a clause (Exhibit 19-1) that limits the arbitrator's authority to fact finding only.

"Sudden death" offenses are violations that the employer considers serious. They should be limited to only a few (10 at the most). The employee has been forewarned that if caught committing them she or he will be immediately discharged.[73] For sudden death offenses the arbitrator would have no authority under the labor agreement to reinstate, just to determine the facts.

The union in *S.D. Warren*[74] argued that the case was controlled by the *Misco* decision. This was never an issue. In *Misco,* the company did not specifically reserve the right in the labor agreement to discharge for a rule violation. In this respect, *S.D. Warren* was different.

In *S.D. Warren* the contract allowed the arbitrator only to determine a fact, not provide a remedy. The union is not interested in keeping undesirable persons any more than the company is. Some unions will argue that they will be charged with a fair representation case. Since *O'Neil* this is very unlikely. This type of clause is usually not hard to negotiate, but the company must insist upon it. Politically the union leadership must mildly oppose it.

There is always an exposure that the employee will file a fair representation charge with the NLRB when the decision of the union is not based on a contract clause or its interpretation.

Arbitrators' decisions are difficult to overturn,[75] so the best approach is to limit their authority in the labor agreement. This is often in the collective bargaining agreement and should be a company demand at the next bargaining session.

---

[70]Other circuits agree: *Stroehmann Bakeries, Inc.* v. *Local 776 International Brotherhood of Teamsters,* 969 F.2d 1436 (3rd Cir. 1992); *Chrysler Motors Corp.* v. *International Union, Allied Industrial Workers of America AFL-CIO Local 793,* 959 F.2d 685 (7th Cir. 1992).

[71]Federal Mediation and Conciliation Service, Arbitration Statistics, report that over half of all referrals for a panel are for discharge disputes.

[72]For information on arbitration of discharge cases, see Thomas R. Knight, "Impact of Arbitration on the Administration of Disciplinary Policies," *The Arbitration Journal,* 39, no. 1 (1984), 53.

[73]Discharge language for sudden death offenses is found in chapter 12, Exhibit 12-3.

[74]*S.D. Warren Co.* v. *United Paperworkers' International Union, AFL-CIO,* 846 F.2d 827 (11th Cir. 1988).

[75]The vice president of the union once told the author that he told the members that the employer would never grant a certain demand. The members left it on the list and the employer granted it. Now the vice president never tells members how the employer will react.

It is more common in the late 1990s for the courts to overturn arbitration awards[76] than at any previous time since the Steel Trilogy cases in 1960. Slightly less than half of the awards that were contested in the last two decades have been reversed. There is no reason to believe that this trend will not continue.

PROBLEM-SOLVING BARGAINING

Problem-solving bargaining differs from traditional bargaining in that the parties are not adversaries. The bargaining session begins with "What's your problem" rather than with both sides submitting a long list of demands.

The foregoing pages relate to traditional bargaining. There is nothing illegal about problem-solving bargaining. It would be difficult to prove surface bargaining in problem-solving bargaining when the parties are not adversaries and each side is not maneuvering for position.

In adversary bargaining the union exercises its power to get a bigger piece of the pie, while management gives only the amount needed to prevent a strike. If the price is too high, there is a strike. It then becomes a question of who can take the economic impact the longest.

In the late 1980s and early 1990s this process broke down in some labor-management negotiations.[77] Union membership was declining; concession bargaining was common;[78] union members would not strike for fear of losing their jobs through replacements. Management would implement its last offer, refusing to follow selective provisions of the expired contract. The union would carry on an antimanagement campaign by picketing, sabotage, use of harassment, or use of any other type of pressure to get management back to the bargaining table.

Both parties wanted a change.[79] A spirit of cooperation developed. Interest-oriented, problem-solving, nonadversarial bargaining began on a small scale. This type of bargaining does not work in all companies because a certain bargaining history is necessary.[80]

Those labor-management companies that have tried it, even on a small scale, say it has been successful.[81] It is advisable to start this type of bargaining on a small scale and then expand it if successful. This is another option for labor and management that is similar to Alternative Dispute Resolution.

ALTERNATIVE DISPUTE RESOLUTION

Alternative Dispute Resolution (ADR) is a mechanism similar to mediation,[82] settlement negotiations, fact finding, or a minitrial to resolve a dispute between the parties.

The 1991 Civil Rights Act (Section 118) provides for ADR procedures. The incentives have never been greater to use a procedure to settle a dispute out of court. It is not uncommon for a lawsuit involving a wrongful discharge to cost more than $100,000. With the advent of the CRA91 and ADA there is no doubt that the frequency of lawsuits will increase.

Court decisions have suggested that ADR will be fully accepted by the courts.[83] Judicial attitudes about ADA have changed drastically since *Alexander* v. *Gardner-Denver,* 415 US. 36 (1974). The vast backlog of cases, the lack of arbitrators to resolve statutory claims, and Congress's intent that statutory claims do not have to be resolved in

---

[76]See *Lee* v. *Chica,* 983 F.2d 889 (8th Cir. 1993).

[77]See "The Joint Leadership at Sartell," *Home Companion Publications,* (Dec. 1, 1995), 5.

[78]In 1992 there were about 481 strikes in the United States, compared to 3,111 in 1977.

[79]If the parties didn't play all their cards when they had them, then the other side might get them!

[80]The Federal Mediation and Conciliation Service has started a program called relationship by objective (RBO), a form of problem-solving bargaining. It is patterned after corporate management by objective programs. There is a great demand for the program, and it promises to reduce the bitter and protracted strikes that were common in the 1980s.

[81]Formed a committee called Joint Leadership Teams.

[82]For a good discussion of mediation and settlement, see D. Reder, "Mediation as a Settlement Tool for Employment Disputes," *Labor Law Journal,* 43, no. 9 (September 1992), 602.

[83]*Gilmer* v. *Interstate/Johnson Lane Corp.,* 111 S.Ct. 1647 (1991).

judicial forums are probably the reasons for this change in attitude. A well-drafted ADR procedure is very much in order and can avoid expensive lawsuits. It appears from all the statutes, attitude of the courts, and cost of lawsuits that the time for ADR has come.

There Is Not a Settlement

In any human endeavor there is always possibility of failure. In ADR, if there is no settlement the process will still be worth the effort. If ADR fails, then the parties must go to court to get the matter resolved. After ADR, the issues will be narrowed, the witnesses will be better informed, and there is still the possibility that it can be settled with the judge's help. The negotiation process has been started and the parties probably have made concrete offers. Maybe another ADR method will work, such as a minitrial, after which a better risk analysis may be made. The court proceedings can start from there. Scheduling for the discovery process starts at the unsuccessful meeting. All of the above factors will save management time and legal fees when the parties go to court. The time and money spent on ADR will be returned many times over.

Unions and employers must find some way to avoid delays in getting a dispute resolved, expensive court procedures, and conservation of lawyers' fees and management's time. Mediation of employment-related disputes is one method that is worth a trial.

CHAPTER
20
MANAGEMENT MALPRACTICE

Use of the Term Malpractice
Malpractice in Management
Invasion of Privacy as a Form of Malpractice
Individual Liability When Acting in Behalf of Employer
Failure to Provide a Safe Place to Work
Prevention of Exposure to Malpractice

USE OF THE TERM *MALPRACTICE*

Malpractice in the Professions

The oldest and most common use of the term *malpractice* is in the medical profession where the doctor is negligent in the treatment of the patient. This is usually considered professional conduct that is below what is expected of a doctor,[1] which also includes judgment. The law requires professional competence of a doctor when he or she undertakes to treat a patient.

Malpractice suits are also common in the legal profession.[2] It is malpractice when the client loses rights or is denied monetary recovery because the attorney failed to act. Legal malpractice also occurs when the attorney gives advice without adequate research and such advice adversely affects the client. For example, if the attorney tells a client that she or he does not have a legal basis to sue when upon research the law is clear that there is a remedy, this would be malpractice. If the attorney had used care and researched the problem before advising the client, the advice would be poor judgment.[3] This is not legal malpractice.

Malpractice suits against accountants, consultants, and other professionals are on the increase, but far from approaching the frequency of those in the medical profession. However, attorneys are catching up to doctors in the frequency of lawsuits.

---

[1] Failure to warn patient of violence is not malpractice
[2] See *Dzivbak v. Mott,* 503 N.W.2d 771 (Minn. Ct. 1993).

[3] As a disgusted client said to the lawyer, "Use your judgment. You haven't used much lately, so you ought to have a lot left."

Malpractice in Business Relationships

Management malpractice can be related to business conduct other than the treatment of employees. Customer mistreatment, unethical conduct between competitors, tax fraud, ruthless pricing practices, or fraud in dealing with the public are all examples of management malpractice that doesn't involve the employee.

In one situation a lower court found that malpractice was committed by the clergy. The pastor of a church described heaven to a 24-year-old man as a very nice place. This person had suicidal tendencies. This is a natural thing for clergy to do, but the man committed suicide. The family sued the church, and both had large legal fees.

MALPRACTICE IN MANAGEMENT

The concept of management malpractice in dealing with employees is different from that in business conduct. The term refers to conduct that is not necessarily negligent or incompetent but includes acts that are unacceptable in American society. The court in *Belanoff* v. *Grayson,* 471 N.Y.S.2d (A.D. 1st Dept. 1984), characterized it as "conduct that exceeds all bounds usually tolerated by society."

Lawsuits for management malpractice are becoming more frequent. Some lawyers have a lucrative practice representing employees in malpractice suits when they are terminated. When employers lose a malpractice case, jury awards average above $100,000, plus employee's attorney fees and their own.

Management uses what it believes to be an effective way to correct unacceptable conduct. The methods used by management to make certain that such employee conduct will not recur are often interpreted to be malpractice. The problem arises when the law decides that the techniques used are not acceptable to society. What may be legitimate conduct to management may not be acceptable to society.

This chapter will examine this area of management liability. It will give insight into those management practices that the courts say society will not accept. To prevent malpractice in management it is first necessary to know what it is. Then one must know the legal consequences when a "short fuse" manager takes action involving an employee. Although malpractice exists in other areas in business, this chapter will deal only with the employer-employee relationship.

Malpractice Defined

Management malpractice is conduct that has serious consequences on the employee's personal or physical well-being. This area of management liability is small, but its growth is being aided by other rapidly expanding areas of employee rights. The courts are taking the position that the employer-employee relationship carries with it certain legal obligations. This position is supported by statutes as well as the common law.

The National Labor Relations Act requires the employer to refrain from certain activities affecting the employee's right to join or not to join a union. Financial protection for job-related injuries is provided under the workers' compensation laws of the various states. The Equal Pay Act requires employers to give equal pay for equal work without regard to sex. Title VII states that an employer cannot make any employment decision that is based on race, color, disbility, nationality, or sex. The Age Discrimination in Employment Act (ADEA) and its amendments and the Americans with Disabilities Act (ADA) also prohibit discrimination.

All these statutory rights have strengthened the belief that an employee has a property right in his or her job. This property right is being expanded so rapidly that in many situations, a person cannot be discharged without a just cause. The erosion of the common law employment-at-will doctrine is resulting in the elimination of another management prerogative. This increases the exposure to malpractice suits.

Change in Employee Attitude

Another important development in the employee relations field is the change in the attitude of the dissatisfied employee. Formerly a dissatisfied employee grumbled for a while, looked to a union for help, or eventually quit.

Today employees use the various agencies established to hear complaints such as the NLRB, EEOC, or the union, or they may go to an adventurous attorney to start a private lawsuit. They often receive large monetary awards from management through the jury system rather than rely upon the relief provided by statute.

Almost all malpractice suits are actions in tort. They differ from the breach of contract suits common in wrongful discharge cases in that they are more serious offenses. The successful prosecution of a malpractice action requires a showing of more extreme behavior by the defendant and results in the awarding of higher damages. In supporting a malpractice claim for emotional distress it is usually necessary to show intent. In other malpractice actions the courts require only evidence that the plaintiff was injured by the defendant's unreasonable conduct.

Examples of Malpractice Lawsuits

A common form of management malpractice is where the employee alleges intentional infliction of emotional distress. This is sometimes called "a contemptuous tort." It is a common allegation in discharge cases. In this type of case the employee alleges that the employer's conduct was intentional, reckless, and contrary to what a civilized society should tolerate.

The effect upon the employee must be severe; we are not yet sure how severe. An employer refused to allow an employee to take a tranquilizer when being questioned about a theft. The court held that this was intentional infliction of emotional distress where the employer had knowledge of the employee's condition.[4]

Where an employer ridiculed, threatened, humiliated, and sexually harassed an employee, the court found a tort of outrageous conduct.[5] An employer demoted a manager to janitor and otherwise set out to humiliate the employee. The

jury, with court approval, awarded $3.4 million for infliction of emotional distress.[6]

Wrongful Employment Action but Not Malpractice

An example of a case where the action was not severe enough to be malpractice is where in *Moye* v. *Gary*, 595 F.Supp. 738 (S.D. N.Y. 1984), the supervisor called an employee a "fag" and a "poor woman." In *Morrison* v. *Sandell et al.*, 466 N.E.2d 290 (Ill. App. 1983), a co-worker put human waste in a file drawer that the plaintiff was about to use. The court held that the conduct was not severe enough and was an "isolated incident that lacked duration." Another example of conduct not severe enough to find emotional distress was in *Vinson* v. *Linn-Mar Community School District*, 360 N.W.2d (Iowa 1984). A former employer was guilty of defamation of character by malice and mistruths, for which damages were awarded, but the court held that this was not an act that was "atrocious and utterly intolerable in a civilized community."

- Suffered embarrassment by his wrongful discharge when he had to tell acquaintances that he was unemployed.
- Stayed awake at night worrying about employment.
- Had unsteady nerves.
- Was depressed most of the time.
- Avoided social contact with his friends.
- Experienced fear about meeting financial obligations.
- Went to a physician as well as a psychologist regarding stress.
- Had no self-confidence when meeting prospective employers.

The court did not consider these effects severe enough to maintain a claim of intentional infliction of emotional distress for the wrongful discharge. It held that the law intervenes only when the

[4]*Tandy Corp.* v. *Bone*, 678 S.W.2d 311 (Ark. 1984).

[5]*Wing* v. *JMB Management Corp.*, 714 P.2d 916 (Colo. App. 1985).

[6]*Wilson* v. *Monarch Paper Co.*, 939 F.2d 1138 (5th Cir. 1991).

employer's action is "so severe that no reasonable man could be expected to bear it." [7]

An employee refused to stop dating a co-worker. The discharge caused severe distress. The court held that the discharge was not severe enough to warrant an action for emotional distress.[8] This rule was also adopted in Missouri where the employer—before the discharge—said, "Dammit, you've done it again," and commented that she "doesn't know a goddamn thing." The employer's conduct at the time of the discharge was alleged to cause the plaintiff suffering in the form of severe mental pain, anguish, embarrassment, stomach problems, and loss of sleep. The court noted that the employer's conduct, although not above reproach, could not be characterized as so extreme and outrageous as to be considered a tort. It further stated that employees must necessarily be hardened to a certain amount of rough language and other action that is inconsiderate and unkind. Although the plaintiff suffered mental stress, it was not sufficient to allow recovery.[9]

The successful prosecution of an emotional distress claim requires the plaintiff to show more extreme action by the defendant than in other malpractice cases. In supporting an allegation of emotional distress it is usually necessary to show intent, but in other malpractice actions the courts only require that the plaintiff was injured by the defendant's unreasonable conduct.

INVASION OF PRIVACY AS A FORM OF MALPRACTICE

An intrusion upon a person's right to seclusion is a tort. To prevail in this type of claim the plaintiff must show that the defendant intentionally intruded, physically or otherwise, upon the plaintiff's private affairs or concerns. The plaintiff must also show that a reasonable person would find this intrusion offensive.

---

[7]*Eklund* v. *Vincent Brass and Aluminum Co.*, 351 N.W.2d 371 (Minn. App. 1984).

[8]*Patton* v. *J.C. Penney Co.*, 719 P.2d 854 (Or. 1986).

[9]*Rooney* v. *Super Markets, Inc.*, 668 S.W.2d 649 (Mo. App. 1984).

In *Leudtke* v. *Nabors Alaska Drilling, Inc.*, 708 P.2d 1123 (Alaska 1989), the employer implemented a drug testing program. The plaintiffs refused to submit to urinalysis pursuant to the program. They were fired. They sued claiming that the test was an intrusion upon their privacy and accordingly their discharge was contrary to public policy.

The court found that there is a sphere of activity in every person's life that is closed to scrutiny by others. The boundaries of that sphere are determined by balancing employees' and employers' competing interests. Employer testing for drugs on an oil rig was for health and safety reasons. These supersede the employees' right of privacy.

CRA91 places certain limits upon the total amount of compensatory and punitive damages that an individual may recover. Some legal scholars believe this applies to infliction of emotional distress. Others disagree because Section 102 of the act applies to intentional discrimination only. If there is a severe wrong the court will find a way to hold defendent guilty.

Case law involving unlawful intrusion upon privacy is relatively rare. It is therefore difficult to determine whether the common law right to privacy constitutes a clearly mandated public policy as required to vacate an arbitrator's award in discharge cases.

Sexual Harassment as Invasion of Privacy

Sexual advances are considered an invasion of privacy under certain conditions. This offense has more potential exposure to lawsuits. In *Eisenstadt, Sheriff* v. *Baird*, 405 U.S. 438 (1972), the U.S. Supreme Court held that in questioning an employee about marriage and her sex life, these are fundamental rights entitled to privacy protection. When questioning about sex with her husband, accompanied by sexual advances, there is a likelihood that this would be an invasion of privacy for which damages would be determined by a jury, as was the case in *Phillips* v. *Smalley Maintenance Services*, 711 F.2d 1524 (11th Cir. 1983). The courts in these cases held that questioning about a person's sex life is an invasion of privacy, whereas touching or other sexual advances are not an invasion of privacy but only a violation of Title VII that has a lesser penalty.

Distinction from Violation of Title VII

Sexual harassment is a tort. It occurs when the employee alleges that failure to submit to sexual advances results in emotional distress or is an invasion of privacy.

The court explained the difference between statutory and common law violation very well in *Lucas* v. *Brown,* 736 F.2d 1202 (8th Cir. 1984). This involved an employee who refused to submit to sexual advances and alleged that she was discharged for that reason. In dismissing a Title VII claim because it was not filed within the time limits, the court allowed the employee to recover punitive damages on the basis that the discharge was a violation of public policy. The court stated that "a woman invited to trade herself for a job is in effect being asked to become a prostitute." The court allowed damages for intentional infliction of emotional distress because "in light of the nature of the employment relationship and the power of the employer," punitive damages would be justified. The courts that allow recovery beyond Title VII for mental anguish and physical symptoms of distress state that back pay and reinstatement would not adequately compensate the employee. In a Title VII suit limitations of CRA91 as to punitive damages may apply. Mental anguish was allowed in *Holien* v. *Sears, Roebuck and Co.,* 677 P.2d 704 (Ore. 1984).[10] This had the effect of allowing a tort recovery in a wrongful discharge.

In some situations the evidence will not prove a violation of Title VII, but the employer still can be liable for sexual assault. Under CRA91 intent would have to be shown. A District of Columbia court in *Clark* v. *World Airways,* 24 F.E.P. Cases (BNA) (D.C. of D.C. 1980), held that the evidence would not allow a Title VII action because the company president never made submission to sexual favors a condition of employment. However, there was sufficient evidence for a jury to find that the president had sexual relations with the plaintiff and while doing so he was serving his employer. The court found that the act was in the course of employment because the employer provided the opportunity for the offensive conduct and it was an outgrowth of the employment situation; a minority view.

Not all courts will hold that sexual harassment is malpractice. When a fashion director with high performance ratings was discharged allegedly for refusal of sexual favors, the court, in *Wolk* v. *Saks Fifth Avenue, Inc.,* 728 F.2d 221 (3rd Cir. 1984), held that the remedy was under Title VII and did not permit an action for tortious conduct. A Florida court said that mere sexual harassment conduct was not outrageous enough to allow an action for punitive damages.[11]

It is doubtful whether the result would be the same under CRA91 limits. A lawsuit can be filed under Title VII if intentional sexual harassment can be shown. In that case a jury trial and punitive damages (a monetary punishment for a wrong) would be permitted under Section 201 of CRA91. Punitive damages would be determined by a jury and are always greater than back pay.

The common law action for a tort as a result of the sexual advances could be asserted, and if the employee prevailed the remedy would be the same as under CRA91. If the sexual harassment was environmental as opposed to quid pro quo, CRA91 applies.

The problem of sexual harassment in the workplace is not going to be completely solved in the near future. Sexual advances are difficult for some people to control. Management's exposure to litigation very often will extend beyond Title VII. Not all courts agree that sexual harassment can result in a tort, but there is presently enough case law to make the exposure troublesome for the employer. Why be concerned about whether sexual harassment is malpractice? Just have strict enforcement of a nonharassment policy.

---

[10]See also *Ball* v. *Cracking Good Bakeries,* 777 F.2d 1497 (11th Cir. 1986), where the court allowed a claim for malpractice. Also see *Ford* v. *Revlon, Inc.,* 734 P.2d 580 (Ariz. 1987), and *O'Connell* v. *Chasdi,* 400 Mass. 686 (Mass. 1987), where the court found emotional distress in sexual harassment complaints.

[11]*Ponton* v. *Scarfone,* 468 So.2d 1009 (Fla. App. 2 Dist. 1985).

INDIVIDUAL LIABILITY WHEN ACTING IN BEHALF OF EMPLOYER

Can members of management be held personally liable when acting in behalf of their employer? We are living in an era of legal scrutiny of all management activity. The supervisor, manager, or personnel practitioner is often afraid to act in behalf of the employer for fear of personal liability. In an unpublished survey of management personnel by the author, respondents were asked whether they believed they could be held personally liable when acting in behalf of their employer. Almost 80 percent wrongly thought that they could. Few knew the circumstances that might lead to personal liability.

Managers run the risk of personal liability in several different areas of activity, such as price fixing under antitrust laws, misuse of funds or company property, and conflicts of interest. Most directors of any organization, whether profit or nonprofit, have potential personal liability when acting in behalf of the organization.

Officers of corporations are often asked to participate in community activities, which they do on company time and company expense accounts. They could be liable under certain circumstances. Many officers are exposed to information that makes them "insiders" for security transactions. They could be personally liable under some conditions in this area.

This book deals only with the employer-employee relationship in all phases of management activity. Administrative management personnel, when participating in other areas of management activity, might be well advised to get legal counsel to protect their personal liability.

Corporate Veil Protection

The general rule is the manager is not liable for mere mistakes—errors of judgment when acting in behalf of the employer. The courts take the position that a corporate veil of immunity protects the manager from personal liability except for deceit or fraud. If deceit or fraud is present, the manager is usually liable.[12]

There have been rare incidents where employees have caused this corporate veil to be penetrated. In these situations the courts found the manager individually liable to the employee when acting in behalf of the employer.[13]

Court decisions where the manager has been held individually liable are rare.[14] The corporate veil of immunity still prevails. However, unawareness of the exposure may lead to abuses. They will have the effect of making lawsuits against managers as popular in the future as malpractice suits against doctors and lawyers are today.

Where the employer intermingled personal assets with corporate funds and failed to pay wages and benefits, and then dissolved the corporation, NLRB held the owner personally liable.[15]

Liability of Company Officers

Unless an officer participates in deceit or fraud, the courts will not find individual liability. However, where corporate officers knowingly permitted the company to violate the Wage Payment and Collection Act to deny employees their wages, the officers were held individually liable for the unpaid wages when the company filed bankruptcy. The court said in *Mullins* v. *Venable,* 297 S.E.2d 866 (W.Va. 1982), that the

---

[12]Joseph J. Manna, "Personal Liability Under the Civil Rights Act of 1991: Piercing the Corporate Veil." *Temple Politics and Civil Rights Law Review,* 4 (1995), 339.

[13]*Emmert* v. *Drake,* 224 F.2d 299 (5th Cir. 1955).

[14]The Employee Retirement Income Security Act does not permit the court to pierce the corporate veil to find that transaction between union pension plan and non-fiduciary closely related to union is prohibited transaction.

[15]Las Villas Produce, 279 NLRB No. 120 (1986).

---

[12]Joseph J. Manna, "Personal Liability Under the Civil Rights Act of 1991: Piercing the Corporate Veil." *Temple*

officers had a duty to see that the corporation obeyed the law.

As a general rule the courts will inflict a greater degree of responsibility on officers than on other members of management. In a situation similar to the *Mullins* case, the corporate officers had a substantial interest in the corporation and were directly involved in decisions affecting the employees' compensation. They were held personally liable under the Fair Labor Standards Act for failure to pay minimum wages and overtime during the last week of existence of the corporation.[16]

In considering the liability of an officer, the court will look to see if the officer was acting in good faith, within authority, and using the proper degree of prudence and diligence. A manager attempted to hide assets to avoid paying back pay for wages due; the court said the corporation is the alter ego of the manager, who became personally liable.[17] Where corporate officers acting in behalf of the corporation caused damages by willful participation in fraud and deceit, they were held personally liable.[18]

A stockholder-employee asked to inspect the corporate books. He was discharged instead. The court said that the officer-director was personally liable for inducing the corporation to discharge the employee. The discharge was not for the benefit of the corporation.[19] The corporation was not held liable because it had a right to discharge under the employment-at-will doctrine. Normally, officers are not held personally liable for discharge. Most courts hold that it is within their supervisory duties to act in behalf of the corporation. In the case cited here, discharging the employee was not the cause of liability, but refusal for him to see the stockholders list is what caused the personal liability.[20]

---

[16]*Donovan* v. *Agnew*, 712 F.2d 1508 (1st Cir. 1983).

[17]*Donovan* v. *Burgett Greenhouses, Inc.*, 759 F.2d 1483 (10th Cir. 1985).

[18]*Lentz Plumbing Co.* v. *Fee*, 679 P.2d 736 (Kan. 1984).

[19]See also *Restatement (Second) of Agency*, Sect. 439 (1958).

[20]Also *Nordling* v. *Northern States Power Co.*, 465 N.W.2d 81 (Minn. Ct. App. 1991).

Personal Liability under Antidiscrimination Laws

When claims against supervisors or managers for personal liability are brought under the discrimination statutes, the courts have refused to entertain them. CRA91 is silent on this point. When the employee wants to sue a manager, rather than relying upon a discrimination statute she or he will sue for a tortious injury under the common law if the case is good.

Management personnel are often named in discrimination suits for reasons other than personal liability. The plaintiff may wish to have a member of management available to negotiate a settlement or to establish the ultimate liability of the employer. Once the purpose is achieved, the managers are usually dropped as defendants.

There is nothing in the contents or legislative history of Title VII as amended by CRA91 or most other antidiscrimination statutes that indicates that Congress intended managers to be personally liable. Title VII refers to only three kinds of entities: employers, employment agencies, and labor unions. When defining employers, the courts adopt the National Labor Relations Act definition, which states that an employer is anyone who is not an employee. In *Silver* v. *KCA, Inc.*, 586 F.2d 138 (9th Cir. 1978), a supervisor made a remark about an employee, calling her a "jungle bunny." A co-worker overheard the remark and became indignant and demanded an apology. The apology was made to the indignant employee but two days later the co-worker was discharged. She sued, alleging that her termination was a violation of Title VII. The discharge was due to opposition to the supervisor's remark about her black co-worker. The court said that a remark made about a co-worker to another employee is not a violation of the act unless the remark is directed at an employment practice. The court went on to say that Title VII was not intended to stop discrimination by private individuals—reprehensible as that may be. The intent of the act was to eradicate discrimination by employers against employees.

The courts have consistently found the employer and not the offender liable under other antidiscrimination statutes. In *Martin* v. *Easton*

Publishing Co., 478 F.Supp. 796 (E.D. Pa. 1979),[21] the manager was not acting in behalf of the employer when he discriminated under the Equal Pay Act. The court said that "no additional relief can be obtained from individual defendants and no purpose will be served by retaining them in litigation for equal pay."

Liability under the Civil Rights Act of 1866 as Amended

The Civil Rights Act of 1866, as amended in 1871 and 1991, states that all persons have the right to enforce contracts and receive equal benefit of all the laws regardless of their color. The statute was passed to close a loophole in the Thirteenth and Fourteenth Amendments of the Constitution, but is used as an antidiscrimination statute. In effect, this early statute bars intentional discrimination because of race but got little attention in the courts until 1968. Section 1881 of the 1866 statute makes any person who acts under the color or authority of a statute, ordinance, or regulation liable for injury to others. The statute further states that liability is not limited to injury, but includes rights, privileges, or immunities secured by the Constitution. This statute has the effect of making all persons in the public sector or those persons acting under the authority of a law personally liable for their acts.[22] Such acts must involve the making or enforcement of a contract.

This statute has been used extensively in finding public officials personally liable when performing their duties under the authority of a statute, ordinance, or regulation. In a leading case of *Vinard* v. *King,* 728 F.2d 428 (10th Cir. 1984), an employee handbook of a municipally owned hospital stated that a permanent employee could not be discharged without cause. The personnel director of the hospital discharged an employee without a hearing. When the employee brought suit, the court held that the action of the director was a violation of Section 1981 (1871 amend-ment) and the Fourteenth Amendment. The court allowed punitive damages against the director as a municipal official but not against the hospital because this was a municipal organization that couldn't be sued.[23]

Supreme Court Endorsement of Public Employee

The U.S. Supreme Court has endorsed personal liability of a public employee in *Smith* v. *Wade,* 103 S.Ct. 1625 (1983). A prison guard placed the plaintiff in the same cell with another inmate who the guard knew was dangerous. The plaintiff was beaten by his cellmate, and the court allowed punitive damages against the guard. This has been extended to state judges. In *Forrester* v. *White,* 108 S.Ct. 538 (1988), a judge was personally liable under Section 1983 of the U.S. Code when making an administrative decision involving the discharge of a probation officer; he was immune only for judicial activity.

The courts strictly follow the requirement that the defendant must be acting under the authority of a regulation or a statute. The court held that a manager of Kentucky Fried Chicken was not acting under the authority of the state merely because the word "Kentucky" was in the corporate name. The plaintiff argued that the name alone brought the defendant under the statute. The courts require more than a name.[24]

Personal Liability under Antitrust Statutes

The antitrust statutes most often used for personal liability are the Sherman and Clayton acts. All the various antitrust regulations basically state that any act that restricts competition is illegal. Section 2 of the Sherman Antitrust Act states that every person (a corporation is considered a person) who shall make a contract or engage in any combination or conspiracy declared illegal under the act is guilty of a felony. A

---

[21]See also *Padway* v. *Palches,* 665 F.2d 965 (9th Cir. 1982).

[22]In *Hafer* v. *Melo,* 112 S.Ct. 358 (1991), the court held that public officials can be sued individually when acting in behalf of an employer, but the agency cannot.

[23]In *St. Louis* v. *Praprotnik,* 108 S.Ct. 915 (1988), the court held that the city or a governmental unit cannot be sued by the employee unless there is a constitutional issue.

[24]*McCarthy* v. *KFC Corp.,* 667 F.Supp. 343 (D.C. Ky. 1985).

violation is punishable by a fine of up to $1 million for a corporation. For any other person the fine is not more than $100,000 and/or three years in prison at the discretion of the court. Section 2 of the Sherman Act unequivocally imposes personal liability on any member of management, when acting for the benefit of the corporation, as well as on the corporation.

To be in violation the acts or omissions must result in restricting competition and the facts must show implied or actual intent. In the past, courts have given jail sentences to individuals although in most cases the sentences have been suspended or the defendants have been required to perform some community service. In an early case (which the Supreme Court refused to review) there was clear intent to violate the Sherman Act; the court sentenced eight officers and management personnel from 20 to 60 days in jail.[25]

The personnel practitioner has the most exposure to antitrust liability when making wage or cost surveys with competitors. Surveys run afoul of the antitrust laws when the reason for obtaining the information is to formulate future policies as to costs, wages, working conditions, and benefits. This, according to the U.S. Justice Department, has the effect of lessening competition. This is what happened when nonunion stockbrokers sued the New York Stock Exchange for conspiring among its members to reduce their commissions. The court held in *United States of America v. Utah County for Health Care Human Resources Administration,* U.S. LEXIS 1771 (1996), that this exchange of information was a violation of the antitrust laws because it resulted in collusion to fix commissions.

In *Goodspeed* v. *Federated Employers of the Bay Area,* the Justice Department, in an out-of-court settlement, stated that surveys among competitors are in compliance if certain conditions are met:

1. Report only aggregated information.

2. Publish no data as to future intentions.

3. Avoid surveys that have fewer than 10 participants.

4. Avoid discussions with competitors where there is agreement to pay certain rates for certain jobs. This is a sure violation.

Because intent has to be shown to prove an antitrust violation, getting approval from legal counsel for a wage survey with competitors is important. Although the cases involving surveys are few in number, the Antitrust Division of the Justice Department and activist groups are ready to challenge any questionable survey.[26] Whether a particular salary survey is within the antitrust laws is a matter to be determined by legal counsel.

Labor unions are specifically exempted from antitrust laws under both the Sherman Act and the Clayton Act. Section 20 of the Clayton Act states that neither unions nor their members can be sued.[27] Unions lose their antitrust immunity when the activity is designed to control the marketing of goods and services or limit competition for goods and services.[28] They can also lose their exemptions where they coerce nonunion groups to join the union or where they conspire with employers to hire only union contractors.[29] Unions also have no standing in suing their employer under antitrust when the employer diverts work from union to nonunion contractors unless a breach of contract is involved.[30] Normally labor-management relations are not regulated by antitrust laws, nor are they intended to infringe upon the authority of the National Labor Relations Act.

Extent of Liability under Other Statutes

Under the Consolidated Omnibus Budget Reconciliation Act (COBRA) 29 U.S.C. Sect. 601–608 as amended), if a qualifying employee or dependents are not given notice of the right to be covered under the employer's present group health

---

[25]*U.S.* v. *American Radiator and Standard Corp., et al.,* 338 F.2d 201 (3rd Cir. 1967).

[26]See also A. Hamton, J. Tarky, and Vaughn, "Wage Surveys and Antitrust Laws," *Labor Law Journal,* (Dec. 1995).

[27]*United States* v. *Hutcheson,* 312 U.S. 219 (1941).

[28]*Allen-Bradley Co.* v. *Electrical Workers (IBEW) Local No. 3,* 325 U.S. 797 (1945).

[29]*Amalgamated Meat Cutters Local 189* v. *Jewel Tea Co.,* 381 U.S. 676 (1965).

[30]*Associated General Contractors* v. *Calif. State Council of Carpenters,* 103 S.Ct. 897 (1983).

insurance plan, the person responsible is personally liable. The personal liability can be up to $100 per day from the date of failure to give notice.

Under the Employee Retirement Income Security Act (ERISA), the fiduciary can be personally liable for violations, but this usually is an outside professional.

The Immigration Reform and Control Act (IRCA; 8 U.S.C. 1324a) makes the individual liable when acting in behalf of the employer. If the employer or any individual recruits, hires, or employs an undocumented alien, the employer and employee responsible are liable. It also imposes a personal liability if an individual fails to keep records.

There is an exposure to individual liability under the Equal Pay Act as amended in 1990. Cases of this type are rare. There must be intent and willful disregard for the statute.

A manager can be liable for the traditional common law claims if the plaintiff can establish the requisite elements for a tort. Such actions as defamation, intentional infliction of emotional distress, assault and battery, and tortious interference with a contract are all possibilities.

Section 17(e) of the Occupational Safety and Health Act provides for individual criminal liability where a manager or safety official violates a standard, rule, or regulation and causes the death of an employee.[31]

Employer Indemnification for Employees Acting in Employer's Behalf

Managers can perform their assigned duties in good faith and carry out corporate policies and still become insecure. They often fear that unsuccessful job applicants and employees they discipline can sue them individually.[32] The employer, to eliminate this problem, often agrees to indemnify the person acting on behalf of the company for the losses. This practice encourages the innocent manager to resist meritless suits or unjust charges and encourages competent persons to accept responsible positions.

Some states have statutes that require the employer to indemnify if the corporate bylaws are silent. The manager must act in good faith and have no reason to believe that the act was unlawful. Most state courts will permit indemnification where the manager reasonably believes that she or he is acting in the best interests of the corporation. This indemnification includes expenses, attorney fees, settlement costs, judgments, and fines. This principle was endorsed by the U.S. Supreme Court in *Burks* v. *Lasker,* 441 U.S. 471 (1975).

When liability insurance coverage is used to indemnify the manager in discrimination lawsuits, it usually is not effective. There is a well-settled rule that a contract to indemnify a person for damages caused by intentional misconduct is against public policy. The question in all these cases is whether there was intentional misconduct in violation of a statute. Because the courts will not allow personal liability under Title VII, indemnification is a moot question under that statute. In other discrimination statutes, however, such as Equal Pay, Age Discrimination, and Pregnancy Disability Act, whether there is misconduct or intent is important for indemnification coverage.

Sometimes the court will not permit indemnification because of the nature of the offense. In *Kryriazi* v. *Western Electric Co.,* 647 F.2d 388 (3rd Cir. 1981), the plaintiff was allowed to recover from the employer under Title VII for sexual harassment by her co-workers and supervisors. She was allowed to bring a separate action in state court against her supervisor for maliciously interfering with her employment. The corporate immunity veil was pierced, and the supervisor was held personally liable. The court prevented the employer from paying the damages because this would not correct the abusive conduct.

Recommendations for Avoiding Personal Liability

The general rule is that there is no personal liability for persons acting wrongfully in behalf of the employer. The exception to this rule is where the employee is acting under the authority of a statute as a public employee, commits an antitrust

---

[31]*Cedar Construction Co.* v. *OSHRC,* 587 F.2d 1303 (D.C. Cir. 1978).

[32]See Minnesota Statutes Section 302A.521 (1991 Suppl.).

violation, is fraudant, or is deceitful. However, there are enough exceptions to this general rule and the consequences are so catastrophic that it is worthwhile for members of management to take reasonable steps to avoid possible exposure.

The most important factor to prevent exposure is to recognize that the possibility does exist in rare situations. The second point is that the standard of behavior must be what is acceptable in American society. Everyone should know what that standard is.

Individuals sometimes get trapped into an organizational philosophy that is obsolete or otherwise out of step with contemporary thinking on how employees should be treated.

When other employees or the company participates in activity that may result in personal liability, evidence of lack of participation is the best defense. This question frequently comes up in antitrust violations that provide for personal liability. The documentation should include the date of the decision and a brief synopsis of the facts and events surrounding the decision. The manager should not rely upon indemnification insurance because this is of little help where intent is shown or implied and if the act is contrary to what is accepted by society.

Employee-related litigation has made a small start in attempting to obtain damages from the manager or officer involved in an employment decision. Awareness of the increasing trend will cause managers to take preventive steps. These preventive steps will make them feel secure in accepting the responsibilities of their jobs without fear of personal liability.

It should also be noted that there is a trend in Congress to make the individual liable for a violation. COBRA and IRCA, to name a couple of laws, were passed in the late 1980s.

FAILURE TO PROVIDE A SAFE PLACE TO WORK

Workers' Compensation Exclusion

Employers have more immunity from malpractice charges for failure to provide a safe place to work than for most other employment actions. The main reason for this immunity is that workers' compensation statutes provide an exclusive remedy in most states.[33]

Employees who were injured by exposure to toxic chemical in a fiberglass cloth used in constructing airplanes may be able to recover on their claim of outrage against their employer, which allegedly knew that the cloth would make them sick, the Washington Supreme Court ruled. To recover, the employees must show that the employer intentionally inflicted emotional distress, the court said. The employee's allegations of a variety of work-related medical symptoms, oppressive behavior by supervisors, human experimentation, inability to transfer despite medical restrictions, and the employer's cleaning and ventilating of the workplace prior to government testing could establish that emotional distress was inflicted either intentionally or recklessly, it said. Even though an emotional distress claim arising from these circumstances ordinarily would be barred by workers' compensation exclusivity, the court said the alleged employer conduct behind the employees' outrage claim constitutes a "deliberate intent to injure" that is exempt from the exclusivity rule. *Birklid* v. *Boeing Co.,* Individual Employment Rights Cases 97.

There are exceptions to this rule. Failure to inform the employee of a hazard will create an exposure to a lawsuit. A criminal action can be brought under OSHA.[34] In *People* v. *O'Neil,* 550 N.E.2d 1090 (Ill. App. 1990), the court held managers criminally liable because they disregarded the safety of the employees and a fatality resulted. The Ohio statute (Code 4121.80) that limits the worker's right under common law to bring a tort action for a safe work environment was declared unconstitutional.[35]

In *Granite Const. Co.* v. *Superior Ct. of Fresno,* 197 Cal. Rptr. 3 (Cal. App. 5 Dist. 1983), the employer was indicted criminally for manslaughter in the death of seven employees who

---

[33]See chapter 16 for more detail.
[34]*People* v. *Magnetic Wire,* 534 N.E.2d 962 (Ill. App. 1989).
[35]*Brady* v. *Safety Klee Corp.,* 576 N.E.2d 722 (Ohio S.Ct. 1991).

died when their platform cable snapped.[36] In Texas, Virginia, and Pennsylvania the employer must be indifferent to employee welfare and safety in order for the corporation to be liable outside of the workers' compensation laws. Some courts require intent to harm to take it outside of workers' compensation laws.[37]

Personal Liability for Unsafe Conditions

Everyone who has worked in safety programs knows that injuries can occur despite the best efforts of management. In most lawsuits involving personal liability for unsafe conditions, the corporate veil of immunity has been upheld. Most courts will not even allow the employee to sue the employer for an injury, because the workers' compensation statute is the exclusive remedy. Because no one wishes to face even the remote threat of personal liability, the safety practitioner often overreacts to any potential danger. However, there are some indications that the "safety net" of immunity has been pierced and an exposure of personal liability does exist for failure to provide a safe place to work. Section 17(e) under the Occupational Safety and Health Act makes individuals criminally liable under the act when it is shown that they knowingly and intentionally violated the act.[38] One court held the manager liable in a tort action for failure to give safety training.

There is constant pressure from organized labor, some government authorities, and college professors to change the corporation protection of workers' compensation laws.

The Future of Malpractice for Unsafe Conditions

Under present court decisions the risk of corporate or personal liability for failure to provide a safe place to work is increasing. Courts have shown an increasing tendency to hold employers liable both financially and criminally for work-related deaths. In the future they may be held liable for malpractice for failure to use up-to-date techniques, follow regulations, or use accepted practices that prevent accidents. The real issue is going to be whether there was a negligent disregard for the safety of the employees. Failure to act in a reasonable manner and not be sensitized to the vulnerability could change the present level of exposure.

Safety officials or managers have an exposure for lack of professional responsibility in failing to provide a safe place to work if up-to-date techniques are not used to prevent accidents.[39] This exposure is still embryonic but is growing rapidly, particularly if the existence of the exposure is ignored.

PREVENTION OF EXPOSURE TO MALPRACTICE

Management malpractice lawsuits have their roots in the medical, legal, and professional areas. Management malpractice lawsuits are not as common as in medicine or law. However, they are about to explode in the management area as they did a few years ago in other professional groups.

Intentional infliction of emotional distress is yet to be defined in the employer-employee relationship. *Breach of public trust* and *covenant of good faith and fair dealing* are still terms that are legally vague. However, the increasingly common use of these terms by employees and their attorneys means that the employer's exposure to litigation by employees is rapidly growing. Some attorneys are now advertising their "unjust dismissal services."

---

[36]See "Civil and Criminal Law Liability Exposure of the Safety Professional," *Professional Safety* (April 1987), p. 10.

[37]Kendall H. Sage, "The Intentional Tort Exception to the Exclusive Remedy of Workers' Compensation," *Labor Law Journal* (Feb. 4).

[38]See "Living with OSHA," *ABA Journal*, (May 1989), 104; "Soon Corporate Crime May Really Not Pay," *Business Week*, (February 12, 1990), 25; M. Connally and M. Shaye, "Executives Who Cheat on OSHA Can End Up in Jail," *Complete Lawyer ABA, 7,* no. 1 (Winter 1990), 63.

---

[39]The safety director could be held criminally liable under OSHA, with the manager, as an advisor and abettor: *U.S.* v. *Shear,* 962 F.2d 458 (5th Cir. 1992).

The present indications are that management malpractice litigation will get worse, and no legislative relief is on the horizon to change this trend, as there is in product liability and medical malpractice. This increasing trend of exposure to litigation can only be stopped by management action before adverse case law and statutes are developed by bad facts. Progressive management should develop key policies and procedures now. Waiting to experience the ordeal of a malpractice lawsuit before doing something about it is shortsighted management. Management's first step to avoid malpractice is to decide what acts are malpractice according to the law and management philosophy. Policies and procedures to prevent malpractice should be established. Policies should not interfere with the profitability of the operation but where possible should be more strict than what is required under existing law. What is not outrageous conduct today may very well become so in the future. Each year it seems that more "reasonable acts" become "unreasonable."

Drafting Policies on Malpractice

Policies on malpractice should be somewhat different from other policies because of the catastrophic consequences of a lawsuit. They should be a directive from the CEO and not guidelines allowing the option of following them. The only committee needed to draft such policies is the chief operating officer and legal counsel. Indemnification should be granted only when the policy is followed and discharge is the result when it is not. Discharge or discipline of the employee who violates a policy is always a good defense for the corporation, because it shows a good faith effort to enforce.

Recommended Policies to Prevent Malpractice

The purpose of the policies is to make management aware that an exposure exists in these various areas and to give management's position: the requirement that they be complied with. The following policies are recommended:

1. Each member of management above a certain level should be required to become familiar with the term *malpractice.* This could be explained internally along with other training programs.

2. A strong policy against harassment should be drafted to comply with Title VII. If this is enforced, there would be little need to have any policy to prevent invasion of privacy or emotional distress except to inform that such an action is possible in certain situations.

3. An antitrust policy should be drafted requiring strict compliance and stating that corporate and personal liability is possible under the law. The policy should be silent on personal liability in other areas unless the operations are under 1866 or 1871 statutes. Then the policy should make it clear when the personal liability is permitted under the statute.

4. The policy should allow only a few persons who understand the qualified privilege doctrine to release information. Whether externally or internally, information should be released only to those persons who have a business reason to receive it and can do something about it.

5. The policy emphatically should require all members of management to follow an established procedure on discharges.

6. Safety and health programs must be taken seriously.

7. If a certain activity is legally questionable, try to involve another member of management.

8. The policy should note that almost all humans desire equality, stature, and involvement. Any activity should consider these feelings.

Malpractice in Discharge, Negligent Hiring, and Negligent Retention

The most common management actions that result in malpractice are discharge, negligent hiring, and negligent retention, although other situations such as sexual harassment and sexual abuse can be troublesome.

The most important action to prevent malpractice is the establishment of a discharge procedure. Such a procedure should go beyond that which is designed to prevent wrongful discharge for a breach of contract. Exit interviews, investigation, and a joint decision to discharge should be in place under the wrongful discharge policy. To prevent malpractice in discharge the courts require compliance with a discharge policy or the establishment of one. There is little exposure to a malpractice in the discharge process if there is an objective performance appraisal that will stand judicial scrutiny. Also, if those acts that management decides will result in discharge are properly communicated to the employee, there is little exposure to a lawsuit.

For prevention of negligent retention exposure, there should be a rule that requires a co-worker to report all incidents that indicate that the employee has dangerous tendencies. Management should then take necessary action. A substance abuse policy for discovery and treatment should be supported by all members of management. As for negligent hiring exposure, we are not sure how much investigation is required to prevent a lawsuit. What we do know is that at least the police records should be checked as well as any questionable work history information, especially for certain jobs. Reference information that relates to performance, absenteeism, and tardiness is of little value in determining the character of the applicant.

Case law in management malpractice is increasing gradually. It will take time for management malpractice to reach the popularity of medical malpractice.

Malpractice exposure should not be a serious management problem. Malpractice suits will subside if progressive management takes steps to prevent actions toward the employee that are not acceptable in American society. All members of management must comply and understand malpractice.

Management should not depend upon others to solve the malpractice problem. Lawyers can do only so much. They must depend upon convincing testimony and facts created by management. As has so often been said, "Bad facts make bad law."

CHAPTER 21

THE DIRECTION OF PERSONNEL LAW IN THE LATE 1990s AND 2000

Federal Laws Most Encountered in Personnel Management
Bridging the Global Gap
Direction of Antidiscrimination Laws
Labor-Management Relations
Direction of Personnel Law in Discharge
Common Myths in Employment Law Cases
Predictions in Other Areas
High-Priority Tasks in the 1990s
Gaze into the Crystal Ball

This book has discussed the most recent legal intrusions on the personnel function. It is evident by court decisions and statutes that the law does not interfere with personnel administration in carrying out its function. To the contrary, it has caused the personnel practitioner to eliminate many subjective practices that did not always contribute to the profits of the organization. The changes that the laws have forced upon the personnel function in the 1970s and 1980s will not stop in the late 1990s, but the law has matured and the gray areas will continue to decrease. Employers and employees alike have become more sophisticated in using the law to accomplish their objectives. Whereas past lawsuits have been in lower-level jobs, in the future there will be more adversity in the upper levels of management (white or gold collar workers). Because there is no longer a social stigma in suing your employer, policies and procedures will become more sophisticated to avoid exposure to the law. Management resistance to the new laws experienced in the 1970s is rapidly fading as they are learning to live with the law, and legal counsel is becoming better trained in employee relations.[1] Employees in the late 1990s and into 2000 will be more reluctant to sue when employers better understand the law. Management in the late 1990s and into 2000 will develop a painless way to live economically with the law when making employment decisions.

---

[1]Dave Schmidt, "The Future of Labor or Employment Law," 68 Fed. 3rd 685 (1993).

The personnel practitioner in the late 1990s and into 2000, to avoid obsolescence, must be alert when employees use their newly acquired rights, and advise management how to minimize exposure to litigation and still not interfere with organizational goals.

In the late 1990s and into 2000 there will be a profound change in the workforce. More than 20 million new workers will be added. However, only 15 percent of these additions will be white males; the remainder will be minorities or females.[2] (Forty-two percent will be females.)

The workforce will be older. In 1992 the average retirement age was 61, and there is little reason to believe that this will be lower in the 1990s and into 2000. More than 80 percent of the workforce will be employed in the service sector of the economy. These changes in the workforce will result in significant changes in the employer-employee relationships. The increase in women as working mothers will cause a demand for child care and flexible work schedules.[3]

The Family Medical Leave Act (FMLA) is the political response to the changing workforce. The intent of Congress and the president is to assist Americans to balance better the demands of the changing workforce. The act is enforced by the Department of Labor, which issued regulations in June 1993. The FMLA refers mostly to the family as it relates to medical leave.[4]

The new workers must be trained. Job training for displaced workers and the influx of minorities will give an added importance to training.

FEDERAL LAWS MOST ENCOUNTERED IN PERSONNEL MANAGEMENT

In the late 1990s and 2000 the laws that we have been discussing in the preceding chapters will not go away. The only thing that will change is their application to different sets of facts. There is one thing certain in employee relations—management will continually be tested by employees as to their enforcement of policy, compliance with existing laws, and court decisions in those areas where there is no statutory law.

BRIDGING THE GLOBAL GAP

The employer who wants to get some of the lucrative market overseas must decide to train, train, and train. Only 60 percent of the expatriates receive any training before they go overseas.[5] They are expected to train the local workers in two years and return home. In the late 1990s companies will go global with increasing frequency. The company says they are going global, but there is very little training to help the employees understand what that really means. Companies think that this means doing business in a different geographical location and forget about corporate culture information systems, finance, and computer systems.

What is needed is a totally *objective* source to filter out the news and developments important to business, to advise companies on how to meet the challenges they face, and to provide unbiased reviews of products and vendors.

Expenditure of Resources

Training means an expenditure of resources. Some managers believe that training should be only for those who go overseas. What about the assistant purchasing director who deals by fax and phone with suppliers in 50 countries? He has never had orientation on how to deal with the Saudis, Malaysians or Chinese. Everybody must be

---

[2]R. Schuler and V. Huber, *Personnel and Human Resource Management,* 4th ed. (New York: West, 1990).

[3]In 1991 the 26-year pattern of a steady percentage increase of women entering the workforce was stopped: *Issues in Labor Statistics* (Washington, DC: U.S. Department of Labor, Bureau of Labor Statistics, 1992). See most recent issue.

[4]For further provisions of the act, see McGladrey and Pullen, "The Family and Medical Leave Act—A Practical Guide to Cost-Effective Compliance" (New York:Panel Publishers [a Division of Aspen Publishers, Inc.], 1993).

[5]Michael Starr, "Who's the Boss? The Globalization of U.S. Employment Law." *Business Law,* 51 (1996), 635.

trained whenever they go overseas or not. If they deal with companies overseas they must be trained. When the expatriate returns in two years he or she must be oriented into a new life; the expatriate will be like a small island in a large sea. He or she must be a special person to adjust. The markets overseas are great and many companies will go after them, but it is not all gravy. It is a whole new game when we go global. Management must know how to deal with all the ambiguities in the late 1990s or they will be on the outside looking in.

There are other problems that must be solved before a company can have a successful global operation. I put spouse relations at the top of the list. Once you've sent your expatriate overseas, ask yourself whether you've addressed the needs of his or her partner. For an expat's assignment to succeed, you will have to design helpful programs to make their lives meaningful as well. If you're sending a dual-career couple abroad, provide job leads, a social network and volunteer activities so both individuals can reach self-fulfillment.

More than 65 percent of all married couples with children have duel careers.[6] So the person in charge of overseas personnel has the work cut out for him or her.

Legal Problems with the Global Worker

A company has a difficult time doing business in a foreign country without running up against the law. CRA91 makes it clear that the expatriate must follow the law of the country that he or she may be from. In this chapter we see that the laws force the company to make certain policies so as not to be exposed to the laws of the United States. This puts the expatriate in a no-win situation. The laws in the United States say not to discriminate as to sex. Yet in the foreign country the expatriate may be working with women who can't even vote. The expatriate either violates the U.S. law by ignoring it or follows the culture of the country where he or she works.

In South America no one would talk to a woman salesperson. The company discharged her and assigned a male salesperson to sell in that country. She filed a charge in the United States. The court said that as a matter of law it was sex discrimination, a conflict with foreign culture. This would not be so bad, but her company was sued, incurred huge legal fees, and had to pay the woman salesperson. The female expatriate was discharged for getting the company into trouble with the law.

Enforceability of the Law

In some countries the law is passed but not enforced. In Mexico, there is a speed limit for the highway but no highway patrol. When asked why, the officials will say there is no money. As one Spanish attorney once told me, "The laws are so strict that we violate them." The expatriate must find out what laws are enforced against the foreigner. Some countries will hold the foreigner to the law, yet ignore the resident. The law is part of the culture of the country and the expatriate must learn it.[7]

North American Free Trade Agreement (NAFTA)

For more than two years Canada, Mexico, and the United States tried to solve the problem of trade by negotiations. The jury is still out on whether they did. Two charges are filed against U.S. companies doing business in Mexico. The Teamsters charged that Honeywell, Inc., in Chihuahua fired two Mexican workers for attempting to organize a union. A similar charge was filed by UE against General Electric, the largest employer in Mexico. Both charges allege that workers' rights were violated. The NAO agreed to review the charge. The purpose of the review is to report on Mexico's "promotion, compliance and effective enforcement" of Mexico's labor laws. NAFTA was designed to solve problems like this. What will happen if the review board said Mexico is wrong? In the United States there is no question that this would be an

---

[6]Bureau of Labor Statistics monthly report.

[7]See Bety Southard Murphy, "ADR's Impact on International Commerce." *Dispute Resolution Journal,* (Dec. 1993), 68-7.

unfair labor practice if the allegations were correct. In Mexico, so what? What our government is to do about it remains to be seen.

The Honeywell expatriate in Chihuahua did what other Mexican companies would do. Now there has to be a big hearing, legal fees incurred, all because the expatriate followed the culture of that country. Should he follow the laws of the United States? Maybe NAFTA is strong enough to straighten out this mess, but I doubt it.

The global management must recognize that all tasks take longer than expected. It is the job of the expatriate to change this. The change must be gradual and may not always meet the standards of the U.S. worker.

Must Make it Worthwhile. When a worker is moved to a foreign environment, the employer must increase the compensation level to make all the related problems worthwhile. There is nobody to cut the mother-in-law's grass at home, the schools are not up to standard, and the family is bored after the first six months of travel.

Management Involvement is Necessary

More management involvement is necessary than if the global worker was working at home. When the boss visits the plant, both the spouse and the global worker should be taken to dinner. Family problems should be discussed. They are as important as the production problems that will be discussed the next day.

Appraisal of the Global Worker

Management tolerance in achieving goals must be greater for the global worker than for the U.S. worker. The employer should not accept excuses, but should be discreet in criticism. It is the solution of problems, not their presence, that determines results. The global worker's creativity as well as morale must be assessed. The purpose of the transfer must be revisited.

There is no right or wrong way as long as it is recognized that global workers are different— different from U.S. workers and different from each other depending upon the country where they were reared and where they worked. Fear, not the law, prevents the employer from drafting policies

and procedures that will solve the problems of the global worker. The task is not impossible, as long as the differences are recognized and treated accordingly. The one axiom that should be followed in all management policies, especially with global workers, is, *If it works, if it's not illegal—do it.*

Drafting Policy for the Global Worker

It would be a serious mistake to have the same policy for the global worker as for the U.S. worker. It would be just as serious to exclude the global worker in many of the policies that apply to the U.S. workers. The inpatriate's priorities, emotions, and lifestyle must be considered. Often they were not considered in the homeland of the inpatriate. In many countries there are no human rights laws. To attempt to completely change all the habits of the global worker would be a costly management mistake. By intensive training it can be done. However, what is gained? The global worker returns to the homeland where the law is different. If all the habits are retained, the global worker is all alone in an adverse sea. If there is a change back to the old habits, what was gained by the intensive training?

Some Changes Must Be Made. If there are no changes in work habits there would not be any reason to create a global worker. The employer must determine what can be changed and have the wisdom not to try to change those habits that can not be changed. The local customs must not only be considered, but in many situations are controlling.

Employer decisions must be tailored to fit the individual. The employer must recognize that the homeland methods, whether acceptable or not, have been a way of achieving success and survival.

The global worker must be accepted by coworkers in another country. Certain customs in that country must be followed. If the customs are different from company policy, customs should take precedence.

Importance of Personal Characteristics. In many situations personal characteristics are more important than work behavior. In most countries if the expatriate's word is not respected, that person becomes ineffective.

Legal problems become very complicated for global workers. The objective of the human resource manager is to keep the employee from becoming disgruntled enough to see a lawyer. The employer never wins a lawsuit. Only the lawyer wins with huge legal fees.

The personnel laws of the United States and those of the country where the employee works must be followed where possible. Problems created by following U.S. or foreign laws must be resolved on a case-by-case basis.

DIRECTION OF ANTIDISCRIMINATION LAWS

In the early 1970s most discrimination cases dealt with race. Many of the basic principles that apply to sex, age, disability, and religion were developed in racial cases.

There is considerable maturity in the law in racial discrimination. Employers know what is required to validate a test, what is meant by the labor market area, what is required for a prima facie case, what are acceptable recruiting practices. The law permits the employer to hire the best qualified applicant. There is no obligation to maximize the hiring of minorities. In the late 1980s the Supreme Court used the individual relationship on a case-by-case basis to determine discrimination. They scrapped the original presumption of employer guilt.

Age Issues

In the early 1970s budgets of the regulatory agencies were used to resolve the immediate problem of racial discrimination. Age and sex cases were brushed aside. In disputes under the Age Discrimination in Employment Act (ADEA), the Department of Labor until 1979 was the enforcement agency, with a small budget. Few cases of age discrimination were ever brought to court, although the violations existed.

The conditions that prevented active enforcement of age cases in the 1970s will not be present in the 1990s. Budgets have become

adequate. The older worker no longer has a stigma for suing the employer. In the past, persons in lower-level jobs were bringing discrimination lawsuits that consisted mostly of younger workers who were not protected by ADEA. As the stigma of suing the employer diminishes, middle- and upper-level management, almost all over 40, will use the ADEA and other statutes by hiring an attorney and going directly into court. Their financial resources will permit this, rather than depending on a governmental agency. Going through EE will be a formality. This makes the employer extremely vulnerable to age discrimination litigation.

Too few employers have a measurement of performance that will pass judicial review. What other reason is there to terminate an employee of 30 years' service except performance or policy violation (which is rare with middle and upper management)? If poor performance is the reason for discharge, the measurement must be objective and uniformly applied to the extent that a jury will accept. Age cases also have a practical problem in that one does not see many young people on the jury. Furthermore, can anyone imagine going before the U.S. Supreme Court and arguing that an employee is too old to perform the job, without extremely convincing evidence?

The employer's problem with ADEA was increased when Congress lifted the mandatory retirement age of 70. Where many employers could "coast" with the problem until age 70, this option is no longer available. The only solution to the problem of the older worker (other than poor performance or rule violation) is voluntary programs or, in the case of the small company, making a private deal. In the 1970s the most popular cases were race, in the 1980s sex discrimination. In the 1990s, with the baby boom now including persons over 40, age discrimination cases will increase. An increase will come from the Americans with Disabilities Act (ADA) and the Civil Rights Act of 1991 (CRA91), which amended Title VII. Early retirement incentives will be on every employer's menu. Employers will find a legal way to get rid of the older worker.

Where the employer is not sure that a factor other than age can be defended, voluntary retirement programs will be used more often. Each year the employer is winning a larger percentage of age discrimination cases by using some factor other than age or preventing the problem by the use of releases or early retirement programs. This trend will continue, and in the next decade the employer will solve the age discrimination problem by one of two options: using either a factor other than age or voluntary retirement. The key to these programs is to obtain voluntary decisions to retire. Compliance with the Older Workers Benefit Protection Act is a must to ensure that the decision is voluntary.

Sex Issues

During the 1970s the EEOC was too busy with racial problems to spend much effort on sex discrimination. Many of the women's rights groups were using their resources and energy in an unsuccessful attempt to get the Equal Rights Amendment to the Constitution passed.

In the sex discrimination area, most of the original antidiscrimination law as to hiring, promotion, or transfers has matured to the point where the employer knows what the law is.

Sexual Harassment. Sexual harassment under Title VII is a continuing problem.[8] Since the *Meritor* case we know what it is but have to find a way to stop it.

In sexual harassment problems, members of women's groups are active in correcting this form of sex discrimination, which is similar to what occurred in the racial discrimination area in the early 1970s. More than one third of all law students are women.[9] Women are not only accepted in great numbers by law firms (over 16 percent of the practicing bar are women); also, to the surprise of some male attorneys, they are becoming good trial lawyers. Because of the influx of women into the legal profession, women employees are more comfortable going to a

woman lawyer with their problems; as with all lawyers they are anxious to take the case. The employer of the 1990s must prepare for an increase in sexual harassment cases and establish policies and procedures that will prevent exposure in this area. This problem will not go away, but employers will find a way to be relieved of liability.

The Glass Ceiling. The concept of the glass ceiling is not new. There have been many studies that indicate the glass ceiling has not been pierced.[10] There are many corporations, statutes, and governmental agencies that are swinging the hammer to break the ceiling.[11] There is some case law on the subject, but what little law we have favors the breaking of the glass ceiling,[12] even to the extent of bumping the incumbent.[13] There is little question that there will be considerable progress made in the 1990s, and by the year 2000 this will no longer be a problem.[14] The problem of the 1970s was to bring women and minorities into the workforce. In the 1980s the problem was to keep them there. In the 1990s the artificial barriers must be removed to allow upward mobility.[15]

Equal Pay. The wide difference in compensation between the sexes for the same work still remains unsolved. The traditional method of job evaluation and equal pay legislation has failed to

---

[8]See C. King, "Sex, Love Letters and Vicious Remors Anticipating New Statutes Creating Sexually Hostile Environments."

[9]When the author first went to law school, there was one woman in his class of 125 students. When asked what she was doing in law school, her reply was "to marry a lawyer." She did in her junior year and never returned.

[10]*Reporting on Glass Ceiling Door Initiative* (Washington, DC: U.S. Department of Labor, 1991); J. Serling, "Knocking on Congress's Door," *New Woman,* (November 1992), 115; K. Butler, "What Does the Glass Ceiling Cost You?" *Personnel Journal,* 71 (November 1992), 70.

[11]K. Butler, "Melt the Glass Ceiling," *Personnel Journal,* 71, no. 11 (November 1992), 26; *Breaking the Glass Ceiling in the 90's* (Washington, DC: Department of Labor, Women's Bureau, 1992); Civil Rights Act of 1991; K. Springfield, "Chicago Career Queen," *Newsweek,* (June 15 1992), 42.

[12]*Adair* v. *Beech Aircraft Corp.,* 782 F.Supp. 1558 (D.C. Kan. 1992); *Daines* v. *City of Mankato,* 734 F.Supp. 681 (D.C. Minn. 1980).

[13]*Walters* v. *City of Atlanta,* 803 F.2d 1135 (11th Cir. 1986).

[14]L. Dumas, "Hot Careers for 90's," *Working Mother,* 15, no. 8 (August 1992).

[15]Life is like that. When you get up at age 20 you think about sex, at age 30 getting married, at age 40 getting a career, at age 50 making money, at age 60 retiring. When you get up at age 70 you think how many pills you must take. At age 80 you just hope you will get up.

correct the problem. Wage levels established by the marketplace have received judicial acceptance by the majority of the courts, and as more women come into the marketplace, wage differentials in many job categories will be greater. The violation of the equal pay law will continue until there is complete job integration.

In the next decade women in the workforce will become more dominant in American society. The number of women in the workforce already exceeds the 1991 figure of 7 out of 20. They will, with increasing frequency, occupy top-echelon jobs. As they enter top jobs in the 1990s they will become very effective professionals and entrepreneurs. Women have not been deeply influenced by assumptions and practices that have been used in the past to deny them a place in management. Women have the social incentive to succeed; doing well means more to them, because as women they must prove that they are better than or as good as men. This is no easy task when traditionally they have been considered inferior.

There is a light at the end of the tunnel in job integration to solve the equal pay problem. Other methods have failed. Comparable worth was a fad of the 1980s that was doomed at the outset. You cannot compare one job with another by job evaluation when the wage level of one job was not determined by job evaluation. Although comparable worth is legally dead, some state legislatures are trying to revive it.[16] The result of this legislation is to raise the compensation level of female jobs. This will only start a "seesaw action" in the future when the males again decide to rely on the marketplace for their wage levels. Politically, legislation in the comparable worth area is advisable, but it cannot be relied upon to solve the equal pay problem in the future. This does not mean that wage differentials should be accepted by management; it just means that more effective methods should be used.

Affirmative Action and Diversity: Not a Problem

The literature is full of what to do about it. Some entrepreneurs will argue that with the growing number of minorities entering the workforce, it will be good business to have a large percentage of minorities on the payroll. The selection process should favor minorities. They should be identified as minority employees.

This approach is wrong. The minority doesn't want to be treated any differently than anyone else. Hire on merit and forget about diversity training. In the future, programs should be instituted to identify high-potential minority employees in the same manner as the company does for non-minority employees. Management has enough problems without creating more. Train everyone and if the training doesn't work, get rid of the marginal employee. Forget the color of the skin or the gender.

The Handicapped Worker as a Future Problem

The area of dealing with handicapped workers has a potential exposure in the late 1990s and early 2000s.[17] An increasing number of physical conditions and abuses are considered a handicap by most state laws. A person who is physically handicapped doesn't pose a problem if a reasonable attempt is made to accommodate. Employers in the late 1990s and early 2000s will have learned from their mistakes of the 1980s and will be more objective when attempting to accommodate. There will be more tryouts and fewer subjective suppositions that the employee cannot do a certain job. The argument that accommodation affords a danger to others will not stand the judicial test in the late 1990s and early 2000s.[18]

It is in the areas of drug and alcohol abuse that the more serious problems prevail. The employer

---

[16]P. F. Orazem, "Comparable Worth and Factor Point Pay Analysis in State Government," *Industrial Relations, 31* (Winter 1992), 195–215.

[17]The EEOC estimates that ADA will increase their caseload by more than 12,000 per year. The CRA91 will add even more.

[18]Gross obesity will be a Handicap," Rhode Island Dept. of Mental Health, Retardation Hosp., 10 F.3d 17 (1st. Cir. 1993).

can have a policy, but its effect is to drive the activity underground, which causes a more serious problem when it surfaces. A policy alone will not solve the problem; help is needed from the co-workers as well as employee treatment centers that are designed to kill the desire. The employer in the 1990s must recognize that the problem will not go away and a constant vigilance is necessary. No one approach will solve it.

The Smoke-Free Environment

In the late 1990s there will be an increasing number of companies that have a smoke-free environment. A smoke-free environment at the workplace should be a goal. Although sufficient medical evidence now exists to judicially accept the fact that passive smoke is a health hazard,[19] medical opinion is here.[20] There is enough medical evidence and worker opposition to smoking in the workplace to make it advisable for the employer to eliminate the smoking problem as soon as the CEO quits.

The AIDS Problem

The employer who does as little as possible about the AIDS problem will have the least number of scars in the future. There is no relief in sight for an employer solution. Medically AIDS cannot be acquired in a work-related activity. Except for high absenteeism in the final stages, AIDS does not interfere with performance on the job, although health costs increase. All these facts lead to the conclusion that the employer has no need to know if a person has AIDS.

The employment problem arises when a co-worker refuses to work with a known or alleged AIDS patient. Educational programs will give some degree of security, but if the employee has already made up his or her mind, ignoring medical facts, then there is little the employer can do. The AIDS problem is a temporary one that will be solved when a vaccine is found. This is predicted to be sometime in the 1990s. In the meantime the

employer should go into a holding action and deal with each situation on an individual basis, except to continually educate the employees. Transfer, co-worker pressure to terminate, and voluntary quit of co-workers are all considerations. One of the problems with educating the employee is that the media and the government are attempting to educate the public, and this may be contrary to the employer's best interests. A management educational program must be continual and current.

It is advisable for management to make its position on life-threatening diseases known through communication to the employees. The form of communication can be a policy, handbook, memo, payroll stuffer, and so on. The statement should make it clear that management will consider the rights of all the parties involved and will give great weight to medical opinion. The ADA and most state statutes define persons with AIDS as handicapped. They have protection like any other disabled persons under ADA.

Discrimination for Religion

This area of discrimination is continually being tested. Religious belief is strong motivation that will not be compromised without a fight. In the next decade there will be some refinement of what is considered well-settled law. Employers know that they must accommodate, but only a minimum effort is required.[21] The courts have also settled the issue that the employee does not choose accommodation and any reasonable accommodation satisfies the law. What is reasonable will be determined on a case-by-case basis.[22] However, the courts will continue to respect any religious discipline that is acquired before or during employment. The employer's defense is a bona fide attempt to accommodate[23] and not to question the religious belief or the employee's dedication to it. Except for some refinements there will be little change in the late 1990s and early 2000s in this area of personnel law unless ADA has a profound effect upon the courts.

---

[19]See EPA Report on Secondhand Smoke (1993).

[20]See "The Consequences of Involuntary Smoke: A Report of U.S. Surgeon General" (Washington, DC: U.S. Department of Health, 1986).

[21]However, the influence of ADA may cause the courts to change this.

[22]Social Problems 523 (1993).

[23]G. Dotatly, "The Future of Reasonable Accommodations," *Columbia Law Journal,* 26 (1994) 123.

Safety and OSHA

In the late 1990s and early 2000s management will put a higher priority on safety programs. There will be more concentration on unsafe acts. Compliance with OSHA standards is essential to avoid high fines. Compliance will create a safe place to work but will not prevent accidents. It is management's obligation to create safe workers.

Workers' compensation costs will continue to increase to the point where management will concentrate more on safety than on legislation to lower workers' compensation costs. Management accountability for safety will be required by the shareholders and the government.

OSHA will refer more cases to the Department of Justice for criminal prosecution. In its first 20 years of operation the Occupational Safety and Health Review Commission has referred 70 cases for criminal violation, more than one third of these in the last three-year period. This trend will continue. There is a growing trend among state prosecutors to seek criminal conviction of employers who endanger the lives of their workers. Typically, such prosecutions are for violation of state criminal statutes and are not based on violations of specific OSHA standards. State tort action will also increase in view of recent case law that OSHA does not prempt state action in tort.

Egregious penalties will become more common. The increases in fines will cause more litigation because employers will not accept these high penalties. Alternative Dispute Resolution (ADR) will be more common in OSHA cases.

Ergonomics will get a lot of attention in the 1990s and is the coming method to prevent high workers' compensation costs and OSHA citations. Safety directors will become expert ergonomists just as in the 1980s they had to become experts on illness and health. They will not survive as safety directors unless they become professionals in ergonomics.

Employment of Aliens

Congress has made it clear that it is the responsibility of the employer to stop illegal aliens from crossing U.S. borders.[24] The Immigration Reform and Control Act (IRCA) has not removed the acquired rights of undocumented aliens to be protected by antidiscrimination laws or any other statute. If an employee is an undocumented alien the law is saying that there will be no relief until he or she goes home. The employer is liable if she or he does not send the alien home, unless citizenship or a work permit is acquired.[25] It hasn't worked to say to the employer that all that is asked is showing of an intent to comply with the spirit of the law. Congress must find another way.

Compliance with IRCA will not solve the problem in the future, nor will it prevent aliens from coming into the United States. More legislation is forthcoming. It will be another added routine administrative task for which the personnel practitioner is responsible.

The Technology Era

The late 1990s will see technology changing the lifestyle among all workers. The paycheck that is now done by computers will be more accurate and on time. The personnel practitioner will become more concerned with skill level of the workforce than managing a change as they are now. The law as we know it today will become as obsolete as the linotype operator in the printing industry. Shepards citations will be the thing of the past when the lawyer can push a button and get any information at any time that he or she needs.

The Downside of Technology

More lawsuits will result in a greater invasion of privacy. The over 100,000,000 nonunion employees that were given additional rights by Title VII, ADA, OSHA, FMLA, and ADEA will lose some of those by litigation. Downsizing is a

---

[24]In its first years of existence, IRCA has failed to stop illegal aliens from crossing the borders.

[25]Since the passage of IRCA in 1990 it has become much easier for aliens to become documented.

part of our technological society that is not to be forgotten.

LABOR-MANAGEMENT RELATIONS

There will be little increase in unionization in the late 1990s. Only 10 percent of the private sector belongs to unions. The best-educated prediction is that labor will continue to lose a percentage of the workforce.[26] The previous 25 to 30 percent level will not be achieved in the foreseeable future. The 15 to 20 percent level is more realistic. However, the heavy concentration of union membership in auto, paper, steel, aerospace, entertainment, mining, construction, transportation, and communications will continue. Unions are still effective. The average wage in 1992 was $547 per week for union members and $412 for nonmembers.

The Changing Image of Unions

To attract new members, unions are offering a variety of nontraditional benefits. Such benefits include[27]

1. Credit cards requiring no annual fee and charging less interest
2. Free 30-minute legal consultations and document review and a 30 percent discount on subsequent legal charges from a national panel of attorneys
3. Supplemental group health insurance
4. Low-cost travel, including discounts on airfare, hotels, and car rental
5. Tighter arbitration policy to save money

Unions in their organizing efforts will continue to wait for any management action that breeds discontent. Wages and benefits are no longer a big

---

[26]Between 1972 and 1991 more than 31 million new jobs were created, but union membership did not increase in 1991: USDL Release No. 92–61, Bureau of Labor Statistics. The NLRB reported a 20 percent decrease in election cases for 1992. The success rate of union elections dropped from 48 to 45 percent. The trend is continuing. By the year 2000 union membership could be 5 percent of the workforce.

[27]M. Ballet, "New Directions in Union Organizing," *Labor Law Journal* (Dec. 1994).

concern for employees, but layoffs, discharges, security, and fairness in working conditions will still be important.[28]

Unions will continue to increase in their activity in enforcing antidiscrimination laws and safety or health laws. Governmental enforcement agencies will not be able to relax in their enforcement activities as long as union pressure continues.

New Bargaining Approach

The major change in union activities will be an abandonment of the traditional collective bargaining and grievance representation. Studies show that members are no longer interested in seniority issues, nor do they want to strike, the very foundations that unions grew from in the 1950s and 1960s. In addition to increasing benefits, unions and the government are abandoning the traditional adversity in collective bargaining and attempting more labor-management cooperation in all aspects of the employer-employee relationship. The representation will be in many areas other than the traditional working conditions. In such areas as discrimination, workers' compensation, unemployment compensation, and OSHA, laypersons are permitted to represent others. Union professionals can become experts as employee representatives in the same manner as they have acquired expertise in arbitration. The leader who rose through the ranks from a worker to a union leader is being replaced by the educated activist.[29]

Ineffectiveness of the Strike Weapon

In the 1990s the effectiveness of the strike as a technique to achieve economic gains will continue to diminish. This was once a powerful weapon to pressure the employer into submitting to almost any demand. As a union leader once told the author, "We have to decide how much we will take from the employers this year." The employer has

---

[28]In 1995 unions have won as many elections as they lost, but the trend will not continue.

[29]See B. Pisik, "An Organizer's Drive to Lead the Teamsters," *Insight,* 7 no. 42 (October 21, 1991), 28.

found a way to combat the strike weapon by the use of replacements. (They can also be used in case of a legal lockout.) The right to hire replacements and deny the strikers reinstatement until a vacancy occurs has existed for many years but was not used until the middle 1980s. The Supreme Court in *Belknap, Inc.* v. *Hale,* 103 S.Ct. 3172 (1983), held that under certain circumstances a strike replacement had an employment contract that was actionable in a state court when replaced by the striker after the strike was settled. Employers have been surprisingly successful in the use of strike replacements. Many workers were convinced that the employer could not operate without their skills. The striking workers were overwhelmed when they found out the employer could. For many years employers, too, did not think it was possible. Their success in use of replacements has grown to the extent that highly talented professional football players can be replaced when they go out on strike (not so with baseball).[30] The threat of the use of replacements at the bargaining table gives the employer a superior bargaining position. It will also cause the membership to accept the employer's position.[31] When the power to strike is gone, it will be difficult for the union to hold its membership unless there is representation in other areas.

Organized labor problems of survival will also be increased in the 1990s by the changing of the complexion of the workforce. The union-represented workers are not only declining in numbers, but their militancy has disappeared as well. They have become middle class workers who are concerned with individual achievements rather than collective action. Unions will focus on the political process in the late 1990s.[32]

The Rise of the Nonunion Worker

Another substantial change in labor-management relations in the late 1990s will be the increased use of the National Labor Relations Act by nonunion workers. They will become more aware of their rights under the act. The realization that they do not have to belong to a union to be protected under the act will cause many problems for the employer in the 1990s who often does not realize that nonunion employees have protection of the act. Because the workers have rejected the union as a place to go for relief, they will turn to the NLRB. Employer concern that concerted activity has the same protection for the nonunion worker as for the union worker will be on the menu in the 1990s. The employer must be protected and, at the same time, protect employee common law and statutory rights.

Alternative Dispute Resolution (ADR)

The use of ADR will increase. More statutes like CRA91 will provide for the procedure.[33] All types of disputes will rely on mediation processes. Disputes under almost all antidiscrimination statutes, as well as other granting of employee rights, will be expensive in the 1990s if allowed to go to court. The cost of going to trial will exceed $100,000. Alternative Dispute Resolution is cheaper and faster.

As the workplace becomes more diverse and multicultural as a result of new waves of immigration, new and expanded opportunities for the disabled, racial integration, and ever increasing numbers of women in the workforce, alternative dispute resolution, particularly arbitration and mediation, can and indeed must become a vital force and key method and avenue for achieving social stability and harmony in the workplace.

ADR will be the dispute solution of the future, especially as litigation and arbitration costs rise. The EEOC will adopt a procedure of deferring to ADR, as the NLRB did in deferring to arbitration.

---

[30]In the strike of the National Football League in 1987, replacements weakened the bargaining position of players to the extent that it was settled without granting of the major demands that caused the strike. In 1994, 1995 the players were not replaced.

[31]In 1974 there were 424 strikes involving 1,000 or more employees. In 1989 there were 52.

[32]In the 1988 elections unions gave $16 million to candidates.

[33]For good discussion on ADR, see T. Olsen, "Alternative Dispute Resolution," *The Human Resources Year Book, 1992/93,* ed. Mary F. Cook (Englewood Cliffs, NJ: Prentice Hall), p. 16.60.

DIRECTION OF PERSONNEL LAW IN DISCHARGE

The erosion of the employment-at-will doctrine will continue in the late 1990s. It will force more employers to adopt a just-cause policy of their own before their state legislature does it for them.

COMMON MYTHS IN EMPLOYMENT LAW CASES

Myth Number One

If we can prove the employee is scum, we will win.

Truth
Two wrongs do not make a right. Again, all things being equal, a tie will go to the employee. As a corollary to this, the majority does not rule in an employment case. In other words, if an employer can corroborate its story with 20 other people, and an employee can corroborate his or her story with only two other people, the employee will still (in all likelihood) win.

Myth Number Two

A well-documented file will provide a good defense.

Truth
A papered file is worse than no file. A papered file is a file where the employer has decided to fire the employee and then goes about accumulating documents. Many times the employer can avoid being caught, but when the employer is caught, it is a costly situation. Nothing in the file is worse than no file at all. The best course of action for an employer is to make a good faith effort to honestly and sincerely document the employee's work performance. Any more or less and the employer is in trouble.

Myth Number Three

All things being equal, a jury is likely to accept an employer's argument. There is conflict at the beginning.

Truth
The employer behavior is much more closely scrutinized by a jury than an employee's behavior. All things being equal, a tie will go to the employee.

Myth Number Four

Because we treat all our employees the same way, we are fair and legally protected.

Truth
The jury asks what is fair and the right thing to do for the person.

Importance of the Handbook or Policy Manual

The handbook or policy manual will play an increasing role as a contract in the late 1990s. Employers will have to change the traditional handbook to either make it a contract or put in a disclaimer. The disclaimer or release will have limited popularity. If the employer discovers that this false security will create more problems than it will solve, their use will cease. A disclaimer will not be a substitute for a poorly written handbook. The handbook of the future will tell the employees what is expected of them and not what the employer will do for them. It will cease to be a document to sell the company to the worker and will be a document to enforce the company policies and procedures. In the future, management as well as the employee will have to follow the handbook provisions. It will be in a nonunion setting what the collective bargaining agreement is in a union facility.

Remedies in Tort Actions

The most serious change in personnel law in the 1990s will occur in the area of punitive damages (if not limited by statute) and the invasion of privacy, especially by technology.[34] The theory that a violation should make the employee whole is rapidly changing. Members of

---

[34]K. H. Decker, "Employment Privacy Law for the 90's," *Pepperdine Law Review,* 15, no. 4 (1988), 551.

the plaintiff's bar will seize every opportunity to bring an action for punitive damages rather than to rely on the remedy provided in statutes. Most statutes were passed on the theory that a violation is a statutory wrong for which the plaintiff should be made whole.[35] The trend in punitive damages can be stopped through policies and procedures that respect the law and a humane treatment of the employees. In sexual harassment cases and under the ADEA, the plaintiff feels that a greater wrong is done for which he or she wants money. Rather than going to the statute, the plaintiff sues under the common law doctrine of tort. If the court finds that the statute is not an exclusive remedy, the case will be allowed to go to the jury, which can award punitive damages rather than the remedy under the statute. The CRA91 and other statutues will increase the number of jury cases, but awards will be lower.

The plaintiff's bar will push malpractice suits and huge awards to their very limits. The movement to limit the size of the awards by statute will continue in the late 1990s. Many states will have statutes limiting the liability. CRA91 has put a limit on awards that is lower than the average jury award in 1992. When a doctor has to pay up to $200,000 for malpractice insurance, it becomes a social problem that the politician will do something about. The correction of the abuse for the medical profession will also apply to such other areas as legal malpractice and management malpractice.

Under the Employee Retirement Income Security Act[36] (ERISA), the practitioner or manager can, by terms of the statute, be individually liable for a violation. This was followed by the Consolidated Omnibus Budget Reconciliation Act[37] (COBRA), and later the Immigration Reform and Control Act[38] (IRCA). These three major acts in personnel law all made the individual personally liable for violation of a particular provision. In the late 1990s the Congress, in an effort to have a built-in enforcement provision, will include individual liability. The personnel practitioner must not in the future rely upon the "corporate veil" for protection when a particular provision of a statute is violated.

PREDICTIONS IN OTHER AREAS

Trends in Workers' Compensation

The high cost of WC insurance will in the future cause the employer to institute cost control programs the same as cost containment in the health care field. In the late 1990s there will be more deductibles and back-to-work incentives similar to the health care area. Because it is a social insurance program, it is highly unlikely that there will be any co-insurance. The cost of insurance will become competitive among the states, and in this respect, changes will become political.

Iowa, Massachusetts, Michigan, Minnesota, and many other states have incentives built in the law for both the employee and the employer to control costs. This approach will spread in the late 1990s to more states. There will be more pressure to reduce litigation in workers' compensation because this is one objective of the state laws that has badly failed.

There will be a deregulation of the insurance industry that will cause open competition, and then the insurance companies will be interested in claim control in the same way as they have been selling their services because of the cost control programs. State insurance plans to cover workers' compensation benefits will not grow in the 1990s. Many of the existing plans are already broke.

Unemployment Compensation in the 1990s

In the future there will be more revisions of the tax rate, so those industries that have the highest unemployment will be paying higher taxes. These

---

[35]CRA91 allows punitive damages under certain conditions. Because punitive damages are recognized in the statute, there will be more litigation on what they mean. The decision in *Foley* v. *Interactive Data,* 765 P.2d 373 (Calif. S.Ct. 1988), has been replaced by statute.

[36]29 USCA Sect. 1001 et seq.

[37]P.L. 99–509, Title X (1986).

[38]P.L. 99–603, also known as the Simpson-Rodino Act (1986).

revisions will be made by increasing the minimum and maximum tax rate.

Because of higher taxes, employers will be more concerned with reducing their costs and therefore will become more skilled in presenting their appeals. However, the use of legal counsel will increase in cases where the stakes are high. The employer will insist that the only benefits that the employees should receive are when they are out of work "through no fault of their own" and are not available for work while receiving benefits. As more case law is developed in the areas of voluntary quit and misconduct, employers will better understand it. They will develop policies and practices that will clearly define misconduct. There can be no misunderstanding that certain employee actions are voluntary quits. An example would be to refuse treatment for substance abuse; however, an option to return to work after successful treatment must be made clear. When an employee acts in a certain way it will be considered a voluntary quit.

An Increase in Written Policies

In the late 1990s more companies will have more effective written policies than in the past. The larger the organization, the more need for policies. These policies will be for the purpose of communication and preventing exposure to lawsuits.[39] In most cases policies already exist in some form, but all too often they are in a form that the courts will not accept. Policy revision in the late 1990s will get the attention of management when

1. There are attempts by the union to represent the employees.

2. A lack of communication is causing problems.

3. A lawsuit is started because of absence of policy.

4. Present policies are in confict with state or federal law.

5. The organizational structure has changed so much that the old policies are no longer effective.

In some areas, such as sexual harassment, substance abuse searches, privacy through technology, and discharge, policies are essential to avoid liability. In other areas policies are desirable for communication to the employees. The policy manual or handbook in the 1990s will be more carefully written. It will avoid such phrases as "We reserve the right"; "Exceptions may be made for _____"; "You have job security here."

The use of policies by managers to justify a position already taken or to disregard the policy if it is contrary to that position will cease in the 1990s. All provisions of the policy will be followed by all members of management, or there will be a lawsuit and then the policy will be followed.

Increase in privacy suits will correlate with the use of technology.

Relationship with Legal Counsel

The personnel practitioner in the late 1990s must have enough knowledge of the law not only to keep legal costs and damages at a minimum but also to be able to carry out the personnel function as economically as before employee rights legislation.

The legal counsel, to be of service to the personnel practitioner, must be more discreet in giving legal advice in the 1990s. Counsel must do a better job of understanding employee relations consequences of a decision. There may be many policies with which legal counsel does not agree but which are legally sound. "On advice of counsel" must be legal advice and not policy advice on personnel matters unless specifically requested.

The personnel legal counsel of the 1990s must say no[40] less often and assess the exposure to taking a certain action to keep the wheels turning. Saying that a particular employment decision is not legal is easy and safe. The exposure of being

---

[39]See "An Ounce of Prevention," *Inc.*, (October 1984), 153.

[40]When this author was a corporate legal counsel and was called to give an opinion on a problem, the answer was no, it could not be legally done. The practitioner then reminded me of a directive I had written while a personnel executive two years previous directing the requested action. This author's answer was, "Then I was in personnel; now I am legal counsel and I say you can't legally do it."

proven wrong is almost eliminated.[41] An employment decision must be made; one with the least legal exposure should be forthcoming from the legal counsel.[42] There is a duty on the personnel practitioner to demand useful legal advice on how to do something, not advice that it can't be legally accomplished. If such demand is made without success, then a change in legal counsel should be considered.[43]

The legal counsel of the late 1990s must be aware of personnel practitioner problems. Counsel must understand that although there may not be the best evidence to discharge an employee to prevent a wrongful discharge lawsuit, the manager is going to discharge the employee regardless of the legal advice. The task of legal counsel is to advise on the best way to do it to prevent a lawsuit.

Managers are not going to let the law or the courts run the operation; the job of the legal counsel and personnel practitioner is to advise the most legal way to do it.[44] The personnel practitioner must insist on legal advice that tells how to do it, not that one cannot do it. Economically effective use of legal counsel is a must for the 1990s and beyond.[45] There is statistical evidence that management is not prepared to handle the increased number of employee complaints of the late 1990s. To be prepared, management must put preventive law at the top of the priority ladder.[46]

HIGH-PRIORITY TASKS IN THE 1990s

The strains and stresses of the employment relationship are evident in the preceding chapters. OSHA, ADA, and EEOC regulate employment decisions by statute. This trend will continue to grow. Nothing will happen unless action is taken and priorities for this action are set.

This text has an abundance of recommendations to relieve the stress and strain of the employment relationship and suggestions either to prevent litigation or to defend lawsuits. If all were adopted, the personnel practitioner would do nothing else but write and administer policy changes. It would be unrealistic to expect that such recommendations would fit all organizations and all situations. It is, therefore, appropriate at this time to recommend four of the most important actions to be taken that will prevent more than 90 percent of all litigation and not interfere with the objectives of the organization to make a profit or perform a service. They are

A policy on sexual harassment that is effective

A search and seizure statement

A policy on substance abuse

A discharge procedure

Sexual Harassment

Sexual harassment is one of the most difficult employee activities to stop, and the least difficult to avoid liability for. A policy is a must for the 1990s. The statement should give the employer's position on this illegal activity and be effective. Being effective means doing something about it that will prevent the activity from being repeated.

The policy must require the employee to report to any member of management an unwelcome activity. If it is not reported, it is considered welcome. An activity may be welcome today but unwelcome tomorrow. It may be welcome to one co-worker and not to another.

How management is informed is not important as long as they know or should have known. The employee must be assured that the policy on no retaliation will be strictly followed.

---

[41]See W. Albrecht, "The Changing Face of Personnel Law and the Practical Lawyer," *North Dakota Law Review,* 67 (1991), 469.

[42]As the author's superior once said in mild reprimand, "Mismanagement is better than no management at all."

[43]This is sometimes difficult where there is in-house counsel. The best effort is probably to complain to the supervisor, who uses best political judgment on how to correct the situation.

[44]The author once was legal counsel to a manager who always got in trouble with the law. When asked why he did things that tested the law, he replied, "You are smart enough to get me out of it."

[45]R. Reminger, "At Risk," *Personnel Journal,* 70, no. 3 (March 1991), 52.

[46]For the importance of good management to prevent exposure, see C. Santana-Melgoza, "When Discrimination Is Not the Case," *Labor Law Journal,* 42, no. 6 (June 1991), 376–80.

Once informed, management must immediately do something about it. What is immediate depends upon several factors and differs from company to company. Doing something about it means investigating, documenting the investigation, and evaluating the results. The complaint must be accepted at its face value until all the evidence has been evaluated. After evaluation, management must take the steps that are necessary to prevent the activity from being repeated.

In the 1990s there will be sexual harassment litigation even if the procedure described here is followed. Those who do not have a policy will have one after litigation. The activity exists; it will not go away. It may go underground. Only employer policy will prevent liability.

Search and Seizure

Almost every employer in the 1990s will have excessive pilferage of employee's or employer's property. They may not realize it for a period of time, but it is there. With a policy the exposure to litigation is greatly reduced. Most courts will accept the legal principle that once a policy has been communicated and the employee continues to work, the employee is prevented from challenging the policy.

The employer's policy is intended to prevent pilferage, not to catch the employee. The law permits the employer to protect its property and that of its employees. The employer's action should not be because of the law, but to protect property.

Those employers who think that prosecuting the workers will stop pilferage soon will have egg on their face. The police need stronger evidence to prosecute than the employer does to discharge because of a violation of a policy. The policy should not be concerned with changing the social order, but with preventing pilferage at the work site.

In the 1990s, the employer who communicates a search and seizure statement will reduce pilferage, lessen exposure to litigation, and promote good employee relations.

A Policy on Substance Abuse

Before there can be any enforcement of a substance abuse policy, there must be a communicated rule that possession, sale, and being under the influence of any drug or alcohol are prohibited. This rule must be in place before any procedure can be used to determine whether it has been violated.

The purpose of a test is to obtain the facts to determine whether an existing rule has been violated. The U.S. Congress, state legislatures, and court decisions will permit testing in the late 1990s with increasing frequency.

Testing is not the only way to determine whether a policy has been violated. Often observance can be more valid than a test.

The employer never knows when testing will be needed. Some state statutes prevent the use of tests under certain conditions, but most of them allow it when there is a reasonable belief that the policy has been violated. Random testing will become more legal in the 1990s, but the employer must consider the exposure to litigation and the consequences for employee relations. The author is against the use of random testing as such, except to require it as a condition of employment after the job offer has been made.

The problem of substance abuse can be solved by legal procedures to determine whether the rule has been violated; however, the employee's privacy must be respected at all times.

Adoption of Termination Policy

The fourth most important policy to be adopted is a termination policy. The day is gone when the supervisor, while in an emotional state and with shaky hands, goes to the work site and says, "You're fired." Employers must adopt a just-cause policy for discharge before legislation and the courts do it for them.[47] If adopted by the employer, the policy should coordinate with other policies and goals of the organization.

---

[47]Some of the provisions of the Model Termination Act will be adopted by the various states.

There are enough decisions by the courts to know what just cause means. Just cause is the violation of policy or warning for poor performance when the employer has knowledge that the violation would result in discharge. The adoption of a just-cause policy by the employer should be a gradual program starting at certain job levels or job categories and expanding with experience.

In a nonunion plant the blue-collar worker must be familiar with a just-cause policy. The policy in the beginning does not have to be any more than communication of the sudden death reasons for discharge and of the progressive discharge procedure. Many employers feel that adoption of a just-cause policy would eliminate any defense that the common law employment-at-will doctrine affords. This assumption is not necessarily true. The policy could adopt the exceptions to public policy, malice, and bad faith, but not implied contract. Because the United States is the only industrialized country that does not have a federal just-cause policy, it is essential that it is kept that way.

Positive Personnel Administration Policies

Positive personnel administration policies are:

A complaint procedure

Uniform policy administration

An antidiscrimination policy covering all members of the protected class

Objective measurement of performance

The Personnel Function and the Law

During the period of the publication of three editions of this book there has not been a relationship in the United States that is not experiencing stress—relations between men and women, between the employer and the employee, between husband and wife, between executives and their boards, between unions and their members, and between management, employees, and legislative branches of governments. These strains on social and political relationships are evident in the preceding pages. In the 1990s employer and employee will become aware of this stress and, within their ability, directly or indirectly will relieve it. There will be more consideration for the other person's point of view, and restraints in all areas will decrease. Power will be exercised only to relieve the stress and not to create it. Failure in the late 1990s to do something about this situation would be a substantial loss for the personnel function.[48]

Personnel work in the late 1990s should continue to be exciting. One can consider questions on the application form that are meaningful, merit increases that reward performance, tests that will predict performance on the job, performance appraisals that will actually rate performance, uniform criteria for discharge, not having to defend the supervisor's subjective judgment of hiring and promotion, and employees knowing their rights.

GAZE INTO THE CRYSTAL BALL

- The concept of the *job* will fade. Workers will possess a variety of skills and responsibilities, rather than being confined to the parameters of a traditional job description.
- Job performance may be assessed by monitoring electrical activity from the brain, telling an employer whether a worker is busy or fatigued.
- Growth of telecommuting may lead to environmental problems as millions of telecommuters overrun rural areas and spoil the natural beauty.
- Major conflicts are likely to develop in the future as Baby Boomers age and Generation X balks at supporting a growing number of retirees.
- Manufacturing productivity improvement will be bad news for job seekers. U.S. factory output grew 21 percent between 1987 and 1992, but the number of manufacturing jobs fell by 4 percent.

---

[48]This statement is true of any preventive law procedure. The author once had a case where an affirmative action program costing less than $100 could have prevented a charge that cost over $3,000 to settle. To the author's knowledge the employer still doesn't have a plan.

No longer will users of information be forced to come to one central location to obtain the information they need; instead, the information will come to them at any hour of the day or night, regardless of their location (in the office, at home, on the beach). Law firms will be able to cut costs by eliminating the many square feet of prime office space now allocated to book stacks.

The personnel function will become one of the most important functions of management.[49] By hiring qualified applicants the company will grow. Poor performance when objectively measured is always correctable and accordingly does not prevent growth. The workforce will take an interest in the company growth; and, with high-quality people, stock options, profit sharing, and other incentive plans will be easily sold to the board of directors as an effective means to accomplish organizational goals.

The law is in place;[50] the merging of the law and personnel function is basically completed. Since the personnel function has an added ingredient, the law, it has become more professional and very exciting. As a result of the new ingredient, the practitioner has more responsibility and in some cases is overworked.[51]

Case law and the statutes are telling the employer that in the process of investigating an employment complaint the employer may not be found guilty. The employer loses even though there are no monetary damages. Often employees file charges when they do not know what law has been violated. They feel they have been wronged in some way. The law permits the employee to attempt to correct this employer wrongdoing. The focus of this text is on the exposure to litigation. Personnel practices may have to be revised not because they are unlawful, but to prevent the turmoil in the workplace that results when a lawsuit is filed.

This book gives the laws that prohibit wrongful acts by an employer. There is no law that prohibits poor management. The test of the efficiency of any organization is not whether personnel practice falls within the law. Practices and procedures must go beyond the law into the realm of good management. The federal government and the states will not or cannot legislate good management, but nothing prevents the employer from practicing it.

As we close out the 20th century and enter into the 21st, the personnel function has made a complete cycle. From its very beginning it was a necessary management function that was considered administrative. It is now not only an administrative necessity but also a cost-control function. Exposure to lawsuits is abortive to good employee relations. It is not necessary for survival, especially for a small company.

The author's only regret is that he is not beginning his career in personnel and law—what fun it would be! The students—those starting in the field as well as present practitioners—are to be envied. It is only the passive, obsolete personnel practitioner, his or her legal counsel, and those of us who are ending our careers in personnel law that are to be pitied.

---

[49] HR will computerize their operations from midrange and mainframe systems to client/server systems.

[50] See *Federal Labor Laws,* 14th ed. (St. Paul, MN: West, 1992).

[51] According to the Bureau of Labor Statistics, the average worker now spends 49 hours a week on the job. This is a considerable increase since 1980. For the personnel or human resources manager the increase is even greater.

APPENDIX

Case	Number	Pages
Andrews v. *City of Philadelphia*	895 F.2d 1469, 1482 (3rd Cir. 1990)	97, 98
Ansonia Board of Education v. *Philbrook*	107 S.Ct. 376 (1986)	73, 75
APP Parts Co. v. *Auto Workers*	923 F.2d 486 (7th Cir. 1991)	297
Arcadi v. *Nestlé Food Corp.*	38 F.3d 672 (2nd Cir. 1994)	217
Arizona Governing Comm. for Tax Deferred Annuity and Deferred Compensation Plans, Etc., et al. v. *Nathalie Norris, Etc.*	103 S.Ct. 3492 (1983)	108, 146
Armeson v. *Heckler*	946 F.2d 90 (8th Cir. 1991)	73
Arnold v. *Firestone Tire & Rubber Co.*	686 S.W.2d 65 (Tenn. 1984)	78
Associated General Contractors v. *Calif. State Council of Carpenters*	103 S.Ct. 897 (1983)	309
Astroline Communications Co. v. *Sherberg Broadcasting*	110 S.Ct. 997 (1990)	126
AT&T Technologies Inc. v. *Communication Workers of America et al.*	106 S.Ct. 1415 (19986)	296
Automobile Salesmen's Union v. *NLRB*	711 F.2d 383 (D.C. Cir. 1983)	285
Autoworkers v. *Yard-Man, Inc.*	716 F.2d 1476 (6th Cir. 1983)	148
Ayoub v. *Texas A&M Univeristy*	927 F.ed 834 (5th Cir. 1991)	40
Baggs v. *Eagle-Picher Industries, Inc.*	957 F.2d 268 (6th Cir. 1992)	83
Baker v. *Weyerhaeuser Co.*	903 F.2d 1342 (9th Cir. 1991)	100
Ballard v. *Consolidated Steel Corp.*	61 F.Supp. 996 (S.D. Cal. 1945)	214
Ball v. *Cracking Good Bakeries*	777 F.2d 149 (11th Cir. 1986)	305
Banas v. *Matthews International Corp.*	502 A.2d 637 (Pa. Super. 1985)	207
Barnes v. *Gen Corp. Inc.*	896 F.2d 1457 (6th Cir. 1990)	118
Batchelor v. *Sears, Roebuck and Co.*	574 F.Supp. 1480 (E.D. Mich. 1983)	184
Bates v. *State Bar of Arizona*	97 S.Ct. 2691, 433 U.S. 384 (1977)	4
Baxter International Inc. v. *Morris*	976 F.2d 1189 (10th Cir. 1992)	152, 153
Bay v. *Times Mirror Magazines*	936 F.2d 112 (2nd Cir. 1991)	114, 119
Becnel v. *Answer Inc., et al.*	428 So.2d 539 (La. App. 1983)	144
Belanoff v. *Grayson*	471 N.Y.S.2d (A.D. 1st Dept. 1984)	302
Belknap, Inc. v. *Hale*	103 S.Ct. 3172 (1983)	165, 325
Belknap, Inc. v. *Hale*	463 U.S. 491 (1983)	293–94
Benassi v. *Georgia-Pacific*	662 P.2d 760 (Ore. App. 1983)	205
Bender v. *A.G. Edwards & Sons*	971 F.2d 698 (11th Cir. 1992)	296
Berand v. *IMI Systems, Inc.*	8 IER cases 325 (BNA 1993)	164
Beth Israel Hospital v. *NLRB*	437 U.S. 483 (1978)	283
Biderman's of Springfield, Inc. v. *Wright*	322 S.W.2d 892 (Mo. 1959)	199
Biggins v. *Hazen Paper Co.*	953 F.2d 1405 (1st Cir. 1992)	120
Biggs v. *Wilson*	1 F.3d 1537 (9th Cir. 1993)	212
Bill Johnson's Restaurants, Inc. v. *NLRB*	103 S.Ct. 2161 (1983)	282
Birklid v. *Boeing Co.*		311
Birmingham Ornalmental CO. v. *NLRB*	615 F.2d 66 (5th Cir. 1980)	283
Blackmon v. *Brookshire Grocery Co.*	835 F.2d 1135 (5th Cir. 1988)	221
Blaw-Knox Foundry and Mill v. *NLRB*	646 F.2d 113 (4th Cir. 1981)	95
Boem v. *American Bankers Insurance Group, Inc.*	557 So.2d 91 (Fla. App. 3rd Dist. 1990)	199
Bohrer v. *Hanes Corp.*	715 F.2d 213 (5th Cir. 1985)	115, 133
Bolling v. *Baker*	671 S.W.2d 559 (Tex. App. 4 Dist. 1984)	200
Bongiovanni v. *Vanlor Investments*	370 N.W.2d 828 (Minn. App. 1985)	262

Case	Number	Pages
Boothby v. *Atlas Mechanical, Inc.*	8 Cal. Rptr. 600 1992 Cal. App. LEXIS 726 (Cal. 3rd Dist. 1992)	145
Boton v. *Dept. of Human Resources*	(1995)	204
Bourque v. *Powell Electrical Mfg. Co.*	617 F.2d 61 (5th Cir. 1980)	168
Bowen v. *U.S. Postal Service*	103 S.Ct. 588 (1983)	292
Bower v. *AT&T Technologies*	852 F.2d 361 (8th Cir. 1988)	173
Boynton Cab Co. v. *Newbeck*	296 N.W.2d 636 (Wis. 1941)	262
Boys Market v. *Retail Clerks Union*	398 U.S. 235 (1970)	295
Bozemore v. *Friday*	106 S.Ct. 3000 (1986)	119
Braatz v. *Labor Industry Review Comm.*	496 N.W.2d 597 (U.S. Sup.Ct. 1993)	108
Bradley Lumber Co. v. *NLRB*	128 F.2d 768 (8th Cir. 1942)	283
Brady v. *Safety Klee Corp.*	576 N.E.2d 722 (Ohio S.Ct. 1991)	311
Branch v. *G. Bernd Co., et al.*	955 F.2d 574 (11th Cir. 1992)	147
Bratt v. *IBM*	785 F.2d 352 (1st Cir. 1986)	199
Brennan v. *T.M. Fields, Inc.*	488 F.2d 443 (5th Cir. 1973)	107
Bright v. *Houston Northwest Medical Center Survivors, Inc.*	934 F.2d 671 (5th Cir. 1991)	214
Brock v. *Georgia S.W. College*	765 F.2d 1026 (11th Cir. 1985)	107
Brock v. *M.W. Fireworks, Inc.*	871 F.2d 307 (8th Cir. 1989)	218
Brock v. *Norman's Country Market, Inc.*	825 F.2d 823 (11th Cir. 1988)	221
Broderick v. *Ruder*	685 F.Supp. 1269 (D.C. 1988)	95
Brown v. *A.J. Gerard Mfg. Co.*	695 F.2d 1290 (11th Cir. 1983)	259
Brown v. *Polk County*	61 F.3d 650 (8th Cir. 1995)	74
Brown v. *Port of Sunnyside Club, Inc.*	304 N.W.2d 877 (Minn. 1981)	262
Bruno v. *United Steelworkers of America*	784 F. Supp. 1286 (D. Ohio 1992)	147
Buffalo Forge Co. v. *United Steelworkers of America*	428 U.S. 397 (1976)	295
Bullock v. *Auto Club of Michigan*	444 N.W.2d 114 (Mich. S.Ct. 1989)	165
Burch v. *A&G Associates*	333 N.W.2d 140 (1983)	203
Burks v. *Lasker*	441 U.S. 471 (1975)	310
Burne v. *McGregor Electronics, Inc.*	989 F.2d 959 (8th Cir. 1989)	96
Burns v. *McGregor Electric Industries, Inc.*	955 F.2d 559 (8th Cir. 1992)	95
Burns v. *McGregor Electric*	989 F.2d 939 (8th Cir. 1993)	98
Butros v. *Canton Reg. Transit Authority*	997 F.2d 196 (6th Cir. 1992)	63
Byrd v. *Lakeshore Hospital*	30 F.3d 1380 (8th Cir. 1994)	140
Calero v. *Del Chemical Corp.*	228 N.W.2d 737 (Wisc. 1975)	200
California Federal Savings and Loan Assn. v. *Guerra*	107 S.Ct. 683 (1987)	140
California Hospital Assn. v. *Henning*	770 F.2d 856 (9th Cir. 1985)	145
Capellopo v. *FMC Corp.*	50 FEP cases (BNA) 11 57	187
Carpenters Local 1478 v. *Stevens*	743 F.2d 1271 (9th Cir. 1984)	297
Carr v. *General Motors Corp.*	389 N.W.2d 686 (Mich. 1986)	246
Castiglione v. *Johns Hopkins Hospital*	517 F.2d 786 (Md. App. 1986)	178
Cazzola v. *Codman & Shurtleff, Inc.*	751 F.2d 53 (1st Cir. 1984)	169
Cedar Construction Co. v. *OSHRC*	587 F.2d 1303 (D.C. Cir. 1978)	310
Chambless v. *Master, Mates & Pilots Pension Plan*	772 F.2d 1032 (2nd Cir. 1985)	150
Cherry v. *Kelly Services, Inc.*	319 S.E.2d 463 (Ga. App. 1984)	204
Chiari v. *City of league City*	920 F.2d 311 95th Cir. 1991)	71
Chicago Tribune Co. v. *NLRB*	943 F.2d 791 (7th Cir. 1992)	41

Case	Number	Pages
Christenson v. *Iowa*	563 F.2d 353 (8th Cir. 1977)	111
Chrysler Motors Corp. v. *International Union, Allied Industrial Workers of America AFL-CIO Local 793*	959 F.2d 685 (7th Cir. 1992)	298
Cincinnati Newspaper Guild v. *NLRB*	938 F.2d 284 (D.C. Cir. 1991)	288
Circus Circus Hotels v. *Witherspoon*	657 P.2d 101 (Nev. 1983)	200
City of Los Angeles v. *Manhart*	435 U.S. 702 (U.S. S.Ct. 1978)	108, 146
City of Richmond v. *J.A.Croson Co.*	109 S.Ct. 706 (1989)	124, 127
City of Riverside v. *Rivera*	106 S.Ct. 2686 (1986)	43
Clark v. *World Airways*	24 FEP cases (BNA) (D.C. of D.C. 1980)	305
Coble v. *Bonita House, Inc.*	789 F. Supp. 320 (N.D. Cl. 1992)	148
Cockrell v. *Boise Cascade*	(10th Cir. 1986)	168, 170
Cole v. *Farm Fresh Poultry Inc.*	824 F.2d 923 (11th Cir. 1987)	214
Comerford v. *International Harvester Co.*	178 So.2d 894 (Ala. 1932)	157
Communication Workers of America v. *NLRB*	784 F.2d 847 (7th Cr. 1986)	292
Confer v. *Custom Engineering Co.*	952 F.2d 41 (3rd Cir. 1991)	149
Conkwright v. *Westinghouse Electric Co.*	933 F.2d 231 (4th Cir. 1991)	150
Connecticut v. *Teal*	102 S.Ct. 2525 (1982)	38–39, 56, 66, 146
Conner v. *Fort Gordon Bus Co.*	761 F.2d 1493 (11th Cir. 1985)	175
Corning Glass Works v. *Brennan*	417 U.S. 188 (1974)	106
Corp. of Presiding Bishops v. *Amos*	107 S.Ct. 2862 (1987)	74
Cort v. *Bristol-Meyers*	431 N.E.2d 908 (Mass. 1983)	198
Costa v. *Markey*	677 F.2d 1582 (1st Cir. 1982)	62
County of Washington v. *Gunther*	101 S.Ct. 2242 (1981)	111
Cova v. *Coca-Cola Bottling of St. Louis*	574 F.2d 576 (6th Cir. 1978)	133
Crain v. *Burroughs Corp.*	560 F.Supp. 849 (D.C. Cal. 1983)	184
Crain Industries, Inc. v. *Cass*	810 S.W.2d 910 (Ark. S.Ct. 1991)	177
Cunico v. *Pueblo School District No. 60*	917 F.2d 431 (10th Cir. 1990)	127, 131
Daemi v. *Church's Fried Chicken*	931 F.2d 1379 (10th Cir. 1991)	63
Daines v. *City of Mankato*	734 F.Supp. 681 (D.C. Minn. 1980)	320
Dalheim v. *KDFW.TV*	918 F.2d 1220 (5th Cir. 1990)	218
D&D Distributing Co. v. *NLRB*	801 F.2d 636 (3rd Cir. 1986)	272
Danzer v. *Professional Insurers, Inc.*	679 P.2d 1276 (N.M. 1984)	174
Davidson v. *Board of Governors of State Colleges and Universities for Western Ill.*	920 F.2d 441 (7th Cir. 1990)	113, 114
Davis v. *Monsanto Chemical Co.*	858 F.2d 345 (6th Cir. 1988)	98
DeCintio v. *Westchester County Medical Center*	807 F.2d 304 (2nd Cir. 1986)	94, 95
Department of Human Resources of Oregon v. *Alfred L. Smith*	110 S.Ct. 1595 (1990)	259
Despear v. *Milwaukee County*	63 F.3d 635 (7th Cir. 1995)	83
Devine v. *Pastre*	732 F.2d 213 (D.C. Cir. 1984)	297
Diaz v. *Pan American Airways, Inc.*	442 F.2d 389 (5th Cir. 1970)	86
Diggs v. *Western Electric*	587 F.2d 1070 (10th Cir. 1978)	48
Dillon v. *Frank*	752 F.2d 403 (6th Cir. 1992)	90
Dingess v. *SuperFresh Food Markets*	93 BNA Reports 1995	71
Diversified Industries v. *Meredith*	572 F.2d 596 (8th Cir. 1977)	23
Dole v. *Snell*	875 F.2d 802 (6th Cir. 1989)	218
Donnellon v. *Fruehauf Corp.*	796 F.2d 598 (11th Cir. 1986)	39
Donovan v. *Agnew*	712 F.2d 1508 (1st Cir. 1983)	307

Case	Number	Pages
Donovan v. *American Airlines*	686 F.2d 267 (5th Cir. 1982)	217
Donovan v. *Burger King*	672 F.2d 221 (1st Cir. 1982)	221
Donovan v. *Burgett Greenhouses, Inc.*	759 F.2d 1483 (10th Cir. 1985)	307
Donovan v. *Hahner, Foreman, Harness, Inc.*	736 F.2d 1421 (10th Cir. 1984)	237
Donovan v. *Sureway Cleaners*	656 F.2d 1368 (9th Cir. 1981)	226
Donovan v. *Techo, Inc.*	642 F.2d 141 (5th Cir. 1981)	226
Donovan v. *United Video, Inc.*	725 F.2d 577 (10th Cir. 1984)	219
Dumas v. *Kessler & Maguire Funeral Home*	380 N.W.2d 544 (Minn. App. 1986)	173
Dunlop v. *City Electric*	527 F.2d 394 (5th Cir. 1976)	215
Dzivbak v. *Mott*	503 N.W.2d 771 (Minn. Ct. 1993)	301
Ebling v. *Masco Corp.*	292 N.W.2d 801 (Mich. 1980)	165
EEOC v. *AIO Security Investigations*	55 F.3d 1276 (7th Cir. 1995)	69, 70
EEOC v. *American Arabian Oil Co.*	111 S.Ct. 1227 (1991)	36
EEOC v. *Chicago Miniature Lamp Works*	947 F.2d 292 (7th Cir. 1991)	48
EEOC v. *City Colleges of Chicago*	944 F.2d 339 (7th Cir. 1991)	36
EEOC v. *Consolidated Service Systems, Inc.*	No. 91-3530 and 92-1879, unpublished opinion (7th Cir. 1993)	48
EEOC v. *Detroit Edison Co.*	512 F.2d 301 (6th Cir. 1975)	48
EEOC v. *Enterprise Assn. Steamfitters Local 638*	542 F.2d 579 (2nd Cir. 1979)	259
EEOC v. *Ithaca Industries, Inc.*	847 F.2d 116 (8th Cir. 1988)	75
EEOC v. *Madison Community Unit School Dist. No. 12*	816 F.2d 577 (7th Cir. 1987)	107
EEOC v. *McCarthy*	768 F.2d 1 (1st Cir. 1985)	106
EEOC v. *Mississippi State Tax Commission*	873 F.2d 97, 99 (5th Cir. 1989)	134
EEOC v. *Mt. Vermon Mills*	58 FEP cases 73(BNA) (D. Ga. 1992)	101
EEOC v. *Ohio Edison*	1 F.3d 541 (6th Cir. 1993)	39
EEOC v. *Spokane Concrete Products*	534 F.Supp. 518 (E.D. Wash. 1982)	60
EEOC v. *Tortilleria "La Mejor,"*	758 F.Supp. 585 (ED. Cal. 1991)	64
EEOC v. *Universal Mf. Corp.*	914 F.2d 71 95th Cir. 1990)	74
E.I. duPont de Nemours and Co. v. *Finklea*	422 F.Supp. 821 (S.D. W.Va. 1977)	189
Eisenstadt, Sheriff v. *Baird*	405 U.S. 438 (1972)	190, 304
Eklund v. *Vincent Brass and Aluminum Co.*	351 N.W.2d 371 (Minn. App. 1984)	304
Eliel v. *Sears, Roebuck and Co.*	387 N.W.2d 842 (Mich. App. 1985)	184
Ellison v. *Brady*	924 F.2d 872 (9th Cir. 1991)	97
El Rey Sausage, Inc. v. *INS*	925 F.2d 1153 (9th Cir. 1991)	64
Emmert v. *Drake*	224 F.2d 299 (5th Cir. 1955)	306
Emporium Capwell Co. and Western Addition Community Organization v. *NLRB*	420 U.S. 50 (1973)	41
Enis v. *Continental Ill. Nat. Bank & Trust*	582 F.Supp. 876 (N.D. Ill. E.D. 1984)	166
Evans v. *Morsell*	95 A.2d 480 (Md. 1978)	203
Ewing v. *NLRB*	861 F.2d 353 (2nd Cir. 1988)	273
Farr v. *US West Communications*	58 F.3d 1361 (9th Cir. 1995)	149
Faulkner v. *Maryland*	564 A.2d 785 (Md. 1989)	197
Fernandez v. *Wynn Oil Co.*	653 F.2d 1275 (9th Cir. 1982)	42, 92
Fibreboard Paper Products Corp v. *NLRB*	379 U.S. 203 (1964)	289
Firefighters Local Union No. 1784 v. *Stotts*	467 U.S. 561 (1984)	126
First Options of Chicago, Inc. v. *Caplan*	(6th Cir. 1994)	297
First Options of Chicago, Inc. v. *Manual Caplan*	72 F.3d 1920 (7th Cir. 1995)	296

Case	Number	Pages
Hunt v. *Mid-American Employees Credit Union*	384 N.W.2d 853 (Minn. 1986)	103
Hutchinson v. *McDonald's Corp.*	110 S.Ct. 57 (1989)	204, 205
Idaho Dept. of Employment v. *Smith*	434 U.S. 100 (1977)	259
Ingersoll-Rand Co. v. *McClendon*	111 S.Ct. 478 (1990)	149, 150
International Brotherhood of Teamsters v. *U.S.*	431 U.S. 324 (1977)	131
International Union UAW v. *Johnson Controls*	111 S.Ct. 1196 (1991)	42
Intlekofer v. *Turnage*	973 F.2d 773 (9th Cir. 1992)	100
Irving Chute Co. v. *NLRB*	350 F.2d 176 (2nd Cir. 1965)	275
Ives v. *South Buffalo Railway Co.*	94 N.E.2d 431 (N.Y. App. 1911)	238, 239
Jacobson v. *U.S.*	112 S.Ct. 1535 (1992)	195
Johnson v. *Allied Stores Corp.*	679 P.2d 640 (Idaho 1984)	8
Johnson v. *Columbia, S.C.*	949 F.2d 127 (4th Cir. 1991)	214
Johnson v. *Honeywell Systems*	955 F.2d 409 (6th Cir. 1992)	51
Johnson v. *St. Francis Hospital*	759 S.W.2d 925 (Tenn. App. 1988)	246
Johnson v. *Shalala*	998 F.2d 121 (4th Cir. 1993)	68
Johnson v. *Transportation Agency*	107 S.Ct. 1442 (1987)	62, 128
Jones v. *Anchor Motor Freight, Inc.*	424 U.S. 554 (1976)	292
Joyner v. *AAA Cooper Transportation*	597 F.Supp. 537 (Ala. 1983)	94
J.P. Stevens & Co. v. *NLRB*	461 F.2d 490 (4th Cir. 1972)	167
Justin v. *Martin* affirmed 113 S.Ct. 55 (1992)	951 F.2d 121 (7th Cir. 1991),	23
Kaiser Aluminum and Chemical Corp. v. *Weber*	443 U.S. 193 (1979)	126
Kamrath v. *Suburban National Bank*	363 N.W.2d 108 (Minn. 1985)	194
Karnes v. *Milo Beauty and Barber Supply* *Co., Inc.*	441 N.W.2d 565, 568 (Minn. Ct. App. 1989)	206
Kass v. *Brown Boveri Corp.*	488 A.2d 242 (N.J. Super. 1985)	167, 169
Kassman v. *Busfield Enterprise, Inc.*	639 P.2d 353 (1981)	203
Katz v. *Dole*	790 F.2d 251, 255 (4th Cir. 1983)	95
Katz v. *School Dist. of Clayton Missouri*	557 F.2d 153 (8th Cir. 1977)	105
Kay v. *Peter Motor Co.*	483 N.W.2d 481 (Minn. App. 1992)	101
King v. *General Electric*	906 F.2d 107 (7th Cir. 1992)	119
King v. *Vincent's Hospital*	112 S.Ct. 570 (1991)	143
Kinney v. *State Industrial Commission*	423 P.2d 186 (Ore. 1967)	242
K-Mart Corp. Store No. 7441 v. *Trotti*	667 So.2d 6329 (Tex. App. 1984)	197
Knee v. *School Dist. No. 139 in Canyon City*	676 P.2d 727 (Idaho App. 1984)	170
Kopp v. *Samaritan health Systems*	13 F.3d 264 at 269	98
Kristoffel v. *Hangman Ford Service Co.*	985 F.2d 364 (7th Cir. 1993)	114
Kryriazi v. *Western Electric Co.*	647 F.2d 388 (3rd Cir. 1981)	310
Lamp v. *American Prosthetics, Inc.*	379 N.W.2d 909 (Iowa 1986)	152, 153
Laniok v. *Advisory Committee of Brainard* *Mfg. Co. Pension Plan*	935 F.2d 1360 (2nd Cir. 1991)	146, 149
Larson v. *Employment Appeal Board*	474 N.W.2d 570 (Iowa 1991)	261
Larson v. *Homet Aluminum*	449 N.W.2d 1172 (Ind. App. 3rd Dist. 1983)	206
Leathem Research Foundation of CUNY	658 F.Supp. 651 (S.D. N.Y. 1987)	172
Lechmere Inc. v. *NLRB*	112 S.Ct. 841 (1992)	281, 283
Leckelt v. *Board of Commissioners of Hospital* *Dist. No. 1*	909 F.2d 820 (5th Cir. 1990)	74, 85, 86

Case	Number	Pages
U.S. v. *Utah County for Health Care Human Resources Administration*	U.S. LEXIS 1771 (1996)	309
U.S. v. *Westinghouse*	638 F.2d 570 (3rd Cir. 1980)	189
United Steelworkers of America v. *American Mfg. Co.*	363 U.S. 564 (1960)	291, 296
United Steelworkers of America v. *Enterprise Wheel and Car Corp.*	363, 297 U.S. 593 (1960)	291, 295
United Steelworkers of America v. *Warrior and Gulf Navigation Co.*	363 U.S. 574 (1960)	291, 295
University of Pennsylvania v. *EEOC*	850 F.2d 969 (3rd Cir. 1988)	157, 188
University of Pennsylvania v. *EEOC*	110 S.Ct. 577 (1990)	279
Upjohn v. *U.S.*	101 S.Ct. 677 (1981)	25
Vaughan v. *Edel*	918 F.2d 517 (8th Cir. 1990)	174
Vickers v. *Veterans Administration*	549 F.Supp. 85 (D.C. Wash. 1982)	77
Vinard v. *King*	728 F.2d 428 (10th Cir. 1984)	34, 308
Vinson v. *Linn-Mar Community School Dist.*	360 N.W.2d (Iowa 1984)	303
Vinson v. *Taylor*	753 F.2d 141 (D.C. 1985)	96
Visser v. *Packer Engineering Assoc. Inc.*	924 F.2d 655 (7th Cir. 1993)	114
Wallace v. *Dunn Construction Co. Inc.*	62 F.2d 374 (11th Cir. 1995)	51
Walling v. *Belo Corp.*	317 U.S. 706 (1941)	222
Walling v. *Portland Terminal Co.*	330 U.S. 148 (1947)	216
Walter Myer v. *Aluminum Co. of America*	804 F.2d 821 (3rd Cir. 1986)	141
Walters v. *City of Atlanta*	803 F.2d 1135 (11th Cir. 1986)	320
Waltman v. *International Paper Co.*	875 F.2d 468 (5th Cir. 1989)	100
Wamsley v. *Champlin Refining and Chemicals, Inc.*	37 F.3d 634 (5th Cir. 1994)	117
Wards Cove Packing Co. v. *Atonio*	409 U.S. 642 (1989)	36
Watson v. *Fort Worth Bank & Trust*	108 S.Ct. 2777 (1988)	38
Wayne Adams Buick Inc. v. *Ference*	421 N.E.2d 733 (Ind. 1981)	243
Weaver v. *Minnesota Valley Laboratories, Inc.*	470 N.W.2d 131 (Minn. App. 1991)	103
Weeks v. *Southern Bell Telephone and Telegraph Co.*	408 F.2d 228 (5th Cir. 1959)	73
Weiner v. *McGraw-Hill*	443 N.E.2d 441 (N.Y. 1982)	165, 172
Welch Mfg. Co. v. *Pinkerton's*	474 A.2d 436 (R.I. 1984)	203
Welch v. *Liberty Machine Works, Inc.*	23 F.3d 1403 (8th Cir. 1994)	50
West Virginia University Hospitals, Inc. v. *Casey*	111 S.Ct. 1138 (1991)	36
Whirlpool Corp. v. *Marshall*	445 U.S. 1 (1980)	233, 237
White v. *New York Central Railroad*	343 U.S. 188 (1917)	239
Whittaker v. *Care-more, Inc.*	621 S.W.2d 395 (Tenn. 1981)	184
Wicken v. *Morris*	523 N.W. 2d 415 (Minn. 1995)	15
Wigginess v. *Fruchtman*	482 F.Supp. 681 (S.D. N.Y. 1979)	86
Wilcf Transportaiton Inc. v. *NLRB*	949 F.2d 1308 (7th Cir. 1991)	282
Wilis v. *Roche Biochem Laboratories, Inc.*	21 F.3d 1768 (1994)	82
Williams v. *Katten, Muchin & Zavis*	837 F. Supp. 1430 (N.D. Ill. 1993)	31
Williams v. *Saxbe*	413 F.Supp. 654 (D.C. 1976)	93
Williams v. *Tri-County Growers, Inc.*	747 F.2d 121 (3rd Cir. 1984)	212
Wilson v. *Monarch Paper Co.*	939 F.2d 1138 (5th Cir. 1991)	114, 115, 303
Wilson v. *NLRB*	920 F.2d 1282 (6th Cir. 1990)	76
Wilson v. *US West Communications*	58 F.3d 1337 (8th Cir. 1995)	75

Case	Number	Pages
Wimberly v. *Labor and Industrial Relations Commission*	107 S.Ct. 821 (1987)	140, 259
Wing v. *JMB Management Corp.*	714 P.2d 916 (Colo. App. 1985)	303
Wisner v. *Saunder Leasing Systems*	784 F.2d 1571 (11th Cir. 1986)	75
Wolk v. *Saks Fifth Avenue, Inc.*	728 F.2d 221 (3rd Cir. 1984)	305
W.R. Grace v. *Rubber Works Local 759*	103 S.Ct. 2177 (1983)	291, 297
Wright v. *Methodist Youth Services*	511 F.Supp. 307 (Ill. 1981)	94
Wygant v. *Jackson Board of Education*	106 S.Ct. 1842 (1986)	127
Yates v. *Avco Corp.*	819 F.2d 630 (6th Cir. 1987)	101
Young v. *Southwestern Savings & Loan Association*	509 F.2d 140 (5th Cir. 1975)	168
Yuhas v. *Libbey-Owens-Food Co.*	562 F.2d 496 (7th Cir. 1977), cert. denied	92

GLOSSARY

Adverse impact. A term used interchangeably with disparate impact, which alludes to group discrimination.

Applicant pool. A technique to have qualified candidates available when a vacancy exists. Often used in affirmative action programs.

Belo contract. A guaranteed wage contract for nonexempt employees that, under certain conditions, is permissible under the FLSA.

Bona Fide Occupational Qualification. As defined in Sect. 703(a)(e)(1) of Title VII, means that it is in compliance to discriminate because of sex if sex is a qualifying factor to perform all the duties of the job.

Business necessity. A decision that is reasonably necessary for the safe and efficient operation of the business.

Collyer Doctrine. Position of the NLRB that wherever possible a dispute should be arbitrated rather than processed by the board as an unfair labor practice.

Common law. As distinguished from statutes, it is a body of law that derives its authority from customs, rules of action, and decrees of the courts enforcing such customs and rules. It is the unwritten law of England, statutory and case law of the American colonies before the American Revolution.

Comparable worth. A wage theory that requires equal pay for comparable work even if job content or job categories are different.

Compensatory damages. Damages that compensate for actual loss caused by the defendant's wrongful act or omission of an act.

Complaint. When used in nonlegal context it is an employee's disagreement over a management policy or action concerning working conditions or wages. In a legal context it is an allegation of wrongdoing and a request for remedy.

Concerted activity. A protected activity under the NLRA where a group of employees are involved in an activity concerning work conditions or where an individual action affects working conditions of others and she or he is acting in behalf and under the request and authority of others.

Constructive discharge. When an employer creates conditions that a reasonable person cannot endure so she or he quits, but the action is treated by the courts as a discharge.

Contemptuous tort. A form of malpractice where intentional conduct by the employer is contrary to what civilized society should tolerate.

Defamation. A written or oral statement that has the effect of damaging the reputation or social stature of another person.

Deposition. A pretrial discovery procedure whereby testimony is given under oath outside of open court.

Dictum. Court language in a decision that does not relate specifically to the issue. The statement, remark, or observation that is not necessary in deciding the issue.

Discharge. An employer action that indicates to the employee that his or her services are no longer wanted.

Discrimination. Where there is different treatment in violation of a statute.

Disparate impact. A situation where as a result of a qualifying criteria the persons protected by statute are disproportionately selected as compared to groups who are not included in the protected class. (Usually if under 80 percent, it is considered a disparate impact.)

Disparate treatment. Where an employee is treated less favorably than other employees in violation of a statute.

Employee benefit. Something of a monetary value to the employee that is not related to work performed and is paid for either partially or wholly by the employer.

Employer. Anyone for whom an employee works.

Employment-at-will. A common law doctrine that an employee can be terminated for good cause, for no cause, or even for a cause morally wrong.

Equal work standard. A term used in applying the Equal Pay Act to determine whether two jobs performed by persons of different sex have equal skills, and have equal responsibility, and require equal effort under similar working conditions.

Exposure to litigation. A potential lawsuit that has sufficient facts to incite an attorney to represent the employee on a contingency.

Financial core member. Where a union member cannot be disciplined for crossing the picket line during a strike as long as she or he tenders dues to remain a member of the union.

Gray areas. An uncertainty as to the application of a statute or legal principle.

Grievance. A procedure under a labor agreement where the employee alleges that the agreement is not being followed.

Hostile environment. Conduct permissible by the employer whereby an environment is created that is offensive and abusive to a reasonable person. This is most often used in sexual harassment situations, where "reasonable woman" is the standard.

Insubordination. Where an employee refuses to obey a reasonable order from the employer.

Interrogatories. Written questions asked in a discovery procedure to a party having information of interest in the case.

Intentional infliction of emotional distress. A tort allegation that an employer intended to inflict emotional distress.

Just cause. Used in connection with discharge where the employee has been informed of a certain rule violation or poor performance that will result in discharge.

Legal paradox. Where courts grant immunity from liability for disclosing employee information and employer refuses because of fear of being sued.

Liquidated damages. Statutory damages based on actual loss but increased two or more times to compensate for a violation of the statute.

Litigation-happy society. That urge to sue everybody regardless of whether there is merit to the offense.

Lodester. A court-approved method of determining reasonable attorney fees.

Management malpractice. Where the conduct of the employer toward the employee is such that it exceeds the bounds that society will tolerate.

Manager. An employee who directly or indirectly manages the work of others.

Mixed discharge. Where an employee is engaged in a protected activity and in an unrelated action violates a rule or policy or has poor performance.

Moonlighting. Where an employee has two jobs that may be competing with each other.

Negligent hiring. The employer is liable for injury to third persons where employer knew or should have known of an applicant's dangerous tendencies. The employer's negligence is the proximate cause of the injury to those persons that employer could reasonably expect would come in contact with the dangerous employee.

Negligent retention. Where employer is aware of or should have been aware of an employee's dangerous propensity for violence or maliciousness (regardless of the cause) and did not do anything about it.

Per se. As used in legal context, without any other facts, it is a violation.

Personnel documents. All information kept by an employer that is received about an employee in the course of employment.

Practitioner. A person who has part-time or full-time responsibility for all or part of the personnel function.

Prima facie case. There are sufficient facts for the action to prevail until it is contradicted and overcome by other evidence.

Protected activity. An employee activity that is protected by statute from retaliation by the employer.

Protected class. That group of individuals who are protected from discrimination by a federal, state, or local statute.

Punitive damages. Monetary damages above the actual loss, which are given for punishment for wrongful behavior.

Qualified privilege doctrine. Where under certain conditions the employer is immune from liability when disclosing employee information to another person who has a business right to receive it.

Quid pro quo. Something for something. As used in the text, giving one thing of value to one person for another thing considered valuable to another person.

Reasonable accommodation. An effort on the part of the employer to give consideration for job placement to an employee as required by statute.

Red circle rate. Where an employee retains the rate of his or her old job when performing a job that has a lesser rate.

Retaliation. An adverse action by an employer against an employee for exercising a right under a statute or the common law.

Statute of Frauds. A statute that provides that an enforceable agreement must be in writing unless it can be performed within one year.

Subpoena. A court order directed to a person to appear at a certain time and place and give testimony on a certain matter.

Subpoena duces tecum. A court order to appear as a witness and bring certain documents related to the issue at trial.

Sudden death discharge. A discharge where the employee has been warned that when she or he commits the offense immediate discharge is mandatory.

Summary judgment. A motion to dismiss the action because there is no genuine issue of material fact to be determined by a judge or jury.

Summons. A document that commences a civil action or proceeding that asserts jurisdiction, and requires an appearance or an answer.

Supervisor. A person who directly supervises the activity of others.

Tort. When one person causes injury (physical or otherwise) to another, for which a court will allow a civil action.

Undue hardship. The result from accommodating that affects the employer to the point that no accommodation is necessary to comply with a statute.

Use it or lose it. A term used in connection with vacation time off. You take the time or lose it.

Voluntary quit. When an employee exercises directly or indirectly a free choice to terminate the employment relationship.

Weighted application blank. A structured method for determining which characteristics will predict job retention.

Weingarten Doctrine. The right of an employee to have representation in an investigative interview.

Writ of Certiorari. A discretionary device used by the U.S. Supreme Court to choose cases it wishes to hear.

INDEX